ARCHAEOLOGY IN THE LEVANT

Essays for Kathleen Kenyon

Kathleen Kenyon: Jericho 1952.

ARCHAEOLOGY

IN THE LEVANT

Essays for Kathleen Kenyon

Edited by Roger Moorey and Peter Parr

ARIS & PHILLIPS LTD
Warminster, England

ISBN 0 85668 084 2

Published by:
Aris & Phillips Ltd., Warminster, England.

Printed in England by:
Biddles Ltd., Guildford, Surrey.

CONTENTS AND LIST OF PLATES

ABBREVIATIONS

AASOR	Annual of the American Schools of Oriental Research
Acta.Arch.	Acta Archaeologica
ADAJ	Annual of the Department of Antiquities of Jordan
AfO	Archiv für Orientforschung
AJ	Antiquaries Journal
AJA	American Journal of Archaeology
Am. Ant,	American Antiquity
Ant.	Antiquity
ANET	J.B. Pritchard : Ancient Near Eastern Texts (Princeton, 1955)
Arch.J	Archaeological Journal
Arch. NL	Archaeological News-Letter (London)
ASOR	American Schools of Oriental Research
AUSS	Andrews University Seminary Studies
BASOR	Bulletin of the American Schools of Oriental Research
Bib. Arch.	Biblical Archaeologist
BIES	Bulletin of the Israel Exploration Society
BJPES	Bulletin of the Jewish Palestine Exploration Society
BM Beyr	Bulletin du Musée de Beyrouth
BSAE	British School of Archaeology in Egypt
Bull.Inst.Arch.	Bulletin of the Institute of Archaeology (London)
CAH	Cambridge Ancient History
Chambers Enc.	Chambers Encyclopedia
Corpus Script. Chr. Or., [Script. Arab.]	Corpus Scriptorum Christianorum Orientalium;
Corp. Script. Eccl. Lat.	Corpus Scriptorum Ecclesiasticorum Latinorum
Enc.Brit.	Encyclopedia Britannica
FAO	Food & Agriculture Organization (United Nations)
HTR	Harvard Theological Review
HUCA	Hebrew Union College Annual
IEJ	Israel Exploration Journal
ILN	Illustrated London News
Institute of Archaeology Ann. Rep.	Institute of Archaeology Annual Reports. (London)
JAOS	Journal of the American Oriental Society
JdI	Jahrbuch des Deutschen Archäologischen Instituts
JEA	Journal of Egyptian Archaeology
JBL	Journal of Biblical Literature
JCS	Journal of Cuneiform Studies
JNES	Journal of Near Eastern Studies
JPOS	Journal of the Palestine Oriental Society
JRAI	Journal of the Royal Anthropological Institute
JRAS	Journal of the Royal Asiatic Society
JRS	Journal of Roman Studies
JSS	Journal of Semitic Studies
LAAA	Liverpool Annals of Archaeology & Anthropology
MDAIK	Mitteilunger des deutschen archäologischen Instituts : Abteilung Kairo
MUSJ	Mélanges de l'Université Saint-Joseph de Beyrouth
Nat. Geog. Mag.	National Geographic Magazine
Nat. Geog. Soc. Research Reports	National Geographic Society Research Reports
NTS	Nimrud : Texts Series
OIP	Oriental Institute, Chicago : Publications
P.E.F. Annual	Palestine Exploration Fund. Annual
PEFQS	Palestine Exploration Fund, Quarterly Statement
PEQ	Palestine Exploration Quarterly
PPS	Proceedings of the Prehistoric Society
QDAP	Quarterly of the Department of Antiquities of Palestine
RA	Revue Archéologique
RB	Révue Biblique
ZAW	Zeitschrift für die Alttestamentische Wissenschaft
ZDPV	Zeitschrift des Deutschen Palästina - Vereins

EDITORIAL PREFACE

Volumes of commemorative essays are notoriously subject to delay. This was no exception. It was originally planned in 1972 to appear at the beginning of 1976 at the time of Dame Kathleen's seventieth birthday. Though our contributors were almost all unfailingly prompt, and subsequently sympathetic to our problems, inflationary pressures had restrained publishers in the meanwhile as they had everyone else. For sometime it looked as if this volume might never go beyond the typescripts. At the party held in Oxford in January 1976 to mark Dame Kathleen's birthday we were only able to offer her a list of the essays sent in her honour and a finely handwritten copy of the personal tribute by Dr. and Mrs. Tushingham printed here. Happily, soon afterwards, Messrs. Aris and Phillips offered to help us and we are most grateful for their confidence and support.

Sadly the delays have depleted the ranks of our contributors in two notable instances, though we have at least the compensation of the fine essays they submitted to us in 1974. Sir Mortimer Wheeler played a crucial part in Dame Kathleen's career as teacher and friend, counsellor and critic: roles to which she herself paid due tribute in *Levant* IX. Through the appropriately named 'Wheeler-Kenyon' method a quiet revolution was wrought in Palestinian field archaeology. Perhaps no other scholar contributed so much constructive criticism to its evolution in Palestine as Professor G. Ernest Wright, an offspring of the equally influential school of Palestinian archaeologists and Biblical scholars nurtured by Professor W. F. Albright. All that is best in Palestinian archaeology today derives much of its strength from these two strands of applied archaeological scholarship.

No problem in planning a *Festschrift* volume is quite so acute as the initial one - whom to invite. It is all the more trying when restrictions of length and subject are pressing. At the very outset one crucial aspect of Dame Kathleen's career in archaeology had to be set aside. The archaeology of Britain in the Iron Age and Roman period, to which she made considerable contributions between 1930 and 1950, had to be ignored, save in the bibliography. No less painful was the decision to exclude all those who as students had worked at Sabratha, Jericho or Jerusalem, or on Palestinian archaeology in the Institute of Archaeology in London, but had subsequently moved on to make their names in areas or aspects of archaeology that even so broad a term as 'Levant' could not encompass. But even with these draconian exclusions our troubles were not at an end, for potential essayists still greatly outnumbered the scale of the planned volume. In the event we concentrated primarily on Dame Kathleen's closest working colleagues over more than a generation's involvement with Palestinian archaeology and on students who by 1971 had gained doctorates under her supervision. Yet we remain well aware that some distinguished colleagues were even then only narrowly barred from an invitation. We hope that they will forgive us and accept the wisdom and general equity of our final selection, if only because the fairest application of our criteria firmly excluded one of the editors.

March, 1977.

Roger Moorey.
Peter Parr.

DAME KATHLEEN KENYON
A Personal Appreciation

In the essays which make up the bulk of this book, Dame Kathleen's colleagues and students pay their tribute to one of the leading archaeologists of our day. Yet, we are all aware that by concentrating our attention on her professional and academic accomplishments, we are losing something of the woman, the friend, and the leader who won and has held our respect over many years. We write this note on behalf of the many who have shared the experience of working on a Kenyon expedition.

We feel that this experience had its fullest expression in the Jericho excavations, but it is difficult to spell out, for those who were not there, the elements which made it unique. Some of us were seeing, for the first time, an excavation which was well-organized, whose purposes were well-defined, and whose method satisfied our subconscious desire for a logical, rational approach to stratigraphy. Moreover, we were serving under a director who obviously knew what she was doing and what she required of us, but who also, just as clearly, could make the process of learning a new discipline a pleasant and rewarding experience by her own zeal, modesty and naturalness. There was the romance of the site itself, situated a thousand feet below sea level, on the edge of a rich oasis scented with citrus blossom and flanked by the towering rusty slopes of the Judaean desert immediately to the west. It was a place identified, for most of us, with the Biblical stories of Joshua, replete with adventure and miracle. Here, too, our German and British archaeological predecessors had found important remains of early cities going back thousands of years, and their great trenches and dumps were visible in every direction. We lived among thousands of Arab refugees from what had only five years before become the State of Israel; the manner and strangeness of their lives, though now impoverished, had for us the glamour of the exotic; many of them worked for us and went on to become the most skilled excavators in Palestine as well as personal friends.

These factors, however, were largely external. It was our life, at work and at play, which came to have special significance. We were filled with wonder, shared openly and delightedly by K, at the surprises which Jericho produced almost every day. We were digging into a past beyond anyone's imagination at the time; the great brick defensive works, built and rebuilt over scores of generations; the houses, and particularly the neat, standardized, but well-appointed abodes of eight and ten thousand years ago; the plastered skulls and the great tombs filled with most wonderfully preserved furniture, tools, weapons, pottery, textiles and jewellery; a stone city wall which predated the Egyptian Old Kingdom pyramids by three thousand years, and, below it, an even older one complete with great round stone tower and rock-cut fosse. It was a treasure-trove of an undreamed antiquity and sophistication and Kathleen was the leader who held the key to it.

She was indefatigable; she worked up to twenty hours a day and left many of us feeling guilty because we could work only sixteen. She claimed no special insight, no unique ability to interpret the new discoveries; she consulted us, as equals, and tried out her ideas on us, encouraging us to suggest counter-explanations if we disagreed with her. We were a band of searchers, joined together in an exciting exploration of a past which challenged us at every step. No wonder we felt privileged, a "chosen few", fortunate to be engaged in this great venture.

But, no matter how excited and involved we were, rest and recreation were needed. Perhaps, not unexpectedly, our social life shared much of the enchantment of our work. Because of our location, we had to make most of our own entertainment, and our adventures are still the subject of fond memories and recollections. There was the lavish picnic at the citrus plantation of the late Dr. Awni Dajani (at the time of his death Director of the Jordan Department of Antiquities, but at this time in his twenties), when the perils of riding horses with little or no harness and camels with the hardest of wooden saddles produced enough falls, bruises, and stiff joints to cripple the staff for several days (but not to stop the work). There were the fantasias, or dances, held around the dig house, in which staff and workers participated. There was the spontaneous party to celebrate George Washington's birthday (a mere hint of the international nature of K's expeditions), which was such a great success that another to mark George the Third's birthday was held (even though no one could remember the right date, and anyway it didn't matter). There was, finally, the "lowest Boat Race on record", timed to coincide with the famous Oxford-Cambridge event on the Thames, but in every other respect bizarre, for it was rowed on the Dead Sea, in punts which could hardly be kept afloat, by crews whose identification with the universities in question was often exceedingly slight or non-existent, and which ended in celebrations on the shore paralleled in England only on Guy Fawkes Day. In all of these events, K participated with great zest.

Of course, one must admit that the Jericho experience has taken on a legendary glow as time has passed; we have forgotten the cold and rain, the wet beds and the lack of hot water, the weariness and the hard slogging work day in and day out. Even so, we are surely not wrong in remembering it as something unique, and in attributing that special quality to two factors: the site itself and the character of the director.

Those who did not share the Jericho experience, but have worked with K at other sites - particularly in the Old City of Jerusalem from 1961-67 - will recognize that much of the spirit which characterized the earlier dig was also present at Jerusalem. There was the same sense of adventure in our work, and the same camaraderie in dances on the roof. Where the spirit was less concentrated, the reason was probably our presence in a large city, surrounded with crowds and all the appurtenances of civilization. Where it continued to pervade our work and play there is no doubt that the source and embodiment was the director herself. Her knowledge, experience, diligence and enthusiasm, her high standards and the patience and skill with which she inculcated them, her modesty, friendliness, sense of humour and tolerance - all of these qualities have entitled her to the honours she has received, and the love and respect which she has engendered in all those who have been privileged to know and work with her. May she go from strength to strength.

MMT and ADT

A BIBLIOGRAPHY OF KATHLEEN M. KENYON UP TO 1975
by N. J. H. Lord and A. C. Western

Books and Monographs

The Buildings at Samaria. (Samaria-Sebaste 1). (With J. W. Crowfoot and E. L. Sukenik). London, 1942.

Excavations at Jewry Wall Site, Leicester. (Report of Res. Com. of Soc. of Antiquaries No. XV). Oxford, 1948.

Guide to Wroxeter Roman City. London, 1949.

Beginning in Archaeology. London, 1952.

Beginning in Archaeology. (2nd ed.). London, 1953.

Guide to Ancient Jericho. Jerusalem, 1954.

Digging up Jericho. London, 1957. (Foreign editions in Swedish, Italian, Dutch, Hebrew and Spanish).

The Objects from Samaria. (Samaria-Sebaste 3). (With J. W. and G. M. Crowfoot). 1957.

Excavations at Southwark. (Research Papers of Surrey Arch. Soc. No. 5). 1959.

Archaeology in the Holy Land. London, 1960.

Excavations at Jericho. Vol. I. Tombs Excavated in 1952-4. London, 1960.

Beginning in Archaeology. (Revised ed.). London, 1961.

Archaeology in the Holy Land. (2nd ed.). London, 1965.

Excavations at Jericho. Vol. 2. Tombs Excavated in 1955-8. London, 1965.

Amorites and Canaanites. (Schweich Lecture for 1963). London, 1966.

Jerusalem - Excavating 3000 Years of History. (New Aspects of Antiquity). London, 1967. (Foreign edition in German).

Archaeology in the Holy Land. (3rd ed.) London, 1970. (Foreign editions in Swedish, Danish, German, Dutch, and Spanish).

Royal Cities of the Old Testament. London, 1971.

Digging up Jerusalem. London, 1974.

Articles in Periodicals and Composite Volumes

"Sketch of the Exploration and Settlement of the East Coast of Africa", *The Zimbabwe Culture* by G. Caton Thompson, (Oxford 1931), 260-74.

"Roman Theatre at Verulamium, St. Albans", *Transactions St. Albans & Herts. Architectural and Archaeological Soc.* (1934), 133-42.

"Roman Theatre at Verulamium, St. Albans", *Archaeologia* 84 (1935), 213-61.

"Excavations at Jewry Wall site, Leicester, 1936 Season", *Transactions Leicester Literary & Philosophical Soc.* 38 (1937), 20-61.

"Excavations at Viroconium, 1936-37", *Archaeologia* 88 (1938), 175-227.

"Excavation Methods in Palestine", *PEQ* (1939), 29-37.

"Excavations on the Wrekin, Shropshire, 1939", *Arch J* 99 (1943), 91-109.

"Problems of the Central and West Midlands", *Arch NL* i (1948), 17-18.

"Excavations at Breedon-on-the-Hill, Leicestershire, 1946", *Transactions Leicester Archaeological & Historical Soc.,* 26 (1950), 17-82.

"Excavations at Sutton Walls Camp, Herefordshire, 1948-50", *Transactions Woolhope Club,* (1949-51), 148-54.

"British School of Archaeology in Jerusalem", *Arch NL* 4 (1951), 1-2.

"Some Notes on the History of Jericho in the Second Millennium B.C.", *PEQ* (1951), 101-38.

"Excavations at Jericho", Interim Rep., *PEQ* (1952), 4-5.

"A Survey of the Evidence concerning the Chronology and Origins of Iron Age A in Southern and Midland Britain", *Institute of Archaeology Ann. Rep.* 8 (1952), 29-78.

"Excavations at Jericho, 1952", *PEQ* (1952), 62-82.

"Phoenician, Roman, Byzantine - the three cities of Tripolitanian Sabratha. The rise and fall of an ancient city revealed", *ILN* (29 March 1952), 538-9.

"La Plus Vieille Ville du Monde", *Samedi Soir* (12 July 1952), 6.

"Early Jericho", *Ant* 26 (1952), 116-22.

"The Newly-found Tombs of the Lords of Jericho, 3600 years ago", *ILN* (3 October 1953), 520-2.

"Mankind's earliest walled town; uncovering the walls and towers of Jericho from Neolithic times to the sack of Joshua", *ILN* (17 October 1953), 603-4.

"Jericho before Joshua", *Listener* (4 June 1953), 928-30.

"Jericho gives up its secrets", *Nat. Geog. Mag.* (December 1953), 853-70. (With A.D. Tushingham).

"Die Ur-mauern von Jericho", *Welt am Sonntag* (22 November 1953), 7.

"Neolithic Portrait Skulls from Jericho", *Ant* 27 (1953), 105-7.

"Archaeology", *Odhams Encyclopaedia Illustrated,* London (1953).

"Stone Age Man Builds a City", *Daily Telegraph* (28 December 1953).

"Ancient Jericho", *Scientific American* 190, 4 (1954), 76-82.

"Jericho in 5000 B.C. New Discoveries from the Dawn of Civilisation", *Times* (6 April 1954), 9.

"Excavations at Sutton Walls, Herefordshire, 1948-51", *Arch J* 105 (1954), 1-87.

"Excavations at Jericho", *JRAI* 84 (1954), 103-10.

"Excavations at Jericho, 1954", *PEQ* (1954), 45-63.

"Excavations at Jericho, 1955", *PEQ* (1955), 108-17.

"A crescentic Axehead from Jericho and a Group of Weapons from Tell-el-Hesi", *Institute of Archaeology Ann. Rep.* 11 (1955), 10-18.

"Excavations at Jericho, 1956", *PEQ* (1956), 67-82.

"Tombs of the Intermediate Early Bronze-Middle Bronze Age at Tell Ajjul", *ADAJ* 3 (1956), 41-55.

"The World's Oldest known township: Excavating the Jericho of 7000 years ago and earlier", *ILN* (12 May 1956), 504-6.

"The Jericho of Abraham's time, and the city which Joshua destroyed. Bronze Age levels of the world's oldest excavated city", *ILN* (19 May 1956) , 552-5.

"Jericho, the world's oldest town: a tower with an interior stair thousands of years older than the pyramids, and other discoveries", *ILN* (13 October 1956), 611-3.

"Jericho and its setting in Near Eastern history", *Ant* 30 (1956), 184-95.

"Excavations at Jericho, 1957", *PEQ* (1957), 101-7.

"The British School of Archaeology in Jerusalem: the new School building", *PEQ* (1957), 97-100.

"Reply to Professor Braidwood", *Ant* 31 (1957), 82-4.

"The Oldest Town in the World", *Times* (22 August 1958), 9.

"Ancient Jericho", *Arab World* (October 1958), 7-10.

"Some Notes on the Early and Middle Bronze Age Strata of Megiddo", *Eretz Israel* 5 (1958), 51-60.

"Some observations on the Beginnings of Settlement in the Near East", *JRAI* 89 (1959), 35-43.

"Earliest Jericho", *Ant* 33 (1959), 5-9.

"We dug back 9,700 years in History", *Toronto Globe Magazine* (21 March 1959), 8-10.

"Excavations at Jericho, 1957-8", *PEQ* (1960), 88-108.

"Jericho and the Origins of Agriculture", *Advancement of Science* 66 (1960), 118-20.

"Excavations in Jerusalem, 1961", *PEQ* (1962), 72-89.

"Ancient Jerusalem", *Discovery* (1962), 18-23.

"Excavations at Jerusalem, 1961", *Ant* 36 (1962), 93-6.

"Biblical Jerusalem", *Expedition* (Bull. of Univ. Mus. of Pensylvania) 5 (1962), 32-5.

"Archaeology of Palestine I - Prehistoric and Early Phases", *Peake's Commentary on the Bible* (1962), 42-9.

"Archaeology", *Hastings Dictionary of the Bible* (1963), revised ed., 50-51.

"Jericho", *Hastings Dictionary of the Bible* (1963) , revised ed., 470-1.

"Jerusalem", *Hastings Dictionary of the Bible* (1963), revised ed., 471-6.

"British Archaeology Abroad - Jerusalem", *Ant* 37 (1963), 39-40.

"British Archaeology Abroad - Jerusalem", *Ant* 38 (1964), 9-10.

"Excavations in Jerusalem, 1962", *PEQ* (1963), 7-21.

"Megiddo, Hazor, Samaria and Chronology", *Institute of Archaeology Bull.* 4 (1964), 143-57.

"Excavations in Jerusalem", *Bib Arch* 27, 2 (1964), 34-52.

"Excavations in Jerusalem, 1963", *PEQ* (1964), 7-18.

"Ancient Jerusalem", *Scientific American* 213, 1 (1965) , 84-91.

"Syria and Palestine c. 2160-1780 B.C.", revised *CAH* 1, 2, Fasc. 29 (1965).

"Excavations in Jerusalem, 1964", *PEQ* (1965), 9-20.

"Jericho", *Enc Brit* (1965-8), 14th ed.

"British Archaeology Abroad - Jerusalem", *Ant* 39 (1965), 36-7.

"Archaeology", *Chambers Enc.* 1 (1966), 535-43.

"Jericho", *Chambers Enc.* 8 (1966), 74.

"British Archaeology Abroad - Jerusalem", *Ant* 40 (1966), 90-1.

"Palestine in the Middle Bronze Age", revised *CAH* 2, 3, Fasc. 48 (1966).

"Excavations in Jerusalem, 1965", *PEQ* (1966), 73-88.

"Palestine" (in part) *Enc. Brit.* (1966-73), 14th ed.

"Excavations in Jerusalem, 1966", *PEQ* (1967), 65-73.

"Jericho", *Archaeology* 20 (1967), 268-75.

"Jericho", D. Winton Thomas (ed.) *Archaeology and Old Testament Study,* (Oxford, 1967), 264-75.

"Excavations in Jerusalem, 1967", *PEQ* (1968), 97-109.

"Jerusalem" (in part) *Enc. Brit.* (1968-73), 14th ed.

"Middle and Late Bronze Age Strata at Megiddo", *Levant* 1 (1969), 25-60.

"Jericho" (in part) *Enc. Brit.* (1969-73), 14th ed.

"Israelite Jerusalem", J. H. Sanders (ed.) *Near Eastern Archaeology in the 20th Century* Essays in Honour of Nelson Glueck, (New York, 1970), 232-53.

"Women in Academic Life", *Journal of Biosociological Science,* Suppl. 2 (1970), 107-18. (The Galton Lecture 1969).

"New Evidence on Solomon's Temple, *MUSJ* 46, 9 (1970), 137-49.

"The Origins of the Neolithic", *Advancement of Science* 26 (1970), 1-17.

"Some Aspects of the Impact of Rome on Palestine", *JRAS* (1970), 181-91.

"An Essay on Archaeological Technique: The Publication of Results from the Excavation of a Tell", *HTR* 64 (1971), 271-9.

"Syria and Palestine c. 2160-1780 B.C.", *CAH* 1, 2, (1971) 3rd ed., 567-94.

"Archaeology and the Old Testament", *Perspective,* Journal of Pittsburgh Theological Seminary (Memorial to Paul Lapp) (1971), 3rd ed. 11-22.

"Palestine in the time of the 18th Dynasty", revised *CAH* 2, 2, Fasc. 69 (1971).

"Archaeological Excavations in Jerusalem, 1964-67", *Nat. Geog. Soc. Research Reports, 1965 Projects,* (Washington, 1971), 141-52.

"Palestine in the Middle Bronze Age", *CAH* 2, 1, 3 (1973) 3rd ed., 77-116.

"Palestine in the time of the Eighteenth Dynasty", CAH 2, 1, 11 (1973) 3rd ed., 526-56.

"Jericho", *Enc. Brit.* (1974) 15th ed.

"History of Syria and Palestine", (in part) *Enc. Brit.* (1974) 15th ed.

"Tombs of the Intermediate Early Bronze - Middle Bronze Age at Tell 'Ajjul", in J. R. Stewart *"Tell el Ajjul - The Middle Bronze Age Remains",* App. 2. Studies in Mediterranean Archaeology (Göteborg, 1974), 76-85.

Reviews

"La Neuvième Campagne de Fouilles à Ras Shamra-Ugarit", C. Schaeffer, *Arch J* 95 (1939), 355-6.

"Megiddo I, Seasons of 1925-34, Strata I-V", R. S. Lamon and G. M. Shipton, (Chicago, 1939) *Arch J* 96 (1940), 180-2.

"Explorations in Eastern Palestine III", N. Glueck, (AASOR 18-19, 1937-9) *Arch J* 97 (1941), 186-8.

"Report on Excavations at Wroxeter (the Roman City of Viroconium) in the County of Salop 1923-7", D. Atkinson, (Oxford, 1942) *AJ* 23 (1943), 66-7.

"Lachisch II; The Fosse Temple", O. Tufnell, C. H. Inge, G. L. Harding, (The Wellcome Marston Archaeological Research Expedition to the Near East Publication Vol. II Oxford, 1940) *AJ* 24 (1944), 156-7.

"The River Jordan", N. Glueck, (Philadelphia, 1946) *PEQ* (1948), 66-7.

"Manual of Archaeological Surveying", A. H. Detweiler, (ASOR Publications of Jerusalem School, Archaeology II, 1948) *JRS* 39 (1949), 186-7.

"Bethshan II. Four Canaanite Temples Pt. I. The Temples and Cult Objects", A. Rowe, (Philadelphia, 1940) "Megiddo II. Seasons of 1935-9", G. Loud, (Chicago, 1948) "Excavations at Tell en Nasbeh I-II", C.C. McCown and I. C. Wampler (Palestine Institute of Pacific School of Religion and ASOR, 1947) *Ant* 24 (1950), 196-200.

"Arretinische Reliefkeramik mit Beschreibung der Sammlung in Tübingen", H. Dragendorff, (Reutlingen, 1948) *JRS* 40 (1950), 161-2.

"Israel Exploration Journal Vol. I", (Jerusalem, 1950-1) *Ant* 25 (1951), 110-11.

"Ancient Hebrew Seals", A. Reifenberg, (London, 1950) *AJ* 32 (1952), 85.

"The Roman Town and Villa at Great Casterton, Rutland", P. Corder, (Nottingham, 1951) *Arch J* 108 (1952), 198.

"Anatolian Studies Vol. I", *Ant* 26 (1952), 218.

"City of Shepherd Kings", W. M. Flinders Petrie, and "Ancient Gaza V", E. J. Mackay and M. Murray, (BSAE 64 1952) *AJ* 33 (1953), 81-2.

"Manuel d'Archéologie Biblique Vol. II. Faits Socieux Religieuse", A. G. Barrois, (Paris, 1953) *Ant* 29 (1955), 190-1.

"Photography for Archaeologists', M. B. Cookson, (London, 1954) *AJ* 34 (1956), 135-6.

"Offa's Dyke: a Field Survey of the Western Frontier Works of Mercia in the 7th and 8th centuries A.D.", C. Fox, (London, 1955) *Arch J* 113 (1957), 166-7.

"Jerusalem de l'Ancien Testament. Recherches d'Archéologie et de l'histoire. Part II Archéologie du Temple. Part III Evolution historique et d'histoire", L. Hugues Vincent and M. A. Steve, (Paris, 1956) *AJ* 39 (1959), 293-4.

"Lachish IV. The Bronze Age", O. Tufnell, (Oxford, 1958) *Ant* 33 (1959), 231-4.

"The Ancient Library of Qumran and modern Biblical Studies", F. M. Cross, (London, 1958) *Library Review*, Glasgow (1959), 132-3.

"Hazor I", Y. Yadin et al., (Jerusalem, 1958) *Ant* 33 (1959), 231-4.

"Hazor I. An Account of the First Season of Excavations 1955", Y. Yadin et al., (Jerusalem, 1958) *JSS* 4 (1959), 374-6.

"Archaeology and its Problems", S. J. de Laet, (London, 1957) *JRS* 49 (1959), 193-4.

"Excavations at New Testament Jericho and Khirbet en-Nitla", J. K. Kelso, (AASOR 29-30, 1955) *JSS* 4 (1959), 61-3.

"The Excavations at Herodian Jericho, 1951", J. B. Pritchard, (AASOR 32-33, 1958) *Ant* 33 (1959), 231-4.

"Antiquities of Jordan", G. L. Harding, (London, 1959) *AJ* 40 (1960) 78-9.

"The People of the Dead Sea Scrolls", J. M. Allegro, (London, 1959) *AJ* 41 (1961), 98-9.

"The Excavations at Herodian Jericho, 1951", J. B. Pritchard, (AASOR 32-33, 1958) *JSS* 6 (1961), 283-4.

"Hazor II. An Account of the Second Season of Excavation 1956", Y. Yadin et al., (Oxford, 1960) *Ant* 36 (1962), 142-4.

"Mounds of the Near East", S. Lloyd, (Edinburgh, 1963) *PEQ* (1965), 171-2.

"Mounds of the Near East", S. Lloyd, (Edinburgh, 1963) *AJ* 45 (1965), 267-8.

"Nimrud and its Remains", M. E. L. Mallowan, (London, 1965) *Manchester Guardian* (1966).

"The Canaanites", J. Gray, (London, 1964) *JSS* 12 (1967), 281-2.

"Ancient Pottery from the Holy Land", R. Amiran, (Jerusalem, 1969) *AJ* 52 (1972), 369-70.

"The Bible and the Ancient Near East", R. de Vaux, (London, 1972) *Bible Lands* (Summer 1972), 210-11.

"Gezer I: Preliminary Report of the 1964-6 Seasons", W. G. Dever, H. D. Lance and G. E. W. Wright, (Jerusalem, 1970) *PEQ* (1973), 170-1.

"Biblical Archaeology and History", P. W. Lapp, (New York and Cleveland, 1969) *Ant* 48 (1974), 155-6.

"The Church of the Holy Sepulchre in Jerusalem", C. Couasnon, (London, 1974) *Bible Lands* (Autumn 1974).

"L'Epoque Pré-Urbaine en Palestine", P. R. de Miroschedji, (Paris, 1971) *Ant* 48 (1974), 235-6.

"L'Epoque Pré-Urbaine en Palestine", P. R. de Miroschedji, (Paris, 1971) *Biblica* 55 (1974), 88-90.

"Hazor. The Schweich Lectures 1970", Y. Yadin, (Oxford, 1972) *Journ. Theological Studies* 26 (1975), 437-9.

"Hazor. The Schweich Lectures 1970", Y. Yadin, (Oxford, 1972) *AJ* 55 (1975), 420-1.

"Hazor. The Schweich Lectures 1970", Y. Yadin, (Oxford, 1972) *PEQ* (1975), 167-9.

"Beer-Sheba I. Excavations at Tel Beer-Sheba", Y. Aharoni et al., (Tel Aviv University, 1973) *Ant* 49 (1975), 318-9.

Obituaries

"Sir David Russell". *PEQ* (1956), 60.

"G. M. Crowfoot". *PEQ* (1957), 154.

"J. W. Crowfoot". *PEQ* (1960), 161-3.

"Awni Khalil Dajani". *PEQ* (1968), 78-9.

"Father Roland de Vaux, O.P.". *Levant* 4 (1972), 5-8.

"W. F. Albright (1891-1971)". *Levant* 5 (1973), 6.

"G. Ernest Wright". *PEQ* (1975), 81.

"Sir Mortimer Wheeler". *Levant* 9 (1977), i-ii.

THE ESSAYS

THE NEOLITHIC IN WADI RUMM: 'AIN ABU NEKHEILEH.
by Diana Kirkbride.

Although the sequence of Neolithic cultures at Jericho was first uncovered by the German expedition of Sellin and Watzinger before the First World War, and again by Professor Garstang in the 1930's, the significance of the early finds did not appear to dawn on any of the participants, or indeed on the archaeological world as a whole. Perhaps the time was not ripe or, more probably, the emphasis of the dig was placed so firmly on the biblical aspects of the site that full appreciation was not feasible at that time. Nevertheless, fifteen years after the end of Garstang's excavations Dame Kathleen Kenyon led her own expedition to Jericho and this time the revelation of those astonishing early cultures was not only fully and highly appreciated everywhere, but others were prompted to specialise in the study of these early periods. Writing as one of those members of the Jericho team who, in my case, turned from Egyptology and concentrated on widening our scanty knowledge of the earliest settled communities, I am glad to have been given this opportunity to acknowledge the help given me by Dame Kathleen. Help that entailed not only her support and field training, but, not least, the incentive that led to my own specialisation.

* * * * * * * * * * * * * * *

Wadi Rumm lies in that part of the Hisma that forms the south-east corner of Jordan. The wadi is justly famous for its great red sandstone mountains resting on their granite plinths, its pink sands and cool springs that line the east side of Jebel Rumm. The springs' emergence along this is caused by a geological fault: a rising and tilting of the Pre-Cambrian granite from west to east. About 25 miles west of Rumm the mountains along Wadi Ytm are entirely of granite while as one goes eastwards the granite gets lower and is capped by Cambrian sandstone. In Jebel Rumm itself the granite is twice as high on its west flank and tilts sharply to the east. The huge, mainly Cambrian sandstone mass of this mountain forms a vast catchment that rests on the harder rock. Water percolates through the porous sandstones until it reaches the impermeable granite then runs down the slope to emerge in many springs well over 100 feet above the wadi sands. Along this line of springs a comparatively luxurious vegetation grows, grasses, ferns and mosses with even pistachio, wild fig and palm Trees also cling to unlikely cracks in the rocks as they do, for example, at Petra, and a few live at the junction of sand and granite at the foot of the mountain. The broad and sandy wadi bed of Rumm supports large stands of white broom in addition to desert scrub, and stunted grasses grow in the bays on the east side of Jebel Rumm below the springs.

A few years ago the fauna was still fairly varied, and probably is much the same now: Ibex and gazelle, hares, foxes and hyrax, a few leopards, cheetahs and wild and ferral cats as well as small rodents live in the mountains and sands. The wadi is very hot in summer when sandstorms blow up and down the main bed from south to north in the mornings and back again in the afternoons, but the rock-armed bays in the mountainside below the springs protected, and still do, both ancient and modern settlements from the blown sands. For the rest of the year the weather is kind, broken only by occasional terrific thunderstorms when cascades of water pour down well-worn courses in the vertical mountain sides with a reverberating roar that once heard can never be forgotten. The resultant spates turn small, if deep, dried-up sandy wadi beds into raging torrents that pour out of the bays into the main Wadi Rumm and there eventually lose themselves in its sandy vastness.

'Ain Abu Nekheileh, one of those springs nearly 200 feet above the sands of Wadi Rumm, is situated at the centre of the next bay, about 5 kilometres south of the one where the famous Nabataean remains and modern Police Post lie. It erupts into a little cool pool with grass and its overhanging guardian palm which gives the spring its name, Father of the Little Date Palm, and lies on a small, cul-de-sac ledge in the mountain side. A steep climb up a rock track worn in the granite over the millennia by man and his animals is the only means of access. At the foot of the mountain and about 50 metres away from the place where the track begins its ascent lies a small Neolithic settlement. Found by Sir Alec Kirkbride and G. Lankester Harding when they were surveying the Hisma, the site was named by them after the spring upon which the inhabitants depended.[1] During my subsequent survey of Rumm, I decided to make a very small sounding at Abu Nekheileh to obtain additional material to confirm or deny Stekelis' typological, though tentative, correlation of the site with Jericho VIII/PNB, made on the results of the original surface survey.[2] With the help of Professor John Carswell, who joined the team as surveyor/draughtsman, a very small sounding was put down.[3]

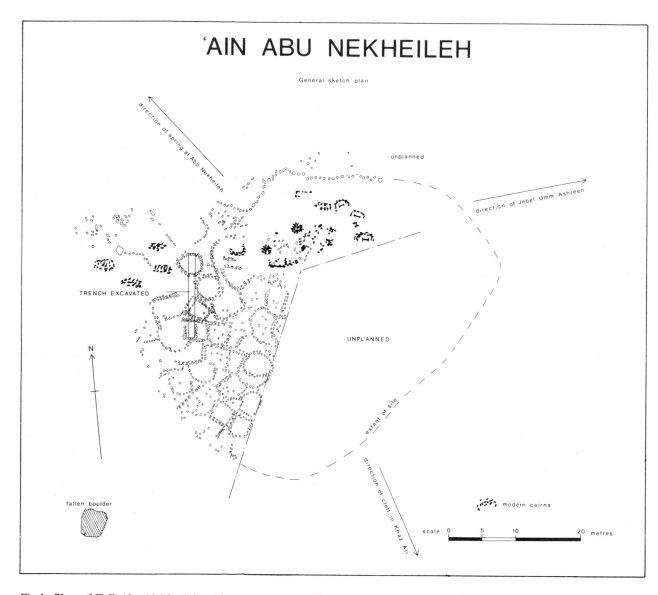

Fig 1: Plan of Tell Abu Nekheileh without excavation. Note position of sounding.

The settlement is marked by a very low, roughly oval, stone-covered mound with various cairns and graves along its northern perimeter. Walls of both round and rectangular buildings can be seen on the surface with comparative clarity; so much so that we were able to plan part of the settlement without digging (Fig. 1).

The Sounding. Abu Nekheileh is about 50 x 45 metres, an irregular oval, with a deposit of only about 75 cm. The trench, 12 x 1 metres, was sited towards the western perimeter and laid down to include parts of both round and rectangular buildings. It was finally enlarged at the north end to include the whole of House IV. The work was carried out in four parts: I, the rectangular building between walls A and B; II, across the corner of two more buildings; III, a space between II and round house IV.

The deposit was essentially sandy with only slight traces of hardened floors, so the stratification was guided mainly by the colour of the sand. Five buildings all of slightly different phases were touched by the sounding.

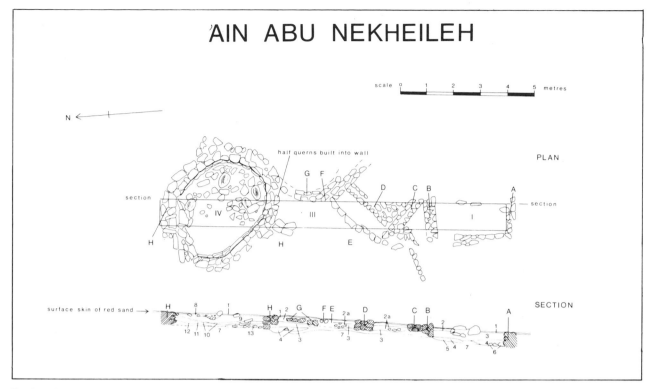

Fig 2: Abu Nekheileh – plan and section of sounding.

Section Description. (Fig. 2).

I. Contained by walls **A** & **B**.
1. Red surface sand.
2. Purple sand. Superficial level 2.
3. Blackish sandy occupation.
4. Reddish sandy with some black, goes to both walls. 1 broken rubber.
5. Red Sand with hearth patches on other side of room from 6.
6. Stony area. ? Working platform, with black in and around it. 1 grinder and a sandstone pounder.
7. Sterile red sand = virgin soil.

II. Between walls **B** & **E**.
1 + 2 Surface.
2a. Stony area resting on blackish sand ? work platform.
3. Blackish sand.

III. From wall **E** to **H**.
1 + 2 surface.
3. Blackish, sandy.
4. Reddish with traces of grey from above.

IV. House IV. Walls **H**.
1. Surface
8. Thick black sandy with many stones and a broken granite quern. Possibly a late phase now eroded.
9. Very black and powdery.
10. Reddish sandy.
11. Black powdery.

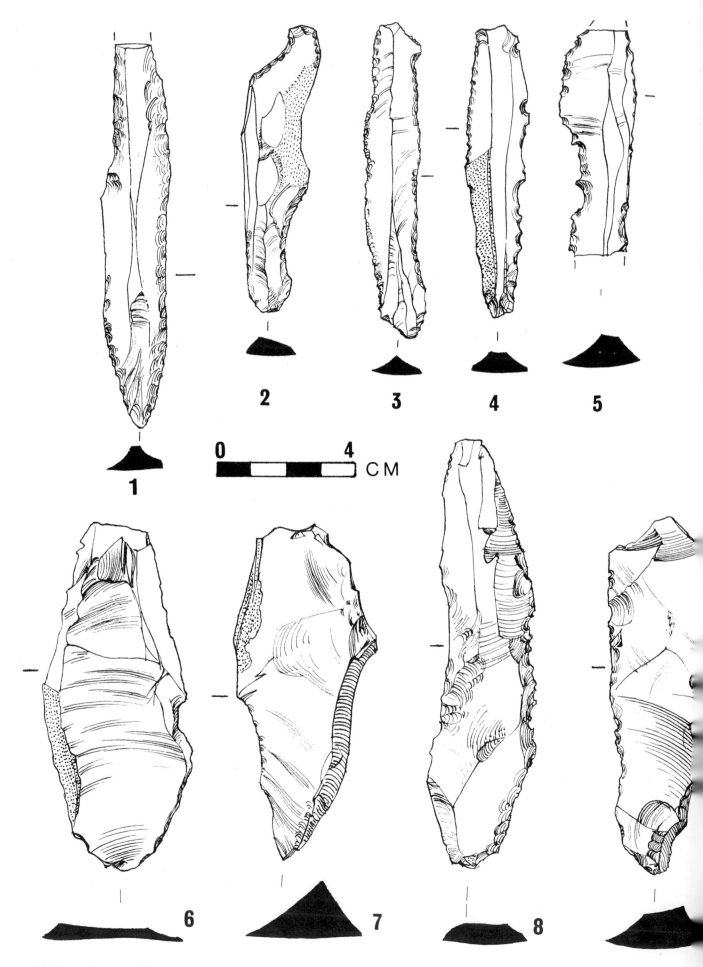

Fig 3: A selection of flint implements.

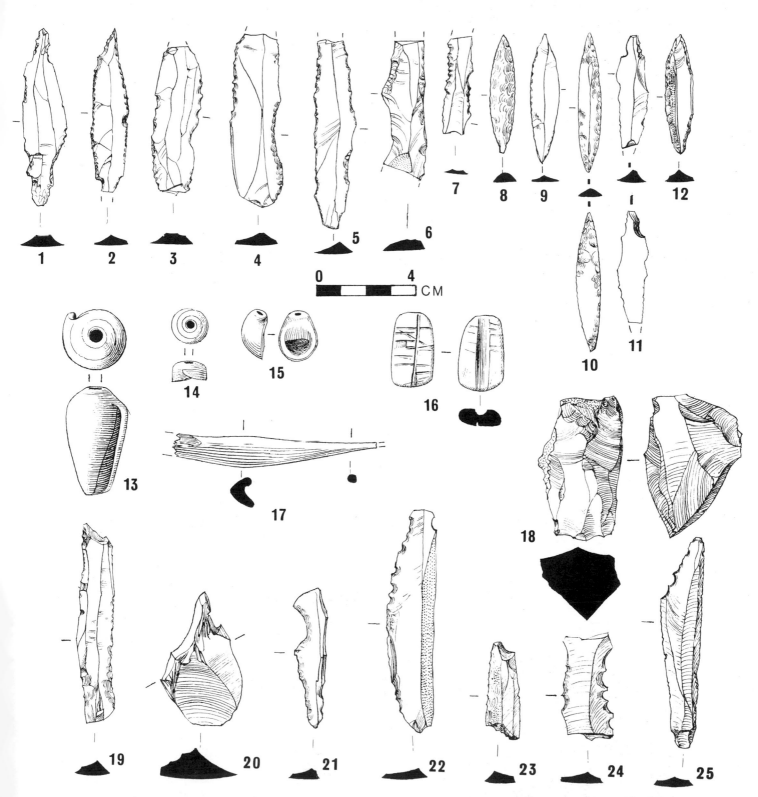

Fig 4: Flint implements: Nos. 1–12, 18–25. Bone beads: Nos. 13–15. Bead-Polisher ?No. 16. Bone-Point No. 17.

Plate Ia. House IV. The rough rebuilding of the North Wall inside the older line may conceal a doorway.

Plate Ib. House IV. Disturbed work platform and querns. Cache of flints and shells against wall behind central quern.

12.   Grey powdery, from above and counts as one with 11.
13.   Many stone slabs, ?fallen querns. Could be working platform.
7.   Sterile red sand.

In short, the black and grey sandy layers, really one entity, are those of the living floors. With the exception of House IV only one occupation layer is found in each building, and in IV the upper black stony layer, 8 and the black below it and in it could well indicate a secondary occupation. The red sand, 10, represents a period of desertion after the original occupation comprised by 11 - 13.

Obviously a deposit of only 75 cm does not allow much time lag between the different buildings, so the phasing, already difficult for this reason, is rendered more so by the fact that I and IV seem to have been slightly semi-subterranean. In each case the exterior wall faces are founded at a slightly higher level than the interior ones, as, for example at Beidha. Whether or not I and IV were contemporary remains an open question especially as they represent two different types of architecture. The round house, IV, seems to be the earliest with its neighbour, represented by Wall G slightly later. House I was founded away from the round buildings leaving room for the altered rectangular house represented by walls E/F & D to be squeezed in between it and the round ones, but our very small trench failed to supply a firm answer.

House IV, the only excavated one, presents a familiar plan recalling Beidha VI, but without the post sockets in the wall (Fig. 2). No definite doorway was found although a large stone in the western arc might have been a high step. The northern arc had suffered some damage and been roughly rebuilt with a wall of large stones somewhat inside the original one. Here again there might have been a doorway (Pl. Ia). The eastern half of the house contained many slabs of stone lying untidily on the floor. They give the impression of tumble, but may equally have been the disturbed remains of a stone foundation providing a firm base for grinding without the querns sinking into the soft sand below.

Five querns were found on these stones, but they also give the impression of having fallen, or been thrown in (Pl. Ib).

Apart from the querns, seven grinders, one with a groove (Fig. 5. No. 1), a flint hammerstone and a pebble polisher were scattered among the stones, while close against the wall behind the central quern lay a large cache of flints, shells and shell beads (Figs. 3 & 4). In view of these significant finds it is more likely that this was indeed the working floor, and when the house was deserted for a time probably nomadic tribesmen went in and turned everything over looking for loot, but missing the flint cache. The presence of similar rough stones at the foot of wall A in House I would seem to bear out this interpretation rather than the theory of tumble, especially as grinders were found in the stones of I and nowhere else except in a similar position in IV. In both I and IV the other halves of the floors were of blackened sand with the pink sterile sand immediately below.

The Stone Industries (Figs. 3-5).

As no flint is available in Wadi Rumm the nearest source must be somewhere on the limestone desert plateau about 25 miles north. The very fine material used for some of the chipped stone industry must have been imported, or fetched, from outside the immediate surroundings. The other main material was quarzite which is obtainable locally. As expected, the granite and sandstone, also available in quantity locally, provided the material for the ground stone tools, the querns, grinders and so on.

The most characteristic implement of Abu Nekheileh is the arrowhead. These fine objects lie on the surface in profusion and were collected by Kirkbride and Harding in number when they found the site. We were fortunate in finding some in House IV.

Most of the chipped stone from the cache consisted of unretouched blades and some débitage. The raw material is of very fine quality, and the blades are straight with flat reverse faces.

Although the arrowheads are predominantly leaf-shaped, ranging in size from 4 to 12 cm. or more, a few are of the tanged variety. The overwhelming majority are leaf-shaped with their obverse faces bearing fine squamous pressure-flaking. Usually the retouch is confined to the obverse, but in a minority of examples the reverse is retouched under the ends and sometimes trimmed along one or both edges (Fig. 3. No. 1 & Fig. 4. Nos. 8-10, 12). As a type they

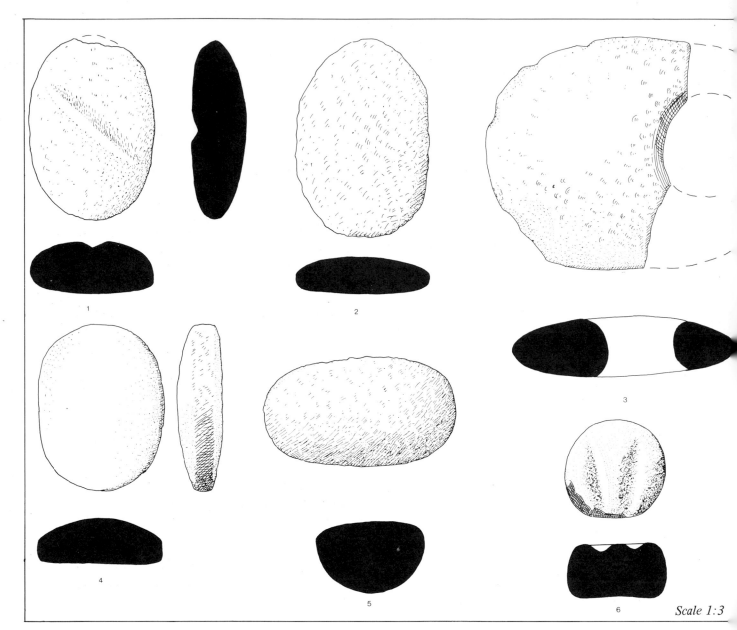

Fig. 5: Ground stone objects.

come into the PPNB at rather a late period and continue into the Pottery Neolithic where the evolved type becomes known in Syria, Palestine and Lebanon as 'Amuq points. At Beidha they are found first in Level IV and increase in number to the latest level, I. The arrowheads at Beidha are earlier than Abu Nekheileh, but the 'Amuq points seem to derive from the Pre-Pottery specimens. At Beidha they were not very numerous, they are described by Mortensen as Type 14a[4] and mentioned by Kirkbride.[5] This type also occurs in the later PPNB levels at Munhata[6] and during the same period at el-Khiam.[7] Fig. 3. No. 1, perhaps an unfinished spearhead, is the largest specimen from the sounding, but larger ones were found during the initial survey. Two tanged arrowheads were present, a broken specimen (Fig. 4. No. 11) which seems unfinished and re-used as a borer when the tip broke, and Fig. 4. No. 2, the latter akin to Mortensen's Type 19 of Beidha, but with unifacial retouch on the obverse edges only.

Several cores were found of which one is illustrated (Fig. 4. No. 18) all are the double-ended type common to the PPNB. The notched blades, borers, oblique points, blades and flakes illustrated all show affinities with the PPNB and need no detailed description. However, the saw-edged blade (Fig. 4. No. 24) is of a later type prevalent in the Pottery Neolithic. The conclusion that may be drawn from the flint industry of Abu Nekheileh is that it is later than, for example, Beidha, and, though still mainly in the Pre-Pottery tradition certain later elements are to be found. The leaf-shaped arrowheads, of which more perfect specimens were found on the surface than in the sounding, are a development and refinement of specimens appearing during the later part of the PPNB. They eventually become known as the 'Amuq points of the early Pottery cultures of the Levant.

The Finds are unexceptional. Rubbers, grinders, pounders and so on are perfectly ordinary (Fig. 5. Nos. 2, 4, 5). A single grinder (Fig. 5. No. 1) was used as a 'shaft-straightener', with a single diagonal groove across one surface: a common feature of the PPNB and indeed earlier. The stone counterpoise weight (Fig. 5. No. 3) is also known from the PPNB, for example at Beidha[8] and Munhatta.[9] The querns of Abu Nekheileh are of the usual simple oval type as found at Beidha and Jericho. A single flat circular rubber had two grooves across one surface (Fig. 5. No. 6): another feature that can be matched at Beidha. The single broken point (Fig. 4. No. 17) is undiagnostic. Many shells from the cache were not pierced, though a minority were finished beads and others were sawn across and cut off near the apex (Fig. 4. Nos. 13-15).

One class of object deserves special mention (Fig. 4. No. 16), a small grooved (?) bead-polisher. Roughly rectangular in shape with a polished groove down the centre of the long axis of one face with, in this case, a few lightly incised lines cut at right-angles from the groove. The reverse side bears a thick, rather deeply incised line down the centre with less deeply cut lines crossing it. This specimen is made of an unidentified micaceous stone. It represents another class of object that occurs in the PPNB and continues into the early Pottery Neolithic. At Beidha the specimens are larger, rougher, and always of micaceous material, but have not yet been analysed. They are roughly square or rectangular, really simply small flat slabs, with the central polished groove across one face, and, in almost every case, on the reverse a series of incised lines, some straight and regular and others not. It seems as if the lines could have been to provide a gripping, or non-skid, surface to prevent the slab from moving when used as a polisher - if indeed that was their function. Examples close to thos of Beidha in size, shape and material (larger than the Abu Nekeileh specimen), but of superior workmanship and decoration, have now been found at Abu Hureireh; another site with PPNB affinities in northern Syria[10]. These polishers became more refined as time went on. They became smaller, high-sided, made of hard stones and more amuletic in character. One specimen, though from PPNB levels, is recorded for Munhatta,[11] but although it does not appear to bear the characteristic incisions it is identical in shape to one found by the writer at Labweh in the Beqa'a of Lebanon.[12] The latter is decorated all over, except for the groove, with intricate incised designs. In short, from the evidence at Labweh, these objects seem to have reached their zenith in about 5900 B.C.; a time just before true pottery was introduced at that site. The specimen from Abu Nekheileh indicates again that this site was occupied during the transition period between the so-called Pre-Pottery and Pottery Neolithic.

Summary & Conclusion. Abu Nekheileh was not occupied for a very long time, or for long at a time, despite the fact that two forms of architecture are present. It was probably more in the nature of a base rather than a permanent settlement, to which an extended family returned seasonally, probably when the pistachio and acorns were ready for collection, and perhaps to gather a cereal harvest. No evidence is available for the latter. No sickle-blades were found, but, like the beduin today, the crops may have been taken by hand-pulling. The presence of very many querns, grinders and so on does not necessarily mean grinding cereals, but the possibility must be borne in mind in view of the prevalence of agriculture by this time. Further excavation would help here. The inhabitants undoubtedly relied heavily on hunting, the evidence of the large numbers of arrowheads shows that. Equally undoubtedly game was abundant in those days. Here again further excavation would produce faunal remains for analysis. The houses, both round and rectangular, seem to have been provided with rough stone working platforms covering about half the floor space in a room. In House IV there is evidence that grinding, flint working and bead-making took place on these platforms, an observation borne out by the fact that grinders were also found among similar stones in House I. Unfortunately the working platform in House IV together with its contents of querns, grinders and so on seems to have been rifled during the absence of the owners and everything is thrown about and out of place. House IV is alone in the tiny part of the settlement covered by the sounding in having more than one period of occupation.

The results of this very small sounding place Abu Nekheileh more firmly in its chronological setting than was possible when the site was first found. Stekelis had little comparative material to work with, but his tentative suggestion that Abu Nekheileh was contemporary with Jericho VIII/PNB must be refuted. Too many parallels with the PPNB are present, even with this small amount of material, to allow us to place the site so late. The arrowheads, close to the 'Amuq points, the saw-edged blade, and the refined (?) bead-polisher all point to a later date than the PPNB as represented, for example, at Beidha. On the other hand the parallels with the earlier sites are stronger than these. Abu Nekheileh must have been occupied for a fairly short time during the transition between the earlier and later Neolithic, a date in the last quarter of the 7th Millennium B.C. should not be too far out. As a transitional site its importance lies in the fact that it was occupied during the 1500 year gap in occupation between Pre-Pottery and Pottery Neolithic mooted for Palestine and Jordan. As one who does not agree that there was such a vast gap it is comforting to know that life was going on in Jordan during this period. It is possible that further excavation of this site would produce more parallels on which to work, and the missing faunal, botanical and carbon remains, but in the meantime even such a small sounding has given us enough to place Abu Nekheileh in that important transitional stage.

References.

1. A. S. Kirkbride, and G. Lankester Harding, *PEQ* (1947), pp. 7-27.
2. M. Stekelis, in Kirkbride & Harding, op. cit. p. 26.
3. D. Kirkbride, "Chronique Archéologique" *RB* (1960), p. 67.
4. P. Mortensen, *Acta Arch.* XLI (1970), Type A14., p. 25, fig. 16. i-k.
5. D. Kirkbride, *PEQ* (1966), fig. 11, nos. 5-7, p. 39.
6. J. Perrot, *Syria* XLIII (1966), fig. 2, nos 5, 6.
7. J. G. Echegaray, *Excavaciones on la Terraza de al Khiam* (Jordanian) II (Madrid, 1964), fig. XXXIV. 32, 33.
8. D. Kirkbride, op. cit., p. 36, fig. 9, nos. 5, 6.
9. J. Perrot, op. cit., fig. 5, no. 2.
10. A. Moore, Verbal communication.
11. J. Perrot op. cit., fig. 5, no. 8.
12. D. Kirkbride, Monograph for *Berytus*(in preparation).

THE UNIQUENESS OF JERICHO
By Peter Dorell

During the excavation and subsequent debate on the earliest occupation levels of Jericho, a view that seemed unquestionable was that Jericho could not be unique. If one sizeable walled settlement of PPNA date existed, there must surely be others; the rather fruitless controversies about whether or not the site was "urban" or "a city"[1] need not be considered in this context. The form of the settlement, the developed technology of the building, especially of the defences, and the implicit stability of the social organization, all seemed to denote the existence of other such towns, even of a hierarchy of villages, and of a long period of technical evolution. Archaeologists in the area were on the whole confident that such would emerge in subsequent surveys and excavations, although it was likely that much of the expected evidence would lie in the basal levels of large tells in the Levant. Numbers of PPNA sites, of different sizes and complexity, have of course since been discovered, but none, it seems fair to say, have been comparable with Jericho.

Now, twenty years after the Jericho excavations, the original premise can perhaps be questioned. Was Jericho, after all, *sui generis*? And if so, what unique set of circumstances allowed its generations of inhabitants, unlike others of their period, the time and energy and impetus to make such investment of labour in buildings?

The first and most obvious circumstance to examine was its proximity to the perennial spring of 'Ain es Sultan. It can be assumed that in some form or other it was flowing then as now. If there was no active spring, the position of the settlement makes no sense at all. It can also be assumed that its point of emergence had changed little before it was displaced eastward by the construction of the present road skirting and partially cutting through the eastern flank of the tell. A photograph of about 1890 shows it emerging from a niche at the base of the eastern side of the tell[2]. No doubt a deep sounding in or near Site H would show whether its original point of emergence was within the PPNA walls, as seems likely, but such an excavation might change the position of its present emergence, and even perhaps its flow, and would certainly be extremely unpopular locally.

How far the spring's output, and the variations in its flow, have changed or fluctuated over nine or ten thousand years is much more difficult to estimate. Nowadays at least the flow reflects the rainfall in the Judaean Hills with an interval of only one or two days, rising to a maximum of about 0.37 cubic metres per second after heavy rain. However, even at the end of the dry season, its flow is still about 0.26 cubic metres per second[3]. It may be assumed therefore that maximum flow conditions result from an over-topping of a larger reservoir aquifer from which the base-flow is maintained. This aquifer, it is believed, runs right up to the watershed of the hills through strata of Sennonian chalk and limestones,[4] being thereby replenished by the higher and less variable rainfall of the summits. Periods of comparative aridity of the sort suggested by Butzer[5], and used by Blake[6] to explain some early changes in settlement patterns in Palestine, might therefore have had little effect on average flow conditions, diminishing only the volumes of maximum flow. Periods of less rainfall would mean that isohyets would migrate uphill, and the summits, and thus the aquifer, would be the last places to be affected; and the size of the aquifer itself might serve to smooth out the effects of small scale climatic variations on the stream-flow.

If these suppositions are valid, they attest the existence of a constant water supply at Jericho, one requisite for its stability over long periods of its occupation, at a time when elsewhere in the Levant and in the Near East generally, settlement was still relatively ephemeral.

Another factor which might have had a considerable effect on the conomy of the early town was the way the original stream emerged and dispersed. 'Ain Duk and the Wadi Qilt, the neighbouring water courses, are both occasionally reinforced by direct run-off from the slopes of the Judaean hills which 'Ain es Sultan is not. Although these slopes are within a rain shadow, they attain present day rainfall averages of 200 to 500 mm, much of it in the form of violent downpours. Where these springs debouch down the hill-foot fans, they run in deeply incised beds. There seems to be no such incision associated with the spring of 'Ain es Sultan, although evidence may have been destroyed during the millennia of ploughing and levelling in the oasis. Nor are there any crenellations in the contour lines downstream of the spring to suggest the vestige of incisions. The combination of the rate of bank-full discharge and of the local gradient (50 m over 1.5 km, i.e. 0.03 m per m or 1:30) classifies the stream as a type characterised by straight or braided, rather than meandering, flow[7]. Of the two, braiding seems more likely. Apart from the lack of any sign of an incised channel and the lack of reinforcment by direct run-off, there is a relatively low ratio, 7 to 5, of maximum to minimum flow. It is therefore difficult to envisage the sort of devastating flood-flows which can carve deep channels in desert wadis.

The spring then might well have issued in much the same way as it does today - with considerable force and carrying little sediment except at maximum flow. The ground downstream of the spring slopes quite evenly in a direction 13º–15º south of east, and across this slope the stream might have spread out, splitting and rejoining. Some channels no doubt would have become lost through percolation and evaporation, and others perhaps would have formed open pools and swamps, although the slope of the ground was surely too steep to have allowed anything more than very local stretches of standing water. Admittedly, standing spring-pools are found in quite steeply sloping wadi beds, e.g. in the Wad Ghazzeh[8], but these seem to occupy scour hollows resulting from massive flash floods, which it is suggested above could not have occurred at Jericho. Some part of the stream would no doubt have found its way to the Jordan, especially in winter when local rains, at present about 140 mm average per annum, and lowered evaporation would have swollen the stream and reduced losses to the air en route.

It is not easy to make even a guess at the extent of the oasis that the waters of the spring, if they took the form suggested above, would create. Vita-Finzi and Higgs[9] estimate an area of approximately 980 hectares of irrigated land around Jericho at the present time. This is of course achieved by sophisticated and carefully controlled gravity irrigation; but to counter-balance this, allowance must be made for the vastly greater proportion of the water that is drawn off for domestic purposes by the modern population. It is interesting to note also in their diagram that the furthest limit of irrigation lies almost exactly in the direction, a few degrees south of east, which was calculated above as lying across the generalised contours downstream of the spring. They also show an extension of irrigation south-wards almost along the -250m contour. This may well have been engineered in order to water the modern town of Jericho, the position of which was probably influenced by the position of the Roman road which reached the valley south of the Wadi Qilt. With little or no physical traces remaining as evidence, one can only say that the oasis water-ed by 'Ain es Sultan in Neolithic times must have been smaller than that now formed by artificial irrigation, even perhaps less than half the size.

There are however many other perennial springs in the Levant, and many other fans in the valley with non-saline soils covering the sterile Lisan marls (10, 11). What is uncommon, if not unique, is the combination of a fresh water supply without great annual variation, and of a topography whereby the waters might have spread over a considerable local area.

What then might have been the effect of these circumstances on early settlement? In the first place, it is a well-established principle that in a hunting and gathering economy the greater the diversity of types of territory that can be exploited the better. Jericho had such diversity to a marked degree. During its early phases, the site would have commanded, within a few kilometres, stretches of shaded riverine country; open wadi-cut steppe country along the flanks of the hills; and, to the west, the rocky and precipitous hills of Judaea. All the food animals whose bones have been identified from the PPNA levels are native to one or other of these habitats.

More important than this, however, is what could be called a 'reverse-transhumance' effect among the wild population. In much of the Near East the hungry season is in the summer. Water is scarce, vegetation dries up, and game animals not only become more elusive and difficult to catch, partly because the females no longer have very young offspring, but also yield leaner carcases. This need not have applied at Jericho. The water supply was constant, and although hill and steppe vegetation would have withered in summer, the oasis plants and trees should not have suffered in the same way, and would therefore have attracted more of the normally peripheral animals. During the hottest and most exhausting months of the year, hunting might have been easier rather than more difficult.

Much has been written in recent years about the history and processes of the domestication of both plants and animals, and many accepted theories have been challenged if not overthrown. In some cases the arguments seem to be no more than attempts to replace simple unproven theories by complicated but equally unproved theories. At Jericho however some of the requirements usually postulated for domestication need not have applied. The territory of food animals for at least a part of the year may have been limited to a small area; even animals of the open steppe and the hills could have been brought to within easy hunting or trapping range by the need for water and the attractions of shade and vegetation. An element of natural control over the movements of animals was thus present, a control which could have been extended by man without any great revolution in economy or technology. For instance, an obvious first step might have been to capture and retain a number of animals during the winter and spring when grass and water on the steppe and hills began to attract game away from the oasis. Since this is the breeding season for some of the species, this could have led on to retention of the young to form a domesticated nucleus, topped up by annual capture.

Such speculations are of course not susceptible of proof. However, they suggest a mechanism whereby, in the particular environment of Jericho, a hunting and collecting economy might have passed into one with elements of domestication in a sedentary situation. A degree of protection for the domesticants is naturally implied in this process, a problem surely of no great difficulty in a community with the techniques of building and with a tradition of hunting. Clutton-Brock[12] in fact remarks on the scarcity of the bones of large predators at Jericho. This may be because the bones of such animals were not brought within the walls, but an additional reason might have been that their numbers were kept down by purposeful killing.

The element of selective breeding often taken as one of the criteria of domestication would naturally be minimal during a process of partial control, and would have become effective only during later periods when full domestication became widespread. Whether the known changes in average size, and in fact diminution of average size, of most domesticants between the early Neolithic and the Bronze Age is necessarily an effect of domestication has been challenged. [13] However this is resolved, one consideration that might have influenced the process should be borne in mind. In the Levant lowlands, especially in summer, killed meat stays edible, by modern standards, only for a day or two. There is no way of judging the Neolithic or Bronze Age palate nor resistance to potentially toxic micro-organisms, but most of the higher animals, apart from a few specialised species, prefer fresh meat; some, as any owner of a domestic cat knows, insist on it. The optimum size of a killed animal might therefore have been strongly influenced by the size of the group normally sharing one carcass. The often referred-to Kung bushmen solve what is a similar problem by an extensive gift relationship, but this is in a hunting community where the labour of hunting a large animal might not be very different from that needed to hunt a small one. Flannery[14] quotes figures that show that an auroch, one of the animals hunted in Neolithic Jericho, would have divided into 400 edible portions of 1 kilogram each - a formidable amount of meat, surely needing a very extended group to dispose of it or a great deal of wastage. With full domestication, however, a beast would come to represent a certain amount of time and labour, and, presumably, a known proportion of the food reserve. It might therefore have become economically desirable for a grazing area to support a large number of small animals rather than a small number of larger ones, an obvious incentive to breeding selectively for smaller size. A similar incentive came into being at the unknown time when domestic animals became not only a reservoir of food but also units of value or exchange.*

Consideration of the remains of food animals, of plant remains, and of carbonised material from early Jericho has led to the conclusion that "the Pre-pottery Neolithic was largely, though not entirely, dependent upon hunted wild animals, with some local cultivation and the use of existing vegetation. By the time of the Early Bronze Age there was great expansion of herds of domesticated animals, extensive cultivation, and the need to travel farther afield for supplies of fuel and structural timber". [15] This statement remains true for the Neolithic even if, as I have suggested, the line between 'wild' and 'domesticated' might be shaded to include 'wild but seasonally concentrated', 'wild but with a part of the flocks or herds kept in captivity annually', and 'wild but with a reservoir of young captive animals topped up annually from the wild stock'.

As elsewhere in the Near East, the domestication of plants went on at the same time as the domestication of animals.[16] A few grains of emmer and of two-rowed hulled barley, some fig pips and three broken pieces of legume were recovered from the PPNA levels. [17] (It must be remembered that the excavations took place before techniques of total seed and organic fragment recovery had been developed. The discovery of such small objects depended entirely on the sharp eyes of the workmen and supervisors. In fact is is remarkable that any were noticed at all).

As with animals, the process of domestication of plants might have been aided by the particular circumstances of Jericho. Given the pattern of banks, back-swamps, and even natural levees which could have occurred if the stream were braided, a rich and varied flora might be expected. Moreover such a pattern would have provided plant habitats of differing degrees of ground moisture, shade, and soil texture, such that any naturally or deliberately introduced

---

* A well-known story among African anthropologists concerns a herdsman of the Masai being urged by a veterinary officer to reduce his large herd of semi-starved cattle, and to concentrate on quality rather than quantity. The herdsman's retort was "if I give you one brand-new pound note, will you give me two old and crumpled ones in exchange?"

species might have found a suitable niche in the environment, a niche which might have been artificially extended without great labour if the plant proved valuable.

Van Zeist[18] maintains that Jericho should be excluded from discussion of early agriculture because dry farming was impossible due to the low rainfall, artificial irrigation had not been developed until long after the early phases, and food grains could therefore only have been obtained by trade. However, there seems to be as little reason for trying to put a date to the 'invention' of irrigation as there does to put one to the 'invention' of agriculture. Given a natural system of stream distributaries, it would surely not call for inventiveness of a high order to extend these distributaries laterally, and thus to increase the amount of fertile land if only by increasing the stream bank areas. The process in the Jericho setting has none of the complexity and organisation necessary for the low-gradient diversions of Mesopotamia, nor for the basin irrigation of the Nile valley.

Jericho must always have offered high fertility and an equable winter climate. Farmers there today can harvest two or three crops a year of many plants, especially vegetables, and the seasonality of agriculture so marked in the rainfall areas of the Levant, is far less apparent. If this were so, even to a lesser degree, in Neolithic times, two major problems of early farming might have been less severe. Firstly the rigidity of the "farmers' calendar" would have been less marked; and secondly, there would have been less need to develop the techniques and facilities for storage of harvested or collected food grains and seed.

One can suggest, then, that the uniqueness of Jericho may partly be explained by the opportunities the site offered for securing animal and vegetable foodstuffs, not by new or revolutionary economic techniques but because of the comparative ease with which food production could have been introduced without drastic change in a pre-existing social or economic framework, and the food supply increased without a great initial or continuing input of labour.

It has been suggested by Anati[19] and by others, that Jericho's apparent prosperity and stability were largely a result of trade. Anati suggests three commodities in which the settlement might have traded - salt, bitumen, and sulphur. Trade may certainly have played a part in the settlement's economy; but although the three commodities suggested might have been important in the general Neolithic economy, it is difficult to envisage them as the basis of the settlement's economy, nor is Jericho particularly well placed for their exploitation. Sodium chloride can be extracted from the Lisan marls, together with a group of other salts, simply by mixing the marl with water and evaporating the resultant solution.[20] A simpler way of obtaining it however would have been to scrape the rocks around the edge of the Dead Sea, or of course to construct simple salt pans, although these would not have been so easily made, nor so productive, as pans at the southern end of the Sea, which is shallower and more saline.

Bitumen and sulphur could also, Anati suggests, have been found at or near the shores of the Sea. But Jericho is twelve kilometres from the nearest shore, a considerable distance to carry bulky commodities. The Sea may have been larger in Neolithic times, but transport problems would still have been great. If trade were the main basis of the economy, the settlement would surely have been more conveniently sited five or six kilometres to the south-east - still on the 'Ain es Sultan stream but considerably closer to the source of raw materials. Moreover, at least some of the bituminous material found at Jericho was in the form of bituminous limestone, the most accessible outcrop of which is at Nebi Musa, some eight kilometres to the south. More important than these arguments is the fact that, sited as it was, Jericho neither had easier access to, nor could better control the sources of commodities, than could a foraging expedition from any settlement on the area. It is easy to suppose that Jericho, firmly established upon a basis of food collection and production, could collect these commodities for its own use and as a medium of exchange for desirable goods from far away. Or it might very well have acted as an entrepot for these or other commodities. It is rather more difficult to envisage its obviously stable economy as having relied predominantly on such trade.

If the availability, through the exploited advantages, of plentiful food and drink is indeed a principal cause of the uniqueness of Jericho, it is necessary to examine what the demands of the population would be. This requires first some evidence of the size of that population in early Neolithic times. Unfortunately, both questions involve calculations for which there are few data and for which the methods of calculation themselves are in dispute. What can be done is to approach the two problems, which are of course complementary, from several directions, using whatever evidence there is, and to hope thus to arrive at upper and lower limits for population size, and to estimate whether potential food supplies would have supported such a population.

The walled Pre-pottery site covers some four hectares (10 acres). There is no way of knowing whether or how far settlement spread beyond the walls: there was certainly some such spread in PPNB times. Nothing of any significance has been found west or north of the tell, but there might have been extra-mural settlement to the south or east, all traces of which have been lost under later intensive agriculture. For the walled area Kathleen Kenyon [21] estimates a population of two or three thousand, i.e. 500 - 750 per hectare, basing this figure on population densities of modern Arab villages. On the other hand, Adams, [22] after discussing the complexity of the problem, estimates population figures of only 100 per hectare for early walled towns in the Uruq region, admittedly in quite different natural and economic environments. This estimate allows for the fact that during the periods he is considering, Late Uruq to Early Dynastic I, excavation has shown that a considerable proportion of the areas of the larger towns was occupied by public and ceremonial buildings; the proportions might have been quite different at Jericho, as is discussed below. For smaller, unwalled settlements he estimates a population density of 150 per hectare.

An attempt to base estimates of population upon the Jericho excavations themselves brings one up against the fact that no complete house plan of the PPNA was exposed. Apparently the most complete house plan revealed of the PPNA is the nearly circular dwelling in Site M.[23] This had an approximate diameter of 5 metres, and therefore an area of about 20 square metres. Doubling this area to allow for yard space and immediate outbuildings gives 40 square metres. Thus a space of 4 hectares would allow for about 1,000 dwellings close-packed. Allowing a modest one-third of the total enclosed area for roads, open spaces, pens, and towers, this total would fall to 660 dwellings. If each dwelling were occupied by a nuclear family of five (and there is of course not the least proof that this was the case) the total population would have been of the order of 3,000 to 3,500, i.e. 750 to 850 per hectare. For purposes of comparison, the Greater London Council aim for a nett residential density of 336 persons per hectare in the more densely populated parts of London.[24]

Obviously numerical data from such diverse sources, that by different methods of calculation can produce results ranging from 100 to 850 per hectare and a total population from 400 to 3,500, are open to considerable doubt. But with the limited aim of assessing the feasibility of a self-sufficient Neolithic community at Jericho, the figures might be taken as representing the probable minimum and maximum population. During the long occupation of the tell, even during the Neolithic, the population may in fact have fluctuated between, or even beyond, these extremes.

Certainly the impression given by the amount of building during the life of the tower at Jericho is of a fairly closely-packed community, its population perhaps to be measured in thousands rather than in hundreds. There is also the matter of the extent of defensive building, and of the labour force involved. Even the first phase of the PPNA wall was a substantial affair more than 2 metres thick, and on the west side it is still preserved to a height of about 4 metres.[23] If its circuit were completed only as far east as the present spring, its length would have been about 600 metres. At a constant minimum height of 4 metres, this would represent about 4,500 cubic metres of limestone (allowing 10% for interstices), or, at limestone's average specific gravity of 2.7, something over 12,000 metric tons.

A modern builder of dry-stone walls expects to construct 4.5 to 5m of 1.4m high wall in a working day given good stone.[25] At an average thickness of 50 cm, this amounts to about 3.3 cubic metres. By this standard 4,500 cubic metres would require 1360 man/days. This is a surprisingly modest requirement - about a week's work for 200 able-bodied men - and clearly well within the capabilities of even the minimum population estimate. To plan and organize the enterprise, to clear the site and quarry the stone, must have called for considerably greater numbers, but, it seems likely, still of the same order of magnitude.*

The complementary question of estimating what size of population the oasis and the surrounding country could have supported presents equally large areas of doubt. In the first place, there is no clear agreement about aptimum food intake and energy expenditure even in modern populations.[26] Secondly there is a scarcity of the basic information needed to calculate such figures for modern peasant farmers.[27] Thirdly, the evidence of the

---

* The same considerations apply to the walls of the later phases. It is interesting to note that the volume of the ditch, which is associated with the second phase, were it to have followed the same circuit, would be more than 6500 cubic metres, i.e. about 18,000 tons. This would have supplied more than enough material to complete the second and third phases, so there is the possibility that the ditch was as much a quarry as an addition to the defensive system. It is not known where the rock for the first phase of the wall was quarried, but if more of the boulders were found to be water-worn in this than in later phases, it would suggest that some of the material was collected rather than quarried. Local minor wadis, and the upper parts of the fan, are still strewn with such rocks, so it is not impossible that for the first phase the material was collected rather than quarried.

nature of the food resources of Neolithic man based on animal and vegetable remains must be far from complete. For example, few if any bird bones were found in the early levels at Jericho: yet today in such an area as Tell Fara, where shooting is now forbidden, game birds such as partridge (*Alectoris barbara*), quail (*Coturnix coturnix*), and bustard (*Chlamydotis undulata*) abound, [28] any of which could be caught by traditional trapping methods. And fourthly, for the reasons discussed earlier, it is difficult to make even an informed guess at the site's area of exploitation of vegetable resources (domesticated or not) or at the population of game animals within hunting distance. So any estimates must again be regarded as bracketing possibilities rather than as probabilities.

Modern opinion gives the optimum gross calorie intake of an adult engaged in heavy manual work as between 3500 and 4000 per day.[29] If allowance is made for a proportion of lighter work, for the slightly lower requirements in hot climates and possibly smaller stature, [27] the lower figure might be assumed. Using the range of population estimates taken above, 400 to 3000, and allowing for 50% of the population being juvenile or for other reasons needing only half the adult average, total daily Calorie requirements fall between one and eight million.

The proportion of meat to vegetable food in the diet of the Neolithic population can, again, only be guessed at; a one-to-one ratio on a calorie basis is assumed here for the sake of simplicity, although this is a somewhat higher proportion of meat than is enjoyed by modern hunting populations in the same sort of country. Again using the figures quoted by Flannery, [14] wheat and barley supply about 3400 Calories per kilogram of edible material, while goat, gazelle, auroch and pig supply an average of something over 2000. Within this rough outline, equal nourishment values per calorie might be assumed, since although meat contains more fat and slightly more protein, cereal alone contains carbohydrate.

Total daily meat intake on this basis would therefore be of the order of 250 kg for the lower estimated population and 2000 for the upper. For cereal food, the figures would be about 150 and 1200 kg. Using the flimsy evidence of the small sample represented by animal skeletons found in the Pre-pottery A and B, [30] the meat diet consisted of 8% goat flesh, 6% gazelle, 73% Bos, and 13% pig (goat and gazelle provide about 25 kg of edible meat per carcase, auroch 400 and pig 70.) [4]

A population of 400, then, would consume in rounded figures 300 goat, 200 gazelle, 160 bos, and 170 pig per annum, while a population of 3000 would need 2500 goat, 1700 gazelle, 1300 bos and 1400 pig (the figures in each case representing half the total Calorie needs of the population). At most, this means that the smaller population would have to catch fewer than three animals a day, and the larger fewer than 19. Assuming, as previously suggested, that the circumstances of Jericho would allow of hunting and trapping nearby, rather than necessitating extensive long-range running-down and stalking, these bags might have been achieved by quite small numbers of hunters. Allowing ten to an average hunting party, some 30 for the smaller population and 200 for the larger, i.e. about 15% of the active population, would have been involved.

These figures represent minima. In a great many societies, past and present, hunting and the hunting group play an important part in the social structure of the community, and cannot be considered exclusively in economic terms. This may, for all we know, have been true of Jericho, but at least it can be seen that the provision of animal food was well within the capabilities of the community, so long as the animals were there to be hunted.

On the question of the extent of the hunting territory, and the animal populations, the imponderables become so great and the information so uncertain, that it seems better not to attempt a guess. On the basis of site catchment analysis, Vita Finzi and Higgs[9] suggest that the area within reach of the site would have been so unproductive of game that the inhabitants, before animal domestication, must have lived largely on a vegetable diet. This may have been so, but if account is taken of the compensatory nature of the local regime as suggested earlier, and of the possibility of retention of animals during the winter, local productivity might have been considerably higher.

The vegetable part of the diet would presumably have consisted of wild and cultivated cereals, nuts, fruits, seeds, tubers, and the leaves and non-woody parts of a wide variety of plants. Of all these, it is possible to make a rough estimate of cereal quantities only, bearing in mind that these might have formed only a small part of the total food resource. If cereal were the main vegetable food, then the daily requirement for populations of 400 and 3000 would be, as suggested earlier, 150 and 1200 kg, or about 55 and 440 tons per annum respectively. Zohary [31] records that stands of wild cereals in Galilee yield, in rainy years, 500 to 800 kg per hectare, while unmechanised plough cultivation yields 500 to 1500 kg. Taking the lower figure, a population of 400 would need about 100 hectares to provide half their food requirements, and a population of 3000, 880 hectares. Under early Mesopotamian conditions, Adams [32] calculated a yield of about 600 kg per hectare from irrigated land. 500 kg per hectare would therefore represent a low figure in this quite different regime.

These estimates would be further modified when considering Jericho if one takes into account the possibility mentioned earlier of two or three crops per year. In the simplest terms, two crops a year would reduce the necessary areas to support the two postulated populations to 50 and 440 hectares, three crops a year to 33 and 290. As usual, these estimates are of the crudest. However, since all have been based on minimum resources and maximum requirements, they at least represent evidence that possible available land resources and possible populations are of the same order of magnitude. For purposes of comparison, it might be mentioned that in 1939, before very much mechanisation had taken place, the population of the Jericho area was 4200, [33] and it was a net exporter of food crops. By 1948 'Ain es Sultan not only irrigated rather more land, but provided domestic water for 22,000 refugees in the nearby camp.

The several lines of reasoning discussed suggest that the site could have supported a population substantially higher than the minimum figure of four hundred during the earlier phases of the walled town. The precise number is unimportant but a population of the order of two thousand seems a reasonable estimate by any of the criteria used. Only a massive lateral excavation of the tell could settle the question, an enterprise not at all to be justified on any other grounds. More important than precise figures however are the possibilities that the site could have supported a settled population without great seasonal variations in food supply, or in the labour needed to win it. Moreover the particular geomorphological, climatic, and hydrological circumstances of the area might have allowed of the introduction or development of a food producing economy by a series of fairly minor innovations, none, it may be surmised, of a sufficiently large or revolutionary character to demand a qualitative change in the economic way of life or social structure of the community. It has often been assumed that the establishment of sedentary, food-producing communities, particularly where this involves irrigation and fortification, implies social structures different from those existing in hunting and collecting economies. But the line between the two sorts of economy is no longer regarded as so definite as was once thought, and while very little is known of the structure of Neolithic society, even less, surely, is known of the society of earlier periods. There is little reason to think that their systems of social relationships, kinship, and governance were less complete and binding than in later times, or that the allegiances and responsibilities of the one sort of economy would not extend into the other. Early Jericho must have existed at one of the hinge-points of this change and its early date and complexity - in fact its uniqueness - may have reflected the impetus given it by its particular environment.

London, February 1975.

References
1.   R. J. Braidwood, *Antiquity*, xxxi (1957), pp. 73ff.
2.   H. A. Harper, *Walks in Palestine* (The Religious Tract Society, London, 1894).
3.   G. S. Blake, *Geology and Water Resources of Palestine* (Jerusalem, 1928).
4.   *Atlas of Israel* (Jerusalem, 1970).
5.   K. W. Butzer, *Erdkunde* xi (1957), pp.
6.   I. Blake, *Advancement of Science* (June 1969),
7.   L. B. Leopold, M. G. Wolman, and J. P. Miller. *Fluvial Processes in Geomorphology* (San Francisco, 1964).
8.   D. Price Williams, *British Western Negev Expedition Report* (duplicated, 1973).
9.   C. Vita Finzi and E. S. Higgs, *PPS* xxxvi (1970), pp. 1ff.
10.   C. Vita Finzi, *PEQ* (Jan-June, 1964), pp. 19ff.
11.   A. Reifenberg, *The Soils of Palestine* (London, 1947).
12.   J. Clutton-Brock *in The Domestication and Exploitation of Plants and Animals*. (*eds* P. J. Ucko and G. W. Dimbleby. London, 1969), pp. 337 ff.
13.   M. R. Jarman and P. F. Wilkinson, *in Papers in Economic Prehistory* (*ed* E. S. Higgs, Cambridge, 1972), pp.
14.   K. V. Flannery, *in The Domestication and Exploitation of Plants and Animals* pp. 73 ff.
15.   A. C. Western, *Levant III,* 1971, pp. 31 ff.
16.   K. M. Kenyon, *Advancement of Science* 26 (1969-70), pp. 1 ff.
17.   M. Hopf, *in The Domestication and Exploitation of Plants and Animals,* pp. 355 ff.
18.   W. van Zeist in *The Domestication and Exploitation of Plants and Animals,* pp. 35 ff.
19.   E. Anati, *B.A.S.O.R.,* 167 (1962), pp. 25 ff.
20.   I. W. Cornwall. Personal communication.
21.   K. M. Kenyon, *Advancement of Science,* (July 1960), pp. 118 ff.

22.   R. McC. Adams and H. J. Nissen, *The Uruk Countryside* (Chicago, 1972).

23.   K. M. Kenyon, *Archaeology in the Holy Land* (London, 1960), Pl. 5B.

24.   P. Hall, *The World Cities* (London, 1966).

25.   Miss Audland, Secretary, Stewartry of Kirkcudbright Dry Stane Dyking Committee, Personal Communication.

26.   J. V. G. A. Durnin, et al, *Nature,* Vol. 242, 1973.

27.   J. V. G. A. Durnin and R. Passmore, *Energy, Work and Leisure* (London, 1967).

28.   Personal observation.

29.   *F.A.O. Calorie Requirements* (London, 1950).

30.   J. Clutton-Brock, *Levant III* (1971), pp. 41 ff.

31.   D. Zohary in *The Domestication and Exploitation of Plants and Animals,* pp. 47 ff.

32.   R. McC. Adams, 136 (1962), *Science.*

33.   *Admiralty Handbook to Palestine and Transjordan* (London, 1939-45).

A HOARD OF FLINT KNIVES FROM THE NEGEV
By Joan Crowfoot Payne

I have been meaning to publish the flints described below for almost as many years as I have known Kathleen Kenyon; they were found in Palestine during the years before the war, when she began her work in the Near East, and this volume seems a proper vehicle. My note is offered with much admiration and affection.

In 1935 three magnificent flint knives were brought into the Rockefeller Museum in Jerusalem; they were said to have been found by Bedu in the Negev. In the same year, I visited the area, and was shown the find-spot by the local Bedu. It was planned at the time to make further investigations, but the political situation deteriorated, and a further visit was not possible. The knives remained in the Museum, but have not previously been published. Through the very kind and efficient help of the late Miss Ephrath Yeivin, of Tel Aviv University, and Mr Dan Gazit, of Kibutz Gevuloth, I was able to revisit the district in 1974, and to re-identify the site. The Department of Antiquities and Museums of Israel has kindly given me permission to publish the knives.

Tell Tuwail is a small fairly steep hill, about 2 km. west of Bir el Mu'alaqa (Be'er Osnath), in the Wadi Gaza (Nahal Habsor). The knives were found at the foot of this hill, where it rises from a small terrace towards the south. We found no early pottery on the surface on or near the hill, and the few flints that we collected are not diagnostic. There are numerous surface sites dating from the Chalcolithic period onwards in the district, and the lack of any such indications on and near Tell Tuwail suggests that the group of knives were buried together intentionally in a convenient hillside, a suggestion supported by the fact that they show no signs of use.

The knives (Pl. II) are made from tabular flint, light greyish-brown, fairly coarse-grained. They are identical in form, lanceolate, and exceptionally large, measuring 42.2 x 8.7 cm., 34. 1x8.7 cm., and 33. 7x7.6 cm. The sides taper to rounded ends, one end, the tip, being much broader than the other; the cross-sections are a very thin pointed oval, slightly thicker at the narrower end, the butt. One face is almost entirely covered by cortex, ground down until the flint is beginning to show through in places near the edge; marks of grinding in various directions, most clearly diagonal or longitudinal, are easily visible. The other face is entirely covered by flat retouch, not very carefully done, worked from both edges, with a final fine retouch round the edge along both sides and round the tip. The narrower thicker butt, presumably for tang or handle, has no final edge retouch. In all three knives, the edge shows no trace of use.

There are, as yet, no precise parallels for these remarkable knives, and it is not possible to date them with certainty. There is, however, one closely comparable dagger or knife. It was found by Bedu while clearing out deposits from the cave of Umm Qala'a, in the Wadi Khareitun.[1] This knife, measuring 31. 8x7.0xl.0cm., is lanceolate, pointed at both ends, slightly thicker at the butt than at the tip. It is made on tabular flint. One face is largely covered by cortex, and is retouched along one edge and round the tip. The other face is covered by rather coarse flat retouch, with finer retouch along both edges stopping 8cm. above the butt. There is no trace of grinding on this knife, but in other respects it closely resembles the specimens from Tell Tuwail. Neuville made a sounding in the cave of Umm Qala'a in 1928, to try to establish the date of the knife; no other specimens were found, but Chalcolithic pottery was found both in the remaining deposit and outside the cave, where it had presumably been thrown by the Bedu.[2]

A Chalcolithic date for the Tuwail knives would be entirely consistent with the use of tabular flint on such a massive scale. Very large flakes, struck from tabular flint, with cortex entirely covering the dorsal face, were used for fan scrapers, a factory site for the production of which is known in the Wadi Gaza.[3]

Two more daggers or knives are known, both of which, from their contexts, could date from the Chalcolithic period. One was found in the cave of et-Taouamin,[4] the other at Byblos.[5] Both are relatively small, measuring a little more than 10cm. in length. Both are partly polished, one has a straight base, the other is tanged, neither is made on tabular flint.

The size of the Tell Tuwail knives immediately suggests a connection with Egypt, where lanceolate knives or daggers of a comparable magnitude were made throughout the Predynastic period.[6] There are certainly close resemblances, though the forms are not precisely the same. The cortex is generally entirely removed from Egyptian knives, but tabular flint was certainly used.[7] In Egypt, the largest knives, some nearly 40cm. long, date from the Amratian (Naqada I) period; here too the rather coarse retouch of the Tuwail knives would be more in place than later in the Predynastic period. The exquisite serially flaked knives, made by grinding the surface before the final flaking, belong to the Gerzean (Naqada II) period.[8] In both periods, fine retouch round the edge, usually producing a minute serration, extends to just above the butt, which is slightly thicker than the body and forms a tang or handle. Thus, while the Tell Tuwail knives are certainly not Egyptian imports, they may well have been inspired by Egyptian models, at a time when Egypt and the Negev are known to have been in contact.

References

1.   R. Neuville, *Syria,* XII (1931), pp. 26-9.
2.   R. Neuville, op. cit., pp. 28-9; R. de Vaux, "Palestine during the Neolithic and Chalcolithic periods", *CAH* fasc. 47 (1966), p. 31.
3.   E. MACDONALD, *Beth Pelet* II, p. 10.
4.   R. Neuville, *JPOS,* X (1930), pp. 64-75.
5.   J. Cauvin, "Les Outillages Néolithiques de Byblos et du Littoral Libanais", in M. DUNAND, *Fouilles de Byblos* IV, pp. 180-1.
6.   e.g. W.M.F. PETRIE & J.E. QUIBELL, *Naqada & Ballas,* pl. LXXII.
7.   Bruce A. Bradley, "Predynastic Egyptian Flint Implements - an Inductive Technological Sequence", *Newsletter of Lithic Technology,* I, 3 (1972), p. 3.
8.   F.J.C. Spurrell, "The Flint Implements of Naqada", in W.M.F. PETRIE & J.E. QUIBELL, op. cit., pp. 57-8; W. M. F. PETRIE, *Diospolis Parva,* pp. 23-4; E. J. BAUMGARTEL, *The Cultures of Prehistoric Egypt* II, pp. 32, 38-41.

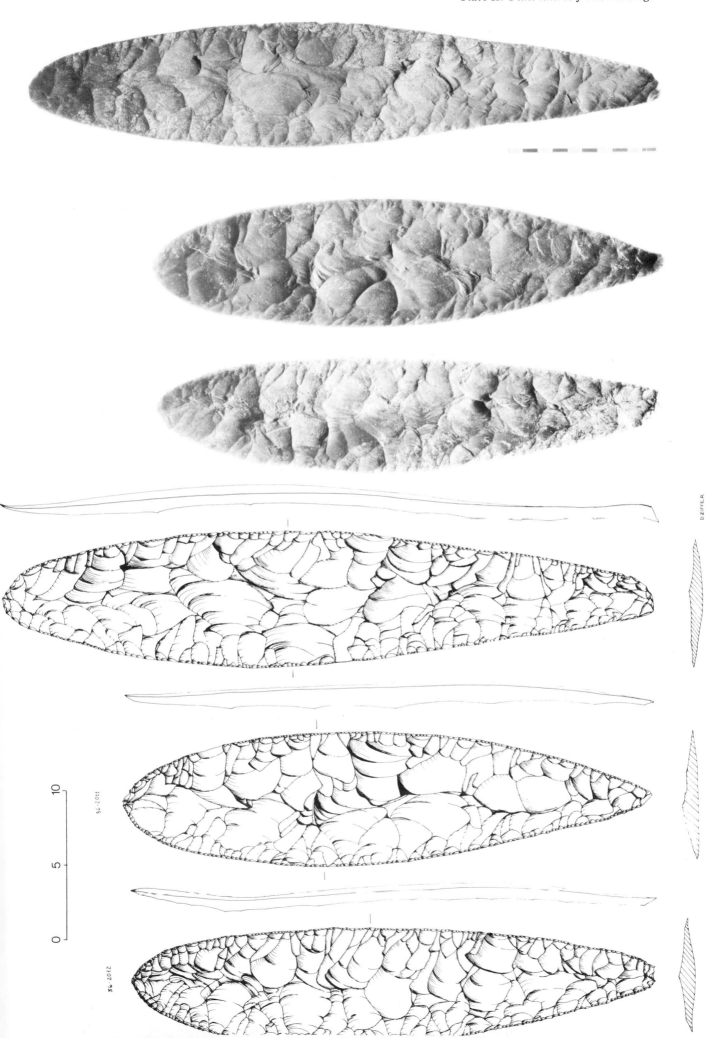

Plate II: Flint knives from the Negev.

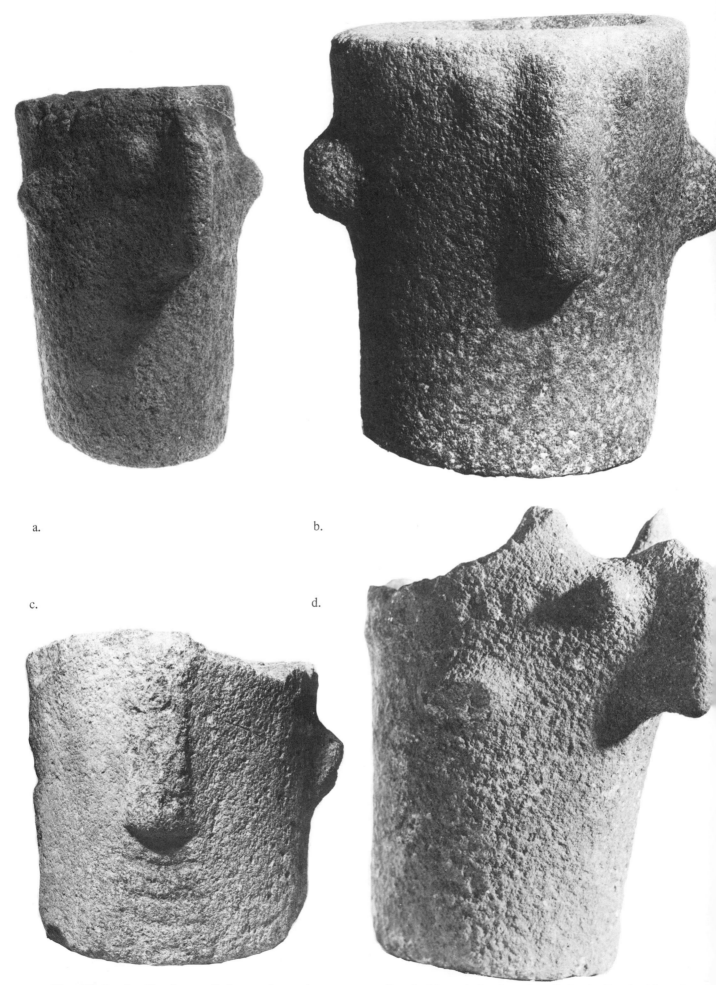

a.

b.

c.

d.

*Plate III: Basalt pillar figures, Golan: a. from a house context (height 28 cm.): b–d. surface finds : b. (height 40 cm.)
c. (height 28 cm.); d. (height 30 cm.)*

ASPECTS OF SYMBOLISM IN CHALCOLITHIC PALESTINE
by Claire Epstein.

It has long been accepted that the Chalcolithic age in Palestine was a period in which agriculture and stock-breeding had become basic to the economy. Ghassul was essentially a village of farmers, while at Beersheba the inhabitants likewise engaged in agriculture.[1] Recent excavations in the Golan have revealed a similar pattern.[2] At the same time there is abundant evidence of expertise in the arts at all the sites: painting, metal-working, ivory-carving and the like, to which sculpture in the round may be added. All of these were inspired by cultic beliefs, as was the case in contemporary Mesopotamia.[3] This axiom must constantly be borne in mind when attempting to evaluate the artistic expression of the period, no matter what the material to which craftsmanship was applied: everything had its own accepted inner meaning, including ossuaries for the dead, ceremonial equipment for temple rites, frescoed walls, propitious house-gods and on occasions the decoration on vessels in everyday use.

In the course of excavations at a number of sites in the Golan carried out during 1973-1976, schematic basalt figures were discovered, similar in type to others previously found on the surface in the same general area (Fig. 1: 1–2 and Plate III).[4] All are in the form of a short pillar, the top of which is modelled as a bowl, while on most there is a very prominent nose which commences high up below the bowl rim and extends to as much as half the height of the pillar, the ears frequently being shown in the form of knobs on either side of the head. On some of the smaller figures the nose is not unduly emphasised, but it is the sole facial feature shown. The excavated statues were found in Chalcolithic house complexes built close to the cultivated fields and the wide range of artifacts in the buildings points clearly to agriculture and allied pursuits. The finding of a similar pillar figure at the Chalcolithic site of Tell Turmus, in the Huleh Valley at the foot of the Golan scarp in the north[5] and also at Khirbet Ḥūtiyyc in the Wadi Samak in the south (Plate IIIb) lends added weight to the suggestion that this was a commonly-used form. Some pillar figures are portrayed with horns and other animal features, clearly associating them with sheep and goats and were no doubt believed to exert protective power over flocks and herds, while a naturalistically conceived basalt figure of a ram with a bowl on its back, likewise found at Tell Turmus (see above, note 5) can be similarly interpreted.

The figures, which are essentially stylised, almost certainly represent a tutelary godhead portrayed in what was an accepted manner, namely in the form of a circular pillar with the addition of an offering bowl at the top, the latter indicating their essentially cultic character. To this basically circular conception specific features were added, such as nose, eyes, horns, hair, mouth or beard; while from the emphasis placed upon the nose, it is clear that great importance was attached to it and it may well have been regarded as the seat of the breath of life[6] so necessary when the bene-ficient powers of the house-gods were invoked to ensure protection for men and flocks alike.

A further point to be noted is the use of basalt as the material in which the figures are sculpted. This hard volcanic rock is indeed difficult to work and its carving requires a high degree of technical skill.[7] But it should be remembered that it is the most common and often the only stone available over wide areas of the Hauran and the Golan. Excavations have shown that it was used extensively, not only for building purposes but also for agricultural tools and household utensils (see above, note 2) and its very hardness may have dictated the way in which certain features were wont to be rendered plastically, such as the ear-knobs on either side of the head, the globular eyes and a similar treatment of mouth and goatee beard (in contrast to the linear manner of indicating the beard on one of the humanising figures - see Plate IIIc).

The importance attached to the nose which can be inferred from the pillar figures, is further demonstrated by the way in which it was emphasised on different kinds of artifacts. This is examplified by the ivory figurines from the Beersheba culture,[8] on which attention is directed to the sexual traits. On the male figures, however, there is also a large and extremely prominent nose, commencing high on the forehead and reaching to the chin, the eyes (but not the mouth) being likewise indicated. When viewed in profile, not only is it evident that the head is disproportionately large in relation to the body, but the juxtaposition of the sexual member and the protruding nose is particularly striking (Plate IV)[9]. Other heads, probably also from male figurines,[10] likewise have an unusually large nose, while on female heads the nose is smaller.[11] As compared with the schematic circular form of the pillar figures, the approach to the ivory figurines is essentially a naturalistic one since the actual human form is

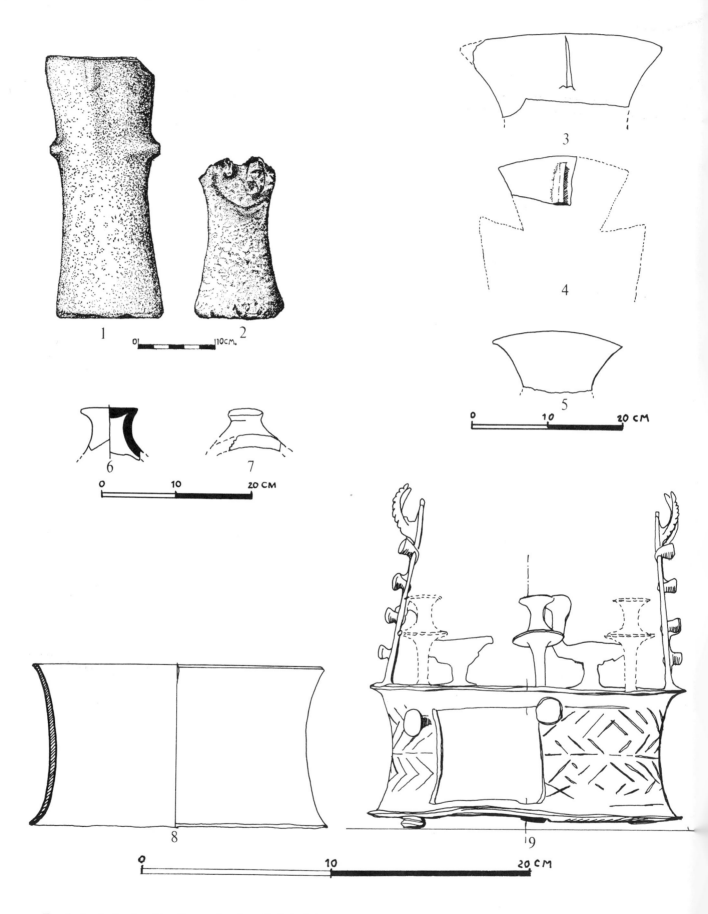

Fig. 1: 1–2, Basalt pillar figures (surface finds), Golan; 3–5, curved ossuary frontons, Azor and Benei Beraq; 6–7, jar ossuaries terminating in discs, Azor and Giv'atayim; 8–9, metal "crowns", Judean Desert Hoard.

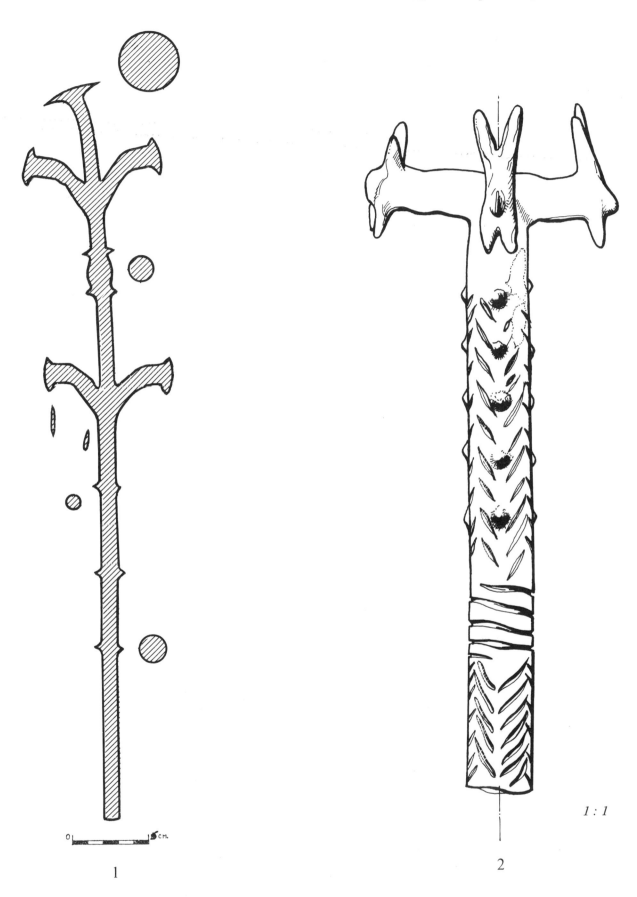

Fig. 2: Metal standards, Judean Desert Hoard: 1. (height 49.4 cm.); 2. (height 18.2 cm.)

1

2

1 : 1

depicted, even if in a conventionalised manner. On both, however, the nose is treated as a dominant feature and there are other shared characteristics. Moreover, by analogy with the bowl on top of the house-god figures, it would appear that the intentional hollowing out of the top of the head of the ivory figurines (Plate V) was for a similar purpose and that in the bowl-like hollow a small offering was placed, such as seeds or grains of corn, whereby it was hoped to ensure the success of the crops. Such an interpretation is borne out by the distinctly cultic character of the assemblage in which one of the full-length male figurines was found, which included two large basalt offering bowls, a votive or ceremonial ivory sickle (clearly connected with crops and harvests) [12] and a tusk decorated with vegetal and fertility symbols [13] widely current in contemporary Mesopotamia. [14]

The above two types of figures were differently conceived and fashioned in completely different media, one in the north and the other in the south. Nevertheless, they have a number of traits in common which point to their having been inspired by the same basic approach. Moreover, both were connected with ritual and the practice of the cult and both were rendered with a prominent nose which can be plausibly understood as representing the seat of the breath of life. There are thus good grounds for interpreting the schematised pillar-form figures on the one hand and the conventionalised human-form figures on the other, as epitomising - each in its own way - the concept of the life-giving force, in other words, a deity. Further, the circularity of the house-gods is seen to be intrinsic to them and not merely the result of a haphazard choice of form. If this be so, then the circularity expressed through the columnar shape should likewise be interpreted as symbolising the godhead.

The above two criteria of a well-marked nose and circularity of form can now be applied to other contemporary artifacts found in entirely different regions. Thus, on many of the ossuaries from the Coastal Plain a prominent nose is rendered plastically on the pediment which rises above the opening, particularly on those found at Azor [15] and at Benei Beraq [16] as well as at the other sites. [17] In almost every case the nose is placed high up on the fronton (Fig. 1: 3—4), as on the pillar figures and on the ivory figurines. There can be little doubt, then, that the nose shown on many of the ossuaries should be interpreted in exactly in the same sense as the nose on the pillar-form house-gods and on the Beersheba figurines and that in all three contexts it denotes an attribute of the deity whose protection was sought, in death as in life. At the same time it should be noted that circularity is expressed through the curved form of the pediment which rises above the ossuary roof. [18] Excluding ossuaries modelled in the form of a house, [19] in the form of a jar [20] or in the form of an animal (see under), a large number of those found at Azor and Benei Beraq are equipped with pediments which splay out in a marked curve above (Fig. 1: 3—5), giving in silhouette the same impression as the widening top of many of the pillar figures and it can be concluded from the recurrence of this type of distinctly curved fronton on ossuary after ossuary that its shape was not accidental and that, as in other contexts, the idea of the deity was implicit in the circularity of form. [21]

It has been plausibly suggested by Bar-Adon that many of the ossuaries were fashioned in the form of a temple or shrine and this is a view with which the writer is in complete agreement. This would explain the application to the pediment above the ossuary doorway of emblems representing different attributes of the godhead [22] - among them a prominent nose - which were doubtless believed to be endowed with apotropaic powers, their very portrayal being a guarantee of protection, especially in the case of the ossuaries in which were placed the bones of the dead. It has been likewise suggested that part of the fragmentary fresco from Ghassul be completed so as to form a temple doorway with pediment above; [23] but the restoration should be surely made, not with the angled corners as shown but with the same curved outline as on the ossuary frontons and the pediments surmounting the temple doorways which rise above the "crown" from the Cave of the Treasure (Fig. 1:9), [24] the latter having prompted the suggested comparison.

Once the significance of the circular form has been understood in terms of Chalcolithic iconography, many hitherto puzzling representations become clearer. Thus not only is the curve of the pediment seen to be emblematic, but the circular shape of the so-called "crowns" found in the Cave of the Treasure [25] can be similarly interpreted (Fig. 1: 8). This is expressed even more explicitly by a "crown" decorated with a prominent nose and eyes (Plate VIa) [26] in addition to other well-known cultic symbols; [27] it is further borne out by the "crown" already referred to (Fig. 1: 9), which is a complete symbiosis between the idea of the deity expressed through circularity of form and the related idea of the temple, since the "crown" wall is itself pierced by a doorway flanked on either side by circular emblems.

Among the hundreds of cult objects comprising the Judean Desert Hoard - which may well have originated in the Ein Gedi sanctuary and have been taken for safety to the cave in which they were discovered [28] - there were some eighty tube-like metal standards, the majority of which terminate above in a circular disc. [29] Others are rend-

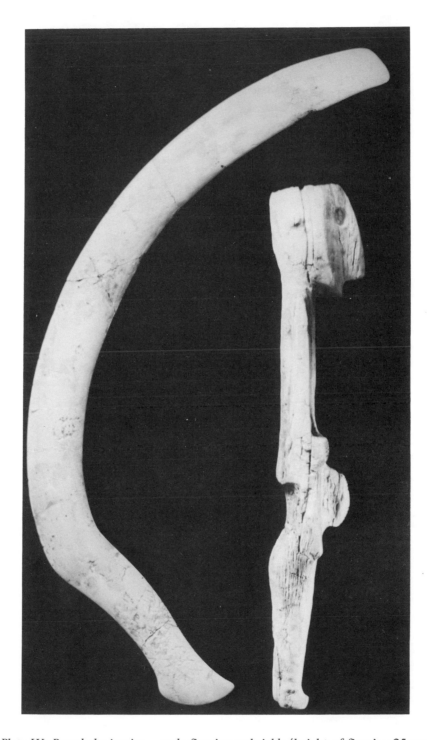

Plate IV: Beersheba ivories — male figurine and sickle (height of figurine 25 cm.)

Plate V: Hollowed head of male ivory figurine, Beersheba culture

ered in a flower-like manner (possibly intended to represent corn) on which the same circular head is shown in profile at the top of the branching stalks (Fig. 2:1),[30] while a similar profile rendering occurs on a number of ceremonial axe-heads, possibly used in rites connected with the practice of the cult.[31] The circular disc at the top of the standards can thus be understood as a variant of the idea of circularity expressed through the pillar-form basalt figures. This is especially striking in the case of a standard which in effect is the metal counterpart of several basalt statues (Plate VIb).[32] Here the upper part terminates in the usual circular disc (which takes the place of the bowl on the pillar figures), while below it are globular eyes, a prominent nose, the hint of a mouth and markedly protruding ear-knobs on either side of the head. Despite the difference in the size and the material used for the standard and the house-god figures, the essential features are the same on both the metal and stone forms and both are clearly cultic in function. Here, then, is further substantiation of the submission that the circular discs on so many of the standards should likewise be understood as symbolising the godhead and that in all probability they were regarded as being imbued with a special potency. By the same token related disc-like forms occurring in contemporary contexts may be similarly interpreted. This applies equally to the circular bosses placed one above the other round the plastically-rendered temple doorways which rise from the rim of the "crown" already referred to (Fig. 1:9), while the same meaning is implicit in the discs on the façades and at the base of the pediments of the temple-form ossuaries,[33] or round the doorways of the house-shaped ossuaries,[34] or as the culminating feature on so many of the jar ossuaries (Fig. 1: 6 7 and see above, note 20). The same disc-like symbol is used on the top of long shafts placed one on either side of the opening of an ossuary on which the fronton is angled but the ossuary itself circular in shape (Plate VId).[35] This treatment of the entrance was doubtless inspired by the tradition current over wide areas of Mesopotamia whereby it was customary to indicate the temple and the presence of the god by ringed gate-posts which were his recognised symbol.[36] On the ossuary, the addition of an agricultural tool, held in position between two protruding discs, implies a specific association with fields and crops. At the same time the two flanking shafted symbols rising above the pediment recall the standards from the Cave of the Treasure, while their juxta-position may be compared not only to that of the ringed gate-post symbols, but also to that of the shafted projection (one of a probable pair) which, terminating above in two concentric discs, one above the other, rises from the doorway on the metal "crown" already discussed (Fig. 1: 9). This same circular symbol is likewise used for pierced metal discs found in the Cave of the Treasure[37] together with one which is triangular in shape. It has been suggested that the latter symbolises the fertility goddess;[38] if this be so, then the two differently-shaped metal objects are seen to be complimentary in their connotation.

Having seen that in Chalcolithic terms circularity of form expressed the idea of a tutelary godhead, those pillar figures which are characterised by traits clearly associating them with animals may now be considered. The larger figures in this group conform to the general type in that they are columnar in shape, terminate in a sculpted bowl above and are shown with a prominent nose and with knobs on either side of the head; but in addition the figures are horned. On one, there are small globular eyes and a divided blob beard below a similarly-rendered mouth, the divided beard indicating that a caprid is intended. These same features - including the prominent nose emphasising the life-giving quality which was so important for ensuring the fecundity of the flocks - are shown on four goats' heads placed round the top of a standard (found in the Cave of the Treasure) in exactly the position in which the circular disc usually occurs (Fig. 2:2).[39] The implication is clear: the goats heads which take the place of the disc associate this standard specifically with flocks and herds and it may well have been used in rites to invoke protection for them and to guarantee their increase. Although the eyes are not shown, all four heads have horns (much shorter than those on cerfian figures on other standards) and likewise a divided goatee beard.[40] Another horned pillar figure (Plate IIId) has protruding eyes and hair, the latter being indicated in a stylised manner round the head and reaching to the eyes. The representation of hair on the hard basalt, in conjunction with well-marked horns further emphasises the association with sheep and goats. A smaller horned figure is so schematic that it is uncertain what animal is intended (Fig. 1: 2). The relatively small size of this and other figures made them easily portable, enabling them to be set up as occasion demanded in suitable positions in house or courtyard. Here, then, is further evidence in support of the interpretation of the pillar figures as house-gods.

A preoccupation with flocks and herds is likewise apparent at Azor where a number of ossuaries are modelled in the form of an animal.[41] One of these has eight feet, but this does not detract from the overall impression given that it is intended to represent a sheep.[42] Another painted ossuary is likewise modelled as an animal (Plate VIc)[43] and it has been suggested that it was made to represent a monster.[44] The façade, however, is far more reminiscent of a couchant sheep[45] and such an interpretation not only seems closer to the way in which the pediment is treated, but closer to the reality of those who made it.

If horns symbolised the godhead as protector of the flocks, then other pediment fragments from Azor,[46] as well as a distinctly rounded fronton from Benei Beraq[47], can probably be similarly interpreted; but it must be

a.

b.

c.

d.

Plate VI: a. Metal "crown", Judean Desert Hoard, (height 9 cm. diameter 18 cm.); b. Standard decorated with facial features, Judean Desert Hoard, (height 13.2 cm.); c. Ossuary, Azor, (length c. 62 cm.; d. Ossuary, Azor, (height 61.2 cm.)

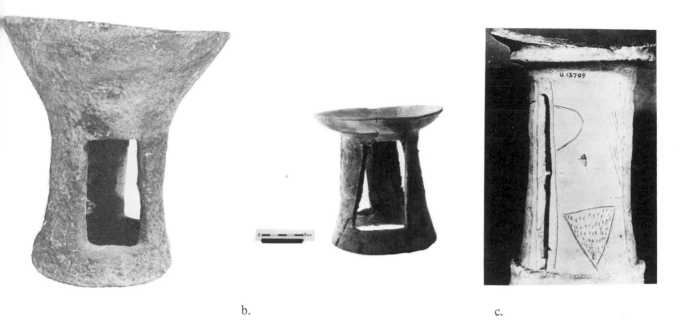

b.   c.

e.   f.

*VII: a. High-footed basalt bowl, Tiberias, (height 50-52 cm.); b. High-footed pottery bowl, Azor, (height 16.5 cm.);
c. Broken clay offering table, Ur, (height 45 cm.); d. Large storage jar, decorated with non-functional discs
(house context), Golan, (extant height 75 cm.); e. Bowl decorated with facial features and discs, unknown
Palestinian provenance, (height 5.1 cm., diameter 7.5 cm.); f. Handle treated as a face, with eyes and modelled
forehead, South Golan, (size of sherd 13x9 cm.).*

admitted that it is not always easy to identify the animal intended from schematic and often fragmentary remains. Other well-known motifs, clearly having a cultic significance, are also found on different types of artifacts at all the major sites; but since they do not occur in the repertoire of the pillar figures found to date (which have been used as a yard-stick for the suggestions put forward in this paper), they will not be discussed here.

Finally, we would consider briefly an artifact in stone which was made also in pottery (Plate VIIb),[48] the ceramic version continuing in use until much later times. This is the so-called "chalice" or high-footed bowl made of basalt which has openings in the base, examples of which occur at many different sites. The largest known vessel of this kind is 50 cm. high and was found at Tiberias (Plate VIIa).[49] This massive piece recalls the basalt pillar figures and illustrates the relationship between the two artifacts which incorporate the same basic elements: a bowl above and a columnar shape below. In the case of the "chalice", the circular form is without human or animal features of any kind. This is no doubt due to the added emphasis placed on the bowl as a recipient for offerings, its greater importance being conveyed by its increased size (compared to the bowls at the top of the pillar figures) and to its having been meticulously worked and sometimes also decorated. Another shared characteristic is the use of basalt as the material in which both kinds of artifacts were made; and this may be due to an earlier regional tradition. A further point to be noted is that, whereas the house-god figure is made in the form of a solid pillar, the "chalice" is set upon a hollow columnar base, pierced by what are frequently referred to as "windows". These rectangular openings (often with rounded corners) recall the doorways in the temple façades which rise from the rim of the "crown" discussed above (Fig. 1: 9) and this association is heightened by comparison with the hollow "crown" itself, which is likewise pierced by an opening symbolising the temple doorway. A similar treatment of the base of offering stands occurs at Ur at a somewhat later date (Early Dynastic II-III), on which the rectangular slits in the stem are clearly intended to represent temple doorways, being flanked on either side by a ringed gate-post, as well as by other well-known fertility symbols (Plate VIIc).[50] There are thus good grounds for interpreting the circular base of the "chalice" as having originally been fashioned to represent a shrine and this ties in well with its function. When reassessed in this light, this type of vessel is seen to fall into place among a whole series of artifacts, each having a specific cultic meaning which in contemporary contexts was readily understood.[51]

Reviewing the above, a number of points emerge: despite regional differences during the Chalcolithic period, it is apparent that all forms of creative art were ultimately cultic, both in inspiration and purpose. Knowledge of the bearers of this culture is based on material found at relatively few sites; and although a certain amount of parallelism of detail had previously been recognised in assemblages from different parts of the country, there was a lack of a common denominator relating the various forms of artistic expression. The basalt pillar figures, whose true purpose and function only became apparent once they had been found *in situ,* have to no small extent contributed towards filling this gap; and it is now evident that there was a common approach, perhaps pointing to an earlier common origin elsewhere. This was diversely expressed through different objects, some of which were made expressly for use in religious rites and ceremonies, but many of which were closely connected with the everyday pursuits carried out in the houses and courtyards in which the people lived and worked.

An important aspect of the pillar figures is their intrinsic circularity of form through which was expressed the idea of the godhead and, by association, the idea of the temple and the practice of the cult.[52] Thus it appears that not only was circularity identified with the deity, but by extension, everything circular was regarded as being imbued with a special potency and, by reason of its apotropaic qualities, a circular symbol was frequently applied to different kinds of artifacts (Plate VIId-e).[53] In the same way a nose, symbolising the breath of life, was used as a life-fertility talisman on all kinds of objects, including on vessels in everyday use (Plate VIIf). Thus by a process of diversification the idea conveyed through the columnar form of the house-gods could be expressed equally by the curve of an ossuary pediment or a button-headed standard, by protruding discs round the representation of a shrine doorway or on an ossuary façade. Moreover, the addition of a prominent nose served to highlight the promise of fertility through the association of the godhead with the object on which it was portrayed, in the expectation that increase and prosperity would thereby be ensured.

In conclusion, it cannot be too often reiterated that cultic traditions and symbols are long-lived and enduring, continuing in use in a variety of forms for many hundreds and even thousands of years, until long after their first meaning has been forgotten.[54] In time they come to be considered as accepted cultic symbols and motifs and are used as such conventionally on ritual objects of all kinds. Thus there are good grounds for postulating that those aspects of Chalcolithic iconography which have been discussed in this paper - as well as others not dealt with here - had their origin in beliefs current in much earlier times, being introduced by related but not necessarily contemporary groups settling in different parts of Palestine during the fourth millennium B.C.[55] This would account for regional differences in the media used and the forms taken by the same widely-accepted range of symbols, whether on the basalt artifacts of the north, on the clay ossuaries of the coastal region, on the ivory figures of the Beersheba culture, on the wall frescoes of Ghassul or on the magnificent array of metal objects from the Cave of the Treasure in the Judean Desert. All were inter-related; all ultimately derived their inspiration from the same sources, probably already then shrouded in antiquity.*

* Since this paper was first written in the winter of 1974, excavations at a number of Chalcolithic sites have brought to light additional material which substantiates the theses put forward here. Corroboration of the suggested function of the basalt pillar figures was obtained at two separate sites in the summers of 1974 and 1976; while the figures of the Woman with the Churn and the Ram carrying Cornets, excavated by Alon at Gilat in the northern Negev in 1975 (D. Alon, "Two cult vessels from Gilat," '*Atiqot*' XI(1976), p. 116–118) fit admirably into the suggested scheme. There is every likelihood, then, that additional evidence confirming the premises presented will be forthcoming before publication date.

C.E.

References

1.   J. Perrot, "La préhistoire palestinienne", *Supplément au Dictionnaire de la Bible,* VIII, col. 437; R. de Vaux, "Palestine during the Neolithic and Chalcolithic periods", in *Cambridge Ancient History* I, 3rd ed., pp. 523, 525.

2.   C. Epstein, "Notes and News", *IEJ* 23(1973), pp. 239-241, Vol. 24 (1974), pp. 254-257, Vol. 25 (1975), pp. 255-257 and Vol. 27 (1977), pp. 43–45.

3.   B. L. GOFF, *Symbols of Prehistoric Mesopotamia,* pp. 139, 169.

4.   C. Epstein, *IEJ* 25(1975), pp. 193-201.

5.   To be published by M. Prausnitz. For a short description of soundings at Tell Turmus, see Y. Dayan, *IEJ* 19 (1969), pp. 65-78.

6.   Compare J. Perrot, '*Atiqot* III (1961), p. 34.

7.   Perrot, *Supplément au Dictionnaire de la Bible,* VIII, col. 431.

8.   J. Perrot, *Syria* XXXVI (1959), pp. 8-10 and Pls. II-III; *idem, Eretz Israel* 7 (1964), pp. 93* - 94* and Pls. L-LII.

9.   *Ibid.,* Pl. LI:1.

10.   Perrot, *Syria* XXXVI, Pl. III: 1-2; *idem, Eretz Israel* 7, Pl. LIII:2.

11.   *Idem, Syria* XXXVI, p. 9 and Pl. III:3-4; *idem, IEJ* 5(1955), Pl. 22:A.

12.   *Idem, Eretz Israel,* 7, p. 92*.

13.   *Ibid.,* Pl. L.

14.   GOFF, *Symbols of Prehistoric Mesopotamia,* p. 62.

15.   Perrot, '*Atiqot* III, pp. 13, 32 and Fig. 19.

16.   J. Kaplan, *IEJ* 13(1963), Fig. 7:5, 7,8.

17.   E. L. Sukenik, *JPOS* XVII (1937), p. 16 and Pl. IV:2; V. Sussman and S. Ben-Arieh, '*Atiqot* 3 - Hebrew Series - (1966), Fig. 4:3,4; J. Perrot, *Eretz Israel* 8 (1967), p. 47* and Pl. XII:4.

18.   Y. Yadin, '*Atiqot* XI (1976), p. 121.

19.   Perrot, '*Atiqot* III, Figs. 25:3, 32:6 and 33:1. At Ben Shemen one of the ossuaries was modelled in the form of a house, *idem, Eretz Israel* 8, Pl. XII;3.

20.   Perrot, '*Atiqot* III, Figs. 35-36; Kaplan, *IEJ* 13, Fig. 4:10. For jar-shaped ossuaries at Ben Shemen, see Perrot, *Eretz Israel* 8, Pls. XII:2 and XIII.

21.   In this connection it may be recalled that among the many oculi pendants from Ghassul, Beersheba and elsewhere - all with distinctly rounded top - is a tiny bone pendant from Ḥorvat Beter which terminates above in a miniature pediment, similar to the temple doorways rising from the rim of the "crown" and the front-ons on the ossuaries. Its shape, which is clearly intentional, is entirely in keeping with its amuletic character and it may well be that the rows of incised dots between the "eyes", which run from top to bottom, were intended to indicate the nose. M. Dothan, '*Atiqot* II(1959), p. 31 and Fig. 18:3.

22.   Compare the widespread use of symbols on temple pediments in Mesopotamia. E.D. VAN BUREN, *Symbols of the Gods in Mesopotamian Art,* p. 4.

23.   P.BAR-ADON, *The Cave of the Treasure* (Hebrew) - henceforth Bar-Adon, *CT* - p. 139; *idem,* "Expedition C ", in *The Expedition to the Judean Desert,* 1961, *IEJ* 12(1962), p. 224 and Fig. 1.

24.   Bar-Adon, *CT,* pp. 28-32; *idem, IEJ* 12, Pl. 40.

25.   Bar-Adon, *CT,* pp. 28-43.

26.   *Ibid.,* pp. 34-35; Bar-Adon, *IEJ* 12, Pl. 41.

27.   The decorative elements on the "crowns", as on many of the standards, are well-known from Mesopotamia

where they are frequently associated with the fertility goddess. It does not necessarily follow that the "crowns" should be interpreted as representing the goddess, since all symbols were interchangeable and frequently replaced one another, being identified sometimes with the god and sometimes with the goddess. GOFF, *Symbols of Prehistoric Mesopotamia,* p. 88.

28.   D. Ussishkin, *Bib. Arch.* XXXIV (1971), pp. 37-38.

29.   Bar-Adon, *CT,* pp. 54-97: Nos. 22-26, 28-57, 59-77, 79-113, 116-119, 122-129; p. 121; No. 177; *idem, IEJ* 12, Pls. 32, 42.

30.   Bar-Adon, *CT,* pp. 54-55: No. 22; p. 93: No. 119.

31.   *Ibid.,* p. 100: Nos. 142-143; p. 117: Nos. 158, 161-163; p. 119; No. 172; *idem, IEJ* 12, Pl. 37: B. It should be noted that some of the axes are blunt and on others the blade is too thin for use.

32.   Bar-Adon, *CT,* p. 53; *idem, IEJ* 12, Pl. 39:A.

33.   Perrot, *'Atiqot* III, Figs. 23:2, 24:5, 6, 30:9; Kaplan, *IEJ* 13, Fig. 7:2,6,7; Sussman and Ben-Arieh, *'Atiqot* 3, Fig. 4:5. The similarity of the "crown" and the ossuary façades was pointed out by Bar-Adon, *CT,* pp. 138-139 and *IEJ* 12, p. 222.

34.   Perrot, *'Atiqot* III, Fig. 33:1,7, where it seems unlikely that these are beams, as suggested. See, *idem, Eretz Israel* 8, p. 48.

35.   Perrot, *'Atiqot* III, Fig. 21:1 and Pl. III:1-2.

36.   VAN BUREN, *Symbols of the Gods in Mesopotamian Art,* p. 44; E. C. During-Caspers, *Jaarbericht Ex Oriente Lux* 22 (1971-1972), pp. 211-227.

37.   Bar-Adon, *CT,* pp. 98-99: Nos. 130, 132-141; *idem, IEJ* 12, p. 223 and Pl. 36:C.

38.   Bar-Adon, *CT,* p. 99: No. 131.

39.   *Ibid.,* p. 51, No. 19.

40.   Compare the horns on standard No. 17, *ibid.,* pp. 46-49; Bar-Adon, *IEJ* 12, Pl. 42. - The animal head on standard No. 18 may also be intended for a goat, though a goatee beard is not indicated and the horns are large and branching. Bar-Adon, *CT,* p. 50.

41.   Perrot, *'Atiqot* III, p. 13, Type 2 and p. 31.

42.   *Ibid.,* Fig. 26:2 and Pl. V:4,5.

43.   *Ibid.,* Fig. 26:3.

44.   *Ibid.,* p. 14.

45.   Compare the basalt figure of a sheep, as in note 5.

46.   Perrot, *'Atiqot* III, Fig. 32:9, 15.

47.   *Ibid.,* Fig. 16:D.

48.   *Ibid.,* Pl. IX:20.

49.   D. Ussishkin, *IEJ* 18(1968), pp. 45-46.

50.   L. WOOLLEY, *Ur excavations,* IV, p. 78 and Fig. 17:b; p. 176: No. U. 13709.

51.   In addition to chalices, basalt votive bowls also occur, these, too, being frequently connected with the practice of the cult (see the Beersheba context as in note 12, above). Carefully worked and sometimes decorated, they lack the pierced columnar base clearly associating them with the godhead and, by implication, with the shrine.

52.   It is worth recalling that the only Chalcolithic temple known to date is the Sacred Enclosure at Ein Gedi, which may well have been regional. In its sanctuary, the altar was marked by a semi-circular row of stones built against the centre of the back wall. On the right was a carefully dressed flat-topped base made of white limestone, standing some 25 cm. high, upon which a cult statue may have stood. The base resembles and is about the same height as many of the pillar figures; in the sanctuary it stood out on account of its circular shape and contrasting colour. D. Ussishkin, *Bib. Arch.* XXXIV, pp. 29-30 and Figs. 1 and 13.

53.   The non-functional discs and knobs used in the decoration of different kinds of vessels were almost certainly regarded as apotropaic. M. F. Zayadine, *Bible et Terre Sainte* 49(1962), p. 7, No. 9; A. MALLON, R. KOEPPEL *et al., Teleilat Ghassul,* I, Fig. 56:3; J. Ory, *QDAP* XII (1946), pp. 46-47 and Pl. XVI:33; on storage vessels from the Golan - see Pl. VIId.

54.   E. D. VAN BUREN, *Clay Figurines from Babylonia and Assyria,* p. xiii. From among a wide range of artifacts from different periods and regions illustrating the continuance of earlier forms long after the original meaning had become lost in oblivion, the following may be cited: on two shrine models from Nippur, dating to the Ur III period, a god is shown standing in the temple entrance. On one example the door is flanked on either side by a large spear (a later version of the ringed gate-post symbol), while above is a fronton similar to those on the ossuaries. On both models a row of clay discs encircle the shrine doorway, these being placed one above the other in exactly the same way as the metal discs

round the temple doorways which rise from the rim of the "crown" from the Judean Desert. *Ibid.,* Fig. 159: No. 593; D.E. Mc COWAN, R.C. HAINES *et al., Nippur I - Temple of Enlil, Scribal Quarters and Soundings,* p. 91 and Pl. 129:6.

55.   Perrot, *Supplément au Dictionnaire de la Bible,* VIII, col. 438; J. MELLAART, *The Chalcolithic and Early Bronze Ages in the Near East and Anatolia,* pp. 22-23.

PHOTOGRAPHIC ACKNOWLEDGEMENTS

The photographs used for the illustrations are reproduced by courtesy of:
    J. Perrot, Director, French Archaeological Mission to Israel (Plates IV, V, VIc and VIIb).
    D. Ussishkin, Institute of Archaeology, Tel-Aviv University (Plate VIIa).
    The Trustees of the British Museum (Plate VIIc).
    Leconte Collection, Lyons (Plate VIIe).
All other photographs by courtesy of the Israel Department of Antiquities and Museums.

SILVER IN THE LEVANT IN THE FOURTH MILLENNIUM B.C.
by Kay Prag.

As a student of Dame Kathleen's I am aware not just of her contribution to archaeology in the Levant, both in advancing field techniques and analysis and in the clarity and honesty of principle which is fundamental to all her undertakings, but also of her generosity with both time and help to those associated with her. It thus gives me great pleasure to contribute to this *Festschrift* honouring her achievements.

I have been attracted in recent months to one aspect of the material cultures of the Levant in the second half of the fourth millennium. This is the surprisingly widespread use (and preservation) of silver objects, which have been found in relatively large numbers, relatively that is in metallurgical terms, in Egypt, the Levant and in Anatolia. When one considers that the statistical availability of native silver as opposed to native gold or copper is estimated at 20% as abundant as gold and 0.2% as abundant as copper[1] the fact that 233+ silver objects have been found at Byblos in the 'énéolithique' graves, 23+ objects in late pre-dynastic contexts in Egypt, 7 objects in Palestine in Proto-Urban graves and 9 objects in Anatolia (now dated *c.* 3000 B.C. by radio carbon), that these numbers far exceed the number of gold objects known in the same period and at Byblos even the number of copper finds, and that little silver has been found in archaeological contexts in Egypt[2] and the Levant in the succeeding third millennium, the situation seemed to merit investigation.

A good deal has been written on early silver metallurgy. Most writers base their assessments of early developments on analogies with present knowledge of mineral resources and technological requirements, on rare analyses of ancient objects and admit the sparseness of the evidence. Little is known of the ancient mines. The resulting hypotheses tend to be somewhat speculative. It is generally accepted that native silver is of rare occurrence, partly because of its tendency to be reduced by the chlorides in rain and ground water; and because it normally has to be mined at some depth where it was beyond the reach of the earliest smiths.[3]

The great expansion of silver production in the late third millennium is generally associated with technological advances involved in the reduction of lead ores and the beginnings of cupellation processes. Wertime[4] has pointed to the silver cupel buttons from Mahmatlar in Turkey, dating to this period, as 'the first convincing evidence of the production of silver from lead ores'. With this later phase of silver production I shall not be concerned.[5]

Silver Objects From Byblos

The numerous objects from the 'énéolithique' cemetery at Byblos form the largest group of silver objects of the early period known to us. The exact number of such objects found in this cemetery between 1922 and 1962 is unknown, for only a small number of the graves are yet fully published.[6]

The total number of graves of the period which were excavated is noted as 2101,[7] mostly jar burials though there are about 14 cave tombs. All were dated by the excavator to 3800-3200 B.C.[8] and although the date of some of these graves, in particular the cave tombs, has occasionally been questioned[9] I believe it to be substantially correct for both cave and jar burials. The silver objects seem to date from the later group of tombs, perhaps to be generally dated in the second half of the fourth millennium; but detailed assessment will have to await the full publication.[10]

The published silver objects consist of:

Beads (95+), all made of thin hammered foil. The shapes vary considerably and include biconical (some with rolled edges and one facetted), long barrel, cylindrical, oblong and globular types.[11]

Rings (33+), the dimensions of which are rarely given, though one was made of a round strip of twisted wire 3 mm. in diameter. Some of these appear to be ornaments for the hair, or from headdresses made up with the silver bands. One, in T.30, was a finger ring.[12]

Earrings (53+), like the rings are all made of thick wire, in one case listed as 3.7 mm. in diameter. The rings are usually single with overlapping ends, though in a few cases there were pairs of double earrings (each made up of two engaged rings). The sizes range between 1.7 cm. and 4.2 cm. in diameter. Two earrings were ornamented with carnelian beads.[13]

Head bands (22+), many of which were found in fragmentary condition, consist of thin, hammered strips of metal, usually undecorated, though a few have *repoussé* dots. The usual size is 30 - 35 cm. long, about 12 mm. wide, and there are one or two small holes at the ends to allow tying with a fine thread. Occasionally two or even three were found on one head, and associated with rings, making an elaborate head ornament.[14]

Bracelets (11). T.222 had a bracelet of twisted silver wire, square sectioned at the ends.[15] The usual type is plain, resembling the earrings but larger.[16]

Three sets of casings and cappings for ceremonial maces or sceptres.

These objects distinguished only three tombs, and deserve individual attention.

T.630: a silver tube, 12 cm. long, lay on the fingers of the left hand of the dead person; the ends were thickened or rolled and the shaft was decorated with four groups of seven incised circles. This originally formed the decorative grip for a wooden handle which was (at least partly) covered with bands of silver, and supported a spheroidal polished haematite macehead with silver cappings at top and bottom which was found by the head. A copper rivet appears to have been associated with this object.

T.631: another silver tube, as in T.630, and associated with an unidentified silver object, perhaps a support for a now perished object.[17]

T.1674: a ceremonial piriform ivory macehead with its base set in silver and mounted on a silver-ornamented handle with a silver pommel.[18]

All of these objects are relatively small and all of hammered sheet metal or wire. None were necessarily cast in any sort of mould.[19] The technology is thus simple though the varied shapes show skill. In the same graves gold and copper were exceedingly rare. Though one or more silver objects occurred in 28 of the first 273 tombs published, copper occurred only in five and gold in none. Of those tombs so far referred to in preliminary publication only, gold occurred in only three, in the form of one ring and 13 beads;[20] copper always occurred as daggers and rivets except for four hooks (probably fish-hooks).[21] There are 24 copper daggers referred to in all,[22] mostly with one or three rivet holes, rarely five, and in some cases the copper rivets are preserved, occasionally with traces of wood or bone handles. The daggers are of sophisticated type, frequently with midribs as well as rivets, and have been somewhat neglected in studies of early weapons.[23]

The emphasis on silver in the graves may of course simply show a bias of grave offerings, with gold too valuable to bury and copper too much valued for weapons and tools. It is notable that all the silver objects are ornamental or ceremonial - for the silver-capped maceheads and the unidentified object probably fit into the latter category.

Dunand publishes two sets of analyses for the silver objects,[24] which indicate mostly silver chloride. Nearly all the metal occurred in the jar burials. Although jar burials are also found in the cave tombs, the cave burials, on the evidence of their contents as published, have a slightly different ceramic repertoire[25] and almost no metal. The pottery is definitely of a similar chronological horizon (i.e. second half of fourth millennium), but whether the cave tombs represent a minority group in the population or a slightly later chronological period is difficult to say on present evidence. The point of interest to us is the reference to 'une coupelle' (no. 5644) in Cave Tomb 7 which suggests that the silver was at least imported into Byblos in crude form and subsequently shaped into objects on the site. This object is now supported by three others from jar burials published in *Byblos* V, in T. 1128 which contained two small "coupelles coniques" (though no bones or other objects) and T. 1216 which had "une coupelle"[26].

Silver objects in Palestine

In 1950 Père de Vaux discovered a small silver dish of rather sophisticated shape in a tomb at Tell Far'ah.[27] It is nearly 5 cm. high and nearly 12 cm. in diameter. As the tomb was reused in the Middle Bronze Age - although the bowl was found in the 'énéolithique' level - a certain caution has surrounded the find and is probably the reason why it has not been given much prominence in studies of early metallurgy.[28] De Vaux however pointed out that although the vase was unique in the Levant, its occurrence was not surprising in view of the quantity of silver at Byblos, and also was able to parallel the shape in the contemporary ceramics of Palestine. The shape is also paralleled reasonably among the pottery from the tombs at Byblos:[29] de Vaux's account of the vase also states that 'la coupe du profil montre clairement la technique d'emboutissage', which also links it with the Byblos objects. There is still no parallel elsewhere in these countries for such a metal vessel. However there has recently been a most interesting find in two tombs at Azor where the objects recovered from Proto-Urban burials include a number of silver earrings, three complete and three fragmentary, one of which has been analysed. [30] They are not identical to those from Byblos, for although they are also made of wire, the ends have been hammered flat and in two cases at least, the rings were coiled. The latter could perhaps be compared stylistically with the 'engaged rings' from Byblos. These silver objects were accompanied by one gold bead and various items of copper - two daggers and one javelin with two to four rivet holes and midribs, rivets and two copper needles, which can generally be compared in style, quality and technique with objects from Egypt and Byblos although they are not identical. An important point is that here also analysis indicates a very pure silver with no gold content.

The number of silver objects thus far known (in Palestine) is therefore few in proportion to the known number of graves and excavated sites. It is notable that Azor is a site on the coastal plain, perhaps more in contact either by land or sea with the Byblos region than some of the well-known inland sites such as Jericho.

Relatively few metal objects are known from the Proto-Urban cultures of Palestine - daggers, adzes and flat axes are the best known, [31] but the standard of metallurgy among the Ghassulian-Beersheba groups of the mid-fourth millennium was very high - the example par excellence being of course the Nahal Mishmar hoard of copper objects for which advanced casting and alloying techniques are attested. [32]

There is no doubt therefore that casting of rivetted daggers was possible in the fourth millennium in the Levant. This is confirmed by the evidence of the copper dagger found in Naqada Grave 836 by Petrie. The rivets of this were not found, but the advanced form of the dagger with its three rivet holes and strong midrib bears some relation to those at Byblos and Azor, though it is not identical, and Petrie suggested that it was an import as it is unlike any other from predynastic Egypt. Petrie stated that despite its developed form it was not possible for this dagger to be later than the undisturbed grave in which he found it, and dated it to SD 63. [33]

It seems likely that this can be regarded as an import into Egypt from the Palestine-Byblos area.

Silver objects in Egypt

Although the forms in silver objects, as in copper daggers, differ in Egypt from those we have seen in the Syria-Palestine region, silver was also popular in the second half of the fourth millennium. Though many of the objects are made of foil or wire as at Byblos, there are also a number of quite heavy cast tools. As the shapes are characteristic of the Naqada 2 period, whatever the sources of the raw material they were undoubtedly manufactured locally. They range in date right through this period.

As most of these objects come from graves they have been given sequence dates according to the objects, especially the pottery, found with them; the following list therefore still requires detailed support from stratified excavation. Those marked with an asterisk have been analysed: see below.

SD 38: thin hollow silver bead from Naqada Grave 1547. [34]

SD 32-48: 'an armlet of a hard white metal . . . not yet analysed, but may be a silver-copper alloy' from Naqada Grave 1635. [35]

*SD 42: thin hammered silver lid from Naqada Grave 1257. [36]

SD 42: thin hollow globular beads (two?) from Naqada Grave 1257 (with lid). [37]

*SD 44-64: hollow silver model hawk from Naqada Grave 721, once attached to a ?wooden core by means of copper pins, two of which still remain in position beneath the eyes and one is loose in the box - the latter being about 4 mm. in length. [38]

SD 46-52: 'silver in fused buttons' from Naqada Grave 1760. [39]

*SD 50: silver dagger from el Amra Grave b.230. [40]

SD 55-56: silver wire handle on a jar said to be from a shaft grave at Homra Dom. [41]

?SD 55-56: silver and gold foil ?pendant from Homra Dom. [42]

SD 55-56: silver knife from Homra Dom. [43]

SD 55-56: silver dagger from Homra Dom. [44]

Before SD 56: 11+ hollow silver beads, of barrel, ring and conical shapes, from Grave h.41 at el Mahasna. [45]

SD 57-64: silver spoon, with twisted handle and circular bowl from a tomb at Naqada. [46]

**SD 60: silver adze* from a tomb at Ballas. [47]

SD 60-66: spoon with silver bowl and copper stem from el Amra Grave b.233. [48]

SD 61: thin silver ring from Naqada Grave 1770. [49]

As at Byblos there is therefore a reference to what seem to be cupel buttons of silver, in Petrie's reference to the 'fused buttons' from Naqada Grave 1760. Unfortunately, these buttons are not at present to be found. The fact that Petrie listed them in *Prehistoric Egypt* in his section on materials, not among the objects, furthers the supposition that these are not finished objects. [50]

Relatively few analyses of these objects have been carried out, and almost no detailed analyses exist. Lucas and Harris list only one early analysis, which refers to Amélineau's discovery at Abydos of an ornamental binding for a wooden beam of the archaic period. [51] It is not therefore particularly relevant to a study of predynastic silver finds occurring from SD 38 onwards. Lucas and Harris were of the opinion, based on this evidence, that the earliest Egyptian silver was in all probability a naturally occurring silver-rich gold. [52] Modern surveys in Egypt have shown that the occurrence of silver in a natural gold product can be as high as 76%. However, they concluded that 'in no case is the percentage of gold as low as that recorded for some examples of Egyptian silver, and unless it is assumed that specimens with a very much lower gold content were found anciently, it seems possible that silver may have been imported as early as the Old Kingdom at least'. [53] They also suggested that some ancient gold-silver sources richer in silver may have been worked out, but rule out other local sources of silver such as the galena ores which have a very low silver content.

Very little serious work has been done on predynastic silver, but it seems clear that this silver has a significantly lower gold content than that of most analysed Old Kingdom material.

The only other analyses referred to in the literature are those listed by Williams and Baumgartel. Williams published the analysis of the el Mahasna beads. [54] Mishara and Meyers comment that this bead is possibly of native silver. [55] Mrs. Baumgartel had some objects tested [56] and in addition the el Amra dagger was shown to be silver during cleaning in Cairo Museum, as was the Ballas adze during cleaning at the British Museum; no other details of these analyses seem to be available. These objects vary considerably in present appearance - the lid and beads from Naqada being reduced to a dark matt purple corrosion product; the hawk has a mottled pale grey appearance and was originally thought to be lead; the Ballas adze, heavy and highly metallic still, has the dull grey shine of pewter.

Petrie and Mrs. Baumgartel both suggest that the silver came from outside Egypt, Petrie suggesting north Syria as the source. [57] Mrs. Baumgartel pointed out that 'if we knew the source of pre-dynastic Egyptian silver it would cast some light on foreign connexions and trading'. [58]

Silver objects in Anatolia

Considering its rich silver resources surprisingly few silver objects of the fourth millennium have yet been recovered in Anatolia. The silver ring from Beycesultan Level XXXIV [59] has held the place of honour for some years though its date has now been lowered on radio-carbon evidence by nearly a millennium to *c.* 3000-2900 B.C. [60] and now fits well with the two silver earrings from Alishar Hüyük Level 14, [61] and the two very rich graves recently found at Koruçutepe and dated *c.* 3000, which contained silver necklets, hairrings, headband (cf. Byblos), wristlet and stamp seal on a wristlet, again associated with copper daggers and stone macheads. [62]

The range of these objects has a certain amount in common with those at Byblos, and jar burials in Chalcolithic and Early Bronze Age Anatolia have frequently been noted.[63]

Silver objects in Mesopotamia

Although it is not my intention to list objects from Mesopotamia or further east in detail the use of both silver and lead with fairly advanced techniques is well attested in the Jemdat Nasr period - there is the lead bowl from Ur,[64] a number of cylinder seals ornamented with silver or base silver animals,[65] a silver vase from Warka[66] and a limestone bull with silver legs also from Warka.[67]

Sources

Apart from the silver-rich gold deposits in Egypt the only major silver sources noted today in the Levant are those in Anatolia. They are conveniently shown by Ryan.[68] It is notable that a source is shown in the Amanus Range, only 300 km. to the north of Byblos; and it is this region that is probably referred to as the 'silver mountain' in the time of Sargon of Akkad in the Mesopotamian texts of the second half of the third millennium. This is the earliest reference to a silver source in a text.[69]

Silver occurs particularly in the Malatya to Trebizond region of eastern Anatolia, although there are some sources to the west in the region of Izmir. Undoubtedly these areas were tapped for the much greater quantity of silver known during the third millennium in Anatolia and Mesopotamia, in particular the ingots from Troy II and the treasures at Ur. These objects seem to fall into a later category than those of the fourth millennium and at present the distribution pattern in the south is a curious one. In Egypt there is relatively little from the first six dynasties and the few analyses suggest native gold/silver.[70] In Palestine and Syria none is yet known from the Early Bronze Age. Thus all of the northern production in the third millennium appears to have stayed in an Anatolian-Mesopotamian axis.

Chéhab refers to Dunand's earlier view that the silver at Byblos derived from Armenia and the Caucasus;[71] latterly Dunand himself has suggested that although the 'énéolithique' copper at Byblos may have an Anatolian or northern origin,[72] the 'énéolithique' silver may have a more local origin. He refers to the galena deposits at Zibbata ez-Zeit in the Hermon region of Lebanon, which analysis has shown yields a little silver.[73] This would imply a considerable technical competence in retrieving silver from galena ores.

Views on the derivation of fourth millennium Egyptian silver have been referred to above.

Gowland[74] and Patterson[75] have both suggested that the rare cerargyrite (silver chloride) or native crystals were the source of the earliest silver objects, but Wertime inclines to the view that silver was discovered in course of the accidental cupellation of lead ores, in particular the rarer silver-rich cerussites rather than galena.[76] He comments on a connection in the use of lead and silver, but there may be a longer gap between the first recorded appearances of these metals than he implies: the first occurrence of lead is far earlier than any of silver, that from Catal Hüyük being dated to the seventh millennium[77] while the earliest silver perhaps occurs some time in the middle of the fourth millennium. However his view that silver might have been discovered in the course of accidental cupellation of lead is not affected - rather supported by a suggestion that lead had long been experimented with by the smiths before the appearance of silver objects. The occurrence of lead objects is not very frequently attested however. As well as Catal Hüyük, there is Arpachiyeh in the fifth millennium, and now perhaps a thin lead strip from Byblos, T.388,[78] of the same date as the silver. However, it is very rare in the south and there seems to be none in Palestine. The number of predynastic lead objects known in Egypt is almost a non-existent quantity, apart from the use of galena as eye paint from Badarian times. In fact the only object still so described is the leaden figurine in University College, London, purchased by Petrie.[79] Mrs Baumgartel is cautious both of the date and the authenticity of this object.[80] It certainly stands alone if it is a round cast object of this period; on the other hand it has all the characteristics of 'pin' figurines of the Naqada 2 period, and Ucko has pointed to the fact that this class of figurines falls into a special category that often merited expensive materials.[81] The substance of which it is made, not analysed so far as I know, is curiously whitish-mottled and clay-like with metallic inclusions, and is very heavy.

A link between silver and lead in the south Levant and Egypt is therefore not well supported so far, depending on very little lead and a few 'cupel buttons', and if such a link is to be maintained as in Wertime's hypothesis, it throws the onus for the source back on the Anatolian region. The lack of silver objects in the south from the end of the fourth millennium perhaps lends emphasis to the suggestion that some rich source was worked out by this date, but only a series of detailed analyses is likely to clarify the issue.

The concentration of silver at Byblos in itself tends to suggest that the region may have played a central role in a silver trade in the Levant in the fourth millennium. That goods were brought from Byblos and the Levant to Egypt in the Naqada 2 period has long been known. [82] The 'énéolithique' cemetery at Byblos suggests such a trade was not one-sided, for a number of objects from the jar burials show direct links with Egypt. These include an ivory vase pulled by a quadruped,[83] a bone figurine[84] and, although they do not come from the tombs, a number of flint knives must be of Egyptian inspiration if not origin. [85] Could the Biblites have received these items as exchange for their silver as well as their timber and resin, the silver being exported in the partly prepared form of 'cupel' buttons? Considering the rarity of gold at Byblos there is also a temptation to consider whether the Egyptians did not also pay in gold. But as Dunand notes, there is so little gold at Byblos that a local source cannot be excluded.

As to Palestine, the links that can be noted between 'Proto-Urban C' type pottery shapes and those from Byblos, as well as a general comparison between the Palestinian coastal preference for burial in pottery ossuaries within caves compared to Biblite jar burials in caves leaves little difficulty in the way of suggesting a source for the Azor silver earrings and the Far'ah vase.

Regardless of the implications for metallurgical history, the distribution of silver objects at present appears to conform to a pattern, similar in type to that of lapis lazuli distribution in the late fourth and early third millennia. In the case of lapis, political factors far to the east in Iran are thought to be the reason for the interruption of distribution to Mesopotamia and Egypt at the beginning of the third millennium. [86]

In the case of silver, it might be suggested that at the end of the fourth millennium the Levantine source of supply (perhaps a rich and accessible cerussite as Wertime suggests) was worked out either in the Amanus or more doubtfully in Anti-Lebanon, and the trade came to an end. The products of subsequent exploitation further to the north requiring a more advanced technology in working galena ores, and developing a few centuries later, were distributed to the west (Troy) and to the south-east (Mesopotamia), rather than to the Levant and Egypt where the craft of the smith seems to have gone through a different and rather slower development until late in the third millennium.

References

1.   T. A. Wertime, 'The Beginnings of Metallurgy: A New Look', *Science,* 182 (1973), p. 883.
2.   A. Lucas and J. R. Harris, *Ancient Egyptian Materials and Industries* (4th ed.), p. 246 (hereafter *Lucas and Harris*); G. Brunton, *Qau and Badari* I, p. 69, pl. XVIII.10, II, p. 20; W. B. Emery, *Archaic Egypt*, p. 224.
3.   Wertime, op. cit., p. 883; *Lucas and Harris*, pp. 245ff.; W. Gowland, 'Silver in Roman and Earlier Times: I. Prehistoric and Proto-historic Times', *Archaeologia* 69 (1920), pp. 121-160; J. R. Partington, *Origins and Development of Applied Chemistry,* under 'Silver'.
4.   Op. cit. p. 883.
5.   R. J. Forbes, in C. Singer, E. J. Holmyard and A. R. Hall, *A History of Technology* I, pp. 575, 582, has suggested that cupellation first came into use in the Near East and Asia Minor in the first half of the third millennium, basing this on the purity of the Troy II ingots. K. R. Maxwell Hyslop, *Western Asiatic Jewellery c. 3000 - 612 B.C.* also refers to this in her introduction; J. Mishara and P. Meyers, 'Ancient Egyptian Silver. A Review' (Second Cairo Solid State Conference: Recent Advances in Science and Technology of Materials 21-26 April, 1973), summarize the state of knowledge for Egyptian silver as native silver in use in the fifth and fourth millennia, sulfide ores in the third or 'possibly even earlier' (p. 2); K. Branigan, 'Silver and Lead in Prepalatial Crete', *AJA* 72 (1968), pp. 219-229 suggests cupellation in the Aegean not till EB2.
6.   Tomb 1: C. Virolleaud, 'Decouverte à Byblos d'un Hypogée de la douzieme dynastie Egyptienne', *Syria.* III (1922), pp. 273-290, esp. p. 289 and pl. LXIII.(2), 4, 6; Tombs 2 - 2 *bis:* P. Montet, *Byblos et l'Egypte,* pp. 239-240 and pl. LXXIV; Tombs 3-206: M. Dunand, *Fouilles de Byblos* I (hereafter *Byblos* I); Tombs 207-275, 292, 306 and references to 528, 582, 585, 587, 589, M. Dunand, *Fouilles de Byblos* II (hereafter *Byblos* II); M. Dunand, *Fouilles de Byblos* V refers to a number of tombs; preliminary reports on the cemeteries appeared in *BMBeyr* I (1937), pp. 23-33; III (1939), p. 77; V (1941), p. 21 ff.; VIII (1946-8), p. 159; IX (1949), pp. 53-64, 65-74, 75ff., 107; XII (1955), pp. 7-12, 13-20, 21-23, 47; XIII (1956), pp. 73-78, 79-86; XVI (1961), pp. 69-73, 75ff.; XVII (1964), pp. 21ff., 25-27, 29-35; XIX (1966), p. 95ff.
7.   *Byblos* V, p. 214.

8. *BMBeyr* XVII (1964), pp. 29-35; in *Byblos* V, p. 216 he reaffirms this date (39/3800-3200 B.C.) with the succeeding period contemporary with Dynasty I in Egypt.

9. R. Amiran, 'The Pottery of the Middle Bronze Age I in Palestine', *IEJ* 10 (1960), pp. 221-223, pl. 26A-F; E. D. Oren, 'The Early Bronze IV Period in Northern Palestine and its Cultural and Chronological Setting', *BASOR* 210 (1973), 33-4.

10. Only two copper objects are noted as coming from the small early section of the cemetery to which 78 burials have been attributed, *Byblos* V, p. 181.

11. They are noted from Tombs 4 *bis,* 117, 153, 216, 222, 230, 236, 272, 630, 631, 889, 1081, 1106, 1191, 1266, 1314, 1424, 1555, 1566, 1567, 1580, 1670, 1671, 1674, 1675. *BMBeyr* XVI (1961), pp. 78-79 refers to 1566 and 1674. See *Byblos* V, p. 319, fig. 191.

12. Noted in Tombs 14, 30, 42, 210, 216, 230, 247, 272, 689, 1424, 1563, 1580, 1670, 1671, 1675.

13. Tombs 19, 23, 29, 35, 77, 97, 115, 117, 119, 145, 147, 153, 163, 174, 196, 203, 240, 249, 1020, 1191, 1546, 1566, 1608, 1960. See *Byblos* V, p. 319, fig. 191 and p. 320, fig. 193.

14. Tombs 77, 145, 163, 222, 230, 247, 272, 630, 631, 1191, 1566, 1567, 1671, 1674, 1675. Those in 1191, 1566 and 1674 were described in *BMBeyr* XII (1955) p. 22 and XVI (1961), pp. 78-79. The best preserved, from T.631, is illustrated by Chéhab in *BMBeyr* IX (1949), p. 75ff. pls. I-II. See also *Byblos* V, p. 320, fig. 192.

15. But cf. *Byblos* V, p. 320, fig. 193, no. 16851, where it is shown as an earring. The list given in *Byblos* II.2, p. 867 is a bit difficult to reconcile with the objects shown in *Byblos* V, fig. 193. The facetted bead, not mentioned in *Byblos* II, where two oblong silver beads are listed, is shown on fig. 193, and referred to on p. 318 as being from Tomb 8241 (an impossible tomb number, and not the registration number either in this case). Its provenance at present must remain uncertain.

16. From Tombs 1546 *bis,* 1563, 1668, 1670, 1671, 1675. See *Byblos* V, p. 321, fig. 194.

17. For these tombs, see Chéhab, *BMBeyr,* IX (1949), p. 75ff., pls. I-III; cf. *BMBeyr,* VIII (1946-48), p. 159; *Byblos* V, p. 305.

18. See *BMBeyr* XVI (1961) pp. 78-79, pl. IV.2; *Byblos* V, pp. 305-306, fig. 182, no. 30597.

19. Dunand notes the facetted bead as a possible exception, see note 15 above; *Byblos* V, p. 318.

20. Tombs 631, 1566, 1674.

21. Tombs 1380, 1669.

22. Tombs 46, 84 (5), 169, 179, 240, 653 (2), 944 (2), 1075, 1144, 1483, 1887, 2016.

23. Noted by J. Mellaart, *The Chalcolithic and Early Bronze Ages in the Near East and Anatolia,* p. 46, fig. 17A; but barely included in K. R. Maxwell-Hyslop, 'Daggers and Swords in Western Asia', *Iraq* VIII (1946), cf. p. 22 n.1, Type 20 (p. 23) and Type 22a (p. 24), and e.g. Type 1 (p. 3).

24. *Byblos* I, following p. 449:

    4. - Fragment du bandeau de la tombe énéolithique 77. Chlorure d'argent altérée par chloruration.

    5. - Boucle d'oreilles (no. 5636 *bis*) de la tombe énéolithique 35. Même consideration que pour le fragment précédent. Traces de cuivre.

    Analyses of copper objects are also given:

    6. - Lame de poignard no. 5699 de la tombe énéolithique 46. Cuivre seulement; toutefois ce seulement n'est que probable en raison de l'exiguité de l'échantillon.

    Also in *BMBeyr,* XII (1955), p. 14 there is an analysis of a copper dagger with triangular tang and three rivets: 'cuivre mélange de quelques impuretés (cuivre rosette) provenant en grand partie de la fusion directe des pyrites sur les charbons d'un foyer . . . une origine chypriote du minerai est à envisager, car les impuretés de ce cuivre resemblent à celles qui sont associées aux scories anciennes d l'île fraitées à nouveau par une companie anglaise'. The analyses were made by Professor Fillon in Beirut.

25. There appears to be more incised decoration on the pottery in the caves than in the jars, and more vessels with handles; but identical types *do* also occur in the jars.

26. *Byblos* V, pp. 251-252.

27. R. de Vaux, 'La Troisième Campagne de Fouilles à Tell el-Far'ah près Naplouse' *RB,* 58 (1951), p. 587, fig. 13 and pl. XXVIIa.

28. Again J. Mellaart, op. cit., p. 50, fig. 20, is one of the few who refer to it.

29. No. 5673 from T.50 and no. 5922 from T.189, both jar burials.

30. *RB,* 65 (1972), p. 418; A. Ben-Tor, "Two Burial Caves of the Proto-Urban Period at Azor, 1971", *Qedem* I (1975) p. 24, fig. 12.10-12, pl. 22.6. The analysis of one fragmentary earring is given p. 24, n. 26: Ag 92.57%, Cu 1.72%, As, Pb, Sn $\langle 0.02\%$, Sb $\langle 0.03\%$, Ni 0.0043%, Zn 0.0028%, Fe 0.012%, I.R. 4.60%. I am most grateful to Dr Moorey for drawing the *Qedem* publication to my attention.

31. Meṣer II, see P.R. Miroschedji, *L'Epoque Pré-Urbaine en Palestine* (Cahiers de la Revue Biblique 13, Paris 1971), p. 41, fig. 16.1; and two flat axes, one dagger with a single rivet hole and two chisels?, from Beth Shan XVI, see G. M. Fitzgerald, 'The Earliest Pottery of Beth Shan', *Museum Journal* 24 (1935), 5-32, pl. III.21-25.

32. D. Ussishkin, *Bib. Arch,* 34 (1971), 23; C. A. Key, *IEJ* 8 (1963), 289; *Science* 146 (1964), 1578.

33. W. M. F. Petrie and J. E. Quibell, *Naqada and Ballas,* pp. 22, 48 and pl. LXV.3. Ashmolean Museum no. 1895 - 968.

34. University College, London no. 4999, now fragments only; E. J. Baumgartel, *Cultures of Prehistoric Egypt,* II, p. 7 (hereafter Baumgartel, *CPE* II); id., *Petrie's Naqada Excavation, A Supplement* (hereafter Baumgartel, *Supplement*).

35. W.M.F. Petrie and J.E. Quibell, *Naqada and Ballas,* p. 45; Petrie, *Diospolis Parva,* p. 25; not listed in Baumgartel, *Supplement;* whereabouts unknown.

36. Ashmolean Museum 1895.987, dimensions H. 8 mm., D. 4.5 cm., perhaps from stone jar, Ashmolean Museum 1895.167; Petrie and Quibell, *Naqada and Ballas,* p. 45, pl. LXV.2; Petrie, *Prehistoric Egypt,* p. 27; Baumgartel, *CPE* II, p. 7; *Lucas and Harris,* p. 246 n.6.

37. Ashmolean Museum 1895.987, few small fragments only remaining; references as for preceding, except Petrie and Quibell, *Naqada and Ballas,* p. 48, pl. LXV.1; C. R. Williams, *Gold and Silver Jewellery and Related Objects* (New York Historical Society, N.Y. 1924), p. 20. The appearance of the metal now is very similar to that of the lid, i.e. very thin, matt dark purple.

38. Ashmolean Museum 1895.137; Petrie and Quibell, *Naqada and Ballas,* p. 26, pl. LX.14; Baumgartel, *CPE* II, pp. 22, 75; Petrie, *Prehistoric Egypt,* p. 27; *Lucas and Harris,* p. 244, n. 1; Petrie, *Diospolis Parva,* p. 25.

39. Petrie, *Prehistoric Egypt,* p. 43; not listed in Baumgartel, *Supplement*; not in UCL; whereabouts unknown.

40. D. Randall MacIver, A.C. Mace and F. Ll. Griffith, *el Amrah and Abydos,* p. 42, pl. VI.1.2; Petrie, *Tools and Weapons,* p. 28, pl. XXXIII.1; Cairo Museum Entrance Journal, 35158; Baumgartel, *CPE* II, pp. 9-10, pl. II.1-2. Dimensions: 16.6 x 4.1 cm.

41. Quibell, *Archaic Objects* 14341; Baumgartel, *CPE* II, p. 9 and pl. I.4; Cairo Museum, Entrance Journal.

42. Quibell, *Archaic Objects* 14516, pl. 58; Cairo Museum Entrance Journal; Baumgartel, *CPE* II, p. 9, pl. II.8.

43. Quibell, *Archaic Objects* 14515; Cairo Museum Entrance Journal, 31562; Baumgartel, *CPE* II, p. 9. Dimensions 12 x 3.3 cm.

44. Quibell, *Archaic Objects* 14514; Baumgartel, *CPE* II, p. 9, pl. II.4. Dimensions 17.9 x 5.1 cm.

45. Musée du Cinquantenaire, Brussels; E. R. Ayrton and W.L.S. Loat, *Predynastic Cemetery at el Mahasna,* pp. 16, 30 and pl. XVI.3; Baumgartel, *CPE* II, pp. 7-8; *Lucas and Harris,* p. 246 n. 6; C. R. Williams, op. cit., pp. 28 and 20.

46. Vanished shortly after excavation; Petrie and Quibell, *Naqada and Ballas,* p. 46, and cf. pl. LXI.8; Petrie, *Prehistoric Egypt,* p. 27; Baumgartel, *CPE* II, p. 7; id., *Diospolis Parva,* p. 25; *Lucas and Harris,* p. 246 n.6; C. R. Williams, op. cit., p. 20.

47. UCL 5477; Petrie and Quibell, *Naqada and Ballas,* pp. 14, 48; Petrie, *Tools and Weapons,* p. 16 and pl. XVI. 65; Baumgartel, *CPE* II, p. 8.

48. D. Randall MacIver, A.C. Mace, F.Ll. Griffith, *el Amrah and Abydos,* pp. 24, 46; Baumgartel, *CPE* II, p. 7.

49. Petrie and Quibell, *Naqada and Ballas,* p. 45; Petrie, *Prehistoric Egypt,* p. 27; id., *Diospolis Parva,* p. 25; Baumgartel, *CPE* II, p. 7; *Lucas and Harris,* p. 246 n. 6; C. R. Williams, op. cit., p. 20. Present whereabouts unknown, once University College, London?

50. I am most grateful for Dr. P.R.S. Moorey's advice over these objects, as indeed for discussing the subject generally and drawing a number of relevant articles to my attention; also for allowing me to examine the objects in his care at the Ashmolean Museum.

51. *Lucas and Harris,* p. 491, no. 1. See E. Amélineau, *Les nouvelles fouilles d'Abydos 1895-96,* p. 274, and also pp. 216, 218, 234 and pl. IX. Gold was actually visible in this object; it contained 38.1% gold and 60.4% silver.

52. *Lucas and Harris,* p. 248.

53. *Lucas and Harris,* p. 249.

54. As silica 2.55%, metallic silver 4.07%, ferric oxide 2.55% corresponding to 1.67% of Fe, some traces of calcium in the form of the carbonate, chloride of silver 90.83%, carbonate of silver deriving from the alteration of the silver (C.R. Williams, op. cit., p. 20; analysis done by M. Huybrechts, University of Liège).

55. Mishara and Meyers, op. cit., p. 6.

56. The lid, which proved to be of nearly pure silver - 98%?, the hawk (*CPE* II, p. 22) 'pure silver'.

57. Petrie, *Prehistoric Egypt,* p. 27.

58. Baumgartel, *CPE* II, pp; 6-10.

59.   S. Lloyd and J. Mellaart, *Beycesultan* I, pp. 280-283.

60.   R. C. dates for Level XXXVI = $3010^{\pm} 58$ b.c (P-298); for XXVIII = $2740^{\pm} 62$ b.c. (P-297); I am most grateful to Mr. A. G. Sherrat for pointing this out and for discussing aspects of ancient metallurgy with me. He is by no means to be held responsible for any errors of mine in this direction, however. See also Wertime, op. cit., p. 878, Table 1, who lists the original date in the second half of the fifth millennium.

61.   These may date a little later: Mellaart suggests EB2; H. H. von der Osten, *The Alishar Hüyük Seasons of 1931-32,* I (OIP XXVIII), p. 51, fig. 43. They form part of a group from pot burial eX19 which also contained two copper bracelets, one flint blade and a fragment of a serpentine macehead.

62.   M. van Loon, 'The excavations at Koruçutepe, Turkey, 1968-70. Preliminary Report', *JNES,* 32 (1973), pp. 357-444; for the graves, see pp. 359-361, fig. 3, pls. 3, 4, 5.

63.   E.g. chalcolithic Tarsus: see H. Goldman, *Excavations at Gözlu Küle, Tarsus,* II, pp. 6-8.

64.   Ashmolean Museum 1935.769.

65.   Ashmolean Museum 1964.744; two from the Warka 'Sammelfund' in the late protoliterate levels - E. Heinrich, *Kleinfunde aus den archaischen Tempelschichten in Uruk; Ausgrabungen der Deutschen Forschungsgemeinschaft in Uruk-Warka,* I (Leipzig, 1936), pp. 28-29, pl. 17, nos. W14722c1 and W14766f.

66.   Late Proto-literate period, E. Heinrich, op. cit., pl. 29, W15260.

67.   *Vorläufiger Bericht über die von der Notgemeinschaft der Deutschen Wissenschaft in Uruk-Warka unternommener Ausgrabungen,* 7 (1935), pl. 24.b and pp. 15-16; also illustrated in E. Porada, *JAOS,* 70 (1950), p. 223ff. and fig. 5; cf. also the ?Elamite example of a silver animal, D. Hansen, *Metropolitan Museum Journal,* 3 (1970), pp. 5-14. This latter object has been analysed as almost pure silver, including 0.6 - 1.7% copper, 0.006 - 0.04% gold - native silver?

68.   C. M. Ryan, *A Guide to the Known Minerals of Turkey,* (Maden Tetkik ve Arama Enstitusu and the United States Operations Mission in Turkey, Ankara 1960): see map.

69.   C. J. Gadd, 'The Dynasty of Agade and the Gutian Invasion', Revised CAH fasc. 17, pp. 12-13.

70.   See nn. 2 and 51.

71.   'Tombes de chefs d'époque énéolithique trouvées à Byblos', *BMBeyr* IX (1949), p. 75ff.

72.   *Byblos* V, p. 212 and cf. n. 24 above.

73.   *Byblos* V, pp. 311-312.

74.   W. Gowland, 'Silver in Roman and Earlier Times: I. Pre-historic and Proto-historic Times', *Archaeologia,* 69 (1920), pp. 121-160, esp. 123; see also *Lucas and Harris,* p. 248 n.2.

75.   C.C. Patterson, *Am. Ant,* 36 (1971), p. 286.

76.   Wertime, op. cit., p. 883.

77.   Wertime, op. cit., p. 878, Table I.

78.   *Byblos* V, p. 317.

79.   U.C. no. 15125, Ht. 7 cm. Petrie, *Prehistoric Egypt,* pl. II.7 and pp. 9 and 27. For references to predynastic lead objects, see *Lucas and Harris,* p. 244; the hawk is silver, as noted above. I am most grateful to Mrs. Barbara Adams for allowing me to examine the figurine and other objects in University College.

80.   I am most grateful to Mrs. Baumgartel for her help and advice on the Egyptian predynastic objects and for general discussion about the use of silver, to which she early drew attention as being an important class of predynastic material.

81.   P. J. Ucko, *Anthropomorphic Figurines of Predynastic Egypt and Neolithic Crete with Comparative Material from the Prehistoric Near East and Mainland Greece* (London, 1968), pp. 427-8.

82.   H.J. Kantor, *JNES,* 11 (1952), p. 239ff.; id., in *Chronologies in Old World Archaeology,* ed. R.W. Ehrich, pp. 1-46; W. Stevenson Smith, *Interconnections in the Ancient Near East,* pp. 5-6; *Lucas and Harris,* p. 430 n. 6 note the timbers found in Egypt as cedar (Lebanon, Asia Minor), cypress (Syria) and pine (probably Syria, also Asia Minor and south Levant).

83.   No. 18549, from T.272, *Byblos* II, pl. CLXXXVII; cf. Ayrton and Loat, *Predynastic Cemetery at el Mahasna,* Grave H29 has a comparable but separate ivory animal and stone vase; the arrangement of animal and container can be compared with well known Egyptian spoons, e.g. Petrie and Quibell, *Naqada and Ballas,* pl. LXI.2.

84.   No. 5740 from T.146, *Byblos* I, pl. CLXXXIX and p. 385, fig. 295. Cf. Ayrton and Loat, *Predynastic Cemetery at el Mahasna,* pl. XVI.1, Grave H41 (which also contained silver beads) had a clay figurine; the closest parallel to the Byblos figure was bought by Petrie, said to have been found at Ballas, published in *Prehistoric Egypt,* pl. II.24; pl. II.23, though a male figure, has very similar prominent ears; related bone figures also come from the main deposit at Hierakonpolis.

85.   Nos. 3056, 3098, 3349, 3597, 3883, 3905, 5266, 5267 and 6066 in *Byblos* I. I would like to thank Mrs. J. Crowfoot Payne for her help over this, and especially for her kind loan of a copy of *Byblos* V in advance of

this volume's reaching the libraries.
86.   G. Herrmann, 'Lapis Lazuli: the Early Phases of its Trade'; J. Crowfoot Payne, 'Lapis Lazuli in Early Egypt',
      both in *Iraq*, XXX (1968), pp. 21-61, esp. p. 37.

NEW PERSPECTIVES ON EARLY BRONZE III IN CANAAN
Joseph A. Callaway

I.   Introduction

Historical interpretation of the Early Bronze Age[1] in Canaan has advanced dramatically since World War II as a result of major excavations at Beth-yerah, Tell el-Far‘ah (N), Jericho, Arad, Ai, Taanach and Bab edh-Dhra. Dame Kathleen Kenyon has been at the fore-front of this advance since she began the epochal excavation at Jericho in 1952. She has inspired more excellent techniques of excavation by the example of careful and controlled removal of strata,[2] and has provoked much scholarly discussion by introducing new interpretations and nomenclature for periods such as the "Proto-Urban" transition from Chalcolithic to the EB urban age.[3] Many students and professors have been influenced in their professional careers by Dame Kathleen, among whom the writer is glad to be included, because it was at her suggestion that a study of the tombs at Ai was undertaken in 1961.[4] This led to a decade of excavations at Ai, beginning in 1964, and eventually to development of the new perspectives on EB III outlined in the following discussion.

Recent Studies. Summary studies of EB in Palestine have appeared regularly since about 1960, when Wright outlined briefly his interpretation of major developments since his initial pioneering study in 1937.[5] The "low" chronology of EB followed by Albright and his pupils was outlined in the same *Festschrift* volume with Wright's article by Freedman and Campbell,[6] and Albright himself published a revision of his chronology in 1965.[7] Lapp, a pupil of Wright's, summarized the state of EB studies at the end of the 1960's from the perspective of his work at Bab edh-Dhra and indicated his preferred "solutions" to outstanding problems at the time.[8]

The most important contribution during the 1960's was a masterly synthetic summary prepared by de Vaux for the Third Edition of *The Cambridge Ancient History*.[9] Rising above partisan arguments about chronology, nomenclature and classification, de Vaux managed to gather into one brief fascicle just about all that was worth knowing about EB in the mid-1960's. Wright's review article of the fascicle by de Vaux updated his own views in 1971.[10]

More limited and technical studies of EB have appeared along with the summaries. Hennessy, in a dissertation under Kenyon's direction, analyzed the materials from Areas E III-IV at Jericho and introduced the first phasing of EB on the *tell* from the Kenyon excavations.[11] His major contribution is a reconstruction of foreign relations during the period based upon the evidence of pottery and other artifacts. Amiran published a very useful handbook on pottery in the Holy Land with a long section on EB pottery in 1963, translated into English in 1969.[12] And the writer has now published a report on the sanctuary at Ai which interprets the phasing of the site and relates the major strata to parallels in Canaan and elsewhere. [13]

Numerous short specialized studies have appeared in journals and at professional meetings. The focus of interest in these articles has been largely EB I-II or the transition from Chalcolithic to EB. Even Lapp's summary paper deals mainly with the transition from Chalcolithic to EB because the most dramatic new evidence from Bab edh-Dhra related to that period.[14] One reason for the extraordinary interest in the early phases is that discussions of the later phases were relatively free of controversy. Albright observed in 1965 that "Early Bronze III is the best known and best dated period of EB," [15] and most scholars agreed with him. In any case, recent studies have largely by-passed EB III except in a very general and summary fashion.

The Significance of EB III. One result of recent research is that EB III appears to be less well known and dated than was supposed. Albright's sequence of three phases, viz., "(A) before the introduction of Khirbet Kerak ware; (B) during the domination of Khirbet Kerak ware in the north; (C) after the decline of the Khirbet Kerak culture and during the Egyptian Sixth Dynasty" [16] is not longer precise enough.

With regard to his Phase A, Hennessy argued persuasively that the Khirbet Kerak culture appeared at Beth-yerah and Beth-shan in the north at the beginning of EB III, [17] and Khirbet Kerak-type vessels have been identified as far south as Ai in EB IIIA.[18] The domination of Khirbet Kerak culture in Phase B can now be extended south as far as

Ai, during the time of Sanctuary A. Amiran has identified Khirbet Kerak ware in Sanctuary A, [19] and the nature and location of the vessels leads the writer to believe a Khirbet Kerak-oriented regime was in power at Ai during EB IIIB.[20] Albright's Phase C is somewhat ambiguous. Recent efforts to designate an EB IV classification by Dever, Schaub and others seem to be aimed at resolving this ambiguity. [21] In any case, Phase C belongs in the post-urban age of EB after the great cities had fallen and should, therefore, be separated from EB III as is now being done.

The Khirbet Kerak culture at Beth-yerah and Beth-shan in EB IIIA represents an intrusion or migration of new-comers from the north similar to the increments of newcomers who periodically entered the land during EB I-II. Their influence in shaping the history of EB III is now well-known.

A lesser-known but equally significant influence from Egypt appears at the same time in the south at Ai. Evidence of this presence has been known for a generation, since the collection of imported alabaster and stone vessels was excavated at Sanctuary A in 1934. [22] However, the nature of the Egyptian intrusion and its chronology have not been properly evaluated in view of the international context at the beginning of EB III. Lapp's statement that "outside the sanctuary there is nothing to suggest Egyptian occupation or control of Ai, . . . "[23] comes short of what now seems to be required by the evidence.

Actually, present indications are that Egypt did control Ai in some kind of political or economic relationship, or both. The Egyptian presence is evident in the temple-palace complex on the acropolis, the water reservoir inside the city wall at the Corner Gate, and in Sanctuary A.[24] These are all public buildings. Domestic houses do not reflect the same influence, suggesting surrogate control of the city and not a settlement of migrants on the order of those at Beth-yerah in the north.

Historically, Egypt has always gained footholds in Canaan through surrogates or vassals, beginning with the first effort in EB IC some 300 years before the second attempt at Ai in EB IIIA. The Egyptian base in EB IC was established at Gath, at the southwest edge of the foothills leading into the central highlands. Lapp interprets the evidence in Stratum V at Gath as indicating a conquest, not a raid, for the purpose of making the city "a protected base from which Egypt exploited its economic interests."[25] A security interest also may be attributed because more of the wares of the newcomers to Canaan from the north are found in Egypt than are Egyptian wares in Canaan in EB IC. [26] The rulers of Egypt must have recognized a pattern of settlements following closely on the heels of trade with the northerners.

The stage is set in Canaan at the beginning of EB III, therefore, for a developing conflict between two kinds of outside influences. On the one hand, Egypt attempts a second time to establish an imperialistic base in the country, this time at Ai, while on the other, major increments of settlers from the north have a foothold in the cities of Beth-yerah and Beth-shan. The conflict is a type that becomes classic in later times, i.e., between an imposed foreign influence and what appears to be essentially a process of infiltration and settlement. The struggle between these influences is the story of EB III in Canaan.

II. The Phases of EB III

Some Problems in Interpretation. The two most important EB III sites in Canaan, Khirbet Kerak and Ai, have served very poorly as type-sites because of incomplete publication of the former and some wrong interpretations in the case of the latter. The writer contributed his share of wrong interpretations of the evidence at Ai during the years from 1964 to 1969. In retrospect, most of the difficulty resulted from conclusions based upon insufficient evidence.[27] There is constant pressure on the director of an excavation to put out comprehensive historical reconstructions in oral and preliminary reports from the very beginning of a project, and it is easy to get locked into an inadequate reconstruction which predisposes one to overlook any evidence to the contrary.

Marquet-Krause had the same difficulty at Ai. The stratification of her Sanctuaries A-C, excavated in 1934, became the pattern for interpreting strata elsewhere. [28] When an additional city wall phase was discovered in the lower city in 1935, it was not recognized as evidence of a fourth phase of the city.[29] The writer subscribed to the Marquet-Krause reconstruction of three major city phases during the first three seasons of excavations with the result that evidence of the fourth phase found in the first season at Site C in 1964 made no significant impression, although it was recorded. [30] Preliminary reports carried reconstructions based upon a theory of three major city wall phases, and other writers incorporated the erroneous data in their articles. The result has been a confusion of EB II and EB III evidence at Ai, and, consequently, an inability to use it properly in understanding EB III in Canaan.

An effort has been made in recent publications to set forth the present understanding of the phases at Ai, [31] and because of its significance for interpretation of EB III, a summary is included below.

The EB IIIA-IIIB City Phases at Ai. The first undisputed evidence of two major EB III city phases at Ai emerged in the analysis of sections from Site A, the sanctuary. Sanctuary A was found to be the EB IIIB phase of a building that apparently served as a domestic house in EB IIIA. [32] Both phases were associated with the monumental citadel tower constructed over the remains of the EB IC and EB II citadels. The buildings designated Sanctuaries B and C by Marquet-Krause were associated with the earlier citadels, and preceded the two EB III phases.[33] The EB IIIA phase of the Sanctuary A building was, therefore, overlooked by Marquet-Krause.

Discovery of a missing phase at Site A led to a closer examination of the city wall phases. A small excavation at the north end of the citadel in 1970 uncovered the Citadel Gate, dating to EB IC and contemporary with the Postern Gate at Site L, the Corner Gate at Site K, and the Wadi Gate at Site J. [34] The Citadel Gate was blocked in the EB II strengthening and widening of the city wall, and Citadel B was constructed over the ruins of Citadel C and the approach road leading to the gate. The EB IC and EB II city walls were, therefore, the original Wall C built c. 3000 B.C. and its widened version designated Wall B, constructed c. 2860 B.C. [35]

This same construction was found at Site L, where the Postern Gate was blocked by the Wall B builders in EB II, and the Lower City Gate was constructed in the widened version of the same wall just east of the Postern Gate. [36] At Site C, the Wall B addition to Wall C was found on the inside of Wall C, [37] and at Site K, the round corner tower was rebuilt of smaller stones over the foundations of the EB IC tower, utilizing the same gate and city wall in both EB IC and EB II.

The consequence of these identifications was that two major city walls, the middle and outer walls of Marquet-Krause, were left for EB IIIA and EB IIIB respectively. Subsequent excavation at Site L provided stratigraphic proof that these assignments were correct, [38] and support was found at Site K, where the EB IIIA water reservoir blocked the EB II Corner Gate, and both EB IIIA and EB IIIB walls were found associated with the reservoir. [39] Here, then, were the remains extensive enough to fill the long span of time in EB III from c. 2700 to 2350 B.C., a span which hitherto was so lacking in material evidence that Wright called it an "embarrassment" to the Palestinian archaeologist. [40]

Since the four city-wall phases were identified after considerable use of the Marquet-Krause A-B-C sequence, a decision was made to keep the designations already known and add designation "A^1" for the additional phase. The two phases of the inner wall dating to EB IC-II became Walls C and B respectively, the middle wall became Wall A, and the outer wall A^1. A correlation of city phases with those of the sanctuary, along with the suggested chronology, is as follows: [41]

Ai Stratum	Sanctuary Stratum	City Wall Features	Period	Chronology
Pre-Urban	Building R	Unwalled village	EB IB	ca. 3100-3000 B.C.
Urban C	Building C	First major walled city	EB IC	ca. 3000-2860 B.C.
Urban B	Building B	Urban C walls rebuilt and widened .75 to 1.00 m.	EB II	ca. 2860-2700 B.C.
Urban A	Building A	New city walls built against outside Urban C/B walls	EB IIIA	ca. 2700-2550 B.C.
Urban A^1	Sanctuary A	Urban A walls rebuilt and doubled in width	EB IIIB	ca. 2550-2350 B.C.

The Phases of EB III in Canaan. EB III at Ai, as noted above, includes two major city building phases dating from ca. 2700 to 2350 B.C., and the EB IIIB phase has evidence of sub-phase modifications in the strengthening of the citadel at Site A and remodelling of houses at Site C. This accounts for the longer period of time assigned to EB IIIB. Two major periods are identified also at Jericho by Hennessy. His Phases F-D of Areas E III-IV are assigned to EB IIIA and correspond to Building A of the sanctuary site and Urban A of the general stratification at Ai. Phases C-A comprise the final occupation layers of Jericho in EB IIIB and correlate with Sanctuary A and the Urban A^1 city at Ai.[42]

Imitation Khirbet Kerak ware appears in Phase VI at Ai, and the forms associate this phase, dated to EB IIIA, with Beth-shan XII, or the initial EB III settlement at Beth-shan. [43] Both imitation and exemplar

Khirbet Kerak pottery and associated artifacts occur in the EB IIIB stratum at Ai. These have their parallels in both Beth-shan XII and XI, indicating a comparable phasing at Beth-shan with perhaps regional variations.[44] Level IV at Beth-yerah is more difficult to correlate with the sites of Ai, Jericho and Beth-shan, although the brief report available states that "the Khirbet Kerak period lasted a very long time" and "four stages of building may be discerned on this level."[45] This seems to mean successive building phases, and would, therefore, hold the potential for close correlation with the other sites.

Outside of Canaan, the EB IIIA phase is associated with Phase H at Judeideh in North Syria, where Khirbet Kerak ware may be related to imitations in Phase VI at Ai.[46] It follows that EB IIIB is related to Phase I of the Amuq stratification, as Wright indicated.[47] Egyptian parallels of the pottery and stone vessels of EB IIIA at Ai are found in both Second and Third Dynasty remains,[48] and architectural parallels of Temple A on the acropolis at Ai, contemporary with Building A (EB IIIA) of the sanctuary site, are found in the tomb of Hesy and the pyramid complex of Zoser, both of the early Third Dynasty.[49] Rebuilding of the city of Ai in EB IIIA seems to have been completed early in the Third Dynasty, therefore, at least by the reign of Zoser. Associations of EB IIIB remains with the Egyptian Fourth and Fifth Dynasties are not as direct as those of EB IIIA with the earlier dynasties, but the total evidence suggests a transition during the Fourth Dynasty to EB IIIB at Ai, and a termination sometime during the Fifth Dynasty.[50] A suggested correlation of EB III phases in Canaan may be arranged as follows:

Period	Ai	Jericho	Beth-shan	Beth-yerah	Syria	Egypt	Chronology
EB IIIA	Phases VIA-B	Phases F-D	Stratum XII	Level IV	Phase H	Dynasties III-IV	2700-2550 B.C.
EB IIIB	Phases VII-VIII	Phases C-A	Strata XII-XI	Level IV	Phase I	Dynasties IV-V	2550-2350 B.C.

III. The Egyptian Presence at Ai in EB IIIA.

Introduction. The relation of Sanctuary A to the acropolis buildings at Ai in EB III has resisted a satisfactory explanation because of confusion in phasing EB III. Now that the basic phases are defined, the problem of the sanctuary may be taken up again. Marquet-Krause, as is well known, identified the building containing a collection of Egyptian alabaster and stone vessels as a sanctuary, and she designated the large rectangular building on the acropolis as the palace.[51] Albright did not accept the "palace" designation, arguing that the structure was a temple on the evidence of architectural form,[52] and Wright recently documented this view with an impressive array of parallels cited from Palestine and Syria.[53]

Both views had their problems because of inadequate evidence. Marquet-Krause had the anomaly of beautiful imported Egyptian alabaster cult vessels installed in a nondescript domestic-type house, and, furthermore, the alabasters seemed to be much earlier in date than some of the pottery and artifacts with which they were found. Wright, on the other hand, could not demonstrate any cultic objects from the acropolis building, and could not locate the royal quarter if his temple identification was sustained. A satisfactory resolution of the problem, therefore, should account for the missing royal quarter, a temple devoid of cult vessels, a more-or-less *ad hoc* sanctuary building, and a unique collection of imported Egyptian vessels out of chronological context. Wright suggested that the sanctuary was more like a domestic house than a cultic shrine, and that it served merely as a storage place for vessels used in the temple.[54] His direction was accurate, and conclusions beyond this could not be drawn without more evidence. Fortunately, the evidence appears to be in hand now, and Wright's view can be supplemented and, in substance, sustained.

The Temple and Sanctuary A. A reconstruction of the temple-sanctuary relationship became possible as bits and pieces of evidence accumulated. The first significant discovery was that Sanctuary A was actually an EB IIIB phase of a building erected in EB IIIA. A careful study of the succession of buildings on the site led the writer to conclude that each one up to Sanctuary A, the final structure, was a private house with features comparable to those known at Ai and elsewhere.[55] Not one artifact in any of the phases preceding Sanctuary A suggested a cultic function of the buildings.

The second conclusion reached in the study of Site A was that a domestic house built in EB IIIA was remodeled in EB IIIB using the same foundations and room arrangement for the shrine that we know as Sanctuary A.[56] The shrine did not follow a tradition of sanctuaries through the previous periods. Neither did the architecture of the building have significance because it was an *ad hoc* installation, with the altar placed against the inner wall of the citadel in what had formerly been a courtyard and the main room of the house converted into a "holy of holies" that contained the major collection of cultic artifacts. Entrance to the sanctuary was gained through the now-partitioned court in Marquet-Krause ch. 120, and the cultic room, her ch. 116, was entered through a doorway opening from the courtyard. [57]

If the sanctuary was moved to Site A in EB IIIB, where was it located in EB IIIA? The answer, of course, is the acropolis area, but two items of missing evidence still made the identification somewhat uncertain. First, there was the missing royal quarter which should be somewhere near the acropolis; and second, some evidence that the central rectangular building was a temple should remain among its ruins.

An important section in the corridor along the west wall of the central structure led to identification of the missing royal quarter. [58] This section indicated that the foundations of the earliest central building preceded the enclosure wall around it characterized by apsidal corners. A spacious building on the west side of the central room with its five roof-support piers actually was built in the initial complex, and this building had two rows of small roof-support columns parallel with the single row of large piers in the central room. [59] The wall with apsidal corners belonged with the second phase of the western building.

This large building west of the central rectangular room is the best candidate for the missing royal quarter. An enclosure wall built in jointed segments of about 10 m. each surrounded the royal quarter on the west, and joined the central structure at its east and west ends. [60] With the temple on the east and the enclosure wall surrounding the north, west and south sides, the royal quarter was effectively walled off from the city and located on the highest part of the acropolis.

A system of sections inside the temple building in the centre of the complex aided in relating the temple phases to those of the royal quarter. Two major architectural phases of the temple were defined, with both using the same foundation and plan of the original structure.

The first temple was built of unworked cyclopean stones still visible in the foundation of the present building. [61] Five piers rested on flat bases lined up in the middle of the building and supported the roof, and since the bases were built flush with a thick plaster floor, the piers had the appearance of resting on the floor. [62]

Succeeding this temple was a second one, now well-known, with its row of four raised pier-bases across the room and having walls of hammer-dressed stones shaped like bricks and laid in mud mortar like a brick wall. [63] The bases were shaped by sawing deep grooves outlining a rectangle on the top, after which the stone outside the grooves was chipped away, leaving a clean raised surface upon which the pier of stones could rest. Some trimming on top of the rectangle indicates that the edges of the pier were set in about three centimetres on top of the base, leaving a sharply-defined projection about three centimetres wide around the base of the pier, and about the same height above the level of the floor. [64] This provided a pleasing break between the smoothly plastered surface of the floor and the pier, and added a unique and significant element to the building.

That this building was, indeed, the original Egyptianized temple of EB IIIA is indicated by the discovery of two alabaster bowls similar to those found in Sanctuary A (EB IIIB) in the EB IIIA rooms of the temple. Amiran examined the bowl fragments and original field records (in Hebrew) and confirmed that Bowl No. 514+692 is from ch. 42 and Bowl No. 344+399 is from ch. 22 of Fouille G, the acropolis. [65] The provenance of No. 344 is given in the French publication as Fouille D, but the original records in Hebrew indicate Fouille G, where the matching piece No. 399 was found, as the correct provenance. [66] Both bowls were found in rooms filled with rubble in the EB IIIB phase of the temple, at the time Sanctuary A was established at the citadel, confirming stratigraphically that they were used in the EB IIIA temple when the Sanctuary A vessels were also used there if our reconstruction is correct. A correlation of sections revealed that the original temple, built of cyclopean stones and with five roof-support piers, was used during the EB IC and EB II phases of the royal quarter. The EB IC phase of the royal quarter had two rows of small columns in the main room and utilized the original enclosure wall built in jointed segments. [67] In EB II, the same enclosure wall was rebuilt and used, but the royal quarter was constricted, using an outer wall characterized by apsidal corners laid between the parallel rows of pillar bases of the former building. [68]

The second temple characterized by raised-top bases and brick-like masonry was built in EB IIIA and continued in use through EB IIIB. But the plan of the royal quarter changed radically. The segmented enclosure wall used in EB IC-II seems to have been abandoned, and the perimeter wall of the EB IC royal building was rebuilt and made into an enclosure wall. This constricted the temple-royal quarter complex still further, and rectangular rooms were added at each end of the temple. [69] Then, in EB IIIB, the spaces around the temple seem to have been filled with rubble, eliminating the royal quarter and leaving only the large rectangular temple open. Because of the prominent Khirbet Kerak evidence in Sanctuary A, my conclusion is that Egyptian influence was downgraded in EB IIIB, the Egyptianized temple was transferred to Site A and made into an *ad hoc* sanctuary, and the new ruler at Ai occupied the former temple building on the acropolis. [70]

The temple, therefore, remained constant in size from EB IC through EB IIIB, but the shape and size of the royal quarter changed in each phase. Generally, the royal quarter became smaller in each succeeding phase, until the temple building itself was taken over in EB IIIB as the royal residence. A summary of the temple and royal quarter phases is as follows:

Temple	Royal Quarter	Location	Features	Stratum	Period
Temple C		Site D	5-pillar temple	Urban C	EB IC
	Building C	Site D	Twin rows of pillars	Urban C	EB IC
Temple B		Site D	5-pillar temple	Urban B	EB II
	Building B	Site D	Apsidal wall, no pillars	Urban B	EB II
Temple A		Site D	4-pillar temple	Urban A	EB IIIA
	Building A	Site D	Rectangular rooms	Urban A	EB IIIA
(Sanctuary A)		Site A	Remodeled residence	Urban A^1	EB IIIB
	Building A^1	Site D	Remodeled temple	Urban A^1	EB IIIB

The Water Storage Reservoir. Perhaps the most surprising discovery at Ai during the recent excavations was an intact water storage pool inside the city walls at the Corner Gate site. [71] The pool was built above ground and not in an excavated pit, utilizing the natural surface of the area for the floor and skillfully constructed dikes around three sides of the sloping site to contain the water. Reaching a depth of 3 m. along the east side and sloping upward with the incline of bedrock to a shallow edge on the west side, the 25 m. wide pool had an estimated capacity of 1815 cubic metres, or about one-half million gallons. [72]

The pool was constructed in EB IIIA, closing off the Corner Gate which had been used in EB IC-II, and was part of the general city-building operation that included a new city wall, Temple A with its Egyptianized artifacts on the acropolis, and a significant erosion-control dam at the Wadi Gate site on the lowest side of the *tell.* Several features of the pool indicate considerable expertise and experience on the part of the builders, suggesting that they were imported for the job. Foremost among these features are the special soil preparation for the dike and floor to minimize seepage loss, the arrangement of stone facing for the dike and floor surfaces, and the safeguards built between the pool and the city wall to prevent water damage of the fortifications.

The floor and dike fill material was the dark reddish-brown *khamra* soil found on and off the site, although it appeared to be darker in color than the present surface soil. One possibility considered was that imported additives of a special nature may have been used in the fill, causing its very dark hue. [73] However, exhaustive separation and analytical testing showed that the special color and physical properties resulted from a concentration of selected portions of certain soil deposits, either from the site itself or the nearby fields. Confinement of the selected material in the fill for an extended time enhanced the darkening, particularly from worm activity, some of which was noted. [74]

The density of the in-place fill material was as high as that obtainable from present-day compaction procedures applied to similar soil materials, namely 1.9 grams per cubic centimetre. Quantitative analysis of particle sizes present in the fill and similar materials within a 2 km. radius of the *tell* indicated that the proportion of finer materials was increased three-fold in the sealant for the pool by its builders. [75] These fine-grained materials, having a particle size of less than .002 mm. and consisting of silt particles and silica resulting from the deterioriation of limestone beds, gave the special properties to the soil used in the dike and floor.

How would such a large quantity of fine-grained sealant material be obtained? The most obvious answer is that pocketed areas were found where surface soil had washed down the terraces and steps in bedrock from higher levels, leaving coarser materials in each successive step downward until the finer particles collected in sedimented pools lower down the slope. This is the method used in separating finer grades of pottery clay from coarser materials. Such pockets of fine clay are found on bedrock on the site, as is reported in Layer 12 of the sanctuary excavation. [76] The major problem, then, in collecting the fill was to find these pockets of fine clay, separate coarser debris from the clay and transport the resulting materials to the construction site.

A surface of this sealant material would not prevent seepage of water, however, because even clay has a certain porosity. To reduce the exposure of porous areas, a stone facing for both the dike and floor was imbedded in the fill with individual stones keyed together closely enough to reduce the area of contact between sealant and water by 90 per cent. A single layer of stones up to 30 centimetres in thickness was imbedded in the dike, apparently to increase its strength, while two layers of flat stones were laid for the floor, one superimposed upon the other.[77] The double layer was arranged with the joints of the lower stones covered by the upper ones, resulting in a further reduction of sealant contact with stored water.

Whether by design or a natural process, the mortar material used in the joints between the stones consisted of a gradation of particle sizes in proportions which would allow progressively smaller flow areas as the interstices between adjacent soil particles were filled. This choice and placement of material was probably based upon previous experience in building dams or ponds, or even experience in reducing the porosity of pottery vessels. In any case, the moistened materials pressed down by the weight of the water would tend to increase compaction, and seepage would tend to fill the space between minute particles with still smaller particles, resulting in maximum blockage to the flow of water through the joints of the stones into the fill material.

One further feature of the stone facing should be mentioned. At the point of juncture between the floor and the dike, the stones of the floor continued some distance underneath the dike,[78] reducing the possibility of a shrinkage crack between the two and giving structural continuity at a weak point in the system. On the uphill side of the pool, the floor surface was extended on bedrock with the sealant continuing between the two, allowing the incoming flow of water to be directed upon the floor and minimizing the chance of the floor being undermined. By continuing the floor underneath the dike on the low side, the flow path was directed to the vertical facing of the dike and the possibility of undermining the dike was also minimized.

Finally, the backside of the dike was constructed against the city wall with a built-in drainage system to carry off any seepage water or leaks and to prevent damage to the fortifications. A balk cut into the southeast corner of the dike shows the thick layer of *khamra* behind the facing stones separated from the city wall by a mass of loose stones laid up at the outer edge of the sealant.[79] These stones allowed any water escaping from the pool through the dike to be directed alongside the city wall to a drainage point probably at the northeast corner of the installation. This drain prevented a collection of water against the inner face of the wall and allowed a monitoring of water loss at all times.

The soundness of the reservoir design and construction is attested by its preservation to the present day without any evidence of a major break or even leak. About 1 meter of silt collected over the floor before it was abandoned at the end of EB IIIB, and no tell-tale erosion ditches or channels are evident in the 25-meter width of the silted layer to suggest a break.

The Egyptian Presence at Ai in EB IIIA. As noted above, the Egyptianized cult vessels of Sanctuary A have indicated a strong tie between Ai and Egypt recognized for a generation. The discussion of the sanctuary and Temple A has sought to place in context the major archaeological facts relating to that tie, and the conclusion was that the cult vessels were introduced in EB IIIA when Temple A was constructed on the acropolis. The temple itself has not been associated with Egypt, although its unique construction features have been well-known for many years. We seem to have reached the point in reconstructing the sequence and nature of events, however, to posit a more serious involvement of Egypt in the affairs of Ai in the rebuilding of the city and, presumably, its administration in EB IIIA.

There is evidence that suggests Egyptian involvement in building Temple A on the acropolis. The writer noted in a preliminary report that the raised-top pier bases of the temple, shaped by sawing grooves in the top of the base outlining a rectangle, were probably made with Egyptian copper saws.[80] Tools of this kind are known in Egypt from the reign of Zer in the First Dynasty, and are numerous by the time of the Third Dynasty. Emery reported a cache of six saws from Tomb 3471 at Saqqara,[81] and saw marks are found on basalt, granite and alabaster architecture and sarcophagi dating to the Fourth Dynasty.[82]

Another feature of the temple is the manner of construction of the 2 m. wall of hammer-dressed stones laid in mud mortar like bricks. This unique way of building a wall without a rubble core has no parallel in Canaan. However, it is an Egyptian method of building in the Third Dynasty. The technique is evident in the pyramid complex of Zoser where the core of the temenos wall enclosing the pyramid is made of "coursed rubble masonry of local limestone set in clay" and faced with "fine paneled masonry of white silicious limestone from the quarries at Tura."[83]

The coursed masonry wall at Ai was faced with plaster, however, instead of worked stone blocks. Actually the plaster application was very carefully planned, reflecting experience and skill on the part of those who did the work not evident in the earlier phases of the temple. An initial base layer of the mud mortar used between the stones was applied in uneven places on the inside face of the wall, apparently to create an even, flat surface. On top of this was applied a layer of red clay plaster mixed with straw for a binder. This plaster became the base for a final layer of white *hunwar* that covered the wall, [84] continued on the floor to the edge of the raised top of the pier bases, and probably coated the piers of stones themselves. This type of finish is found in Egypt in the Tomb of Hesy, where mud brick walls were faced with plaster over a base layer of the mortar used between the bricks. [85] The plastered walls of the Tomb of Hesy were decorated with painted designs, which may also have been the case at Ai if the black patches photographed by Marquet-Krause are remnants of painted areas, as they appear to be. [86]

Temple A, therefore, appears to have prominent Egyptian features in the manner of wall construction, the plaster finish on the walls, and the pier bases inside the main room. Round column bases with a worked ridge between the floor and column of the type found in rectangular shape at Ai are evident in the pyramid complex of Zoser. [87] Thus Temple A as well as its cult furnishings reflects Egyptian involvement more serious and intimate than trade relations alone would imply. With this kind of investment in the focal public building of the new city, an assumption of political ties approaching vassalage must not be ruled out.

Egyptian engineering of the water storage reservoir described above cannot be proved at this time, because there are no other reservoirs known in Canaan in EB IIIA, nor are parallels to be found in Egypt. We may theorize that the quality of planning and construction of the reservoir matches the unique quality of Temple A on the acropolis, and that this kind of engineering is found only in Egypt in EB IIIA. The erosion control dam constructed at the Wadi Gate site at the same time has some of the same engineering features as the reservoir, [88] and must be considered a part of the total project of rebuilding the city. But more direct evidence of Egyptian connections cannot be cited at this time.

One observation is relevant here. All of the projects cited as Egyptian-related are for the ruler of the city and the public, and no projects for private citizens can be identified in the excavated areas. This implies an Egyptian interest in controlling the city as a base for political and economic exploitation of interests in Canaan, and possibly as a first line of defence in securing the approaches to the east border of Egypt against encroachments from the north or from Trans-Jordan where Schaub and Rast have recently discovered evidence of very large EB communities in the vicinity of Bab edh-Dhra. [89]

IV. Khirbet Kerak Evidence at Ai in EB IIIB

The Transition to EB IIIB. An assault on the fortifications of the EB IIIA city occurred at the end of the period, evident in blackened, calcined stones on top of the city wall in front of the citadel at Site A[90] and in the destruction of the EB IIIA South Gate at Site C. [91] No evidence of widespread destruction inside the city is found, however, suggesting that changes in the leadership of the city were agreed to by the defenders when the fortifications fell. This would mean the ousting of pro-Egyptian rulers and the installation of new leaders who seem to have had a northern, or Khirbet Kerak, orientation as will be discussed below.

Significant changes were made at Ai at the beginning of EB IIIB in the city fortifications and in the accommodations for the new ruler. As noted earlier, the new ruler seems to have downgraded the Egyptianized cult of Temple A and transferred it to the *ad hoc* sanctuary at Site A. This would be a rather arrogant and offensive move to the ousted pro-Egyptian party, and if, indeed, the royal household was established in Temple A on the acropolis as seems to be the case, the offence would be compounded. The changes involved risk of retaliation from Egypt, so considerable measures were taken to secure the city from attacks.

The South Gate in Wall A at Site C was penetrated in the attack that brought about the overthrow of the city, and a section of city wall north of the gate was broken down. This part of the wall was repaired, eliminating the gate, and a 4 m. addition to the wall was built against its outer face. The most dramatic evidence of the reconstructed wall was found at Site H, near the Corner Gate and water reservoir, where the combined width of the EB IIIA wall and its EB IIIB addition was 8 m., and its height was 7 m. [92] A comment by one of the workmen who helped uncover this stretch of wall captures the mood that must have prevailed in EB IIIB. "The people who lived here," he said, "were afraid."

Khirbet Kerak Evidence in Sanctuary A. There is no evidence of an increment of Khirbet Kerak settlers at Ai in EB IIIB, although Site C yielded persistent evidence of both authentic and imitation Khirbet Kerak vessels in one small area.[93] The major evidence of the new influence comes from the sanctuary, where political rather than ethnic changes would be reflected. Comparative studies of the Sanctuary A artifacts have been made at intervals since 1935,[94] and the identification of Khirbet Kerak artifacts in the sanctuary assemblage is now secure.[95]

Foremost among the artifacts are the pot stand with parallels from Beth-shan, Beth-yerah, Judeidah and Ta'yinat in Syria, and several sites in Anatolia.[96] Decorated bone tubes and cups should be included with the pot stand, in the writer's opinion, as well as some of the pottery votive cups, one of which was found on the altar of Sanctuary A surrounded by five painted stones.[97] These objects were located in the most prominent places in the sanctuary, e.g., on the altar and in the room serving as the "holy of holies", and the conclusion of the writer is that the cult must be viewed as pro-Khirbet Kerak in this phase rather than pro-Egyptian as in EB IIIA.

V.   Egyptian and Khirbet Kerak Influences in Canaan in EB III

The Egyptian Interest in Canaan in EB IIIA. Increasing Egyptian interest in Syria and Canaan is evident at the end of EB II with the emergence of rulers in the Second Dynasty who seem to have had imperialistic inclinations. Inscribed materials belonging to the reign of Khasekheumi are found at Byblos in Stratum VI, indicating trade with Syria via the sea route at the transition to EB IIIA.[98] Some decorated pottery forms discovered inland in both Canaan and Syria suggest a trade route by land as well.

Among Amiran's "Abydos" ware forms are juglets and jars decorated with geometric designs of Egyptian origin.[99] This decoration is characterized by triangles alternately plain and dotted, or hatched; diamond-shaped patterns with similar designs; undulating horizontal lines; chevrons inside parallel horizontal lines; and alternating straight and wavy horizontal lines.[100] The lines are painted in black, red or brown on "light-faced or white-slipped" ware. Vessels with this decoration are found at Arad, Stratum II,[101] Tomb A127 at Jericho,[102] the EB IIB destruction debris of Site A at Ai,[103] the Kinnereth tomb in Galilee,[104] and as far north as Judeideh in north Syria.[105] Two vessels with the same type of decoration are found at Saqqara with bird "signatures."[106] The spread of these painted forms, therefore, is from Abydos in Egypt via Canaan to Judeideh in north Syria, with most examples occurring in Egypt, an increasing number in Canaan, and a few at Judeideh.

There seems to have been a strong Egyptian interest in a trade route by land, therefore, at the end of EB II. Whether the Egyptians were responsible for the wave of destructions that overwhelmed EB II cities such as Gath, Arad, Tell en-Nasbeh, Ai, Tell el-Far'ah and others is not clear. Some evidence at Ai favors a theory of destruction there by earthquake in EB IIB, but this may prove to be untenable. What we do know is that Egypt established a foothold at Ai at the beginning of EB IIIA, with the result that no major threat to the land route across Sinai remained between the Canaanite outpost and the Egyptian frontier.[107] The city at Ai faced toward Trans-Jordan, where a potential threat in the newly-discovered cities east of the Dead Sea did exist. The Egyptian interest in Ai, therefore, seems to have been an imperialistic one, to secure trade and military routes by land between Egypt and Syria.

Another link in the developing chain of Egyptian influence in EB IIIA may be Megiddo, where Temples 5192 and 5269 appear to belong in EB III.[108] The evidence is confused, but Kenyon's effort to work out a sequence of phases resulted in ascribing the twin temples with a single enclosure wall to "Phase E," preceding Temple 4040 in "Phase F" both of which could be attributed to EB III.[109] The rebuild of Temple 4040, her "Phase G," would be attributed to the first phase of EB-MB, recently designated EB IV as noted earlier. If this sequence is accepted, Temples 5192 and 5269 belong in EB IIIA and may reflect Egyptian influence similar to that at Ai aimed in this instance at securing the strategic gateway to north Canaan and Syria.

Khirbet Kerak Penetration of Canaan in EB IIIB. De Vaux noted that in addition to the major sites of Beth-shan and Beth-yerah, there are traces of Khirbet Kerak ware "on almost all the sites of the plain of Esdraelon and further north. South of the plain of Esdraelon it is rare . . ."[110] This may indicate an effective Egyptian control of the region south of Megiddo in EB IIIA. However, the northern ware eventually appeared in the southern hill country and coastal plain, evident in sherds at Ras el-Ain, Gezer, Tell el-Hesi, Lachish, Ai and Jericho,[111] as well as at Megiddo itself.[112]

At Ai and Jericho, a case can be made to assign the spread of Khirbet Kerak ware to EB IIIB, and the same may be true at Tell el-Hesi, Ras el-Ain, Gezer and Lachish. All of these sites except Ras el-Ain seem to have been settled at the end of EB, suggesting that settlements were established on unoccupied locations after Egyptian control over Ai, and probably Megiddo, was broken. The scant Khirbet Kerak evidence at Megiddo is not attributable to a secure stratum, but it does occur in the upper layers that are mixed with Middle Bronze materials.[113]

The penetration of Khirbet Kerak ware south of Esdraelon was limited, but it does imply that Egyptian influence weakened considerably in EB IIIB, and that the more-or-less people's movement that began with the settlement of Beth-yerah and Beth-shan at the beginning of EB IIIA eventually triumphed over the second attempt by Egypt to gain control of Canaan and, presumably, Syria.

VI. The Termination of EB III in Canaan

A brief word concerning the destruction of the great EB III cities in Canaan seems to be required in closing this discussion. Some writers have attributed the wave of disasters that overcame the EB IIIB cities to nomadic invaders who introduced the period now designated EB IV.[114] This seems implausible to the writer in view of three considerations.

First, the fortifications of cities like Ai, with an east wall 8 m wide and at least 7 m high, would most likely hold against the onslaughts of unsophisticated and probably unorganized nomadic raids. And to attribute organized military expeditions to nomads from the Trans-Jordan or the Negeb would be scarcely credible, because no organized army can be proved to have invaded Canaan from the east until the Roman Tenth Legion advanced on Jerusalem via Jericho in A.D. 68, and this invasion was not from Trans-Jordan.[115] The termination of EB IIIB in Canaan, therefore, must have been brought about by other people than Kenyon's "Amorites."

Second, there is evidence of Egyptian military campaigns into Canaan during the Fifth and Sixth Dynasties. De Vaux notes that a scene in the tomb of Inti at Dishasha depicts the capture of a Canaanite city during the Fifth Dynasty.[116] If we terminate EB IIIB not later than c. 2350 B.C., as is done in this study, the great Canaanite cities would fall before the end of the Fifth Dynasty. However, there is evidence of more military activity in Canaan during the Sixth Dynasty,[117] which could well account for the destruction of any cities that survived the Fifth Dynasty campaigns.

The motive for Egyptian campaigns against cities in Canaan is a third consideration. If the Egyptian presence in Canaan was forcibly removed at the beginning of EB IIIB, as seems to have been the case at Ai, the Egyptians would have a motive for retaliation when there arose another ruler who had imperialistic ambitions. De Vaux observes that "it is possible to discern an attempt to establish — or re-establish — Egyptian domination over this country," meaning Canaan, and he discounts the motive of defensive action against new pressures from the north which threatened Egypt.[118] Most likely the motive was to re-establish Egyptian influence in Canaan, and we may assume that the nomads flooding into the land laid desolate by Egyptian military power thwarted that attempt.

VII. The Chronology of EB III

Hennessy dated the introduction of Khirbet Kerak ware associated with the EB IIIA settlers at Beth-yerah and Beth-shan to c. 2700 B.C., or at the end of the Second Dynasty on two lines of evidence.[119] First, the inscribed materials in Byblos VI from the reign of Khasekheumi are in an EB IIIA context indicating a beginning in north Syria at the end of that dynasty. And second, a C14 date for local Khirbet Kerak ware in south Russia of 2800 B.C. ± 90 gives a beginning point for the migration of newcomers who settled in north Canaan. Allowing 100 years for the migration, which seems to be generous, the date of c. 2700 B.C. is supported.

The date of 2700 B.C. is compatible with the results of C14 dates from Ai. Four assays of samples taken from the EB IIB destruction layers at Ai yielded an average of 2712 B.C., based upon a half-life of 5570 years.[120] The weight of the evidence at Ai favors a higher rather than lower date, but a round number of 2700 is used here since even that date is higher than most published chronologies.[121]

Only one other C14 assay of EB III samples at Ai was taken. Wood from the construction of the second EB IIIB phase of a house at Site G yielded a date of c. 2450 B.C., based upon a 5570 year half-life.[122] This wood was burned in the terminal destruction of the city at the end of EB IIIB, but its date must be reckoned from the time the house was built, not when it was destroyed. Allowing 100 years for the duration of the phase, which may be generous, a terminal date of c. 2350 B.C. can be assigned to the termination of EB IIIB at Ai.

The chronology of EB III at Ai covers a period from c. 2700 to 2350 B.C., with a division between EB IIIA and EB IIIB placed arbitrarily c. 2550 B.C. These limits are not far from a chronology for EB III in all of Canaan. The terminal date of some sites may be as late as 2300 B.C., and the beginning of some may have varied as much as 50 years. What we need more precise information on is the transition point from EB IIIA to EB IIIB, and that is not available at this writing. [123]

References

1.   Abbreviated henceforth as EB.
2.   For instance, the grid of 5-meter squares introduced by Kenyon at Jericho has become a common feature of excavations in the Near East. However, Kenyon's method of using vertical profiles to control excavation of layers is not common.
3.   *Vide* Paul W. Lapp, in *Near Eastern Archaeology in the Twentieth Century* (James A. Sanders, ed.), p. 102; abbreviated henceforth as "Palestine . . . "
4.   Joseph A. Callaway, *Pottery from the Tombs at Ai (et-Tell)* (1964).
5.   G. Ernest Wright, in *The Bible and the Ancient Near East* (G. Ernest Wright,ed.), pp. 81-85; *vide* Wright, *The Pottery of Palestine from the Earliest Times to the End of the Early Bronze Age* (1937), pp. 56-102.
6.   "The Chronology of Israel and the Ancient Near East," pp. 201-28.
7.   "Some Remarks on the Archaeological Chronology of Palestine before about 1500 B.C.," *Chronologies in Old World Archaeology* (Robert W. Ehrich, ed.), pp. 47-60.
8.   Lapp, "Palestine . . . ," pp. 101-31.
9.   "Palestine in the Early Bronze Age," C.A.H. (3rd edition), 1971, I, 2, pp. 208-37.
10.   "The Archaeology of Palestine from the Neolithic Through the Middle Bronze Age," *JAOS*, 91 (1971), pp. 276-86.
11.   J. B. Hennessy, *The Foreign Relations of Palestine during the Early Bronze Age* (1967).
12.   Ruth Amiran, *Ancient Pottery of the Holy Land*, pp. 35-77.
13.   Callaway, *The Early Bronze Age Sanctuary at Ai (et-Tell)* (1972), abbreviated henceforth as *Sanctuary*.
14.   Paul W. Lapp, *BASOR* 189 (1968), pp. 12-41.
15.   Albright, op. cit., p. 51.
16.   Ibid., pp. 51-52.
17.   Op. cit., p. 23.
18.   Callaway, *Sanctuary*, p. 266, fig. 60:11.
19.   *IEJ*, 17 (1967), pp. 185-86.
20.   Callaway, *Sanctuary*, pp. 302-305.
21.   *BASOR* 210 (1973), pp. 2-66.
22.   J. Marquet-Krause; *Syria* 16 (1935), pp. 325-45.
23.   "Palestine . . . ," p. 121.
24.   Callaway, *Sanctuary*, pp. 247-49; 292-93.
25.   Lapp, "Palestine . . . ," p. 121.
26.   Ibid., pp. 122-23.
27.   Insufficient evidence is that not corroborated or supported by a second independent witness.
28.   See Callaway, *Sanctuary*, pp. 20-22.
29.   The addition to the inner city wall is drawn in J. Marquet-Krause, *Les fouilles de 'Ay (et-Tell)*, Pl. C, in Fouille V$_4$–V$_3$ between Loci 144 and 242. Marquet-Krause probably would have discovered the additional phase had she lived to continue excavation in 1936.
30.   Joseph A. Callaway, *BASOR* 178 (1965), p. 28, in the discussion of Wall C.
31.   Callaway, *Sanctuary*, pp. 28-37; Callaway and Norman E. Wagner, *PEQ*, July-Dec., 1974.
32.   Callaway, *Sanctuary*, p. 253.
33.   Callaway and Kermit Schoonover, *BASOR* 207 (1972), pp. 41-50.
34.   Ibid., pp. 44-46.
35.   Ibid., p. 44, n. 9.
36.   See Marquet-Krause, *Les fouilles* . . . , Pl. C, Locus 242; also Callaway and Wagner, op. cit., Pl. XXVIII B.
37.   This feature will be shown in a photograph and plans to be published in *The Early Bronze Age Citadel and Lower City at Ai (et-Tell)* by the writer.

38. See Callaway and Wagner, op. cit.
39. Callaway, *BASOR* 198 (1970), pp. 25-31.
40. "Archaeology of Palestine," op. cit., p. 84.
41. The chronology of c. 2550-2400 B.C. assigned to EB IIIB in Callaway, *Sanctuary,* p. 330, now seems too short a period for the two sub-phases noted in the next section of this paper, and therefore is lengthened to 2550-2350 B.C. in the forthcoming report on the citadel and lower city and in the table given here.
42. Hennessy, op. cit., pp. 22-25; Callaway, *Sanctuary,* pp. 259-60; 305.
43. Callaway, *Sanctuary,* pp. 257-58.
44. Ibid., pp. 303-304.
45. B. Maisler, M. Stekelis and M. Avi-Yonah, *IEJ* 2 (1952), p. 171.
46. Callaway, *Sanctuary,* pp. 259-60.
47. "The Archaeology of Palestine," op. cit., p. 85, Chart 3.
48. Hennessy, op. cit., 69-70; R. Amiran, *IEJ* 20 (1970), pp. 170-79; Callaway, *Sanctuary,* pp. 300-302.
49. Callaway, *Sanctuary,* pp. 247-49; 253-54.
50. Ibid., pp. 306-307.
51. Marquet-Krause, "La deuxième campagne . . . ," pp. 325-35.
52. W. F. Albright, *The Archaeology of Palestine,* rev. ed. (1960), p. 76.
53. G. Ernest Wright in *Archäologie und Altes Testament: Festschrift für Kurt Galling,* (A. Kuschke und E. Kutsch, eds. (1970), pp. 299-319.
54. Ibid., p. 306.
55. Callaway, *Sanctuary,* pp. 62; 69-71; 104-105; 149-50; 253-54.
56. Ibid., p. 297.
57. Ibid., Fig. 87.
58. See Callaway, *BASOR* 178 (1965), p. 33, Fig. 13.
59. Ibid., p. 32, Fig.12 and p. 33, Fig. 13. A base for one of the twin rows of pillars is at the lower right of the scale in Fig. 13, against Wall B; the pillar bases are located on each side of Wall B in Fig. 12, as, for instance, the one marked by Elevation 853.97 and a corresponding one not drawn across Wall B on the opposite side. Wall K marks the line of the outer wall of the Royal Quarter on the west side of the temple.
60. The enclosure wall is not published, because it was discovered in the final stage of the Ai excavations. Its location is indicated by the line of the inner face drawn in Marquet-Krause, *Les fouilles* . . . , Pl. XCII, Elevation 12. The wall averages about 2 m. in width.
61. Callaway, *BASOR* 178 (1965), p. 35, Fig. 14. The base of cyclopean stones is under the brick-like stones of the wall on the left side of the photograph.
62. Ibid. A flat base is in the foreground, behind the half-metre scale and a small balk. The plaster surface in the balk runs to the top edge of the base.
63. Ibid., p. 37.
64. Ibid., p. 36, Fig. 15.
65. Amiran, *IEJ* 20 (1970), p. 177.
66. Ibid., see also Marquet-Krause, *Les fouilles . . . ,* p. 53, No. 344.
67. See note 60 above.
68. Ibid., p. 32, Fig. 12, Wall B.
69. Ibid. One rectangular room is drawn north of Walls A and G in the plan.
70. Callaway, *Sanctuary,* p. 305.
71. Callaway, BASOR 198 (1970), pp. 26ff.; see p. 9, Fig. 1 for the location of the Corner Gate at Site K.
72. Dr. George R. Glenn of the School of Engineering, Rutgers University, made the calculation as part of a technical study of the pool in 1970. Much of the information given here is taken from his study.
73. Note the contrast in the *khamra* and the triangle of grey soil in Fig. 15 of n. 71 above.
74. Glenn noted in his unpublished report that though worm activity was evident, it was not extensive.
75. A combined hydrometer-sieve analysis method was used to obtain this information.
76. Callaway, *Sanctuary,* pp. 30-31.
77. A photograph of the stone facing is in Callaway, BASOR 198 (1970), p. 29, Fig. 16.
78. Ibid.; note especially the floor stones under the bend of the dike.
79. Ibid., p. 28, Fig. 15, between the dark fill and the large stones of the city wall on the right.
80. Callaway, BASOR 178 (1965), p. 37.
81. Walter B. Emery, *Great Tombs of the First Dynasty,* Vol. I, p. 19, Pl. 5B.
82. A. Lucas, *Ancient Egyptian Materials and Industries,* p. 85.
83. C. M. Firth and J. E. Quibell, *The Step Pyramid,* Vol. II, p. 1, Pl. 73. See also S. Clark and R. Engelbach, *Ancient Egyptian Masonry,* Figs. 1-4.

84. See Callaway, BASOR 178 (1965), p. 38, Fig. 16.
85. J. E. Quibell, *Excavations at Saqqara (1911-1912): The Tomb of Hesy,* (1913), Pl. IV:1, 2.
86. Marquet-Krause, *Les fouilles . . . ,* Pl. VI: 2.
87. See n. 83 above.
88. Callaway, BASOR 198 (1970), pp 23-24.
89. Walter E. Rast, *Newsletter,* American Schools of Oriental Research, No. 8 (1973-74), pp. 1-7.
90. Callaway and Schoonover, BASOR 207 (1972), p. 51, Fig. 7. Wall A in the photograph is badly calcined on top of the ridge back of the 2-metre scale.
91. Callaway, *BASOR* 196 (1969), p. 11, Fig. 7. The wall is now designated "A," and the face under the metre scale is the east side of the South Gate. Details on the gate and Wall A will be published in *The Citadel and Lower City at Ai (et-Tell).*
92. Callaway, BASOR 198 (1970) pp. 25f., Fig. 13.
93. Area C IX, to be published in *The Early Bronze Age Citadel . . . .*
94. See Callaway, *Sanctuary,* p. 299.
95. Ibid., pp. 302-304.
96. Ibid., p. 303.
97. Ibid., pp. 302ff.
98. Hennessy, op. cit., p. 88.
99. Amiran, *Ancient Pottery . . . ,* pp. 59, 62, 65; Pl. 17:6-10; also H. Kantor, *Chronologies in Old World Archaeology,* Robert W. Erich, ed., p. 15; Hennessy, op. cit., Pl. XLIV: 1-3.
100. Amiran, *Ancient Pottery,* p. 62.
101. Ibid., p. 66, Photo 61.
102. Ibid., p. 65, Pl. 17:9.
103. Callaway, *Sanctuary,* p. 207, Fig. 45:10, 11.
104. Amiran, *Ancient Pottery,* p. 65, Pl. 17:7, 8.
105. Hennessy, op. cit., Pl. L:8.
106. Amiran, *IEJ,* 18 (1968) p. 242, Pl. 26C-D.
107. Arad and Gath were not rebuilt after their destruction at the end of EB II. Hennessy, op. cit., p. 88, conjectures that these cities were destroyed by Egyptians.
108. K. M. Kenyon, *Eretz-Israel* V, (1958) pp. 55*-58*.
109. Ibid., p. 57*.
110. De Vaux, op. cit., p. 7.
111. Ibid,; de Vaux does not mention the evidence from Ai which has been referred to by the writer in the foregoing discussion.
112. Amiran, *Ancient Pottery . . . ,* p. 73, Pl. 19:2, cited from Megiddo XVII.
113. This bowl from Megiddo XVII is closely paralleled by one from Site C at Ai in the EB IIIB stratum, to be published in *The Early Bronze Age Citadel . . . ,* Fig. 66:40.
114. Thus Hennessy, op. cit., p. 25; Kenyon, *Archaeology in the Holy Land,* pp. 135ff.
115. The traditional Israelite invasion of Canaan related in Josh. 1-12 is included in this assertion; see Callaway, *JBL,* LXXXVII (1968), pp. 312-20.
116. De Vaux, op. cit., p. 29.
117. Ibid.
118. Ibid.
119. Hennessy, op. cit., p. 88. The half-life used in calculating the C14 date was presumably 5570 years.
120. Callaway, *Sanctuary,* pp. 200-201; 260.
121. See Freedman and Campbell, op. cit., chart on p. 220: c. 2615-2315 B.C.; also Lapp, "Palestine in the Early Bronze Age," p. 124: c. 2550-2275 B.C.
122. Callaway, *Sanctuary,* pp. 305-306. The date of c. 2400 to 2370 B.C. should be lowered to c. 2350 B.C.
123. August 7th, 1974.

AN EB-MB BILOBATE TOMB AT AMMAN
by F. Zayadine.

On September 2nd 1972, a bulldozer widening the Amman-Sweilih road, broke open two caves situated 5 km north-west of Amman and about 1 km from the Hussein Sports City, on the property of Muhammed Ali Jilani. The Department of Antiquities was immediately informed and when the author arrived on the spot, early in the morning, the work on the road was stopped, but one of the chambers (Tomb 2) was severely damaged as half of it had been smashed by the bulldozer. Chamber 1, however, was almost untouched, except for a hole about 1.60m by 1.0m in the roof. A large chunk of rock had fallen down in the cave, without disturbing the tomb contents.

a.   b.

Plate VIII: a. General view of the Tomb, b. Deposit of Chamber 1.

The area where the tomb was found is a rocky hill, built over by scattered modern houses (Pl. VIIIa). A careful survey of the mound showed that it was dug with many caves, some of them being reused by the local people. A rock-cut tomb of the loculi type was also discovered to the south-east of the EB-MB burial. It was cleaned by the Department of Antiquities but no object of any kind was found inside. About 2 km north of the hill, in a small ravine, lies a square megalithic tower called Rujm el-Kharabsheh, probably dating to the Iron Age. On the hill itself, fragmentary structures could be noticed but no striking remains.

The Tomb

Chamber 1 The tomb, as shown on Pl. VIIIa, was situated at the foot of the hill. Chamber 1 was first entered through the hole made by the bulldozer. No dump or rock fall had disturbed the tomb deposit, which was perfectly preserved in its original position (Pls. VIIIb, IXb and Fig 1). The roughly circular opening of the chamber was situated on the north-eastern side and was blocked by a rounded stone, chinked with small rubble (Fig 2).

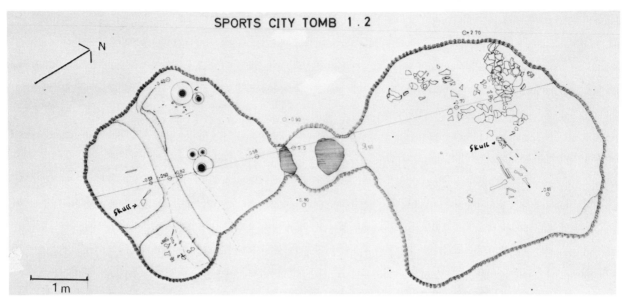

Fig 1:   Plan of tomb.

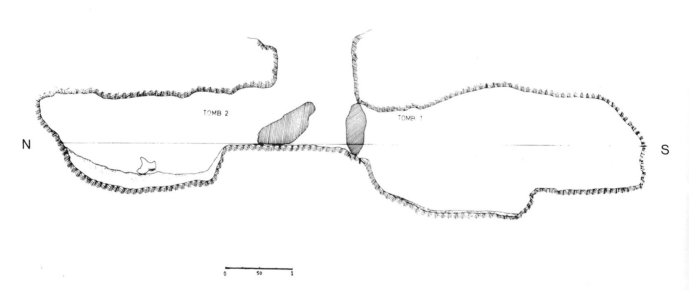

Fig 2:   Section of tomb.

Though the opening was tightly closed a small heap of brown soil had filtered through the interstices but had not reached the tomb material. The chamber, which was roughly square, measuring 3.10m east-west and 2.75 north-south, had a dome-shaped ceiling cut with a blade about 2 cm. wide. An instrument of the same size was also used at Dhar Mirzbaneh, as noticed by Lapp[1]. On the southern side a bench, 2.90 by 1.35 m. and 0.15 to o.30m high above floor level, was prepared from the rock (Fig 2). It was divided into two shallow basins by a ridge about 0.20m wide and 0.10m high.

In the smaller eastern basin were scattered some long bones, belonging to an adult, without a skull. A broken lamp (No. 9, Pl. IXc and Fig. 4) was found with the bones, but this had probably been originally deposited in a niche where another lamp was found (No 8, Pl. IXc and Fig 4), and had fallen down when the bulldozer hit the cave.

*Plate IX: a. Jars of Chamber 1 and 2; b. Deposit of Chamber 1;
c. Lamps from Chamber 1 and 2.*

A copper pin 3 cm long and a few greenish paste beads were also collected from the same basin.

The second, western, basin, which was larger than the first (1.38m by 1.70m) was covered by disintegrated bones mixed with *huwwar* flecks. The most prominent bones were a skull fragment, a vertebra and probably a piece of tibia. A rivetted copper dagger was lying between the vertebra and the skull, its point toward the skull. Rivets and two beads were mixed with the bones.

The hall of the chamber was covered by a layer of soft *huwwar* about 5 cms thick and contained the pottery deposit. As shown in Pls VIIIb & IXb and Fig 1, the pottery was arranged in two different groups. The first, in the north-western corner, comprised a jar and a jug; all around the pottery were deposited adult bones, and a javelin was lying about 20 cm south of the jar. The best recognisable bones were: phalanges, tibia, ulna, ribs, humerus, astragalus, patella, all mingled in confusion. The jar (No 5) contained the complete skeleton of a rodent and the jug (No 4) a few human and probably animal bones.

The second group of pottery consisted of a jar and two jugs (Pl. IXb). The jar (No. 1), which was slightly leaning to the west, contained rodent bones, and the jug (No. 2) fragments of human bones.

To my knowledge, the bench of chamber 1 is unique in the EB-MB period of Transjordan and I have failed to find any clear parallel to it in Palestine. The two basins, together with the two groups of pottery and the two lamps, suggest two different burials, though the skeletal remains provide no obvious evidence for this conclusion. At any rate, there is no doubt that the burial was a secondary one, as indicated by the bones found in Jugs Nos. 2 and 4. Why rodent bones were discovered in the two jars (Nos. 1 and 5) is not understandable; probably the small animals, seeking food, fell down into the jars and were not able to escape. But this means that the tomb was left open at one time, for it is improbable that the rodents could penetrate into it when the shaft and the entryway were tightly sealed.

A rounded shaft, measuring 1.40m high, 1.05m E-W and 1.20m N-S, led to the entrances of chambers 1 and 2. It was filled with soft brown soil. When this soil was removed, it was seen that the blocking of chamber 2, a rounded stone of about 0.80m by 0.70m, was pushed back from the entryway (see plan, Fig. 1). This was not a modern disturbance of the tomb since the shaft was still blocked by earth. Many sherds thrown in the passageway and anciently broken, indicate that the tomb had been looted in ancient times.

Chamber 2

Since this chamber was half destroyed by the bulldozer, a thick layer of fallen rock and dump had to be removed. When this operation was completed, it was decided to dig the chamber in three strips, about 1.0m wide and 2.70m long. In the first strip, on the south-western side, a layer of soft brown soil appeared, apparently washed in from the entryway. The upper part of a jug (no. 11) was found in this layer and other fragments of the same pot were in the entryway. But what was surprising was to discover some other fragments of the same vessel in a different layer, about 40 cm. below the brown soil. This was obviously the result of an ancient disturbance of the burial, as indicated above. When the tomb was robbed, Jug No. 11 was broken and part of it thrown in the entryway but was washed in later with the brown soil. The other pots were also smashed by the robbers and heaped in the north-eastern side of the cave. Three of them were restored in the Jordan Museum by Mr. Abu Mustafa. A lamp, which had originally been placed in a niche, was complete but had been removed from its original place by the bulldozer driver.

Because of the roof collapse and of the looting of the tomb, the skeletal remains in Chamber 2 were badly preserved. Nevertheless a careful removal of the debris revealed the original position of the bones. The skeleton of a single adult was laid on a bedding of fine *huwwar* about 3 cm thick. A smashed skull was found with jar fragments. The other recognisable bones are: a fragmentary femur, a tibia, metatarsal bones, ulna, phalanges, ribs and a few vertebrae. If the position of the bones is undisturbed, then it may be deduced that the single burial was in the flexed position, (Fig 1). This is in clear contrast with the secondary inhumation of chamber 1.

Except for a little copper plaque with holes found near the skull, no metal objects were collected from chamber 2. They were probably robbed in antiquity, for metal plaques are generally associated with daggers.

The Finds

The Pottery: Eleven vessels were collected from the two chambers. They include four jars, four jugs and three lamps. Two of the jars (Nos 1 and 5, Pl. IXa and Fig 3) have a rounded body, while No 12 (Pl. IXa) is rather more oval. The ledge handles have all overlapping flaps, a characteristic of later types.[2] Jars Nos 1 and 12 are decorated at the base of the neck by a clay rope indented by pressing the clay with the thumb and index finger at regular intervals. This decoration is usually supposed to be added to conceal the attachment of the wheel-made neck with the hand-made body, and is obviously different from the common band of slashes incised on the jugs. It appears on jars from Dhar Mirzbaneh[3] and from Transjordan.[4] The general shape of the three jars is widely known from the Jericho, Dhar Mirzbaneh, Husn and Jebel et-Taj (Amman) tombs. Two of the Jebel et-Taj[5] jars have both ledge and vertical handles from neck to shoulder. This uncommon feature should be interpreted as indicating a transitional phase. Jar No 13 (Pl. X Fig. 3) has a globular shape, with a diameter larger than its height. It has no

Plate X: Pottery

ledge handles, but since part of the rim is missing it could have been provided with a loop handle. A jar from Jericho[6] provides a good parallel to this vessel.

Three of the four jugs, Nos 2, 3 and 4, (Fig. 3 and Pl. X) came from chamber 1 and only No 11 from chamber 2. Each of them has a globular body, a flat base and a flat loop handle. Nos 2 and 4 are decorated with oblique slashes at the base of the neck and No 2 has an X pattern on the handle. It is to be noticed that No 4 has a groove around the neck and No 3 two grooves on the mid-body. These grooves were probably made on a wheel.

The best parallels to these jugs were found at Jebel et-Taj (Amman),[7] where the X pattern is incised on the flat loop handle, but also at Jericho[8] and Husn.[9] No loop handled pots were found at Dhar Mirzbaneh, where lug and ledge handles occur.

Two of the three lamps (Pl IXc and Fig. 4) were found in chamber 1. No 8, which was cracked, was deposited in a niche about 1 m. above ground level, in the south-eastern corner of the cave; No 9 was probably deposited in the same place but fell down on the bench when the cave was hit by the bulldozer. Traces of burning were observed on both of them. The presence of these two lamps may be considered as further evidence of two burials in the same cave. All of the lamps, which are four-spouted and have rounded bases, are well paralleled from other sites, such as Dhar Mirzbaneh, Jericho and Megiddo.

Metal Objects:

The significant metal objects are a dagger with four rivets and mid-rib, and a javelin with hooked tang and 'poker' head (Fig 4). Both of them came from chamber No 1, the dagger from the bench and the javelin from the hall. Tombs with both javelin and dagger are reported at Jericho, Dhar Mirzbaneh, el-Jib and Lachish.[10] The close association of dagger and javelin suggested to Lapp 'that a war hero or tribal chief carried both a dagger and a javelin.[11,] It is likely that the bench of chamber 1 was prepared for some outstanding person or persons.

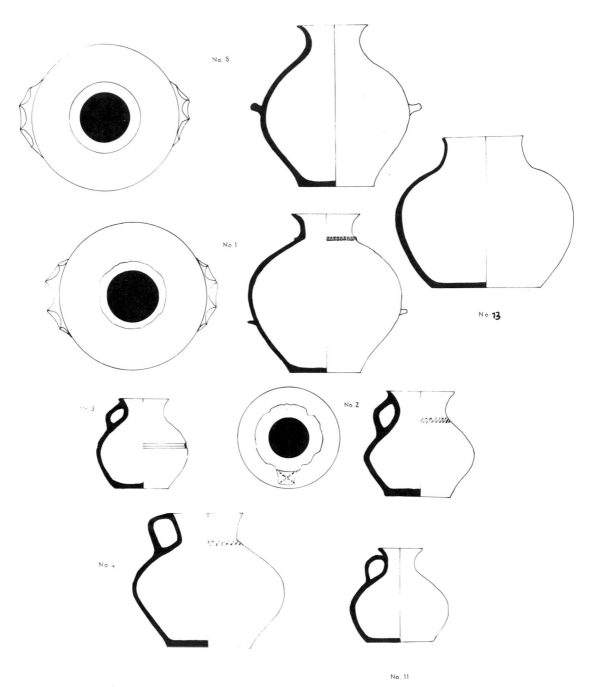

Fig 3:   Pottery

A pointed pin about 3 cm long was found in chamber 1, and a plaque with holes in chamber 2; neither are published. Similar objects to both of these occur in the Dhar Mirzbaneh tombs. Although not analysed, all these metal objects are presumably of copper.

Conclusion:

Although well documented by archaeological finds in Palestine and Transjordan, the chronology of the EB-MB period is still conjectural. This situation arises from the fact that most of the material comes from tombs and not from stratified excavations. Nevertheless, excavations at sites like Ader,[12] Khirbet Iskander,[13] Aro'er[14] and Tell Iktanu[15] in East Jordan allow the distinction of at least two archaeological periods. At Aro'er, on the northern ridge of the Arnon Valley, there is no clear architectural evidence, but the two periods are distinguishable. At Tell Iktanu, in the Jordan Valley, recent excavations have revealed two building phases. Unfortunately, the material from the Amman area (Jebel et-Taj and Sports City) is not sufficiently distinctive or prolific to permit a clear definition of the period to which it belongs. The absence of cups, plates and bowls is rather embarrassing for a comparative study

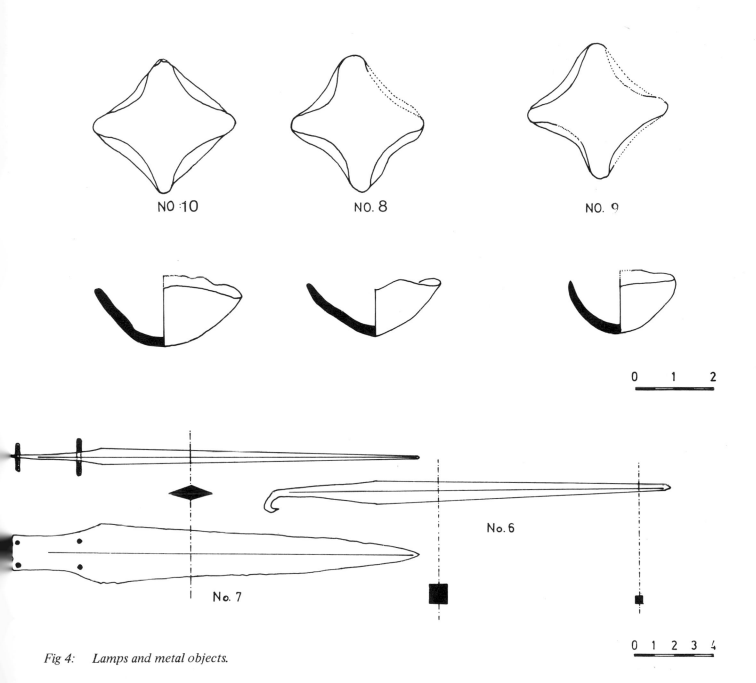

NO. 10   NO. 8   NO. 9

0   1   2

No. 6

No. 7

0 1 2 3 4

Fig 4:   Lamps and metal objects.

of the pottery deposit. But other features may help to fix the period of the material, namely, the absence of paint or slip, the absence of lug handles and the use of flat loop handles, the overlapping flaps of the ledge handles, the general roundness of the forms instead of the elongated shapes inherited from the EB period. The appearance in the Jebel et-Taj group of both ledge and loop handles is probably an indication of a transitional period in which EB traditions tend to be abandoned. On the other hand, the javelin head with hooked tang is related by Lapp to the second phase of the EB-MB period (IB II). [16]   In this case, it is reasonable to date our tomb to the end of the EB-MB period. But if we accept the statement made by some scholars [17] that the end of the EB-MB period is characterized by the penetration of caliciform vessels brought by the Amorites from Syria, then the absence of this type of pottery from the Amman tombs becomes problematic. It may indicate either the absence of Syrian influence in the Ammonite area or a date of the tombs prior to the Amorite invasion. [18]   Until more material is brought to light the latter solution seems to me the more probable. At any rate, it is tempting to relate the two tombs of Amman to a transitional period, later than level VIb of Aro'er, and before the destruction of the EB-MB culture in Transjordan. A date of the two groups around 1950 B.C. could be acceptable.

Description of the Finds

No	Provenance	Description
1	Chamber 1	Globular jar, ledge handles with five flaps, moulded rope at the base of the neck. Dark grey and tan ware, dark core. Rodent bones inside. H. 36 cm (Pl IXa and Fig 3).
2	,,	Jug, globular body, flat loop handles from neck to shoulder. Slashes around neck and X incisions on handle. Yellowish ware inside and grey outside. H. 16 cm (Pl. X and Fig 3). Contained human and rodent bones.
3	,,	Jug, globular body, flat loop handle from neck to shoulder, two grooves at mid-body. Dark grey ware. A human tooth and rodent bones inside. H. 20cm (Pl. X Fig 3).
4	,,	Jug, globular body, loop handle from rim to shoulder. Slashes and groove around neck. Lime deposit inside and outside. Dark grey ware. Human and animal (?) bones inside. H.20 cm (Pl. X and Fig 3).
5	,,	Jar, globular body, ledge envelope handle with three overlapping flaps. Buff ware. Rodent bones inside. H.39 cm (Fig 3 and Pl. IXa).
6	,,	Javelin head; rounded hooked tang, square section of body. L.20.5 cm. (Fig 4).
7	,,	Dagger with midrib; four rivets to attach wooden handle. L.21.5 cm (Fig 4).
8	,,	Four-spouted lamp, rounded base, buff ware, traces of burning. H. 5cm (Pl. IXc and Fig 4).
9	,,	Four-spouted lamp, rounded base, red-brown ware, traces of burning. Broken. (Pl. IXc and Fig 4).
10	Chamber 2	Four-spouted lamp, rounded base, brown to grey ware. Complete (Pl. IXc and Fig 4).
11	,,	Globular jug, loop handle from neck to shoulder. Buff ware, grey to dark-grey core. H.20cm. Incomplete (Pl. X and Fig 3).
12	,,	Jar, oval body, envelope ledge handle, moulded rope around neck. Ochre ware; mended. H.36cm. (Pl. IXa).
13	,,	Jar, rounded body, handleless (?) Buff to grey ware, dark core. Incomplete. H.20.5 cm. (Pl. X and Fig 3).

References

1. P. Lapp, *Dhar Mirzbaneh Tombs,* (1966) p. 78
2. K. Prag, 'The Intermediate Early Bronze-Middle Bronze Age', *Levant* VI (1974) p. 78.
3. P. Lapp, op. cit. Fig. 33, 21.
4. K. Prag, *Levant,* VI.
5. R. Dajani, *ADAJ,* XII-XIII (1967-1968), Pl. XL, 2-3.
6. K. Kenyon, *Jericho* II, Fig. 89, 9.
7. R. Dajani, *ADAJ,* XII-XIII, (1967-68) Pl. XL, 1 and 4.
8. *Jericho II,* Fig. 29-11; 89, 7.
9. G. L. Harding, *Palestine Exploration Fund Annual,* VI (1953), Fig 1, 17.
10. *Dhar Mirzbaneh Tombs,* p. 53, with references.
11. Idem, p. 53.
12. *AASOR,* XXXIV-XXXV (1960), p. 79-97.
13. P. J. Parr, *ADAJ* IV-V (1960) p. 128-133.
14. E. Olivarri *RB* LXVI (1969) p. 240-259.
15. K. Prag, *Levant,* VI (1974) pp. 77 ff.
16. Op. cit. p. 53.
17. De Vaux, *RB,* LXXIV (1967) p. 474: E. Olivarri, *RB* LXXVI (1969) p. 258.
18. The hypothesis of the Amorite invasion undergoes criticism by T. L. Thompson in *The Historicity of the Patriarchal Narratives,* (1974) p. 144 ff.

POTTERY FROM A MIDDLE BRONZE AGE TOMB NEAR TELL HADIDI ON THE EUPHRATES.
by H. J. Franken.

The pottery described here was excavated by an expedition from the University of Leiden in 1973, headed by Drs. S. E. van der Leeuw and the present writer, near Tell Hadidi. This is one of the sites that is threatened with inundation by the Euphrates Lake in the Tabqa region of North Syria.[1]

The Leiden expedition has aimed at collecting large samples of pottery from as many cultural periods as possible found in a small area in order to study the relation between clay composition and different pottery manufacturing methods. This technological study is not in the first place based on research with the aid of modern electronic equipment but it bridges a gap that still exists between research into ancient ceramic materials and typological studies in archaeology. In the search for a more scientific and theoretical basis for typological studies it was found that the analysis of the method in which a given type of pottery was made, opens up more possibilities for comparative studies, for sorting pottery into types and for laboratory research than existing typologies do. This analysis is not specifically the work of the ceramic chemist, nor of the archaeologist, but of the experienced potter who is not in the first place interested in chemical composition but in aspects of the quality of clay for practical purposes, added tempering materials, and what that means for making certain shapes and other practical problems. It is a study of pottery as seen by professional potters. The present paper is offered as an example of such an analytical study.

The reader will look in vain for a comparative study or attempts to date the pottery. This however can wait until the M.B. pottery from Hadidi and Selenkahiye is published.

The Find.

On both banks of the Euphrates in the area that will be inundated by the lake of the Tabqa Dam, ancient tombs are being robbed of their contents. One such tomb (or possibly two), situated at the base of Tell Hadidi on the west side, had suffered from a roof collapse before it was opened in 1973 by tomb robbers. The tomb had been dug in the conglomerate near the flood plain of the Euphrates. It turned out that the tomb had been thoroughly excavated and the fill was dumped on two sides. It consisted of pebbles, cobbles and a mixture of earth and ashes from an accumulation of medieval occupation on the rock surface, the remains of totally smashed skeletons and pottery fragments. The tomb was not lined with boulders and covered with flat slabs of limestone, as some other tombs in the area are. In those cases the robbers remove only one of the covering stones and leave the rest of the structure intact. The contents of the tomb as found by us consisted only of pottery and smashed bones. Any other objects if present originally must have been taken away. We excavated the dump completely and all pottery fragments were collected. Eighteen large plastic bags were filled with sherds and more than half of the sherds made up sixty-four complete sections of bowls and jars. This dump partially overlaid another dump from the excavation of an adjacent tomb. The earlier dump did not contain sherds. A number of sherds turned out to date from medieval times. The plan of the tomb or tombs can roughly be indicated, largely from a supposed similarity to other holes found. These were also clearly tombs, slightly longer than wide, with rounded corners and not more than two metres long. The floor was about two metres below the present surface of the rock, which may have been somewhat eroded since the tomb was made. Assuming that these measurements are correct, there may have been two tombs (the later one being partly cut into the earlier one) at a slightly different angle and on different level. The shaft of the collapsed tomb was then on the west side. But since the cement of the conglomerate here is no longer as hard as it is in other places, the tomb robbers may easily have enlarged the original shape of both shaft and tomb. The fact that the dump contained well over a hundred fragments of different bases, undoubtedly from the Middle Bronze Age, and our estimate that at least four individuals had been buried there makes it doubtful whether this could have been the contents of one tomb only.

To begin with we assume that this pottery can be treated as one group. Only those fragments that when mended made up complete sections will be extensively treated here but all the other fragments were incorporated in our study. From these sherds samples were taken for kiln tests and for thin slide analysis. The mended pottery is the property of the National Museum in Aleppo and could not be used for tests.

The characteristics of the raw materials, colour and hardness.

Seventeen thin slides were made from selected sherds. These sherds were compared for clay paste with a number of slides made from pottery from Tell Ta'as and Tell Selenkahiye. These sites are found to the south-west of Tell Hadidi, situated on the edge of the flood plain of the Euphrates on chalk rock and conglomerate at a distance of 7.5 and 20 km. (as the crow flies) respectively.

In most cases we find very sandy clay. The sand is composed of granite minerals: fine quartz grains, muscovite, (sometimes in large quantities) alkali felspar, plagioclase and iron oxides: haematite and limonite. Occasionally a grain of basalt occurs or coarse lime grains. The texture is very fine (《0.10mm.) to fine (《0.25mm.); medium sized grains are rare. The density can vary from 5 to 10 grains per 0.25mm^2; but sometimes the grains are less dense. The amount of fine carbonate can vary considerably. If we assume that the clay was taken at some depth from the flood plain of the river, the presence of lime in different quantities can be explained from the many side-wadis that regularly deposit lime in the flood plain. One finds these lime deposits in alluvial clays in the little deltas at the end of these wadis. The Euphrates deposits also consist of layers containing different sizes of mineral grains in the clays. When this clay is dug to make bricks or pottery these thin deposits are mixed and, depending on the extension of the quarry and the depth from where the clay is taken, each mixture may have a different texture and lime content. There does not seem to be a good reason to make a distinction in this pottery based on either grain size or density of the grains or on the amount of lime contained by the clay. The sand, including quartz grains, present in the clay was not added by the potters. It acts as a temper and it makes it possible to use the clay for coiling and for throwing.

This pottery can be fired well above 1000°C., unless there happen to be coarse lime impurities, or a very strong lime component. From a number of sherds fired to 1050° for a short time in an electric kiln only one showed cracks afterwards, but the temperature was not high enough for vitrification. Many sherds from this tomb group were originally fired to higher temperatures. Evidence for this is the greenish colour often found. In our kiln tests some sherds became vitrified at 1100° and some had started to melt. Fifty-six sherds were fired to 1050° and here a clear distinction was found which cannot be related as yet to the typology. Two colour groups emerged from this test. A number of sherds became light brown and the others pale yellow. Pottery found with reddish brown colours will invariably become pale brown. Yellowish or greyish coloured sherds may become light brown or pale yellow. This feature is possibly again due to the relation between iron and the amount of carbonates present in the clay.

There is a considerable amount of scum formation due to the salt content of the clay substance. Where the pot has been scraped in a half-dry state, most of the scum was also removed. The colour of the scum is near-white unless the layer is very thin. On the refired sherds one often finds a secondary, thin iron crust which looks like a blackish fleck on the surface before firing. This is probably caused by organic material with which the sherd was in contact during the period before excavation.

Some small vessels were fired in a reducing atmosphere. These vessels were placed inside a larger vessel, the mouth of which was then closed by another pot on top of it. The potters were certainly aware of this effect because they sometimes purposely put a bowl or wide cup over the rim and neck of a jar in the kiln. This bowl rested on the shoulder of the jar. Consequently the area covered by the bowl is grey whereas the uncovered part of the jar is reddish. The grey is near 10YR 5/1 (Munsell, 1954). The inside of the jar is then invariably the same grey. If it can be demonstrated from a larger collection than the one available to us that this was only done in case of red-firing clay, the potters were able to judge from the colour of the unfired clay whether it was red-firing or not. Cups used to cover the upper part of these jars were not found in this group. There are no cup fragments with a grey colour inside.

The colours have been named according to the Munsell Soil Color Charts, 1954. They can be summarized in the following manner. The hues are mostly from 5 to 10YR. Higher temperatures may produce 5Y. The values are mostly from 3-8, but exceptionally 0-2 for greys. The only colour found once in the red hues is 7.5R 6/8, light red. Thus we find colours from white to light (or very pale) -yellow, -brown, -pink and -grey. Colours in the 5Y hues tend to be pale yellow to pale olive and they indicate nearly vitrified and very hard pottery. Most sherds are hard and according to some kiln tests most of the pottery may well have been fired above 900°C. There are no dark cores except in cases where part of a jar was fired on purpose in a reducing atmosphere, as has been described already. The surface colours on the outside and inside (cups and bowls) are strongly influenced by scum formation during firing in the kiln except on the dry-scraped areas around the bases. Thirty-seven vessels have scum in patches or evenly over the surface. If salt had been added on purpose one would expect that more would have been added to make uniformly white coloured pottery (on the surface). But it is clear that this was not the purpose of the 'red' jars with grey upper parts. The source of the salts is the clay and probably the water used by the potters.

Thus we have found that there can be a considerable difference in the amount and size of the non-plastic grains which are derived from granite rock. There is also a large variety in the amount of carbonate in the clay. The composition of this mixture depends on how and where the clay was quarried, but not on tempering materials that were added on purpose by the potters. The colour and hardness vary with the composition and with the temperatures reached in the kiln. The only treatment of the clays after they had been dug was mixing thoroughly with water and kneading before the clay was used to make coils. This kneading was done rather thoroughly: there are very few undissolved clay grains in the sherd.

There were no impurities of organic matter (roots, etc.) in the clay as found and this indicates that no clays from near the surface were used. In a few cases the sherd gives the impression that a fine temper was added but this may be caused by the accidental presence of medium sized grains in the clay. No obvious relation could be established between visible grains and certain types. In our experience with many pottery groups, temper groups are distinctive for type groups.

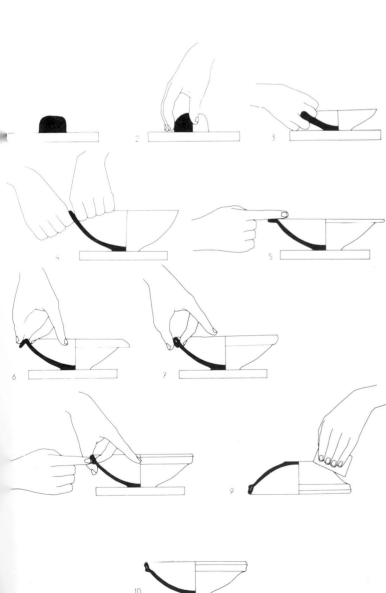

Fig 1:

The method of pot building.

The purpose of this analysis is to see whether a group of pottery which according to the find circumstances belongs together (a repertoire) can be explained from one method of potmaking. When two or more methods are found, the pottery group has to be broken up according to the different methods employed.

With one possible exception all the pots that could be mended and the remaining sherds can be explained in this case by one model.

Either potters used different methods for making pots for special purposes, or the method employed for making small vessels was not suitable for larger pots: storage jars and large vats are often made without the use of a wheel, whereas the smaller vessels are turned on a wheel. Cooking pots often show another method of making than the rest of the group. It depends among other things on the type of wheel used by the potters how large a pot could be made on it. The largest jar found in this group (Fig. 4, 14) represents probably the maximum size to be made on the wheel which the Hadidi potters had. Another limitation was the self-imposed demand for thin-walled pottery. This resulted in a rather laborious method and much loss of clay. The pottery is not thrown in the proper sense of the word. As an illustration of the method construction drawings of a small bowl and a jar (Figs. 1-2) have been added. For thickness of the sherd see the Table below.

The potters began in the same way for all the types. The amount of clay, needed to make a small bowl was attached to the wheel and centred (a), or, as is almost certainly the case, the small bowls were turned from a cone of clay. The wheel was turned clockwise (b) or counter-clockwise (c). From this small group it cannot be ascertained whether this difference has any significance for the typology.

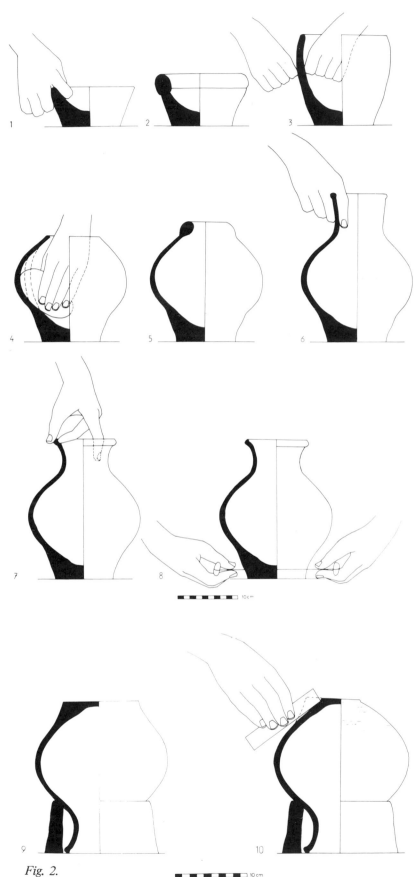

Fig. 2.

From this clay cake the potter could then turn small vessels without having to modify the shape of the wall afterwards, but as a rule he left the lower part thicker than it is in the finished product (d). In two cases only the lower part of the wall around the base on the outside was not thinned down after the potter had finished and dried the upper part. Obviously the lower part of the wall as it is found in the finished products was too thin to carry the weight of the clay when still wet. Vessels not exceeding the height of ca. 7 cms could be made from the original clay cake on the wheel. For the larger vessels one or two coils had to be added (e). It depended largely on the diameter of the rim whether a fold was needed to finish the rim and to give it a profile. The top of the unfinished rim was not pressed down as can be done with more plastic clays, but folded. Nor could this clay be easily cut with a needle. Therefore only small rims (in circumference) could be finished by smoothing the top between the fingers (i). Apart from small cups and bowls all the rims were folded to the outside (j), also if the rim is not thicker than the wall. In this case the clay has been pressed up again: the rim becomes thinner and higher (k). Depending on the direction of the upper part of the wall the rim will become vertical (in cases of bowls) or flaring (in cases of jars where the height of the pot in relation to the position of the hands is also an important factor). The rim was supported on the inside while the fold was pressed against the outside. Sometimes the fold is pressed more firmly against the wall with a finger or a rib (1). The result is a horizontal groove and further profiling of the rim. In some cases (bowls and jars) this is done two to four times (m).

The number of coils used depended on the size of the pot to be made; one or two for larger bowls, and probably three for the largest jars. The reason that joints are rarely found with the sherds are (1) the adhesive quality of the clay and (2) the method of joining. In cases of thick-walled vessels one often finds flat horizontal joints or wedge shaped joints but in this case the joint is oblique in section as a result of subsequent thinning of the wall. This gives a large area of contact between the coils.

When making jars the potter started in the same way as making a bowl, then coils were added to make the spherical shape of the body but less spherical than the finished product shows. He then added a coil to make a neck (h) which he could make vertical (f). Before the last coil was added the pot was widened in the middle in order to obtain the required shape, which is evidenced by the stretch marks at the widest circumference of the body on the inside. As a rule the lower parts of the pots and the bases were reworked after the rims were finished. The vessel was cut loose from the turning base with a needle or with string and put aside in a sheltered place where the upper part was allowed to dry until it was leather-hard. It became strong enough to support the lower half of the pot which was left thick and therefore still wet. Then the pot was put back on the wheel on a cone of clay wrapped in some material in order to keep the pot centered, or in a clay ring. Next, the surplus clay was scraped away from the lower part with the rib in a turning movement (o) and the base was shaped. The scraped part of the wall can always be seen. In the case of jars this was usually done to the widest circumference of the vessel. In the case of-shallow bowls the marks of scraping reach to about half way up the wall. This scraping can easily have the effect of a slight carination. The potters did not as a rule take away clay from the inside. Usually the impression of the fingers made while opening the clay cake on the wheel (Fig. 3/2) are still visible also with the bowls. The base was given its circumference while the side was scraped. Hence the base sometimes looks like a disc base owing to the shape of the rib and depending on how much the base was thinned. Then the base was finished. Two methods of finishing jar and bowl bases were found. The base was made flat with a rib (p) and often smoothed with the fingers, sometimes resulting in a slightly concave base (partly due also to subsequent shrinkage). Or a ring-base was cut out of the surplus clay (q). The ring was not separately made and added. The clay inside the projected ring was scraped away and often the ring was wet-smoothed between the fingers. Sometimes the base became dangerously thin by this treatment but on the whole the potters had a good feeling for this work. In two cases the base had become too thin and had to be mended with clay added on the inside to the base. Occasionally the rib was used on the inside to thin down the base (n). The work must have been done on a turning base because the bases are centred and the majority of the vessels have a really horizontal rim.

Occasionally a bowl or jar was burnished. Spiral (t) and vertical (u) burnishing was applied. Often this burnishing is merely intended to smooth the surface of a pot after treatment with the rib. In this case however it was no longer functional. It is very likely that it was functional at an earlier stage. When the grain size (texture) is slightly coarse the marks of scraping with a rib make a rough surface which has to be reworked with a hard, smooth object (shell, rib) which may have a burnishing effect. The spiral and vertical burnishing found on some of these pots and not on other similar shapes can be taken as rudimentary. The strokes are not continuous but widely spaced.

Often rough areas on the surface were slightly smoothed with wet fingers and occasionally one finds on vertical necks of jars and on cups the so-called reserved slip technique. This also seems to be rudimentary in so far as it was no longer normal practice. While the pot is turning a wet finger is slightly pressed on the wet surface and moved up toward the rim. As a result of this pressure very fine slip from the surface is moved up and forms a band in a spiral immediately above the finger impression. In this way the pot is decorated with a fine slip band.

Some very small handles were found, but not on the reconstructed pottery. One of the reconstructed vessels had presumably three lug handles (w) and one had a spout (v). In one case three small clay pipes were added to make short legs (x) and once the short neck of a deep bowl was accentuated by pressure of a finger on the inside (y) probably while the rim was folded. In one case a pedestal base was found which was made as a separate piece and added to a bowl (r). Once a separately made neck and rim were found (z).

All this can be considered coherent from the potter's point of view. The potters were aware of the necessity to make the thickness of the bases the same as that of the pot wall. Otherwise the base may crack during drying or firing. In later times this problem is often solved by applying a different method. The upper part of the vessel is thrown first, cut loose from the wheel with a lot of surplus clay, then allowed to dry. Next the half finished pot is put back on the wheel upside-down, and from the still wet thick clay which is now turned up the base is thrown closed. Until the moment of closing the thickness of the wall can be controlled. Often a base ring is then pinched from the clay around the centre of the base or the base is left round. The method became fairly common in the Iron Age in Palestine; well into medieval times even bowls and wide cooking pots were made this way, apart from many jars. It is rather surprising that we find in the group of mended pottery from this tomb a small bottle (Fig. 3, 31-32) which shows that this method was already known and used (s). Whether it was made by the same potters who made the other vessels or whether this small 'pilgrims bottle' was obtained from elsewhere cannot be decided. The bottle was made 'sideways'. A shallow bowl was made in the manner already described above with enough surplus clay left for the potter to be able to make a shoulder. Instead of making a proper shoulder, he continues until there is only room for one finger left. At this point the clay of the small neck is pressed together and the shape is closed in a turning movement. While still wet the side was pierced and a separately made neck was inserted and fixed with some clay on the outside against the wall. The shape was then allowed to dry and the original base was scraped and rounded with a rib. The potter took great care to make a symmetrical shape. Often, when this technique is applied, one finds that the original bowl part of the flask is less bulging than the part that was thrown closed. A further development was that both sides were closed: first the one half is made (dome shaped) and then the shape is turned upside down with enough surplus clay attached to it to allow for throwing the second half closed. By itself there is no reason to conclude that this flask does not belong to the period of the tomb.

In this survey of the methods employed by the potters size is taken into consideration in one way only. Standard size seems to be attributable to the amount of clay that could be worked without adding a coil. The quality of the clay used in combination with the demand for thin-walled pottery were limiting factors within the method. To make larger pots would have demanded a different way of making them.

The thickness of the wall of each pot was measured at three points, (a) below the rim, (b) near the base, and (c) in the centre of the base.

Cms.	0.2	0.3	0.4	0.5	0.6	0.7	0.8	0.9	1.0
(a)	2	12	21	14	13		1	1	
(b)	1	7	11	13	15	8	5	2	1
(c)	5	7	10	16	9	5	3	3	3

This means that thin-walled pottery was made on purpose with great care. It also explains why there are few cracked bases. Thirty eight bases are 0.5cm. or less in thickness.

Within these limits pots made in exactly the same way have not been distinguished according to size. Some cups may be smaller than others but they are grouped here in one type. Hence we find that once or twice a type has an identical code; the difference lies only in the size or in a slightly different shape, as for instance bowls with straight or round walls. Furthermore, only when large quantities of this pottery are found, will we be in a position to determine whether the potters intended to make two different looking shapes or not. Except for these few instances all the types can be distinguished by their code.

Summary

a — turning base with or without a cone
b — turning clockwise
c — turning counter-clockwise
d — base left unfinished
e — one or two coils
f — upper part vertical
g — cylindrical shape widened
h — coil for neck and rim
i — rim smoothed unprofiled
j — rim folded outside
k — rim folded and pressed up
l — rim pressed with finger or rib
m — two to four grooves on the rim
n — inside scraped
o — lower part of the outside wall scraped
p — base smoothed with rib
q — ring-base cut with rib
r — pedestal base added
s — base closed upside down
t — spiral burnishing
u — vertical burnishing
v — spout added
w — lug handles added
x — three legs added
y — neck accentuated
z — neck plus rim added

The catalogue of the mended pottery contains the drawing number, type and formula, tomb and register number, and references to notes on individual pots.

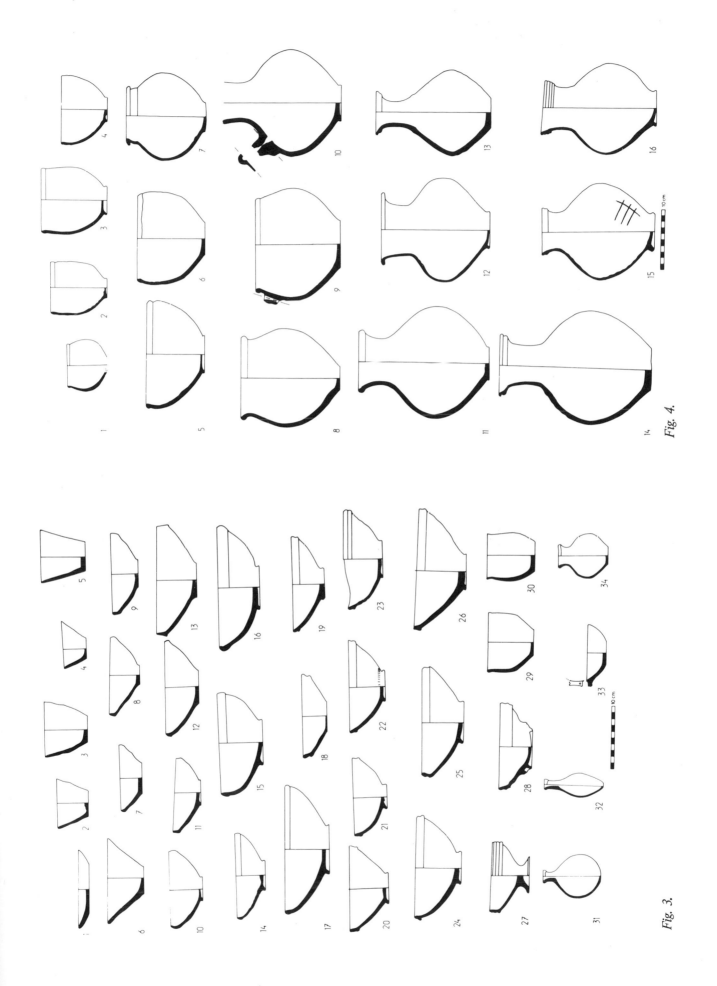

Fig. 4.

Fig. 3.

Figure 3

Drawing no.	Type	Formula	Tomb no.	Register no.	Note
1	1	ab/ciop	48	223	
2	2a	abip	6	181	
3	2b	abdiop	51	226	1
4	2b	abdiop	7	182	
5	2b	abdiop	49	224	2
6	3	abi	8	183	3
	3	abi	34	209	
7	4a	abdjp	47	222	
8	4b	abdkop	25	200	
9	4b	abdkop	39	214	4
	4b	abdkop	35	210	5
	4b	abdkop	32	207	6
10	5	abdkoq	28	203	7
11	5	abdkoq	18	193	8
12	6	ab/cdjop	20	195	
	6	ab/cdjop	23	198	
13	6	ab/cdjop	13	188	4
14	7a	abdj(n)op	10	185	9
	7a	abdj(n)op	46	221	
15	7a	abdj(n)op	14	189	10
16	7b	abd(e)joq	29	204	
	7b	abd(e)joq	33	208	
17	7b	abd(e)joq	42	217	11
	7b	abd(e)joq	31	206	12
	7b	abd(e)joq	15	190	
18	8	abdjlop	36	211	
	8	abdjlop	38	213	13
19	8	abdjlop	45	220	
20	9a	ab/cdjloq	43	218	
21	9a	ab/cdjloq	44	219	14
	9a	ab/cdjloq	19	194	
	9a	ab/cdjloq	16	191	
22	9a	ab/cdjloq	41	216	15
23	9a	ab/cdjloq	26	201	
24	9a	ab/cdjloq	37	212	
	9a	ab/cdjloq	21	196	
25	9b	acdjloqt	40	215	16
26	9c	abdejloq	11	186	
	9c	abdejloq	12	187	
27	10	abdkmort	2	177	17
28	11	abdklox	53	128	
29	12	ab/cdfiop	50	225	
	12	ab/cdfiop	27	202	
30	12	ab/cdfiop	17	192	18
31/32	27	a(b)dostuz	5	180	27
33		(hand-made)	54	229	28
34	28	abdiop	4	179	

Figure 4

Drawing no.	Type	Formula	Tomb no.	Register no.	Note
1	13	abfio	9	184	19
2	14	abdfkop	3	178	
3	15	abd(e)fkoq	30	205	
4	16a	ab/cdfkoq	24	199	
	16a	ab/cdfkoq	52	227	
5	16b	ab/cdefjoq	22	197	
6	17	abdefjop	64	239	
7	18	acdegjpy	61	236	20
8	19	a(b)degjop	55	230	21
9	20	acdegjopw	65	240	
10	21	acdefgh-oqv	60	235	
12	23	a(b)defghjnoqt	62	237	22
13	24	a(b)defghlop	57	232	23
14	24	a(b)defghlop	59	234	24
15	25	acdegloqtu	1	176	25
16	26	abdefgmoqtu	63	238	26

Notes

At least twenty four vessels showed worn bases. Pottery in the colour group 5 Y which is also the hardest pottery does not wear easily so the number of used pots is probably higher.

1 — The angle between base and wall should be taken into consideration.
      Then types 2 and 34 can be distinguished. If more pottery is available finer technological distinctions can be made.
2 — Very carefully finished cup.
3 — The base shows the characteristic mark of needle cut from a cone.
4 — The base is slightly concave.
5 — The clay was worked in a fairly dry state.
6 — During scraping the pot turned counter-clockwise.
7 — Scum formation only on the inside of the bowl.
8 — The bowl is lobsided, the base is not in the center and scraping the base was not done on the wheel.
9 — The bowl rested on the rim of another bowl during firing.
10 — The inside of the bowl was also scraped.
11 — One of the rare cases where the sherd is not fired to the same colour right through.
12 — Overheated and badly warped.
13 — Needle cut base.
14 — Note the profile of the base.
15 — 'Nail' impression around the base.
16 — The outside is spiral burnished. There is a distance of 0.4 to 0.6cm. between the lines of burnishing. The width of this line is 0.4cm. near the base, 0.2cm. near the rim. On the inside the base was wet smoothed.
17 — Burnished inside and outside, with a space of 1-3mm. between the burnished lines.
18 — A 'potter's' mark on the base.
19 — Reserved slip.
20 — The pot was fired in a reducing atmosphere in two degrees. The vessel is near-black inside and has a dark grey patch around the base. In the kiln the pot was stacked in a bowl and another bowl covered the rim.
21 — Obviously too much clay was scraped away, because the inside near the base had to be re-enforced with clay smoothed out in all directions.
22 — The burnishing spiral runs thirty-nine times round from base to rim. The neck was treated with reserved slip technique.
23 — Reserved slip on the neck. The pot is tar stained near the base. The upper part is probably wider than shown in the drawing. The discrepancy between description and drawing may be due to the fragmentary state of the reconstructed pot.
24 — The upper part of the jar was treated with reserved slip technique.
25 — Spiral burnishing on the upper half. The lower half was burnished in oblique direction down to the base in five fields. The upper part was covered by a cup during firing. A 'potter's' mark near the base.
26 — Spiral burnished like 22.
27 — The method of construction has been described already. One side is entirely dry-scraped and the other partially.
28 — Irregular burnishing on both sides all over the surface. Most likely made without the aid of a wheel.

References

Henk J. Franken, *In Search of the Potters' Craft at Ancient Jericho,* Vol. I. North-Holland Ceramic Studies in Archaeology, Amsterdam, 1974.

Pottery from the Euphrates area will be published in this Series in 1978.

Footnote

1.   The excavations in Syria, from 1972-1974 are financed by the Netherlands Organization for the Advancement of Pure Research in The Hague.

GRAVES AT TELL EL-YEHUDIYEH: reviewed after a life-time
by Olga Tufnell.

Introduction

Nearly a century has elapsed since Naville and Griffith began and Petrie continued excavations at the 'Hyksos' camp site at Tell el-Yehudiyeh, some twenty miles north of Cairo. At that time, little was known of the place or period. Griffith had found scarabs naming Sesostris I and Ammenemes II (1971-1895 B.C.), which probably derived from deposits prior to the construction of the camp, if they had not survived as 'heirlooms' among the inhabitants. He also recovered scarabs naming a queen and an official, apparently of the Thirteenth Dynasty or later. Petrie's excavations, on the other hand, provided scarabs 'believed to belong to the age' of the Thirteenth to Seventeenth Dynasties; they were inscribed with the names of Merneferre, Khyan, Sekhaenre and Apepa (Auserre Apophis). Though these scarabs were not found in graves, they indicated a main range for the occupation of the site covering the end of the Thirteenth and part of the Fifteenth-Sixteenth Dynasties.[1]

Within these limits, Petrie singled out a dozen graves found inside the camp and in the eastern cemetery. He considered that the scarabs were 'the most varied and distinctive of the contents and are linked to known forms of the XIIth. dynasty'. He therefore used them to set up a sequence for the relevant graves, based on the details of design, starting from those showing the best and most regular work.[2] The contents of the graves are republished in the present paper with new drawings, whenever it has been possible to locate the whereabouts of the objects concerned. They are widely dispersed and special acknowledgement is due to the Directors of the Ashmolean Museum, Oxford, the University Museums in Manchester and Philadelphia and the Musées Royaux d'Art et d'Histoire in Brussels and their staffs, who gave permission for republication.[3]

Petrie was the first to attempt sequence dating of graves on the basis of scarab design alone, a system which has not found favour since then. Certainly, other factors must also be considered, such as the relative size of each piece, and the style used to reproduce the natural features of the beetle. Given a number of examples from the same deposit, I am personally convinced that a sequence can be constructed showing a logical progression, which William A. Ward and I hope to demonstrate more fully in due course.[4] Meanwhile, it is necessary to reconstruct the grave-goods of certain cemeteries, at least in part, in order to establish the relative order of the deposits, and the collection from Tell el-Yehudiyeh takes an important place towards the end of the period with which we are concerned.

Graves and burials (*HIC* double vol., pp. 10-14, pl. XII.

The best preserved 'Hyksos' graves were long narrow rectangular pits, originally intended for the interment of one body; they were unlined, but at least two were covered with brick vaulting, a feature also seen at Tell el-Dab'a.[5] There was no special orientation to the graves, and the position of the bodies in them was inconsistent. All the burials were at least partially disturbed, not necessarily by tomb robbers, as it appeared at that time, but perhaps because they were of a secondary nature, like many of the interments of the period in Palestine. The condition of the incomplete skeletons in Graves 407 and 5 was perhaps significant; the juvenile in Grave 3 was buried in a coffin of thin boards, with the knees originally drawn up, another reminder of Palestinian burial custom. In the case of the child in Grave 4, the jaw had been set upright at right angles to the head.

Scarab-seals (*HIC* pp. 10-14 and pls. VI-VIII).

Materials All the engraved scarabs in the graves were made of 'steatite', a term in common archaeological use, though the proper mineralogical definition frequently differs. There were besides three uninscribed amethyst scarabs, Fig. 1: 7 and Figs. 2: 14 and 27. On the use of amethyst, see below under *Beads*.

Classes of Design Before considering the place of the scarabs in the chronological progression it is worth indicating what classes are present in the two collections found singly or bought on the site.[6] Much the same elements are present in both, and they are those which occur most frequently after the period of pottery Group II at Jericho.

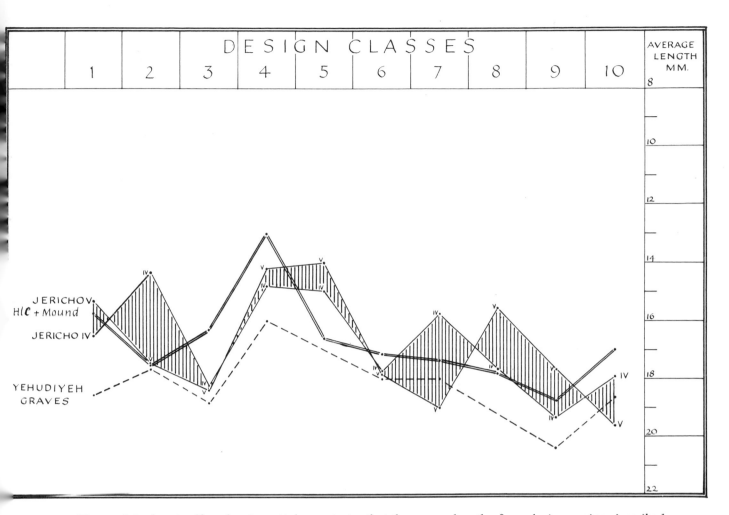

The graph is almost self-explanatory. It demonstrates that the average length of scarabs impressions inscribed with motifs in the ten design classes are largest in the Yehudiyeh graves and therefore earlier than the combined averages of the same designs from general collections made on the site, as published in *Hyksos and Israelite Cities* and in *Mound of the Jew*. The Yehudiyeh material is shown against the background of the same classes of design found at Jericho in pottery Groups IV-V, and it will be seen that the bulk of the scarabs from the Delta site fall clearly between the two. As one would expect, the earlier classes 1-5 tend to get smaller, whereas the later classes 6-10 increase in average length.

Design class 1, **Linear patterns** are characteristic of the First Intermediate Period in Egypt (before 2,000 B.C.), though the geometric versions survive at Jericho in Group V, and especially at Tell Fara and at Tell el-'Ajjul. Floral motifs drawn with two or three stems are also present, providing parallels at the same sites, and an unusual 'flower' is matched in a stratified context.[7]

Design class 2, **Scrolls and spirals,** is not numerically strong at Yehudiyeh; in its first phase it is confined to a single example of the Z-S-C-scroll, following the decline of this motif at Megiddo and Jericho.[8]

Design class 3, **Egyptian signs and symbols**, requires several sub-divisions. **Monograms and varia** (3A) are rooted in the First Intermediate Period, though examples occur at Yehudiyeh (3A1-2). Designs which are not classified in the present survey are numbered together (3A3). **Horus hawk with *ntr* and other signs (3A4)** is present only in small and debased versions. **Symmetric patterns** (3B) with several motifs paired on either side of a vertical row in the centre are well-represented at Yehudiyeh as elsewhere, though the elements are markedly different from those at Megiddo and Jericho. Most of the versions of the **cobra** (3B1) are missing. The **nsw-bit** (3B2) combination symbolising the unity of Upper and Lower Egypt occurs once at Yehudiyeh, though it was common at Jericho in tombs of Group II. **Red crowns** (3B3) of Lower Egypt are rare, like the once popular **Horus eyes** (3B4). The place of all these is taken at Yehudiyeh by the **sedge plant** (3B5), representing Upper Egypt, and **Nbw(GOLD-sign) in longitudinal setting** (3B6), which sometimes occur together on one and same scarab, a combination which does not arise at Megiddo or Jericho.[9]

The large class of low broad signs in Egyptian script, which do not seem to make sense in the Egyptian language are grouped together under the heading **formulae** (3C). At Jericho, the average length for them is constant at 18 mm. for Groups II-IV, dipping to 15.5 mm. in Group V. A progressive decrease in average length is also manifest at Yehudiyeh, see ref. 21 below. Examples of the **cartouche** (3D) depend on the existence of royal or pseudo-royal names in a particular deposit, and here they do not add much to the discussion.

The placing of true hieroglyphs or formulae within panels (3E) is a development which was outlined at Megiddo. At that site they were introduced no earlier than Stratum XIIIA-B = Kenyon's MB II ph. C continuing into phase E and only the first two kinds of panel were used.[10] A plain panel with three or more signs in the margin (3E1) is characteristic of scarabs naming Seuserenre Khyan. Panels with two signs (3E2) name Mayebre Sheshi, Khauserre Amu and Ykb; these varieties were not present at Yehudiyeh though one example of 3E3 composed of **ntr signs opposed** enshrined the name of Sekhaenre. A significant omission in the Yehudiyeh collections is the absence of the last variety of **panels with cross-bars** (3E4) present for these same kings but especially characteristic of Sekhaenre and Ahetepre; from this last fact we can infer that the Yehudiyeh site reached its zenith before the reigns of these two kings. Though the name of the last important king of the Fifteenth Dynasty was never placed between panels as far as I know, one scarab from the site records the name of Auserre, whose long reign was partly contemporary with conclusion of Kamose's life, the predecessor and brother of Amosis, founder of the Eighteenth Dynasty.[11] In the excavated series, panel designs only appear at the end of Group II or early III at Jericho; panels 3E2-3 are missing and there is a single significant item for 3E4, from the top layer of Tomb G 73 in Group IV. All forms of panel designs are rare at Fara, and at 'Ajjul the greatest emphasis is concentrated on panels with cross-bars (3E4).[12] The conclusion seems to be that Tell el-Yehudiyeh - like Jericho itself - was no longer fully occupied by the end of the Middle Bronze Age. which was the most flourishing period at 'Ajjul.

Design class 4, **concentric circles,** enjoyed its main popularity at the close of the First Intermediate Period, and it lingers on thereafter, as seen in two small examples from Yehudiyeh.

Design class 5, **cross pattern,** was often made up in its earlier phases of concentric circles, but towards the end of the Megiddo series and in Groups II-III at Jericho, the design had assumed its final form with curled diagonals. An equation can therefore be set up which may indicate the starting point for the Yehudiyeh assemblages:

Average lengths

mm.	Megiddo *Levant* V	Müller	Kenyon	mm.	Jericho Groups II-III	mm.	Yehudiyeh *Mound + HIC*
15	no: 60		stra.XI = MB II ph.E	16	283:2,16;286:1;292:3	18	X:39 IX:140

Design class 6, **Coiled and 'woven' patterns,** presents another link between Megiddo and Yehudiyeh in a rare example of a knot-like pattern (6B).[13] These beautiful designs soon gave place to less sophisticated patterns (6C) each of which is represented at Yehudiyeh.

Design class 7, **Scroll borders,** is just present in its earliest continuous form (7A). Of three examples of paired scrolls, the smallest at 19 mm. has two pairs each side; two other pieces have three pairs, though the sides are open at one end, an improvement possibly introduced in the first place as a space-saving device (7B2-7C3). The idea goes back at least to the reigns of Sesostris III and Ammenemes III; it regained favour in the reigns of Seuserenre Khyan, of which the scarab in a gold mount from Yehudiyeh is a striking example (see ref. 25). The same device is adopted for scarabs of Meruserre Yakubher and Mayebre Sheshi though it seldom appears thereafter.

Design class 8, **Rope borders,** were in short supply at Yehudiyeh, though they were never placed around scroll borders, as they had been at Jericho. Among the few examples surrounding animals (9B-9C), one scarab provides a close analogy, extending contacts into Group V at Jericho.[14]

Design class 9, **Animals and heraldic beasts,** was popular, except for antelopes (9B), though of two examples one is well-matched in a room of Level II at Tell el-'Ajjul.[15] Among several varieties of **cobras confronted**, those with a beetle or a hawk between, were preferred to designs with a figure or a heraldic beast in the central place (9C1-9C5). A duplicate from a room ascribed by the excavators to Stra. X at Megiddo is matched as Yehudiyeh at a larger size.[16] The favoured animals in the Yehudiyeh collections were undoubtedly the **crocodile** and the **lion** (9D-9E), with eight representations of each. When the two appear together the lion seems to dominate. The lone example of a crocodile at Megiddo points to the fact that the burials on the mound end at about the point in time when the Yehudiyeh collections began.[17] As Miss Kirkbride remarked, the crocodile was curiously rare at Jericho;

of two true examples, one came from the final use of Tomb J 14, attributed to the period of Group IV, with another from an unclassified tomb probably contemporary with Group V.[18] On all these counts, the Yehudiyeh assemblage fits in between the two.

Design class 10, **Human and mythical figures,** is interesting for figures of both kinds holding a flower more often than a cobra (10A1-2). The **nude goddess** links with Jericho Group IV,[19] with the **Hathor symbol** spread more widely in Groups III-V (10D1-2), though there are no perfect examples for the latter at Jericho, Fara or 'Ajjul. Kneeling figures and twin figures (10C and 10B) are missing in the general collections, though both kinds occur in the graves.

Design class 11, **Names and titles,** the scarabs inscribed with royal names from Yehudiyeh were discussed at the beginning of this paper in order to set the approximate limits of the collections (11A). Two officials are also commemorated, the famous Chancellor Ḥar, and a lesser-known 'Great Administrator of the city' named Senaa.[20] Of over a hundred scarabs naming the chancellor, only eight are known to have come from excavations, but even these reflect the wide range of his influence, from Kerma and Debeira in the Sudan, to Rifeh and Yehudiyeh in Egypt, and to Tell Fara and Tell el-'Ajjul, on the natural frontier of the Wadi Ghuzzeh (or Besor) between Egypt and Palestine. Judging from the style of back, Chancellor Ḥar should have been in power during the reign of Mayebre Sheshi, but it is noticeable that his scarabs displayed a larger average length than those of that ruler, and are more in line on that detail with scarabs of Thirteenth Dynasty kings.

Design class 12, **Unclassified and uninscribed,** apart from a New Kingdom scarab and an Iron Age seal, there is little to record under the first category (12A). Under the second, there were three amethyst scarabs and one of dark green stone (probably jasper), with two more plain scarabs, the material of which is unknown (12B).

The general collections compared to scarabs in the graves

Turning from the classes of design represented in the general collections found at Yehudiyeh, to focus on those which were recovered in the graves, certain differences stand out. These are best appreciated by a comparison between classes 1-10 as seen in the three collections. In Petrie's view, the graves illustrated on pls. VI-VIII were among the earliest on the site, and this opinion is confirmed by the average lengths calculated for them, which are consistently longer than those illustrated in the general collections, the indication being that the scarabs were slowly reducing in average length from the Thirteenth Dynasty onwards. Petrie himself had distinguished an earlier and a later set of graves, both on the decline in standards of design, and on changes in the shape of the pottery, a view which can be substantiated. Very briefly, and taking the classes one by one, the following points are worth noting.

Design class 1, **Linear patterns,** only the floral motif 1E3 is present at 18-19 mm. filling a gap between the two other collections. Design class 2, **Scrolls and spirals,** the emphasis here lies on the earlier versions of the scroll. Design class 3, **Egyptian signs and symbols,** contains more formulae (3C) at a greater average length than either of the larger collections.[21] Design class 4, **Concentric circles,** the motif is missing in the latest collection. Design class 5, **Cross pattern,** is only present in the general collections in a late formal version. Design class 6, **Coiled and 'woven' patterns,** occurs once in the graves, the forerunner of several more somewhat debased renderings of a once skilful design. Design class 7, **Scroll borders,** is confined in the graves to two examples of 3-pair scrolls (7B3) once so popular at Jericho; later the same scrolls are left open at one end (7C3). Design class 8, **Rope borders,** are missing in the graves, and show a big drop in average between the two general collections. At about this point a division is apparent between the earlier and later set of graves. Design class 9, **Animals and heraldic beasts,** display all the usual elements in the animal kingdom, including the traditional sphinx. As for Design class 10, **Human and mythical figures,** twins either side of a tree are so poorly cut, that it is difficult to decide if they have human heads, and it is clear that these and kneeling figures are in the last stages of degradation (10B-C).

Comparisons at Megiddo, Jericho and Tell el-'Ajjul

The individual comparisons listed below, suggest how the contents of the graves at Yehudiyeh relate to the scarabs at other basic excavated sites. It will be seen that Megiddo ends as Yehudiyeh begins. The latter lies almost wholly within the period of Group IV at Jericho, and contacts with the upper layers in Tomb G 73 indicate a place towards the end of the group. With regard to Tell el-'Ajjul, the comparisons lie between 740"-820" a.s.l. in area A near the s-w corner, where Petrie observed a layer of burning between 726-744" a.s.l.[22] The inference is therefore, that these particular scarabs were deposited at about the time of this burning or slightly afterwards. There is already

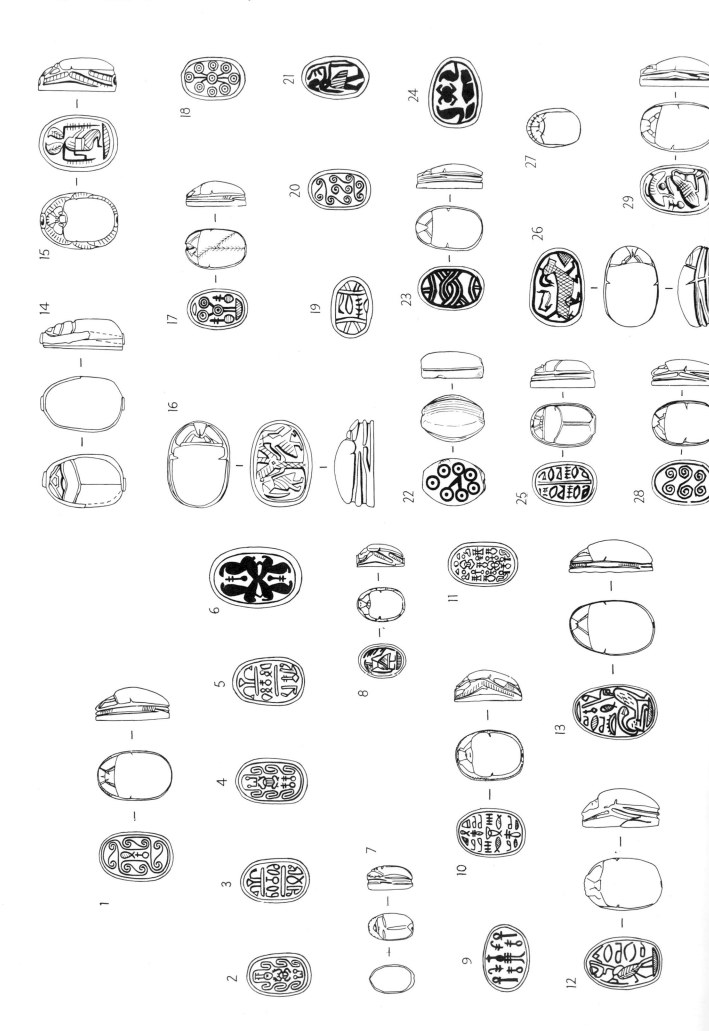

some evidence to suggest that the round pits with loculi, intended for 'horse' burials and the rectangular pits, dug for the same purpose, occupied much the same position in time.

Pit 445 in the northern cemetery at 'Ajjul for instance, provided scarabs resembling others from the general collections at Yehudiyeh.[23] That the occupation at the Delta site impinges on the jewellery period at 'Ajjul is indicated by at least two scarabs which have parallels in tombs containing earrings and beads of gold.[24] Moreover, Petrie reported that 'a plain band of gold, perhaps a head fillet was found in a grave already dug over by the natives' together with a gold-mounted scarab of Khyan.[25] In that connection, Dr. Kenyon stated that Tomb J 14 'stands out from all others excavated at Jericho . . . in the presence of a modicum of gold.[26] That particular tomb was used in two phases, and it would appear that the gold-mounted scarabs were deposited at some time between the two. For two collections of sealings from Egypt and the Sudan, both of which predate in the main the Yehudiyeh assemblage see *J.E.A.* 61(1975), 67-90.

Conclusions on scarabs

The evidence presented so far suggests that the 'Hyksos' camp as a whole was occupied during a relatively short period of little more than a century, say between 1700-1600 B.C., with contacts on the one hand with Twelfth Dynasty scarab tradition, and on the other with the period of prosperity indicated by a lavish use of gold seen in its opening stage at Yehudiyeh, which was to become the hall-mark of the great coastal emporium at Tell el-'Ajjul.

Scarabs from the graves at Tell el-Yehudiyeh
listed according to

CLASSES OF DESIGN

1. LINEAR PATTERNS

1E3: floral motif, 3-stems

Fig. no.	Dimensions mm.	Publication HIC pls. VI-VIII	Grave	Classification Head Back Side	Designs
1 : 3	18x12	9	407	- -	1E3+3B3b+3C
1 : 5	19x12	8	407	- -	1E3+3B3b+3C

Total = 2   Average length = 18.5 mm.

2. SCROLLS AND SPIRALS

2A: Z-S-C scrolls 2B1: interlocking spirals with ends
2B2: interlocking spirals unending

Fig. no.	Dimensions	Publication	Grave	Classification	Designs
2 : 20	16x11	42	37	- -	2A+2B1
2 : 28	17x12x7	55	6	D9 - 0 - d5	2A
1 : 1	20x13x9	1	2	D6 - 0 - e9	2B2

Total = 3   Average length - 17.6 mm.

3. EGYPTIAN SIGNS AND SYMBOLS
(for sub-divisions see text)

Fig. no.	Dimensions	Publication	Grave	Classification	Designs
2 : 19	15x11	44	37	- -	3C
1 : 9	17x12	20	3	- -	3B5
2 : 25	17x12x8	4	1	A5 - II - ell*	3C
1 : 3	18x12	9	407	- -	1E3+3B3b+3C
1 : 10	18x14x8	14	3	A4 - 0 - d6*	3C
1 : 11	18.5x12	15	3	- -	3B1a
1 : 3	19x12	8	407	- -	1E3+3B3b+3C
1 : 12	20x14x10	17	3	B2 - 0 - d5	3A4+3C
1 : 13	22x15x8	16	3	D5 - 0 - e9	3C+9F
1 : 6	24x16	10	407	- -	3B1c repeated thrice

Total = 10   Average length = 18.8 mm.

4. CONCENTRIC CIRCLES

Fig. no.	Dimensions	Publication	Grave	Classification	Designs
2 : 17	15x11x7	53	19	D? - S - c9	4B2
2 : 18	16x11	34	4	- -	4B2
2 : 22	17x13x8	47	47	ovoid	4C1

Total = 3   Average length = 16.0 mm.

5. CROSS PATTERN

NIL

6. COILED AND 'WOVEN' PATTERNS

Fig. no.	Dimensions mm.	Publication HIC pls. VI-VIII	Grave	Classification Head Back Side	Designs
2 : 23	18x12x7	46	37	D5 - 0 - d5	6C2

Total = 1   Average length = 18 mm.

7. SCROLL BORDERS

Fig. no.	Dimensions	Publication	Grave	Classification	Designs
1 : 2	17x11	7	407	- -	7B3a
1 : 4	19x12	6	407	- -	7B3a

Total = 2   Average length = 18 mm.

8. ROPE BORDERS

NIL

9. ANIMALS AND HERALDIC BEASTS

Fig. no.	Dimensions	Publication	Grave	Classification	Designs
2 : 24	19x14	43	37	- -	9C1+9D
2 : 29	20x14x8	53	6	D9 - 0 - d5	9E+10C2 ?
2 : 15	20x15x9	28	5	A7 - 0 - d6*	9C4+10C2c
2 : 26	21x15x10	5	1	D7 - 0 - d5	9B
1 : 13	22x15x8	16	3	D5 - 0 - e9	3C+9F

Total = 5   Average length = 20.4 mm.

10. HUMAN AND MYTHICAL FIGURES

Fig. no.	Dimensions	Publication	Grave	Classification	Designs
1 : 8	13x9x6	18	3	B8 - 0 - d6*	10A2a
2 : 21	17x12	45	37	- -	10A2b
2 : 29	20x14x8	53	6	D9 - 0 - d5	9E+10C2
2 : 15	20x15x9	28	5	A7 - 0 - d6*	9C4+10C2c
2 : 16	23x17x11	27	5	D5 - 0 - d5	10B

Total = 5   Average length = 18.6 mm.

* see note 22

11. NAMES AND TITLES

NIL

12. UNCLASSIFIED AND UNINSCRIBED

12A: unclassified   *12B: uninscribed*

1 : 7	12x8x6.5	19	3	D - I - d5	12B
2 : 27	14x10	54	6	B7 - 0 - ?	12B
2 : 14	20x14x9	29	5	A - I - ?	12B

Total = 3   Average length = 15.3 mm.

Comparisons

Length mm.	Publication			Length mm.	Publication	Designs

| | Megiddo | | | | *Yehudiyeh* | |
| | *Levant* V Müller Kenyon | | | | Figs. 1-2 | |

| 16 | no. 18 | XII = MB II ph. B | | 18 | 3 | 1E3+3B3b +3C |
| 17 | no. 92 | XI-IX ph. G | | 19 | 24 | 9C1+9D |

Total = 2 Average length = 16.5 mm.   Total = 2 Average length = 18.5 mm.

| | Jericho | | | | | |
| | *JT* II Fig. | Group | Tomb | | | |

14	290: 26	III	D 13	17	9	3B5
15	298: 2	IV	J 1	18	23	6C2
17	298: 14	IV	J 1	20	15	9C4+ 10C2c
18	295: 8	IV	G 73(2)	20	1	2B2
18	288: 16 (II)	IV	J 14	21	26	9B
22	295: 19	IV	G 73(2)	19	5	1E3+ 3B3b+3c

Total = 6 Average length = 17.3 mm.   Total = 6 Average length = 19.1 mm.

| | *Ancient Gaza* I-V | | | | *Yehudiyeh* | |
| | Tell el-'Ajjul | Tomb | Level | | Figs. 1-2 | |

16	*AG* I, pl. XIV: 111 445 *cf.* 15			19	3C
16	*AG* IV, pl. VII: 227 TCU 820" *cf.* 17			28	2A
16	*AG* III, pl III: 19 AT 740" *cf.* 20			15	9C4+ 10C2c
17	*AG* III, pl. III: 31 AR 752" *cf.* 18			24	9C1+*nb* 9C1+9D
18	*AG* I, pl. XIV: 89 187 *cf.* 17			25	3C
19	*AG* IV, pl. IX: 283 1553 *cf.* 21			26	9B
20	*AG* I, pl. XIV: 103 407c cf. 20			1	2B2
20	*AG* IV, pl. XI: 461 x cf. 17			25	3C

Total = 8 Average length = 17.7 mm.   Total = 8 Average length = 18.1 mm.

CLASSES OF DESIGN
1. LINEAR PATTERNS
1B: geometric; 1E1-3: floral motifs

TELL EL-YEHUDIYEH

Hyksos and Israelite Cities (1906)

Seal number	Dimensions mm.	Publication	Designs
1	10x7	IX:187	1B
2	16x10	IX:176	1E2+*nb*
3	16x12	IX:188	1B
4	16x12	IX:189	1B
5	17x12	IX:170	1E3+3C
6	20x15	IX:128	1E2+3B 3b
7	23x17	IX:148	1E3+3A3

Total = 7 Average length = 16.8 mm

TELL EL-YEHUDIYEH

Mound of the Jew (1891)

Seal number	Dimensions mm.	Publication	Designs
8	10x9	X:44	1E1
9	11x8	X:43	1B
10	15x12	X:40	1E3
11	15x12	X:36	1E3
12	17x12	X:37	1E2+*nb*
13	20x16	X:38	1E2+1E3

Total = 6 Average length = 14.6 mm

2. SCROLLS AND SPIRALS
2A: Z-S-C- scrolls: 2B1: interlocking spirals with ends;
2B2: interlocking spirals unending

Hyksos and Israelite Cities (1906)

Seal number	Dimensions mm.	Publication	Designs
14	15x11	IX:175	2A
15	15x11	IX:109	2B2
16	16x11	IX:127	2B2
17	18x12	IX:119	2B1
18	21x13	IX:110	2B2

Total = 5 Average length = 17 mm.

Mound of the Jew (1891)

Seal number	Dimensions mm.	Publication	Designs
19	18x13	X:48	2B1

Total = 1 Average length = 18 mm.

3. EGYPTIAN SIGNS AND SYMBOLS
(for sub-divisions, see text)

Hyksos and Israelite Cities (1906)

Seal number	Dimensions mm.	Publication	Designs
20	11x10	IX:150	3A3
21	12x8	IX:133	3A4
22	13x9	IX:165	3C
23	13x10	IX:177	3A3
24	15x10	IX:149	3A3
25	15x10	IX:130	3B4
26	15x11	IX:117	3A4
27	15x11	IX:180	3A1+3B5
28	16x11	IX:123	3B5+*nb*
29	16x11	IX:136	3A2
30	16x11	IX:172	3A3
31	16x11	IX:126	3B5
32	16x11	IX:122	3B5
33	16x12	IX:151	3B6
34	16x12	IX:143	3E3+11A
35	16x12	IX:144	3D1+*nb*+11A
36	17x12	IX:166	3C
37	17x12	IX:170	1E3+3C
38	19x12	IX:125	3B5+3B6
39	19x12	IX:112	3A1+3B2+*nb*
40	19x12	IX:171	3A3
41	20x13	IX:111	3A1
42	20x14	IX:129	3B3b+3C

Mound of the Jew (1891)

Seal number	Dimensions mm.	Publication	Designs
52	9x6	X:30	3C
53	10x7	X:15	3A4
54	11x6	X:29	3C
55	11x8	X:26	3B6
56	12x8	X:28	3B3b+3C
57	12x9	X:17	3A4
58	13x9	X:32	3A3+*nb*
59	13x10	X:22	3B5
60	14x9	X:27	3B5
61	15x10	X:25	3A3
62	?16x10	X:21	3B5+3B6
63	16x14	X:35	3A2
64	17x9	X:20	3B6
65	17x11	X:19	3B5
66	17x12	X:23	3B3e
67	17x12	X:31	3C
68	18x13	X:34	3B3b+10D2
69	19x12	X:18	3B1c+3B5

Hyksos and Israelite Cities (1906)

Seal number	Dimensions mm.	Publication	Designs
43	20x15	IX:128	1E2+3B 3b
44	21x14	IX:168	3A3
45	21x14	IX:169	3A3
46	21x14	IX:124	3D2+7C3a
47	21x15	IX:116	3D4+11A
48	22x15	IX:121	3B1a+9C1 +*nb*
49	23x17	IX:148	1E3+3A3
50	41x?29	IX:142	3B1a+6C3
51	24x16	IX:147	3A3

Total = 32 Average length = 18.2 mm.

Mound of the Jew (1891)

Seal number	Dimensions mm.	Publication	Designs
70	19x14	X: 3	3D1+11A

Total = 19 Average length = 14.5 mm

4. CONCENTRIC CIRCLES

Hyksos and Israelite Cities (1906)

Seal number	Dimensions mm.	Publication	Designs
71	11x8	IX:173	4B2
72	15x11	IX:145	4B2+5

Total = 2 Average length = 13 mm.

Mound of the Jew (1891)

NIL

Total = 0

5. CROSS PATTERN

Hyksos and Israelite Cities (1906)

Seal number	Dimensions mm.	Publication	Designs
73	15x11	IX:145	4B2+5
74	16x11	IX:141	5+6B1
75	18x13	IX:139	5
76	20x14	IX:140	5

Total = 4 Average length = 17.2 mm.

Mound of the Jew (1891)

Seal number	Dimensions mm.	Publication	Designs
77	16x11	X:39	5

Total = 1 Average length = 16 mm.

6. COILED AND 'WOVEN' PATTERNS

Hyksos and Israelite Cities (1906)

Seal number	Dimensions mm.	Publication	Designs
78	11x9	IX:186	6C1
79	15x11	IX:178	6C2
80	16x?11	IX:141	5+6B1
81	16x12	IX:185	6C1
82	16x12	IX:184	6B2a
83	17x13	IX:183	6C3
84	41x?19	IX:142	3B1a+6C3

Total = 7 Average length = 18.8 mm.

Mound of the Jew (1891)

Seal number	Dimensions mm.	Publication	Designs
85	12x9	X:46	6C2
86	13x9	X:45	6C2
87	16x11	X:41	6B2b
88	16x11	X:47	6C1
89	20x14	X:42	6B1

Total = 5 Average length = 15.4 mm

7. SCROLL BORDERS

Hyksos and Israelite Cities (1906)				*Mound of the Jew (1891)*			
Seal number	Dimensions mm.	Publication	Designs	Seal number	Dimensions mm.	Publication	Designs
90	19x14x10	IX:131	7B2a	93	13x10	X:24	7A1a
91	21x14	IX:124	3D2+7C 3a+11A				
92	25x18	IX:113	7C3b+11B				

Total = 3 Average length = 21.6 mm.   Total = 1 Average length = 13 mm.

8. ROPE BORDERS

Hyksos and Israelite Cities (1906)				*Mound of the Jew (1891)*			
Seal number	Dimensions mm.	Publication	Designs	Seal number	Dimensions mm.	Publication	Designs
94	17x12	IX:120	8A+9C1	97	15x10	X:11	8A+9B
95	21x15	IX:114	8A				
96	24x17	IX:146	8A+9C1				

Total = 3 Average length = 20.6 mm.   Total = 1 Average length = 15 mm.

9. ANIMALS AND HERALDIC BEASTS

Hyksos and Israelite Cities (1906)				*Mound of the Jew (1891)*			
Seal number	Dimensions mm.	Publication	Designs	Seal number	Dimensions mm.	Publication	Designs
98	11x9	IX:157	9D	112	15x10	X:11	8A+9B
99	15x11	IX:167	9F	113	15x11	X:16	9C3
100	15x11	IX:154	9C3				
101	?15x12	IX:134	9E	114	17x10	X:9	9F
102	17x12	IX:135	9E	115	19x13	X:13	9D
103	17x12	IX:120	8A+9C1				
104	17x12	IX:155	9B	116	20x14	X:14	9C3
105	19x14	IX:160	9D+10A 2f+nb	117	22x14	X:12	9D+nb
106	19x14	IX:159	9D+10A 2f+nb	118	22x15	X:10	9E
				119	22x16	X:8	9D+9E
107	20x14	IX:158	9D+9E				
108	20x14	IX:156	9C1a+ vulture	120	27x19	X:7	9D+9E
109	20x15	IX:152	9E+10A1f				
110	22x15	IX:121	3B1a+ 9C1+nb				
111	24x17	IX:146	8A+9C1				

Total = 14 Average length = 17.9 mm.   Total = 9 Average length 19.8 mm

10. HUMAN AND MYTHICAL FIGURES

Hyksos and Israelite Cities (1906)				*Mound of the Jew (1891)*			
Seal number	Dimensions mm.	Publication	Designs	Seal number	Dimensions mm.	Publication	Designs
121	13x8	IX:138	10D1	131	15x10	X:6	10A1f+nb
122	16x11	IX:162	10A1b	132	16x11	X:5	10A1b
123	16x11	IX:118	10A1c+ nb				
				133	18x13	X:34	3B3b+10D2
124	16x12	IX:137	10D1+ nb				
125	17x12	IX:164	10A1b				
126	19x14	IX:160	9D+10 A2f+nb				
127	19x14	IX:159	9D+10 A2f+nb				
128	19x14	IX:163	10A2b +nb				
129	20x15	IX:152	9E+10 A1f				
130	23x17	IX:161	10A1+ nb				

Total = 10 Average length = 17.8 mm.   Total = 3 Average length = 16.3 mm.

11. NAMES AND TITLES

11A: royal names; 11B: private names and title; 11C: doubtful readings.

Hyksos and Israelite Cities (1906)				*Mound of the Jew (1891)*			
Seal number	Dimensions mm.	Publication	Designs	Seal number	Dimensions mm.	Publication	Designs
					omitted from statistics		
				134	15x10	X:2	Nubkara Ammenemes II 7A1a+11A
					omitted from statistics		
				135	19x14	X:1	Kheperkare Sesostris I 3D5+7B3a+ 11A
136	16x12	IX:143	Sekhae-nre 3E 3+11A	142	19x14	X:3	Queen 3D1+11A
137	16x12	IX:144	Auserre 3D1+11 A+nb	143	24x16	X:4	Chancellor Har 11B
138	21x15	IX:116	Merneferre Iy 3D4+11A				
139	21x15	IX:124	Khyan 3D2+7C3a +11A				
140	25x18	IX:113	Senaa 7C3b +11B				
141	26x17	IX:115	? 11C				

Total = 6 Average length = 20.8 mm.   Total = 2 Average length = 21.5 mm

12. UNCLASSIFIED AND UNINSCRIBED

12A: unclassified; 12B: uninscribed

Hyksos and Israelite Cities (1906)				*Mound of the Jew (1891)*		
Seal number	Dimensions mm.	Publication	Designs	Seal number	Dimensions mm.	Publication Designs
144	? x 6	IX:132	New Kingdom			
145	16x7	IX:153	Iron Age			
146	13x9	IX:181	12A	150	13x9 amethyst	X:52 B5- 0- ? 12B
147	16x12	IX:179	12A			
148	17x11	IX:182	B- 0-? 12B	151	14x10 amethyst	X:51 D8- 0- ? 12B
				152	14x10	X:33 ? - ? - ? 12A+nb
149	19x13	IX:174	D8-9-? 12B	153	15x10 dk. gn. stone	X:49 B2 - 0 - ? 12B
				154	20x12 amethyst	X:50 D8 - 0 - ? 12B

Total = 4 Average length = 16.2 mm.   Total = 5 Average length = 15.5 mm

Beads and pendants

The only substantial find was 'a necklace of small white disk beads, probably blue originally and of small black globular beads coloured with manganese' shown in two strings on fig. 4:23-4.[27] Apart from these, there were two barrel beads in carnelian somewhat larger than those illustrated under type 73 in Brunton's *Qau and Badari* III, pl. IV. There were besides two amethyst spheroid or ball beads of the general type 79 in the same publication. It is noteworthy that some dozen graves at Yehudiyeh should produce even this amount of the material together with three uninscribed scarabs, whereas nearly three hundred graves of the Second Intermediate Period, including the Pangrave phase could only muster about nine occurrences of amethyst beads and three uninscribed scaraboids. In fact the beads were mostly associated with the girl's burial 3712, the earliest date for which is set by a scarab naming Neferhotep's son.[28]

A tiny drop pendant from Grave 407 is not now available in Brussels; it could well be an Old Kingdom or Middle Kingdom type re-used.[29] One bead drawn with the scarabs in Grave 5 has not been identified in Philadelphia[30]. The same tomb produced two eye amulets, which Petrie was inclined to explain as intrusions in the Twenty-second Dynasty, but subsequent excavations have shown that eye amulets occur in Twelfth and Eighteenth Dynasty contexts, though they are apparently missing from Second Intermediate and Pangrave registers.[31]

Stone kohl-pot (*HIC* p. 11 and pl. VII:21)

Presumably made of alabaster, the surface of this pot is much worn, so that the outer contours are unreliable, like many of the stone vases buried in Second Intermediate graves at Qau, where larger kohl-pots of similar shape were found. Brunton made a point that Twelfth Dynasty shapes tended to be hollowed out inside to conform with the outer contour, and that later examples, particularly in the Eighteenth Dynasty were drilled with a tubular hole. The Yehudiyeh example does show a slight hollowing, but in general proportions it conforms more to the pots of the Second Intermediate Period.[32]

Pottery (*HIC* pls. VI-VIII, X, XIVA)

'Foreign ware'. The three excavators all found sherds of 'black incised' pottery under town remains, and they recovered complete juglets from tombs and by purchase locally; it is this 'peculiar' pottery which has become generally known as 'Tell el-Yehudiych' ware.[33] By publishing the contents of individual tombs, Petrie was more precise on the relationship of the 'black' to the local 'red' ware, and he sketched a possible development within the groups. Examples have since come to light from places in Upper, Middle and Lower Egypt, but many more have been excavated in the Syro-Palestinian region and in Cyprus, and studies have been made on them too numerous to name.[34]

Juglets (Figs. 3-4). There were about twenty juglets in the graves with globular, piriform or cylindrical bodies. The ware was grey, almost black, and the surface was pitted with comb-impressed chevrons applied in a somewhat haphazard manner, the indentations often filled with traces of a white substance.

Concentrating on the basic sites to be discussed in the study on scarabs, the quantity of 'Yehudiyeh' juglets was often insufficient to permit a convincing appraisal of their place in time. A few carefully decorated piriforms came from Megiddo, but a better collection all but two piriform in shape centered on pottery Group III at Jericho.[35] At Tell el-'Ajjul, three piriforms came from burials in the Courtyard Cemetery, and there was a piriform below a cylindrical juglet in superimposed burials in the latest grave in that region, which cannot be earlier than the reign of Ammenemes IV.[36] Following the order proposed by Petrie for the Yehudiyeh grave groups, it will be seen that the juglets from the type site gain in size what they lose in precision and amount of comb-impressed decoration throughout the sequence. The rims are always rolled, never stepped, as at Megiddo, and the handles are invariably 'strap' or roughly square in section, never 'twin' of which there were a good number both at Megiddo and Jericho.[37] The piriform shape was still paramount at Yehudiyeh, but the introduction of three cylindrical forms show that the graves under discussion were as late as Group III at Jericho, when the latter began to take over from piriform shapes, completely surplanting them in Group V. However, further speculation is best delayed until the publication of the rich and varied collection of these wares from stratified contexts found by Dr. Manfred Bietak of the Austrian Mission to Tell el-Dab'a, on the eastern Delta of the Nile, only a few miles from Yehudiyeh itself.[38]

Painted juglets (Figs. 3:2, 4:20, 22). From the first it was recognised that the buff or drab ware juglets with painted decoration in red, black or purple, were as foreign to Egypt as the comb-impressed 'black' ware. That Cyprus was also within its sphere was also evident.[39] The three juglets from Graves 2, 37 and 43 span the occupation period of the graves, and they exhibit an increase in size. It would prove rewarding to undertake a study of standard sizes in this and other industries of the past, though it cannot be discussed at present.

Egyptian 'red' ware. Besides the 'foreign' pottery, most graves contained a selection of simple bowls, cups, jars and potstands, of which new drawings are provided whenever possible, for they may come in useful when these wares are examined in detail. [40] Most of the pottery is wheel-made, but on the jars in particular there is clear evidence that both hand and wheel methods were employed.

Bowls (Fig. 5). The ware of the bowls is reddish-brown with some admixture of dark grits. The surface is often partially covered with red slip. The bowls have only the slightest flare close to the plain rim, and the sides are often lop-sided or undulating from use of the wheel, the marks of which are visible. There appear to be two standard sizes, the larger ranging between 0.20-0.24 m., the smaller between 0.13 and 0.17 m. seen only from Grave 5 onwards. The two exceptions in the collection have thinner curved sides, rising from a concave disk base to a plain rim. Among later examples, one bowl shows some thickening at the rim and a deep oblique ring base (Fig. 5:38).

Cups (Fig. 6:40-44). The ware of the cups is brown or yellowish, containing dark grits, and in one case at least shiny particles, possibly mica. The earliest cup (from Grave 5) was probably hand-made ('pinched'), and it retained a whitish surface inside and out. Larger cups from the later graves 19 and 43 were wheel-made and preserved traces of red slip. The sides curved inwards slightly and the bases were flat disks. In this respect they follow the tradition of certain cups from the Courtyard Cemetery at Tell el-'Ajjul.[41]

Jars (Figs. 6:45-51; 7:52-56). The ware of the jars is reddish-brown with dark grits and a red slip outside, which may extend over the rim. There seems to be a difference between jars from Graves 407 and 5 and those from Graves 19 and 43, the latter registering a decrease in diameter and an increase in height. The curvaceous drop-shape gives way to almost parallel sides, a detail which Petrie did not fail to notice in his assessment of the pottery.[42] Careful measurements would be necessary in order to discover whether there was a deliberate attempt on the part of the potter to reduce capacity.

Potstands (Fig. 7:57-69). The ware is reddish-brown, partly red-slipped. The stands are wheel-made with strongly rolled rims. Petrie considered that the tallest pedestal was nearest to Twelfth Dynasty forms, and it may be that a reduction in height was a functional improvement to increase the stability of the vessel placed upon it. Presumably these were the drop-shaped jars, as seen in Graves 2, 407, 5, 19, and 43, where the number of stands was about equal. The imprint of a thumb on the soft clay of an unfired stand makes a human contact across the centuries. [43]

Metal

Weapons (Fig. 8:71-74). Three daggers and a knife were the only indications of martial equipment, though they could have equally well served domestic purposes; of these the dagger in Oxford is the sole survivor in extant collections. The longest dagger, no. 71 came from Grave 407; judging from the relationship of the blade in the grave to a 'ring' below, the 'thin casting of bronze over an ash core' must have formed the pommel.[44] No. 73 is much corroded and damaged with part of the tang missing. However, since cleaning, two rivet holes are visible in the blade, with a third possibly in the shortened tang. On analysis, the blade proved to be of arsenical copper, and it is not a tin-bronze.[45]

The dagger, no. 73 and the knife, no. 74 were found in Grave 5, the former near the isolated head, with the knife thrown into the contemporary annex containing sheep and lamb bones.[46] The daggers are of the general type found at Jericho in Groups I-IV, though no close parallel can be cited. A point of difference there is the sharper angle where the tang is hammered out and broadened to become the blade. Some of the daggers from Tell el'Ajjul and Tell Fara have lost these precise angles, but nonetheless there are no near comparisons.

Toggle-pins (Fig. 9). Of the actual pins, only fragments have survived the effects of corrosion through the years. The six examples outlined on pl. VI range between 0.045 and 0.105 m. in length, assuming that the scale of 2:3 applies to them. If details are not hidden by corrosion, they all have a plain shaft with little or no thickening to the head. Comparing these pins to the same simple type at Jericho, where the average length is greater, the Yehudiyeh pins are getting smaller and find good parallels in the graves immediately above the lower city in Block G at Tell el 'Ajjul. [47]

Conclusions

What can we learn about the people buried in the graves at Yehudiyeh? The needs of about thirteen individuals in the after life were very simple, and the graves in which they lay were unlined, and protected in two cases only by a brick vault. At least one young person was buried in a wooden coffin, following Egyptian custom. The attitudes of some bodies were disturbed, with limbs missing or redundant, and this evidence suggests burial after partial decomposition had taken place, which would be consistent with observations made in Palestine, in contrast to the situation in Egypt, where the preservation of the body was a major concern. When the bodies were reasonably intact, they lay on their sides, arms bent up towards the mouth, and with knees flexed.

Personal attire seems to have been a toga-like wrap secured on the left shoulder by a metal pin, leaving the right arm bare, conforming in this instance to Palestinian rather than Egyptian costume. Occasionally a dagger was carried, and here again, it is unusual to find them in poorer Egyptian graves. One grave produced a substantial number of roughly-made beads, but otherwise only a very few carnelian or amethyst beads of better quality remained. Like their neighbours in Palestine at this time, bangles, bracelets and earrings were not worn.

The presence of sheep bones in and around the graves suggests that this was a poor community of shepherds, celebrating the customary funeral feasts, served in bowls and cups, washed down with draughts from tubular jars set upright on ring stands. In this respect, the balance was towards Egypt, for none of the two-handled storage jars were found, which were so common in Palestine throughout the Middle Bronze Age. As far as the source of the pottery is concerned, there were about the same number of 'foreign' and 'red' ware vessels, and it is possible that both kinds were made locally. Certainly, the standard of production was low compared to the more elaborate and often inspired designs occasionally found elsewhere, particularly at nearby Tell el-Dab'a.

But the possessions which distinguish these people are the scarabs, proving contact with Egypt, though it does not necessarily imply even a rudimentary knowledge of the written language. It is the scarabs, moreover, which provide a means of comparison to certain other excavated sites in Palestine on the one hand, and with the series of Egyptian royal names of the Middle Kingdom and the Second Intermediate Period on the other. Extending the slight evidence acquired from the individual graves to the collections of scarabs bought on the site, it seems that the great camp was founded either late in the Thirteenth Dynasty, or more likely by the 'prince of the deserts' Seuserenre Khyan. The graves just discussed may have been dug later than his reign, though it seems doubtful that they date from the reigns of Sekhaenre or Apophis, when the general average length of royal scarabs had fallen from 20 mm. registered for Khyan and Mayebre Sheshi to 16 mm. for the last kings of the Fifteenth-Sixteenth Dynasties. A scarab of Auserre (Apophis) came from the site which brings the pre-New Kingdom history of the place down to this reign of over three decades. It was Auserre who exchanged insults with the ruler of Thebes which led to the eventual expulsion of the 'Hyksos' at a much disputed date around 1560 B.C.[48] The recorded movements of the Abrahamic tribes could be placed just before and after this event, moving over the same border lands, and it is surely no coincidence that some lesser kings commemorated on scarabs retained true Semitic personal names.

Petrie discussed the period in 1906, and summarised the succession of kings and vassals in a tabulation which holds good in its main features today.[49] Little systematic excavation had taken place in Palestine when he wrote, apart from his own sounding with those of Bliss at Tell Hesy, and Macalister's extensive excavations at Gezer. Throughout Petrie's long campaign to forge more links between the archaeology of Egypt and Palestine, he adhered to the 'long' chronology based on Manetho's history, which can no longer be entertained, any more than it is possible to accept the length of Bible history, as calculated by Bishop Ussher.[50] Dame Kathleen's own work at Jericho was crucial in extending our view of history far into the past, and it is now clear that only a 'short' chronology of about a century can fit the facts on the ground for that moment in time known as the 'Hyksos' period. [51]

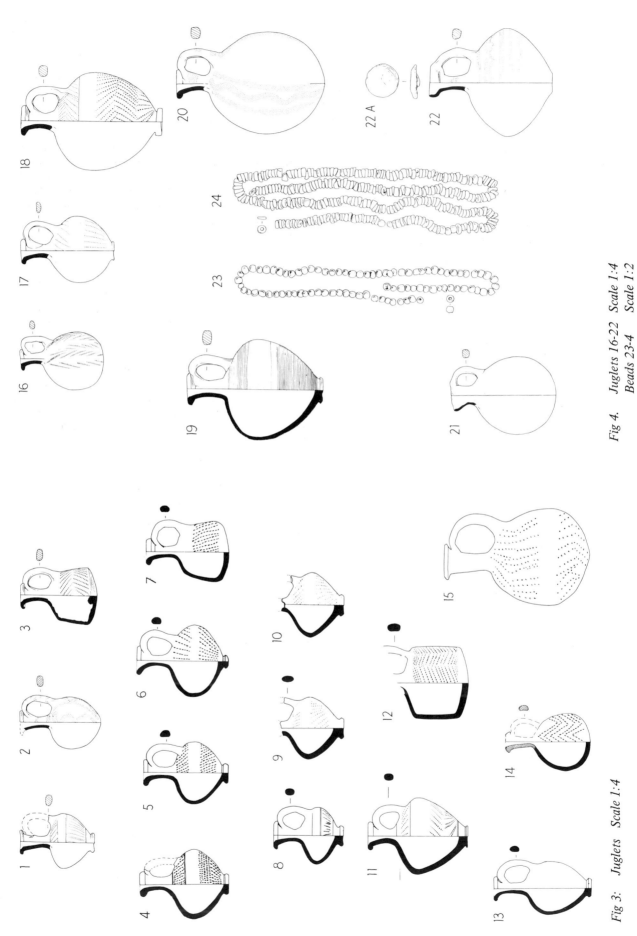

Fig. 4. Juglets 16-22 Scale 1:4
         Beads 23-4   Scale 1:2

Fig. 3: Juglets Scale 1:4

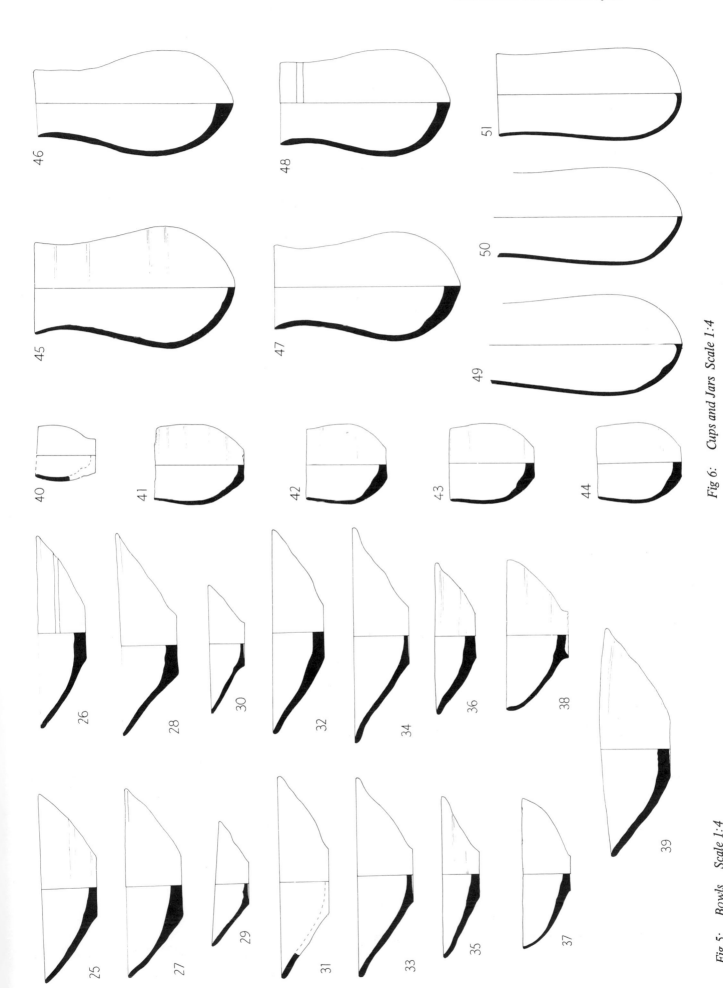

Fig 6:   Cups and Jars Scale 1:4

Fig 5:   Bowls   Scale 1:4

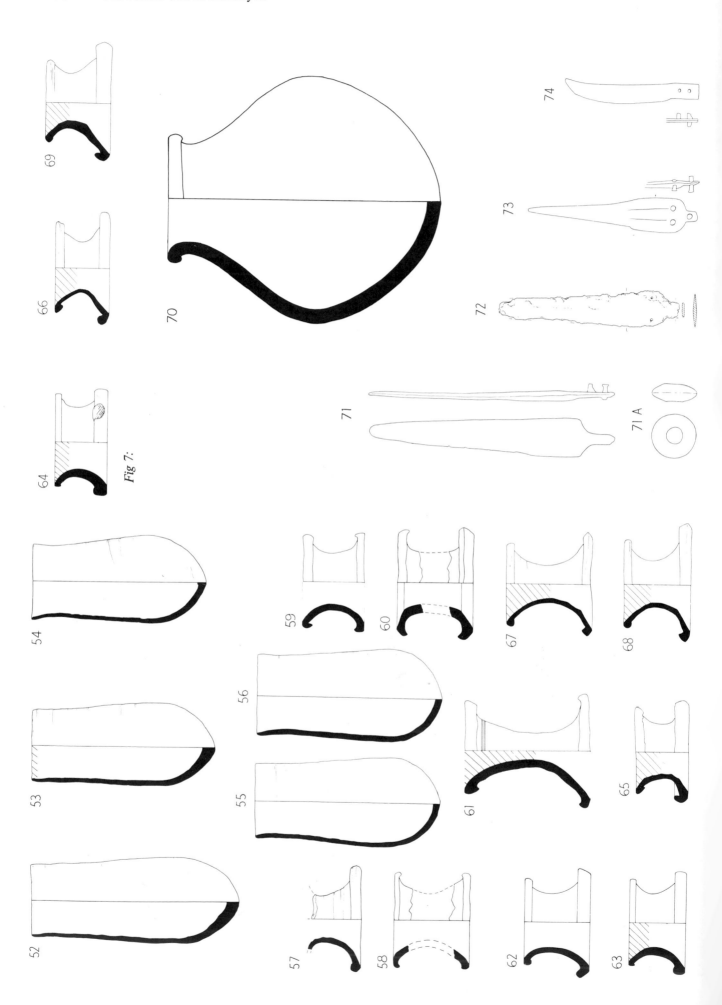

Fig 7:

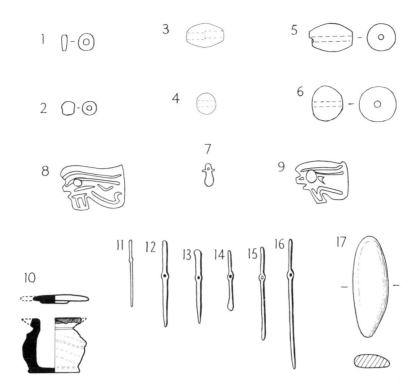

Fig 9.   Beads 1-6   Scale 1:1
Amulets, toggle-pins, stone
sizes uncertain

INVENTORY
TELL EL-YEHUDIYEH
GRAVE 2

Scarab

Dimensions mm.	Publication	Classification Head Back Side	Designs	Museum number
Fig. 1: 1 20x13x9	*HIC* pl. VII: 1	D6 - 0 - e9	2B2	OxAsh. E. 3536A

Pottery

diam. ht.		Description	Museum number
Fig. 3:1 0.060 0.079	*HIC* pl. VII:3 & p.11	*Juglet:* squat piriform, slightly concave disk base, rolled rim, strap handle *Ware:* black. Wheel-made. *Decoration:* comb-impressed oblique lines on shoulder with vertical lines below plain zone, within delimiting bands. Traces of white filling.	OxAsh. E. 3553
Fig. 3:2 0.055 0.084	*HIC* pl. VII:2 & p.11	*Juglet:* globular. Rolled rim, strap handle. *Ware:* buff, cream slip *Decoration:* painted red wavy lines, alternating with straight vertical bands on body, other bands around neck and on handle. Repaired, incomplete.	OxAsh. E. 3554
Fig. 3:3 0.059 0.080	*HIC* pl. VII:5 & p.12	*Juglet:* cylindrical splayed body, rounded base. Rolled rim, strap handle. *Ware:* black. Wheel-made. *Decoration:* comb-impressed chevrons around body with white filling. Repaired, incomplete.	OxAsh. E. 3510
- - - -	*HIC* pl. VII:4	*Juglet:* globular. Rolled rim, strap handle. *Ware:* black ? *Decoration:* comb-impressed chevrons with plain vertical zones between.	- -
Fig. 5: 25 0.203 0.060	*HIC* pl. X:1 & p.12	*Bowl:* slightly curved walls, flat base, Plain rim. *Ware:* brown, red slip inside and over rim. Wheel-made.	OxAsh. E. 3556
Fig. 6: 45 0.130 0.215	*HIC* pl. X:52 & p. 12	*Jar:* drop-shape, slightly pointed base. Plain upright rim. *Ware:* brown, red slip. Wheel-made.	OxAsh. E. 3535

** For two juglets now identified as coming from Grave 407, see fig. 3:13, 14.

INVENTORY
TELL EL-YEHUDIYEH
GRAVE 2 (cont.)

Pottery (cont.)

diam. ht.	Publication	Description	Museum number
Fig. 7: 57 0.0114 0.057+	*HIC* pl. X:36 & p.12	*Potstand:* low ring, rolled rims. *Ware:* brown, red slip. Wheel-made. Incomplete.	OxAsh. E. 3555

Metal

	Publication	Description	Museum number
Text fig. 9: 11 ?o.052	*HIC* pl. VI:3	*Toggle-pin:*	OxAsh. ?

GRAVE 407

Scarabs

Dimensions mm.	Publication	Classification Head Back Side	Designs	Museum number
Fig.1:2 17x11	*HIC* pl. VII:7		7B3a	*Brussels Mus.Roy. E. 2564
Fig.1:3 18x12	*HIC* pl. VII:9		1E3+3B+ 3b+3C	Brussels Mus.Roy. E. 2566
Fig.1:4 19x12	*HIC* pl. VII:6		7B3a	Brussels Mus.Roy. E. 2563
Fig.1:5 19x12	*HIC* pl. VII:8		1E3+3B- 3b+3C	Brussels Mus.Roy. E. 2565
Fig.1:6 24x16	*HIC* pl. VII:10		3B1c repeated thrice.	Brussels Mus.Roy. E. 2567

Bead

	Publication	Description	Museum number
Text fig. 9: 7 7x4	*HIC* pl. VII:10A	Drop pendant ? carnelian	Brussels Mus.Roy. E. 2568

Pottery

diam. ht.	Publication	Description	Museum number
Fig.3:4 0.075 0.093	*HIC* pl. VII:12 & p. 12	*Juglet:* piriform, solid disk base. Rolled rim on slender neck. *Ware:* light brown clay with greyish-black surface, without slip. Lightly burnished outside. Neck, handle & part of body restored. *Decoration:* comb-impressed oblique lines on shoulder, between delimiting grooves, continued in vertical lines below plain zone.	Brussels Mus.Roy. E. 2570

* None of the following items are at present available in the museum collections

INVENTORY

TELL EL-YEHUDIYEH

GRAVE 407 (cont.)

Pottery (cont.)

diam.	ht.	Publication	Description	Museum number
Fig.3:5				
0.065	0.089	*HIC* pl.VII: 11 & p.12	*Juglet:* piriform, solid disk base. Rolled rim on slender neck. Strap handle. *Ware:* greyish-black clay without slip, very porous Wheel-made. *Decoration:* comb-impressed oblique lines on shoulder, continued after plain zone below.	Brussels Mus.Roy. E. 2569
Fig.3:6				
0.075	0.095	unpublished	*Juglet:* piriform, pronounced button base. Rolled rim on slender neck. Strap handle *Ware:* greyish-black clay without slip, but well burnished outside, Button base is badly made and distorted. Wheel-made. *Decoration:* comb-impressed irregular oblique lines on shoulder continued after plain zone below.	Brussels Mus.Roy. E. 2572
Fig.3:7				
0.064	0.087	*HIC* pl.VII: 13	*Juglet:* cylindrical splayed body, rounded base. Rolled rim on slender neck. Strap handle. *Ware:* greyish-black clay, very porous. Wheel-made. *Decoration:* comb-impressed oblique lines around body.	Brussels Mus.Roy. E. 2571
Fig.5:26				
0.202	0.050	*HIC* pl.X:4	*Bowl:* slightly flared, flat base. Plain rim. *Ware:* reddish-brown, red slip outside only; traces of black near the base. Tournette or wheel-made. Restored.	Brussels Mus.Roy. E. 2581
Fig.5:27				
0.202	0.060	*HIC* pl.X:5	*Bowl:* slightly flared, flat base. Plain rim. *Ware:* reddish-brown, traces of red slip inside only; black marks outside. Tournette or wheel-made. Restored.	Brussels Mus.Roy. E. 2579
Fig.5:28				
0.215	0.060	*HIC* pl.X:3	*Bowl:* slightly flared, flat base. Plain rim. *Ware:* light brown, red slip outside only. Wheel-made. Restored.	Brussels Mus.Roy. E. 2582

INVENTORY

TELL EL-YEHUDIYEH

GRAVE 407 (cont.)

Pottery (cont.)

diam.	ht.	Publication	Description	Museum number
Fig.6:46				
0.112	0.207	*HIC* pl.X:53	*Jar:* drop-shape, slightly pointed base. Plain upright rim. *Ware:* reddish-brown, traces slip outside. Hand-made. Restored.	Brussels Mus.Roy. E. 2583
Fig.6:47				
0.114	0.195	*HIC* pl. X:55	*Jar:* drop-shape, slightly pointed base. Plain upright rim. *Ware:* orange-brown, traces of reddish-brown slip outside. Clearly wheel-made. Almost intact.	Brussels Mus.Roy. E. 2587
Fig.6:48				
0.113	0.180	*HIC* pl.X:54	*Jar:* drop-shape, slightly pointed base. Plain upright rim. *Ware:* reddish-brown, red slip outside only. Hand-made. Traces of use of tool for smoothing exterior surface, resembling herring-bone pattern. (Not indicated on drawing.)	Brussels Mus.Roy. E. 2584
Fig.8:70				
0.260	0.287	*HIC* pl.XIV A	*Jar:* large, globular, rounded base. Thick rolled rim. *Ware:* reddish-brown, self-coloured slip. Large black mark on base, due to firing in reducing atmosphere. Wheel-made. Restored from fragments.	Brussels Mus.Roy. E. 2589
Fig.7:58				
0.103	0.080	*HIC* pl.X:29	*Pot-stand:* medium ring, folded rims. *Ware:* reddish-brown, red slip. Wheel-made. Restored.	Brussels Mus.Roy. E. 2578
Fig.7:59				
0.104	0.065	*HIC* pl.X:29	*Pot-stand:* medium ring, folded rims. *Ware:* light brown; red slip all over except for inner surface of base. Wheel-made.	Brussels Mus.Roy. E. 2576
Fig.7:60				
0.118	0.080	*HIC* pl.X:28	*Pot-stand:* medium ring, folded rims. *Ware:* reddish-brown, red slip, Wheel-made. Restored.	Brussels Mus.Roy. E. 2577

INVENTORY

TELL EL-YEHUDIYEH

GRAVE 407 (cont.)

Pottery (cont.)

	diam.	ht.	Publication	Description	Museum number
Fig.7:61					
	0.120	0.133	*HIC* pl. XIV A	*Pot-stand:* pedestal, folded rims. *Ware:* beige-brown; red slip all over except for inner surface of base. Restored.	Brussels Mus.Roy. E. 2575
- -	0.156	0.210	*HIC* pl. X:30	*Potstand:* pedestal folded rims. *Ware:* ?	?

Metal

	diam.	ht.	Publication	Description	Museum number
Fig.8:71					
	? 0	? 0	*HIC* pl.VI.1	*Dagger:* with pommel not now available in museum.	Brussels Mus.Roy. E. 2588

GRAVE 3

Scarabs

	Dimensions mm.	Publication	Classification Head Back Side	Designs	Museum number
Fig.1:7	13x8x6.5 amethyst	*HIC* pl.VII: 19	D8 - I - d5	12	M/c 3457
Fig.1:8	13x9x6	*HIC* pl.VII: 18	B8 - 0 - d6*	10A2a	M/c 3453
Fig.1:9	17x12	*HIC* pl.VII: 20	- -	3B5	M/c 3451 not found
Fig.1:10	18x14x8	*HIC* pl.VII: 14	A4 - 0 - d6*	3C	M/c 3449
Fig.1:11	18.5x12	*HIC* pl.VII: 15	- -	3B1a	M/c not found
Fig.1:12	20x14x10	*HIC* pl.VII: 17	B2 - 0 - d5	3A4+ 3C	M/c 3452
Fig.1:13	22x15x8	*HIC* pl.VII: 16	D5 - 0 - e9	3C+9F	M/c 3450

Beads

		Publication			Museum number
Text fig. 9:4	10x11 amethyst	unpublished	spheroid		M/c 3457b
Text fig. 9:3	20x13 carnelian	unpublished	long barrel		M/c 3457c

Kohl-pot with lid

36x32 approx. *HIC* pl.VII:21   M/c 3448

Text fig. 9:10

Pottery

	diam.	ht.	Publication	Description	Museum number
Fig.3:8					
	0.062	0.073	*HIC* pl.VII: 22 & p.12	*Juglet:* squat piriform, slightly concave disk base. Rolled rim. Strap handle.	M/c 3447

INVENTORY

TELL EL-YEHUDIYEH

GRAVE 3 (cont.)

Pottery (cont.)

	diam.	ht.	Publication	Description	Museum number
Fig.3:8 (cont.)				*Ware:* greyish-black, traces of burnishing outside. *Decoration:* comb-impressed vertical lines, white filling below carination, between wheel-made grooves.	
Fig.3:9					
	0.067	0.090?	*HIC* pl.VII: 23 & p. 12	*Juglet:* piriform, slightly concave disk base. Rolled rim ? Strap handle. *Ware:* greyish-black, surface worn *Decoration:* comb-impressed oblique lines on shoulder, white filling, continued below plain zone, between delimiting grooves.	M/c 3443
Fig.3:10					
	0.069	0.090?	*HIC* pl.VII: 24 & p.12	*Juglet:* piriform, slightly concave disk base. Rim and most of strap handle missing. *Ware:* greyish-black, traces of burnish on surface. *Decoration:* comb-impressed oblique lines on shoulder, continued below plain zone, between delimiting grooves, white filling.	M/c 3444
Fig.3:11					
	0.083	0.105	*HIC* pl.VII: 25 & p.12	*Juglet:* piriform, neat disk base, slightly concave. Rolled rim. Strap handle. *Ware:* greyish-black, traces of burnish on surface. *Decoration:* comb-impressed oblique lines on shoulder, between delimiting grooves. Roughly applied chevrons near base, white filled, above grooves.	M/c 3446
Fig.3:12					
	0.077	0.100?	*HIC* pl.VII: 26 & p.12	*Juglet:* straight-sided cylindrical body. Rim & most of neck and strap handle missing. *Ware:* greyish-black; surface worn. *Decoration:* comb-impressed chevrons placed vertically on body, white filled.	M/c 3445

INVENTORY

TELL EL-YEHUDIYEH

GRAVE 5

Scarabs

Dimensions mm.	Publication	Classification Head Back Side	Designs	Museum number
Fig.2:14				
20x14x9	*HIC* pl.VII:29	A - I - ?	12B	Phila.Univ. Mus. E. 2828
amethyst in gold mount				
Fig.2:15				
20x15x9	*HIC* pl.VII:28	A7 - 0 - d6*	9C4+ 10C2c	Phila.Univ. Mus. E. 2827
Fig.2:16				
23x17x11	*HIC* pl.VII:27	D5 - 0 - d5	10B	Phila.Univ. Mus. E. 2826

Bead & pendants

- -	6x5	*HIC* pl.VII:30		?
Text fig. 9:8				
	14x ?	*HIC* pl.VII:31		Phila.Univ.
	faience	& p.11		Mus. E.2829B
Text fig. 9:9				
	17x ?	*HIC* pl.VII:32		Phila.Univ.
	faience	& p.11		Mus. E.2829A

Metal

diam.	ht.	Publication	Description	Museum number
Fig.8:73				
0.037	0.180	*HIC* pl.VI:7	*Dagger:* tapering blade, thick midrib, short tang (broken) with one rivet, two more in blade.	Phila.Univ. Mus. not found.
Fig.8:74				
0.020	0.140	*HIC* pl.VI:9 & p.13	*Knife:* curved blade, square ended butt, pierced by two rivets.	Phila.Univ. Mus. not found.
Text fig. 9:12				
	0.067?	*HIC* pl.VI: 10 & p. 13	*Toggle-pin:* plain shank, pierced.	Phila.Univ. Mus. not found.
Text fig. 9:13				
	0.060?	*HIC* pl.VI: 11 & p.13	*Toggle-pin:* plain shank, pierced	Phila.Univ. Mus. not found.

Mud figure

-		*HIC* pl.VI: 8 & p. 13		Phila.Univ. Mus. not found.

Pottery

diam.	ht.	Publication	Description	Museum number
Fig.5:29				
0.135	0.035	*HIC* pl.X:7	*Bowl:* slightly splayed & slight concave flat base. Plain rim. Lop-sided. Wheel-made. *Ware:* reddish-brown red wash inside, yellowish exterior. Thick black grits. Distinct finger marks inside.	Phila.Univ. Mus. E. 15580

INVENTORY

TELL EL-YEHUDIYEH

GRAVE 5 (cont.)

Pottery (cont.)

diam.	ht.	Publication	Description	Museum number
Fig. 5:30				
0.135	0.037	*HIC* pl.X:6	*Bowl:* slightly splayed & slight concave flat base. Plain rim. Lop-sided, Wheel-made *Ware:* reddish-brown, yellowish exterior, reddish-black slip interior, firing brown at core, black grits. Distinct finger marks inside.	Phila.Univ. Mus. E. 15581
Fig. 5:31				
0.216	0.050	*HIC* pl.X:5	*Bowl:* slightly splayed & flat base. Plain rim. Wheel-made. *Ware:* reddish-brown red slip inside yellowish exterior. Black grits and black spotty discoloura-tion inside.	Phila.Univ. Mus. E. 2837
Fig. 5:32				
0.215	0.053	*HIC cf.* pl.X: 5	*Bowl:* slightly splayed & flat base. Plain rim. *Ware:* reddish-brown, red slip inside, yellowish exterior. Black grits. Fired black at core, discoloured surface inside.	Phila.Univ. Mus. E. 2838
Fig.5:33				
0.213	0.059	*HIC cf.* pl.X: 5	*Bowl:* splayed and slightly concave flat base. Plain rim. *Ware:* reddish-brown, red slip inside, yellowish exterior. Black grits, discoloured surface inside.	Phila.Univ. Mus. E. 15583
Fig.5:34				
0.226	0.058	*HIC cf.* pl.X: 5	*Bowl:* splayed and slightly concave flat base. Plain rim. Wheel-made. *Ware:* reddish-brown red slip inside, yellowish exterior with red slip splashes. Black grits. Traces of black discol-ouration.	Phila.Univ. Mus. E. 15582
Fig. - -				
0.240	0.120	*HIC* pl.X: 19	*Bowl:* deep and slightly flared sided. Disk (?) base. Plain rim (?).	?
Fig.6:40				
0.059	0.063	*HIC* pl.X: 18	*Bowl:* small cup, incurved, flat base. Plain rim. Hand-made ? *Ware:* yellowish-brown. Traces of white inside and out. Black grits.	Phila.Univ. Mus. E. 2839
Fig.6:49				
0.105	?	unpublished	*Jar:* drop-shape, rounded base. Rim missing. *Ware:* reddish-brown, red slip outside, with scant traces of burning. Black grits.	Phila.Univ. Mus. no number

INVENTORY
TELL EL-YEHUDIYEH
GRAVE 5 (cont.)

Pottery (cont.)

	diam.	ht.	Publication	Description	Museum number
Fig.6:50					
	0.102	?	unpublished	*Jar:* drop-shape, rounded base. Rim missing. *Ware:* reddish-brown, red slip outside and traces of black. Black grits.	Phila.Univ. Mus. no number
Fig.6:51					
	0.099	0.190	*HIC* pl.X: 58	*Jar:* drop-shape, rounded base. Plain rim. *Ware:* reddish-brown, red slip outside, yellowish surface inside. Black grits.	Phila.Univ. Mus. no number.
Fig.7:62					
	0.115	0.070	*HIC* pl.X: 31	*Potstand:* low ring, rolled rims. *Ware:* reddish-brown fired black at core. Black grits.	Phila.Univ. Mus. no number.
Fig.7:63					
	0.110	0.060	*HIC* pl.X: 34	*Potstand:* low ring, rolled rims. *Ware:* reddish-brown, traces of red wash outside & partly inside.	Phila.Univ. Mus. E. 15603
Fig.7:64					
	0.110	0.055	*HIC* pl.X: 32	*Potstand:* medium ring, rolled rims. *Ware:* reddish-brown, red slip outside & partly inside. Black grits. Finger-print on exterior rim.	

GRAVE 19

Scarab

	Dimensions mm.	Publication	Classification Head Back Side	Designs	Museum number
Fig.2:17					
	15x11x7	*HIC* pl. VII: 33 & p. 11	D? - S - e9	4B2	OxAsh. E.3490A

Pottery

	diam.	ht.		Description	Museum number
Fig.5:35					
	0.172	0.039	*HIC* pl.X:11 & p. 13	*Bowl:* undulating sides rising from flat base. Plain rim. *Ware:* coarse brown, red slip inside only. Black grits & mica? Wheel-made.	OxAsh. E. 3525

INVENTORY
TELL EL-YEHUDIYEH
GRAVE 19 (cont.)

Pottery (cont.)

	diam.	ht.	Publication	Description	Museum number
Fig.5:36					
	0.159	0.043	*HIC* pl.X:10 & p.13	*Bowl:* undulating sides rising from slightly concave disk base. *Ware:* coarse brown, red slip inside only. Black grits & mica? Wheel-made.	OxAsh. E. 3526
Fig.5:37					
	0.160	0.050	unpublished	*Bowl:* curved sides, rising from slightly concave disk base. Plain rim. *Ware:* brown, red slip all over, including base.	OxAsh. E. 3524
Fig.6:41					
	0.085	0.093	*HIC* pl.X:22 & p.13	*Bowl:* small cup, in-curved, flat base. Plain rim.	OxAsh. E. 3490
Fig.7:52					
	0.090	0.220	*HIC* pl.X:67 & p.13	*Jar:* drop-shape, curving out to plain rim *Ware:* coarse brown, red slip outside. Wheel-made.	OxAsh. E. 3528
Fig.7:53					
	0.087	0.194	*HIC* pl.X:66 & p.13.	*Jar:* drop-shape, curving out to plain rim. *Ware:* coarse brown, red slip outside. Base scraped. Wheel-made?	OxAsh. E. 3529
Fig.7:54					
	0.091	0.183	unpublished	*Jar:* drop-shape, curving out to plain rim. *Ware:* coarse brown, red slip outside. Base scraped. Wheel-made?	Ox.Ash E. 3530
Fig.7:65					
	0.106	0.056	*HIC* pl.X:36 & p.13	*Potstand:* low ring, rolled rims. *Ware:* brown, red slip outside, patchy surface. Wheel-made.	OxAsh. E. 3527
Fig.7:66					
	0.117	0.055	*HIC* pl.X:38 & p.13.	*Potstand:* low ring, rolled rims. *Ware:* brown, red slip. Wheel-made.	OxAsh. E. 3532

GRAVE 4

Scarab

	Dimensions mm.	Publication	Classification Head Back Side	Designs	Museum number
Fig.2:18					
	16x11	*HIC* pl.VII: 34	- -	4B2	?

INVENTORY
TELL EL-YEHUDIYEH
GRAVE 4 (cont.)

Pottery

diam.	ht.	Publication	Description	Museum number
? 0.060	0.096	*HIC* pl. VII: 35	*Juglet:* globular, rolled rim: ?Strap handle. *Ware:*	?
? 0.222	0.060	*HIC* pl. X: 8	*Bowl:* slightly flared, flat base. Plain rim. *Ware:*	?
? 0.222	0.072	*HIC* pl. X: 9	*Bowl:* slightly flared, flat base. Plain rim. *Ware:*	?
?	0.080	*HIC* pl. X: 21	*Bowl:* small cup, incurved. Flat base. *Ware:*	?
? 0.108	?	*HIC* pl. X: 63	*Jar:* drop-shape ? rounded base, Plain rim *Ware:*	?
? 0.120	0.060	*HIC* pl. X: 41	*Potstand:* medium ring, rolled rims.	?
? 0.120	0.072	*HIC* pl. X: 45	*Potstand:* medium ring. Rolled rims. *Ware:*	

GRAVE 16

Pottery

diam.	ht.	Publication	Description	Museum number
Fig.3:13				
0.096	0.165	*cf. HIC* pl. VIII: 36	*Juglet:* piriform, elongated, angular flat disk base. Rolled rim. Strap handle. *Ware:* reddish-brown, light brown slip outside; very porous. Wheel-made, Restored from several fragments.	* Brussels Mus. Roy. E 2574
Fig.3:14				
0.102 ?	0.162	*cf. HIC* pl. VIII: 39	*Juglet:* globular. Rolled rim. Strap handle. Restored. *Ware:* greyish-black, without slip; very porous. Hand-made *Decoration:* comb-impressed chevrons placed vertically around body.	*Brussels Mus. Roy. E. 2573
0.105	0.154	*cf. HIC* pl. VIII: 38	*Juglet:* piriform, marked shoulder disk base ? Rolled rim. Strap handle *Ware:* *Decoration:* comb-impressed chevrons on shoulder, repeated below plain zone.	?

* From Petrie's field note-book (p.106) it appears that these two juglets were found in Grave 407, though they are missing from the pottery on pl. VII. They are both smaller than the similar juglets registered in Grave 16 the actual measurements of the Brussels juglets being 0.060 diam. for E. 2573 and 0.057 diam. and 0.102 ht. for E. 2574. I am grateful to Miss J. Bourriau for this reference.

INVENTORY
TELL EL-YEHUDIYEH
GRAVE 16 (cont.)

Pottery (cont.)

diam.	ht.	Publication	Description	Museum number
0.099	0.162	*cf. HIC* pl. VIII: 40	*Juglet:* globular, Rolled rim. Strap handle. *Ware:* *Decoration:* comb-impressed chevrons placed vertically, with plain zones between.	?
- - ?	?	HIC pl. VIII: 37	*Juglet:* part of neck only. *Ware:* ? buff *Decoration:* painted band around neck.	?
- - 0.210	0.048	*HIC* pl. X: 10	*Bowl:* slightly splayed, ? disk base. ?Plain rim. *Ware:*	?
- - 0.192	0.066	*HIC* pl. X: 12	*Bowl:* slightly splayed, ? disk base. ?Plain rim. *Ware:*	?
- - 0.084	0.186	*HIC* pl. X: 68	*Jar:* drop-shape, curving out to plain rim *Ware:*	?
- - 0.078	0.198	*HIC* pl. X: 69	*Jar:* drop-shape, almost straight-sided, rounded base.	?
- - 0.108	0.079	*HIC* pl. X: 40	*Potstand:* medium ring, wide base, lower rim rolled *Ware:*	?

GRAVE 20

diam.	ht.	Publication	Description	Museum number
Fig.3:15				
0.102	0.150	*HIC* pl. VIII: 41 & p.13	*Juglet:* globular, Rolled rim. ?Strap handle. Copied from *HIC.*	Munich Staatlichen Saamlung ES 4427
- - 0.180	0.048	*HIC* pl. X: 13 & p.13.	*Bowl:* splayed, ?disk base. Plain rim *Ware:*	?
- - 0.084	0.090	*HIC* pl. X: 24 & p.13.	*Bowl:* small cup. ?flat base. Plain rim. *Ware:*	?
- - 0.090	0.196	*HIC* pl. X: 72 & p.13.	*Jar:* drop-shape, rounded base. Plain rim. *Ware:* *Decoration:* rim painted red.	
- - 0.090	0.196	*HIC* pl. X: 73	*Jar:* drop-shape, rounded base. Plain rim. *Ware:* *Decoration:* rim painted red.	
- - 0.108	0.054	*HIC* pl. X: 43	*Potstand:* low ring, rolled rims. *Ware:*	?

INVENTORY

TEL EL-YEHUDIYEH

GRAVE 37

Scarabs

Dimensions mm.	Publication	Classification Head Back Side	Designs	Museum number
Fig.2:19				
15x11	*HIC* pl.VIII: 44		3C	OxAsh. not seen
Fig.2:20				
16x11	*HIC* pl.VIII: 42		2A+ 2B1	OxAsh. not seen
Fig.2:21				
17x12	*HIC* pl.VIII: 45		10A2b	OxAsh. not seen.
Fig.2:22				
17x13x8	*HIC* pl.VIII: 47	ovoid	4C1	OxAsh. EE 657
Fig.2:23				
18x12x7	*HIC* pl.VIII: 46	D5 - 0 - d5	6C2	OxAsh. EE 640
Fig.2:24				
19x14	*HIC* pl.VIII: 43		9C1+ 9D	OxAsh. not seen.

Beads

diam. ht.	Publication	Description	Museum number
Fig.4:23			
each bead 8x7 approx. See also fig.9:2	*HIC* p.13	String of black globular beads, composition, coloured with manganese.	OxAsh. EE 659
Fig.4:24			
each bead 9x9x3 mm. approx. See also fig.9:1	*HIC* p.13	String of white disk beads, composition, probably blue originally.	OxAsh. EE 660
Text fig. 9:17			
0.053x0.019 x0.007	*HIC* p.13	Slate rubber, found under right humerus.	OxAsh. E 3517

Metal

Text fig. 9:16			
incomplete fragment corroded	*HIC* p.13	Toggle-pin 'The bronze Pin was found near the place of the neck, as in Grave 2'	OxAsh. E 4307

Pottery

Fig.4:16			
0.060 0.090	*HIC* pl.VIII: 48 & p.13	*Juglet:* globular Rolled rim. Strap handle, badly attached. *Ware:* greyish-black. *Decoration:* comb-impressed chevrons in vertical bands, white filled.	OxAsh. E 3501
Fig.4:17			
0.070 0.100	*HIC* pl.VIII: 49 & p.13	*Juglet:* globular, slightly concave disk base. Rolled rim. Strap handle, badly attached.	OxAsh. E 3500

INVENTORY

TEL EL-YEHUDIYEH

GRAVE 37 (cont.)

Pottery (cont.)

diam. ht.	Publication	Description	Museum Number
		Ware: greyish-black. *Decoration:* comb-impressed sparse oblique lines on shoulder, vertical lines below plain zone.	
Fig.4:18			
0.105 0.150	*HIC* pl.VIII: 50	*Juglet:* piriform, rounded shoulder. Pronounced disk base, slightly concave. Rolled rim. Squared handle, badly attached. *Ware:* greyish-black *Decoration:* comb-impressed chevrons on shoulder, above delimiting line, more chevrons below plain zone down to base.	OxAsh. E. 3499
Fig.4:19			
0.107 0.143	*HIC* pl.VIII: 52 & p.13	*Juglet:* piriform, rounded shoulder. Concave disk base. Rolled rim. Squared handle, badly attached. *Ware:* greyish-black. *Decoration:* Wheel-made grooves on shoulder, continuing after plain zone below.	OxAsh. E. 3498
Fig.4:20			
0.110 0.155	*HIC* pl.VIII: 51 & p.13	*Juglet:* deep globular, high shoulder. Rolled rim. Squared handle, badly attached. *Ware:* brown, cream slip flaking off. *Decoration:* vertical wavy lines between straight bands, painted in black.	OxAsh. E. 3491
Fig. 5:38			
0.158 0.064	*HIC* p.13	*Bowl:* curved, oblique disk base. Slightly thickened rim. *Ware:* coarse brown, red slip. Wheel-made.	OxAsh. E. 3492
Fig.7:67			
0.127 0.068	*HIC* pl.X:45 & p.13	*Potstand:* medium ring, wide base. Pronounced rolled rims. *Ware:* brown, red slip. Wheel-made.	OxAsh. E. 3536
Fig.7:68			
0.125 0.070	*HIC* pl.X:49 & pp.13-4	*Potstand:* medium ring, wide base. Pronounced rolled rims. *Ware:* reddish-brown, red slip. Wheel-made.	OxAsh. E. 3538

INVENTORY
TELL EL-YEHUDIYEH
GRAVE 37 (cont.)

Pottery (cont.)

	diam.	ht.	Publication	Description	Museum number
Fig. 7:69					
	0.108	0.090	*HIC* pl. X:47 & pp.13-4	*Potstand:* tall ring, wide base. Pronounced rolled rims. *Ware:* brown, red slip. Wheel-made.	Ox Ash. E.3523+3489
	0.120	0.066	*HIC* pl. X:41	*Potstand:* medium ring, wide base. Rolled rims. *Ware:*	Ox Ash. not seen.

GRAVE 1

Scarabs

	Dimensions mm.	Publication	Classification Head Back Side	Designs	Museum number
Fig. 2:25					
	17x12x8	*HIC* pl. VI:4 & pp. 11, 13	A5 - II - e12*	3C	Ox Ash. EE.635
Fig. 2:26					
	21x15x10	*HIC* pl. VI:5 & pp.11,13	D7 - 0 - d5	9B	Ox Ash. EE.634

Bead

Text fig. 9:5					
	11x8 amethyst	*HIC* pl. VI:6	barrel		Ox Ash. EE.636

Metal

Fig. 8:72					
	0.193x0.039	*HIC* pl. VI:3 & p.13	*Dagger-blade* arsenical copper, corroded. Tip and part of tang missing. Two rivet holes in blade, possibly a third in tang.		Ox Ash. E.3514

GRAVE 6

Scarabs

Fig. 2:27					
	14x10 amethyst	*HIC* pl. VIII: 54	B7 - 0 - ?	12B	Ox Ash.
Fig. 2:28					
	17x12x7	*HIC* pl. VIII: 55	D6 - 0 - d5	2A	Ox Ash. EE.638
Fig. 2:29					
	20x14x8	*HIC* pl. VIII: 53	D6 - 0 - d5	9E+ 10C2	Ox Ash. EE.637

Bead

Text fig. 9:6					
	8x10 amethyst	*HIC* pl. VIII: 56	Spheroid		Ox Ash. EE.639

INVENTORY
TELL EL-YEHUDIYEH
GRAVE 6 (cont.)

Pottery

	diam.	ht.	Publication	Description	Museum number
Fig. 4:21					
	0.082	0.110	*HIC* pl. VIII: 57 & pp.13-4	*Juglet:* globular, incurved rim on short neck. Squared handle, badly attached. *Ware:* black, surface worn, but no trace of decoration visible.	Ox Ash. E.3495

GRAVE 43

Pottery

	diam.	ht.	Publication	Description	Museum number
Fig. 4:22					
	0.116	0.130	*HIC* pl. VIII: 58	*Juglet:* piriform, flat base. Upturned rim on short neck. Squared handle, badly attached. *Ware:* drab under drab slip, showing vertical burnish. Wheel-made. *Decoration:* Band of purple paint around neck. Five bands around body, with one wavy line between.	Ox Ash. E.3484 ?
Fig. 4:22A					
	0.035	0.010	*HIC* p.14	*Lid* circular, with domed projection inside. *Ware:* drab. Hand-made.	Ox Ash. E.3487
Fig. 5:39					
	0.242	0.070	*HIC* pl. X:15 & p.12	*Bowl:* undulating sides, flat base, slightly concave. Plain rim. *Ware:* brown, red slip inside. Wheel-made.	Ox Ash. E.3486
Fig. 6:42					
	0.084	0.084	*HIC* pl. X:25-27	*Bowl:* small cup, slightly incurved, flat base. Plain rim. *Ware:* coarse brown, red slip. Wheel-made.	Ox Ash. E.3485C
Fig. 6:43					
	0.084	0.088	*HIC* pl. X:25-27	*Bowl:* small cup, slightly incurved, flat base. Plain rim. *Ware:* coarse brown, red slip Wheel-made.	Ox Ash. E.3485A
Fig. 6:44					
	0.086	0.084	*HIC* pl. X:25-27	*Bowl:* small cup, slightly incurved, flat base. Plain rim. *Ware:* coarse brown with grits, red slip outside and on rim. Wheel-made.	Ox Ash. E.3485B

INVENTORY

TELL EL-YEHUDIYEH

GRAVE 43 (cont.)

Fig. 7:56

diam.	ht.	Publication	Description	Museum number
0.095	0.195	HIC pl. X: 76	*Jar:* drop-shape, curving out to plain rim. Slightly pointed base. *Ware:* reddish-brown, red slip. Wheel-made.	Ox Ash. E.3533

Pottery (cont.)

diam.	ht.	Publication	Description	Museum number		diam.	ht.	Publication	Description	

Fig. 7:55

diam.	ht.	Publication	Description	Museum number
0.095	0.195	HIC pl. X: 75	*Jar:* drop-shape curving out to plain rim. Slightly pointed base. *Ware:* reddish-brown, red slip. Wheel-made	Ox Ash. E.3522
– –	0.120	0.092	HIC pl. X: 49	*Potstand:* medium ring. Rolled rims. *Ware:*	?
– –	0.108	0.090	HIC pl. X: 51	*Potstand:* medium ring. Rolled rims. *Ware:*	?

References

1. E. Naville, I *Mound of the Jew and the City of Onias*; F.Ll. Griffith, II *Antiquities of Tell el-Yehudiyeh* (1890). W.M.F. Petrie, *Hyksos and Israelite Cities,* double vol. (1906), hereafter abbreviated *Mound* and *HIC.*

2. *HIC,* pp. 10-16.

3. The pottery was described by Mrs. J. Crowfoot-Payne, Dr. Rosalie David, Dr. Frances James and Mr. B. Van den Driessche, who also made the drawings in Brussels. Other drawings were the work of Miss Phyllis Anderson, Mr. George Bridge and Mrs. M. E. Cox. Errors and omissions are my responsibility and I am most grateful to them all for their assistance in reassembling descriptions of these grave groups. My thanks are also due to the G. A. Wainwright Fund and Manchester University for help in covering the costs.

4. O. Tufnell and W. A. Ward, *Studies on Scarab-seals* 2 vols. (in preparation, hereafter abbreviated *StSc*).

5. MDAIK 23 (1968) pl. XXV b; 26 (1970) e.g. pl. X:2

6. *Mound,* pl. X; *HIC* pl. IX. For fuller classification, see O. Tufnell in *JEA* 61 (1975) pp. 67-90.

7. For reference to this and other items see the list on pp. 83f.

8. *Levant* V (1973), pp. 73-4 and note 9.

9. *Ibid.,* p. 76 and note 32.

10. *Ibid.,* pp. 76-7, no. 37, 45, 64, 96.

11. E.J.H. Mackay and M.A. Murray, *Ancient Gaza* V (1951), pl. IX: 5, 8, and 9 show scarabs naming Sheshi, Sekhaenre and Ahetepre, all with the panel border with cross-bars 3E4.

12. *CAH* vol. II, Chap. II (1962), pp. 62ff.

13. *Levant* V, no. 89; *cf. Mound,* pl. X:42

14. *HIC,* pl. IX:120 *cf. JT* II, fig. 300:31

15. *Mound,* pl. X:11 *cf.* Petrie, *Ancient Gaza* I, pl. XIII: 1

16. *Levant* V, no. 122; *cf. HIC* pl. IX:121

17. *Ibid.,* no. 92 (Müller's Stra. XI-IX = Kenyon's MB II ph. G).

18. K.M. Kenyon, *Jericho Tombs* II (1965), (hereafter *JT*), Appendix E: *Scarabs* by Diana Kirkbride, pp. 589-590.

19. *Ibid.,* fig. 296:14.

20. G.T. Martin, *Egyptian Administrative and Private-name Seals* (1971), nos. 1038 and 1473.

21. Average length: graves = 18.2 mm.; *HIC* = 16.7 mm.; *Mound* = 12.2 mm.

22. *Ancient Gaza* I, p. 3, a destruction then attributed either to the 'Hyksos' conquest, or rather perhaps to the raid of Sesostris III, when his troops reached Shechem. The recorded level in Area T is reduced by 100" to compensate for the rise in bedrock. The figure is underlined in this and subsequent references, see O. Negbi, *Hoards of Goldwork from Tell el-'Ajjul.* (1970) p. 16 n. 21.

23. *Ancient Gaza* I, pl. XIV: 108-111 and plan on pl. LV; for 109 *cf. Mound* pl. X:47 and for 110 see *HIC* pl. IX:122.

24. See Individual comparisons p.   and Graves 187 and 1553.

25. *HIC,* p.   15.

26. *JT* II, p. 315, i.e. four scarabs set in gold mounts.

27. *HIC,* p. 13.

28.   G. Brunton, *Qau and Badari* III (1930) (hereafter *QB*), pp. 3, 8 and pls. IV, XIX also registers pls. VI-VIII. It is now known that the scarab naming Si-hathor does not refer to Neferhotep's son: G. Reisner, *Kerma* II, fig. 59, but the style clearly indicates at XIIIth. Dynasty date.

29.   *HIC,* pl. VII 10A; *cf. QB* II, pl. CIII 89C6 and R. Engelbach, *Harageh* (1923), pl. LI type 44R.

30.   *HIC,* pl. VII:30.

31.   *HIC,* pp. 11, 13, pl. VII 31-32; *cf. Harageh,* pl. L and *QB* III, pl. IV type 38.

32.   *QB* III, pp. 3, 11 and pls. XX: 1-2 and pl. XXI.

33.   *Mound,* pp. 9, 39, 56-7.

34.   R. Amiran, *Ancient Pottery of the Holy Land* (1969), pl. 36 and pp. 118-120. Some recent notes are contributed by Drs. K. Prag and R. S. Merrillees in *Levant* V (1973), pp. 128-131 and VI (1974), pp. 192-195.

35.   K.M. Kenyon, *Levant* I (1969), figs. 4:20; 7: 7 and fig. 9: 8 = Kenyon's MB II ph. A-B and E at Megiddo; *cf JT* I chap 5 *passim* and JT II chap 4.

36.   O. Tufnell, *Bull. Inst. Arch.* 3 (1962), fig. 12:36, 41 and fig. 13:52. for the same ware in Tomb 303, see *AG* III, pl. XXXVIII 60M5 and pl. XXXIX 74 0 15' and sketch on pl. XLIX. The *terminus ante* is established by the scarab bearing the abbreviated Horus-name of Ammenemes IV (*AG* III, pl. IV:116). See my study of Tomb 303. *Atiqot* XIII (forthcoming).

37.   *Levant* I (1969), figs. 4-7: Kenyon's MB II ph. A-E.

38.   Writing specifically about my draft of this article in June 1976, Dr. Bietak considered that the material 'corresponds to Tell el-Dab'a, str. E/1, D/3, the Egyptian pottery is even represented in str. D/2 (e.g. fig. 5/32-34, fig. 6/49, 50, 52) which also came . . . partly from contexts of burials without Tell el-Yahudiya-ware'. He added that this ware is not definitely represented in Str. D/2, which has to be dated to the end of the Hyksos period. For preliminary reports see *MDAIK* 23 (1968) and 26 (1970).

39.   *HIC,* pp. 11, 15.

40.   Miss J. Bourriau is completing a thesis on "The comparative dating of Egyptian tomb groups of the Second Intermediate Period".

41.   *Bull. Inst. Arch.* 3 (1962), figs. 9: 2, 5A and 10: 7

42.   *HIC,* p. 14.

43.   Fig. 7:64,

44.   *HIC,* p. 12.

45.   I am grateful to Dr. Hugh McKerrell of the National Museum of Antiquities of Scotland, who allows me to mention his analysis of dagger E. 3514, which forms part of a major programme of surface analysis by radio-isotope non-dispersive X-ray fluorescence. The result shows that the working of copper continued in the Delta well into the period so inaccurately but universally known as the 'Bronze' Age. For analysis of a comparable but shorter tanged dagger from Tomb 1552, see *Lachish* IV (1958), p. 331.

46.   *HIC,* p. 13. For knives, see *JT* II, fig. 111, though there are no close comparisons.

47.   *AG* V, pl. XIV: 97-8, 100, 107. Another small pin came from a rectangular pit of the 'horse' burial type, *AG* I, pl. XXI:94.

48.   T.G.H. James in *CAH* vol. II, Chap. VIII (1973), pp. 289-296.

49.   *HIC,* chap. XI and pl. LI.

50.   F. Petrie, *Beth-Pelet* I (1930), chap II.

51.   These Asiatic intruders were named by the Egyptians *Hikau khoswet* 'Princes of the Desert Uplands' or 'Rulers of Foreign Countries', from which the Greek historian Manetho probably derived the term 'Hyksos' (*CAH* vol. II Chap. II (1973) pp. 54-5.

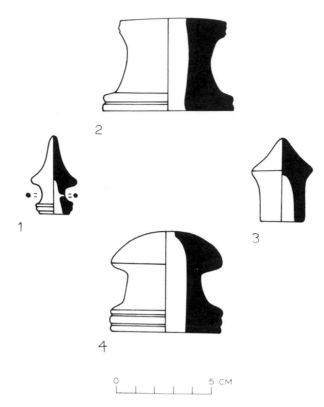

Fig 1: Alabaster chariot fittings from Beth Shan and Memphis: 1. Memphis 6081, limestone, P.29.70.202.
2. Beth Shan locus 1601, level x-a, alabaster ?, no field no., no museum no. 3. Memphis 6111, alabaster,
P.29.70.203. 4. Memphis 2828, alabaster, P.29.74.565.

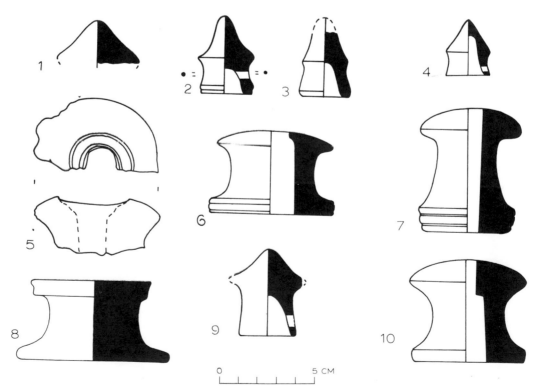

Fig 2. Alabaster chariot fittings from Beth Shan Level ix: 1. 28.9.21, glassy white stone, locus 1333,
P.29.105.854. 2. 27.10.385, marble, locus 1240, P.29.107.845. 3. 27.10.479, alabaster ?,locus
1236, Disposition unknown. 4. 28.11.55, quartzite, locus 1400, P.29.107.844, 5. 28.8.37,
alabaster ?, locus 1332, disposition unknown. 6. 28.8.78, narble, locus 1333, P.29.107.848.
7. 28.9.7, gypsum, locus 1339, P.29.107.849. 8. 28.11.423, alabaster ?, locus 1339, discarded.
9. 28.9.24, marble, locus 1339, P.29.107.845, 10. 27.12.283, limestone, locus 1234, P.29.107.833.

CHARIOT FITTINGS FROM LATE BRONZE AGE BETH SHAN
by Frances James

Dame Kathleen Kenyon has always emphasized the importance to Palestinian archaeology of the great site of Beth Shan in the Jezreel Valley; thus it was thanks to her inspiration that in the 1960's I began to work on the essentially unpublished Beisan materials which had lain in the University Museum in Philadelphia since the 1930's. Recently, work on the Late Bronze Age levels of Beisan has yielded an identification of stone chariot fittings which I hope may help us not only to detect the presence of the chariot in Canaan during this period, but to trace the geographical route and date of its introduction to Egypt and the Levant - as well as its dispersal elsewhere - much more precisely than is at present possible.

It is with much affection for and gratitude to Dame Kathleen that I present my findings on this subject on her 70th anniversary.

These findings concern a group of not-very-impressive white stone knobs (figs. 1 - 4 and pls. XIa-XIIb, which run through Beisan Levels ix-vii. It is possible to identify them as chariot fittings, probably of Egyptian military chariots, having exact parallels on the state chariots of Tutankhamun (pls. XIIIa-XIVb). This article presents the Beth Shan findings as fully as possible and examines the evidence for chariotry in Bronze and Iron Age Canaan. Space limitations obviously will not allow for a study of this matter over all of the ancient Near East and material from other areas is considered here only insofar as it is relevant to the argument, though I hope at a later date to make a fuller survey of the topic.

Background

While the immediate provenance of the knobs at Beth Shan is, in all three levels noted, that of Egyptian military installations, Canaanite chariots may also be represented by these knobs, as there is no particular reason why the latter should not appear also in this context. We know that the chariot, entering the Levant from the east, must have reached Palestine before it reached Egypt and that it was probably the chariot as adapted in Canaan from a still earlier prototype which became the prototype of the Egyptian. Certainly the records of the early xviiith dynasty list literally hundreds of chariots captured by the militarily minded pharaohs on each campaign through Djahi.

At Beth Shan, the knobs run through three of the four levels which produced firm archaeological evidence of Egyptian military installations between c. 1,350 and 1,200 B.C. Level vi, the latest of these four, produced no alabaster knobs though it yielded the best epigraphic evidence for Egyptian presence at Beth Shan. Some of the Level vi houses were of the typical plan with central hall as found at Amarna and had had stone-cut inscriptions, one of a "Commander of Troops of the Lord of the Two Lands, great Steward and Overseer of Foreign Countries and Fan Bearer on the Right of the King," the king being Rameses III.[1]

The absence of the alabaster chariot fittings in this level is probably mere accident, especially as vi is a straight-forward reconstruction of the Levels viii-vii military complex with buildings of the latter more-or-less duplicated.

In Beth Shan Levels viii and vii the knobs are found in the street and among the houses of the Egyptian garrison village to the east of the "temple" and, in Level vii, also among some large military installations to the west of the "temple."[2] The Level viii-vii complex ends, apparently, early in the reign of Ranesses iii, with a destruction which must have had something to do with the invasion of the Sea Peoples, c. 1,170 B.C.

One of the knobs to be attributed to ix (fig. 1, 2) in fact comes from one of the small buildings which appeared on the plan of x-a which seem certainly to have belonged to an early phase of ix. In the main phase of ix, the knobs were found along the streeet ringing the tell and in the small buildings south and east of the large structure which Rowe called the southern temple.[3]

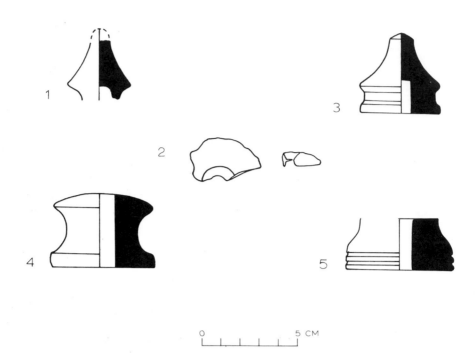

Fig 3: Alabaster chariot fittings from Beth Shan level viii: 1. 27.11.385, marble ?, locus 1313, discarded.
2. 26.11.34, alabaster ?, locus 1108, disposition unknown. 3. 26.11.33, alabaster ?, locus 1108, disposition
unknown. 4. 26.11.57, marble, locus 1108, P.29.107.847. 5. 27.12.6, marble ?, locus 1319, discarded.

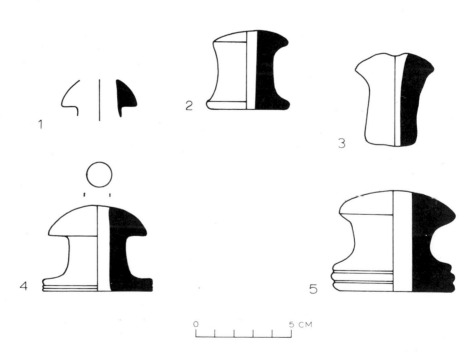

Fig 4: Alabaster chariot fittings from Beth Shan level vii: 1. 28.10.146, alabaster ?, locus 1381, discarded.
2. 28.10.206, gypsum, locus 1381, P.29.107.830. 3. 28.10.33, alabaster ?, locus 1374, discarded.
4. 27.10.640, gypsum, locus 1243, P.29.107.852. 5. 27.10.640, gypsum, locus 1253, P.29.107.852.

The Knobs

The Beisan knobs are of the local alabaster; gypsum; marble; limestone and quartzite. In the illustrations (figs. 1-4 and pls. XI and XII), they are arranged by level. Only Level ix contained examples of all shapes.

Type A-1 (Fig. 1, 2; fig. 2, 6; fig. 3, 5; fig. 4, 4 and 5). This is a spool-shaped knob about 5 cm. high and 6 or 7 cm. in diameter with one end flat and the other domed. A flange 0.5 to 1.0 cm. in width runs around the base, divided into two or three ridges by grooves. A vertical boring runs through the knob; in some cases, as fig. 2, 6, this narrows toward the upper or rounded end. A variant of the A-1 shape is a longer, thinner knob, as, fig. 2, 7.

Type B-1 (fig. 2, 2; fig. 3, 1) is a smaller knob perhaps 2 cm. wide and 5 cm. high, of a shape often described in English as a finial. Some examples have grooving, or at least a beveled edge, around the base. These knobs, too, are bored vertically for attachment but the boring does not penetrate the pointed end. A number of the B-1 knobs have small holes for cross fastenings horizontally pierced across the open end.

Type A-2 (fig. 2, 10; fig. 3, 4; fig. 4, 2). These are almost exactly like the A-1 knob in size and general shape but lack the horizontal grooves and ridges on the flange around the flat end.

Type B-2 (fig. 2, 1 and 9). This is of the same general shape as the B-1 knob, possibly a bit wider overall. The pointed end tends to be an isosceles triangle while the waist below the solid point is less pinched than in the B-1 finial. One example from Level ix (fig. 2, 9) has horizontal borings for cross attachment at the open end. Also in Level ix are two knobs which seem to provide a transition between the B-1 and B-2 shapes (fig. 2, 3 and 4).

Uses

The use of the A-1 and B-1 type of knobs is clearly established by comparison with those found in the tomb of Tutankhamun. That they were not limited to royal use is (presumably) demonstrated by unstratified examples from Memphis (fig. 1, 1 and 4).

Type A-1 proves to be the boss used as a mount for the harness saddle; equipment found in the burial of Tutankhamun included examples using both the shorter knob, (pl. XIIIa) and the longer, (pl. XIIIb).

The Type B-1 knob seems satisfactorily to be identified as a yoke terminal, as seen on the yokes of Tutankhumun's state chariots, pls XIIIa and XIIIb. The A-1 and B-1 knobs would seem to appear together in the relief of the royal family visiting the temple of the Aten at Amarna (pl. XVII).[*] In one of the loci in each of the Beisan levels where the knobs occurred, at least one A-1 and one B-1 knob were found together.

How the Type A-2 knob differs functionally or chronologically from the A-1 knob is hard to say. There may be no real difference, but, as the A-2 knob lacks the decorative grooving and as that shown in fig. 2, 10, has a narrower boring than many of the A-1 knobs, I suggest that it might be the knob used as a boss at the joint of the side and rear crosspieces of the chariot body, as pl. XVa. The boss here not only appears to be of stone but has a boring which seems to be narrower than those on the saddle bosses. In his notes regarding another of Tutankhamun's chariots, a medium-sized chariot " . . . not of finished workmanship . . . probably intended for ordinary purposes . . . " Howard Carter notes calcite bosses at the junction of lower rear body and side cross bar.

What seems also to be a stone boss occurs at this point on the life-size, or nearly life-size, funerary model chariot of Yuya, the grandfather of Tutankhamun, buried some 50 years earlier (pl. XVb).[5] Admittedly the boss of Yuya's chariot is so tightly bound (in leather?) that it is hard to be sure that white stone is the material used here, though this is rather more strongly suggested in the detail (pl. XVIa).[6]

Even if the bosses at this point on the chariot are not exactly of the A-2 shape as suggested, they can hardly differ from it too drastically. They add two more imperishable stone knobs to the four already identified to represent the fittings of a single chariot.

The type B-2 knob is the most difficult of the four to explain. I suggest that, like the B-1 type, it is a yoke terminal, perhaps typologically earlier than the B-1 knob. In Beisan Level ix, there are termini which provide satisfactory transitional types, between the B-1 and B-2, (fig. 2, 3 and 4), suggesting that the latter is indeed a yoke terminal.

A B-1 knob also comes from the unstratified Egyptian materials from Memphis excavated by Clarence Fisher (fig. 1, 3). This one has no holes at its base for cross fastenings, but Anthes figures another example from Memphis which does have the holes. [7]

Something like the B-2 knob, with rather flatter, rounder head, is used as noted below, on the two chariots surviving to us which are earlier than Tutankhamun's. On the chariot of Yuya (pl. XVb), [8] the yoke terminals are much closer to the B-2 than the B-1 shape, though they spread out further horizontally and are flatter than our B-2 example (fig. 2, 9).

On the second surviving chariot, the one in the Museo egezio in Florence, the yoke terminals again seem much more rounded than the B-1 type and very like the ones on Yuya's chariot though, in the only illustration available to me of the Florence chariot, the view of this knob is not very clear. [9]

The B-2 knob also seems to be fairly close to those shown on chariots carried by the tribute bearers in some of the tomb paintings of the earlier part of the xviiith dynasty; for example, in the tomb of Ken-Amun, [10] where the yoke termini are so rounded as to be egg-shaped, and the tomb of Rekhmire; where they seem to be of a rounded lozenge shape. [11] On many of the reliefs, really including the Amarna example noted above and the Medinet Habu reliefs, [12] the lozenge-shaped yoke terminals are a bit more pointed than those in the earlier tomb paintings just noted, but it is difficult to say whether they are B-1 or B-2 types.

Alternately, the B-2 terminals may differ from the B-1 terminals simply in being the product of different workshops. The stratified Beth Shan material possibly suggests this, as both the B-1 and B-2 types, plus transitional examples, occur in Level ix. However, the pottery of ix contains not only material which would seem to belong to the real period of its occupation, but also of the late 17th, 16th and 15th centuries B.C., derived from a fill laid down to level up for the Egyptian layout of ix, so materials from here cannot be used to fix a chronology.

The B-2 knob, or something very close to it, is often published as a staff head and indeed, judging by the staff of Yuya (pl. XVIb), [13] Egyptian staff heads were of this general shape. Knobs of this sort would make very nice little terminals for many kinds of object and their publication heretofore as staff heads, dagger pommels, furniture joints, sceptre heads or stoppers is not surprising and must sometimes be accurate. In fact, as "Chippendale" finials, the B-1 type occurs in our own time on as diverse objects as clocks, desks, beds and bureaus and is incorporated into architecture as well.

On the basis of the distribution of the saddle bosses and yoke termini at Beisan, I suggest that wherever and whatever the stables, some part of the chariots may have been kept in the quarters of their crews or houses of their owners, or at least taken there at times. We know from the tomb paintings that chariot bodies were light enough to be carried by a man. Some reinforcement for this interpretation comes from an almost parallel collection of knobs of Mosul marble found at Nuzi in what their excavator calls "relative abundance" which were *restricted* to private houses. [14]

On the other hand, if chariots seem too large to have been comfortably kept in the small buildings of a tell, workshops might be indicated. This would seem especially applicable at Beth Shan which could very logically have been the site of Egyptian chariot repair shops, and a number of the knobs *are* of the local gypsum. Against workshops is the immediate distribution of the knobs at Beisan where they are scattered throughout the levels in which they occur, rather than being concentrated in a workroom or two. Such evidence as there is from other Palestinian sites with one exception does not reinforce the idea of the chariots being kept on the tell top.

Earlier and Later Fittings

As noted, no alabaster knobs occur in Beisan vi. Indeed, I have found no examples whatsoever of these in any Palestinian Iron Age level, though far more footage of this period has been excavated than of the Bronze Age. While the absence of the alabaster fittings in Beisan vi is in all probability an archaeological accident, other explanations of this are certainly possible. For one thing, the use of alabaster may have been tied to the Egyptian tradition; hence, in Canaan, just after the upheavals caused by the appearance of the Sea Peoples, a new material, perhaps organic, may have been introduced for the knobs. Wood in any case would have been better than stone, but would have left no trace.

Alternatively, the shape could have changed so that the knobs are not typologically identifiable on the basis of the Late Bronze Age prototypes. This does not seem very likely, however, and certainly the Medinet Habu reliefs [15] show elongated saddle bosses, rather like fig. 2, 7, and a lozenge-shaped yoke terminal, though these fittings might have no longer applied to Syria.

The reliefs of Ashurnasirpal (883-859 B.C.) from Nimrud show knobs on both yoke and saddle. The saddle boss is much like our A-1 or A-2 knob but in at least two reliefs the yoke termini seem to have become animal heads, [16] a conceit no doubt suggested by the original muzzle-shape of the finials when placed horizontally. If so, this might suggest that they were cast of bronze and the saddle boss perhaps as well. Certainly this is not an unexpected development in this part of the ancient world.

The Balawat gates of Shalmaneser iii (858-824 B.C.) also show the saddle boss clearly; the yoke terminals here too *suggest* an animal head, but are not altogether convincing. [17] On some of the later reliefs, as from the palace of Sennacherib (704-681 B.C.) at Nineveh, the saddle boss seems to have disappeared and the yoke termini become truncated pyramids. [18] On one relief from the palace of Ashurbanipal in Nineveh, the yoke terminal is shown as changed into essentially the shape of the lower end of the A-1 boss, with the ridges outermost. [19] These latter two are, interestingly enough, very close to the termini on the yoke from Waldalgesheim figured by Piggott. [20] The disappearance of the saddle boss is confirmed in Mrs. Littauer's study of saddles in which she points out that these go out of use in the latter part of the Assyrian period in both Assyria and Egypt. [21]

Professor Piggott has pointed out that yoke termini which are obviously related to those described here survived in Europe in most conservative fashion as late as the European Iron Age. [22] So fittings of the general shape of some of the Beisan examples would seem to continue at least for a millennium, though perhaps not in Canaan and perhaps in materials more up-to-date or more easily available than alabaster in areas to which the chariot diffused.

As to earlier examples of chariot fittings in the Levant: a marble B-2 yoke terminal occurs at Megiddo in Tomb 911-D. [23] The tomb furniture in loculus D is certainly Middle Bronze, but whether the B-2 knob really belongs with it is open to question. T. 911 is an EB-MB "architectural" tomb with four chambers, several of which were reused in the Late Bronze. Other objections are that Chamber D had a hole in its roof and perhaps also that no where else in Palestine have chariot fittings of this period or type (or any other), with minor exceptions from Gaza, been found in burials.

On the other hand, none of the dagger blades found in 911-D would have fitted onto the knob; in fact, nothing whatsoever of the B-2 (or B-1) shape is figured as a dagger pommel by Mrs. Maxwell-Hyslop in her extensive survey of daggers in the ancient Near East. [24]

A more satisfactory stone fitment antedating Beisan ix is a Type A-1 saddle boss from Alalakh, [25] said to have been found in the Level vi-v levelling up over the Yarim Lim palace, dating from the end of the 18th to the middle of the 16th centuries B.C. This example from Alalakh differs from the Beisan examples just enough to suggest some time differential. Alalakh has also produced A-1 bosses paralleling those from Beisan, attributed to Levels iv and iii, dating from 1447 to 1350 B.C. [26]

A Census of Chariotry in Canaan

Finally, there is the group from Nuzi [27] comprising two of our A-1 saddle bosses; one B-2 terminal and another large knob which could be a variant of the A group and finds parallels at Gaza. [28] All belong to Level ii dated to *c.* 1475 B.C. by a letter from Shaushshattar, King of Mittani.

Whatever their numbers in Canaan in the Middle Bronze Age, chariots must have been quite numerous not much later. Tuthmosis iii lists 893 captured at the battle of Megiddo in 1479 B.C. [29] Amenophis ii lists 730 Canaanite chariots taken in the campaign of his 7th year [30] and 1,092 in his 9th year, toward the end of the century. [31] In the Iron Age, we know that Solomon, in the 10th century B.C., dealt in chariots on a large scale [32] and that Ahab of Israel stood at the Battle of Qarqar in 853 B.C. with 2,000 chariots and that Ahab's allies, Hadadezer of Damascus, and Irhuleni of Hamath had 1,200 and 700 chariots respectively. [33]

Gaza and Gezer are two sites which figure prominently in the Egyptian records both as important Canaanite cities and as the site of Egyptian military installations. It is not surprising, therefore, to find that Gezer produced an indefinite, but apparently considerable, number of both types of our knobs. [34]

Macalister publishes one of the A-1 saddle bosses as a " . . . knob with which furniture was decorated." No scale is given in his figure, but the form is unmistakeable. He says in the text, "Many of the knobs of quartzite or alabaster with which furniture was decorated came to light in all Semitic strata. These are flat with a rounded top and concave sides. A hole runs vertically through the axis . . ." and, indeed, the bosses are not unlike some of the furniture of the Assyrian and later periods. [35]

In his discussion on daggers, in the same volume of the Gezer report, Macalister figures two of the B-1 terminals and the caption tells us that " . . . large numbers of ornamental dagger pommels in polished white stone came to light in all strata. It is curious how often these ornaments were found to have been burnt. They are never found in association with the dagger to which they belonged."[36]

Neither the A-2 nor the B-2 type of knob seems to have occurred at Gezer.

Gaza also produced a number of the alabaster chariot fittings, though far fewer than one would expect from as important an Egyptian military centre as "The Canaan," where, in addition, the excavation was extensive and the Late Bronze Age levels uppermost. The immediate context of the Gaza knobs is difficult to determine but seems to be Late Bronze. There is apparently no concentration of them, as at Beisan and Gezer, however.

Two definite A-2 knobs, one definite A-1 knob and one definite B-2 knob are illustrated. Of the A type knobs, two are said to have been of alabaster and one of limestone. The first A-2 example is noted as being found at level 1060 feet, [37] the second was found in top soil. [38] An inverted A-1 knob came from Locus LX at 1039 feet. [39] The B-2 knob has no provenance, but is noted as being xviiith dynasty. [40]

A knob from G 920 near enough to the B-2 terminal to be a possible variant is shown as made of bone. [41] Alternately, this may have been a real staff head. Possible variants of the A-2 knob are one in bone, from LAB 1031, [42] and one in ivory from CO 947 [43] very much like knob K at Nuzi. [44] In neither case in these possible A-2 knobs does the boring go all the way through the knob; in the case of the second example, the boring is squared.

None of the published knobs from Gaza, or additional, unpublished, examples are among the materials from this site now at the Institute of Archaeology in London. What is even more curious is that none at all, whether rightly or wrongly described, appear in Petrie's several volumes of Egyptian objects, though connecting the actual fittings, of which he must have dug up many examples, with their representation in the tomb paintings is the kind of thing Petrie had great flair for, as in the case of the Assyrian governor's dinner ware from Tell Jemmeh.

At Megiddo, in addition to the B-2 terminal doubtfully belonging to Tomb 911—D, we have a single saddle boss, M-2588. [45] Unfortunately, it is totally unstratified, having been found in Sq. W-17 at the southeastern foot of the slope. As at Gaza, it is curious that, with the great horizontal clearance of the tell which took place down into Megiddo level v, no more chariot fittings than this were discovered. These knobs should still have been in use in the Solomonic level v, and probably in Ahab's level, iv, as well and one would have thought that some Assyrian examples, whether in stone or bronze, would have occurred in Megiddo strata iii and ii.

At Hazor, no saddle bosses seem to have been found. A B-2 yoke terminal is figured, however, [46] from Locus 363, Stratum xiii, Area A, at level 226.80. This seems to be in a Late Bronze context. The example is described as an alabaster stopper and is drawn without horizontal cross borings at base. The photograph of this knob, however, shows it broken in such a way as to suggest the boring existed and contributed to the breakage. [47]

Lachish produces a single B-2 yoke terminal. [48] It comes from Pit 1006 in Sq. D-27 where it was associated with white slip ii and basering ware and a galaxy of Late Bronze Age bowls, all dated by Miss Tufnell to c. 1425-1375, B.C.

The upper half of a B-1 yoke terminal comes from Ashdod, [49] where it is said to be of alabaster and described as a pommel. It is almost certainly broken at the rivet holes. Its immediate context is Locus 507, which is a court-yard in stratum 2 in Area B-- at the base of the tell at the southeast. The published pottery from stratum 2 here is close to that of the Beisan levels involved in this study.

Tell Jemmeh has produced one knob in shape very much like that of fig. 4, 1. It is said to have come from Locus JR 180, an unstratified open space which yielded little but this knob.[50] Very Late Bronze Age and early Philistine pottery comes from some of the walled loci on the J plan which, if really associated with the knob, would give it a chronological context roughly paralleling the setting of the Beisan chariot fittings. The material of this knob is bronze, but size, shape and boring pattern seem to be satisfactory and it may suggest a point of departure for a different manifestation of the saddle boss in the Iron Age. Alternately it could be an Assyrian knob which has worked its way down from the upper levels.

No alabaster fittings of either A or B types are figured from Tell Abu Hawam, Tell Fara, Tell Beit Mersim, Ain Shems, Jericho, Samaria, Nasbeh or Gibeon.

The alabaster termini discussed here must have been fastened into place with bronze fittings. Probably one or two rivets held the yoke termini in position. The saddle bosses were more elaborately put together and a long nail held the boss to the leather-covered wooden saddle, as in pl. XIIIb. On at least one of Tutankhamun's state chariots, a red-gold rosette served as a washer between the stone boss and the bronze nail.[51] If bronze rosettes were used in ordinary military chariotry, they should have been from 3 - 4 cm. in diameter. Nothing of this description occurs among the Beth Shan bronzes in the levels in question, nor do any of the saddle bosses in the collection show a wear pattern of this diameter, though the smaller wear pattern from the nail head can be seen on the bosses in pl. XI, b-i, and pl. XII a.

On this basis, the nail heads had diameters of about 1.5 cm. A number of nails with heads this size occur in the Late Bronze and Early Iron Age materials at Beth Shan. These nails, however, are now no more than 6 or 7 cm. in length and seem never to have been longer and it would have taken some 14-15 cm. to fasten the boss to the saddle, as on Tutankhamun's chariot. However, nails of this size and length might cautiously be used as an indication of chariots in the Egyptian and Levantine areas, though other types of fittings really need to be found with them.

In conclusion, considering how many stone knobs were used per chariot and how many chariots the ancient records (even if exaggerated) suggest were present in the armies of both Canaanite princes and pharaohs, it is curious that so few of the knobs have been found on Palestinian tells to date. This is especially true of extensively cleared sites, as Gaza and Megiddo and Beisan vi and v. Admittedly, when in use and probably at their final destruction, the chariot is not to be expected on the tell, but one would nevertheless predict more lost and fragmentary knobs, especially on the sites just noted. Much the same is true of bronze bits and other trappings, though bronze is more likely to have been salvaged for a reuse than stone; in fact, the bits were one of the items taken from the Tutankhamun burial by ancient Egyptian robbers.[52]

These points, plus the fact that chariot fittings at Ashdod, Lachish and Megiddo were found near the base of the tell may suggest that the chariot corps had their quarters off the mound. Getting water for, say 50 horses up a steep tell even only occasionally could have been no small chore. Further, streets would have been like many in the old city of Jerusalem with innumerable steps. Continuous bumping up and down topography of this sort would cause a modern Land Rover to fall apart, let alone the handmade chariot. Further, off-tell stabling would have allowed a much more rapid mobilization. It might be worth looking around the bases of some of the mounds to see if any stables or their defences can be located.

Against this is the apparent destruction of many chariots on the tell at Gezer and the concentration of the fittings at Beisan, though at the latter site we have suggested that their presence was perhaps in workshops.

A final thought is that it seems time to consider just what the chariot *did* for people of the various countries to which it diffused over and above its obvious military uses. Or is the chariots' *floreat* due simply to the concentrations of available surplus and the burgeoning of Empires? In any case, orientalists have been taking its appearance far too casually for far too long. "Yes, yes," we mutter, "The chariot appears at such-and-such a place at such-and-such a time," as if the advent of this first of the world's really very complex mechanisms with the speed and power and magnification of certain human qualities which it brought were not going to change the course of human life and behavior forever more.

References

1.   For plan of vi, see FRANCES JAMES, *The Iron Age at Beth Shan* (hereafter *BS* vi), fig. 77.

2.   For plans of viii and vii, insofar as they have been published, see ALAN ROWE, *Four Canaanite Temples* (hereafter *BS* ii, ii), pl. v and *Topography and History of Beth Shan* (hereafter *BS* i), p. 20, fig. 2.

3.   For plan of ix, see *BS* i, p.12, fig. 1.

4.   N. de G. DAVIES, *The Rock Tombs of Amarna,* pt. iv, pl. iv.

5.   T. M. DAVIS, *The Tomb of Iouiya and Touiyou,* (hereafter *Iouiya*), pl. xxxii.

6.   J. E. Quibell, *Tomb of Yuaa and Thuiu,* pl. lvi.

7.   R. ANTHES, *Mit Rahineh,* p. 107, fig. 15, 82.

8.   T. H. DAVIS, loc. cit.

9.   G. BOTTI, *Aegyptus* 31 (1951), pp. 192 ff.

10.   N. de G. DAVIES, *The Tomb of Ken-Amun at Thebes,* pl. xxii.

11.   N. de G. DAVIES, *The Tomb of Rekh-mi-re at Thebes,* pl. xxii.

12.   H. NELSON, *Medinet Habu* i, pl. 32.

13.   T. H. DAVIS, op. cit., pl. xliii.

14.   F. R. S. STARR, *Nuzi,* p. 468 and pl. 121, k, q, v and w. In this Starr notes some of the Beisan knobs and also the parallel with Tutankhamun's chariot. Nevertheless he published the Nuzi knobs as staff heads, concluding that these shapes were only later used as chariot fitments. I owe this reference to Miss. Munn-Rankin.

15.   e.g. H. NELSON, loc. cit.

16.   R. D. BARNETT, *Assyrian Palace Reliefs,* pls. 24 and 25.

17.   ibid., pls. 140-142; 144-150; 154-157; 159-164; 167-173.

18.   ibid., pls 121; 126.

19.   ibid., pl. 96.

20.   STUART PIGGOTT, *Antiquaries Journal* xlix, (1969), p. 380, fig. 1, 1.

21.   M. A. LITTAUER, *Antiquity,* xlii (1958), p. 28.

22.   Personal communication.

23.   P. L. O. GUY and R. E. ENGBERG, *Megiddo Tombs,* pl. 122, 3.

24.   R. MAXWELL-HYSLOP, *Iraq,* viii (1946), pls. 1-vi.

25.   L. WOOLLEY, *Alalakh,* p. 296 and pl. lxxxii, 27.

26.   ibid., p. 296 and pl. lxxxii, 28 and 29.

27.   STARR, op. cit., pl.121.

28.   see p. 16 below.

29.   J. B. PRITCHARD, *Ancient Near Eastern Texts,* p. 237.

30.   ibid., p. 246.

31.   ibid., p. 247.

32.   I Kings x: 26-29.

33.   PRITCHARD, op. cit., p. 279.

34.   R. A. S. MACALISTER, *Gezer,* v. ii, p. 252, fig. 401.

35.   e.g. W. M. F. PETRIE, *Beth Pelet,* pl. lxvi.

36.   MACALISTER, op. cit., fig. 474, p. 376,

37.   W. M. F. PETRIE, *Ancient Gaza* iii, pl. xxvii, 82.

38.   PETRIE, *Ancient Gaza* iv, pl. xli, 120.

39.   PETRIE, *AG* iii, pl. xxvii, 83.

40.   ibid, pl. xxvii, 65.

41.   PETRIE, *AG* iv, pl. xxxvii, 51.

42.   ibid, pl. xxxvii, 52.

43.   PETRIE, MACKAY AND MURRAY, *Ancient Gaza* v, pl. xviii, 17.

44.   STARR, op. cit., pl. 121, k.

45.   R. LAMON and G. SHIPMAN, *Megiddo,* i, pl. 107, 13.

46.   Y. YADIN, et al, *Hazor* iii-iv, pl clxiii, 26.

47.   ibid., pl. cccxxxv, 12.

48.   O. TUFNELL, *Lachish,* iv, pl. 26, 44.

49.   M. DOTHAN, "*Ashdod* i," *'Atiqot* vii (1967), p. 91, fig. 18, 8.

50.   W. M. F. PETRIE, *Gerar,* pl. xxiv, 62.

51.   H. CARTER, *Tomb of Tut-ankh-amun,* pl. xlii, c.

52.   H. CARTER, op. cit., p. 59.

Plate XI   *a. Early Yoke Termini (University of Pennsylvania)*
           b. Saddle Bosses & Yoke Termini (University of Pennsylvania)

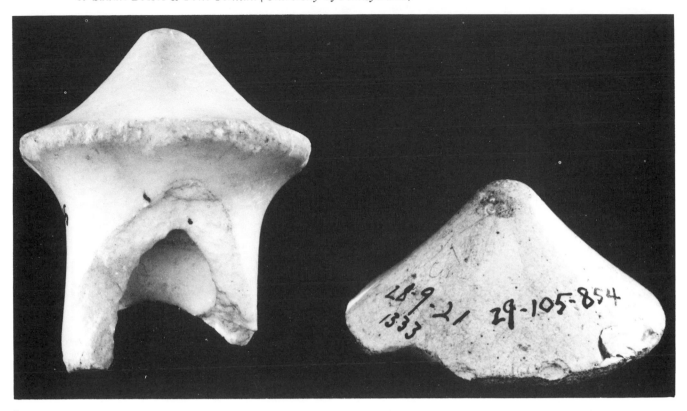

a.

Plate XII   a. *Saddle Boss (University of Pennsylvania)*
          b. *Saddle Bosses and Knob (University of Pennsylvania)*

a.

b.

Plate XIII   a.   Saddles with bosses - State chariot of Tutankhamun.
b.   Saddle with long boss - State chariot of Tutankhamun.

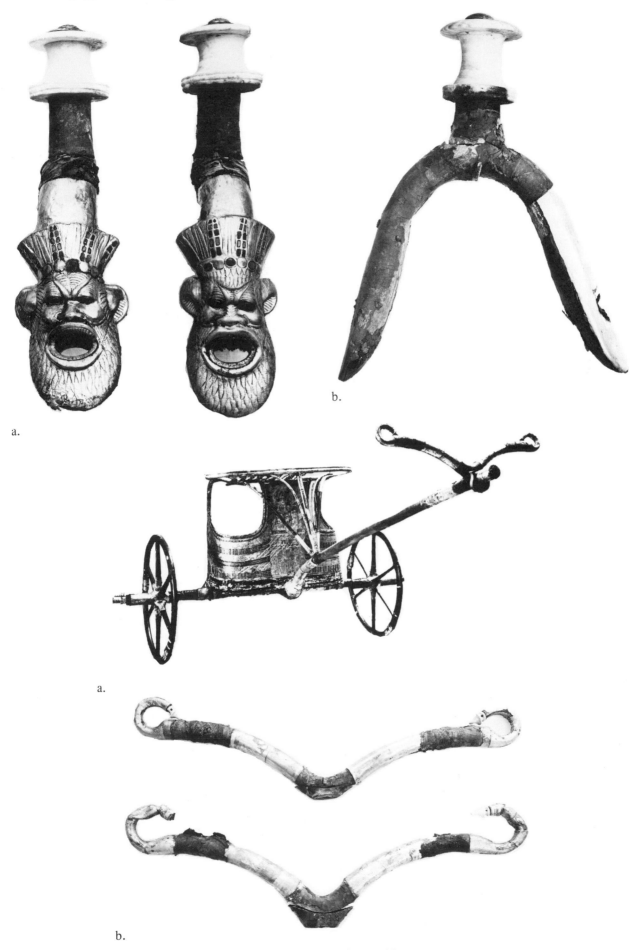

a.

b.

a.

b.

Plate XIV   a.   Yoke with alabaster Terminals - State chariot of Tutankhamun
b.   Yokes with alabaster Terminals - State chariot of Tutankhamun

Plate XV   a. Stone boss at join of side & rear brace - State chariot of Tutankhamun
        b. Yoke Terminals and stone? bosses at join of side & rear braces - Chariot of Yuua

a.

b.

b.   a.

Plate XVI   a. Detail of join of side & rear Braces - Chariot of Yuua
          b. Staff of Yuua.

Plate XVII   Chariots and grooms - Tomb of Peutu at Amarna (N. deG. Davies)

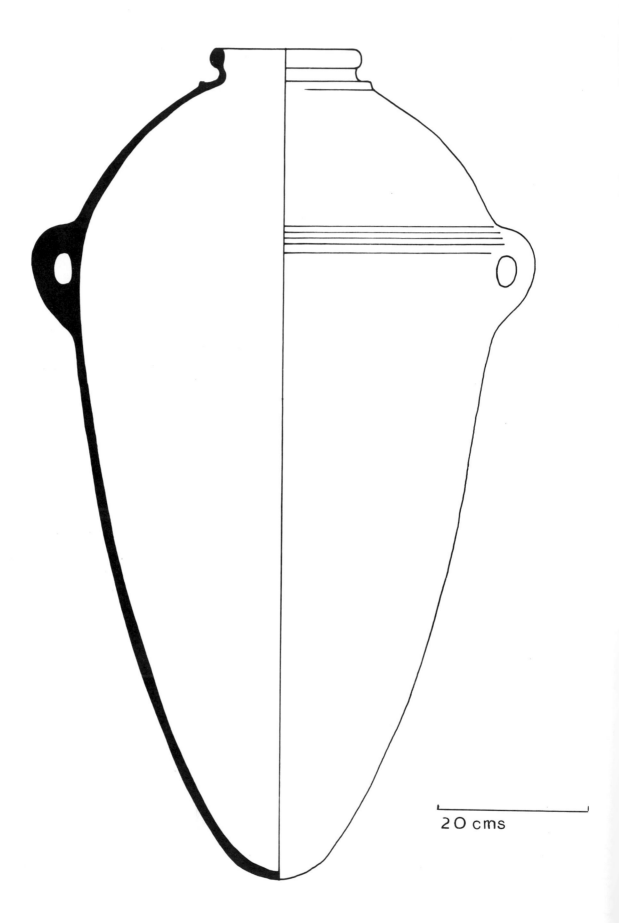

20 cms

Fig 1:   Typical Collared-rim jar from Sahab.

THE COLLARED-RIM JAR OF THE EARLY IRON AGE*
Moawiyah M. Ibrahim

W. F. Albright was the first to identify the jar type under discussion. As early as the excavations of Tell Beit Mirsim and Tell el-Ful, it was designated the collared-rim jar (or pithos). Albright proposed that these jars were the work of the early Israelite settlers in Palestine,[1] This proposal was, and still is, supported or adopted by other biblical archaeologists.[2] Even after *Ancient Pottery of the Holy Land* was published by Ruth Amiran, the presence of the collared-rim jar was thought to be restricted to some sites on the western side of the Jordan river.

It will be shown below that the distribution of this jar type extended to East Jordan. The material we have does not allow one to assign it to a certain ethnic group. Where it is possible we will try to locate the appearance of this type within its stratified context. The function of this pithos seems to be important for the understanding of its makers and the way of agricultural life which was practiced at the beginning of the Early Iron Age of Palestine and East Jordan.

General Description of the Jar (pl. XIX and Fig 1). The jar is typically ovoid rounded, but sometimes with cut-off base. The two handles are attached vertically above the middle of the body, joining the shoulder. The neck is very short and ends with a folded thickened rim (either rounded or ribbed). A plastic ridge from the same clay is applied to the transition between neck and shoulder. The shoulder is wide and slightly convex. Two to five grooves on the angle between shoulder and body show that the two parts were made separately. The height ranges from 1.10 to 1.15m. Most examples are covered with a flakey white or greenish slip on a reddish to dark brown ware. The slip has worn off on many of the sherds or parts of the jars so that one can see white and dark particles and small to large sized grits. The core is grey or blackened in most cases. Straw, sand and lime seemed to be necessary for the tempering of such large vessels. Some of the examples are distorted in various places of the body, caused by the high firing temperature. Rim, handles and bases have been smoothed by a special instrument. The manufacturing process corresponds with the technical characteristics of the Deir 'Alla storage jars discussed by H. Franken.[3] The jars were hand-made with coils. After that a slow wheel was used to smooth the vessel. The potter needed experience and skill to form the pithos to the desired size and shape. The mixture of the clay used by the potter, the size, and the use of these jars have a long tradition going back to the LB and MB periods. Franken notes that 'these jars were still made in the same way in the 8th and 7th century B.C. in some parts of Palestine, as well as thrown jars'.[4]

The excavations of Sahab, carried out in 1972/3 by the Department of Antiquities of Jordan,[5] yielded a large number of pithoi, corresponding with the above description, which are the reason of this article. Stratified jars and sherds belonging to this type were identified in large quantities in two areas (A and B) in the northern part of the *tell*. The first phase, found in the two areas, dates from the Iron I period. Owing to the fact that the two excavated areas are located in different parts of the *tell* (in addition to evidence from Area D and other sections) it is reasonable to assume that Sahab was extensively inhabited during the Early Iron Age, and it is during this period that the settlement reached its largest extention. This is further indicated by the fact that the Iron II period is to be found only in the central area of Sahab.

In Area B sherds were found in association with a house complex. So far three rooms and a long corridor of this complex have been excavated. The walls of the rooms were constructed of stones and bricks. The floor of one room was plastered, while the others were paved with flat rough stones.

In Area A (Pl. XVIIIa-b) we excavated numerous collared-rim jars *in situ* upon a plastered stone pavement. The location of these jars and the fact that all of them had been broken indicates that a swift destruction occurred. Indeed we found burnt roof-beams and other debris which had collapsed upon the jars. No walls were found in association with the pavement. No definite evidence for the function of the pavement has been found. The presence of the jars may suggest that it was a storage area. A large cistern, next to the pavement, still used by the local people, is probably to be associated with the jars and the pavement. Below the Iron I phase, a cave was investigated. This cave was inhabited as early as the late fourth millennium B.C. and re-used in the MB period as a tomb.

Some of the jars are now restored. Most of them bear seal or thumb impressions either on the rim or handle. A seal impression (Pl. XXb), identified on two jars, shows an animal with long horns (probably a goat) followed by

Plate XVIII   *a. Area A at Sahab, Showing Iron 1 Broken jars and Deposit.*
　　　　　　　　b. Area A, Sq. 1, showing collared-rim jars above Iron 1 Stone Pavement.

a.

b.

Plate XIX   Collared-rim variants from Sahab - below is Thumb-indented example.

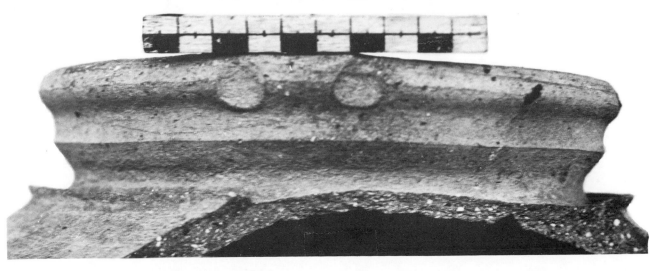

Plate XX   Seal Impressions on Collared-rims.

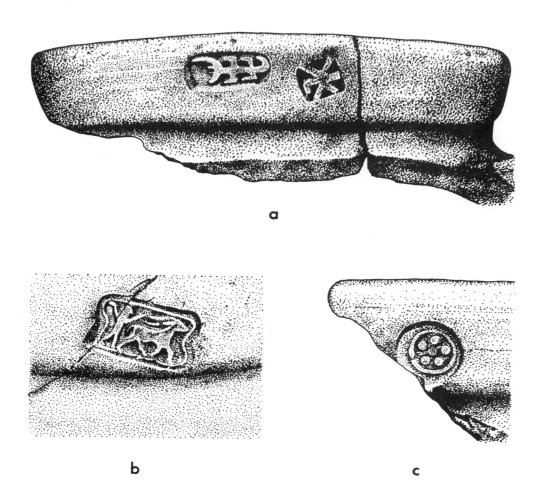

a

b   c

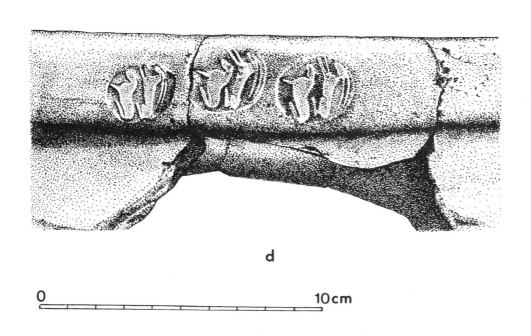

d

0 ⊢————————————————————⊣ 10cm

a human figure. The latter raises his hands and has one leg drawn back trying to catch the animal. Both figures are surrounded by a rectangular frame curved on both narrow sides. Two other jars have on their rims a rounded seal impression, repeated three times on each (Pl. XXd). This shows two running animals, an ibex (or a gazelle) above a lion. Judging from other parallels on seals and cylinders one would expect the lion above the other animal. Other impressions are: a rosette in a rounded frame (Pl. XXc) and a scorpion on the handle of a jar. Two other impressions (Pl. XXa) of a scorpion and a spider simply engraved appear on a collared-rim.

The frequency of the jars and the seal impressions may indicate that they were made in Sahab or its vicinity. Seal impressions on pots from the Early Iron Age are rare, in contrast to their frequent occurrence in the Iron II period.[6] Direct parallels to the Sahab impressions were not found in other Palestinian or East Jordanian sites. Similar designs and motifs remind one of those found on seals and cylinders of the so-called "Second Syrian Group". Some of these have been identified in an Iron I context.[7] But such simple and common designs appear also in archaic levels and seal groups of ancient Near Eastern sites.

The traditional interpretation of these seal impressions, as trade or potters' marks, though not very satisfactory, is momentarily the only explanation the author can offer. If this is the case, it is possible that the jars were made in different workshops. Another possible suggestion is that the jars were made on special order and the seal impressions refer to the owners of the jars. The possibility that the findspot is part of a pottery workshop is not to be excluded. Modern houses surrounding the excavations at Sahab make it difficult to complete investigations in Area A.

Discussion and Comparative Study

Whatever the definition of the periods or the levels where the collared-rim jars appear, most of the specimens from stratified contexts have to be assigned to the beginning of the Early Iron Age. Evidence from Megiddo, et-Tell, Tell el-Ful, Tell Beit Mirsim, Tell Deir 'Alla, Sahab, and others suggest a late thirteenth-twelfth century dating. The ware and the shape of the jar is very distinctive, so that fragments from the surface, especially rims, can be easily identified. No final judgement can be made about the distribution of the collared-rim jar, since little attention was paid to its presence by the scholars who made the major surface explorations in East Jordan and other parts of the area. The references given here show at least that it was present in a much larger geographical area than thought.

"A storage jar with collared rim from the period of the Judges (about 1100 B.C.)", as noted by Kelso, seems to be a common type in Beitin (identified as Bethel).[8] This type of jar was found in a level designated as "Iron I" which followed the Late Bronze phase. The Iron I period was followed by another phase (not emphasized by the excavators) and then followed by the so-called "transition into Iron II". A group of jars, corresponding with this type was found in a house (house A) and other excavated areas at Tell Sailun (identified with Shiloh). The jars contained earth and roof material, but the excavator suggests that they were originally filled with wine. The jars seem to have been broken as a result of fire-destruction. The interpretation of the material is not based on internal evidence, but on conservative biblical tradition, which can hardly be accepted: "Through the excavations thus far undertaken we have on important points been able to reconcile archaeological facts with the accounts of the Old Testament with surprising accuracy. We have caught a glimpse of a town, Shiloh, which in any case existed between 1200 and 1050 B.C. and its destruction through fire (by the Philistines) about 1050; and thus we see the reason why the Ark of the Covenant did not later return to Shiloh; the town did not exist any longer."[9] The early excavations of Tell Sailun were, however, not carried out in a way which enables us to understand the whole stratigraphical context. The approach of these excavations was based on relating and confirming the account of the Old Testament. This kind of work is very confusing and does not help in solving the chronological questions. Such unfounded conclusions related to hypothetical historical events is the kind of thing archaeologists should avoid.

At Megiddo the collared-rim jars are limited to levels VIIB - VI.[10] In Ain Shems they were found only in level III (Iron Ia-B),[11] but they were not common in relation to other storage jars. The date and designation of the period in which the collared-rim jars were found was based on Albright's proposal.[12] There are a few examples from Beisan (Beth-Shan) - Stratum VI - which are smaller but similar in shape. It is not clear whether they have a ridge on the shoulder or not.[13] At Affulah one specimen of the collared-rim with ridged shoulder was found in Stratum IIIB, but some of the body sherds and handles may belong to the same type of jar.[14] There is clear evidence for the presence of such jars in Tell en-Nasbeh.[15] At Tell Beit Mirsim it was recognized in Stratum B and considered to be characteristic of the Early Iron I.[16] The type under discussion has been found at Tell el-Ful (identified by Albright as Gibeah of Saul) in the first and second periods (late thirteenth to eleventh century B.C.), but not in the third period.[17] After the destruction of the first town, as has been suggested by Albright, large pithoi were used to store wine, oil, and grain and kept in store-rooms. [18] Several collared-rims and handles were found during the early excavations of et-Tell, [19] and in definite Iron I (Phase I-II) levels during the excavations of 1964-70, which were carried out under the supervision of J. Callaway. [20] Here again the distribution of the collared-rim was thought to be restricted to a limited area, although its dating and ethnic relationship differs somewhat from Albright's proposal: "The long collared rim is found in the geographical area between 'Afula and Tell Beit Mirsim' with a concentration in the Bethel-'Ai region, while the short collared rim of Phase II is found as far north as Hazor . . . . Phase II at 'Ai may very well be Israelite, but Phase I seems to reflect the presence of pre-Israelite inhabitants". [21]

The pithoi found at Tell el-Qedah (Hazor) show many rim variants which remind one of examples from other sites with regard to ware and form, but some of el-Qedah specimens have a wider mouth and a ridge or raised band around the shoulder. Nevertheless, these jars were considered by the excavators as LB II. [22] Very similar examples to those found at Sahab were recognized in el-Qedah Area A, Stratum V; [23] many storage jars of this type alongside other pots were found in Area C, Building 6063 (LB II-III). Part of the building had been used as a potter's workshop, indicated by the large number of vessels and the potter's wheels found inside one of the rooms. [24] At Tell Zeror, near the coast, there is one example from Stratum IX which may fall under this type. [25] Typical for Tell Qasile, Stratum IX (so-called Post-Philistine or pre-Israelite) is a jar with ribbed rim and a ridge on the shoulder, similar to a variant from Sahab; but the shoulder of the jar from Tell Qasile seems to be shorter and narrower. [26] A fragment of a collared-rim jar with wide shoulder, like those of Sahab, was found in a later Stratum VIII. [27] The earliest Iron Age phase at Raddana, in Bireh, begins with the appearance of the collared-rim jars, which continue to exist in the second phase of Iron Age I. A large number of jars with collared rims were found in storage rooms of a building complex. The jars were broken during the destruction of the settlement "evidenced by the ashes which covered the broken jars". [28] Contemporary with the jars is an inscribed jar handle. Judging from the stratigraphy and the epigraphic evidence, the handle has been dated to the early twelfth century B.C. [29]

Collared-rims have been recognized in several East Jordanian sites, not only in Sahab. Stratified and surface specimens appeared at: Tell Deir 'Alla (Phase A) in the Jordan Valley; [30] Tell el-Mazar just to the north of Deir 'Alla; [31] the Citadel of Amman, during the excavations of 1972 (not yet published); Khirbet el-Hajjar (Iron I, levels and surface). [32] During his survey in northern East Jordan Siegfried Mittmann found at Khirbet el-Hedamus, north of Ajlun, an interesting rim of the same type with incised disarticulated letters of the so-called old (or proto-) Canaanite type (unpublished). The published pottery of Nelson Glueck's survey in East Jordan shows just a few sherds which may fall into the collared-rim type. [33]

At Sahab, pithoi of the same type as those of Area A were used as burial jars. In Area C, Cave (Tomb) 1, on the western slope of the mound, burial jars were found together with rich Iron I deposits including scarabs, alabaster vases, pottery and metal objects. These finds suggest a twelfth century dating. [34] Eight burial jars with their mouths broken off were arranged with every two jars facing each other and in such a way as to form an M-shape. A smaller jar, also with broken off mouth, containing an infant was also found. Some of the jars have thumb impressions and one has an incised cross on the handle. It is quite possible that this tomb belongs to the Iron I settlement in which the collared-rim pithoi were found.

This custom of burying people in jars is known during the Iron I period from other sites of the country. In East Jordan, the burial jars with cut off mouths of Jabal el-Qusur, north east of Amman, are very similar to those of the Sahab tomb. [35] A burial of this type was found in Yazur (Azor), which has been described by the excavator: "Skeletons were found interred within two storage jars cut at their shoulder and joined mouth to mouth". [36] Burial jars arranged in the same way were found in Kfar Yehoshua, [37] and in Tel Zeror. [38]

The burial jars found at Gezer are probably to be identified with the same custom. [39] The resemblance of all these burials to the much earlier burial custom at Alishar Huyuk (Period I-II) in Anatolia is astonishing. [40]

Pithoi: Storage and Trade.

The distribution and use of the pithoi as storage vessels reminds one of the present situation in East Jordan and Palestine. During the last two centuries, or even earlier, villagers and some town-people have been using a particular type of vessel, uniform in size and form, to store oil. It was also sometimes used for the carrying of water. Another type of jar (zir), similar in shape to that of the Iron Age, was used for the storage of drinking water. Elongated juglets, mainly in two sizes, were used as containers for milk and yoghurt. These vessels are accepted by communities, distributed over a rather large area, as units for storage or trade. This necessitated the organization of larger but fewer pottery workshops in order to fulfil the needs of these extended areas.

It is probable that the same thing occurred in earlier periods. The form of production and the functional role of these vessels were much influenced by the social and economic structure of a particular community, the needs and products of the people, as well as the demands of the market. The determining factor for cultural change is mainly to be found in the developing forms and means of production. The arrival of a new ethnic group in a society, even when recognized, is not necessarily the explanation of any change in that society. The discussion of this important problem is, however, not the purpose of this article.

Pithoi as Burial Jars.

In certain cases, referred to earlier in this article, adults and infants were buried in large jars of the Iron I period. This is a custom in the Near East which occurs as early as the Chalcolithic period, continues in the Middle Bronze and Late Bronze periods, and lasts into Iron I-II. It appears that burial jars of the Early Iron Age were in use alongside anthropoid coffins made of clay, which are found in a number of sites both west and east of the Jordan River. Together with the burial jars from Sahab, a wooden coffin of an adult and another of an infant were excavated. Of course other, simpler, burial forms such as those found in shaft tombs and rock-caves are more common in this period.

The facts that the burial jars, which occurred at the sites mentioned above, were with cut-off mouths and that they are of the same type as the storage jars found in the houses, may well indicate that they were not made specifically for burial purposes. It is possible that this custom was practised by a group of people who were distributed in different parts of Palestine and East Jordan and who were accustomed to bury their dead either in jars or clay coffins, and who simply made use of those pithoi which were available in the country. We do not know whether this has to do with a new group of people or whether it was a traditional burial custom, as mentioned above. The influence of Hittite burial customs on those found in Palestine and East Jordan, as noted by M. Dothan, [41] is not clear to the present writer.

Even without the information gained at Sahab it would be necessary critically to examine the use and interpretation of archaeological materials of these periods. Kathleen Kenyon, to whom this contribution is dedicated, is the teacher of many Palestinian archaeologists of this generation. The influence of Gordon Childe's interpretation of material culture can be sensed in Kenyon's work. She knows the importance of linking archaeological material with historical records, but she also warns her students not to let the biblical account dominate the archaeological evidence, as traditional biblical archaeology did. The goal of the so-called "biblical archaeologists" was not only to provide a background for the biblical tradition, but to confirm it. Although still in this tradition, Martin Noth, without being a field archaeologist, was one of the first who raised the question of looking at the archaeological material with a critical eye: "welche archäologischen Funde sind geeignet, auf dieses oder jenes stück der uns literarisch überlieferten Geschichte bezogen zu werden? Bei welchen Funden ist eine solche Beziehung vielleicht ohne weiteres evident? Welche im Alten Testament literarisch überlieferten geschichtlichen Nachrichten sind überhaupt geeignet zur Deutung archäologischer Funde herangezogen zu werden, und welche sind es ihrer Natur nach nicht?" [42]

It is not the purpose of this article to set hard and fast rules for Palestinian archaeology. However it is important that the archaeological evidence should not be influenced by political and religious bias.

The peaceful penetration of the Hebrew tribes into Palestine, during the 14th - 12th centuries, has been variously explained by different scholars. They have attempted to follow and explain these hypothetical events by tracing the archaeological artifacts, with special emphasis upon new elements in the material culture. Thus one of Albright's main criteria for the arrival of the early Israelites was the appearance of the collared-rim jar. This criterion was simply accepted by several scholars, without any real discussion of the supporting evidence. This was, and still is, used as a basis for the early Israelite settlements. The distribution of the collared rims was assumed to be restricted to the geographical area between Hazor in the north and Tell Beit Mirsim in the south. This was exactly the area which was believed to have been settled by some of the early Israelites. The appearance of this pottery in the Jordan Valley and the Ammonite region, as well as north of that area, may be disappointing for those who adopted the Albright proposal. Martin Noth and Henk Franken have already pointed to the dangers of making conclusions without a firm factual basis;[43] such conclusions also divert scholars from dealing with the information actually provided by archaeological finds.

One wonders why Albright, Glueck, Aharoni, Wright and others were so concerned with determining the arrival of the Israelites, and not with defining the early Edomites, Moabites, and Ammonites. According to the Old Testament, the history of the Israelite penetration pre-supposes that the earlier inhabitants had already developed a society of cities and states. However, the excavations of the British School of Archaeology (Jerusalem) at Umm el-Biyara, Tawilan, and Buseirah, as well as others in the southern part of East Jordan show no archaeological evidence of the Exodus. A few sites in Palestine and East Jordan show signs of destruction associated stratigraphically with the appearance of the collared rim jar. Whether these destruction levels represent enemy attacks or were the result of natural causes, such as earthquakes, is still to be determined. If these levels were caused by military action, it is not necessary to assume that only the Israelites could have been the attackers. Kathleen Kenyon in her *Archaeology in the Holy Land,* [44] and Martin Noth in his 'Grundsätzaliches zur geschichtlichen Deutung archäologischer Befunde auf dem Boden Palästinas', [45] remind us that the so-called Israelite Conquest was not the only historical event to be associated with the transition between the LB and the Iron I.

The appearance and wide distribution of the collared-rim jars is not accidental, but it is to be associated with a potter's tradition, and the needs of people in a particular agricultural and industrial context, as well as with commercial contacts among Near Eastern communities, though contemporary analogies remain to be investigated. The uniformity in size, shape and technical process, suggests a kind of agreement among pottery workshops in order to fulfill the demands made upon them by society, namely to produce particular vessels according to functionary and unitary conceptions. Storage vessels of the earlier MB and LB periods, which are close in general shape, appear to have played a similar role. In a recent study Parr has drawn attention to the origin, function and development of the so-called Canaanite jar, which made its appearance at the beginning of the Middle Bronze Age and continued to exist, 'having become widely popular throughout the Eastern Mediterranean region during the following two thousand years'. [46] Size and quality may slightly change according to period, but this can also occur within a particular archaeological period. Practicability of shape for transport and improved methods of manufacture, as have been discussed by Parr, are important aspects for understanding the role and wide distribution of these pithoi. Other aspects, like their duration and their influence on Egyptian and Aegean examples, as well as the use of these jars as shown on Egyptian tomb-scenes from the 15th-14th centuries, have been considered by Virginia Grace. [47]

The presence of the collared-rim jar during the late 13th-12th centuries cannot be attributed to one single ethnic group. The origin and the long use of the type under discussion, whenever and wherever, ought to be considered in connection with a social-economic tradition.

References

*   The author would like to express his thanks to Allen Zagarell who assisted in the translation of this article, and offered helpful observations.

1.   W. F. Albright, *AASOR* 4 (1923), 10; 'The Kyle Memorial Excavation at Bethel,' *BASOR* 56 (1934), 2ff; 'Further Light on the History of Israel from Lachish and Megiddo', *BASOR* 68 (1937), p. 25. Albright refers here to the collared-rim found at Tell el-Mutasallim: 'This new culture is characterized by a pottery which is almost indistinguishable from contemporary Israelite pottery in Shechem, Shiloh, Bethel, Ai, Gibeah, and Beth-Zur, etc., and must be Israelite.' See also *BASOR* 78 (1940), 8; *AJA* 41 (1937), p. 147; *The Archaeology of Palestine*, p. 118.
2.   Y. Aharoni, *The Settlement of the Israelite Tribes in Upper Galilee,* (1957) p. 79ff (Hebr.); *Antiquity and Survival* 2 (1957), p. 146ff; *The Land of the* Bible, (1968), p. 174ff; 'New Aspects of the Israelite Occupation in the North', in *Near Eastern Archaeology in the Twentieth Century, Essays in Honour of Nelson Gluek,* J. Sanders, ed.(1970), p. 254ff, especially p. 263: 'Today, in the light of various excavations and surveys, we know that the definition of the collared-rim jars as most typical of the Israelite settlement during the period of the settlement is surely justified'. See also R. Amiran, *Ancient Pottery of the Holy Land* (1970), p. 232f: 'The ethnic identification of the makers of these vessels, as proposed by Albright and confirmed by Aharoni's surveys seems to be in accordance with other evidence in this period'.
3.   H. Franken and J. Kalsbeek, *Excavations at Deir 'Alla,* vol. I, Leiden(1968), p. 161, fig. 42.
4.   Ibid, 162.
5.   M. Ibrahim, 'Archaeological Excavations at Sahab, 1972', *ADAJ,* XVII (1972), p. 23ff. A second excavation report is to be published in *ADAJ* XVIII.

6. A detailed study of the Iron II stamps and seal impressions has been published by P. Welten, *Die Konigsstempel*, (1969). Two articles appeared by A. D. Tushingham, 'A Royal Israelite Seal (?) and the Royal Jar Handle Stamps', *BASOR* 200 (1970), p. 71ff; *BASOR* 201 (1971), p. 23ff; see also A. R. Millard, 'An Israelite Royal Seal?', *BASOR* 208 (1972), p. 5ff.

7. G. A. Eisen, *Ancient Oriental and other Seals,* (*OIP* 47, 1940), nos. 73, 153, 168 (rosettes); 185, 189, 191, 196 (human with animal figures); 171, 181, 183, 188 (animal figures above each other). A similar human figure to that of Sahab was engraved on a seal found at Tell Sippor (Stratum I= 12th century), A. Biran and Ora Negbi, 'The Stratigraphical Sequence at Tell Sippor,' *IEJ* 1 (1950-1951), p. 160ff, pl. 22: c. See also Macalister, *Gezer* II, fig. 437: 12, 438: b1; *Gezer* III, pl. CCXIV: 8, CC: 33.

8. J. Kelso, 'The Second Campaign at Bethel,' *BASOR* 137 (1955), p. 5ff, fig.2; W. Albright and J. Kelso, 'The Excavation of Bethel,' *AASOR* XXXIX (1968), p. 63, pl. 56, 57: 1-10, 117; see also *BASOR* 56 (1934), p. 2ff.

9. Hans Kjer, 'The Excavation of Shiloh,' *JPOS* X (1930), p. 87ff, esp. p. 173f, figs. 6-11. See also Shiloh, *The Danish Excavations at Tell Sailun, Palestine,* (1969), fig. 1: 6, 8: 86-90, 10: 123, 15, 16, 18: 243; see also pls. I:6, III:31, X:77, XV: 123, XXII, XXIII, XXX:243.

10. *Mcgiddo II,* pl. 83: 1, 4; G. Schumacher, *Tell el-Mutesellim,* (1908), Taf. XLVI: d, Abb. 215.

11. *Ain Shems* IV, pl. LXI: 1-3.

12. Ibid, 129.

13. *Beth Shan Pottery* II, pl. XLVI: 6-8.

14. *Atiqot* I, 43, fig. 16: 4, 18-31.

15. *Tell en-Nasbeh* II, pl. 2.

16. *Tell Beit Mirsim* I, 59, fig. 10:8(?), pl. 26: 18 (some of the handles belong to the same type).

17. *AASOR* IV, 12, pl. XXVIII.

18. Ibid, 50f.

19. *Les Fouilles de 'Ay (Et-Tell),* pl. LXXX: several examples of the upper six rows.

20. J. Callaway, 'The 1966 'Ai (et-Tell) Excavations', *BASOR* 196, (1969), p. 5ff, fig. 5.

21. Dorothea Harvey, *BASOR* 196 (1969), 9: J. Callaway, *BASOR* 198 (1970), p. 18f; 'New Evidence on the Conquest of 'Ai', *Journal of Biblical Literature* 87 (1968), p. 312 ff. The identification of 'Ai has been discussed by M. Noth, 'Bethel and Ai', *Aufsätze zur biblishchen Landes-und Altertumskunde* I (1971), p.210ff; J. M. Grinz, ' 'Ai which is beside Beth-Aven,' *Biblica* 42 (1961), p. 201ff. More recent discussion by A. Kuschke, 'Hwwiter in ha-'Ai?' *Wort und Geschichtc, Festschrift für Karl Elliger zum 70. Geburtstag* (1973), p. 115ff.

22. *Hazor* I, p 154, pl. CXXXIV: 8-11, CIX: 7-9, LXXXVIII: 11-12.

23. Ibid, pl. LVII: 5, 6, 8.

24. Y. Yadin, *Hazor* (Schweich Lectures), London (1972), p. 33f, pl. 11b.
     Further examples with a less pronounced ridge from Stratum XII are published in: *Hazor* III-IV (Plates), pl. CLXVII: 1-7. According to Yadin (Schweich Lectures, p. 135), Stratum XII is below the Iron Age city.

25. *Tel Zeror* III, pl. XV:12 (Late Iron Age).

26. B. Maisler, 'The Excavations at Tell Qasile', *IEJ* 1 (1950-1951), p. 123ff, pl. 26:2, 30:c.

27. Ibid, p. 194ff, fig. 10:c.

28. J. A. Callaway and R. E. Cooley, 'A Salvage Excavation at Raddana, in Bireh,' *BASOR* 201 (1971), p. 11ff. fig. 2.

29. Ibid; see also F. M. Cross and D. N. Freedman, 'An Inscribed Jar from Raddana,' *BASOR* 201 (1971), p. 19ff, figs. 1-3.

30. Franken and Kalsbeek, op. cit., fig. 47: 12, pl. XIV: 1.

31. The author collected a few collared-rims of greenish ware from the surface of Tell el-Mazar early in 1973.

32. Sherds of this type were found in Areas C and B, in association with walls C.1 and B. 2, which date from 11-12th centuries B.C. Collared-rim jars were also found on the surface; for further information see: H. O. Thompson 'The 1972 Excavation of Khirbet al-Hajjar', *ADAJ* XVII (1972), b47 ff; M. M. Ibrahim, 'Two Ammonite Statuettes from Khirbet el-Hajjar,' *ADAJ* XVI (1971), p. 91ff.

33. N. Gluek, *Explorations in Eastern Palestine* IV, pl. 25: 6, 8 (Khirbet Sheikh Mohammad).

34. M. Ibrahim, *ADAJ,* XVII (1972), 31 ff. The author is preparing an article on this tomb for *ZDPV*.

35. The tomb of Jabal el-Qusur has been investigated by the Department of Antiquities of Jordan. The finds were deposited in the Amman Museum and are still to be published.

36. M. Dothan, 'Excavations at Azor', *IEJ* 11, p. 173, pl. 35:3.

37. Ibid; *RB* 69 (1962), p. 397.

38. *Tel Zeror* III, pl. LVI. 1-4.

39.   *Gezer* II, 431f, fig. 513.

40.   E. F. Schmidt, *The Alishar Hüyük,* Seasons of 1928 and 1929, Part I, (OIP XIX), 72ff, 181ff, figs. 88-92, 239-245.

41.   Dothan, op.cit.

42.   M. Noth, *Aufsatze zur biblischen Landes-und Altertumskunde,* Band I (1971), herausgegeben von Hans Walter Wolf, 3ff.

43.   Ibid; H. J. Franken, 'Palestine in the Time of the Nineteenth Dynasty, (b) Archaeological Evidence , *CAH* Vol. 11 Part 2 (1975), p. 331ff.

44.   K. Kenyon, *Archaeology in the Holy Land* (1970), p. 195 ff.

45.   Noth, op. cit.

46.   P. J. Parr, 'The Origin of the Canaanite Jar', in D. E. Strong (ed), *Archaeological Theory and Practice, Essays Presented to Prof. W. F. Grimes,* (1973), p. 173f. Thanks are herewith expressed to Peter Parr for sending a reprint of his study, which was not known to me, and for referring to the essay of V. Grace.

47.   Virginia R. Grace, 'The Canaanite Jar,' in Saul S. Weinberg (ed) *The Aegean and the Near East - Studies Presented to Hetty Goldmann,* 80ff, figs. 2-4.

THE 'HOUSE OF BA'AL' OF AHAB AND JEZEBEL IN SAMARIA, AND THAT OF ATHALIA IN JUDAH.
by Yigael Yadin

The House of Ba'al in Samaria

For many of us - brought up on the scathing exhortations of the prophets - Samaria is associated with the seat of Ba'al's abominable cult and Zion with the eternal city of Yahweh. Yet, during one period, and one only, it was Samaria who led the way in purifying itself from the Ba'al cult, and even taught Zion how to follow suit.

It was Jehu, son of Nimshi, who eliminated the cult of Ba'al in a most dramatic and original - albeit cruel - method (2 *Kings,* IX-X) to be followed, several years later, by Jehoiada the priest, who in nearly the same way killed Athaliah, daughter of Ahab and destroyed the House of Ba'al which she erected in Judah (ibid. XI). In the following discussion an effort is made to probe generally into the nature of these two acts and in particular into the problem of the exact locations of these Houses of Ba'al.

The Biblical narrative of the acts of Jehu is so well-known, that quite often some of the crucial details embedded in the description are overlooked by Biblical scholars and several conventional views are absorbed in recent treatments of the subject, without a fresh effort to re-examine the original text. In view of the above, we should refresh our memory and recapitulate the very act of Jehu and the immediate circumstances which led to it.

Our story begins with the marriage of Ahab to Jezebel, daughter of Ethba'al, king of the Sidonians, as a result of which Ahab served and worshipped Ba'al (1 *Kings,* XVI, 31 f.). A severe famine followed (ibid., XVIII) and Ahab was compelled to survey all the springs and valleys looking for pastures for his horses and other animals. Interestingly enough, in this he was assisted by Obadiah 'who was over the household' - i.e., his prime-minister - who not only carried a Yahweh-theophoric name, but actually 'revered Yahweh greatly'. Jezebel's efforts to eliminate the prophets of Yahweh, prompted Obadiah to hide one hundred of them in caves and provide them with bread and water. Then occurred the famous and unprecedented test on Mt. Carmel. Ahab agreed to gather hundreds of the prophets of Ba'al and Asherah, 'who eat of Jezebel's table'. After the failure of the prophets of Ba'al to invoke Ba'al through their shoutings 'O Ba'al, answer us!', Elijah ' repaired the altar of Yahweh, that had been thrown down'. This indicates that before the site was turned into a Ba'al cult place, an old Yahweh cult place existed there. Elijah's following massacre of the prophets of Ba'al, was done, no doubt, with the tacit agreement of Ahab. One should compare the following order of Elijah, to the gathered people: "Seize the prophets of Ba'al; let not one of them escape" (ibid., XVIII,40) with that issued later on by Jehu: "Let not a man escape" (2 *Kings,* X, 25). It appears that Ahab's departure place to Mt. Carmel was the nearby Jezreel (vs., 45), where he returned only to be met by Jezebel's wrath and her order to seize Elijah: "So may the gods do to me and more also, if I do not make your life as the life of one of them by this time tomorrow" (1 *Kings,* XIX,2). From now on it becomes clear that Jezebel is the one who rules the country from her abode in Jezreel. At this time we are told about the infamous event with Naboth's Vineyard (ibid, XXI,1 f) which must actually have occurred sometime earlier. The whole story emphasises the importance of Jezreel and the 'palace of Ahab' which existed there. Again, Jezebel is the main interested party, and it is she who utters one of the most humiliating words against a king of Israel: "Do you now govern Israel? Arise, and eat bread, and let your heart be cheerful; I will give thee the vinyard of Naboth the Jezreelite" (vs.7). From then on the whole *raison d'être* of the Biblical narrative is to show that the curse of Yahweh had fallen on Ahab and Jezebel in *Jezreel.* The essence of Elijah's curse, is: "In the place where dogs licked up the blood of Naboth shall dogs lick your own blood" (vs.19). And also to Jezebel: "The dogs shall eat Jezebel within the bounds of Jezreel" (vs.23). It is essential that Naboth's blood will be avenged at exactly the same place where he was murdered; *there* must the dogs lick the blood of Ahab and Jezebel.

Ahab was killed in battle in Ramoth-Gilead in Transjordan. Now comes a strange verse and, in a way, an anti-climax to Elijah's prophecy: "So the king died, and was brought to Samaria; and they buried the king in Samaria. And they washed the chariot by the pool of Samaria, and the dogs licked up his blood, and the harlots washed themselves in it, according to the word of the Lord which he had spoken" (ibid, XXII, 37-38). Was this indeed according to the word of the Lord? It is obvious that Ahab's blood had to be licked in *Jezreel* and not in Samaria, as indeed happened later on with Jezebel's blood. Is it possible then, that the name *Samaria* in the Biblical text may designate sometimes not the capital city, but the state of Samaria? We shall discuss this problem soon. Let us now return to Jehu, who is, after all, the hero of our story, and single out some salient points which seem to be relevant to our subject.

A fate similar to that of Ahab and Jehoshaphat befell Joram, son of Ahab, king of Israel and Ahaziah, son of Jehoram (and Athaliah) king of Judah. They are defeated in the same Ramoth-Gilead: Joram is wounded and "returned to be healed in Jezreel" (2 *Kings,* VIII,29). Ahaziah goes down to Jezreel to visit the wounded Joram (ibid.,). Jezreel now becomes the main objective of vengeance by the newly crowned Jehu, who was vigorously supported by Elijah's and Elisha's followers; Jehu arrives in Jezreel and the confrontation between him and the wounded Joram is precisely "at the property of Naboth the Jezreelite" (ibid, IX,21). Joram is killed and again the whole purpose of the Biblical narrative is to emphasise the fulfilment of Elijah's prophecy: "Take him up and cast him on the plot of ground belonging to Naboth the Jezreelite,   for remember, when you and I rode side by side behind Ahab his father, how the Lord uttered this oracle against him: 'As surely as I saw yesterday, the blood of Nabboth and the blood of his sons - says the Lord - I will requite you on this plot of ground! Now therefore take him up and cast him on the plot of ground, in accordance with the word of the Lord" (ibid IX, 25-26). Jezebel, after having "looked out of the window" - most probably a window similar to the one depicted in the Samaria and other ivories - was killed, and again the main point of the story is: "But when they went to bury her, they found no more of her than the skull and the feet and the palms of her hands . . . this is the word of the Lord, which he spoke by his servant Elijah the Tisbite. In the territory of Jezreel the dogs shall eat the flesh of Jezebel" (ibid., 35-37). Again the problem of Ahab's death in Samaria rather than in Jezreel becomes more acute. But here, the Bible gives us perhaps the clue we searched for. Ahaziah, seeing the fate of Joram "fled in the direction of Beth-Haggan. And Jehu pursued him and said 'Shoot him also' and they shot him in the chariot at the ascent of Gur, which is by Ibleam. And he fled to Megiddo, and died there" (ibid., 27). However, the same incident is described thus in 2 Chronicles XXII,9: "He searched for Ahaziah and he was captured while hiding in Samaria". Obviously, for the chronicler, Ibleam and Megiddo are *Samaria.* In fact, were it not for 2 Kings, we would have concluded that Ahaziah was captured in the city of Samaria.

Having eliminated the king and queen, Jehu turns his attention to all members of the royal family and the 'establishment': "they took the king's sons and slew them, seventy persons, and put their heads in baskets, and sent them to him at Jezreel". This act, too, and particularly the presentation of the heads at the entrance of the gate of Jezreel, was performed in order to fulfil the prophecy of Elijah concerning the House of Ahab and Jezreel: "for the Lord has done what he said by his servant Elijah" (ibid, X,10). And now came the final blow to Ahab's 'entourage' at Jezreel, including the *priests:* "So Jehu slew all that remained of the house of Ahab in Jezreel, all his great men, and his familiar friends, and his priests, until he left him none remaining" (vs.11).

Jehu turned now to the city of Samaria; on his way he killed the kinsmen of Ahaziah, who - unaware of the course of events - were on their way to Jezreel "to visit the royal princes and the sons of the queen mother" (vs. 13). On arriving at Samaria, Jehu "slew all that remained to Ahab in Samaria, till he wiped them out" (vs. 17). Up to then, the Biblical narration does not mention any hostile action against the House of Ba'al at Samaria or against its prophets and priests. In order to achieve this aim, Jehu had to resort to what the Bible calls 'cunning   an action which brings the narration to its dramatic climax. Jehu orders the preparation of "a great sacrifice to offer to Ba'al"; he proclaims punishment of death to any absentee; simultaneously he stations "eighty men outside the Ba'al precinct with an order - similar to the one given by Elijah on Mt. Carmel - to slay anyone who may try and escape. Then came the turn of the "guard and the officers" to slay the worshippers, to burn the holy furniture and to demolish the house of Ba'al. The destroyed house was turned into "a latrine to this day" (vss., 24-27). Where was the location of this house of Ba'al? Was it inside the capital city, Samaria?

In order to answer these questions, we must clarify two problems: what was the 'official' religion of Israel under Ahab and the status of Jezreel and its 'palace'. As for the first question, there can be no doubt that Yahweh was the paramount god of the royal family, the capital and the state of Israel. Ahab's children bear names with Yahweh as their theophoric element: Yehoram, Ahaziahu and even Athaliah herself. Furthermore, as mentioned above, Obadiah "who was over the house - i.e., the prime-minister - was a man who "revered Yahweh greatly" (1 Kings XVIII, 3).

Into this *milieu* was thrust Jezebel, daughter of Ethba'al king of the Sidonians - a queen of strong-character, whose main deity was Ba'al and whose whole upbringing was centered around this cult. This obviously constituted a serious problem for Ahab: where should he establish the premises for the foreign way-of-life of Jezebel and her entourage? Could it be right in the heart of the capital city whose official god is Yahweh, the god of Israel? This brings us to the second question: the purpose and status of Jezreel. A. Alt first raised the question of how to explain the existence of two capitals with two palaces: one in the city of Samaria and one in Jezreel; was this just a matter of luxury, keeping a summer and winter palace? [1] Alt was right in raising the issue, but his explanation seems rather strange. According to him Omri and Ahab deliberately established two capitals - in Samaria, the 'Canaanite' capital, and in Jezreel, the 'Israelite' capital - to express a political and cultic dualism: Samaria, the 'Canaanite', served as a center of Ba'al worship, while Jezreel was intended as the centre of Yahweh worship. Alt based his theory, among other things, on the accepted view that the center of Ba'al cult - indeed the very house of Ba'al - was, according to the Bible, in the city of Samaria. Acceptance of Alt's theory resulted in the illogical conclusion that the center of Ba'al worship was in the city of Samaria, the main capital of the kings, whose official deity was Yahweh! Indeed, the Biblical narratives discussed above, contradict such an assumption; Jezebel's main activity - hers and that of those who ate of her table - was centered in Jezreel and the neighbouring Mount Carmel. The Biblical narrative leaves little doubt that one of Ahab's main building activities was in Jezreel, where he built a palace. Enlarging this palace was very close to the heart of Jezebel, and it was this interest which led to the tragic event of Naboth's death, the kernel of the whole Biblical story in relation to Jezebel. It seems that what Ahab built for Jezebel in Jezreel, was a sort of *Petit Trianon*; contrary to Alt's assumption, it seems that Jezreel was chosen for Jezebel's main seat of activities, because it was inconceivable that a palace be built for her foreign cult and way of life in the capital of Israel. This was the cause for the 'phenomenon' - to use Alt's terminology - of two residential palaces of Ahab. Obviously, Jezreel was chosen for various reasons, including tribal traditions connected with the place, climatic and strategic considerations, and - last, but not least - its proximity to the important cultic center of Mount Carmel. [2] The universal agreement among scholars that the House of Ba'al, erected by Ahab, was in the city of Samaria, is based on one Biblical passage - a passage which in its present form is obviously annotated by a gloss of the Deuteronomist: "He erected an altar for Ba'al - *the House of Ba'al, which he built in Samaria;- And Ahab made an Asherah*" (1 Kings, XVI, 32-33). [3] What was Ahab's main guilt? The building of the altar or the House of Ba'al? Obviously, if Ahab built a temple for Ba'al it comprised an altar. It seems, therefore, that the original text here indicated the building of an altar and an Asherah; the editor, who knew about the House of Ba'al, which was the pivot of the Jehu story, added the explanation that the altar and Asherah mentioned here, refer to that temple. Grammatically the gloss is rather crudely inserted. In any event, as we have seen, Samaria without further indications, might refer, in the Biblical parlance, to the state as well as the city. The only relevant text to the temple of Ba'al, which Jehu destroyed, is therefore the one which describes this event. It is interesting that this text, so rich with details, does not mention - directly or indirectly - that the temple of Ba'al was erected in the *city* of Samaria. On the contrary, the circumstantial evidence weighs heavily against such a possibility. This temple must have been a large building within a huge *temenos,* with a large altar (2 kings, X,18-21). Whatever the case, the 'clinching' data is to be found at the end of the narrative - its climax; when all the Ba'al worshippers were assembled, Jehu ordered the guard and the officers to kill the lot and to destroy the building: The guard and officers then "went to the city of the House of Ba'al". Here the location of the temple is clear: the *city* of the house of Ba'al!

This phrase, miraculously saved from being harmonised by the hands of ancient editors, indicates quite clearly that the temple was not in the city of Samaria, and therefore modern Biblical commentators changed it arbitrarily, either by deleting the word 'city' or by changing it to 'the inner room'. [4] Thus we read in the R.S.V: "and went into the *inner room* of the house of Ba'al", with a footnote: "Heb. *city*". However, it is a well-known rule in textual criticism that the *lec.diff.,* should be maintained, unless there is a decisive case against it. In our case the Massoretic text is supported also by the LXX. [5]

Thus we have to look for a city of the House of Ba'al, in which there stood a huge temple and altar. No remains of such a sacred city were found within the acropolis of Samaria, and one may doubt whether such a complex ever stood there, turned into a "latrine to this day" (ibid., vs.27).

Where then, was the 'city of the House of Ba'al'? It could have been in Jezreel - the center of activities of Jezebel and her entourage, where - as the Bible states - Ahab built a *Hēkal.* [6] It is more likely though, that it was on a nearby mountain; [7] if so, Mount Carmel - the main and indeed the only venerated cult place in Samaria at the time of the Omrides - is probably the site of the House of Ba'al. This suggestion is further strengthened if we accept Eissfeldt's proposal [8] to identify the Ba'al of Jezebel with Ba'al Šamêm, the cosmic deity of the Phoenicians and the patron of shipping. [9] In summing up this section one may conclude that Jezebel and Ahab built the place of Jezreel to enable Jezebel to indulge in the Ba'al cult, the centre of which was the nearby Mount Carmel. The House of Ba'al built there and destroyed by Jehu, was known to the people of Judah as the House of Ba'al of the state of Samaria. [10]

The House of Ba'al in Judah

Now we can discuss the problem of the other House of Ba'al - in Judah - which was destroyed in a similar manner. This event is described in the Bible, immediately after the narrative of the destruction of the House of Ba'al in Samaria (2 Kings 1). Indeed the two events are strikingly similar. Judah at that time was ruled *de facto,* by Athaliah, Ahab's and Jezebel's daughter. In fact, on hearing of Jehu's *coup* and particularly of the murder of her son Ahaziah, Athaliah realised that her position in Judah was precarious. Therefore "she arose and destroyed all the royal family" of Judah (2 *Kings,* XI, 1), and "reigned over the land" (ibid, vs.3). Athaliah would have been successful in eliminating the royal seed, were it not for Jehosheba, sister of Ahaziah, who managed to hide the infant Joash and save him from the wrath of Athaliah. Jehosheba's motivation and success were due to the fact that she was the wife of Jehoiada the priest (2 *Chronicles* XXII, 11), the devout and zealous servant of Yahweh. The infant Joash, was hidden in the 'House of Yahweh' for six years, while Athaliah reigned over Judah. This fact indicates that Athaliah with all her power, had practically no control over the temple, which was still the stronghold of the followers of Yahweh, Jehoiada and the captains of the guards, the Levites and the priests. Jehoiada secretly planned his plot to overthrow Athaliah and eradicate her cult, in a manner similar to Jehu's. First, he proclaimed Joash king - and did so in the Temple courts, in the presence of all the guards and priests, who "clapped their hands and said 'long live the king' " (ibid, vs.12). Now comes the turn of Athaliah. Having no control of the Temple, Athaliah realises, only too late, the plot of the Yahwists and the Judean diehards. She cries: 'Treason! Treason!' only to be dragged *outside* and slain, together with her followers. Jehoiada, then, made a covenant between the king and the people. and prepared the scene for the last act - strikingly similar to the one of Jehu: the elimination of the Ba'al cult and its followers, introduced into Judah by Athaliah the daughter of Ahab: "Then all the people of the land went to the House of Ba'al, and tore it down; his altars and his images they broke in pieces, and they slew Mattan the priest of Ba'al before the altars" (ibid, vs.18). This is the first time - indeed the only time - that we hear of the fact that Athaliah built a House of Ba'al and installed a priest in it. Where was this temple?

As with the case of Ahab's and Jezebel's House of Ba'al, scholars agreed, axiomatically, that this Temple was within the boundaries of the city of Jerusalem. This conclusion seems to be unwarranted, for three main reasons:

   a. The Biblical text does not say that the House of Ba'al was in Jerusalem.
   b. The crowded built-up area of Jerusalem in the 9th century, would hardly accommodate an additional temple with altars;
   c. It is inconceivable that such a temple was built within the courts of the Temple of Yahweh. Such an act would not have been tolerated by the Yahweh worshipping Judeans. It is true that the Bible mentions from time to time that some elements of idolatry were introduced into the Temple of Yahweh[11] - but nowhere is there any record that an actual *temple* to a foreign deity was erected within the temple's *temenos.* Even Solomon, who built cult places for his foreign wives, made them 'east of Jerusalem, to the south of the mount of corruption' (2 *Kings,* XXII,13).

It seems therefore, that Athaliah, like her mother Jezebel, had to build her temple outside the city. It should have been a place, preferably connected by tradition with a Ba'al cult; there she could build not only a temple for Ba'al but also a residence to accommodate her and the Ba'al followers.

In trying to locate the site of Athaliah's House of Ba'al, we should look for a nearby mountain, with remains of a monumental building, fashioned architectually like the buildings of Samaria, for there can be little doubt, that Athaliah, like Jezebel, was assisted in her project by Israelite-Tyrian masons.

These requirements fit admirably the interesting remains discovered by Aharoni at Ramath-Raḥel, *c.,* three kilometres south of Jerusalem.[12] The *tell* is on the summit of a mountain (819 m. above sea level) which is the highest point in the region. Here were discovered remains of a monumental temenos-like structure, strikingly similar - although on a smaller scale - to the enclosure of the Samaria acropolis; as in Samaria, the walls of the enclosure are of the casemate type, the stones (both smoothly dressed and with marginal drafting) are laid in headers and stretchers, and the building was adorned by Proto-Ionic capitals. The similarity between the building at Ramath-Raḥel and those of Samaria was of course noted by the excavator. This is particularly clear from his first preliminary report, when as yet he had no theory about the exact date of the building and its identification. It is worthwhile quoting some of his remarks:[13] "The inner wall is only 1.10 m. wide, but it is a beautiful example of the best Israelite workmanship, almost exactly similar to the 'inner wall' of Samaria"[14]; "The resemblance to the palace of Samaria in all these details is so strong that the building technique is obviously the same".[15] At this time, the building was dated as follows: "From the material so far discovered it may be dated not earlier than the eighth century B.C., *but it is not impossible that some of the finds belong to the ninth century B.C.*" [16] (my italics - Y.Y.); "It would be premature to try and date its foundation exactly, but it seems that it was somewhat later than the palace of Samaria". [17]

A most surprising find was discovered in the fifth season of excavation: parts of a window balustrade, made of miniature Proto-Ionic capitals, [18] identical with the one depicted on Phoenician ivories, also discovered at Samaria, and commonly called 'the woman at the window' type. [19] The discovery of the mass of cult clay-figurines should also be mentioned. [20]

All the above-mentioned architectual data should have led the excavator to the conclusion - had it occurred to him - that the building belonged to the period of Athaliah. Her days were the only time that Judah was actually ruled by an offspring of Ahab, who according to the Bible, was responsible for erecting a monumental building. At the time, the excavator concluded his report cautiously: "The purpose of the royal citadel at Ramath-Raḥel and the circumstances of its foundation remain a riddle." [21]

Alas, the correct observations about the striking similarity to Samaria, and the cautiously worded dating, soon gave way to two theories attributing the building to the eighth and the end of the seventh centuries respectively. The first was that the building should be identified with the obscure 'separate house' of the leprosy-afflicted king Uzziah (2 *Kings*, XV,5). [22] This well-publicised theory [23] was soon replaced by another, attributing the building to Jehoiakim King of Judah, who ruled one hundred and fifty years after Uzziah (608-597 B.C.). The drastic shift in the dating was caused, according to the excavator, by a new discovery in the fill of the floor of the building; [24] while the attribution to Jehoiakim was based on a biblical text related by scholars to this king: [25] "Woe to him who builds his house by unrighteousness, and his upper rooms by injustice; who says 'I will build myself a great house with spacious upper rooms' and cut out windows for it, panelling it with cedar and painting it with vermillion" (*Jer.*, XXII, 13-14). This attractive suggestion is met with two serious difficulties:

a. It is not stated that the building was outside Jerusalem. [26] If the text refers indeed to a new building, and not to a reconstruction of the upper chambers of the existing palace, then it is more probable that it was erected on the western hill (Mazar's oral suggestion), where recently Avigad discovered a massive wall of the Monarchy period. [27] It is most improbable that Jehoiakim, with the imminent threat of a Babylonian invasion, would build a sumptuous palace outside the fortified capital.

b. It is hardly credible that a building erected *c.* 600 B.C. in Judah, would be identical in plan, technique and other architectual features, with the buildings of Samaria, two hundred and fifty years earlier, including a gap of one hundred and twenty years since the end of the Northern Kingdom of Israel after the destruction of Samaria. [28]

Having adhered to his view that the Ramath-Raḥel building was to be dated to *c.* 600 and that there were no earlier monumental elements there, the excavator then reported a new discovery. South of, and parallel to the previously discussed casemate wall, a new casemate wall was found, [29] also built of ashlar. This new wall was ascribed to an earlier stratum, although "the resemblance between the ashlar built royal edifices of the *two strata* (italics are mine - Y.Y.) is indeed remarkable". [30] The striking resemblance between the two walls should have sounded the alarm that something was wrong in the stratigraphical analysis. Instead, the excavator resorted to a vicious circle argument: "Actually, however, there is nothing really surprising about this (the striking resemblance - Y.Y.), when we remember that they are not separated by any great distance of time and that similar constructional work with ashlars has also been found in royal citadels of still earlier date, such as those at Samaria and Megiddo." [31] The attribution of the new element to an earlier stratum (designated VB) was forced upon the excavator, also by the fact that older pottery was found in abundance in the area and in the fills of the nearby structures.

The newly-discovered casemate wall, was considered to be part of an earlier [32] royal citadel "well-built, though not particularly large". [33] The conclusion that this wall represented another citadel, [34] smaller in size, was forced upon the excavator by the discovery of a very crude, one-course wide, curved wall, under the floor of the main building. [35] This 'wall' was explained away as an agricultural terrace, part of the "garden-girt citadel" [36] - which according to the excavator should be identified with Biblical Bethha-Kerem. However the 'terrace' wall could represent anything from a primitive sheep-enclosure to a terrace wall of heaps of building material, and can be very old indeed. [37]

It is obvious that if the excavator had concluded that the main building as found, represents a number of phases in its development, many of the apparent difficulties would have disappeared: originally there was a monumental public building of the 9th century, built in Samarian style, only to be repaired and re-constructed in later periods, to which the main finds belonged.

It is difficult to analyze the stratigraphy of the Ramath-Raḥel excavations, because the preliminary reports lack the proper discussions of the sections, foundation trenches etc., Nevertheless, it is quite clear that the plan of the building in its latest stage, is the result of many changes, additions and deletions, an indication of its long history. [38] The pottery found on the floors, or in the fills of the latest stage, do not indicate the date of the original building, but rather its later developments. [39] It seems, therefore, that the monumental building of Ramat-Raḥel was first built in the 9th century B.C. probably representing a royal palace including the House of Ba'al, built by Athaliah, [40] and utterly destroyed by Jehoiada. Later the building must have been completely reconstructed, probably by King Menasseh, who reigned for fifty-five years and was the only king of Judah, who "erected altars for Ba'al and made an Asherah, as *Ahab king of Israel had done*" (2 Kings, XXI, 3) and of whom the Lord said: "I will stretch over Jerusalem the measuring line of Samaria and the plummet of the house of Ahab" (ibid, vs., 13). This date fits very well the nature of the fill under the existing floor.

The hill of modern Ramath Raḥel, was chosen for the erection of the House of Ba'al (if my suggestion is accepted) not only for its dominating position, but perhaps also for its long association with the Ba'al cult. G. Dalman and others have already suggested that Ba'al-Perazim (2 Sam., V,20) was located in this area. [41] Mazar, [42] followed Dalman and in associating the place with Mount Perazim as well ("For the Lord will rise up as on Mount Perazim" - Is. XXVIII,21), concluded that on this site there existed an ancient cult place of Ba'al. The cultic tradition was never forgotten, and even in the Byzantine period a church and a monastery were erected on the spot (The church of the Kathisma).

References.

*   The essence of this article was read by me during the Israel Exploration Society's annual conference in 1972, in Samaria. It gives me great pleasure to present this discussion in a volume dedicated to Dame Kathleen Kenyon, whose important contributions to the archaeology of Samaria and Judah are discerned also herein.

1.   A. Alt, "Der Stadtstaat Samaria", *Kleine Schriften, III,* (München, 1959), pp. 258 ff.
2.   It is even conceivable that the revival of Mount Carmel as a center for the Ba'al cult, was the responsibility of Ahab and Jezebel. This may explain Elijah's crusade against its cult, which replaced the "altar of Yahweh that had been (previously) thrown down" (1 Kings XVIII,30 ff). On the Ba'al of Mount Carmel, see A. Alt, "Des Gottesurteil auf dem Karmel", *Kleine Schriften, II* pp. 135 ff.; W. F. ALBRIGHT, *Archeology and the Religion of Israel,* pp. 156 ff.; cf., also M. Avi-Yonah, *I.E.J.,* 2 (1952), pp. 128 ff.
3.   This is how the Hebrew text should be translated and not as in the R.S.V., which is an effort to overcome the difficulty, and a compromise between the Hebrew and the LXX: "He erected an altar for Ba'al *in* the house of Ba'al, which he built in Samaria. And Ahab made an Asherah". The LXX version is: καὶ ἔστησε θυσιαστήριον τῷ Βάαλ ἐν οἴκῳ τῶν προσοχθισμάτων αὐτοῦ, ὃν ᾠκοδόμησεν ἐν Σαμαρείᾳ καὶ ἐποίησεν Ἀχαὰβ ἄλσος.
4.   דביר instead of עיר.
5.   πόλεῳ οἴκου τοῦ Βάαλ
6.   Which could mean either a 'palace' or a 'temple'. In the Biblical text, Ahab's *hekal* (1 Kings, XXI, 1) points rather towards a 'palace'; However it is interesting to note that the LXX (Cod.Alex., and Vat.,) has here ΑΛΩ which is considered by some scholars to be a corruption of ΝΑΩ, i.e. 'temple', cf., *Biblia Hebraica.*
7.   The cult of the Ba'al was frequently associated with high mountains cf., e.g. Ba'al of Lebanon, Ba'al Hermon and Ba'al Zaphon.
8.   O. Eissfeldt, *Z.A.W.* 57, (1939) pp.1.ff.
9.   See B. Mazar, "The Philistines and the Rise of Israel and Tyre", *The Israel Academy of Sciences and Humanities, Proceedings*, I, 7 (1964) pp. 19 ff. For other views see W. F. ALBRIGHT, *Archaeology and the Religion of Israel,* pp. 156 ff; F. M. CROSS, *Canaanite Myth and Hebrew Epic,* p.7., n.13. On the cult of Mt. Carmel, see in particular A.Alt, "Das Gottesurteil auf dem Karmel", *Kleine Schriften* II, pp. 135 ff.

10.   In addition to the data mentioned above proving that the name Samaria in the Biblical texts indicates the country as well, and not only the city, cf., in particular: "Then the word of the Lord came to Elijah the Tishbite, saying: 'arise, go down to meet Ahab king of Israel, who is in Samaria; behold, he is in the vinyard of Naboth' " (1 *Kings*, XXI, 17-18).

11.   Such as an Asherah, Nehushtan, Incense altars, etc.

12.   Y. AHARONI, *Excavations at Ramath Rahel - Seasons 1959 and 1960,* (Roma, 1962) (Hereafter R.R.I.); idem, *Seasons of 1961 and 1962,* (Roma, 1964) (hereafter R.R.II.). The final report has, unfortunately, not yet been published. The above volumes, lavishly illustrated, consist mainly of the preliminary reports.

13.   *I.E.J.* 6, (1956) pp. 102 ff; 137 ff.

14.   Ibid, p. 138. In another place he writes: "Quiconque regarde la photographie du 'mur interieur' de Samarie, construit par Achabe et la compare à celle du 'mur Intérieur' de la fortresse de Ramat-Rachel, a du mal à les distinguer l'une de l'autre". (*Bible et Terre Sainte,* 37 (1961) p.4.

15.   p. 140. cf., also p. 144. cf. also "Most significant is the resemblance of the Ramath Rahel citadel to Samaria, not only in its plan but also in its history. Both were founded in Iron Age II on uninhabited hills" (p. 151).

16.   Cf. also: . . . "was built during Iron Age II, but not earlier than the ninth century and possibly only in the eighth century B.C." (p. 151) Or in a later report: "or, at the very earliest, (not) prior to the middle of the 9th century" (*R.R.II.,* p. 122).

17.   p. 144

18.   *R.R.II.* p. 55, Fig. 38., pls., 44-48, and jacket.

19.   J. W. CROWFOOT AND OTHERS, *Early Ivories from Samaria,* p. 29. The same is believed by some scholars to be associated with Ashtart and her sacred harlots (ibid).

20.   *R.R.II,* pp. 95 ff., Fig. 36; Pls. 35-37.

21.   *I.E.J.* 6, p. 155.

22.   *R.R.I.,* p. 50-51.

23.   *Bible et Terre Sainte,* 37 (1961), p. 10 and the sub-caption of the article "le palais-fortresses . . . . où se serait retiré le roi lepreux Ozias".

24.   According to Aharoni (*R.R.I.* pp. 59 ff.,) in the fourth season "royal seal impressions of all classes, have been discovered not only beneath the floor of the courtyard . . . but also in the filling beneath the floors of the various buildings and rooms which have been excavated. This furnishes now conclusive proof that the citadel could not have been built earlier than the second half of the seventh century B.C." It should be noted, though, that the royal seal impressions (of the late two-winged emblem) were found under the floors of rooms, even before the Uzziah dating was proposed. (See e.g. *R.R.I.* p. 41, finds in locus 297). It was then taken as proof that the dates of these stamps should be pushed back ("it seems that this fact points to an earlier date for all the types of royal stamps, though Ramat Rahel gives us only a *terminus a quo* in the 8th century B.C." - *R.R.I,* p.51). In another place - *B.I.E.S.,* 24, (1960) p. 93 - this phenomenon was explained as perhaps the result of "the floor (having been) repaired here and there during the lifetime of the citadel, when this fill and pottery was inserted under it". In any case, as we shall see later, this evidence is not relevant to the dating of the original building, since Aharoni's dating was based on the wrong assumption that the remains consist of one phase only.

25.   *R.R.I,* p.60; *R.R.II,* pp. 123-124.

26.   Aharoni quotes the words "beyond the gates of Jerusalem" in vs. 19 as a possible hint to the location of the building. But these words are taken out of context, which describes the burial place of the king . . . . . . " with the burial of an ass he shall be buried, dragged and cast forth beyond the gates of Jerusalem". (Cf. also 2 *Chr.,* XXXVI.6).

27.   *I.E.J.,* 22 (1972), p. 193.

28.   It is appropriate here to comment on the discovery in Jerusalem by Kathleen Kenyon of a Proto-Ionic capital identical to the last detail (two little circles, three triangles) with the ones discovered in Ramath-Rahel. This discovery is very important and relevant to the dating problems since it is quite clear that the capital dates from the same time and may have even been made by the same stone artisans. Unlike the ones of Ramat Rahel, the newly found capital was discovered in a stratigraphic context which permits its dating, or at least its latest possible date. Here is what Kenyon writes about it: "It was found broken at the foot of the scarp on the eastern crest of the eastern ridge, with a tumble of ashlar blocks which could have formed part of a wall in the Samaria style" (K. Kenyon, *Jerusalem - Excavating 3000 Years of History,* London, (1967) p. 46). Concerning the fill in which the capital was found, she writes: "The actual date of the wall is given a *terminus ante* by the fill against it, which, on the preliminary field examination of the pottery, should be eighth century B.C." (*P.E.Q.,* 1968, p. 104). Even if one does not concur with Kenyon's

view that the capital and ashlar blocks are derived from a Solomonic building, 350 years before
Jehoiakim - the archaeological evidence shows that the Ramath-Raḥel original structure was built
before the eighth century - a *terminus* which would fit precisely the period of Athaliah.

29. *R.R.II,* p. 59
30. Ibid.
31. Ibid.
32. "From the 8th century, or at the very earliest from the second half of the 9th century B.C.", Ibid. p.119;
    or "at the very earliest . . . middle of the 9th century", Ibid. p. 122. The date was fixed with the aid of the
    earliest pottery found in the fills, which clearly goes back to the 9th century B.C. Cf., *R.R.I.* pp. 40-41.
33. *R.R.II.* p. 119.
34. Another of the excavator's arguments that this wall belonged to another, earlier, building is that "it is hardly
    conceivable that there was a second casemate wall in this region in stratum VA" - ibid, p. 59.
35. Ibid. Pl. 27, 1.
36. Ibid. p. 119
37. This wall is built directly on virgin soil and no pottery was associated with it.
38. The excavator was clearly aware of the fact that several walls were built in different techniques and that their
    foundations were at various levels of altitude. These facts alone are sufficient, normally, to indicate that
    they belong to different strata or phases. However, the "one phase" theory led the excavator to suggest
    the following explanation to some of the more salient "anomalies":
    a. The dressing and style of the stones of the southern casemate inner wall differ basically from those
       of the northern casemate inner wall; while the former wall is built of finely-dressed smooth ashlar, the
       latter is built of crude stones. This phenomenon is explained thus by the excavator: "The reason is
       clear: since the southern wall faces the citadel court, and was exposed to the viewer, it was adorned by
       a nice facade; the northern wall, on the other hand, was hidden by adjacent rooms, and therefore there
       was no reason to embellish it with special stone dressing" (*B.J.P.E.S.* 24 (1960), p. 86 (Hebrew).
       However, later on, during the later seasons of the excavations, it became clear, that precisely in the
       southern wall, there were discovered, under the level of the floor, two more courses of smoothly
       dressed stones ("superb ashlar masonry" (R.R.II, p. 50)). This indicates that the present floor does not
       belong to the original phase of the building, in which these two courses were intended to have been
       exposed to the viewers' eyes.
    b. The different technique of the wall masonry and the various levels of their foundations are attributed
       to different gangs of masons: "It would therefore seem that the building was heterogeneously
       constructed from the start, perhaps by different teams of builders" (ibid, p. 28).
    c. The "one phase" theory was actually shattered by the excavations near the building gate. This is clear
       when one compares the excavator's observations in *R.R.I.* (p. 35 ff.,) with those of *R.R.II* (p.25 ff.).
       The finds indicated the existence of two structural phases at least; nevertheless, this is how the data
       were explained away: "It is now clear why the pier of the gateway (which, as already stated is as much
       as 2 m. thick) was constructed *in two parts* (italics are mine, here and below - Y.Y.). The gateway was
       actually *let into the casemate wall,* so that the inner part of the pier is flush with the line of the outer
       defence-wall, the foundations of which *extended under the portal of the gateway too.* To the outer
       side of this wall the imposing structure of massive stones *was then added,* both to strengthen the
       defences of the gateway and also to add to the grandeur of its appearance (ibid, p. 26).
    d. Even the lack of a well-conceived plan for the building's inner units did not deter the excavator from
       the one phase idea; instead we are just told that "the constructional work is not uniform, and the
       building was, so to speak, a composite made up of various disparate units" (ibid, p. 27).
    e. The stratigraphical conclusion of the excavator becomes completely incomprehensible and, in fact,
       desparate, when he tries to present a homogenous and continuous line of what he calls the wall of
       the "outer citadel" (of which the discovery was "the great surprise of this (1962 - Y.Y.) season"
       (*R.R.II,* p. 51). The thickness of this 'homogeneous' line varies (see ibid., plan in fig. 6) and the
       building technique and stone dressing of its various sections are radically different from each other.
       When a well-built section of fine ashlar was found, in contrast to the very crude stones of other
       sections ("unusual in the outer defence wall" - ibid, p. 52) it is explained by the possibility that "an
       outer gateway stood here" (ibid). Under the thick fill (containing 'lamelekh' stamp impressions)
       contemporary - according to the excavator - with the wall, an ancient quarry was found "with some
       of the quarried stones still *in situ.* The stones resemble in size and workmanship the blocks of the
       Iron Age citadel; however the situation of the quarry below the filling of the wall shows that it
       antedates the construction of the latter" (ibid. p. 52). The "one phase" idea leaves the excavator no

way out but to say that it "belongs with most probability to stratum VB" (ibid). As noticed above, the "stratum VB" is in fact the original stratum of the main (and only) monumental building. In fact the discovery of the stones in the quarry suggests that the construction of the building in its original phase, was perhaps never finished (see below).

   f. Last, but not least: we already mentioned the important discovery of the window balustrade with the Proto-Ionic capitals. In the 1960 season, a pillar of this balustrade was found "in the filling under the floor of room 329" (R.R.I p. 39). At that time - before the discovery of the other parts of the balustrade with the decorative motif - it reminded the excavator of "the bases of incense-burners made of stone or clay" (ibid). The fact that the columns was found in the filling under the floor of the "one phase" building, compelled the excavator to suggest that it was "thrown in amongst the rubble of the filling" because it was "seemingly not completed, perhaps because of a mistake or break that occured during the work" (ibid). This desperate suggestion, is even more awkward than it sounds, because this column is the only one which was found "more or less intact". If indeed the finish of this more or less complete column was not completed, it may suggest rather, that the original building was not fully finished, when it was destroyed abruptly and its decorative architectural elements were broken and scattered. This possibility is strengthened also by the fact that most of the elements of the balustrade, which were found not in the filling, and are made of soft limestone, looked brand new when found (ibid, p. 57) and that the finish of another column was not completed since it lacked the hole for securing the abacus (ibid). The short reign of Athaliah, and the probability that the House of Ba'al was built in the latter part of her reign when her grip on the throne was consolidated, might have caused the building not to have been completely finished, when it was utterly destroyed by Jehoiada.

39.   This may explain the fact that in the fill of the floor, *lamelekh* impressions of both types, were found. On the dating problems of the stamps and the stratigraphy of Lachish and Ramath-Rahel, see now H. Darrel Lance, "The Royal Stamps and the Kingdom of Josia", *H.T.R.,* 84 (1971) pp. 315-332. The excavator of Ramath-Rahel does not use the *sherds* found *on* the floor for dating purposes, objectively, but rather on historical grounds. Thus a seal impression bearing the name *tnhm mgn* (of which seven identical ones were found in Lachish, Stratum III, which according to one school of thought - with which the excavator is in accord - is of the 8th century B.C.) was found in locus 468 "in which many objects from stratum VA were unearthed" (*R.R.II,* p. 32) Nevertheless, the excavator ascribes it (obviously because of the Lachish finds) to stratum VB "since the find in question is only a fragment of a handle and not a complete vessel *in situ*" (ibid, and see also p. 33). Yet, the broken handle bearing the impression of *'lyqm* the valet of *ywkn* - also found on the floor, is ascribed to stratum VA; the reasoning for this conclusion is a typical example of the vicious circle created by first fixing a date for a stratum on historical arguments, then ascribing an artifact to this stratum, and finally seeing in this object a confirmation for the date of the stratum in question: "Once again it must be borne in mind that the find in question (i.e. the impression - Y.Y.) is not a whole vessel, but only a fragment of a handle, which makes it difficult to assign it with absolute certainty to a definite stratum. However, in view of Albright's suggestion (that Elyaqim was an official in the entourage of King Jehoiachin - a suggestion which is in no way absolutely proven - Y.Y.) this stamp must be dated to the years immediately preceding the destruction of the First Temple, and in that case it may be safely assigned to stratum VA" (ibid.).

40.   Particularly "suspicious" as being a temple, is the large ashlar-built rectangular structure (whose main locus is 758) which is oriented north-south, and consisted in all probability of a court and (at least) two inner elements - see the plan in *RRII,* Fig. 6 and ibid. p. 49. It is interesting to note that near this building "the scarp of the rock remained about 2 m. higher" (ibid. p. 55). Could it be a platform for an altar? This locus is connected with an underground water reservoir and channels. Although the reservoir was later re-used in the Roman period (as ascertained in a recent visit on the spot, where Roman sherds were found in the plaster) it may have been hewn during Iron Age periods. It is worthwhile noting that most of the portions of the window balustrade, were found in this area - although clearly thrown in during later periods as attested by the context of the fill (ibid).

41.   G. Dalman, *Orte und Wege Jesu,* (3rd Ed.) p.21.

42.   B. Maisler (=Mazar) *Journal of the Jewish Palestine Exploration Society,* Jerusalem (1934) pp. 9-10 (Hebrew).

SCRIBES ET GRAVEURS A JERUSALEM VERS 700 AV. J.–C.
by Jean Prignaud

"It is true that a certain amount of epigraphic material of the period of Hebrew kingdoms has been found. None in itself, however, provides dating for a phase in the history of a site, for it so happens that none providing exact chronological data has been found *in situ* on a site, and the knowledge of ancient Hebrew epigraphy is not yet exact; the epigraphic material has to be dated from its find-spot, and not vice versa."

(Kathleen M. KENYON, *Archaeology in the Holy Land,* London,[3] 1970, p. 33)

Depuis que ces lignes ont été écrites[1], les fouilles archéologiques poursuivies dans le pays ont mis au jour une quantité notable de nouveau matériel épigraphique en hébreu ancien, souvent associé à un contexte stratigraphique (sinon chronologique) précis. Le travail de Miss Kenyon à Jérusalem entre 1961 et 1967 a fourni dans ce domaine une contribution non négligeable.[2] En 1967, les toutes dernières semaines de la dernière campagne ont été marquées par la découverte d'une grotte qui contenait près de 1300 pièces de poterie, dont plusieurs en bon état de conservation. Certains de ces vases portent des épigraphes qui font l'objet de la présente étude. Dès le rapport préliminaire qui a suivi cette campagne Miss Kenyon a donné des indications chronologiques assez précises pour l'ensemble de ce matériel:[3] autour de 700 avant J.–C. et sûrement pas plus bas que 650: en tout cas, on peut supposer que le dépôt des vases dans ce qui semble avoir été une *favissa*[4] s'est poursuivi sur une période relativement étendue. On peut donc supposer, en attendant la publication définitive, que le matériel de "Jerusalem Cave I" est sensiblement contemporain du règne d'Ezéchias en Juda, de l'activité du prophète Isaïe, et de l'inscription du canal de Siloé.

Le matériel provenant de la grotte I et proposé à l'examen épigraphique comporte seize numéros qui se répartissent ainsi:[5] trois inscriptions complètes (nº 127, 213, 757), cinq inscriptions fragmentaires (nº 175, 1097, 1098, 1099, 1199), quatre "marques" de propriétaire ou de destination, signes ou symboles plutôt que lettres (nº 346, 543, 1040, 1069); quatre autres tessons (nº 1196, 1197, 1198, 1200) portent des incisions ou des éraflures peut-être accidentelles, trop fragmentaires pour qu'on en puisse rien tirer; une dix-septième pièce, nº 750, est un très beau décor floral incisé qui relève à coup sûr de l'art de la gravure mais pas de l'épigraphie.[6]

Tous ces épigraphes ont été exécutés après cuisson du vase, et sur le vase complet: ce ne sont pas des ostraca.[7] Deux pièces ont été gravées au trait ou incisées (nº 127 et 757). La troisième inscription complète, nº 213, a été gravée par piquetage: c'est la même technique qui a servi à l'exécution des nº 175, 1097, 1098, 1099, 1199. Nous limiterons à ces huit pièces la présente publication. Les marques sur anses se répartissent, du point de vue de la gravure, entre le piquetage (nº 543, 1069) et l'incision au trait (nº 346, 1040): elles feront l'objet d'une autre publication, avec du matériel comparable provenant également des fouilles de Miss Kenyon à Jérusalem.

Inventaire des pièces épigraphiques.

nº 127.[8] Figure 1, planche XXIa.

Le profil dessiné après recollage des deux tessons suggère de classer le vase avec un type de cruche à haut col allant en se resserrant vers l'ouverture.[9] L'inscription est complète, tout entière sur l'un des fragments préservés, à la panse du vase. L'incision est assez profonde pour avoir enlevé toute la couverte lustrée et sombre, et entamé la pâte plus claire.

L'inscription comporte trois lettres suivies d'un point en haut. Son déchiffrement ne fait aucune difficulté: *ṣ f n ·*

Ce nom ne se lit pas tel quel dans la Bible, où l'on trouve la forme théophore Sophonie, *ṣ f n y h w* ; il est, en revanche, déjà bien attesté dans l'épigraphie du pays biblique.[10] Martin Noth l'a inclus dans son étude classique[11] et il renvoie à deux passages bibliques pour la signification de ce "Dankname": Ps 27, 5 et 31, 21.

nº 757.[12] Figure 2, planche XXIb.

Bien que restaurée à partir de plusieurs fragments, cette cruchette est complète à l'exception d'une partie du

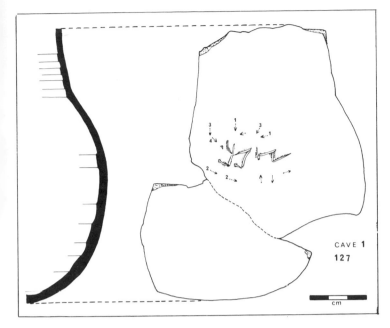

Fig 1.

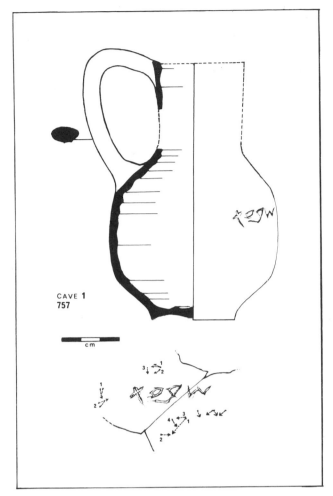

Fig 2.

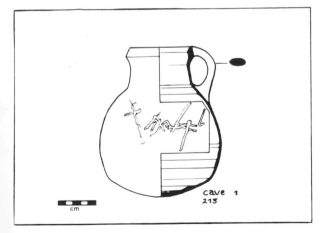

Fig 3.

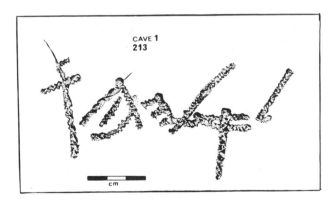

Fig 4.

col. Bien que traversée par une cassure, l'inscription à la panse du vase est, elle aussi, complète. Elle comporte quatre lettres, sans difficulté de déchiffrement: š b ʿ t et non suivies d'un trait ou d'un point comme l'inscription nº 127.

L'onomastique biblique connait la forme š b ʿ[13]: Diringer[14] a proposé d'en voir une variante dans la forme que porte notre cruchette et qu'il avait trouvée sur un sceau de provenance incertaine.

nº 213.[15] Figures 3, 4, planche XXIc XXIIa, b.

Cette cruche est intacte, sauf pour une écaille enlevée à la lèvre. L'inscription à la panse comporte six lettres: l ' l y h w non suivies d'une ponctuation.

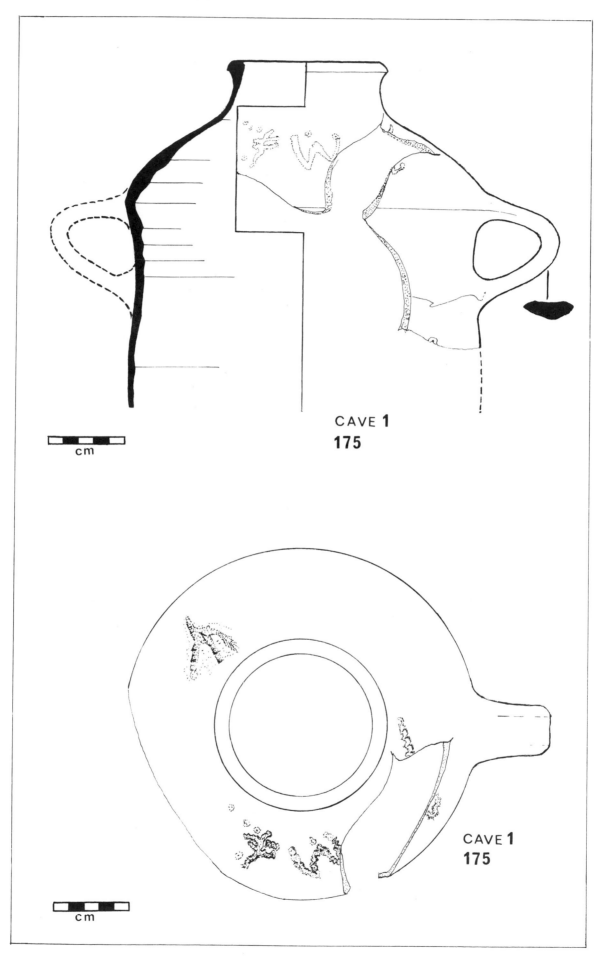

CAVE **1**
175

CAVE **1**
175

Fig 5.

Le nom d'Elie est trop connu pour qu'il soit nécessaire de proposer ici des références bibliques. Mais c'est peut-être la première fois qu'il est attesté dans l'épigraphie locale. On notera surtout la forme théophore, par contraste avec l'hypocoristique du n° 127.

A la différence des deux pièces précédentes, le nom est précédé ici d'un *lamed* d'appartenance.[16]

n° 175.[17] Figure 5, planche XXIIc.

La partie supérieure de cette jarre a été restaurée à partir de nombreux fragments; des lacunes subsistent, dont une, malheureusement, affecte l'inscription gravée au piqueté sur l'épaule. Cette inscription comprend deux parties distinctes, de part et d'autre des anses.

La première partie de l'inscription comprend trois lettres de lecture certaine, même si la première est incomplète: *l[ ] š '* sans ponctuation finale. L'espace vide qui suit le *lamed,* dans la cassure, laisse la place pour une autre lettre du format de cette inscription et on proposera d'y restituer un *alef*: le nom *'s '* est bien attesté dans les ostraca de Samarie.[18]

La seconde partie de l'inscription se compose d'un seul signe, isolé de l'autre coté de l'anse manquante. La forme peut évoquer un *kaf* archaïque ou un *shin* tardif: c'est une palmette simple. Ce motif décoratif ou symbolique n'est pas rare sur les anses de vases en particulier. Nous en avons deux exemples dans ce même lot de la Grotte I, n° 543 et 1069. Comme on l'a dit plus haut, ce matériel fait, avec des pièces semblables, l'objet d'une publication distincte.

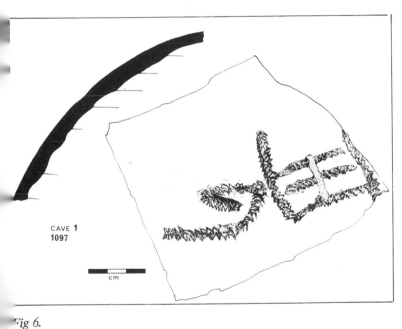

Fig 6.

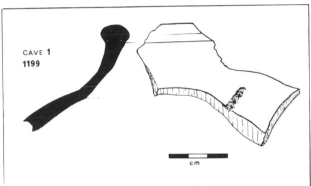

Fig 7.

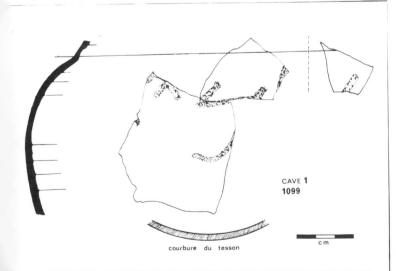

Fig 8.

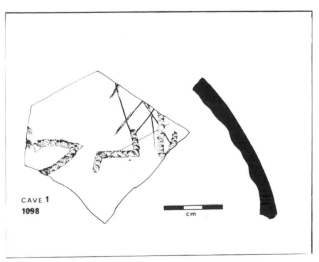

Fig 9.

140

Plate XXI

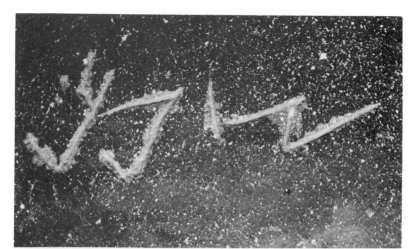

a.

b.

c.

Plate XXII

a.

b.

c.

Plate XXIII

a.

b.

c.

d.

n° 1097. [19] Figure 6, planche XXIIIa.

La disposition adoptée sur le dessin pour ce tesson de grosse jarre est celle suggérée par les marques du faconnage. L'inscription figurait donc sans doute sur une épaule très arrondie.

Les deux lettres préservées sont claires: *ḥ b*. Au milieu de la lettre *ḥet* un trait vertical d'un tracé profond (alors que la gravure des lettres est assez superficielle) a été exécuté avant la cuisson du vase.

n° 1199. [20] Figure 7, planche XXIIIb.

A l'intérieur de ce fragment de col de jarre et sur la lèvre, il y a des traces de feu; la couleur de la pâte à la section a été modifiée aussi profondément par ce feu qui, selon toute probabilité, a été allumé à l'intérieur du vase encore entier.

Le fragment de lettre gravé qui subsiste seul est disposé de telle sorte qu'il ne peut s'agir que de la partie supérieure de la hampe d'un *lamed*.

n° 1099. [21] Figure 8, planche XXIIIc.

Deux des trois tessons préservés de ce vase indiquent la naissance du col, mais la position du plus petit, par rapport aux deux autres tessons qui se raccordent entre eux, n'est pas assurée: il pourrait figurer sur le dessin aussi bien à gauche qu'à droite du reste.

On notera que l'inscription est gravée cette fois non pas sur la panse d'une cruche, mais à la base du col. La portion de lettre qui apparait sur le petit tesson isolé appartient à un *lamed,* cf. les remarques sur le n° 1199, ci-dessus. La grande lettre à cheval sur la cassure entre les deux autres tessons est un *noun,* et ce qui la suit représente vraisemblablement la partie inférieure d'un *hé*. A la cassure, tout à gauche, une trace signale une hampe ou un jambage inférieur rectiligne et incliné vers la droite, c'est-à-dire une lettre du type *gimel,* etc. Tout à droite, sur l'autre tesson, au-dessus du *noun,* une trace à la cassure suggère un *lamed*.

n° 1098. [22] Figure 9, planche XXIIId.

Ce tesson est disposé sur le dessin en fonction des marques du faconnage: il semble s'agir, comme pour le n° 1099, d'une inscription sur l'épaule arrondie d'une jarre. Le treillis qu'on observe dans la partie supérieure droite est incisé assez superficiellement après la cuisson, mais il est visiblement antérieur à la gravure des signes. Les marques à gauche à la cassure sont légères et pas de la même technique que les signes. Il y a donc trois signes conservés, dont celui du milieu est seul complet.

Nous avons présenté ces huit épigraphes ou fragments d'épigraphes selon l'ordre croissant de difficulté de lecture. Avant de revenir sur la paléographie de ces inscriptions, nous voudrions proposer quelques réflexions sur leur technique d'exécution.

L'art de la gravure.

Il est évident au premier coup d'oeil que nous avons affaire à deux techniques de gravure absolument différentes: les deux premières pièces sont incisées au trait (avec d'ailleurs entre elles des différences notables), tandis que les six autres présentent un aspect discontinu du tracé, un "piqueté".

Les n° 127 et 757 ont été incisés semble-t-il avec une pointe. Cette technique de gravure sur argile, lorsqu'elle est appliquée à la surface du vase entre le faconnage et la cuisson, pendant la période de séchage durant laquelle la pâte perd progressivement sa malléabilité, peut permettre à un scripteur habile des effets calligraphiques recherchés, imitant par exemple les pleins et les déliés de l'écriture à la "plume".[23] Mais dans le groupe d'épigraphes sorti de la Grotte I en 1967, nous n'avons trouvé qu'un seul tracé exécuté ainsi avant la cuisson: sur le n° 1097, et nous avons vu qu'il n'appartenait d'ailleurs pas à l'écriture, gravée plus tard, après cuisson, à la surface de la jarre. Après la cuisson du vase, la surface de l'argile présente un support d'écriture relativement dur et paradoxalement fragile. Il est encore possible, cependant, d'obtenir dans ces conditions un effet calligraphique imité de la "plume", avec pleins et déliés.[24] Les scripteurs des deux inscriptions examinées à présent se sont contentés de reproduire des formes de lettres, sans chercher d'effet calligraphique particulier. Mais ce ne sont pas de simples graffiti hâtivement tracés. On peut observer le résultat d'un certain nombre de gestes: l'amincissement d'un trait, éventuellement un trait de fuite si la pointe a quelque peu glissé, indiquent probablement la direction d'un tracé (voyez dans le n° 127, le trait horizontal inférieur du *çadé,* la tête du *pé*); inversement, une attaque peut être signalée par épaississement du trait (n° 127, le trait à la base du *pé* qui revient sur le jambage), parfois par un éclat enlevé à la surface; il y a aussi des "repentirs" (n° 757, le *cain* et le *taw*) qui révèlent le souci d'arriver à une forme bien précise, qu'on a dans l'oeil ou peut-être sous les yeux.[25] Les scripteurs des n° 127 et 757 étaient-ils des gens qui savaient écrire ou copiaient-ils un modèle, une "minute"? La comparaison paléographique aidera peut-être à répondre à cette question, mais nous allons voir en revanche que, dans le cas du second groupe d'épigraphes, l'observation de la technique de gravure apporte une réponse intéressante.

En passant au nº 213, la différence de technique est frappante: au lieu d'un tracé délié et fin (nº 127) ou encore d'un tracé apparemment moins sur (nº 757) puisqu'il comporte des repentirs pour arriver à la forme souhaitée, mais qui demeure un tracé continu, nous avons ici l'apparence d'un pointillé [26]. De nombreuses petites écailles ont été enlevées de la surface du vase, à petits coups obliques, presque tangents à cette surface. Les coups sont généralement très rapprochés mais demeurent pratiquement toujours distincts, et le dessinateur [27] a consacré un soin considérable à reproduire tous les impacts de l'outil. En aucun cas la profondeur de la gravure ne dépasse trois dixièmes de millimètres.

La hampe de la lettre *alef* et celle de la lettre *waw* montrent clairement la disposition des impacts légèrement obliques par rapport à la direction générale du trait; ils ont été sans doute appliqués de haut en bas et de gauche à droite. A première vue, la hampe des deux *lamed* peut donner l'impression d'un double impact, suggérant une gravure en épis ou l'utilisation d'un outil à deux dents. Il est plus probable que le même outil a été utilisé pour toute l'inscription, une sorte de ciselet sans doute et que la différence réside dans un espacement moindre des impacts dans le cas des *lamed.* Un angle de frappe légèrement différent a pu influer aussi sur l'effet produit.

On pense que la même technique de piquetage a été utilisée pour les nº 175, 1098, 1099 et 1199. Une pâte à plus gros grain (175) donne évidemment une impression un peu différente d'une pâte plus fine (1099). En revanche, le nº 1097 appelle d'autres observations [28].

Le fragment 1097 cumule trois techniques différentes:
1- un trait vertical incisé avant cuisson a servi d'axe de symétrie au graveur pour disposer le *ḥet*:
2- les trois barres horizontales du *ḥet* ont été gravées de la même façon, le stylet dirigé du bas vers le haut et de la droite vers la gauche, l'outil incliné de 45 degrés par rapport à l'horizontalité du trait; la gravure a été accomplie de la droite vers la gauche; l'arête supérieure du trait est plus vive; les coups de stylet obliques sont très rapprochés et souvent se superposent.
3- Les barres verticales du *ḥet* et le *bet* en son entier témoignent d'une autre technique de gravure. Le stylet, très vraisemblablement, est le même: il n'y a pas de raison objective qu'il soit différent. Les gestes du graveur sont cependant plus longs, plus aérés, moins serrés. On y reconnaît que le stylet utilisé fut, d'une part, très pointu, et, d'autre part, en métal très résistant, capable sans s'émousser trop vite d'entamer la matière dure qu'est la terre cuite.

La barre verticale gauche du *ḥet* et la queue du *bet* ont été gravées sans percuteur sur le stylet. En effet, le tracé est composé de "griffures" en lignes brisées continues, ce qui exclut le geste de relever l'outil. La largeur du tracé est obtenue par superposition des lignes brisées, ce qui donne l'aspect enchevêtré de griffures. [29]

La symétrie est telle parfois entre deux lignes brisées contiguës que nous sommes invités à nous demander si le graveur n'a pas utilisé un stylet à deux pointes [30] Le trait inférieur de la tete du *bet* a été "griffé" de la manière que nous avons décrite, mais l'angle de brisure des lignes est très aigu; le geste du graveur redevient très serré et rapide; les "griffures" sont superficielles, la pression sur le stylet ayant été plus légère qu'ailleurs. C'est pour cela que le bord supérieur du trait inférieur de la tête du *bet* est marqué par une accentuation rectiligne qui vise à accuser un relief jugé insuffisant en cet endroit.

Je voudrais revenir un instant au nº 213 pour une dernière observation. En haut et à droite de deux lettres, le *hé* et le *waw,* on remarque deux traits longs et minces comme des traits de fuite. On pourrait penser à un raté du graveur, mais un même outil pourrait-il produire des effets de gouge, comme à la hampe du *waw,* et un "dérapage" effilé comme à sa tête? Ces traits sont bien plutôt d'authentiques maladresses imputables non pas au graveur, mais à celui qui a d'avance incisé au trait, d'un tracé très léger, le dessin des lettres à exécuter ensuite par l'artisan. Le trait en haut du *hé* est particulièrement léger; celui au sommet du *waw* est assez profond: le graveur n'a pas réussi à en effacer complètement la marque même dans la partie supérieure de la tête du *waw,* où on la distingue nettement sur la droite du piqueté. Cette dernière observation sur la gravure du nº 213 suggère que celui qui a dessiné au trait le modèle à reproduire et le graveur sont deux personnes distinctes. Le premier est un scribe, un calligraphe habitué à la "plume" (l'analyse paléographique le confirmera): il n'a pas nécessairement l'habileté du second, artisan graveur capable de travailler la surface dure d'un vase fragile.

Car ces inscriptions sont d'abord des oeuvres d'art. Le travail en est comparable à celui du graveur sur pierre ou sur métal, peut-etre mieux connu. [31] Il y fallait bien sûr une main plus légère, car si la surface oppose une résistance, le vase lui-même est un volume fragile: un coup de percuteur trop violent, une inclinaison fautive de l'outil suffisait à le faire voler en éclat ou du moins à le fêler.[32] Même si les vases d'argile sont souvent produits en série et sont peu coûteux, les réalisations de cet art de la gravure qui nous sont parvenues sont assez peu nombreuses: peu de gens devaient être capables de les exécuter. A coup sûr, un vase quelconque prenait un surcroit de valeur lorsqu'il sortait des mains du graveur.

On vient de dire que ces pièces sont, en somme, assez rares. Le professeur Avigad qui, sauf erreur, a été le premier à attirer l'attention sur cette technique de gravure,[33] a paru exprimer une opinion contraire.[34] Il énumère successivement: une "carafe" qui est une des deux pièces inédites qu'il publie dans cet article; une autre carafe provenant aussi de la région d'Hébron;[35] une troisième, encore inédite, provenant de Tel Arad;[36] puis, notre pièce nº 213;[37] enfin, un certain nombre de tessons provenant de fouilles récentes à Jérusalem;[38] nous y ajouterons donc les six pièces présentées ici (cinq, puisque 213 est déjà compté!) et un certain nombre de fragments d'anses, dont nous avons parlé et qui font l'objet d'une publication distincte: tout cela de même technique d'exécution, et tout cela de Jérusalem. Cela fait au total une trentaine de pièces; ce n'est peut-être pas "beaucoup" dans l'absolu, mais c'est beaucoup pour Jérusalem où, à trois exceptions près, toutes les pièces mentionnées ont été trouvées. Le professeur Avigad a sûrement raison de dire que c'est une technique judéenne, et je suis tenté de dire: peut-être même une technique hiérosolomytaine, car les trois pièces de la région d'Hébron et d'Arad peuvent bien venir de Jerusalem.[39]

Paléographie

Nos deux groupes d'épigraphes, les nº 127 et 757 d'un côté (le groupe incisé) et les six autres numéros de l'autre (le groupe piqueté) ne se distinguent pas seulement par la façon de la gravure: ils diffèrent aussi par la forme des lettres. Déjà on aura noté d'un côté le tracé rectiligne et anguleux, de l'autre la tendance aux courbes (le *hé* du nº 213!). On peut dans quelques cas pousser la comparaison lettre à lettre. Comparez le jambage inférieur du *bet* de 1097 et celui de 757, le jambage du *noun* de 1099 et celui de 127 (et aussi celui du *pé*, morphologiquement comparable), le tracé du *shin* de 175 et celui de 757. D'un côté, un tracé continu, incurvé; de l'autre, un tracé discontinu et anguleux. On ne pourrait trouver une meilleure illustration du passage dans lequel Diringer attire l'attention sur les différences entre écriture incisée et écriture à la "plume" en fonction de la résistance différente des supports.[40]

En effet, les graveurs du second groupe ne s'efforcent pas de reproduire une image mentale des lettres: ils suivent avec le ciseau un modèle tracé d'avance à la surface du vase; tracé légèrement à la pointe (nº 213), il garde toute la souplesse de l'écriture à la plume, le ductus cursif du scribe. Dès lors, les épigraphes de la Grotte I apportent du matériel comparatif aussi bien au corpus des inscriptions incisées, lapidaires, etc., qu'à celui des ostraca à l'encre des VIIIème-VIIème siècles.

Cette observation du caractère "secondaire" de ces inscriptions gravées contribuera peut-être à préciser ce qu'on entend en épigraphie hébraïque par écriture lapidaire. Un monument d'écriture lapidaire peut être fort normalement réalisé en deux temps: c'est-à-dire que le lapicide ou le graveur copie un modèle qu'il a sous les yeux, à côté, ou directement en place sur la surface à graver. C'est une opération très différente de celle qui consiste à reproduire par incision, directement, l'image mentale qu'on a des lettres. Le graveur d'une inscription "secondaire" n'est pas nécessairement un illettré. Ce qui importe, c'est que le modèle qui s'impose à lui n'a pas été exécuté vraiment dans les conditions du travail lapidaire, et que dès lors le type d'écriture est, comme on le voit bien ici, susceptible d'un ductus beaucoup plus cursif.[41] Il n'est sans doute pas exagéré de dire que le style lapidaire est mieux représenté par le groupe incisé (nº 127 et 757) que par le groupe piqueté.

Le *bet* de 757 est plus archaïque que celui de 1097, toute question de gravure mise à part. Le *çadé* de 127 n'a pas de petit crochet revenant vers la gauche, à l'extrémité droite du trait horizontal inférieur; en revanche, le *yod* de 213 a ce crochet. Le nom *ç f n* (nº 127) est une forme hypocoristique, tandis que le nom *' l y h w* (nº 213) est un théophore pleinement développé. On a donc peut-être quelques indices pour placer le groupe incisé avant le groupe piqueté, à l'intérieur de la période "passablement longue" que Miss Kenyon supposait pour le dépôt des vases dans la grotte.[42]

L'inscription nº 1098 nous a laissé jusqu'ici avec un problème de déchiffrement. On peut suggérer que le premier signe, à droite, est un *lamed*, et le troisième, à gauche, est un *pé*. Le signe central pourrait être un *zayin*: l'ensemble de l'inscription n'est pas couché sur la "ligne" d'écriture de façon très habituelle (on aura noté la verticalité du *lamed*); on trouve des parallèles à une telle forme dans le développement de l'écriture araméenne[43] ainsi que dans le domaine phénicien.[44] Il demeure que le nº 1098 détonne paléographiquement dans le groupe des épigraphes de la grotte I.

Dès sa découverte [45] Miss Kenyon a suggéré de voir, dans cette grotte remplie de poterie, une *favissa.* Cette interprétation n'est pas contredite par la présence de ces épigraphes. Les noms gravés sont ceux de propriétaires, ou, mieux, de donateurs d'offrandes. Une fois le rite accompli, les vases étaient soustraits à l'usage profane et ils se sont entassés ici pendant peut-etre plus d'un siècle.

References

1. La première édition de *Archaeology in the Holy Land,* (London, 1960).

2. Les lecteurs de langue française ont pu suivre le déroulement de ces sept campagnes de fouilles dans la *Chronique archéologique* de la *Revue Biblique,* ainsi que dans un cahier de *Bible et Terre Sainte,* n° 114, sept.-oct. 1969, en particulier: "Jérusalem dans l'Ancien Testament", par M. le professeur Jacques Briend, de l'Institut catholique de Paris.

3. K. M. Kenyon, "Excavations in Jerusalem 1967", *P.E.Q.,* 100 (1968), pp. 108-109: "The pottery suggests a date of ± 700 B.C. It certainly does not belong to the latter part of the seventh century B.C., but seventh-century forms are beginning to appear. It is of course difficult to say how long deposits of vessels continued to be made. It is therefore advisable at the present stage in the study of the finds to allow a fairly wide margin."

4. Cf. *RB.* LXXV (1968), p. 423.

5. La numérotation est celle du catalogue d' enregistrement des fouilles, *Jerusalem Register for Cave I,* 1967. Nous donnerons en note pour chaque pièce analysée la description de l'objet empruntée à ce catalogue.

6. A l'exception de la pièce n° 346, tout le matériel énuméré ci-dessus se trouve au Département des Antiquités à Jérusalem.

7. Contre RB. LXXV (1968), p. 423.

8. *Register,* p. 21: "Jug. Sherd with inscription. Red ware, fairly close. Some small and some large white grits, wheel-made, dull red slip outside. Hard smooth surface. Inscription incised. Shoulder sherd only. Mended."

9. Type qui est aussi celui du n° 750, anépigraphe non publié ici. C'est, me semble-t-il, le type représenté par le n° 14 de la figure 7, p. 81, dans K. M. KENYON, *Jerusalem. Excavating 3000 Years of History* (London 1967); voir aussi la planche en couleurs XVII, face à la p. 158.

10. David DIRINGER, *Le iscrizioni antico-ebraiche palestinesi,* (Firenze, 1934), pp. 120-122: une estampille de Tell Zakariya et trois estampilles de Tell Judeideh; Sabatino MOSCATI, *L'epigrafia ebraica antica 1935-1950,* (Roma, 1951), pp. 73-75: deux estampilles de Tell ed-Duweir et une estampille de Tell er-Rumeileh.

11. Martin NOTH, *Die israelitischen Personennamen im Rahmen der gemeinsemitischen Namengebung,* (Stuttgart, 1928), p. 178.

12. *Register,* p. 143: "Juglet with inscription. Pink ware with grey exterior at one side, rest pink through, close, some white grits, wheelmade. Creamy wash. Inscription scratched after firing. Complete handle to rim, complete section."

13. M. NOTH, *op. cit.,* p. 146.

14. *D. Diringer, op. cit.,* p. 233.

15. *Register,* p. 37: "Jug. Light red ware, with many fine grey and some white grits. Wheel-made. Complete. Incised inscription on body on one side." - Une photographie de cette cruche a paru dans le rapport préliminaire, *PEQ,* 100 (1968), pl. XXXV, C et le vase a figuré dans l'exposition "*Inscriptions Reveal-Documents from the time of the Bible, the Mishna and the Talmud*" au musée de Jérusalem, hiver 1973-printemps 1974.

16. Les inscriptions sur vases complets du nom du possesseur (ou du dédicataire?) semblent s'écrire indifféremment avec ou sans le *lamed.* Un autre exemple, avec *lamed,* provenant aussi des fouilles de Miss Kenyon à Jérusalem, a fait naguère l'objet d'une analyse calligraphique: *RB.,* LXXVII (1970), pp. 59-67 et pl. Ib. La controverse récente sur la signification du *lamed* dans les ostraca de Samarie ne concerne pas directement le type d'inscriptions dont nous nous occupons ici; on en retrouvera aisément la bibliographie à partir du dernier article paru, à ma connaissance, sur le sujet: A. F. RAINEY, *PEQ.,* CII (1970), pp. 45-51.

17. *Register,* p. 30: "Small storage jar, plus sherds marked. Pink-red ware, grey core, close ware, many small grits. Wheel-made, wet smooth. Rim and part of neck, shoulder with handle. Much of body and all base missing. Mended. Inscription on shoulder."

18. Voir par exemple, D. DIRINGER, *op. cit.,* pp. 42-43, et cf. M NOTH, *op. cit., sub verbo.* Dans sa thèse encore inédite, que j'ai pu consulter a la bibliothèque de L'Ecole biblique de Jérusalem, M. André Lemaire relève des parallèles punique et araméen à ce nom, qu'il rapproche aussi des formes 'š b ' l et 'š y h w: André LEMAIRE, *Les ostraca hébreux de l'époque royale israélite,* Thèse de doctorat de IIIème cycle présentée à la Faculté des Lettres de l'Université de Paris III, juin 1973; une partie au moins de cet important

travail doit paraître prochainement dans la collection L.A.P.O. (Littératures anciennes du Proche Orient, Paris, éditions du Cerf).

19. *Register,* p. 215: "Storage jar (incised sherd). Ware: pinkish buff on outside. Core and inside grey. Medium sized white grits. Wheel-made. Two incised Hebrew characters complete."

20. *Register,* p. 236: "Storage jar rim/body sherd (incised). Ware: outside fired buff coloured with inner layer of core and inside charcoal. Fairly smooth ware with fine white grits. Wheel-made. Only a portion of one Hebrew (?) character incised remains. Small section of rim and neck but many sherds of same material which don't make up."

21. *Register.* p. 216: "Jug sherds (inscribed). Ware: red on outside (slip?). Core and inside orange. Clay fairly fine. Wheel-made. Body sherds only. Incised Hebrew characters, not complete."

22. *Register,* p. 215: "Storage jar (inscribed sherd). Ware: brown outside. Core grey to the inside. Very fine white grits in outer brown layer of clay changing to more coarse material in grey section of core. Wheel-made. One incised Hebrew character complete, others broken."

23. Nous avons souligné cet effet calligraphique à propos d'une anse provenant des fouilles de Miss Kenyon à Jérusalem et qui porte une curieuse inscription incisée avant la cuisson: N Q M . G D L , cf. *RB,* LXXVII (1970), pp. 50-59 et pl. I a.

24. Cf. l'inscription L Y S M ' ' L . , également de Jérusalem, *RB,* LXXVII (1970), pp. 59-67 et pl. I b.

25. Le résultat de ces observations a été reporté graphiquement sur les dessins en fac-similé des inscriptions, les flèches indiquant la direction du tracé (une double flèche signalant un "repentir") et les chiffres l'ordre dans lequel les différents traits ont pu être tracés (ordre suggéré par des chevauchements et des dépassements).

26. D'un "piqueté", si l'on évoque le tailleur de pierre qui "pique" un moellon, c'est-à-dire qui le taille de telle sorte que chaque coup y laisse sa trace. "Un texte *inscrit* a u *ciseau* ou au *burin* est un *piqueté,* si les *graphismes* s'y présentent sous la forme de trous espacés (. . .), ou un *gravé,* s'ils sont tracés en sillons continus (. . .); il peut arriver que les *graphismes* soient réalisés à la fois en *piqueté* et en *gravé,* en *piqueté-gravé,* dirons-nous, si des sillons relient les trous entre eux" (André BATAILLE, *Pour une terminologie en paléographie grecque,* (Paris, Librairie C. Klincsieck, 1954) p. 4.

27. Mon confrère Jean-Baptiste Humbert avec qui j'ai longuement discuté les observations présentées ici. Ma gratitude va aussi à Jean-Michel de Tarragon, qui a préparé plusieurs des photographies.

28. Les paragraphes consacrés au n° 1097 sont tout entiers de Jean-Baptiste Humbert.

29. Après expérimentation, nous avons obtenu un résultat similaire en tenant un stylet comme on tient un crayon entre les doigts et en faisant jouer le poignet.

30. Voir surtout la partie inférieure de la barre verticale gauche du *ḥet,* le jambage final du *bet* et les deux tracés de la tête du *bet.*

31. Voir par exemple les représentations égyptiennes de graveurs sur métal et de tailleurs de pierre: Norman de Garis Davies, *The Tomb of Rekhmiré at Thebes* (The Metropolitan Museum of Art Egyptian Expedition, vol. XI), II, (New York, 1943), pl. LV et LX.

32. Je suggère aux épigraphistes d'essayer avec la potiche du salon.

33. N. Avigad, "Two Hebrew Inscriptions on Wine-Jars," *IEJ,* XXII, (1972), pp. 1-9 et pl. 1 à 3. Dans cet article, le professeur Avigad publie une belle "carafe" qui porte sur l'épaule une inscription originale par son texte et exécutée au piqueté.

34. *IEJ,* XXII (1972), pp. 2: "The letters were incised by chiselling after the firing of the vessel. Traces of this process are clearly visible in each stroke of the letters, which show continuous notches caused by the impact of chisel and mallet. This peculiar chiselling-technique was used in many inscriptions incised in broad, bold letters on pottery vessels of this period." Et, après avoir mentionné les exemples que nous reprenons après lui, le savant épigraphiste conclut, p. 10: "There are, presumably, many other such examples. The practice of chiselling letters seems therefore to have been a common one in Judea. Considerable skill must have been required to apply this technique to so brittle a material as pottery." On voit que le seul point où nous divergeons est l'emploi du mot "many".

35. William G. Dever, "Iron Age Epigraphic Material from the Area of Khirbet El-Kôm", *HUCA* XL-XLI (1969-1970), pp. 139-204; plus spécialement pp. 169-172, fig. 13 et pl. VIII A. Le Dr. Dever dit seulement de l'inscription: "rather crudely scratched after firing."

36. *IEJ* XXII (1972), p 3 note 6: "(. . . mentioned by Y. Aharoni in *Proceedings of the Fourth World Congress of Jewish Studies,* I (Jerusalem, 1967), p. 13 (Hebrew)."

37. Cf. 1a note (15) supra.

38. *IEJ,* XXII (1972), p. 3: "A few fragmentary inscribed sherds recently found in the excavations of the Jewish Quarter in the Old City of Jerusalem also share this characteristic."

39. L'érudition du professeur Avigad m'a un peu découragé d'entreprendre la recherche d'autres exemples de cette technique. Bien entendu, en disant qu'elle est "judéenne", voire de Jérusalem, nous ne prétendons pas qu'elle y ait été inventée, nous constatons simplement qu'elle y a été pratiquée et l'état actuel de notre information suggère que le centre de cet artisanat artistique de gravure sur poterie se trouvait à Jérusalem.

40. David Diringer, "Early Hebrew Writing", *Bib Arch* XIII (1950), pp. 88-89: "Different writing materials and tools favour different kinds of pen-stroke in the quick writer, and set different artistic ideals before the calligraphers. Inscribed or incised on stone, letters tended to be made up of independant strokes or scratches of the chisel, with possibly few curves . . . " Bien sûr, des courbes de jambages, peuvent être réalisées par le graveur sur pierre, cf. les *noun, mem* ou *pé* de l'inscription du Canal de Siloé.

41. Le professeur Avigad qualifie ainsi l'écriture gravée au piqueté sur la carafe qu'il publie: "Having been incised with a chisel, the script has a lapidary appearance" (*IEJ* XXII (1972), p. 5), mais il ne vise peut-être pas par là un "style" d'écriture. Les remarques du Dr. William Dever à propos de la première inscription funéraire de khirbet el-Kôm paraissent aller dans le sens de la copie d'un modèle cursif: " . . . Inscription I is incised in good lapidary style. The letters are deeply cut with a vee-shaped chisel used with a mallet, as the series of chevron-like marks in the grooves attest. (It may be significant that certain cursive features - especially the "tics" on one *waw* (line 2) and on the *zayn* - while clear enough, are much less deliberate" (*HUCA* XL-XLI, (1969-1970), p. 153).

42. Cf. ci-dessus, note (3).

43. J. NAVEH, *The Development of the Aramaic Script* (Jerusalem, 1970).

44. J. Brian PECKHAM, *The Development of the Late Phoenician Scripts,* (Harvard University Press, 1968).

45. Cf. ci-dessus p. 1 et note (4).

46. This paper was written in the early summer of 1974.

A CHARACTERISTIC NORTH ISRAELITE HOUSE
G. Ernest Wright

During the late 1920's three singular houses of striking and precisely similar design were found by the Pacific School of Religion's Expedition at Tell en-Nasbeh, between the Jerusalem airport and Ramallah (Fig. 2 bottom). When the first was unearthed in the campaign of 1927, it was promptly interpreted as a temple, and the Director, Professor William F. Bade, held a church service in its ruins.[1] It is difficult to understand the features of the buildings that would suggest the type as a temple. Perhaps a fancied resemblance to a modern cathedral form was seen: a nave, two aisles and a chancel! More probably it was the remnant of a tendency to identify almost any important building as a temple, though the many arguments still underway in Germany, and even in the *Ecole Biblique,* about the identity of the Migdal-Shechem and its supposed courtyard "watering troughs" marked the end of that tendency.[2] Furthermore, however, the number of pillars employed in these buildings may have led to a sacred interpretation as in the case of Building IA of the Solomonic Stratum IV A at Megiddo.[3] Yet that such pillars were structural elements common in Iron II houses, beginning in Iron I, meant, unless all other explanations failed, that they were not *massebot.* W. F. Albright had proved that such pillars were characteristic of Iron II buildings during his first two seasons at Tell Beit Mirsim in 1926 and 1928.

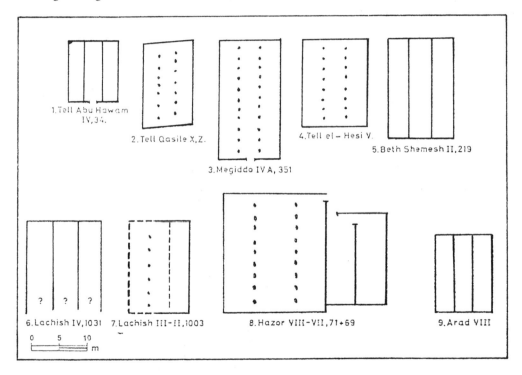

Fig 1:   Long-room Building types, from Y. Shiloh.

The temple interpretation of these buildings quickly evaporated. W. F. Albright in his attempt to interpret the Nasbeh buildings in context with newly found structures at Beth-shemesh and Lachish suggested that the long rooms would fit well with an interpretation of the structures as granaries, Hebrew *miskenot.* This interpretation has held up without serious attack, though with many private reservations,[5] until a fairly definitive article appeared by Yigal Shiloh of the Hebrew University in the *Israel Exploration Journal* 20 (1970), 180-190, with its comparatively ample citation of the literature.

The purpose of this brief discussion is to draw further distinctions beyond those of Shiloh's excellent article in order to see whether others can accept the conclusions.

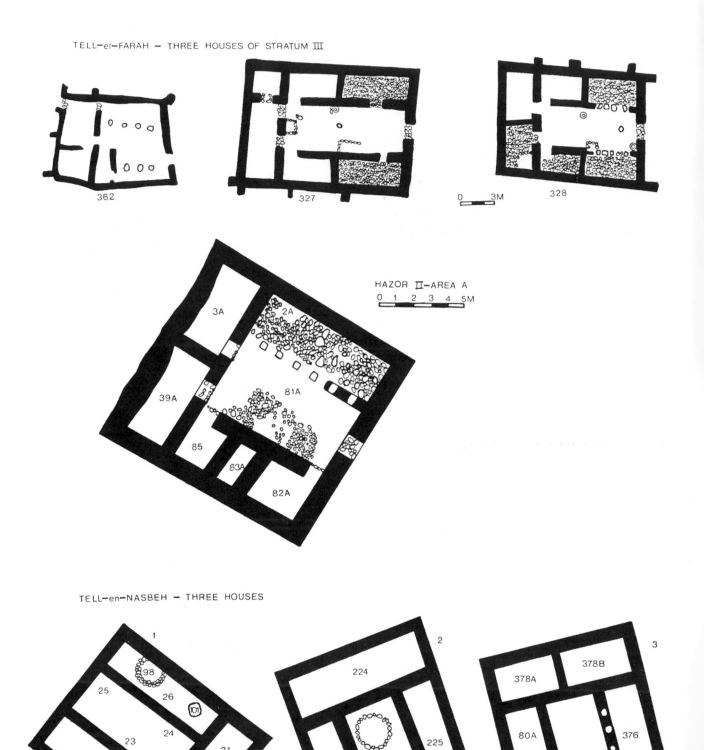

TELL-el-FARAH — THREE HOUSES OF STRATUM III

362

327

328

0   3M

HAZOR II—AREA A

0 1 2 3 4 5M

3A

2A

39A

81A

85

83A

82A

TELL-en-NASBEH — THREE HOUSES

1

98

25

26

23

24

22

21

20

2

224

227

226

225

3

378B

378A

80A

376

379

80B

Fig 2:   *Examples of the 'three sided' "casemate" type of Israelites House with Central Court and Door on Street.*

The first important distinction which Shiloh draws in his article is to single out of the structures in question what he calls "the four-room house and its subtypes," the characteristic feature of which is a back room the width of the building. That feature must be used to separate such a building from the typically three-room long buildings which do not have this cross-room at the back. The published structure of the other type, the long three-room building without the cross-room, seem at this time confined to the 10th and following centuries, of which nine are found, in addition to the several found at Beersheba, beginning in 1970 (see Fig. 1).[6] Of these at least two appear to this writer on archaeological and historical-topographical grounds to be Davidic: those at Beth-shemesh and Lachish.[7] Furthermore, there is an official character about them; they are probably governmental structures, mostly granaries for the collection of taxes in kind. Only at Megiddo do the mangers and tie-holes suggest that the same form could be used for stables.

It is when we come to Shiloh's "four-room house" that this writer would wish to introduce further distinction and subdivisions. Among his examples it appears to this writer that too much is lumped together.

In the first place, is the term "four-room house," used for the Tell en-Nasbeh houses by the excavators and adopted by Shiloh in his analysis, a proper term for all of the structures, or does the very name lead to possible confusion?[8] In my own judgment it is an improper title, especially for the number of buildings which were definitely used as dwellings. The fact is that the exact number of *rooms* is unpredictable because the space can be, and was, divided in different ways. Thus, as regards rooms, the number is unpredictable because of individual preferences.

The main characteristic of the house-type is as follows: There are three rectangular spaces - one across the back and two along the wide walls at right angles to that at the rear. These three spaces are the interior dwelling units on the ground floor, and they are always, in the domestic house, of *approximately the same length and width.* The central entrance to the house is in the centre of the outer wall opposite the transverse rear sector. This entrance leads into what has been called the fourth "room", but which from its installations in certain examples, notably the Shechem example (Fig. 3 top), is the courtyard of the house. Three further characteristics are proof that this central space is a court: 1) Its width varies and is rarely as "tidy" as the width of the other spaces. 2) The doors to the various rooms usually lead off it. 3) A portion of one or both sides of the side spaces have roofs, the bottom of the supports for which are *stone pillars.* These have not always been preserved, though in spite of the drawing of the Shechem house (Fig. 3 top), two were actually present between Rooms 1 (forecourt) and 3. 4) A further characteristic of this building is that stone paving rarely is present in the court, but tends to be in the side rooms off the court. In case this seems a peculiarity, it should be remarked that a mixture of marl, earth and ashes makes an excellent moisture-proof, hard-wearing surface. The MB II B Earthen Embankment and the courtyard of the Fortress-temple at Shechem were made of the first two. Wherever left bare by the German excavators decades before, it was a continual surprise to observe how little erosion had taken place. That the technique has not been forgotten was noted as we watched a refugee Arab family make a make-shift shelter in 1956 next to where we were digging at Balatah. Great care was taken with the floor. Marl and earth from Sellin's dump, mixed with ashes, created a floor which when tamped tight not only could be swept clean but even washed.

A simple explanation drawn from modern analogies in the Arab village of Balatah at Shechem is that the pillared rooms of the court are for the family's livestock used daily (donkey, cows, chickens) and for storage. The living quarters were on the second floor and on the roofs. Since no stone stairs have been found (except possibly Nasbeh 379: cf. Fig. 4:7) access to the upper quarters may be assumed to have been wooden ladders which could be drawn up at night.

Actual proof of an upper story was found in Shechem's House 1727. Above broken pots on the original floor in the back quarter of the house were found fallen polished hard plaster floor fragments, hard as cement and highly polished by cleaning and use. Above them and mixed with them in some cases were thick roof chunks of layered straw-filled marly earth. Mixed with these roof fragments at the top of the debris pile were the fragments of storejars which evidently had been sitting on the roof when the Assyrians destroyed the city in 724 B.C. In and under the debris of the first floor ceiling were remains of the ceiling beams. Tree trunks, 15 to 22 cms. in diameter, had been split in half and the two halves laid side by side for roofing beams. We could not tell precisely how far apart each pair was placed.[9]

It is clear from the masonry that Rooms 8-10 were additions to the house, indicating that the family residing there were occupied in commercial ventures. Smoothing ashlar blocks with a large pink quartzite saddle quern (46 cm. long; 49 lbs. 9 oz. in weight) was one industry which took place in the court - this process of making ashlar

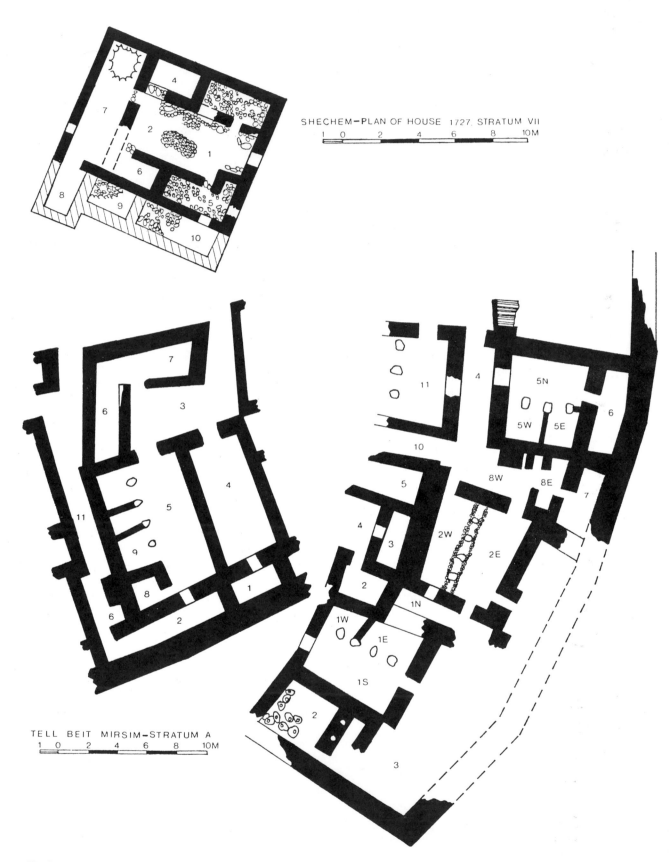

SHECHEM—PLAN OF HOUSE 1727, STRATUM VII

TELL BEIT MIRSIM—STRATUM A

Fig 3:   *Shechem House 1727, and samples of Judean houses at Tell Beit Mirsim.*

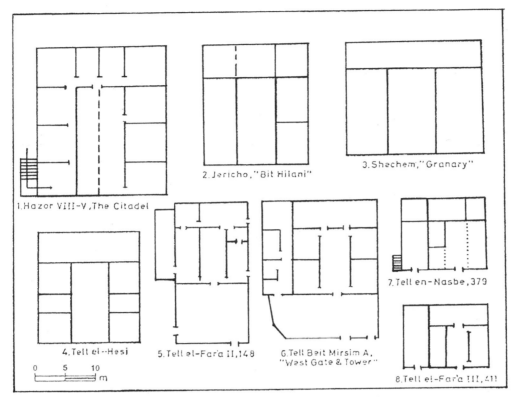

Fig 4:   Examples of Large Public Buildings (except 7 & possibly 8).

blocks so smooth and squared that they could be laid without mortar seems to be the meaning of the Hebrew term *megerah*. [10] Another industry is unclear but may have been connected with the slaking of lime at the large hearth in the court in the final phase of the house's use (Stratum VII A). Beneath the hearth in VII B was a well preserved vine press, the channels cut in the round stone base leading to a whole jar set in place to receive the pressed out juice. Because of the special uses of this court an additional room had been added as the family kitchen (Room 8), with a typical grinding stone and saddle quern for flour in place near a small bin or silo for grain. Rooms 9 and 10 each had a large stone-filled sump connected by an underground drain. What the purpose of this installation was is unclear and suggestions would be very welcome.

The purpose of this detailed digression on the Shechem house is to show that the 'three-sided "casemate" house' with central court can be used and modified at will by a private family. The owners of Houses 23, 226 and 379 at Tell en-Nasbeh and of Houses 327 and 328 at Tell el-Far'ah (Fig. 2) may have been well-to-do families, as was the family of House 1727 at Shechem. Thus Yigal Shiloh's acceptance of McCown's argument that at Nasbeh 'these buildings had some public (administrative) function' [11] is not compelling. As one views the dwellings in the 'wealthy' quarter of Tell el-Far'ah (Tirzah) as they have lain open in the 10th century Niveau III of Pere de Vaux since the completion of his excavations, it is clear that there were at least two rows of them, back to back, with two streets parallel to each other on which the doors from the house courts opened. On the other hand, House 362 (Fig. 2) from the poorer quarter was certainly not built by a wealthy family. Indeed, the Shechem house with walls one wide stone in thickness, widened still further with plaster to support the main wall of mud-brick, would have given a nice surface picture of plastered walls outside and inside. Nevertheless, one has the impression that the structure was erected cheaply by a family bent on 'keeping up appearances.' [12] The Nasbeh houses were much better built.

The adaptation of this house to that of an important administrative official at Hazor during the 8th century (Strata VI-V, Area A) meant an enlargement with much thicker walls and a widening of the whole so that the interior becomes square, in this case approximately 11 m. - not far from c. 30 cubits square in exterior dimensions when plaster is added (Fig. 2). [13] Yet two almost perfect examples of the domestic type were evidently erected for subordinate officials adjacent to the front entrance of the central provincial building in Area B (Houses 3148 and 3169, Stratum V A). [14]

At Tell el-Far'ah (Tirzah) the same type of enlargement occurred in Building 148 of Niveau II (8th cent.) and in its predecessor 411 of the 9th century, the latter being de Vaux's candidate for the "unfinished" palace of Omri, before the latter moved to Samaria (cf. Fig. 4:5 and 8). [15]

In Fig. 4 are Y. Shiloh's interpretations of the form as adapted to larger structures of probable administrative function - though Nasbeh 379 should not be included with these since it is only slightly larger than the others, except for the additional room with stairs on the left side. On the other hand, this addition and another not drawn may indeed separate 379 from the others for more elaborate functions than Houses 23 and 226 (Fig. 2). Fig. 4:8 is from de Vaux's *Niveau Intermediaire* subsequent to his Niveau III of the 10th century. It seems small for the function claimed for it. Yet anyone who has heard de Vaux's eloquent interpretation of every stone on the spot is rendered too emotionally disoriented to deny it outright at this moment in time!

Finally, a great effort has been made by Shiloh to interpret the Iron II house plans of Tell Beit Mirsim as belonging to the same genre as his "four-room house." This writer has found it impossible to follow the argument, and he thus remains unpersuaded by it. In Fig. 3 some typical plans from Tell Beit Mirsim are copied from Albright's *TBM* III, Maps 3 and 5. To the left is a sizable house unit. To the right Room 1 is one unit with the remains of what was once an olive-pressing unit in Room 2 related to it. In the right centre Rooms 2E and 2W, 5 and 11 would appear to be three other units. The use of pillars is ubiquitous, indicating a ground floor court, partially roofed for domestic animal shelter. Family living was on the second floor and roofs. Tell Beit Mirsim is the only Judean town so dug as to provide a sizable view of a later Iron II town plan with a large number of private houses. Not one of them is anything like what has been described here, however inadequately, as 'the house with "casemate" space of roughly equal size on three sides with central court and entrance.' The only exception, as Shiloh indicates in his sketches, is the adaptation of the form for the large West Tower set into the city fortifications (Fig. 4:6).

In other words, thus far in the knowledge of this writer, the house-form in question has not been found south of Tell en-Nasbeh, except for major adaptations for public buildings at Tell Beit Mirsim and probably at Tell el-Hesi (Fig. 4:4 and 6) and Tell Jemmeh. [16] Consequently, it is suggested that this is a (North) Israelite type of house, probably borrowed during the 10th century from Phoenicia, though our lack of Phoenician or Syrian domestic architecture in the Iron Age makes the place of origin impossible to prove.

References

1. Personal information from W. F. Albright, who showed me a photograph of the event: see Wm. F. Bade, *Excavations at Tell en-Nasbeh* (1928), p. 31.
2. See the writer, *Shechem, Biography of a Biblical City* (1965), pp. 80-82.
3. H. G. May, *Material Remains of the Megiddo Cult* (1935), p. 10.
4. *Tell Beit Mirsim* III (*AASOR*, Vol. XXI-XXII, 1943), pp. 22-24 and n. 9; and pp. 54-55.
5. Especially since the discoveries at Tell el-Far'ah, Hazor and Shechem, during the 1950's and 60's (see below).
6. See Fig. ; the long rooms of Tell Beit Mirsim which may have served a similar purpose are not included because they do not form a distinct architectural unit; cf. *TBM* III, Map 3, SE 3-4, Rooms 2, 3 and 4. For Beersheba see provisionally, *The Beer-sheba Excavations*, The Institute of Archaeology, Tel-Aviv University, 1972, plan on back cover. [See now the discussion by Z. Herzog, "The Storehouses", in Y. Aharoni (ed.), *Beer-sheba I* (1973), pp. 23-30 and plates 91-2. Eds.]
7. See most recently the writer, 'The Provinces of Solomon,' *Eretz-Israel*, 8 (1967), pp. 64-66.
8. For details about them, see C. C. McCown, *Tell en Nasbeh*, Vol. I (1947), pp. 206-212. For their position in the city, see map of the whole site (near pocket) and Y. Shiloh, op. cit., p. 189, Fig. 5.
9. For these and other details about this house, see Wright, *Shechem*, pp. 158-162. The rear wall of the house in Room 7 is wider than the other walls of the original house (except for additional Rooms 9-10) because it also served as a terrace wall. See Fig. 76 for a stone-by-stone drawing.
10. See the discussion in Wright, *Shechem*, pp. 159-160 *
11. McCown, loc. cit., and Shiloh, op. cit., p. 190.
12. For the Tell el-Far'ah (Tirzah) buildings and their discussion by R. de Vaux, see *RB* LIX (1952), pp. 551-583; and LXII (1952), pp. 582ff. and Pl. VII where the stratigraphic sequence is revised to introduce an "Intermediate Level" and Building 411 (*batiment inacheve*).
13. Yigael Yadin, *et al., Hazor* II (1960), Pls. CCII and CCIII; for air view see *Hazor* III/IV, Plates (1961), Pl. II; cf. Pl. XXIV. See also more recently, Yigael Yadin, *Hazor* (The Schweich Lectures, 1970), p 180, Fig. 48; p. 186, Fig. 50; and Pls. XXIII and XXXIII:a.
14. Yadin, *Hazor*, p. 188, Fig. 52. The eastern House 3169 has been cleared and planned since the conclusion of the main excavations in 1958: See *Hazor* III/IV, Plates, Pl. XXXII, lower right.
15. See references in note 12.
16. F. J. Bliss, *A Mound of Many Cities* (1894), Fig. 113; and Sir Flinders Petrie, *Gerar* (1928), Pl. IX.

SAMARIA AND CALAH NIMRUD: CONJUNCTIONS IN HISTORY AND ARCHAEOLOGY
by Max Mallowan

In dedicating this essay to Kathleen Kenyon, a lifelong friend and colleague, it seems appropriate to recall memories of two ivory cities wherein both of us have excavated, and to quote in full 2 *Kings* 17. 1-6 which dramatically illustrates the end of a period of tension between these two places.

'In the twelfth year of Ahaz king of Judah Hoshea the son of Elah began to reign in Samaria over Israel, and he reigned nine years. [2] And he did what was evil in the sight of the Lord, yet not as the kings of Israel who were before him. [3] Against him came up Shalmaneser king of Assyria; and Hoshea became his vassal, and paid him tribute. [4] But the king of Assyria found treachery in Hoshea; for he had sent messengers to So, king of Egypt, and offered no tribute to the king of Assyria, as he had done year by year; therefore the king of Assyria shut him up, and bound him in prison. [5] Then the king of Assyria invaded all the land and came to Samaria, and for three years he besieged it. [6] In the ninth year of Hoshea the king of Assyria captured Samaria and he carried the Israelites away to Assyria, and placed them in Halah, and on the Habor, the river of Gozan, and in the cities of the Medes.'

Samaria's loss was Calah's gain; 'And this was so, because the people of Israel had sinned against the Lord their God . .' 17-7: their sinful practices consisted in many different forms of idolatry and ironically they were replaced by other men, no less wicked, from Babylon, Cutha and Hamath and elsewhere, deported by the king of Assyria.

The interchange of peoples which resulted from these massive deportations have yielded legacies which are still of poignant interest to the archaeologist and the historian: we shall see later what bearing these events have on the dating of the remarkable ivories which adorned both cities.

However, before discussing the date of the comparable ivories we may note an important *terminus ad quem* namely, the capture and destruction of Samaria by the king of Assyria in the last quarter of the eighth century B.C. For this feat of arms it is usual to give the credit to Sargon II 722-705 B.C., but in fact it may be convincingly demonstrated that it was Shalmaneser V who was responsible.[1] There is no reason to discard the information provided in 2 *Kings* 17.45; 'Against him came up Shalmaneser king of Assyria and Hoshea became his vassal and paid him tribute'. Thereafter it is related that 'the king of Assyria found treachery in Hoshea' and bound him in prison after a three year siege, which must have been terminated in 722 B.C.[2] The entry in the Old Testament corroborates a passage in the Babylonian Chronicle. Not until 720 B.C. did Sargon return to deport its people and rebuild it as the centre of a new province, Samaria.

It is satisfactory that the book of *Kings* fills a lacuna in the Assyrian historical records and corroborates the Babylonian Chronicle in outlining the probable sequence of events concerning the short and obscure reign of Shalmaneser V 727-722 B.C. We know that his predecessor Tiglath-pileser III who reconstructed the Assyrian empire had, after pacifying Babylonia and repelling the aggressive Urartians, set about establishing Assyrian authority in Syria and Palestine. It was he who subordinated both Judah and Israel and, in the latter kingdom, saw to it that a pro-Assyrian vassal Hoshea was given authority. But it was doubtless the weight of the Assyrian yoke which induced this Israeli monarch to rebel after the death of Tiglath-pileser III; that rebellion made it necessary for Shalmaneser V on his ascent to the throne, to reassert Assyrian authority over Samaria. The task of subjugation was brought to completion by Shalmaneser's successor Sargon.

It is characteristic of the usurper, Sargon, that he arrogated to himself solely the merit for the defeat of Samaria, having reaped the reward which had been acquired for him by his predecessor. Such self-glorification is characteristic of the kings of Assyria and easily comprehensible in one who was a usurper. He was, however, no doubt justified in claiming for himself the restoration of that city.

A remarkable statement by Sargon is recorded on a prism discovered at Nimrud in 1952-53 and published by Gadd in 1954.[3] The passage runs as follows:

25. [The man of Sa] maria, who with a king 26-28. [hostile to] me had consorted together not to do service and not to bring tribute - and they did battle: 29. in the strength of the great gods, my lords 30. I clashed with them 31. [2] 7,280 people with [their] chariots 32. and the gods their trust, as spoil 33. I counted 200 chariots (as) my [royal] muster 34. I mustered from among them 35. the rest of them 36. I caused to take their dwelling in the midst of Assyria 37. The city of Samaria I restored, and greater than before 38. I caused it to become. People of lands conquered by my two hands 39. I brought within it; my officer 40. as prefect over them I placed, and 41. together with the people of Assyria I counted them 42. The peoples of the land of Muṣur and the Arabians 43. I caused the blaze of Ashur my lord to overwhelm them. 44. At the mention of my name their hearts 45. palpitated, their arms collapsed 46. [. . . . . . ?] of the country of Muṣur I open the sealed (treasury ?) 47. the people of Assyria and of Muṣur 48. I mingled together 49. and let them bid for [the contents].

The historical importance of this document is considerable for it reveals that Sargon had continued the work of his predecessors in subjugating not only Samaria but also a part of Palestine and the Arabs. It is generally supposed that Muṣur in this context is not Egypt, which was only overcome at a later date, but some territory not far away to which the Arabs were neighbours.

Line 37 makes it clear that Sargon, after the conquest, repaired Samaria, and his activity there can be followed through the stratification of the excavated city. The stratification has been clearly expounded by J.C. Crowfoot and Kathleen Kenyon, and is based on a typological analysis of the pottery.[4] Samaria I and II contain the earliest remains of the new Israelite city founded by Omri as an akropolis on a virgin hill in 872 B.C., after abandoning the older capital at Tirzah. Here he initiated the new royal foundation and was succeeded by his son, Ahab, whose twenty two year reign 874-853 B.C.[5] was a period of high prosperity and is represented by the substantial ruins of Samaria II. To this period we must attribute the earliest specimens of Phoenician style ivories. A break in the sequence occurs after period II which is succeeded in period III by stone walls, shoddily built, but the masonry is still recognisable in the Phoenician style and attributable to Jehu 841-813 B.C. Period IV begins c. 800 B.C.

Samarian periods V and VI are of crucial importance both archaeologically and historically on account of the decisive evidence of the disastrous clash with Assyria. It was the burnt debris over V and VI that contained *inter alia* the remains of beautifully carved ivories, many of them burnt when the city was sacked. It is probable as we have seen, that the burning should be attributed to Shalmaneser V and the rebuilding to Sargon. The big enclosure wall contemporary with period VI filling appears to be immediately subsequent to the burning and represents the building operations of Sargon. This conclusion agrees very well with the rapportage of the Assyrian scribes who as we have seen, represented Sargon not as a destroyer but as a rebuilder.

The destruction of Samaria by Assyria inevitably invites reflection on the enormous disparity of strength and population between that city and Nimrud from which no doubt the victorious Assyrian army set forth: the great military base available to the Assyrians covered, including the Acropolis, a space not far short of 900 acres of ground. In contrast the walls of Samaria enclosed no more than about 18 acres, less than a third of the site of the inner city or Acropolis of Calah. Israel therefore had little hope of repelling the overwhelming might of Assyria once this had been concentrated on it, and indeed if its rulers had been more far-sighted, Samaria would not have provoked so powerful and dangerous an empire.[6] But Samaria itself had become extremely rich and prosperous; possessing a terrain with a sufficiency of corn, wine and oil. Although it was not an industrial city, the elevated and fortified Acropolis which overlooked important trade routes established it as a political centre of gravity. It was here that Omri and then his son Ahab in the course of his twenty two year reign[7] founded and renovated splendid palaces which were endowed with treasures that attracted the covetous eye of the kings of Assyria who must have laid hands on their splendid ivory furniture.

Ahab, whose reign overlapped for seven years with that of Shalmaneser III, had acquired and possibly caused to be manufactured *in situ,* the sumptuous Phoenician style ivories which, in delicacy of execution and gravefulness of composition have not been excelled elsewhere although, as we shall see, some of the Nimrud ivories similar in style and subject, are closely comparable and could well have been contemporary. However that may be, in spite of the Assyrian conquest, Samaria as a focus of tribal concentration and commercial prosperity possessed exceptional recuperative powers which enabled it to weather the storms of war through the ages, and to remain a prosperous centre throughout the Christian era.

In considering the connections between Samaria and Nimrud we must examine their ivories, which bear many points of resemblance. The situation of Samaria on an easy line of access to the manufacturing towns of Phoenicia and Syria enabled it to obtain *objets d'art* from them. On the ivories, the Phoenician or quasi-Egyptian style is dominant and agrees with the statement in I Kings. 22.39 that the king built himself an ivory house (in Samaria). Ahab, the son of Omri, ruled from 874-853 B.C., and married a Phoenician lady, the notorious Jezebel, daughter of the King of Tyre also styled the "Sidonian," who was understandably eager to acquire the finest products of her home town for the *harem.*[8] The ivories discovered at Samaria probably for the most part belong to this period; perhaps some of them originated in Sidon itself. Indeed the Harvard Expedition found four pieces of carved ivory and some plain fragments on the floor of the Ahab courtyard, where an alabaster vase of the Pharaoh Osorkon II 860-837 B.C. was also found.   [9]

This concatenation makes it probable that many of the Phoenician style ivories found by Layard and subsequently by Mallowan and others at Nimrud belong to the same period and were acquired by Shalmaneser III who was in close touch with the west. Here we take the opportunity of illustrating side by side two striking ivories, one from Samaria [10] Pl. XXIVa and the other from Nimrud.[11] Pl. XXV. These ivories illustrate a squatting figure in precisely the same pose, one knee bent, the other raised, arms outspread, each hand grasping the symbol of eternity namely the ribbed palm branches associated in Egypt with Heh: these figures were perhaps intended to represent the god Re-Harakhte. The parallel is indeed striking, but it is significant that the images are not identical and must have emanated from different workshops. It is indeed possible that at Calah the ivory panel in question was executed in a Phoenician workshop on the site itself, although it is more tempting to look for the origin in Phoenicia. I have, however, emphasised elsewhere that at Calah itself where so many foreigners and foreign craftsmen were in residence, many of these ivories in varying styles, may have been executed there. [12] However that may be, these two parallels illustrate the astounding variety of renderings of a precisely similar theme which reflect an artistic *koine* current in the cosmopolitan world of the 9th and 8th centuries B.C.

It is surprising that as yet we have not been able to find any precise parallels to the Isis and Nephthys figures in Samaria, [13] for the peculiar rendering of the wings is common at Calah. The winged sphinx wearing the double Egyptian crown, [14] is also common at Calah. [15] Furthermore *S.S.* II pl. XI No. 1 illustrates a draped and bolstered throne common on similar plaques at Nimrud and this is probably a 9th century type reminiscent of the *ajouré* work attributed at Calah to Adad-nērāri III, end of the 9th century B.C. [16] We must also recall the ivories described by J. C. Crowfoot: [17] 'dainty little works carved at a time when the twenty-first and twenty-second Egyptian dynasties were popular in Syria'. For example there is a beautifully executed little winged sphinx[18] wearing the double Egyptian crown. This type of sphinx clad with the Phoenician apron is also very common at Nimrud, and it is significant that this *penchant* for carving exquisite miniatures was a trait attributed by Mallowan and Davies to the period of Shalmaneser III, a contemporary of Ahab, though all the miniatures at Nimrud were in the Assyrian style. [19] In accord also with 'the ivory house of Ahab' was the throne room of the palace at Nimrud whereon one entire length of wall was covered with plain ivory panelling or screens;[20] this room was a seventh century restoration with ninth century antecedents and contents as is indicated by a winged sphinx on an oliphant found in it.[21]

It is remarkable that to this period belong the frequent representations of the 'Lady at the Window', the sacred harlot, or hierodule[22] illustrated at Samaria and a favourite theme at Arslan-Tash and Nimrud (Pl. XXIVb). In this connection we must recall the passage in 2 *Kings* 9.30 revealing how the Phoenician born queen tried to entice and seduce Jehu who had supplanted her husband. 'When Jehu came to Jezreel, Jezebel heard of it; and she painted her eyes, and adorned her head and looked out at the window' - a historical record of an imagery cherished in the iconography of the ivories. In Babylonia the goddess Ishtar played a similar role, for in the *bit mesiri* ritual she is similarly placed: "at the window sits the wise(?) Ishtar."[23] This libidinous goddess closely connected with prostition thus took up an appropriately seductive position, like the goddess Gula who with her dog was stationed at the outer gate. Perhaps this imagery could be discerned in the ivory plaques.

Once again therefore the Nimrud ivories reflect a *koine* of current art which may be traced back to Phoenician and to Samarian exemplars.

A similar though later expression of this *koine* may also be discerned in the pottery which cannot here be examined in detail but requires at least brief comment. At Nimrud itself there were only a few specimens of what appeared to be Samarian sherds; one of them was a ring-burnished red ware, wheelmade c. 800 B.C. as in Megiddo IV and at Hama: [24] these must have been imports into Assyria from the west, but as far as we know there was in the ninth century hardly any trace of ceramic contact between Assyria and the region of Syria-Phoenicia. This situation was to be expected in a period which preceded direct intervention and control by Assyria. A marked and indeed a striking difference occurred in the eighth and seventh centuries when much pottery both at Samaria and elsewhere in Palestine displays a strongly Assyrian character. Note also an amphora from Samaria period V.[25] It is however important to appreciate the fact that while there is a marked change in typology at various sites in Palestine with the advent of direct Assyrian rule, many of the changes in type would appear to be genetic developments of the older strains and consonant with archaic progenitors. The subject deserves detailed research by a ceramologist.

This change of ceramic character becomes evident in Samaria VII, a period of reconstruction subsequent to the Assyrian conquest by Shalmaneser V and Sargon, and is clearly demonstrated by a perusal of the pot types in *S.S.*, III, fig 11 - the fine Palace wares Nos. 22, 23 might well have come from Nimrud itself but were perhaps made by potters using similar clays and techniques in Samaria - analysis of the clays would be interesting - many other types identical on the two sites may also be discerned *op. cit.* figs 13, 21, 32. Thus some of the amphorae would have been equally at home in Nimrud and indeed one specimen from ZT the northern wing of the N.W. Palace was indistinguishable from Samarian pottery.[26] This demonstration, which needs pursuing in detail, reflects precisely the historical situation from the latter half of the eighth century until the collapse of Assyria in 614-612 B.C. and is a remarkable example of a clear reflection in ceramic of political control by one of the great powers then dominant. Similar influences could doubtless be discerned in the metal work, seals and many other classes of objects.

We come finally to the architecture which may be expected to be the most eloquent expression both of the indigenous way of life and of foreign influences on it.

It is indeed disappointing that while Nimrud can display a wealth of architectural evidence, the remains of comparable buildings at Samaria are defective and, as regards plans, virtually confined to fragments of buildings and broken stretches of the defensive wall on the akropolis. We have unfortunately no means of judging how far, if at all, the Assyrians after the conquest of the eighth century B.C. imposed any building plans on the displaced persons deported to take up residence there: the evidence such as it is, suggests that the old royal akropolis at Samaria then ceased to play any important part in the life of the city, and that the newcomers were confined to comparatively insignificant houses below the citadel. Perhaps more evidence of this period of architecture will be recovered one day.

There remains however one line of architectural evidence which is of considerable interest and provides a comparison with Assyria namely, the use at Samaria of a fine ashlar masonry notable particularly in the earliest periods - I, II and testifying also to Ahab's use of Phoenician masons.[27] The technique consisted of using finely dressed ashlar resting on rusticated masonry which was used for foundations and therefore not exposed to view. J. C. Crowfoot surmised, no doubt rightly, that this technique of stone dressing had a long ancestry and could be traced back to Ugarit in the 13th century B.C.[28] We know that Phoenician masonry was used in the construction of Solomon's temple at Jerusalem[29] - moreover Phoenician techniques of stone dressing persisted for many centuries and were adopted by the Achaemenians when they penetrated the Mediterranean littoral.[30] The degeneracy of the technique is also manifest at Samaria at the end of the ninth century period IV after the Omrid dynasty, under Jehu[31] shortly before the time when Adād-nērari III 808-782 B.C. was using ashlar and rusticated blocks in the construction in Ezida and the Nabu Temple at Nimrud.[32]

This evidence is of particular interest as implying connections both with Samaria and Phoenicia, for it is known that Adad-nērāri III received the tribute of Is'asu, (Jehoash the king of Samaria) as well as from the rulers of Tyre and Sidon,[33] and it is hard to resist the conclusion that the Phoenician style of masonry was a direct result of these incursions.

The same king, Adad-nērāri III built the western facade of the Nabu temple with finely dressed blocks of ashlar and here in the best Phoenician tradition only used the full dressing in the upper limestone course, approximately 80 cm cube. Rustication, the marginal trimming of the block, leaving the centre as a boss was, incidentally, the most economical method of trimming limestone. Similar Phoenician style masonry was used, probably by the same king, on the western quay walls of the akropolis at Nimrud,[34] where the ashlar rested on blocks of rusticated masonry which were only, and properly, used underwater.

These dressed quay walls at Nimrud were a revetment abutted on an older ashlar frontage which had almost certainly been erected by Assur-nasir-pal II (883-859 B.C.) who on his stela relates that from the water level upwards he filled in his base terrain: it is unlikely that he could have done this without using stone in the lower courses as a later monarch, Tiglath-pileser III (745-727 B.C.) did: 'All the skilled craftsmen I employed to the best advantage . . . for a depth of 20 great cubits below the raging waters (of the Tigris) I piled up mighty limestone boulders.[35] It is not improbable that many of these skilled craftsmen were Phoenician, some of whom are likely to have been employed at Nimrud; there is indeed in the Nimrud inscriptions specific mention of a Phoenician craftsman (probably he was a stonemason). [36]

The latest and in one respect the most interesting evidence of the use of masonry at Nimrud is from the reign of Esarhaddon (680-669 B.C.) who erected a stone facade on the south wall of Fort Shalmaneser. This was a pure piece of showmanship which served no good utilitarian purpose and made use of ashlar masonry, some of it inscribed, in the base courses, superimposed with rusticated, the exact reverse of what the procedure would have been in genuine Phoenician building. An illustration of his doorway in the south facade strikingly demonstrates this inverted arrangement. [37] (Pl. XXVI). The masonry survived up to a height of about 7 metres.

The most striking evidence, however, of the use of stone masonry in Assyria in the 7th century can be ascribed to Esarhaddon's predecessor, Sennacherib (705-680 B.C.), who used more than two million blocks of dressed stone in the construction of the great aqueduct of Jerwan, [38] and elsewhere on a more modest scale in the rusticated masonry of his dam at Ajila.[39] Also of the period of Sennacherib is the great round tower built by him at Ashur: a massive bulwark of ashlar masonry, the like of which is not apparent again until the Hellenistic period.[40]

That Sennacherib also made use of Phoenician masons in the construction of his aqueducts and as stone dressers for his new buildings at Nineveh seems most probable when we consider his explicit statement that he employed Tyrian and Sidonian shipwrights and sailors for the construction and manning of his fleet in his sixth campaign. [41] It is tempting to conjecture that his acquisition of skilled Phoenician manpower followed his third campaign in the course of which he overcame the king of Sidon [42] - 'tribute and gifts . . I imposed upon him for all time without ceasing.' The remarkable feat of engineering the Tarbisu-Nineveh canal, like that at Jerwan, required special and rare skills and was appropriately rewarded, [43] 'Those men who dug that canal I clothed with linen and brightly coloured woollen garments. Golden rugs, daggers of gold, I put upon them.' [44]

The new system of defences at Assur, surviving in part on the outside of the Western Gate, supplemented the older defences of Shalmaneser III and provided a formidable bulwark which has been discussed in detail and well illustrated by W. Andrae. [45] The towers were elliptical in plan and must have risen to a considerable height; the masonry was frequently rusticated. On the evidence of discoveries elsewhere Andrae has plausibly attributed them to Sennacherib owing to the similarity with a blocking used in Sennacherib's *akītu* house, p. 51 (these courses varied between 45 and 51 cm. cube), though possibly the work was completed by Esarhaddon. The masonry was considered by Andrae to have been Assyrian, but Phoenician inspiration is obvious. [46]

It is of course true that stone masonry was used at all periods in Assyria, though at some periods sparingly. The Phoenician character displayed in the time of Sennacherib and his successor is however in striking contrast to that of the preceding king Sargon whose limestone masonry was best displayed in his new and unfinished capital, Khorsabad, where stone was rarely used except in the great bridge which joined the terraces of the Palace and the Nabu Temple. A glance at the huge blocks used in that construction reveals [47] that they have nothing in common with the Phoenician style which we have observed at Samaria and under Sennacherib and Esarhaddon at Nimrud: there is no evidence for labelling Sargon's work as anything but Assyrian, and this may be related to the fact that Sargon unlike his successors had no direct contact with Tyre and Sidon. Perhaps this historical pointer may be used to indicate the possibility that Phoenician influence in masonry techniques gained ground when Assyria previously (under Sargon) mainly preoccupied with Urartu, turned its face towards the west. The point need not be laboured further, for in the homeland Assyrian masons must have been available as well as foreigners, but every conquest was liable to be affected by a change of style,[48] either by the conqueror, or by the conquered, or by both, as we have already seen in Assyrian style pottery of the eighth to seventh centuries B.C.

Thus, although proof is lacking from the inscriptions, we may legitimately see here a transfer to Assyria of the skills particularly associated with Phoenician masons at the time of its domination over the west, and in this way there is evidence for the assumption that the constructional methods employed more than two centuries earlier at Samaria in the ninth century were eventually transferred to Nimrud. Incidentally, it is interesting to recall that we also have inscriptional evidence of the employment of men of Samaria at Nimrud as well as brick-makers from Tyre,[49] although at all times there must have been an abundance of Assyrian masons and craftsmen who far outnumbered the foreigners. [50]

This brief collation of some important links between Samaria and Calah Nimrud illustrates decisively the reciprocal influence influence of historical conjunctions which both linked and severed the two cities. The archaeological evidence concerned with the study of buildings, ivories, pottery and masonry techniques reflects the ebb and flow of historical power and could be further supplemented, as we have already remarked, by a study of metal and seals. We may repeat in conclusion that a profounder understanding of the problems involved would certainly be obtained if analytical work were to be done on the pottery of both cities and others related to them.

References

1. H. Tadmor, *JCS* XII (1958), pp. 22-42.
2. E. R. Thiele, *The Mysterious Numbers of the Hebrew Kings,* p. 217 (hereafter *Thiele*) notes that 'the year 723 is used as the date for the fall of Samaria in both Josephus and the Massoretic text'.
3. C. J. Gadd, "Inscribed Prisms of Sargon II from Nimrud", *Iraq.* XVI (1954), p. 180.
4. *Samaria-Sebaste* I, pp. 5ff. (hereafter *S.S.*) and KATHLEEN KENYON, *Royal Cities of the Old Testament,* p. 92. (hereafter *Kenyon, Royal Cities*).
5. Ahab's reign was thus contemporary with the fifteen years of Ashur-nasir-pal II and seven years of Shalmaneser III who reigned 859-824 B.C., *Thiele,* pp. 61, 62 and 283.
6. *Isaiah* 1, 7, 8; danger of relying on Egypt 2 *Kings* 18, 21.
7. 1 *Kings* 16, 29.
8. 1 *Kings* 16.31.
9. *S.S.* II, p. 4 and G. A. Reisner, *Harvard Excavations at Samaria,* p. 368 pls. 56, 66. Revised date of Osorkon according to I.E.S. Edwards in revised CAH (1974).
10. *S.S.* II, pl. II No. 2.
11. M.E.L. MALLOWAN, *Nimrud and its Remains* II.pl. 511 (hereafter *Mallowan, N & R*).
12. J. V. KINNIER WILSON, *The Nimrud Wine Lists,* p. XII (hereafter *Kinnier Wilson, Nimrud Wine Lists*) and MAX MALLOWAN and GEORGINA HERRMANN, *Furniture from SW. 7 Fort Shalmaneser.* (1974), p. 40 n. 1.
13. *S.S.* II, pl. III.
14. *S.S.* II, pl. V No. 3.
15. *Mallowan, N & R* II, pl. 506
16. *Mallowan, N & R* II, pls. 443-448
17. *S.S.* III, p. 2.
18. *S.S.* II, pl. VII No. 7.
19. MAX MALLOWAN and LERI GLYNNE DAVIES, *Ivories in Assyrian Style,* (1970), p. 3 from NTS 4 pls. XI, XII.
20. *Mallowan N & R* I, p. 294.
21. *Mallowan N & R* I, pl. 271.
22. *S.S.,* II pl. XIII No. 2.
23. The passage is quoted in *The Assyrian Dictionary of the Oriental Institute of the University of Chicago* Vol. 1 Part II p. 199c *ina ap-ti bīti ittašab tēlītu Ištar.* I owe this reference to Barbara Parker. For the incantation ritual see Meier in *AfO* 14, (1941-4), 146 line 112.
24. *Mallowan, N & R,* I, p. 208.
25. *S.S.* III, fig 8: No. 1, p. 119.
26. This particular amphora ND 1975 contained within it lumps of Egyptian blue and is mentioned in *Mallowan, N & R,* I, p. 180.
27. *Kenyon, Royal Cities,* p. 76 and pls. 41-45.
28. *S.S.* I, p. 6 and *Syria* XII (1931), pls. XII 1, 3; *Syria* XIII. (1932), pl. XV, 3. A similar style of masonry was also discovered in the Palace at Ugarit; see the clear illustrations in C.F.A. SCHAEFFER, *Ugaritica* IV (1962), figs. 31, 66-68. 86, 88 and pp. 105-106 where it is surmised that this technique could have been borrowed from the Nile valley. If so, the title Phoenician would not be inappropriate.
29. I *Kings* 5.18; 7.13,14.
30. Maurice Dunand, 'La Défense du Front Méditerranéen de l'Empire Achémenide' in *The Role of the Phoenicians in the Interaction of Mediterranean Civilization,* ed. by William Ward (Beirut American University Centennial Publication, 1968). This important paper illustrates striking examples of Phoenician style masonry in use in Achaemenian times and at subsequent periods, especially at the great Phoenician centres such as in the Temple of Eshmun at Sidon, the Temple of Ba'al at Byblos, or fortified sites at Amrith, Banyas and elsewhere. The style is still evident in Herodian Jerusalem; photographs of the masonry on pls. XIII- XVI.
31. *Kenyon, Royal Cities,* pl. 92 and p. 124.

32. *Mallowan, N & R,* I, pl. 186; use of ashlar on the portal of the great hall *N & R,* 1, pl. 243 attendant of Nabu addorsed against rusticated masonry at the entrance of the god's shrine.

33. Stephanie Page, *Iraq* XXX (1968), p. 143 with discussion in Orientalia, NS 38 (1969) pp. 457 ff and revision by J. A. Brinkman in *RA* 63 (1969), p. 96 note 9. There is no reason against dating the campaign in 798 B.C. See also 2 *Kings* 13.9.

34. *Mallowan, N & R,* I, pls. 33, 34 opp. p. 81.

35. *Mallowan, N & R,* I, p. 81.

36. *Kinnier Wilson, Nimrud Wine Lists,* pp. 91-93, see notes 48–50 below.

37. *Mallowan, N & R,* II, pl. 379 opp. p. 464 and pp. 464-466.

38. T. JACOBSEN and SETON LLOYD, *Sennacherib's Aqueduct at Jerwan,* (Oriental Institute Publications Vol. XXIV, 1935).

39. R. CAMPBELL THOMPSON and R. W. HUTCHINSON, *A Century of Exploration at Nineveh* (1929), pp. 139ff., and pl. V. Also illustrated by the same authors in "The Temple of Nabu at Nineveh", *Archaeologia,* 79 (1929), pp. 78 and 114ff, figs. 1, 2, 4 and 5.

40. *Kenyon, Royal Cities,* pl. 45.

41. D.D. LUCKENBILL, *Ancient Records of Assyria and Babylonia,* II, 319. (hereafter, *LAR*).

42. *LAR,* II, 239.

43. *LAR,* II, 337.

44. No doubt the men decorated were the *ashipu* priests and other priestly dignitaries who were in supreme charge of the operation.

45. W. ANDRAE, *Die Festungswerke von Assur* (1913), p. 51 and pl. 26, fig. 68.

46. See also *W. Andrae, op. cit.* pl. LXXIV illustrating height of the ashlar revetment of the 'Muschlal' fronting the ziggurat.

47. LOUD and ALTMAN, *Khorsabad* II (Oriental Institute Publications Vol XL 1938), p. 15 and pl. 12.

48. Thus the masonry used in the Nabu Temple by Adad-nērāri III c. 800 B.C. may be a reflection of his raids on Tyre and Sidon as noted above.

49. *Kinnier Wilson, Nimrud Wine Lists,* pp. 91-93, including the suggestion that foreigners were perhaps employed at Nimrud in stone-cutting. Note also that stone cutting with adzes is still a technique fully understood in recent times by the stone cutters of the town of Mosul, modern descendant of Nineveh.

50. We may note a few examples of purely Assyrian masonry. The stone quay walls of Adad-nērāri I (1307-1275 B.C.) provide striking examples of the use of great cubic stone blocks at Assur, W. ANDRAE, *Das Wiedererstandene Assur,* (1938), pl. 29a, obviously executed by Assyrian masons, and see also pl. 71a paved stone way in the Assur temple. At Nimrud there is abundant evidence for the use of stone footings in the North West Palace of Ashurnasirpal II. These served as plinths for the gypsum reliefs and long lines of standard inscription. In the Throne Room of the same Palace, there was an enormous throne base, as in that of Shalmaneser III, see *Mallowan, N & R,* II, pls. 369-370 pp. 444f, and throughout Assyria there are abundant traces of megalithic foundation blocks as well as stone pavements. In Assyria, apart from wall foundations and quays, the use of stone masonry was predominantly associated with sculpture, for example the vast *lamassu* figures which stood at the entrance to gateways. But the material predominantly used in walls was mud-brick which was manufactured *in situ* and did not involve the heavy problems of transport such as we have noted in Sennacherib's aqueduct at Jerwan.

Plate XXIV

a.

*Samaria.   Ivory plaque illustrating a squatting figure which grasps
the ribbed palm branches associated in Egypt with Ḥeḥ for comparison
with an ivory plaque from Fort Shalmaneser, Nimrud. (After S.S., II, pl. 11:2).
See page 157.*

b.

*Ivory plaque ND 6316 illustrating Lady at the window from Fort Shalmaneser,
Nimrud, room N.W.15.
(After Mallowan, Nimrud and its Remains, II, p. 522 and 523).
See page 157.*

Plate XXV 163

Ivory plaque from Fort Shalmaneser, Nimrud, iconographically comparable with one from Samaria illustrated on pl. XXIVa. (After Mallowan, Nimrud and its Remains, *II, pl. 511.). See page 157.*

Plate XXVI

South entrance to Fort Shalmaneser, Nimrud, illustrating fine stone masonry used by Esarhaddon (680-669 B.C.) (After Mallowan, Nimrud and its Remains, *I, p. 81).*

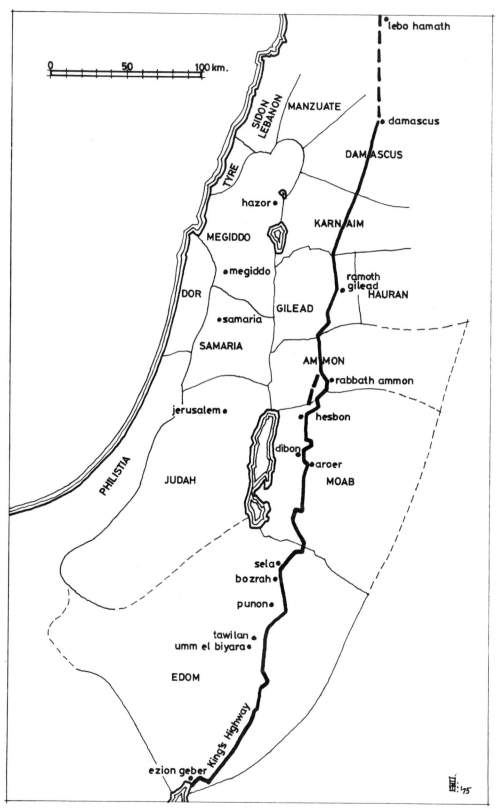

Fig 1.

SOME REFLECTIONS ON NEO-ASSYRIAN INFLUENCE IN TRANSJORDAN.
by Crystal-M. Bennett.

Tiglath Pileser III, King of Assyria (744-27 B.C.), is one of the great figures in history. Due to his genius for administration and his concept of empire, he laid the foundations for a short-lived but brilliantly administered and efficient one. A great politico-economic organisation came into being, whereby much of the Near East came under the one all-mighty king. The empire was split up into provinces, ruled by royally appointed Assyrian governors - (this is documented in the Assyrian Annals[1] and in the Bible[2]), - who had followed in the wake of the successful generals. The governor defined and exacted the amount of tribute due from the conquered area. Attached to each governor was a great hierarchy of civil servants. Tiglath Pileser instituted the policy of "divide and rule", which has been followed by all subsequent empire builders. The important members, and these undoubtedly included crafts-men, particularly skilled metal workers, of a conquered people were deported and in their place were put either other different defeated ethnic groups or veteran soldiers. It is presumed that the ordinary peoples' lives were not affected.

The all-important factor governing the incessant warfare between the kingdoms bounding the Tigris and the Euphrates and that of Egypt and between them the such states as Israel, Judah, Ammon, Moab and Edom, was, of course, economic - the desire to control the vast resources, which lay in Phoenicia, and elsewhere. Tiglath Pileser IIIrd's campaign into Palestine between the years 734 - 732 was almost the final act in this struggle. By 722, Aram-Damascus, Hazor, Megiddo and the Northern Kingdom with its capital at Samaria had fallen. It is very possible that the whole of the north, Qarnini (Qarnaim), Haurina (Hauran) and Gala'za (Gilead), the latter with Ramoth-Gilead as its capital, became typical Assyrian provinces, falling into line with Samaria.[3]

The states of Ammon, Moab and Edom, further south, already existed and, from what little evidence is available both in the Bible and the Assyrian Annals, had treaty agreements with the Assyrians prior to Tiglath-Pileser's campaigns. On a stone slab found at Calah (Nimrud) which records Adad-Nirari III's (810 - 783) expedition to Palestine, reference is made to the countries including Edom, which he intimidated and imposed tribute on.[4] With Tiglath-Pileser IIIrd, however, the names of the Kings are mentioned. We read of him receiving tribute from Sanipu of Bit-Ammon, Salamanu of Moab and Kaush-Malaku of Edom. We know from later references in the Assyrian Annals[5] that it was not only tribute of gold and silver they paid: under Esarhaddon (680-669) subjects of Qaus Gabr, King of Edom, Musuri, King of Moab and Puduil, King of Bit Ammon, together with 19 other kings were employed on transporting various materials to Nineveh for the building of palaces. In Assurbanipal's reign (668-627), these subject peoples were either pressed into or perhaps volunteered for military service. Qaus Gabr of Edom, Musuri of Moab and Amminabdi of Bit Ammon are listed among 22 kings who helped in his wars against Egypt. They also helped in his campaigns against the Arabian king Uate. No passage is more illuminating than that from the Rassam Cylinder describing Assurbanipal's campaigns against the Arabs.[6]

Earlier in this article, reference was made to economics being the driving force behind empire building. One of the essentials in controlling a far flung empire is rapid communication, whereby armies can be moved quickly, reports received of likely dissident movements or incipient rebellions; and trade between the various provinces can be conducted speedily and without hindrance. The map, Fig. 1, shows not only the various provinces, states and towns mentioned in this paper, but also one very important road, marked the King's Highway.[7] This ran from Hamath in Syria down to the northern shore of the Gulf of Aqaba, linking up at strategic points with other main arteries running west-east. There must also have been a whole network of posting houses, camps, look-out posts and signal stations positioned along these roads.

Glueck[8] has noted that "the archaeological survey of Edom, Moab and of the other kingdoms of Transjordan revealed the presence of strong fortresses along their frontiers". In his monumental survey of Eastern Palestine,[9] Glueck plotted many of these buildings and has dated them from Iron I onwards. From the pottery published, the writer can see no reason for such an early date and would prefer to bring them down to the 8th century B.C. as a *terminus post quem.* From the account of Assurbanipal's war against the Arabs, the Assyrians stationed garrison forces along the edge of the desert to check the ever present threat of Arab nomadic incursions. Assurbanipal relates that on his ninth campaign he defeated the king of Arabia throughout the whole length of the region stretching

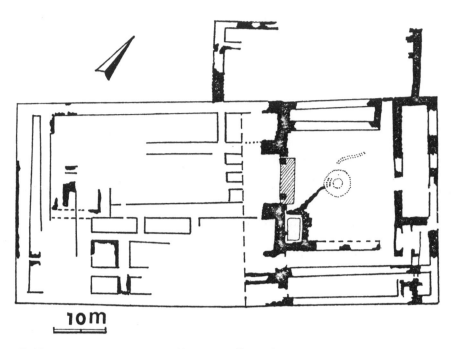

10 M

Fig 2.   General Plan of Early "Acropolis" Buildings
Area A.

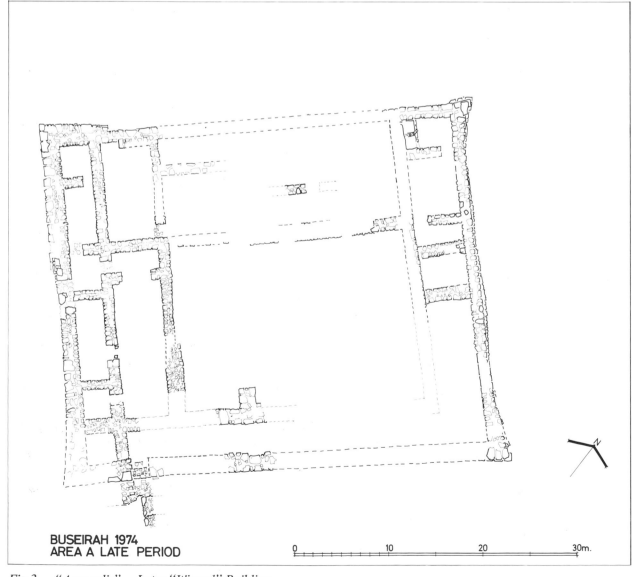

BUSEIRAH 1974
AREA A LATE PERIOD

0   10   20   30m.

Fig 3.   "Acropolis" – Later "Winged" Building

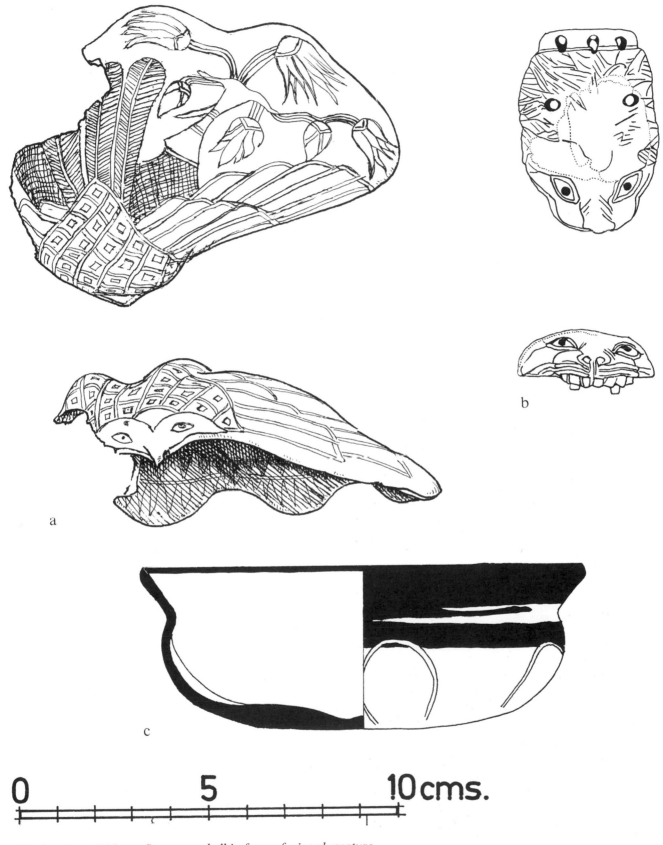

Fig 4. A. *Tridacna Squamosa shell in form of winged creature.*
B. *Ivory Lion's head probably used as a top for a box.*
C. *Dimpled Assyrian type bowl.*

from the pass of Iabrudu (north of Damas) to the land of Edom (*The Rassam Cylinder of Ashurbanipal,* col. VII, 11, 107-15. On the other hand, none has ever been excavated and Glueck may well be right. On the evidence in the Bible, such as in 2 *Samuel.* 8: 13f, J. R. Bartlett[10] has suggested a Davidic date for their beginning. The signal stations within the environs of Buseirah which the writer has visited have yielded no sherds earlier than those found in the excavations at Tawilan (Teman?) and Buseirah (Bozra) in the late 8th - 7th century B.C. levels. A detailed investigation of one of the larger signal stations, such as Khirbet Rumeil in Moabite country (see Fig 1), might be rewarding because from Glueck's description, apart from its location, and the pottery found, the shape and construction of the buildings might have something in common with those at Bozra.

Relatively little archaeological excavation has been done in the relevant areas. In recent years, however, the number of excavations has steadily increased. In a short and general paper such as this reference can only be made to those sites which may have some bearing on the subject; they are marked on the map, Fig. 1., and from north to south are: Ramoth-Gilead (Tell er-Rumeith); Rabbath-Ammon (present day Ammon); Hes'ьan (Tell Heşbān), Dibon (Dhībân) and 'Arð'er ('Aroer) in Moab; and Bozra (Buseirah), Teman(?) (Tawilan), Umm el Biyara and Ezion Geber (Tell el Kheleifeh) in Edom.[11]

The untimely death of Dr. Paul Lapp has delayed inevitably the publication of his excavations at Ramoth-Gilead in 1962 and 1967. From his short reports, in the *Revue Biblique* (Vol. 70 (1963), 406-11; 75 (1968), 98 - 105), it appears that there was a violent destruction at the end of Stratum V, which was probably due to the campaign of Tiglath-Pileser III. After this destruction there was a subsequent re-use of houses with brick floors for a short while. Unfortunately no house plans are available and one wonders if further excavations might not prove a subsequent history similar to that of Samaria, Hazor and Megiddo. The ceramic finds have not yet been published, but Dr. J. Sauer who has been working on the material, and who has seen the material from the writer's three sites in Edom found very little similarity between the pottery from the two regions; he had no neo-Assyrian pottery, but there were affinities between the Tell er Rumeith pottery and that from Samaria/Megiddo and Hazor. In other words, there was a cultural connection between these northern sites, which did not depend on the arrival of the neo-Assyrians.

The picture at Rabbath-Ammon is different. The most recent excavations on the Citadel have been those conducted by Dr. F. Zayadine.[12] The area excavated is insufficient to draw positive conclusions regarding the nature of the buildings, but it is significant that plaster floors which were such a dominating feature in the neo-Assyrian levels at Bozra (see below) have been found. The pottery associated with these plaster floors accords well with that from Bozra. Stratum V has been dated on the basis of pottery, epigraphical material and the double-faced heads (see below) to the 7th century B.C.

Until such time as the area of excavation is extended, the most important area of the Citadel is that on the southern slope, opposite the Roman theatre, where the Tomb of Adoni-Nur was found.[13]

This burial belonged to a servant or minister of Amminabdi (mentioned in the Assyrian Annals during Assurbanipal's reign). With it was pottery, much of it painted, which helps to establish dates for similar pottery from other Transjordanian sites.

From the references to Hesbon in the Bible,[14] it would have been natural to have expected a long sequence of occupation at Heshbon from the time of Sihon, king of the Amorites, down to the 6th century B.C. Excavations have not revealed this and, for our purposes, no buildings have been published which could be assigned definitely to a neo-Assyrian period or could reflect neo-Assyrian influence. According to Dr. J. Sauer,[15] the pottery covers the range 700 to 500 B.C. and confirms definitely the ceramic tradition of the Adoni Nur tomb. His *terminus post quem* is 650, which means that there should be ceramic affinities with the pottery from Umm el Biyara that is dated very securely by a seal impression of the King of Edom, Qos (or Qaus) Gabr.[16]

It is to be hoped that one day there will be a re-excavation of Dibon.[17] Dr. Tushingham has made a valiant effort to present a lucid explanation of the site, which, in view of the Mesha stela is a most important one. His plans of the Iron Age remains are tantalising, because some of the walls resemble closely those from Bozra. According to him, the main periods of occupation paralleled the Samaria periods VA - VIII: that is from shortly before 840 B.C. to 722 B.C. with an extension down into the later 7th or early 6th century B.C. Tushingham makes the interesting point that as there was no evidence of violent destruction anywhere in the area, it might be assumed that the town flourished in spite of political changes, and suffered nothing at Assyrian hands. The successful campaigns of Tiglath-Pileser III and his successors, with the fall of Samaria and the consequent end of Israel, favoured Moab; they were able to win back their lost property and, so long as they paid regular tribute to the Assyrians from 731 onwards, they had nothing to fear. We know that during Assurbanipal's military operations against the Arabs, Kamashaltu, King of Moab "a servant belonging to me" played an important rôle in the campaign. Tushingham has suggested that because of this, the King was given permission to strengthen the defences of his capital, which occurred in his Period 3. Period 2 is also assigned to the neo-Assyrian (slightly earlier perhaps than Tiglath-Pileser III). An examination of the pottery published from both these periods suggests that their background is not very different from that at Bozra.

'Arô'er [18] was a fortress protecting Dibon, but according to the excavator no pottery was found that could be assigned to the neo-Assyrian period and 'Arô'er ended at the same time as the fall of Samaria. Again not enough excavation has been done to get an adequate picture of the fortifications or other buildings. It is possible that important sites such as Dibon and 'Arô'er came under Assyrian influence during Tiglath-Pileser's earlier campaigns; such was his shrewdness that he might well have secured his eastern flank before embarking on his wars against western Palestine.

In Edom four sites have been excavated which have a bearing on our discussion - Bozra, [19] Teman(?),[20] Umm el Biyara[21] and Ezion Geber. [22] It is unfortunate that the plans of the buildings at Ezion Geber which Glueck stated were to be dated to the end of the 8th century B.C. (his period IV) were never published. It is undeniable, however, that Glueck's period IV pottery is identical in many instances with that found at the other three sites mentioned and belongs to the neo-Assyrian period.

Neo-Assyrian influence is not apparent in the buildings discovered on the top of Umm el Biyara, but the situation there was unique: the settlement was pure Edomite and represented a very simple community. At Teman(?) there was a much larger settlement and more sophisticated houses, [23] but they still showed no external influences, even though the pottery and small finds from both Umm el Biyara and Teman(?) reflect the finds from the Tomb of Adoni Nur; and in certain cases perhaps neo-Assyrian influences - to wit, - a scaraboid, (*Levant* III (1971), Pl. IIb), which has been fully commented on by Mlle. A. Spycket in the *Revue Biblique* (1973) 384-395.

The buildings found on the lower terraces surrounding the "Acropolis" or Citadel at Bozra resembled closely those at Teman(?), the walls being made of medium sized, uncut stones, sometimes with a mud plastering, occasionally with a plaster floor, but more often a clay floor. It was on the "Acropolis" that the neo-Assyrian influence became apparent. The whole concept of building changed. Foundations, sometimes to a depth of three metres, were sunk to support massive structures. The walls were still built from roughly hewn stone but they were very well constructed and meant to last. As can be seen in the preliminary report in *Levant* VI (1974), in Area A, i.e. the "Acropolis", there are two major buildings, one overlying the other. Plans of both are illustrated here in Figs 2 and 3., the later being the "winged" building. They are quite unlike any others found by the excavator at other sites and parallels to them must be looked for outside Edom. Two very useful articles for this are those by G. Turner, on "The State Apartments of Late Assyrian Palaces" and "The Palace and Bâtiment aux Ivoires at Arslan Tash". [24] It is worth noting that on a mound to the south-east of the Acropolis, in our Area C (for its location see *Levant VI* (1974), 2, Fig 1.), a type of building very similar to those on the Acropolis was found, with a bathroom. According to Turner, bathrooms first appeared in Assyria in the larger Sargonid palaces at Khorsabad and in Sennacherib's palace at Nineveh. Another point worth mentioning here is that in the earlier building on the Acropolis, we have steps leading up into an inner sanctum with column bases on either side, which were, perhaps, for statues, reminding us of Assyrian temples with stands for deity statues. It is unfortunate that nowhere in the whole excavations did we find any stone fragment which could have been associated with the two columns. It is not definite that the buildings so far excavated at Bozra are palaces or temples. No inscriptions have been found to help with this problem or with that of dating. Even pottery is remarkable for its scarcity in stratified levels. But, with Dame Kathleen Kenyon's example in her brilliant analysis of the pottery at Samaria, we hope we shall succeed. This article has been inspired by her work and is in gratitude for her constant help and advice.

Most of the excavation reports referred to in this paper make some reference to the influence of Assyria on pottery. Undoubtedly the Tomb of Adoni Nur is one of the most important sites for the study of 7th century B.C. pottery, particularly as a conical carnelian seal showing a deity, standing in a crescent, wearing a long garment and with typical Assyrian heavy beard and hairdressing was one of the finds. Miss O. Tufnell remarked that it was natural to find that the seals were influenced by Assyrian motifs and designs. She also commented that the ware of the pottery from this tomb was of very high quality and could be matched for technical ability by the finest sherds from Samaria, (the same could be said of some of the ware from Bozra) but that they could also be the products of Assyrian emporia. That may be true, but a close study of the pottery from Teman(?) and Bozra shows that there is very little pottery that can be said categorically to be an Assyrian import and the probability is that the pottery in both places is locally made and occasionally influenced by Assyria. A most interesting find however, at Bozra was two sherds from different vessels bearing the impressed stamp of a cow and calf motif, which is well known in Assyrian art. The pottery was of a very high quality and almost certainly imported. It is tempting to think of them as sherds from the Assyrian governor or military commander's best dinner service. A drawing of them appeared in *Levant* VII.

A distinctive characteristic of the household ware in Assyrian palaces is a thumb marked or dimple surface. This type was found both at Bozra and Teman(?) and an example from Teman? is shown on Fig. 4. Bowls with rounded bases are also a common Assyrian type and compare with bowls from Period VII at Samaria, following the destruction in 722. Similar bowls have been found at Umm el Biyara, Teman(?) and Bozra. The bi-chrome and band painted pottery, which occurs on so many sites in Ammon, Moab and Edom seems to be indigenous, but with origins in the Late Bronze Age and Early Iron. [25]

A brief reference must be made to two most interesting finds: the first was from Teman(?) in a very burnt pit within an Iron Age II room; it is an ivory lion, probably used as a top for a box, and is illustrated on Fig. 4. It has not been published previously and is illustrated here because of its similarity with other representations of lions found elsewhere in the neo-Assyrian empire. The second object was found on a beaten earth floor in one of the simple houses which covered the terrace between the casemate town wall and the monumental buildings on the "Acropolis" at Bozra. It is a winged creature carved from the upper part of a *Tridacna Squamosa* shell and is illustrated also on Fig. 4. It is probably Syro-Phoenician work and the use of these shells for decorative purposes is known in many places in the 7th C.B.C. in the Near East.

In this connection one should not forget the double faced sculptured heads found in a drain on the Citadel in Amman, [27] which have their similarities in Nimrud, particularly with the famous lady at the window. [28] Whether these sculptures, ivories and carved *Tridacna Squamosa* shells are Egyptian, Syro or Cypro-Phoenician in origin is not really pertinent here. What is interesting is that they turn up on most sites where the neo-Assyrians were in direct control or exercised authority treaties or vassals.

Overall, we may draw, perhaps, certain conclusions. Before Tiglath Pileser III's campaigns against Palestine, he had made sure of the hinterland, represented by such states as Ammon, Moab and Edom. To do this, he entered into treaty agreements with the relevant states. He and his successors ensured the safety of all movement by establishing fortified posts along main roads such as the King's Highway. This was very necessary by the time of Assurbanipal because of the thrusting westwards by the nomadic Eastern Arabic tribes, who posed a big element of danger to the economy of the neo-Assyrian empire. With the acquiescence of some of the kings, such as the one in Edom, the neo-Assyrians installed their own governor or military commander to co-ordinate tactics in the event or threat of invasion. At the same time they brought in architects to erect buildings worthy of them. There is little evidence for a vast import of typically Assyrian pottery, but there is proof of the import of luxury goods, even though they may have been manufactured elsewhere. Culturally, the neo-Assyrians had very little impact on Transjordan.

References

1. See references in H. Tadmor: "The Southern Border of Aram", *I.E.J.*, 12, 1962 pp. 114-122.
2. See references in B. Oded: "Observations on Methods of Assyrian Rule in Transjordania," *J.N.E.S.* 29:1970 p. 177 note 2.
3. Oded, op. cit., p. 179; also E. Forrer, *Die Provinzeinteilung des assyrischen Reiches* (Leipzig, 1920), 69-70.
4. J. B. Pritchard: *A.N.E.T.* col. 281.
5. ibid., Col. 291.
6. ibid., Cols. 297-300.
7. This road is not neo-Assyrian. It was a long established route and is said to be the way taken by the four northern kings under Chedorlaomer, King of Elam, when attacking the southern kings, including the Horites in their Mount Seir (*Genesis* 14: 5-6).
8. N. Glueck, *The Other Side of the Jordan* (A.S.O.R. 1940).
9. N. Glueck: *Survey of Eastern Palestine* (A.A.S.O.R., Vols. XIV, XV, XXVIII and XXIX:. 1933-5 and 1951).
10. J. R. Bartlett: "The Rise and Fall of Edom", *P.E.Q.* (1972), 29.
11. The important sites of Tell es-Saidiyeh, and Tell Deir 'Allā in the Jordan Valley have not been included because I have not been able to consult the relevant publications.

12. F. Zayadine: *"Recent Excavations on the Citadel of Amman."* *A.D.A.J.* XVIII (1973), 17-35.

13. G. L. Harding, "Four Tomb Groups from Jordan", *P.E.F. Annual* VI (1953), 48-72 (including Miss O. Tufnell's Notes and Comparisons).

14. See references cited in R. S. Boraas & S. H. Horn: *Heshbon 1968* (Andrews University Press, Michigan 1969), 99-100.

15. E. N. Lugenbeal & J. A. Sauer: "Pottery from Heshbon" *A.U.S.S.*, X, (1972).

16. C-M Bennett: "Fouilles d'Umm el Biyara: Rapport Préliminaire", *R.B.* 73 (1966), 372-403 and Pl. XXII'b.

17. A.D. Tushingham: *Excavations at Dibon (Dhiban) in Moab* (A.A.S.O.R., XL., 1972).

18. E. Olavarri: "Sondages à 'Arô'er sur l'Arnon," *R.B.* LXXII (1965), 77-94.

19. C-M Bennett: Preliminary Reports in *Levant* V (1973), *Levant* VI (1974) and *Levant* VII (1975).

20. C-M Bennett: "A Brief Note on Excavations at Tawilan, Jordan 1968-70," *Levant* III (1971), V.

21. C-M Bennett, see n. 16.

22. Ezion-Geber-(Tell el Kheleifeh) - for a complete bibliography see E. Vogel: "Bibliography of Holy Land Sites," *H.U.C.A.* XLII (1971), 85-86.

23. op cit in n. 20: Pl. I and IIA.

24. G. Turner: Articles mentioned in the text are in *Iraq* XXXII (1970), 177-214; XXX (1968), 62-69.

25. I am hesitant to say more because Miss M. Oakeshott is preparing a doctorate at the Institute of Archaeology in London on the painted pottery of Transjordan in the Iron II period for which she will use the material from my sites.

26. See my article in *Antiquity* XLI (1967), 197-201.

27. See n. 12 and P. Bordreuil: "Inscriptions des Têtes à Double Face" in the same volume.

28. M. E. L. Mallowan: *Nimrud and its Remains.* II, p. 513, 429 ND 316 (B).

LADY LAYARD'S JEWELRY
by R. D. Barnett.

Sir John Guest, a wealthy industrialist, the great iron-master of Dowlais, near Merthyr Tydfil was one of the new phenomena of the Industrial Age in Britain. In 1833 he married Charlotte Bertie, a daughter of the Earl of Lindsay and a cousin of A. H. Layard. Layard was a frequent and popular visitor at the Guests' country mansion, Canford Manor, at Wimborne in Dorset - it had been a ruin dating back to the reign of King John, which Sir John Guest largely rebuilt.[1] Here was set up in 1847 the 'Nineveh Porch', adorned with Assyrian gateway colossi from Nimrud, and Assyrian reliefs, and equipped with a pair of splendid iron-work gates in the best Victorian-Assyrian style provided by Sir John, in fact housing a miniature museum of Assyrian antiquities from Layard's finds.[2] But after Sir John Guest died in 1852, in 1855 Lady Guest married again, this time espousing - amid some comment - her son's tutor, Dr. Schreiber. Nevertheless, henceforth as Lady Charlotte Schreiber she maintained her own interests, as a woman of scholarship and culture, as translator of the Welsh epic, the *Mabinogion,*[3] and as the possessor of a unique collection of porcelain. In 1869 at the age of 52, Sir Henry Layard - as he was by then - proposed to Enid Guest, then 25, the eighth child of the late Sir John and Lady Charlotte. In spite of the age-gap, the marriage which took place on 9th March, 1869, proved very happy. As a wedding gift to his young bride, the serious-minded scholar-diplomat chose an original, if somewhat bizarre present, ordering a set of jewelry to be made up for her from a selection of his collection of cylinder seals and stamp seals,[4] by Messrs. Phillips of 23, Cockspur Street.[5] 'Today', Enid Layard wrote in her new diary on 23rd March, 1869, 'H. gave me a bracelet, being Esarhaddon's signet w[h]. he had found at Nineveh and had set by Phillips.'[6] The cylinder seal in question is unfortunately not inscribed in cuneiform so we have no other proof than her or his word or fancy that it had belonged to Esarhaddon himself; but it is certainly a very fine seal worthy of a king. The implication seems, however, to be that it was found in the S.W. Palace of Esarhaddon at Nimrud, not Nineveh. Of this I have so far been unable to find any other record, but it is of course perfectly possible.

The set, when complete, consisted of three pieces, (or four, if we count the ear-rings as two). The first was the especially fine cylinder seal, 'Esarhaddon's signet', mounted as the centre piece of a gold bracelet terminating at each end in lion's heads - evidently inspired by the armlets ending in lions' heads worn by Ashurbanipal in his lion-hunt reliefs. It forms however rather an ugly shape and reminds me rather of a manacle than a bracelet. The second item was a pair of earrings, also made from cylinder seals, also with gold caps in the form of lions' heads, and having pendants in the form of pine-cones. The third was a massive necklace made up of eleven cylinder seals and five stamp seals, capped and linked with gold mounts. The whole was kept in a specially made leather covered case lined with red silk. Lady Layard wore these elaborate ornaments on gala occasions when full evening dress was appropriate.[7] The jewelry was for a time mounted on the life-size bust of Lady Layard, by J. Warrington Wood (1881)[8] and was so exhibited for a time in the British Museum. It gave us at least some idea of what it may have looked like when in use. Waterfield describes the necklace as 'covering her white bosom in a heavy row of dull unsparkling browns,[9]' but this is hardly either fair or precise, since it could be seen to cover no more than her white neck, and the predominant colours were not browns, but brown-black, grey and whitish-blue.

This exotic *parure* apparently made a good topic of table conversation when the Layards were willing or desirous for the talk to turn on Sir Henry's unforgettable discoveries in Assyria. No doubt they helped many a diplomatic dinner-party in Layard's long ambassadorial career to success, if it seemed likely to be a little 'sticky'. Whether it would have had the same effect today is an interesting matter for speculation. In 1873, however, the Layards were invited by the Queen to Osborne House in the Isle of Wight, to dine with Her Majesty. "We were ab[t] an hour at dinner" wrote Lady Layard in her diary on July 23rd, 1873, "and the conversation was general. I wore my Nineveh necklace w[h]. was much admired and the bracelet passed round for inspection".[10] Almost fascinating in its combination of ugliness of design and fine craftsmanship, like so much of Victorian art, these weird but historic pieces of jewelry have remained as a valuable reminder of the artistic outlook of a century ago. It was exceedingly difficult to obtain an impression from them, fitted as they are tightly in their modern mounts and this is no doubt one of the reasons why they have not been hitherto studied, much less published.[11] But by the skill of Mr. C.A. Bateman, Senior Conservation Officer in the Department of Western Asiatic Antiquities, this difficulty was overcome, and I am happy to offer them in publication as a tribute to Dame Kathleen Kenyon, in her honour. The seals and stamp seals

Plate XXVII

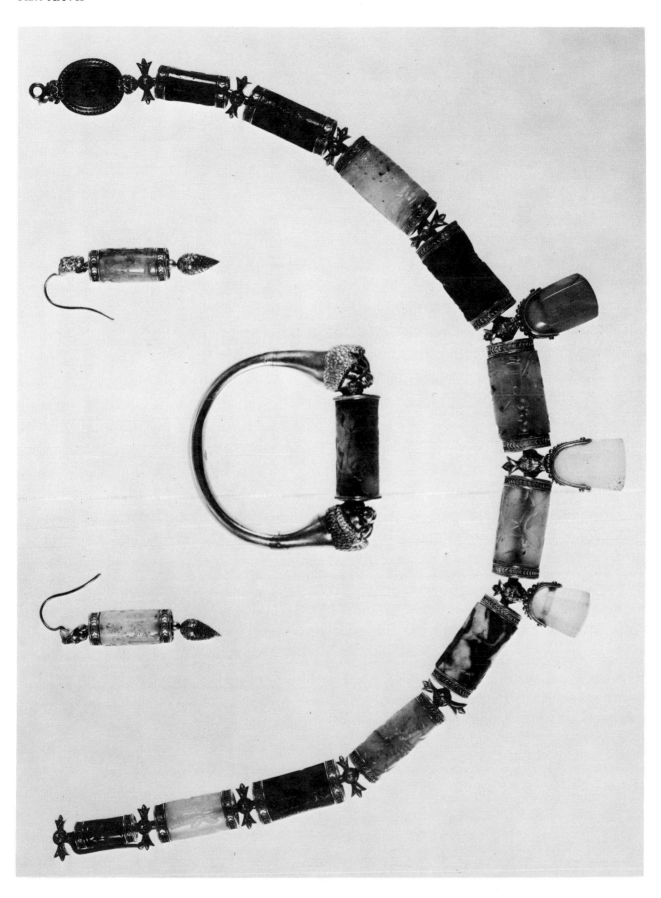

Plate XXVIII

3

1

4

2

5

6

15

17

18

16

Plate XXIX

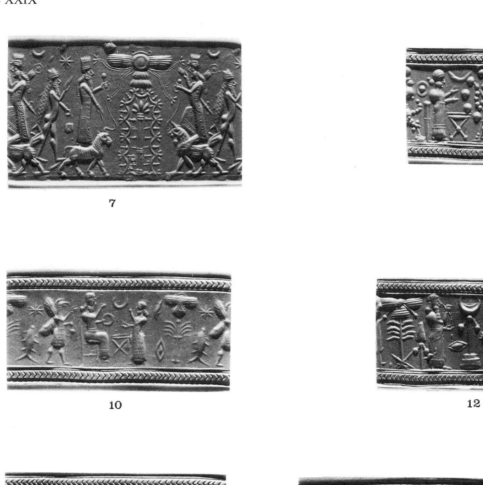

7

11

10

12

14

8

9

13

forming the necklace are for the most part not particularly unusual; but no. 5, an Elamite seal with an Elamite inscription, is of great interest, bearing a royal name; (Pl. XXVIII); and nos. 2 (pl. XXVIII) and 9 (Pl. XXIX), and 18 (pl. XVIII) are fine specimens. The exceptional quality of no. 7, 'the signet of Esarhaddon' (pl. XXIX), hardly needs stressing. It will, however, be noticed that in spite of Mr. Bateman's efforts, the modern gold mounts leave on the top and bottom of each impression a chevron pattern rather like that of a half-track vehicle; but fortunately this does not seriously interfere with the design of any seal, though it occasionally hampers the reading of the inscription.

The jewelry was bequeathed to the British Museum by Lady Layard, and after her death in 1912 was registered in 1913 in the then Dept. of Egyptian and Assyrian Antiquities under the numbers 1913.32 and given the exhibition number 115656.

References

1. Now a public school (Canford School) since 1923.
2. The Nineveh Porch is now the school tuck-shop. The gates are still there, but the 'museum' was long ago dispersed. For my discovery of unpublished Assyrian reliefs there, see my "Canford and Cuneiform; A Century of Assyriology," *Museums Journal,* November 1960. The gateway figures were sold in 1923, being replaced by full-size plaster casts, and were acquired by the New York Historical Society. From there they passed to the Metropolitan Museum of Art. See C. J. Gadd, *The Stones of Assyria* (1936) and E. Porada, *The Great King of Assyria; Assyrian Reliefs in the Metropolitan Museum of Art,* (1945).
3. See David Jones, "Lady Charlotte Guest; Victorian businesswoman; the life of the translator of the Mabinogion". *History Today* April 1970; and Gordon Waterfield, *Layard of Nineveh,* (1963).
4. The remainder of Layard's collection of seals (18 in all) was published by E. Borowski, 'Siegel der Sammlung Layard', *Orientalia,* N.S. XXI, 1922, and by Mrs. E. D. Van Buren "Seals of the 2nd half of the Layard collection" *ibid* XXIII (1924). I am obliged to Miss D. Collon for the second of these references.
5. This firm specialised in reproductions of antique jewelry. They went out of business in about 1927 and are not to be confused with Messrs. S.J. Phillips of Bond Street, founded in 1869. I owe this information to the kindness of Mr. R. J. Norton, former director of Messrs. S. J. Phillips. I have once seen another similar necklace of seals which I understood had been made for a friend of Layard's, Ross.
6. Lady Layard's Journal, British Library, Department of MSS., Add. MS. Vol. 1, Fol. 2, verso. I am obliged to my former colleague Mr. C. F. B. Walker for this and the later reference in n. 10 below, and to Dr. D. Waley, Keeper of the Department of MSS, for permission to quote them.
7. Waterfield, *op. cit.,* p. 310.
8. Born 1839, died 1886. The bust was presented to the Museum by Miss Katherine Wyld.
9. Waterfield, loc. cit.
10. Add.Ms. 46154, vol. 11, fol. 113, verso.
11. Only one (no. 8) appears to have been ever published. An illustration of the jewelry as a whole and a reference to Lady Layard's journal appears in Charlotte Gere, *Victorian Jewellery Design,* 1972, pp. 108 and 275 and pl. 41.

Catalogue

Akkadian

1.[2] * Lion attacking ibex, both rampant, between their hindlegs a criss-cross pattern; the same combat repeated, but with crossed bodies. Between the two groups, a reversed crescent.
2.8 cm h.; 1.7 cm.b. **
Blackish steatite.
cf. R. Boehmer, *Die Entwicklung der Glyptik während der Akkad-Zeit,* (Berlin, 1965) "Akkadisch 1b".
Plate XXVIII, 1

Old Babylonian

2.[6]   Presentation scene. Goddess wearing horned headdress stands with up-raised hands facing r. Man wearing flat cap and long dress, facing r., pours a libation from a cup into a vessel, before a deity facing l., wearing horned headdress and long dress and resting l. foot on a pedestal, (perhaps model of a building) who extends towards the man the rod and ring.

Inscription in four columns: ***
ur-ᵈšul-pa-è   *Ur-Šulpae, son of Za-Èsanum, servant of Šulpae and Ninhursag*

dumu za-É-sa-nu-um   za-Ésanum is probably an Amorite name (otherwise unknown):
                        É could be -bit-, -pit-, -lil-, etc.

ìr ^dšul-pa-è

ù ^dnin-hur-saĝ-ĝá   Haematite.
                       2.7 cm.h.; i.5 cm.b.;

For the introducing goddess in flounced dress with upraised hands, probably LAMA, see A. Spycket 'La déesse Lama,' *Revue d'Assyriologie,* LIV, 1960, and D. J. Wiseman, 'The goddess Lama at Ur', *Iraq,* XXII, 1960.   Plate XXVIII, 2.

3.[8]   Twin figures of goddesses with upraised hands, of type of ^dLAMA, confronted on either side of an inscription.
         Inscription in three columns:

a-na-pa-ni-^dEN.ZU-na-di   (beginning and end of lines partly obliterated by gold mounting)

dumu i-din-eš-tár

ìr ^dšul-pa-è   *Anapani-Sin-nadi, son of Idin-Eštar, servant of Šulpae*

     Variegated red-brown marble, streaked with white. Chipped at top and bottom.
     2.8 cm. h.; 1.3 cm.b.

For this type of inscription and the significance of the twin goddesses, see P. R. Moorey and O. R. Gurney, 'Ancient Near Eastern Seals at Charterhouse', *Iraq* XXXV, 1973, p. 76.
                                                  Plate XXVIII, 3.

4 [14]   Striding bearded man (the 'man with the mace') advances to r. towards figures of interceding goddess (^dLAMA) who faces him, and naked goddess facing to front, holding her breasts.
     Black stone, perhaps limonite. Chipped above and below.
     1.8 cm.h; 1.1 cm.b.

For a discussion of the 'Man with the mace', see Moorey and Gurney, *loc. cit.,* p. 75.   Plate XXVIII, 4.

Elamite

5 [13]   Man dressed in long garment carrying diminutive animal (goat?) faces r. towards goddess on pedestal wearing flounced skirt, who faces l. towards him and raises r. hand in greeting or benediction. Between them, in field, a bird(?) a dagger, a seated monkey
         Inscription in four columns:

li-ba-ar-ma-za-at   *Libar-mazat*
dumu am-ma-me-en-na-ri-[iš]   *son of Ammamenna-rišara*
šà a-ra-a   *servant of Temti-ḫalki*
ìr te-em-ti-ḫal-ki

Dr. Erica Reiner kindly informs me that the first element of the owner's name, Ammamenna, is common in Elamite names, but that the spelling of the second element, rišara, is most unusual.
2.5 cm.h.
Haematite.
17th century B.C. Temti-ḫalki was regent of Susa, 1655-1650 B.C.   Plate XXVIII, 5.

Mitannian (Nuzi)

6 [4]   Naked goddess *en face,* facing l. holds up pair of reversed animals, between (1.) star and (r.) *couchant* sphinx. To r., 'sacred tree' between pair of *couchant* goats. On either side of tree, an upturned crescent.
1.3 cm.h; .9 cm.b.
Blackish stone (limonite?).   Plate XXVIII, 6.

Assyrian- 'Neo-Assyrian Modelled Style'

7 [1]   Adad, standing on a bull, holding mace ring and leash in l. hand, and rod (?) in r., is advancing r. towards 'sacred tree', followed by naked, bearded but sexless man wearing fish-skin, performing act with pine-cone and pail. Above 'sacred tree' is a winged, tailed sun-disc with four streamers ending in buds. Opposite Adad, armed goddess (Ishtar?) standing on winged horned lion with eagle's feet and tail, advances l. towards 'sacred tree', holding mace, ring and leash in r. hand, raises l. in greeting. In field above, a star and crescent.
3.4 cm.h.; 1.6 cm b.
Carnelian.
8th century B.C.

The so-called 'signet of Esarhaddon', evidently found in the palace of Esarhaddon at Nimrud.

Plate XXIX, 7.

'Neo-Assyrian Fine Style'

8 [9]   Bearded hero, wearing kilt and long dress stands facing r. between bearded male sphinxes rampant which he fights, throttling that on r., which has an upright tuft on its cap. To r. is a stylised 'sacred tree', above which hovers moon-god Sin in upturned crescent.
2.8 cm. h; 1.7 cm. b.
Bluish chalcedony, chipped at bottom.
Layard, *Monuments of Nineveh*, II (1853), pl. LXIX, 42.   Plate XXIX, 8.

9 [12]   Bearded winged man wearing kilt and long dress and holding branch of pomegranates in l. hand advances r., saluting with l. Before him bearded fish-man advances r. towards 'sacred tree', above which hovers winged tailed disc with two streamers, one of which he grasps with r. hand. Opposite him, bearded man (king?) wearing long garment and dagger, salutes 'sacred tree' with cupped r. hand. In field, 8-pointed star, seated eagle, lozenge, palmette.
3 cm. h.; 1.3 cm.b.
Whitish chalcedony.
The palmette resembles that on the so-called 'signet of Sennacherib' (now BM 89502) found by Layard at the foot of the bulls in the Great Entrance of the Palace of Sennacherib at Kuyunjik. (Layard, *Nineveh and Babylon* (1853), p. 160). The winged genius with pomegranates occurs in reliefs of Ashurnasirpal, Tiglath-pileser III and Sargon.   Plate XXIX, 9.

'Neo-Assyrian Early Drilled Style'

10 [4]   Eagle-headed winged man wearing kilt advances r. to perform ritual act with cone and pail to goddess who sits on throne facing r. holding ring in r. hand and saluting with l. facing worshipper in front of offering table. He extends l. hand to receive ring and salutes with r. Behind him, 'sacred tree' above which floats winged, tailed disc. In field, 8-pointed star, fish, upturned crescent, a second fish, lozenge.
2.1 cm.h.; 1.2 cm.b.
Whitish chalcedony.   Plate XXIX, 10.

11 [2]   Worshipping woman facing r. over sacrificial table salutes Ishtar advancing to l., surrounded by circle of 8 outer and 15 inner spheres, representing stars. She is followed by scorpion-man advancing l., r. hand raised, l. holding bucket (?). In field, stylus, circle enclosing dot, upturned crescent, fish.
2.2cm.h.; 1.2 cm.b.
Whitish chalcedony.
The scorpion-man supports the throne of Ishtar on the relief at Bavian. For similar scene see G. Eisen, *Ancient Oriental Seals . . . . in the collection of Mrs. W. H. Moore,* (1940), pl. IX, no. 84, where other references are also given. Mounted with gold lion's head and pine-cone to form an earring. Plate XXIX, 11.

12 [3]   Bearded worshipper facing r. extends l. hand and salutes by cracking fingers of r., crescent symbol of Sin of Harran mounted on post and base. To r., 'sacred tree' above which floats winged tailed disc with two streamers. In field, wedge with tassels, lozenge, bull's head, fish, star, mace, stylus (?).
2.1 cm.h.; 1.2 cm.b.
Whitish chalcedony, chipped at top.
For this gesture of salute, see Gadd, *Stones of Assyria*, p. 3.
Mounted as last to form an earring.   Plate XXIX, 12.

13 [10]   Goddess sitting on throne backed with stars facing r. raises r. hand to greet across sacrificial table a bearded, male worshipper, who advances l. also raising hand in salutation. Behind him, a goat looking backwards. In field a 6- pointed star crescent, lozenge.
Above table, a winged tailed disc hovers.
3 cm.h.; 1.5 cm.b.
Grey chalcedony, chipped at top.   Plate XXIX, 13.

14 [7]   Bearded worshipper faces l. towards 'sacred tree' above which a long necked bird appears to be standing. Above floats a winged tailed disc with two streamers. To r. is a figure of the goddess Ishtar with eleven rays encircling her, ending in spheres representing stars. In field, 6-rayed star, fish, vertical shaft on lozenge, upturned crescent.

2.8 cm.h; 1.4 cm.b.
Greyish chalcedony.   Plate XXIX, 9.

Neo-Babylonian

15 [16] Eight-sided conoid stamp seal, engraved on base and two sides. Base. Bearded worshipper wearing headdress
faces r. with upraised r. hand towards smoking altar. Above, upturned crescent.
Side (a) altar with symbols of gods: *marru,* and sickle
Side (b) tripod-table (only two feet shown) with lion's paw feet, supporting lamp of Nusku.
2.6 cm h.; 1.2 cm. b.
Whitish grey agate.   Plate XXVIII, 15.

16 [17] Eight-sided conoid. Bearded worshipper facing l. wearing headdress salutes another bearded figure on
slightly higher level facing r., who returns salutation, standing between two symbols, ball-topped cross and
mace.
2.cm.h.; 1.3 cm.b.   Plate XXVIII, 16.
Coarse disc-cut work.

Achaemenid

17 [18] Persian Great King depicted as Lord of Beasts, holding up a pair of lions by their tails.
2.4 cm. h.; 1.7 cm.b.
Bluish chalcedony.   Plate XXVIII, 17.

18 [15] Ovoid seal with domed back. Wild goat galloping 1.
1.2 cm.h.; 1.8 cm.b.
Greyish chalcedony.   Plate XXVIII, 18.
Fine quality.

---

*   Numbers in brackets indicate the serial number of the item in the arrangement of the seals in the jewellery.

** Sizes are approximate, being the largest visible measurements permitted by the gold mounts.

*** For the reading of this and the following inscriptions I am much indebted to Dr. E. Sollberger.

Plate XXX

Silver earrings (a)   Deve Hüyük.
*   Scale 1:1*

(b. c.) Tell -el Farah. Tomb 725
*   Scale 2:1*

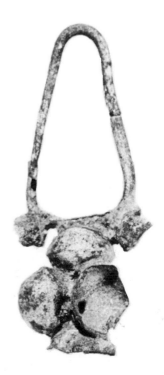

a.   b.   c.

A SILVER EARRING FROM TELL-EL FARAH (South).
by K. R. Maxwell-Hyslop.

A silver earring from Tomb 725 at Tell el-Farah is now in the Petrie collection at the Institute of Archaeology, University of London and in gratitude and appreciation for Dame Kathleen Kenyon's invaluable work on the Palestinian material at the Institute this note on a small, but important, piece of jewellery is contributed by a former colleague.

Tomb 725 contained a necklace of carnelian beads, a stone (? weight), the earring (Pl. XXX b, c,) fragments of a similar earring (possibly the pair) and unfortunately no pottery. It was dated by Petrie to the 26th Dynasty period and recent studies of jewellery dating from the 6th and 5th centuries B.C. demand a reappraisal of this distinctive type.

Description.   Height 4.2 cms.   Width 1.7 cms.

Technique.

The hoop of the earring must have been hammered from a thin strip of silver and then rolled between plates of stone or bronze. The seven balls of sheet silver were probably made by hammering the sheet over a doming block and into semicircular depressions of the size required using a doming punch. This tool could have been made of wood or bronze. The two halves of the globules were then soldered together using a silver alloy of lower melting point than that of the silver used for the earring. Before the two halves were soldered together it would be necessary to pierce one half so that the air could escape and this hole is visible on one of the broken balls.

The condition of the earring precludes the possibility of stating with certainty whether granular decoration, either at the base of the lowest ball, or across the base of the hoop was employed, in similar fashion to the silver earring from Farah tomb 754, which is comparable in shape and technique to the tomb 725 example.[1] A closer parallel, however, can be found in the silver earring from Tomb 19 at Deve Hüyük (Pl. XXXa) which was also composed of seven hollow globules and the dating evidence here is clear; the tomb belongs to the Persian period and the evidence of the coins in the Deve Hüyük cemetery suggests that the date cannot be much earlier than the 5th century B.C.[2]

Additional close parallels with the Farah tomb 725 earring are not easy to find. At Lachish, a gold earring, the high, narrow loop bound with gold and with a comparable arrangement of three hollow balls is remarkably similar. It probably belongs to the Persian period at Lachish,[3] while developed examples of the type with fine granulation occur in the 5th century Jordanian hoard now in the Ashmolean Museum which has been studied in detail by Moorey.[4]

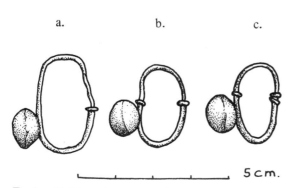

a.   b.   c.

5 cm.

Fig 1.   Gold earrings. Babylon

Fig 2.   Malatya.

The history of this distinctive type of earring begins with examples from Babylon where gold earrings with one large ball or globule made in two parts attached to the loop occurs in tombs of the Kassite period.[5] Three slightly different forms were found (Fig. 1 a - c) but while the simplest form (Fig 1 a) was found in a tomb dated to the earliest Kassite period at Babylon there is no chronological significance in the other two variations. In tomb 32 fourteen examples were found and the excavator considered that the evidence suggests a long period of use for over 300 years from the middle of the 2nd millennium B.C. onwards. At Babylon, this type does not occur in the succeeding 'Babylonian - Assyrian' level, but at Mari, a fine elaborate example in gold with several small balls decorated with minute granules belongs to the Middle Assyrian period.[6]

While it is possible to suggest an Iranian ancestry for the silver Farah earring there is little evidence to prove this hypotheses, beyond a general similarity of technique and design which can be found in gold earrings from Marlik in Gilan, Hasanlu in Azerbaijan and neo-Elamite examples from Susa, notwithstanding the differences such as the use of granulation on the Elamite examples or of pomegranate-shaped balls on the Marlik earring.[7]

Comparable silver earrings from Iran belong to the 8th and 7th centuries B.C. and, while often imitating gold types, show little technical skill. At Sialk Cemetery B (now dated 850 - 650 B.C.) no gold was found; the jewellery was all of bronze, terracotta, silver or silver and iron combined. An earring pendant composed of five large silver globules was attached to a bronze loop, another silver example was made of smaller globules (hollow) with circular loop.[8] Related types can be found both earlier in the Cemetery of War Kabud (8th - 7th centuries B.C.) and at the Median site of Nush-i-Jan, in the remarkable silver hoard considered by the excavator to be part of a silversmith's 'stock in trade'.[9] On this latter piece coarse granulation is employed as a decorative technique and none of these earlier silver pieces display the technical skill shown by the Farah tomb 754 example, where the granulation is finely wrought or approach the standard of work of the silversmith who made the earrings from the Jordanian hoard mentioned above, who could have been working as early as the late 6th or early 5th century B.C.

If the Farah tomb 725 earring was made by a Palestinian silversmith working at Tell Farah and was not imported either from Syria or from a workshop supplying jewellery to a neighbouring Persian governor (such as the occupier of the Persian residence excavated at Lachish) then local characteristics would be expected. It is possible to discern certain features which suggest this may be the case. The high narrow form of the hoop is common among earlier earrings of the Solomonic period at Tell Farah, while a type with solid gold balls soldered to the base of the hoop found in tomb 605, in association with a 'tassel' earring, may well be the prototype for the later silver earring with larger hollow balls.[10] A steatite mould in the British Museum from Kuyundjik (B.M. 1929. 10. 12, 353) shows the Assyrian version of this earlier distinctive type, cast with solid balls, and the final and more elaborate development of both of these types can be found in the Jordanian hoard mentioned above.

None of the earrings discussed here can be found portrayed on Achaemenid or Assyrian reliefs, with the possible exception of Sennacherib's rock reliefs at Hines and here the balls are clearly cut in the shape of pomegranates and are attached to a semi-circular hoop.[11] It is possible, however, that the Farah type of earring is portrayed on sculptured reliefs from South-east Turkey. The lady on the funerary slab from Marash, now in the Adana Museum, wears earrings apparently of this form, with the pin passing through the lobe of the ear, as though the sculptor was intending to indicate an earring with an oblong shaped hoop and pendant globules of which three are carved from the side view. At Malatya another ornament is also shown at the top of the ear, with the wire passing round the lobe to the front. Fig 2. This slab can be dated to the 8th century B.C.[12]

The increasing use of silver for jewellery in Palestine and Syria during the Neo-Babylonian and early part of the Persian periods is indicative of general shortage of gold and unsettled trading conditions and it seems probable that it was not until the organisation of the empire by Darius that gold sources again became easily accessible for merchants supplying the workshops of jewellers, goldsmiths and silversmiths.

It is unfortunate that we know nothing about the extent of Persian occupation at Tell Farah. The rich tomb with the fluted silver bowl and spoon with the handle in the form of a swimming girl, if it is correctly assigned to the Persian period,[13] would indicate that Persian occupation has yet to be identified on the mound. Cemetery 700 apparently contained tombs of differing dates, some as late as Hellenistic times. The earring can therefore only be dated by reference to the similar silver example from Deve Hüyük and the Lachish gold earring with the *caveat* that it is possible that any well dated tomb containing jewellery will always only give a date of when the jewellery was actually in use; it may have been made several generations earlier before it was placed in the tomb. A date in the Neo-Babylonian or latter part of the 6th century B.C. can therefore not be entirely dismissed.

Report on Silver Content.

Examination of two earrings from Tell Fara Tomb 725.

Tests revealed that the larger and more complete earring was of silver of good quality, not base silver.

The more incomplete earring responded very little to tests, owing to the fact that it is almost completely mineralised. However, after considerable careful scraping on the inside of one of the balls an adequate surface was revealed which reacted to the test for good silver.

Ashmolean Museum, Oxford.   A. C. Western
                                                                                                                        11.6.74.

References

1. F. Petrie, *Beth-Pelet*, I, pl. XLVIII, 573, K. R. Maxwell-Hyslop, *Western Asiatic Jewellery* (1971), (hereafter *WAJ*), pl. 210.
2. L. Woolley in *LAAA*, VII, (1914-16) 120, pl. XXIII, 8.
3. O. Tufnell, *Lachish III* 160, Fig 15. This earring was found in the scree below the Persian building associated with inscribed jar handles dated to c. 275 - 250 B.C.
4. P. R. S. Moorey in *Revue Numismatique* X (1969), 198-200.
5. O. Reuther, *Die Innenstadt von Babylon* (1926), Pl. XXII 131, 134.   (Merkes)
6. *WAJ*, pl. 131.
7. The Hasanlu gold earring is made in the form of a pendant *WAJ*, pl. 135. Both parts of the earring, pendant and hoop, Taf. 48, 55, are found on a comparable pair of gold earrings (unstratified) British Museum No. 90.10.11. 1 & 2 (*WAJ* pl. 212) composed of large balls, decorated in granulation attached to a small loop, the balls forming the pendant to the body of the earring. *WAJ*, pls. 144, 211, (Marlik and Susa).
8. R. Ghirshman, *Fouilles de Sialk*, (1939), II, pl. XCV, S. 1476b. pl. XXVII, 8.
9. *WAJ*, pl. 249. D. Stronach in *Iran* VII (1969), pls. VIII-X.
10. K. R. Maxwell-Hyslop *WAJ*, pl. 200.
11. K. R. Maxwell-Hyslop, *WAJ* 243, Fig 135. W. Bachmann. *Felsreliefs in Assyrien*, (1927) Taf. 10.
12. *Hittite Art and Antiquities of Anatolia*. Arts Council (1964) pl. 224.
13. J. H. Iliffe in *QDAP*, IV, (1935), 182; R. D. Barnett in *Iranica Antiqua* II (1962), 90.

Acknowledgements. I am grateful to Mr. H. Hodges of the Institute of Archaeology, University of London and to Mr. P. Lowery, Silversmith, for information concerning the techniques used in the manufacture of this earring. Also to Mrs. Jane MacKay for the drawing, Fig. 1.

YERUSHALAYIM
by A. D. Tushingham.

Yerûshāláyim, as the accepted spelling and pronunciation of the name of the Holy City, has the support of the traditional vocalization of the Hebrew Scriptures and of modern Israeli usage. Yet, as is well known, it is at variance with the original form in both respects. From its foundation, apparently, the name was pronounced something like *Yerûshālēm,* [1] and the evidence from extra-Biblical sources over the centuries is consistent with this. [2] The spelling of the Hebrew Bible (i.e. the *Kethîb,* or "written") assumes a similar pronunciation in both the Hebrew and Aramaic portions, and the versions - particularly the Greek Septuagint [3] of the third-second centuries B.C., the Syriac, and the Latin versions - support it.

In spite of the overwhelming evidence of the Hebrew text, the versions, and the apparently invariable pronunciation by foreigners (at least for the second part of the word), the traditional rendering as established by Jewish scholars and fixed in the vocalization of the *Qerê* ("to be read") was *Yerûshālāyim.* The final syllable was given the form of a dual [4] by the quasi-interpolation of a *yod* or *y,* although the consonant was not inserted into the *textus receptus* (the *Kethîb*). [5] This anomalous situation - a prescribed pronunciation which flies in the face of all the evidence for the original and correct pronunciation, and which has, at the same time, no obvious justification - has remained a *crux interpretum.*

In the hope that an assessment of the evidence now available to us (linguistic, topographic, literary and archaeological) may not only provide a solution to the enigma but also throw light on the architectural history of the ancient city, the present essay is offered as a tribute to Dame Kathleen Kenyon who, for seven hard and decisive years, brought the sharp and incisive tools of modern archaeological theory and method to the fulfilment of the psalmist's exhortation:

"Walk about Zion, and go round about her: tell the towers thereof.
"Mark ye well her bulwarks, consider her palaces;
    that ye may tell it to the generation following." [6]

It is perhaps no accident that one of the early scholars to discuss the puzzle was that dean of Palestinian archaeologists, Père Hugues Vincent. In an article entitled "Les noms de Jérusalem", [7] he pointed out that the rabbinic tradition clung very tightly to the assumption that the second part of the word consisted of the root *sh-l-m;* the scholars who established the traditional pronunciation, therefore, could hardly have made such a mistake as to consider their reading as constituting a dual of the whole word, i.e. "two Jerusalems", which would have had to be something like *Yerûshelemáyim.* Further, the weight of evidence for the ancient and correct pronunciation would have prevented them from introducing such an innovation - at least without some clear and powerful justification. His solution to the problem is that, indeed, the form is intended to be a dual, but it is artificial ("factice"), a "neologisme", and was intended to add dignity to the name of the capital. [8] The rabbis, he thought, justified their innovation on the pretext that the form of the name with a penultimate *yod* was the original form and, in fact, represented a dual; only later, so their argument would have run, was the diphthong contracted into the long vowel attested in the ancient and normal pronunciation of the word.

Vincent's view that the word is not a true dual is supported by most scholars today. [9] KOEHLER-BAUMGARTNER, for instance, consider it "künstlich". A serious attempt to provide a linguistic explanation for the form is given in GKC, [10] and it is necessary for us to consider the validity of the argument. This may be summarized as follows: "Certain place-names were formerly reckoned as dual-forms" viz. those with endings in *áyin, ān,* and *ām.* The view that *ān* and *ām* arise "from a contraction of the dual terminations" *áyin . . .* and *áyim* "seemed to be supported" by the Mesha inscription but because "in many of these supposed duals either a dual sense cannot be detected at all, or it does not agree at any rate with the nature of the Semitic dual, as found elsewhere . . . it can hardly be doubted" that *áyin* and *áyim* "in these place-names only arise from a subsequent expansion of the terminations" *ān* and *ām.* The grammarians then cite the supposed derivation of the *Qerê* form *Yerûshālāyim* from *Yerûshālēm* as "the strongest argument in favour of this opinion", and follow it with other claimed examples of a like process.

Before considering the alleged parallels, we should note that the "strongest argument" is nothing of the sort. As we shall see, the crux of the argument lies in a supposed expansion of proper names ending in *ām* or *ān* into forms with a final *áyim* or *áyin* (i.e. with a penultimate interpolated *yod*) which looks like a dual. But *Yerûshālēm* has a long *ē* not *ā*, and the evidence for an "expanded" form (with penultimate *yod*) in the *Kethîb* - i.e. in the ancient *textus receptus* - is slim and suspect as we have seen. Nevertheless, we must look at the parallels adduced and assay their significance.

The examples given are as follows: *Dōthān* appears in this form twice (Gen. 37:17; II Kings 6:13); once, in pause, and with the locative ending *h*, we have it written as *Dōthāynāh* (Gen. 37:17). A town in Naphtali is spelled *Qartān* in Joshua 21:32 and *Qiryātháyim* in Chronicles 6:61 (note that *two yods* have been added in the second version and the ending is *m*, not *n*). Finally, a place named *Ha'êynām* in Joshua 15:34 is equated with *'Êynáyem* in Genesis 38:21 (but note the peculiar short *e* not *i* vowel in the final syllable and compare Genesis 38:14 and the versions, whose difficulties suggest that this may not be a proper name at all). One can only comment - without attempting to explain them - that these few and idiosyncratic occurrences appear very obscure and weak grounds upon which to build a theory of "expansion" of endings in *ām* and *ān* to *áyim* and *áyin*.

Another element in the argument is the denial that forms of proper names which occur in the Mesha (Moabite) stone with final *n* represent, in fact, original dual endings, even though the same names - when they occur in the Biblical text - have normal dual endings. The examples are: *Qrytn* (Mesha, line 10) and *Qiryātháyim* (Gen. 14:5; Num. 32:37; Josh. 13:19; Jer. 48:1, 23; Ezek. 25:9); *Bt Dbltn* (line 30) and *Bêth Diblātháyim* (Jer. 48:22); *Hwrnn* (lines 31, 32) and *Hōrōnáyim* (II Sam. 13:34 in Septuagint; Isa. 15:5; Jer. 48:3, 5, 34).[11] The Hebrew parallels certainly argue for a reading of the endings in the Moabite proper names as if they were duals - whatever the significance of these endings may be. Whether, however, we assert or deny that the Hebrew and Moabite forms in question are real duals has no bearing or relevance as an explanation of the "dual" form of Jerusalem for, as we have seen, it is essential that the alleged expanded form of *Yerûshālēm* be *Yerûshāláyim* (with penultimate *yod*) and the evidence for such a form in the Biblical period is, at best, meagre and, we believe, non-existent.

GESENIUS-KAUTZSCH-COWLEY also draw a supposed parallel in the form *Shāmráyin* (i.e. Samaria), which appears in the Biblical Aramaic of Ezra 4:10, 17; this apparent dual is considered to be an expanded form of an original, but hypothetical, form *Shāmrān* which is parallel to the Hebrew *Shomrôn*. The cases, however, are not parallel. The Aramaic *Shāmráyin*[12] is written with a penultimate *yod* which assumes a diphthong *ay*.[13] The Hebrew *Yerûshālēm* has no *yod* in the final syllable and was always, on the basis of the versions and foreign transcriptions, pronounced with a final pure vowel, not a diphthong. An expanded version of the name, analogous to Shāmráyin, would have had a penultimate *yod*; yet, as we have seen, the evidence for any occurrence of the form with *yod* in the *textus receptus* is so slight, inconsistent, and undependable as to have no weight against the "unexpanded" form. Even the form as it appears in Biblical Aramaic (in Daniel and Ezra) is *Yerûshlem* - with a short final vowel[14] - and there is no evidence of an expanded form parallel to *Shāmráyin*.

We may go a step further. In Assyrian transcriptions, Jerusalem appears normally as *Ur-sa-li-im-mu.*[15] This represents, probably, *Ursalimmu,* with a short *i*, like the short *e* of the Biblical Aramaic,[16] or, just possibly, *Ursalīmu,* with a long *ī* (representing, perhaps, the tone-long *ē* of the Hebrew or the Biblical Aramaic variant. But, whether the Assyrian represents a vowel still short or, because of the tone, long, it seems clear that the original vowel in the final syllable of the name Jerusalem was short. In contrast with this, the name of Samaria appears in Assyrian transcription as *Sa-mi-ri-na* or *Sa-mir-i-na,*[17] with a long *i* vowel (whether pure-long or tone-long cannot be determined) in the penultimate syllable; this appears to represent an Aramaic (or north Israelite) form of the name of the northern capital rather than the Judahite (or southern) form known in our Bibles (*Shomrôn*). Possibly we must explain the transcription of both proper names in Assyrian as based on Aramaic pronunciations of the two Hebrew words - not an unlikely hypothesis when we consider the extent to which Aramaic was the *lingua franca* of the Near East at this time.[18] However that may be, there is no evidence that the dual form *Shāmráyin* of the Biblical Aramaic (supported, as we have seen, by the Babylonian Chronicle) was "expanded" out of the form attested by the Assyrian transcriptions, and there is likewise no evidence that an "expanded" form of *Yerûshālēm* (Hebrew) or *Yerûshlem* (Biblical Aramaic) ever existed.

Finally, in support of the alleged expansion of proper names into forms which appear to be duals, GKC adduced other supposed examples. Of these, we may say only that, if *Ephráyim* is to be considered an expanded form, there is no unexpanded form extant; that *Naharáyim* is not a dual but a mispointing or misunderstanding of a form which appears in the Amarna letters as *Na-a'-ri-ma, Nārima,* and in Egyptian as *Naharina* (see KOEHLER-

BAUMGARTNER); that *Miṣráyim* may, in fact, be a dual representing the historic union of the Two Lands, Upper and Lower Egypt,[19] for the translations into foreign languages usually favour a singular form with the consonants *m-ṣ-r* with which the Hebrew gentilic (supported by Ugaritic and Nabataean), *miṣrî* "Egyptian", agrees. None of these proper names supports the theory of an "expansion" of an original form into a dual-appearing form.

Our critique of the GKC thesis that all proper names with apparent dual endings are to be explained as "expansions" of earlier forms with *ām* or *ān* may or may not be accepted. However, we believe that enough doubt has been thrown on its validity - or at least on its adequacy as an explanation of the dual form of Yerûshāla̓yim - to warrant our search for another origin of this peculiar vocalization.

We have already noted how infrequent - and unreliable - is the spelling of Jerusalem with a penultimate *yod* in the Hebrew text of the Bible.[20] In the Dead Sea Scrolls, however, it is another matter.[21] In them we find a general distinction between the spelling of the name of Jerusalem in a Biblical quotation and in the commentary (*pesher*) on that text. In the former, the word is spelt, as in the *textus receptus,* without the penultimate *yod* - Yerûshālēm. The *pesher,* however, frequently, but not always, spells the word with this *yod.*[22] Does this usage simply reflect an increasing use of the *matres lectionis* after the third century B.C.?[23] If so, the *yod* should denote a pure-long vowel. The vowel here, however, is merely tone-long - derived, probably, from short *i* as we have seen. Is there any evidence that the vowel letter *yod* was ever used to mark a tone-long *ē*?[24] If not, are we not forced to assume that the *yod* represents a dual or a quasi-dual? Do the *peshārîm,* therefore provide the earliest evidence for that artificial dual pronunciation which was to be canonized by the rabbis?

The coins of the First Revolt[25] provide somewhat more ambiguous evidence. In the spelling of the word Jerusalem, the penultimate *yod* is consistently present in all examples from the Years 2 through 5 but not at all in Year 1. Must we conclude, merely, that the orthography is fluid[26] and we have one pronunciation only: Yerûshālēm (with *yod* marking a tone-long vowel)? Or do we have evidence here for a new pronunciation, as a dual,[27] which is written in the first year defectively and in all other years fully? Or, finally, do we have, in the first year, the old pronunciation and in the other years the "dualized" version? We must, at least, consider the possibility that the form with penultimate *yod* reflects a dual pronunciation.

When we turn to the coins of the Second Revolt (that of Bar Cochba in A.D. 132-35) we note a peculiar change: although the proper name Jerusalem occurs frequently in all three years of the minting, the word never has the penultimate *yod.*[28] This is a reversal of the process of fixing the orthography which we have come to expect,[29] and suggests that the insertion of *yod* in the word *Yerûshāla̓yim* in the *peshārîm* of the roughly 175 years preceding A.D. 70 and in the coins of the First Revolt, and its absence in the coins of the Second Revolt, signify something more than a simple orthographic process.[30]

But, before going further, it is necessary to recognize what, at first sight, appears to throw doubt on the thesis that we are, in fact, dealing here with a dual form (apparent or real). In the inscriptions on the coins of the First Revolt, the word Jerusalem (spelled with or without the penultimate *yod*) is, as we have seen, treated as a feminine, singular noun.[31] It is true that city-names are generally treated as feminine and Jerusalem always is. Further, as there is no dual ending for adjectives, dual nouns are modified by plural adjectives.[32] On logical and grammatical grounds, therefore, the hypothesis that the word Jerusalem is here treated as a dual and not as a feminine singular, appears to collapse.

But was everyday usage, grammatical propriety or, for that matter, rabbinic practice so averse to this apparent discrepancy? We may doubt it on several grounds. As far as practice is concerned, we may note that wherever the word Jerusalem appears in the Hebrew text and an accompanying verbal or adjectival form provides a clue to its gender and number, it is treated as a feminine singular. Yet, it was pronounced, according to the traditional pointing, as a dual. This is true even of the passage, Jeremiah 26:18, where, in the Ben Asher text, the *yod* is inserted as a penultimate letter. Again, in Jeremiah 48:1, the proper name *Qiryāthάyim,* which is certainly pronounced as a dual, has a feminine singular verb. In other words, the ears of the rabbis did not flinch at the juxtaposition and the reason is probably not far to seek. Presumably the grammatical rule or usage, by which city names were treated as feminine singulars, took precedence over the rule by which duals - or apparent duals - must have plural adjectives and verbs. In other words there is no discrepancy between the feminine singular adjective *qedôshāh* and an assumed dual form of Jerusalem. It is possible, also, that the presence or absence of the article - i.e. *qedôshāh* or *haqqedôshāh* - on the coins of the First Revolt has the same significance, or lack of significance.

We have, we believe, given some evidence which may be construed to indicate that in a period extending roughly from 100 B.C. to A.D. 70 the name Jerusalem could have been pronounced as if it were a dual. In this period, only, it seems, do we have a spelling of the word with a penultimate *yod*. If we are correct in our analysis, this cannot be a simple *mater lectionis,* an indication of a pure long vowel, because the final vowel of Jerusalem was originally a short *i* and, at most, was lengthened into a tone-long *ē*. If it is not a pure-long vowel, it seems most logical to conclude that it marks a pronunciation *áyim,* a dual-like ending. It is difficult to imagine a major change in pronunciation occurring and becoming fixed for an important Biblical name apart from, and independent of, the process of fixing the consonantal text. It seems more than fortuitous, therefore, that the period when the use of the penultimate *yod* in *Yerûshāláyim* is attested independently of the sacred text and *can* reflect a pronunciation different from the ancient one should coincide with the roughly two centuries when that text was receiving its definitive form. At no other time does it seem likely that the pronunciation of Jerusalem as a dual could have arisen. If so, it seems logical to seek an explanation of this phenomenon in some peculiarity, some strange or unexpected characteristic, of the city of Jerusalem in that period which could give rise to it.

Several years ago the writer, while preparing a series of maps illustrating the growth of the city of Jerusalem over the centuries, [33] was struck forcibly with the evidence - both literary and archaeological - that the city of Jerusalem under the Hasmonaeans was, in fact, made up of two, separately walled, entities. That publication did not profit from the excavations in the central valley and on the western hill which have been made since 1967, but the results of these have - if anything - strengthened the case.

Before turning to the new evidence, however, it is necessary to consider the conclusions reached by Avi-Yonah [34] who, like the writer, attempted to evaluate and use the new evidence provided by the Kenyon excavations. He supports strongly the view that the Sukenik-Mayer wall is Josephus' Third Wall, and we must admit the cogency of this argument - if we treat it in isolation from all other evidence. He points out that this wall was begun by Agrippa, was abandoned for 22 years and was finished hurriedly only at the beginning of the First Revolt. The evidence produced by the Kenyon excavations does not demonstrate absolutely that the Sukenik-Mayer line fails to meet these requirements. [35]

On the other hand, there is strong evidence in favour of identifying Agrippa's Third Wall with the line of the present north wall of the Old City, and Avi-Yonah fails to deal adequately with this.

The excavations carried out by Robert Hamilton along the north wall of the Old City [36] discovered, beneath the present Damascus Gate, the remains of a triple gateway with an almost obliterated inscription of Aelia Capitolina placed off-centre above the easternmost arch. This gate (more correctly, its destroyed predecessor) formed an integral part of a fine wall which rested on a moulded plinth. Hamilton assumed that the block with the inscription was re-used in its present position. The well-built wall and its triple gateway, therefore, could well be the work of Hadrian for it preceded the patch, or reconstruction, which contained the inscribed block. Hamilton, however, found another, more massive, wall lying below the west tower of the gate and the curtain wall east of it, and he believed that the plinth and triple gate above were built of ashlar robbed from this earlier wall. The latter - the earliest wall on this line - he attributed to Herod the Great on the basis of both the size of the blocks used and their dressing.

The more extensive excavations carried out at this spot by Dr. J. B. Hennessy on behalf of the Jordan Department of Antiquities and the Jerusalem Municipality between November 1964 and September 1966 have provided new data. [37] The plinth below the east tower has been cleared to bed-rock in several places, and the whole of the eastern gate-way of the triple gate exposed. Hennessy, also, considers the inscribed block above this gateway to be later than the original arch and the associated wall but his evidence for dating the latter is stratigraphic rather than typological. He points out that the earliest deposits north of the gate, reaching down to bedrock, are of the first half of the first century A.D., and these contain burials and coins of the procurators to support the pottery dating. Up to the time of Herod Agrippa, therefore, the area immediately in front of Damascus Gate was outside the city. Above these deposits is a series of plastered street surfaces which seal the foundation trench of the wall with the moulded plinth and the triple gate. Two coins of Agrippa I were found embedded in the plaster of the roadway. The fine wall, the original triple gateway and the street, therefore, cannot antedate the time of Agrippa. Hennessy considers Hamilton's more massive "Herodian" wall to be foundational to the wall with the plinth; we can, at least, agree that it must be Agrippan or later.

Avi-Yonah, therefore, is going beyond the evidence when he says that "these remains [i.e. the gate and plinth beneath Damascus Gate] can be only additions to the Second Wall made either by Herod or Agrippa." [38] They cannot be Herod the Great's work and, if Agrippan, they mark the first construction on this line. So, too, if Agrippan, they can hardly be additions to, or in themselves constitute, the Second Wall of Josephus. Avi-Yonah's line for the Second Wall, therefore, is too far north. [39]

This rather long digression has had one purpose: to show that Avi-Yonah's hypothesis for the course of Josephus' Second Wall does not accord with the archaeological evidence at our disposal. That wall's course northward from a point on the First Wall was established by the Kenyon excavations in Site C[40] as lying approximately on the line of the modern Suq Khan ez-Zeit. It probably continued north as far as the present junction with the Via Dolorosa and followed its line eastward toward the site of the ancient Antonia. [41]

Avi-Yonah's dating of the Second Wall is also doubtful. [42] He says, simply: "The Second Wall certainly existed at the time of Herod's siege (37 B.C.), as we learn from *Ant.* XIV, 476. As it covered the northern front of the extension of the city to the western hill, an extension which took place most probably in the Hellenistic-Hasmonean period, it was apparently the work of either John Hyrcanus or Alexander Jannaeus". However, the evidence is not as unequivocal as Avi-Yonah claims.

Josephus (*War* I, 141 ff.) describes Pompey's attack on the city in 63 B.C. thus:[43] "Aristobulus' party, . . . retired into the temple, cut the bridge which connected it with the city, and prepared to hold out to the last. The others admitted the Romans to the city and delivered up the palace." This passage (*War* I, 143) succinctly explains the situation: the temple is on the eastern hill; the "city" with the Palace of the Hasmonaeans lies on the western hill; each has its own circumvallation and they are joined across the central valley by a bridge only - probably the predecessor of that which spanned the valley in Herodian times and is now represented by Wilson's Arch. Pompey, when he besieged the city, built up his earthworks against the north wall of the temple and, perhaps in the central valley itself (see *War* I, 145 ff.) There is not the slightest indication that the valley itself was enclosed within a wall at the time of Pompey's attack.

At the time of the Parthian invasion, in 40 B.C., the followers of Antigonus attacked the forces supporting Herod and his brother Phasael and advanced against the "palace", which may have been the Baris [44] or the Palace of the Hasmonaeans. [45] A battle took place in the "market-place" (*Ant.* XIV, 335), which must have been in the central valley; there is no mention of a siege preceding this battle and the implication is that the "market-place" was open and unwalled. Later, at Pentecost, when the city was crowded with visitors, Herod made a sortie from the palace into the "suburb" (*Ant.* XIV, 399) - the northern end of the central valley which contained the market. [46] The inference is clear: the central valley remained unwalled but served as a suburb between the two fortified hills to the west and east.

When, finally, Herod made his own attack on the city to assert his claim to his kingdom, the details of his campaign are clear from the account given in *War* I, 342-57. It is significant that he purposely followed the pattern of Pompey's attack, pitched his camp north of the temple (343) and raised his earthworks there. Presumably the lines of walls were the same as they had been twenty-five years earlier. There is no suggestion that he had to pierce an outer city wall before he could attack the wall of the temple and there is no mention of fighting in the valley to the west of the temple. It should be noted, also, that the attack and breaching of the north wall of the temple did not require a prior reduction of the Baris, for it was only after the capture of the temple by Herod's and Sossius's troops and the subsequent slaughter that Antigonus "came down from the castle" (i.e. Baris: *War* I, 353; *Ant.* XIV, 481).

The account of the siege given in the *Ant.* is essentially the same as that given in the *War,* except for an interpolation which includes the reference to the First and Second Walls. In this account, too, Herod encamps against the north wall of the temple, following Pompey's example (*Ant.* XIV, 466). It is only when Josephus comes to recount the capture of the city that he introduces new details missing in his earlier account of the same events. Specifically, the First and Second Walls are introduced without any explanation of their course or the parts of the city they covered. Such information is provided in the *War* when he is preparing to describe the siege under Titus and one would have expected him to give similar information before his account of Herod's siege in the *War,* if these two walls had been involved. In the *Ant.* account of Herod's siege, moreover, Josephus appears to have forgotten for the moment that the First Wall protected the Upper City on the western hill, and the Second Wall enclosed the northern end of the central valley; in no way were such walls a barrier to an attack on the temple from the north. It is obvious that Josephus, in his account of Herod's siege in the *Ant.,* nodded and that his earlier account, in the *War,* must be considered more accurate. In his defence, we can only say that, when he wrote the *Ant.* account, he was probably thinking of the city as he knew it years before; he knew that the Third Wall was built by Agrippa and inadvertently fell into the error of assuming that the First and Second Walls were both in existence at the time of Herod's siege. Whatever the reason for the discrepancy in Josephus' account, it is obvious that Avi-Yonah's dependence on the *Ant.* passage for dating the Second Wall is unjustified.

However, the latest excavations have provided more positive evidence that the central valley was not enclosed within a general circumvallation of the city until some time in the reign of Herod. A tomb found by Professor Mazar in the central valley on the lower slopes of the western hill west of the temple was apparently in use down into the reign of Herod the Great. [47] It seems most unlikely that a cemetery could have existed within the walled city, and the obvious conclusion is that Josephus' Second Wall was built by Herod as part of his major architectural programme for the capital city.

Professor Mazar's excavations do not appear to have provided any new evidence on the line of the Second Wall where it crossed the central valley south of the temple area. It seems unlikely, on the basis of his work, that the wall was inside the present line which contains the Dung Gate. Similarly, excavations carried out sixty years ago by J. Germer-Durand [48] on the eastern slopes of the western hill, below the church of St. Pierre en Gallicante, and the soundings of the Kenyon expedition [49] in the same region and further south, suggest strongly that the Herodian settlement on the western hill was confined to its upper parts, including the traditional Mount Zion, the area now occupied by the Dormition, the Cenacle, Tomb of David, etc. [50] On topographic and archaeological grounds, therefore, Herod's wall, joining the western hill to the eastern hill south of the Temple area, could not have been far south of the present Dung Gate line. [51]

If we are correct in our thesis that the Second Wall was built by Herod the Great, we must accept the conclusion that Jerusalem - until that time - consisted of two independently walled communities, which Josephus called the Upper City and the Lower City. That they had their own circumvallations is demonstrated for the earlier period by the quotations we have given above describing the situation at the time of the attacks of Pompey, the Parthians and Herod the Great in 37 B.C. That these walls remained in existence even after the construction of the Second and Third Walls is proved by the fact that, after Titus succeeded in capturing the temple and the eastern hill in A.D. 70, he was still forced to raise earthworks and lay siege to the Upper City (*War* VI, 392 ff.)

In only one passage (*War* V, 144) does Josephus appear to say that a wall, earlier than the Second, crossed the central valley. His First Wall, defending the north side of the Upper City ran as follows: "Beginning on the north at the tower called Hippicus, it extended to the Xystus, and then joining the council-chamber terminated at the western portico of the temple." That the wall extended to the Xystus is understandable and, at this point, or nearby (i.e. at the northeast corner of the Upper City) the wall should have turned south for, as we have seen, the western hill had its own circumvallation. Josephus says nothing of this section of the wall; instead, he continues, "and then joining the council-chamber . . ." it ends at the western side of the temple. This rather lame and vague description suggests that the wall actually ended at (i.e. "extended to") the Xystus but in some way was carried on across the central valley.

That there was a bridge across the central valley at this point is well-attested (*War* II, 344); the great vault known as "Wilson's Arch" was probably one of the supporting elements of the bridge in the Herodian period. The bridge remained in existence, certainly, during the siege of Titus, for we are told that John and the Zealots built a tower at its eastern end (i.e. "above the Xystus") as a protection against Simon who held the Upper City (*War* IV, 581; VI, 191); it was still standing when the Temple had been captured but the survivors were holding out in the Upper City (*War* VI, 325). In fact, there appears to have been a matching tower at the bridge's western end, built by Simon, as a counter to John's construction (*War* VI, 377). But, in all of these references, there is no mention of a wall crossing the central valley anywhere near this point - i.e. in line with the Xystus; if there had been, it would have had to be broken down to prevent its use by the Romans as a causeway or viaduct from the Temple hill to the Upper City and there is no suggestion of this.

We may also note that excavations in the central valley have produced no evidence of a cross-wall. South of Wilson's Arch, at least, the street running along the west wall of the Temple, and excavated by Mazar, appears to continue unbroken. The situation to the north of the Arch is not quite so clear, but Hamilton's excavations immediately north of the Tariq Bab es-Silseleh in 1931, found no evidence of one. [52] A very broad (14 m.) wall crossing the valley was apparently nothing more than a foundation for the vaults of the viaduct above and, in any case, post-dated the Herodian period. The conclusion seems obvious: there was no continuation of Josephus' First

Wall across the central valley, and the city was composed of two separately-walled parts until the construction of Josephus' Second Wall (as we believe) by Herod the Great. [53]

The topographic, archaeological and literary evidence appears to support the view that from a period preceding Pompey's attack (and probably going back to about 100 B.C.) down to the destruction of the city by Titus, the most characteristic feature of the city of Jerusalem was the fact that it consisted of two, independently-walled, parts - the Lower City and the Upper City; these two parts were first joined by the Second Wall built by Herod the Great, and later enclosed within the Third Wall - perhaps only at the outbreak of the First Revolt - but the essential two-fold nature of the city remained. This duality, this doubleness, of the city was, therefore, very apparent for perhaps the first seventy-five years (that is, until Herod built the Second Wall) and was only slightly veiled, after this, down to the destruction of the city in A.D. 70.

We may, then, propose that it is more than a coincidence that, at the very time when a dual or quasi-dual pronunciation of the name of the city could have arisen to describe a clear and observable peculiarity of the city, we have evidence, in the spelling of the name of the city in the *peshārîm* and the coins of the First Revolt, for such a pronunciation. We have, we believe, raised strong arguments against the accepted grammatical explanation of the dual form and have shown that there is no evidence of a dual pronunciation of the name in the Biblical period; we have gone further and shown that a penultimate *yod* could never, according to the generally accepted orthographic rules, have represented a pure-long *î* or *ê*, for the original final vowel was a short *i* or, at most, a tone-long *ē*. We appear, then, to be left with the probability that the *yod* does, in fact, signify a dual or a quasi-dual.

We have attempted, thus far, to suggest no more than that at the critical period with which we are dealing, the name of Jerusalem took on a dual or quasi-dual cast. We are convinced that the pronunciation of the *Qerê* cannot be taken to mean "two Jerusalems", that is, we do not believe that it is in any sense a proper, grammatical dual. Rather, it is, as Vincent said, an artificial form which cannot be explained (or defended) on grammatical grounds. [54] But popular usage in all languages scoffs at grammatical rules and the niceties of word-formation. National academies established to maintain the purity of the language, or to invent "proper" native terms for new ideas, objects or institutions, have never had any notable success, for a living language moves far too quickly. Such a false or artificial dual as is represented by *Yerûshāláyim,* we believe, bore a very clear meaning to the people who coined it - possibly the natives of Jerusalem itself. In their pronunciation of the ancient name they effectively and graphically, if ungrammatically, described their city by reference to its most characteristic feature: it was a "double-town".

Like any other example of ancient or modern "franglais", the dual pronunciation of the ancient name Jerusalem cannot be fitted into the rule-book of the purists but it gives a priceless - because vivid - insight into the minds of the inhabitants of the city two thousand years ago and throws light not only on the historical topography of the city of that time but on the origins of an otherwise inexplicable pronunciation of that city's name.

References

1. The city was founded "about 1800 B.C."; see KATHLEEN M. KENYON, *Jerusalem; Excavating 3000 Years of History,* p. 24. The earliest mention of the city is in the Egyptian Execration texts; see WOLFGANG HELCK, *Die Beziehungen Ägyptens zu Vorderasien im 3. und 2. Jahrtausend v. Chr.* (2nd ed., 1971): p. 48, no. 12 (Sethe texts, probably under Amenemhet III, i.e. late 19th century B.C.); p. 58, no. 45 (Posener texts, under Amenemhet IV or later, into beginning of Dynasty XIII); the Margissa texts, published by Posener in *Syria* 43 (1966), pp. 277 ff., which are apparently contemporary with the Sethe texts, also mention the city by name. On the probability that the final tone-long *e* represents an original short *i* see below. I wish to express here my thanks to members of the Royal Ontario Museum curatorial staff, particularly Dr. Nicholas Millet, and of the Department of Near Eastern Studies in the University of Toronto, particularly Drs. John S. Holladay, Jr., Donald B. Redford, Ronald F. G. Sweet, John W. Wevers and Ronald J. Williams; they are to be exculpated, of course, for any misuse of the information or advice they so generously provided.
2. See, briefly, KOEHLER-BAUMGARTNER, *Lexicon in Veteris Testamenti Libros* (1951 ed.) (hereafter KOEHLER-BAUMGARTNER), under   ירושלים   for the important references, and further discussion below.
3. Ιερουσαλημ. We may disregard the other Greek form, Ιεροσολυμα, which occurs in such later extra-canonical books as I Esdras, I-IV Maccabees, and Tobit, in the Letter of Aristeas, Josephus, and the New Testament (where frequently the normal Septuagint form appears). This strange form, followed by Jerome in his

Latin Vulgate version (*Hierosolyma*), is a Hellenistic creation; declined as a neuter plural, with or without the article, it is simply an archaizing - rather an atticizing - form imitating such declined proper names in classical Greek as Athens, Thebes, Sparta, Corinth, etc.; it was also, probably, influenced by the chance similarity between the first part of the word and the Greek 'ιερος, which would accord with the concept of the "Holy City". It probably has no significance for the original pronunciation of the name of Jerusalem. For the mixture of the two Greek forms in the extra-canonical books in the extant manuscripts, see ALFRED RAHLFS, *Septuaginta* (Stuttgart, 1935), notes on I Esdras 1:37 and I Macc. 1:20, where the editor assumes an original Hellenistic form "corrupted" by the normal Septuagint transliteration.

4. I.e. *aym*, the historical spelling, with a short *i* as a helping vowel; see FRANK MOORE CROSS, JR., and DAVID NOEL FREEDMAN, *Early Hebrew Orthography* (hereafter CROSS and FREEDMAN), p. 51, no. 37 - *bm'tym*, "for two hundred" in the Siloam Inscription, and GESENIUS-KAUTZSCH-COWLEY, *Hebrew Grammar* (2nd English ed. 1910) (hereafter GKC), section 28*e*.

5. See KOEHLER-BAUMGARTNER: the form without an inserted penultimate *yod* occurs more than 640 times in the Ben Asher text of the Old Testament which is the basis for this Hebrew lexicon and for KITTEL, *Biblia Hebraica* (3rd ed.). The five exceptions are Jer. 26:18 (but the parallel verse in Mic. 3:12 has no *yod*), Esther 2:6 (possibly, because of its lateness - perhaps from the time of John Hyrcanus - the earliest evidence for the insertion of the *yod*), I Chron. 3:5 (but the parallel verses in II Sam. 5:14 and I Chron. 14:4 have no *yod*), and II Chron. 25:1 (the parallel in II Kings 14:2 has no *yod*). There is one further exception, I Kings 10:2, in the earlier printed Hebrew texts, but *not* in the Ben Asher text noted above; see KITTEL, *Biblia Hebraica* (1st and 2nd eds.) and GESENIUS-BUHL, *Handwörterbuch* (17th ed.). The evidence appears overwhelming that these few exceptions, with the possible exception of the Esther occurrence, are to be considered pure slips of the copyist, under the influence of the accepted pronunciation of the *Qerê*.

6. Pslam 48:12f.

7. *Memnon. Zeitschrift für die Kunst und Kultur-Geschichte des Alten Orients,* VI (1913), specifically pp. 95 f. I am indebted to Père P. Benoit for this reference.

8. Vincent here quotes Ewald: "une ville double paraît avoir été tenue pour plus honorée et plus grandiose."

9. Although their explanations for it differ. It is most unlikely that the rabbis knew, or even concerned themselves with, such fine points in the evolution and writing of the language as historical orthography. Furthermore, even if they knew enough to use the argument, it is most unlikely that it would have carried any weight beyond their own narrow circle.

10. Section 88*c*.

11. On the vocalization of the final syllable of the Moabite forms, however, see CROSS and FREEDMAN, pp. 39 f., where a preference is shown for *ōn* derived from *ān*, rather than *ēn* derived from *ayn*, on the grounds that, in *ḥwrnn*, the first syllable has an *uncontracted* diphthong *aw* and one would hardly expect a *contracted* diphthong in the final syllable - i.e. *ēn* from *ayn*. Whether such linguistic and orthographic phenomena must move at the same pace and in such closely-yoked concert we may doubt. As for the contraction of the final diphthong itself, CROSS and FREEDMAN give the indisputable example of *m'tn* in line 30 of the Mesha inscription which they transliterate as *ma'tēn*, derived from *ma'tayn*, i.e. Hebrew *mā'táyim*, "two hundred".

12. An interesting substantiation of this pronunciation is to be found in the contemporary Babylonian Chronicle where we have a reading *Sha-ma-ra-'i-in*; see SIMO PARPOLA, *Neo-Assyrian Toponyms*. Veröffentlichungen zur Kultur und Geschichte des Alten Orients und des Alten Testaments, Bd. 5 (Neukirchen-Vluyn: Neukirchener Verlag des Erziehungsvereins, 1970), p. 302 (hereafter PARPOLA). The spelling of the Biblical Aramaic form is identical with that in the Elephantiné papyri: see A. COWLEY, *Aramaic Papyri of the Fifth Century B.C.* no. 30, line 29.

13. CROSS and FREEDMAN, p. 31.

14. This is the consistent pointing in the Ben Asher text as published in KITTEL, *Biblia Hebraica* (3rd ed.), but in the earlier editions, it had a variant with a tone-long *ē* in the last syllable. The spelling is the same in the Elephantiné papyri: see A. Cowley, *op. cit.,* no. 30, line 18.

15. PARPOLA, p. 375.

16. Might this short vowel explain, also, the short *upsilon* in the Hellenistic Greek transliteration (see f.n. 3)?

17. PARPOLA, pp. 302 f.

18. Cf. II Kings 18:26.

19. See Phoenician *mṣrm* (where the diphthong *ay* has become pure long *ê* and the *yod* has disappeared in the orthography) and Aramaic *mṣryn* (where the diphthong with *yod* is still preserved. The form which appears in the Lachish Letters is similar; see CROSS and FREEDMAN, p. 54, no. 66: *mṣrymh* "to Egypt" with the final locative *h*.

20. For completeness, we must mention here the orthography of the name on the seals with the five-pointed star, now generally dated to the third quarter of the third century B.C. Between the points, the name is spelled *Y-r-sh-l-m,* with no indication of the long vowel *û* or the penultimate *yod.* That the former vowel was, in fact, pronounced is demonstrated quite clearly from the Elephantiné papyri, as we have seen (f.n. 14). Its absence in the orthography of these seals may be dictated by the pentagram itself - i.e. the necessity of fitting the name between the five points of the star. Another explanation may well be the fluctuation in practice at this period as to the use of vowel-letters; stamps of the same period, for instance, spell *Yehud* (Judah) as *y-h-d* or *y-h-u-d.* The absence of the *yod* may be explained in the same way, but, because no earlier examples with the *yod* are known, it is more likely to be the normal orthography of the time; see Paul W. Lapp, "Ptolemaic Stamped Handles from Judah", *BASOR* 172 (Dec. 1963), pp. 22 ff., and H. Neil Richardson, "A Stamped Handle from Khirbet Yarmuk", *BASOR* 192 (Dec. 1968), pp. 12 ff.

21. It should be noted that, according to GKC, section 88c, Strack found the form with *yod* even in old MSS of the Mishnah.

22. See KARL GEORGE KUHN, *Konkordanz zu den Qumrantexten* under ירושלם/ירושלים e.g. without the *yod*: IQpH 9.4; 12.7; 4QT 30; IQ Genesis Apocryphon 22.13. With the *yod*: 16 (1Q Frag=DJD I) 9.2 (*pesher* to Ps. 68:30,31); 4QpJs[a] A 11; C 9 (both *peshārîm,* but see A 7=Isa. 10:32, where *yod* has been inserted, presumably under the influence of the *pesher*); 4QpJs[b] 2, 7.10; 4QpJs[c] 11; 4QpNah, lines 2 and 11; M (War Scroll) 1.3; 3.11; 7.4; 12.13, 17.

23. FRANK MOORE CROSS, JR., *The Ancient Library of Qumran and Modern Biblical Studies* (rev. ed. 1961), p. 189, f.n. 40a. (hereafter CROSS).

24. GKC, sections 8b, 9k.

25. LEO KADMAN, *The Coins of the Jewish War of 66-73 C.E.* (Corpus Nummorum Palaestinensium, Second Series, vol. III); see p. 74, where he lists a total of 65 shekels and half shekels from Year 1 of the Revolt and 340 from Years 2-5.

26. In Year 1, not only is Jerusalem written without the penultimate *yod,* but the adjective *qedôshāh* has neither the definite article nor the vowel letter *waw* to mark the pure long vowel *ô.* KADMAN translates: "Jerusalem is holy". In Years 2-5, however, Jerusalem is written with the penultimate *yod,* and the adjective has both the definite article and the vowel-letter *waw* marking the long vowel. The translation is: "Jerusalem the Holy". Is it at least possible that both forms of the inscription mean "Jerusalem the Holy" but that of the first year is defective, not only in its lack of use of the vowel-letter *waw,* and its omission of *yod* in Jerusalem but also in its lack of the definite article?

27. A dual pronunciation is certainly possible; note that the *yod* in the spelled out "year two" (*shenath shetáyim*) on the coins of that year quite clearly signifies the dual; KADMAN, *op. cit.,* p. 98, pp. 124 ff., nos. 10 (base silver), 11-19 (bronze); see, also, next footnote.

28. Y. MESHORER, *Jewish Coins of the Second Temple Period,* pp. 94 ff. The manuscript evidence, to the extent that it has been preserved, appears to agree with this; see P. BENOIT, J.T. MILIK, and R. DE VAUX, *Les Grottes de Murabbaʿât* (Discoveries in the Judaean Desert II). In an Aramaic double deed dated to "year three of the Freedom of Jerusalem" (25.I.1), Jerusalem does not have a penultimate *yod.* There are, however, two Hebrew double documents, 29 and 30, in which a word occurs (*b . . ʾ l y m*) on which Milik comments (see 29.9): "la deuxième lettre conservée [there are two unclear letters after *b,* so this is in fact the fourth letter of the word] ne peut être qu'un aleph, . . . et difficilement un šin." He believes it to be a place name but does not think it can be read "in Jerusalem". If it is so read, there would be a penultimate *yod* but there is no space for a vowel letter "waw" for *û* (which one would consider essential). Strangely, the Index of this publication betrays no doubt whatsoever on the reading and transcribes the word as "in Jerusalem" in both documents, complete with the penultimate *yod* and the long *û* with vowel-letter *waw*! YIGAEL YADIN, *Bar-Kokhba* (New York: Random House, 1971), p. 134, apparently sees no difficulty in reading "in Jerusalem" in these deeds, but the writer must accept Milik's doubts, not only on the basis of the textual difficulties noted, but because nowhere in the documents from Murabbaʿât or Naḥal Ḥever, to his knowledge, is there any reference to Jerusalem except in the dating formulae. We must, therefore, consider the reading of Jerusalem with a penultimate *yod* in documents of the Second Revolt period as, at best, uncertain. However, there can be no doubt that the dual is represented in the normal fashion in these records, as on the coins: the Murabbaʿât document 29 refers twice to "year two" and in each case spells *shetáyim* with the *yod.*

29. CROSS, p. 171: "The evidence from Murabbaʿât indicates that even the principles of orthographic practice (use of vowel letters, *matres lectionis*) became fixed at this time. While minor orthographic variations appear, as well as a few variants of other types, they are no more significant than variants in Tiberian Masoretic manuscripts; the relatively fluid orthographic practice of the Hasmonaean and Herodian periods

known from Qumran has vanished, once and for all." It is true that Cross is speaking here of the Biblical text, but if orthographic development could affect the form of writing *Yerûshāláyim* in the *peshārim* of the first century B.C., and the coins of the first century A.D., one would think that the form with *yod* would have become the standard form of the word in the coins of the second century A.D.

30. KADMAN, op. cit., p. 62, denies this emphatically. "This proves that in the orthography of that time [i.e. the time of the First and Second Revolts] *yod* and *waw* could be either included or omitted from the spelling and that the shortened spelling does not indicate an earlier stage of development."

31. Note the modifying adjectives *qedôshāh* or *haqqedôshāh*.

32. GKC, section 132*f*.

33. DENIS BALY and A.D. TUSHINGHAM, *Atlas of the Biblical World,* pp. 166 ff. (hereafter *Atlas*).

34. M. Avi-Yonah, "The Third and Second Walls of Jerusalem", *IEJ* 18 (1968), pp. 98-125.

35. E. W. Hamrick, "New Excavations at Sukenik's 'Third Wall' ", *BASOR* 183 (Oct. 1966), pp. 19-26; "Further Notes on the 'Third Wall' ", *BASOR* 192 (Dec. 1968), pp. 21-25. The coins of the procurators found in the foundation trench show that this east-west stretch of the wall is to be dated later than Agrippa, but do not require it to be dated later than the beginning of the First Revolt. On the other hand, the negative evidence is also strong: in what other circumstances can we imagine such a wall being built? Its line does not accord with the information provided by Josephus on the course of the Roman siege wall.

36. "Excavations Against the North Wall of Jerusalem, 1937-38", *QDAP* X (1940), pp. 21-26, fig. 2 and pls. I-VI (soundings D and E).

37. Preliminary report in *RB* 75 (1968), pp. 250 f., supplemented by Hamrick, "Further Notes . . . " (see f.n. 35).

38. *Op. cit.,* p. 122.

39. While it is this point which the writer wishes to make, he can point out the ramifications of the argument for Avi-Yonah's identification of the Sukenik-Mayer wall. If the present line of the north wall of the Old City with its original triple gate is the Third Wall, the Sukenik-Mayer line still requires an explanation which accords with its size, character, and the evidence from its foundation trench. If we accept the Sukenik-Mayer line as the Agrippan Third Wall, it is obvious that the more southerly line must be assigned its proper role in the history of the city's fortifications - possibly the wall of Aelia Capitolina. Certainly a triple gate would conform with the architectural practice followed by Hadrian elsewhere in the city; cf. P. Benoit, "L'Antonia d'Hérode le Grand et le Forum Oriental d'Aelia Capitolina", *HTR* 64:2, 3 (April, July 1971), pp. 135 ff. But the dating of this line, and the question of whether Hamilton's underlying wall is separate or foundational, must await the full publication of Hennessy's excavations at Damascus Gate and, particularly, the contents of the foundation trench.
See now (1976) J. B. Hennessy, "Preliminary Report on Excavations at the Damascus Gate, 1964-6" *Levant* II (1970), pp. 22 ff.; D. Bahat and M. Ben-Avi, "Excavations at Tancred's Tower", *Jerusalem Revealed. Archaeology in the Holy City 1968-1974* (Jerusalem: Israel Exploration Society, 1975), pp. 109 ff.; for an excellent review of all the pertinent evidence, see P. Benoit, "Où en est la question du 'Troisième Mur'?, *Studia Hierosolymitana, I partie: "Etudes Archéologiques"*. Collectio Maior du Studium Biblicum Franciscanum, no. 22 (Jerusalem: Franciscan Printing Press, 1976), pp. 111 ff.

40. *Jerusalem,* pp. 151 ff.; see *Atlas,* pp. 170 ff. This line has now received further support from the excavations carried out by Ute Lux of the German Archaeological Institute beneath the Lutheran Church of the Redeemer; see *IEJ* 22 (1972), p. 171 and pl. 34A.

41. The evidence of great fills dating from the early second century A.D., in site C, and from the same (?) period in the German sounding (the statement in the preliminary report - see preceding note - is ambiguous) suggests that the cross-valley leading down to the Central Valley from the west was very wide at this point and was never built up or occupied even when the Third Wall - which must have enclosed the area - was constructed. The situation was otherwise on the north, where the quarter of Bezetha stood until it was set on fire by Cestius (*War* II, 530) and finally destroyed by Titus (*War* V, 302).

42. *Op. cit.,* p. 123.

43. Our references to Josephus, like Avi-Yonah's, derive from the Loeb Classical Library edition, translated by H. ST. J. THACKERAY, RALPH MARCUS and L. H. FELDMAN.

44. The fortified residence or castle adjoining the temple on the north side, first built, according to Josephus (*Ant.* XVIII, 91), by John Hyrcanus and referred to under Queen Alexandra (see *Ant.* XIII, 426: "the fortress overlooking the temple").

45. Also probably built by John Hyrcanus or Alexander Jannaeus but referred to first under Queen Alexandra (see *Ant.* XIII, 411).

46. It is interesting to note that this area was still called the "suburb" even after the Second Wall was built. Of the four gates in the west wall of the temple listed by Josephus in *Ant.* XV, 410, the first is clearly that which

leads by the bridge over Wilson's Arch across the central valley to the Upper City. The fourth, which "led to the other part of the city" by means of steps which descended into the central valley and "from here up again to the hill" can best be identified with that which led out over Robinson's arch; see, now, B. MAZAR, *The Excavations in the Old City of Jerusalem near the Temple Mount* (Jerusalem: Israel Exploration Society, 1971), pp. 13 ff. The other two led to the "suburb" which can then probably be located at the northern end of the western wall - i.e. in the part of the central valley north of Wilson's Arch.

47. MAZAR, *op. cit.,* pp. 28 f. and fig. 17 (tomb 7038).

48. "La maison de Caïphe et l'église Saint-Pierre à Jérusalem", *RB* XI (1914), pp. 71-94, 222-46, particularly pp. 241 ff. He discovered shekels of the Year 4 of the First Revolt, and evidence for an earlier cemetery belonging, apparently, to the Herodian period, for fragments of decorated ossuaries and sarcophagi were found. About a hundred meters north of Germer-Durand's "maison romaine", more recent excavations (reported by Y. Margovsky in the "Chronique Archéologique", *RB* 78 (1971), pp. 597 f.) have discovered, as the earliest occupation in this area, three houses "d'époque hérodienne, sans doute du premier siècle après J. -C."

49. *Jerusalem,* pp. 155 ff., and, for the locations of the sites, see B, D.I, D.II, and E on fig. 5, page 29.

50. Mr. Magen Broshi has excavated this area and reports substantial Herodian remains (personal communication).

51. Miss Kenyon, in fact, accepts the line containing the Dung Gate as representing roughly Herod's southern wall across the central valley; see *Jerusalem,* p. 144 and Fig. 14; also, *Atlas,* map 33 and pp. 170 ff.

52. R. W. Hamilton, "Jerusalem. Ancient Street Levels in the Tyropoeon Valley within the Walls", *QDAP* I (1932), pp. 97 ff., "Street Levels in the Tyropoeon Valley", *ibid.,* pp. 105 ff., "Street Levels in the Tyropoeon Valley, II" *QDAP* II (1933) pp. 34 ff.

53. The rather exiguous amount of the southern part of the central valley included, on our reckoning, within the Second Wall, throws some doubt on the accuracy of the reconstruction of N. Avigad for the late Monarchy period. His brilliant excavations in the Jewish quarter on the western hill (see his preliminary reports in *IEJ* 20 (1970), pp. 1 ff., 129 ff.; 22 (1972), pp. 193 ff.) have revealed a great wall, some 7 m. broad, of which the preserved portion - 40 m. long - runs roughly south, then southwest, then due west; *IEJ* 22 (1972), fig. 2. If this is a true city wall - as Avigad believes - and was intended to include a new quarter (the Mishneh) in the central valley and on the western hill, its continuation should include within the city of the late Monarchy most or all of the central valley from below the Pool of Siloam up to a line roughly corresponding with Josephus' First Wall and the bridge across that valley. But no evidence of the inclusion of this area within the city of the Monarchy period exists; in fact, the soundings of the Kenyon expedition cited above for the course of the southern arm of the Second Wall, argue strongly against the inclusion of the southern part of the central valley within the city before the time of Agrippa. It seems far more likely that Avigad's great wall is part of a "castle" or "fortress" which would provide some protection and even a refuge for the inhabitants of an otherwise unwalled suburb on the western hill and would also dominate the central valley - so threatening the flank of any hostile force seeking to attack the main part of the city (on the eastern hill) from the west.

54. See f.n. 7; it is interesting that Vincent, too, considered that the historical topography of Jerusalem at this period could well have given rise to the artificial dual, although he discarded the possibility.

JERUSALEM : PATTERNS OF HOLINESS
by R. W. Hamilton.

Jerusalem, as everyone knows, has worn from time immemorial the character of a "holy place", a quality not impartially diffused but focussed in particular precincts within the city that have been honoured by Jews, Christians or Muslims each in their turn: Mount Sion, the Tomb of Christ or Golgotha, and the Rock or *Sakhrah* which lies at the centre of the Haram ash Sharif.

In this recurrence of holy places a persistent pattern may be discerned, a pattern of motives. Without exploring in depth either the physical appearance or the cultic use of these places I would like to suggest certain parallels in the motives which impelled first a Jew, then a Christian,[1] then a Muslim to establish shrines in Jerusalem. For it is notable that every one of these places acquired its fame by the act of an individual person. I hope that these reflections may have some slight interest for my old friend, the eminent archaeologist and lover of Jerusalem, to whom they are offered.

Three questions, then, are posed: why did Solomon build the Temple? Why did Constantine build the Martyrium? Why did 'Abdul Malik build the Dome of the Rock ? Each of these questions may be answered in three ways: you may say "he built it to accommodate this or that act of worship or ceremony"; that I would call the "ritual" or "liturgical" answer. Or you may say "he wished to commemorate some historical or supernatural event"; that I call the "mythological" answer. Or, lastly, you may say "he really built it to bring about such-and-such a result in contemporary affairs or to influence men's minds in such-and-such a direction. That is the "political" answer. All three kinds of answers are called for in each of our three cases and we cannot fully explain the matter unless we can identify each of these nine motives.

The best preserved of the three buildings and perhaps the simplest to interpret is the most recent. Accordingly, reversing the chronological order, I shall begin with the Dome of the Rock and work back, as far as may be possible, from 'Abdul Malik to Solomon.

The Dome of the Rock stands on a rocky terrace near the centre of the Haram ash Sharif and on its highest point. The Haram exactly coincides with the latest Jewish temple enclosure. This had lain waste for more than five centuries when 'Abdul Malik began to build. It was a ghostly place full of strange legends: a dungeon where Solomon tortured demons; bloodstains on the pavement; a pinnacle of the temple; and two enigmatic statues of Hadrian. These details were noticed by the earliest of recorded western travellers, the pilgrim from Bordeaux (c. A.D. 333),[2] who continues his tale: "not far from the statues is a rock with an opening in it (*lapis pertusus*) to which Jews come each year and anoint it and lament and tear their clothes, and so depart." That at least is fact not legend.

In the 7th century, soon after the Arabs took Jerusalem, the area was in much the same state; for in A.D. 670 Arculf[3] wrote:

> In that famous place where once the proud temple stood . . . the Saracens now frequent a rectangular (*quadrangulam*) place of prayer which they have roughly built by setting big beams on the remains of some ruins . . .

He does not mention the rock. The rectangular place of prayer is easily recognised as a forerunner of the Aqsa Mosque, the congregational building required in every town for Friday prayers where Muslims form an urban population. The essential feature of such a building was an end wall toward the *qiblah,* extended sideways and without public entrances, so that a congregation might pray before it in the prescribed direction without distraction.

The Dome of the Rock, built twenty years after Arculf's visit, is as different as could be from that. It is an octagon not a rectangle; it has no *qiblah* wall extended sideways; it is concentric not orientated, and has doors in all four directions. A congregation could not easily pray there. Then for what ritual purpose did 'Abdul Malik design it ? The answer lies in the building itself: high central dome on a ring of arches; two surrounding ambulatories; entrance from any direction; at the centre, the Rock. All this denotes a building designed not for prostration toward Mecca but for circulation round a centre of interest. Thus the Dome is a reliquary - or in Christian terminology a martyrium - sheltering and displaying the Rock and inviting the faithful to walk round it. And so indeed for a time it was used; for al Ya'qubi (died c. 900 A.D.) in his *History*[4] writes:

> 'Abdul Malik built a dome over the Rock and hung it about with curtains . . . and the
> people began to walk round it as they walk round the Ka'bah.

Thus the first of our nine answers is easily given: the "ritual" purpose of the Caliph was to sanctify the Rock and provide for a rite of circumambulation about it.

But what was the explanation given - what was told of the Rock ? By what "myth" were the Muslims induced to walk round it ? The sheikhs in the Haram today will reply that the Rock is honoured as the place from which the Prophet ascended into the presence of Abraham on that night wherein he was miraculously translated from the Holy Mosque to the More Distant (*aqsa*) Mosque to receive a revelation of divine mysteries. Their explanation is truly ancient, for it was given by al Ya'qubi: "it was on this rock" he writes "that God's messenger set his foot when he ascended into heaven." That tradition, then, goes back at least to the third century of the *hijrah*; perhaps before. Nevertheless, on the evidence of the building itself it must be false. The Prophet's ascension is indirectly referred to in one sentence only of the Quran, the opening words of the seventeenth chapter entitled The Night Journey: "Praise to Him who caused his servant to go by night from the Holy Mosque to the More Distant Mosque, of which we have blessed the bounds, that we might reveal to him some of our signs." It is hardly conceivable that the foundation text of any building dedicated to the memory of the Night Journey or Ascension of the Prophet should not include those words. So thought the Turkish Sultan Suleiman Salim, who in A.D. 1545 placed them at the head of the monumental inscription with which he crowned the new tilework covering of the Dome of the Rock; and so, too, did the Fatimid Sultan adh Dhahir (A.D. 1035), whose mosaic inscription on the great arch confronting the nave of the Aqsa Mosque begins with the same majestic words. But in all the texts inscribed by 'Abdul Malik on the Dome of the Rock - and they number at least five - not a word is to be found of the Night Journey. Furthermore, there are accounts of the Haram which make it clear that a quite different Dome of the Ascension, which may still be seen, has existed in one form or another from early times side by side with the Dome of the Rock. We may be sure, then, that by whatever story the Caliph explained to Muslims his exceptional honouring of the Rock, it was not that mentioned by al Ya'qubi and believed today.

The true mythology of the Rock is to be sought in the record of events at Jerusalem fifty years before 'Abdul Malik. When the Caliph 'Umar in 638 desired to fix a Muslim place of prayer in Jerusalem, it was not "Muhammad's Footprint" that he sought, nor any relic of the Night Journey. Al Tabari (839 - 923) quotes an eyewitness:[5]

> He arrived at Aylia and proceeded into the *masjid*; then he made toward the *mihrab* of David,
> and the rest of us followed. He went into it then and recited the Prayer of David. Then he
> prostrated himself in prayer and we did likewise.

Theophanes (751 - 818) records the same event with the sour malevolence of a Christian:[6]

> 'Umar entered the holy city wearing filthy camel-hair garments and with devilish hypocrisy
> sought to see the temple of the Jews, which Solomon built, meaning to make it a prayer
> house for his own blasphemous sect.

A better-tempered account, with some fanciful and some factual detail, is worth quoting from Eutychius Patriarch of Alexandria, who died in A.D. 940.[7] He describes how the Caliph was received at Jerusalem by the Patriarch Sophronius and arranged with him the terms of surrender. After praying on the steps of Constantine's Martyrium 'Umar asked the Patriarch for a site to build a mosque. Sophronius replied:

> I will give the Commander of the Faithful a place where the kings of *Rum* were unable to
> build; it is the Rock . . . which Jacob called the gate of heaven. The Israelites called it Holy
> of Holies. It is the middle point of the earth and was their temple . . . When the mother of
> Constantine built the churches in the holy city the Rock and its surroundings were a waste
> of ruins. They would tip rubbish there, until a vast dung heap was formed upon the Rock.

Whereupon Sophronius took 'Umar by the hand and led him to the dung heap. There ensued the famous scene of all the Muslims, led by the Caliph, filling their garments with rubbish and pitching it into Gehinnom "until they had cleared the place and cleaned it, and the Rock was revealed."

This is all too obvious an imitation of the similar story told of Constantine's excavations at Golgotha three centuries before (p.   below). But we need not trouble to sift fact from fiction. It is enough that Eutychius retained a mythology for the Rock already known to Tabari and Theophanes: it was the dim but pious memory of the Prophet David and the Temple of Solomon, that constituted for the Muslim invaders the peculiar interest of *Bayt al Maqdis.*

But it is not to be supposed that Arabs in remote Hijaz knew anything of the Rock, or could locate any single feature in the city of the Prophet's first *qiblah.* It was not until some of them reached Jerusalem that Muslims for the first time learnt the topography of the temple.

We have a nearly contemporary witness to tell us how that came about. An Armenian bishop named Sebeos in the later part of the 7th century wrote a History of Heraclius, which includes the Arab conquests.[8] He writes of Palestine:

> I must again tell of the schemes of rebellious Jews who, having for a certain time received help from the descendants of Hagar, conceived the idea of rebuilding the temple of Solomon. Having discovered the place called Holy of Holies they used the foundations and structures there to build a place of prayer for themselves. The Ishmaelites becoming jealous expelled them and called that place their own house of prayer . . .

That is an oriental Christian's story, spiced with malice but true to life. It agrees with Arculf's contemporary picture. Since the initiative came from the Jews we may be sure that the "holy of holies" was indeed the Rock and no other part of the temple area. For there can hardly be doubt that the *sakhrah,* with its cave below and opening above, is the very *lapis pertusus* that the Bordeaux Pilgrim had seen and which Jews came yearly to anoint. There, surely, was to be found for Jews the Holy of Holies and for Muslims the *Mihrab of David,* the authentic scene of David's prayer, an object of veneration and of pilgrimage.

The Muslims may have been satisfied with that solemn thought; but we must still ask what prompted 'Abdul Malik to institute a pilgrimage not prescribed by the Quran, or to build a martyrium of a kind never to be repeated in Islam. What was the real, the "political" motive in 'Abdul Malik's mind ? Arab historians named two: he intended to divert pilgrims from Mecca and the hostile influence of Ibn az Zubayr; or, he wished to redress a sense of inferiority felt by Muslims when they contemplated the splendour of the great Christian churches. Each of these explanations appears to be supported to some extent by subsequent events; and it was probably subsequent events which gave rise to them. But neither explanation touches the heart of the matter. That is revealed beyond controversy by the building itself. We must turn once again to the great mosaic inscription, which no Arab historian need have read since it was more than two hundred yards long and wrapped in perpetual gloom. Nevertheless it is our sole contemporary and unchallengeable witness. We must give some space to reading the essential first part of it.

The inscription encircles the inner and outer sides of the octagonal wall surmounting the arcade that separates the two ambulatories. A short historical text, bearing the date and naming the Caliph fills, the outer side of the south-eastern section and must be the end of the inscription. Counting back sixteen sides we find the beginning on the inner side of the southern wall. After *bismillah* the text opens with these introductory sentences:

> There is no god but God alone. He hath no partner. To him is the kingdom and to him the praise. He giveth life and giveth death and hath power in all things. Muhammad is the servant of God and his messenger. Verily God and his angels bless the prophet. Ye who believe, bless him and invoke peace upon him.

The text then proceeds with its message:

> People of the Book, go not astray in your religion but speak only the truth of God. The Christ, Jesus son of Mary, was but a messenger of God and his word conveyed into Mary and a spirit from him. So believe in God and his messengers and do not call him three: for your good, refrain. God is one god only. Far be it from him to have a son; heaven and earth are his and need no intermediary. The Christ does not scorn to be the servant of God nor do the angels that are near him, and whosoever scorns his service and is proud these will he sweep away one and all. O God, bless thy messenger and thy servant Jesus son of Mary. Peace be upon him in the day of his birth and the day of his death and the day of his being raised alive. This is Jesus son of Mary, word of truth, about whom they are confused. It was not in God to have a son - praise to him - if he decrees a thing he but says to it "be" and it is. God is my lord and yours, so serve him; that is the straight path.

The text is arrested at that point (and there only) by three vertical stops, beyond which we need not follow it; for thereafter, save for briefly contrasting the fates of believers and backsliders, it consists only of prayers for the Prophet interspersed with repeated declarations of God's unity.

This is the fundamental text, which reveals 'Abdul Malik's purpose in all clarity: the Dome was to embody, in the universal language of architecture, the voice of Islam declaring to the People of the Book the authentic revelation of Christ's humanity and God's indivisible unity. It was addressed to Christians; for Syria, the centre of Umayyad power, was a Christian province. It was built in Jerusalem, for that was the centre of Christendom. It had no separate message for Jews but what they might read into it.

Four other buildings near at hand - the Nativity, Eleona, Anastasis, Ascension - all associated with rocks or caves spelt out in Christian terms the mixed divinity and humanity of Christ. The Dome of the Rock in the same architectural language denounced their polytheism, declared the subordination of Jesus and, by 'Abdul Malik's deft political act, gave to the faith and culture of the Muslims an architectural, theological and social pre-eminence over all others in the land.

So much for the motives of 'Abdul Malik in 691. Let us now travel back in time to Constantine and Golgotha, about 330 A.D. Two contemporary writers tell us what happened. The Bordeaux Pilgrim writes:[9]

> As you go towards the Neapolis gate . . . on your left side is the *monticulus* of Golgotha, where the Lord was crucified. About a stone's throw from there is the *crypta* where his body was laid. There lately by order of the Emperor Constantine a basilica has been built, that is a church, of marvellous beauty having beside it cisterns whence water is drawn and behind it a bath where children are washed.

Eusebius in his biography of Constantine describes events at much greater length.[10] Here is a much condensed paraphrase of his elaborately eloquent account:

> The emperor decided to expose the place of our Saviour's resurrection in Jerusalem, and there to build a church. Now in former times impious men - more like devils - had buried the cave deep out of sight and covered it with a great mound of earth. On this they laid a stone pavement and, finally, built a den of black damnation for Aphrodite, queen of vice. Our emperor divinely inspired commanded the place to be purged. The whole palace of lies, with its idols and contraptions of deceit, was thrown to the ground; its masonry and timbers were broken up and carried away. The very soil and foundations were then dug out to the bottom and cast right away, layer after layer, until the virgin rock was revealed. Whereupon, by a miracle surpassing all men's hopes, the venerable testimony ($\mu\alpha\rho\tau\acute{\upsilon}\rho\iota\upsilon$) of our Saviour's resurrection appeared, the sacred cave, rising from the dead as he had done.

There, then, is the *mythos* of the cave, a $\mu\nu\tilde{\eta}\mu\alpha$ $\dot{\alpha}\theta\alpha\nu\alpha\sigma\acute{\iota}\alpha\varsigma$ seen by all Christians to be the physical proof and vindication of their faith.

Whether the tomb was the right one we cannot know, for more than one was found. Nor can we know whether the discovery was a genuine surprise ($\pi\alpha\rho$' $\dot{\epsilon}\lambda\pi\acute{\iota}\delta\alpha$ $\pi\tilde{\alpha}\sigma\alpha\nu$) or the foreseeable confirmation of an ancient tradition. Again, we cannot tell quite what part the temple of Aphrodite may have played. For notwithstanding contemporary propaganda or later folklore it is at least possible that the site was chosen precisely because a prestigious temple stood there; as John the Baptist in Damascus took over the temple of Jupiter, or as in Bethlehem Christ's nativity was commemorated in an oak wood sacred to Adonis. Religions may detest each other, but still each covet the other's place of worship. Whatever the truth about that, it is certain that for Christians of Aelia the chosen tomb became the authentic memorial of the Resurrection, and Aphrodite's shrine a diabolical attempt to suppress it.

Thus the Christian myth, dimmed for two centuries in pagan Aelia, revived with brilliance to challenge the genius of imperial architects. The mysteries of Golgotha and the holy cave were told amongst the faithful as plain narrative; for Christians, unlike Muslims, based their faith on a literal belief in historical events. From these the ignorant derived hope and comfort, philosophers the concept of a Trinity.

The first article of Christian belief was that Christ had risen, and the tomb was evidence of that. It was Constantine's purpose, accordingly - his "liturgical" aim - to give that evidence a compelling architectural setting, wherein the cycle of events might be re-enacted *in situ* before the people, in hymns and salutary readings, fortifying belief and imprinting emotions of fellowship and adoration.

We know much of how the architects set about that. The tomb was detached from the surrounding rock and enclosed in an edicule, which stood clear under the sky separated from the main church, the martyrium, by the length of a colonnaded courtyard, within which it occupied a recess extending to the west. The martyrium, the Bordeaux Pilgrim's "basilica", lay eastward with its west wall forming the east side of the courtyard. Beyond the basilica to the east was an atrium, to which a flight of steps and portico gave access from the market street. Thus the memorial in its edicule stood at the farthest point of the site from the main street entrance, separated from that by two open spaces and the congregational church.[11]

In a very general way this lay-out foreshadowed that of the Muslim *haram,* separating the sacred rock from the congregational building and leaving much of the area open to the sky. But there was an important difference, which reflected the priestly function of clergy in the Christian rite: the memorial of Christ was not displayed, as the *Sakhrah* was to be, for open inspection and perambulation by the people at large, but was enclosed in its edicule, a sanctum screened from the congregation and reserved in the liturgy for the sole ministrations of the bishop. We shall see that King Solomon had similarly veiled the sacred object of the Jews from vulgar eyes.

It was natural that all planning for the ritual requirements of the church in Aelia should be left to the bishop, Makarios. But the gist of the letter in which Constantine conveyed his wishes is worth briefly summarizing:

> My purpose is to adorn with the finest possible buildings that holy place which by God's command I have disburdened of the foul idols that overlaid it. So pray make all plans and take all steps necessary to provide a basilica which with its appurtenances shall be second to none in the world. My friend Dracilianus and the Governor of your province have my commission for the actual construction and decoration and will instantly provide craftsmen and materials in whatever quantity you require. Let me know about your columns and marble; for, as befits the place, everything is to be of the best. What about the roof? If it is to be coffered, it could also be gilded.

Such lavish partiality in a ruler not formally enrolled as a Christian, who would have admitted no sharp distinction between Jesus Christ and Sol Invictus (whose birthdays and weekly days coincided) must raise the obvious question: Why?

The answer is well known. Christian or no Christian, Constantine beyond question was head of the Christian church. He had lately ensured by his presence at Nicaea an unprecedented consensus of bishops in the formulation of their beliefs. The glorification of Christ's memorial, to the disparagement of Aphrodite, was a demonstration, in language more intelligible than the subtleties of Nicaea, of Christianity's superior truth. Just so in later years the Dome of the Rock was to make manifest the purer monotheism of Islam. Both demonstrations bore the Q.E.D. of imperial command; and of both we must accept the dictum of Gibbon that the counsels of princes are more frequently influenced by views of temporal advantage than by considerations of abstract truth. If the Martyrium of Constantine may fairly be construed as a declaration of faith in the Resurrection, the linch-pin of Christian belief, and the expulsion of Aphrodite as the refutation of idolatry, both must be seen as coordinated acts of imperial strategy, a strategy of pacification and unity, which aspired to impose on the licentious and disruptive passions of a polytheistic world the salutary harness of a single innocuous religion.

To explore the remoter mysteries of Solomon's Temple is a task fraught with every possibility of error. Not a vestige of the shrine itself remains; while from the text of divinely inspired books the zeal of priestly censors must be expected to have expunged all trace of worldly motive from the proverbial wisdom and piety of Solomon. Still, the ritual purpose of the temple is not in doubt: it was neither more nor less than a House, and was so described by Solomon when he invoked Yahweh at its dedication: "Here have I built thee a lofty house, a habitation for thee to occupy for ever" (I Kings, 8).

But how was the invisible to be housed ? The Semitic mind could not easily in those days envisage a god except as located in space, nor dispense with some visible object to give assurance of his presence and attention. For the Israelites, accordingly, the worship of Yahweh required some tangible manifestation of his location: the "Ark of the Covenant" (a portable box decorated with sphinxes); or the effigy of a bull (such as the popular golden figurines of Bethel and Dan); or perhaps a featureless monolith like the stela lately found in the temple of Arad. These venerable relics in shrines up and down the country denoted for Israel and Judah the proximity of Yahweh and his readiness to receive their offerings.

It was the most famous and widely venerated of these objects, the Ark, that Solomon, at the behest of Yahweh and by guidance of his father David, was destined to provide with a house. He followed a simple plan of Bronze Age ancestry, which the texts describe in some detail and of which recognizable examples have been detected in Near Eastern excavations. It was in effect the plan of a royal house enclosed in a vast precinct and designed to veil and enthrone the sacred object, while admitting the ritually qualified by a system of graduated architectural zones. The Ark reposed, as a king might have done, within a relatively small and generally unapproachable sanctum. Before this a larger ante-room, served by priests, contained apparatus for small offerings and incense. Before this, again, a porch flanked by bronze pillars or braziers of monumental size and mystic significance confronted the temple courts; where, under the sky, the beasts and birds of sacrifice might conveniently be slaughtered and dissected, blood flow, and the smoke of fat and burning entrails rise from altars before a suppliant or expectant multitude.

But if the temple was a royal house designed for the residence of Yahweh or his symbol, we have still to ask why the ancient and traditional tent was superseded, and why the seat of Yahweh after its many wanderings had once again to be removed. For it is to be recalled that on its return from the Philistine country the Ark went no more to its ancient home at Shiloh but was carried first to Beth-shemesh; then to Kiriath-jearim (I Sam. 6); then to the house of Obed-edom the Gittite (II Sam. 6); then, finally, with dancing and shouting and blowing of trumpets to the City of David, where it abode in a tent pitched by David beside the spring Gihon in the deep valley outside the eastern wall of the city. It was there, by Gihon, that Solomon was anointed king with oil taken from the tent; and there that the Ark remained for the lifetime of David and for ten years of King Solomon's reign.

But it was not there that Solomon built the temple. In the eleventh year the Ark was removed once more, and carried up from the low ground by the waters to a very different site on the high ridge above the City of David, five hundred yards or more beyond its northern bounds. To explain this migration we must seek the motives, political and mythological, which might have recommended it to the wisdom of Solomon and to the superstitions of the people.

The historians tell us that although it was Solomon who built the temple he did it only as David's heir:

> David gave Solomon his son the plan of the temple and its buildings . . . also plans of all he had in mind for the courts of the house of the Lord . . . He prescribed the weight of gold for the gold vessels . . . and the weight of silver . . 'All this was drafted by the Lord's own hand', said David; 'my part was to consider the detailed working out of the plan' (I Chron., 28).

Thus David played "Bishop Makarios" to Yahweh's "Emperor Constantine". But, more than that, David had personally bought the site, paying 600 shekels of gold to Arauna the Jebusite; and from his private store had set aside three thousand talents of gold and seven thousand of silver for the fabric and ornaments of the temple, beside vast quantities of precious materials from the royal treasury (I Chron., 29). Thus the temple came very near to being the personal possession of the king, like the royal palace which it adjoined.

The installation of the Ark is described in I Kings, 8. The elders of all the tribes were invited. Solomon himself, as chief priest and king, recited the prayers and blessings. The celebrations lasted seven days and the people went home well contented with their share of 22,000 slaughtered oxen and 20,000 sheep, blessing the king and pleased at the god-given prosperity of Solomon. No wonder that in a later generation the dissident Jeroboam at Shechem soliloquized:

> Now shall the kingdom return to the House of David; if this people go up to do sacrifice in the house of the Lord at Jerusalem, then shall the heart of the people turn again unto their lord, unto Rehoboam king of Judah.

Whereupon Jeroboam set up the golden calves at Bethel and Dan, instituting an annual pilgrimage (I Kings, 12) and thus anticipating by sixteen centuries the stratagem attributed (plausibly but I think wrongly) to 'Abdul Malik at Jerusalem.

In the conflict long ago foreseen by the prophet Samuel (I Sam., 8) between tribal independence and the burden of monarchy the prestige of the ark, astutely carried by David to his own city, weighed heavily on the side of monarchy. And when Solomon, dedicating the temple, gave concrete demonstration of the wealth, liberality and divine favour of the House of David the lure of holy festivities in Jerusalem could not easily be resisted.

In our day "national unity" is a cliché readily invoked as a motive in human affairs; and it has been credited to the genius of David and Solomon. But texts unadulterated by editorial hindsight show that David's service to the

Lord was conceived in less modern terms: it was not for the unity of Israel that he prayed but for perpetuation of the House of David. The temple set the seal on a covenant of which the terms are poetically proclaimed in Psalm 132:

> O Lord remember David . . . how he swore to the Lord . . . 'I will not enter my house nor mount my bed . . . until I find a sanctuary for the Lord, a dwelling for the mighty one of Jacob.'

Then, the temple being ready, the ode continues:

> Arise, O Lord, and come to thy resting place, thou and the ark of thy power.

Next comes the Lord's side of the pact:

> The Lord swore to David an oath which he will not break: 'a prince of your line will I set upon your throne. If your sons keep my covenant . . . their sons for all time shall sit upon your throne.'

Just so the spokesman for Yahweh, Nathan the Prophet, had declared on a former occasion (II Sam. 7):

> 'I will set up one of your family, one of your children, to succeed you and I will establish his kingdom. It is he shall build a house in honour of my name, and I will establish his royal house for ever . . . Your family shall be established and your kingdom shall stand for all time in my sight, and your throne shall be established for ever.'

To which David replied with this prayer:

> 'Now, Lord God, perform what thou hast promised for thy servant and his house for ever more . . . saying to thy servant "I will build up your house" . . . Thou hast made these noble promises . . . and thy promises come true; be pleased now to bless thy servant's house that it may continue always before thee.'

Thus the words of the Lord and the importunity of David express unequivocally the vision that inspired King Solomon: the promise of a perpetual succession of priest-kings in the House of David, ruling "in the sight of the Lord" and presiding as founders, benefactors and freeholders over the temple, its endowments and its ceremonies, the enduring symbol of supernatural authority and popular obedience.

The temple once established and its ceremonies proceeding, no man needed to ask what led David to the site; for the answer was: God chose it. Nevertheless, in these matters the will of Yahweh could not be known but by some divine manifestation; and it is the nature of that manifestation, or of its vestiges in tradition, which poses the last of the questions concerning Solomon's temple: its mythology. The problem is not easily to be solved; for the documents combine an unquestioned conviction that Yahweh had chosen Sion with a hardly credible explanation of that belief.

In II Chron., 3 we are told that "Solomon began to build the house of the Lord in Jerusalem on Mount Moriah." That seems at first to recall the Land of Moriah where Abraham once narrowly escaped sacrificing his son Isaac. But Solomon was not thinking of Abraham, for the verse continues: "where the Lord appeared to his father David . . . on the threshing floor of Ornan the Jebusite." The full story of that is told in II Sam., 24 (with added embellishments in I Chron., 21). It tells of a destroying angel bearing pestilence, whose arm was stopped by Yahweh as it stretched toward Jerusalem. Jerusalem was saved, but seventy thousand of Israel from Dan to Beersheba had perished. David, whose unauthorized census had caused the trouble, saw the angel standing by the threshing floor. He said: "This is to be the house of the Lord God"; and with the good will of its foreign owner, Araunah the Jebusite, bought the threshing floor and built an altar upon it.

To the Chronicler, writing centuries later, this seemed an acceptable prehistory for the temple. But could it have seemed so to contemporaries of David and Solomon? Must not the hallowed belief that Yahweh himself had chosen the place "for the honour of his name" - his "Holy Hill" - have had deeper roots in the consciousness of the people than their memories of a recent epidemic? The prehistories of the other great High Places of Israel were all enshrined in tales of the Patriarchs, of the Migration or of the Judges. We may be sure that God's Holy Mountain had a sacred history long before the time of David himself.

Can it be, then, that the Chronicler's mythology of the Temple is a late invention? Later history suggests it may well have been. Just as the Muslims of Jerusalem were quick to forget the Jewish mythology of the Rock, and to substitute the *mi'raj* of Muhammad for the *mihrab* of David; and as the Christians of Aelia lost no time in reinterpreting the pagan past of Golgotha as Satan's antiChristian plot; so, we may surmise, the priests and kings of Judah were swift to repress in official documents its Canaanite prehistory and ascribed to the temple site an innocuous past as a threshing floor, making its owner, though a Jebusite, an amiable nonentity who did obeisance to David and offered generous gifts for the first sacrifice.

But what was the true, the unmentionable past? We have only one clue, the mysterious character of Melchizedek, King of Salem, priest of El-Elyon, who far back in the Bronze Age greeted Abraham with bread and wine and with the auspicious words: "Blessed be Abram by El-Elyon, Creator of Heaven and Earth; and blessed be El-Elyon who has delivered your enemies into your power." And Abraham gave the king a tithe of the spoil.

We need not ask how this strange nugget of Bronze Age history found and kept its place in the Book of Genesis; but there it is, anchored in the prehistory of Jerusalem, the City of Salem's Foundation, by the name of its priest and king, Melchizedek, almost the namesake and surely a predecessor of that Adonizedek, king of Amorite Jerusalem, whom Joshua immured and slaughtered at the cave of Makkedah.

What happened on that occasion to the high place of El-Elyon, Maker of Heaven and Earth? We may be sure that Joshua did not destroy it; for "at Jerusalem" (writes the Jewish historian) "the men of Judah were unable to drive out the Jebusites who lived there, and to this day Jebusites and men of Judah live together in Jerusalem." So El-Elyon retained his ancient seat. Which explains why, for the first decades of the reigns of David and Solomon, the Ark of the Covenant reposed by the waters of Gihon, in the valley. For the Holy Mount was occupied not by a threshing floor but by an altar and high place linked with the Patriarch and inhabited by El, both of them too respected to be disturbed. When in the eleventh year of King Solomon the Ark at last moved up the mountain, the take-over was imperceptible: for El-Elyon, God Most High, Maker of Heaven and Earth, was indistinguishable from Yahweh with the same attributes. Meanwhile Arauna's sons and David's "lived together in Jerusalem", mingling sacrifices as their fathers had done.

So it was in the liberal days of Solomon. But reformers in later years with pious bigotry preferred not to know, still less to teach, that Sion the Holy Mount of Yahweh had been a heathen high place. So a theophany was invented which flattered the royal house and purged the ancient myth, leaving only Arauna the enigmatic owner of a threshing floor, and the King of Judah mysteriously beatified as "priest for ever after the order of Melchizedek" (Ps. 110, 4).

References

1. To call Constantine a Christian is near enough to the truth to be allowable in this context.
2. P. Geyer, *Itinera Hierosolymitana* (*Corp. Script. Eccl. Lat. XXXIX*) 17.
3. P. Geyer, *It. Hier.,* 145.
4. Al Ya'qubi, *History* II, 311.
5. *History* (de Goeje) Ser. I, 2408.
6. *Chronographia* (Migne, *P.G.* CVIII), col. 693, year 6127.
7. *Annals,* 17 (*Corpus Script. Chr. Or., Script. Arab.,* Ser. 3, Tom. vii. Cheikho, 1909).
8. Sebeos, *History of Heraclius* (French translation from the Armenian by Frederic Macler. Leroux, Paris 1904), p. 102.
9. Geyer, *Itinera Hierosolymitana,* p. 18.
10. *Vita Constantini* III, ch. 25 (Migne, *P.G.* XX, col. 1085).
11. The famous rotunda, which enclosed the edicule under a roof, was constructed at a slightly later stage in the 4th century: see Charles Couasnon, O.P., *The Church of the Holy Sepulchre in Jerusalem* (Schweich Lectures for the British Academy, O.U.P., London, 1974), 21-3.

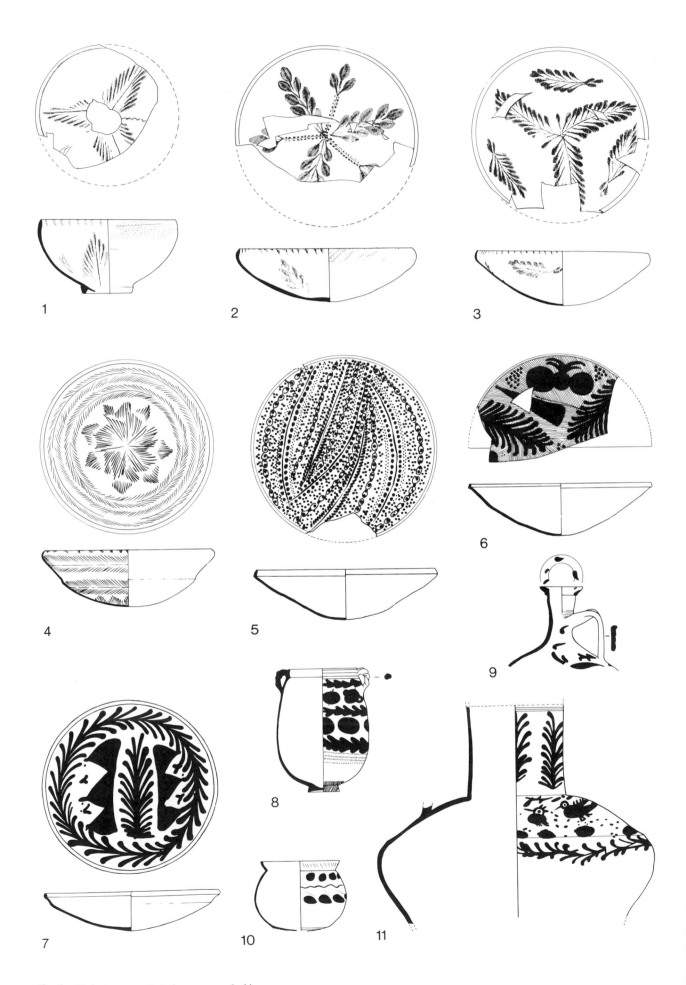

Fig 1: Nabataean painted ware - scale ¼

POTTERY, PEOPLE AND POLITICS
by Peter J. Parr

None of us, surely, would disagree with Sir Mortimer Wheeler's dictum that 'the archaeologist is digging up not things, but people';[1] and yet none of us, either, would doubt the truth of James Deetz's remark, that 'the bridge between artifacts like potsherds and projectile points and the society that made them is the most critical connection in archaeology'.[2] The connection between potsherds and people is always being made, of course, and even if there has been a reaction in recent years against such terms as 'Beaker folk' or 'Hyksos pottery', it is still an important - perhaps the single most important - assumption in archaeological methodology that the movements and activities of specific groups of people can be distinguished in the archaeological record most readily and certainly from a study of ceramic typology. The assumption is undoubtedly correct in many instances; but at a time when archaeologists, both 'new' and 'old', are looking more closely than ever before into their methodology, and when improved laboratory techniques are making it possible to extract more physical data than ever before from potsherds, it will not come amiss to subject the assumption to scrutiny. The purpose of this paper, therefore, is to make a small contribution in this direction. It will look at some aspects of a particular type of pottery, Nabataean painted ware - about which we appear to know a great deal - and ask questions concerning it which may be of more than local Levantine interest.

Although not yet fully worked out, the stratigraphical evidence from the excavations at Petra of the British School of Archaeology in Jerusalem (1958-64)[3] makes it possible to trace a clear development in both the forms and the decoration of Nabataean painted ware, a development which is represented by the examples illustrated in Figure 1. The absolute chronology of the pottery, however, is still uncertain; its origin in the 1st century BC is generally accepted, and the evidence from Petra suggests the earlier rather than the later part of that century. The ware was certainly current in the 1st century AD, but the date of its disappearance is quite unclear, owing largely to the badly eroded and disturbed nature of the latest stratified deposits at Petra and elsewhere. The writer believes that it was still being made as late as the 3rd or even the 4th century AD, but this cannot yet be demonstrated. Fortunately these problems of absolute chronology need not concern us here, although we shall return to the date of its origin.

Since the most distinctive feature of the pottery is its painted decoration, we shall begin our description with this. The designs are overwhelmingly foliate or floral, although other elements occasionally appear, as, for example, the birds on the late jug, Fig. 1, no. 11. The earliest designs seem to be based on a simple radiating palmette motif (Fig. 1, nos. 1-3); the more complex 'feather' design of no. 4 may be contemporary with these or slightly later. The surface of these early vessels is usually creamy-pink, and the paint is light red; the individual brush strokes are visible, and the veins of the leaves are often shown by a slightly thicker application of pigment. The overall effect is one of naturalism and delicacy, and the standards of workmanship and artistry are extremely high.

In what might be termed the 'classic' period of the Nabataean painted ware, beginning perhaps in the early 1st century AD, the motifs become more conventionalized and static and the painting less delicate (Fig. 1, nos. 5-10). The pigment - now deeper in hue, ranging from purplish-red to near black - is applied uniformly on a dark pink or red ground. The patterns include a greater variety of elements than hitherto; side by side with the ubiquitous palmettes appear stylized pomegranates, 'double cones', grapes, 'peacock eyes', etc., all rather rigid and lifeless compared with the earlier designs. A notable feature is the overloading of the decoration; few empty spaces are left on the field, which is also often covered with an all-over shading of fine parallel or reticulate lines (Fig. 1, no. 6). Yet the results are still of considerable elegance and beauty, and it is not until the final stages of development - perhaps in the late 2nd and 3rd centuries AD - that the progression away from naturalism and towards stylization is accompanied by such a deterioration in the quality of the painting that a truly 'debased' or 'degenerate' style can be said to prevail (Fig. 1, no. 11).

Turning now to forms, one of the most remarkable features of the Nabataean painted ware is that the overwhelming majority of the vessels so decorated are either bowls or plates. Painting on other shapes - for example small jars and cups, or jugs (Fig. 1, nos. 8-11) - does occur but never in the earliest period and only relatively occasionally in the 'classic' and later phases. Of the bowls and plates, several variant types may be noted. In the earliest period a deep hemispherical bowl with ring base occurs (no. 1), side by side with a shallower, round-based vessel, with either a gently curving or a slightly carinated 'cyma' profile (nos. 2-4). The round bases are probably commoner than the ring, though actual statistics are not yet available. Ring bases certainly disappear in the following period, as do the gently incurved and carinated profiles, and the standard 'classic' Nabataean painted plate is a round-based vessel with a pronounced short inverted rim (nos. 5 and 6).

Finally, a few words about the fabric of the painted ware. 'Eggshell Ware' is the customary description, and the term is well suited to indicate the thinness and hardness of the majority of the vessels, of all three periods. However, here again a development is discernible. The clay of the earliest pieces is finely levigated and is uniformly fired to a creamy-buff hue; the walls are thin, but not so thin as they usually are in the 'classic' period, when the fired clay is normally brick-red in colour, though often with a black un-oxidized core. Grits occasionally mar the fabric of the later vessels, and the surfaces can sometimes be quite rough. The general impression is of a gradual decline in standards of craftsmanship, accompanying the decline in the artistry of the painting that we have already noted, and perhaps connected with an increase in mass-production techniques.

So much for a description of the Nabataean painted ware. Before turning to the problem of its origin we should perhaps attempt briefly to explain and justify its attribution to the Nabataeans. This may at first sight seem unnecessary - after all, the attribution has never seriously been doubted - but, as we shall see, the relationship of the pottery and the people is by no means straightforward, and is well worth examining for the lessons it might teach us.

First we should bear in mind that the term Nabataean was originally a tribal name (*nbṭw* = *nabaṭu*) applied to themselves by a group of Arabic speaking people in north Arabia in the latter part of the 1st millennium BC.[4] By extension the term is used by modern scholars to refer both to the written language (a variety of Aramaic) and the script used by the *nabaṭu,* and to the political state which, in the course of time, they established. By a further extension the word has been used by archaeologists, as is normal, to designate those cultural traits - pottery, architecture, sculpture, coinage, etc. - actually or supposedly associated with the Nabataeans. As a tribe, the Nabataeans existed at least as early as 312 BC, in which year they were attacked by the Seleucid king Antigonus in their tribal centre, Petra. Perhaps at this time they were still nomadic; but by the middle of the 3rd century they had become sedentary, as excavations at Petra and Avdat, for example, have shown. It was perhaps at this time, and certainly not later than the early 2nd century BC, that the Nabataean leaders assumed the title of king, and they were soon controlling an area which stretched from the Hauran in the north to the Hejaz in the south. From then on the 'kingdom of the Nabataeans' was a political reality which, despite varying fortunes and fluctuating frontiers, survived until 106 AD, when it was incorporated into the Roman Empire.

Now a study of the chronology and distribution of the painted pottery we have been describing shows, on the one hand, that its attribution to the Nabataeans is entirely justified. It is found in abundance at Petra and at dozens of other sites in southern Palestine and Transjordan - the heartland of the Nabataean territories - and dates, in its early and 'classic' phases, to the apogee of Nabataean political fortunes. And yet, on the other hand, it is equally clear that the distribution of Nabataean painted pottery is by no means co-terminus, either in time or in space, with the Nabataean state or with the Nabataean cultural province, as evidenced, for example, by architecture or inscriptions. This is a matter of great interest and importance. As regards time, it is evident that the Nabataeans, as a tribal and political unit, must have existed for a long period - perhaps as much as 250 years - before the first painted pottery appears; and it is equally clear (if the latest examples of the pottery are to be dated to the 2nd century AD and after, as they almost certainly must) that the painted ware continued to be popular well after the extinction of the Nabataean kingdom. In other words, the first two and a half centuries of Nabataean history, the formative period of their political and social development as a sedentary people, can in no way be recognized in the archaeological record by means of this distinctive ceramic; while, conversely, the identification in the archaeological record of examples of the late style of Nabataean painted pottery is quite irrelevant to a study of the Nabataean polity. The importance of these facts for Nabataean studies is obvious enough, but they surely also have a wider significance for archaeological methodology, a point to which we shall return.

As regards the geographical distribution of the painted pottery, the situation is even more interesting. As we have seen the centre of gravity of the distribution map is southern Palestine and Jordan; it has been found also in Sinai and in northern Saudi Arabia, at Meda'in Salih, and al-Jauf, for example.[5] In the north, Glueck's famous 'ceramic frontier' at approximately the latitude of the northern end of the Dead Sea, beyond which he found no surface sherds of the painted ware, has been breached to some extent by its more recent discovery in tombs at Amman and Jerash, and in the excavations of the late Paul Lapp at Tell er-Remith, in the far north of Jordan;[6] but these are perhaps only isolated examples, and there appears to be no trace of the painted ware in the Hauran, despite recent surveys and archaeological clearance at such sites as Bosra. In Palestine, in spite of dubious reports of occasional discoveries of painted Nabataean sherds at, for example, Jerusalem, it seems clear that the major area of distribution is also confined to the south, with a frontier running approximately on a line from Beersheba to Masada.

Now in the south this distribution pattern is largely consistent with those of Nabataean inscriptions and Nabataean architectural forms, but the non-conformity in the north is striking, and has often been noted. For much of the 1st centuries BC and AD - just at the time of the *floruit* of the painted ware - southern Syria is known from historical sources to have been under Nabataean political control, while from architectural and epigraphic evidence it is known to have been the home of people who worshipped Nabataean gods, built in Nabataean styles, and wrote in Nabataean script. Yet the fine Nabataean painted pottery was not used there. Why? The most commonly accepted answer has been that of Glueck, who asserted that "the Nabataeans seemed to have occupied this part of their kingdom in insufficient numbers to warrant manufacturing or even importing their strikingly unique and beautiful pottery, and made use of local wares. They functioned there, it seems, more as colonial overlords than as permanent settlers in completely homogenous communities, and apparently did not form the decisive majority of the native population."[7] This is probably true, though it is necessary to remember that the 'colonial presence' was sufficient to warrant the erection of magnificent temples and other public monuments in the Nabataean style, and that the Hauran was sufficiently an integral part of the Nabataean kingdom for Rabbel II (71-106 AD) to move the capital from Petra to Bosra.

Yet even admitting that the Nabataean presence in the north was one of administrators, commercial agents and priests, and not one of villagers and tribesmen, does not necessarily explain the absence of painted pottery there. After all, this pottery was a luxury item, evidently very popular with wealthy Nabataeans at Petra and other towns in the south, some of them, like Meda'in Salih, more remote from Petra than was the Hauran. It might surely have been expected that the Nabataean merchants and officials in the Hauran would have brought the pottery with them, just as Greek traders had taken Mycenaean pottery to Egypt and Syria, or Roman traders Terra Sigillata to southern India. In fact, looked at in this way, the surprising thing is not just that the Nabataean painted ware did not spread to the Hauran, but that it did not spread even further afield along the Nabataean trade routes. Here was a people whose wealth and reputation were based primarily on trade, and who certainly had commercial contacts as far afield as Delos in the Aegean, and Puteoli on the Bay of Naples, and presumably also in Gerrha on the Arabian Gulf and perhaps Qataban in the Yemen; a people who were an important and integral part of the economic and diplomatic scene in the Levant for several centuries at the turn of the era. Surely it might have been expected that amongst the luxury commodities their merchants were accustomed to handling the delicate and attractive pottery would have been included; would have been exported, if not to the more distant regions, at least to Palestine and Syria. Yet it was not. The suggestion that the pottery was too fragile to travel is not convincing; despite its fineness it is structurally no weaker than, for example, Cypriot base ring ware or Roman sigillata, and both of these travelled. If there had been a demand for the painted ware outside the heart of the Nabataean kingdom, whether amongst the Nabataean merchants and officials in the Hauran or the more distant emporia, or amongst the non-Nabataean local population of the Decapolis, Judaea, Ituraea, etc., we can be sure that the pottery would have got there. There was a demand for glass, and sigillata, and lead glazed wares, and they arrived. The fact that the Nabataean painted pottery was not exported can only mean that, however attractive it was to the Nabataeans at home, it did not appeal to the taste of the majority of the inhabitants of contemporary Palestine and Syria. We should, therefore, look more closely at this matter of taste, so crucial to a study of changing fashion, and thus of archaeological method; but so relevant is this also to the problem of the origin of the Nabataean pottery, that we must turn to this first.

The origin of the painted Nabataean pottery has often been discussed, but only at the level of stylistic analogy. Here there is little problem, and Iliffe's statement, made many years ago,[8] that its parentage was 'by Sigillata out of Hellenistic Painted Wares' is obviously correct. Subsequent discussion has mostly centred on the question of which of the Hellenistic painted styles provided the model for the Nabataean. Iliffe's own preference, for the Alexandrine Hadra vases, seems generally to have prevailed, though it might also be suggested that West Slope ware (despite the differences of technique) or the painted lagynoi,[9] examples of both of which styles have been found in Palestine, provided alternative sources of inspiration.

Yet such formal comparisons, however cogent, do very little to solve the real problems concerning the origin of the Nabataean pottery. This pottery is by no means an imitation, even a remote imitation, of earlier or contemporary Hellenistic/Roman wares. The Nabataean potter was inspired, certainly, by what he had seen elsewhere, but he did not copy it. He borrowed certain elements that appealed to him - or to his clientele - and arranged them into a style which was genuinely and uniquely his own. Why he chose to borrow certain elements and not others, and how he arranged them, are the questions of real interest, the answers to which (can we but know them) are likely to provide more insight into Nabataean culture and psychology than even the most exhaustive catalogue of ceramic comparisons.

The introduction of the word 'psychology' may appear strange, and requires justification. Pottery has seldom been used by archaeologists to provide an insight into the character and spirit of an ancient people, in the way that architecture and sculpture have. Emily Vermeule has referred, somewhat disparagingly, to the way in which the "qualities of rationality, precision, sense of organic design, clarity, authority, and freedom from surface fuss" apparent in Minyan ware have been thought to reflect the 'national psychology' of its makers, supposedly the first Greeks. [10] Less hesitantly, Sir Leonard Woolley has suggested that the reappearance in Level VI at Alalakh of the traditional painted pottery is indicative of a 'nationalistic revival' following the demise of the foreign dynasty of Level VII, under which the painted ware had been deliberately suppressed. [11] But few other archaeologists, intent on their typologies and neutron activation tests, have been tempted in this direction. Yet no less an authority than Herbert Read has said of pottery that it is "so fundamental, so bound up with the elementary needs of civilization, that a national ethos must find its expression in this medium. Judge the art of a country, judge the fineness of its sensibility, by its pottery; it is a sure touchstone". [12] There is no reason why this should be true of only (for example) Greek or Chinese vases; it should be equally true of any genuinely national or popular style of aesthetic merit, and this the Nabataean painted style was. We are therefore justified in using it to throw light on the 'national ethos' of the Nabataeans.

Let us now return to the question of the origin of the Nabataean painted ware, and to the acts of selection and creation which are central to it. The most striking feature of the earliest Nabataean pottery is not the resemblance of its motifs to those of the various Hellenistic wares cited, but the complete difference in the way those motifs are used by the Nabataean painter. In the Hellenistic wares the decoration is normally applied to the outer surfaces of the vessels. This is, of course, necessarily so in the case of closed shapes like the Hadra vases or the lagynoi (which were not adopted by the Nabataean potter), but even the open bowls and plates which occur - though not commonly - among the West Slope forms are, with few exceptions, decorated on the outside, and Thompson surmises that the West Slope artist found the problem involved in decorating the flat surface provided by the bowls and plates largely beyond his capabilities. [13] Yet it was precisely (and initially exclusively) the round concave inner surface of the bowl that the Nabataean potter chose as the field on which to display his talent. There is no obvious reason for this, and it is important to note that there was no locally existing tradition of painted pottery by which he may have been influenced. It is true that some six or seven centuries previously there had flourished in Transjordan an Edomite school of potters who had frequently decorated the inner surfaces of their bowls, though only with geometric patterns; but the difference of date, together with the absence of any connecting tradition during the first centuries of Nabataean settlement in the region, preclude any possibility of direct Edomite influence on the Nabataean potter. Nor is any other oriental - Asiatic or Egyptian - influence visible in the painting. There thus seems no escaping the conclusion that, on the one hand, the Nabataean painted style was an original creation so far as its basic conception and arrangement were concerned, but that, on the other hand, the elements that made up the design were purely Hellenistic. Moreover, the fact that this painted pottery appears suddenly in the Nabataean cultural repertoire, with no evidence for preliminary and hesitant experimentation, leads us to the further conclusion that its introduction was the work of a single individual potter who was entirely at home in the Hellenistic artistic tradition.

We have still to try to explain the reason for its introduction, and in this connection the date of the earliest examples - the earlier part of the 1st. century B.C. - is important. This appears to have been a time of accelerated growth in the political fortunes and the culture of the Nabataeans. It is the period of their furthest expansion north, culminating in the (admittedly short-lived) occupation of Damascus during the reign of Aretas III (c. 84-71 B.C.) The first Nabataean coinage had appeared about the beginning of the century, though it was Aretas III (significantly called 'the Philhellene') who issued from Damascus the first properly inscribed coins, in the Hellenistic manner. It is likely also that the first major urban development of Petra, including its fortification, [14] dates from about this time. It certainly cannot be maintained that all of these developments were contemporary or causally linked, but they are clearly suggestive of a new dynamism, stemming perhaps from new prosperity as the Nabataeans came into closer contact with Syria, in Nabataean culture. With this may well have come a desire for 'cultural respectability', at a time when to be culturally respectable meant to be Hellenized. Writing in connection with Nabataean sculpture, Avi Yonah has remarked how this reflects 'a people detaching itself from its origins', [15] and the same may be said even more emphatically of the painted pottery. Could the introduction of this ware have been a deliberate act of policy by the Nabataeans in order to proclaim to the world their 'Philhellenism', at a time when they were beginning to become ashamed of their Arabian background? Is it too fanciful to suggest that the real factor of importance in the origin of this ware was a political decision of the king (perhaps Aretas the Philhellene himself) and his advisors, acting on much the same principle as, though in contrary fashion to, the rulers of Alalakh VII who (according to Woolley) deliberately suppressed the native painted pottery in order to promote their own political aims?

If it be conceded that the introduction and the popularity of the Nabataean painted ware in the heart of the kingdom can in some way be explained by the desire of its makers to compete with - indeed, to outshine - their neighbours in terms of Hellenization, then the failure of that pottery to have much impact in the neighbouring states can be explained also. The inhabitants of Syria and Palestine had a long tradition of cosmopolitanism behind them, and had been open to Hellenic influences long before Alexander the Great brought them within political reach of the Greek and Roman imperialists. The acceptance of western fashions must have been a more natural process for them than it was for the Nabataeans, who were relative newcomers to the old urban civilisation of the Levant, let alone the new urban civilisation of the Hellenistic *oikoumene*. The need did not arise (it might be suggested) for the rulers and the inhabitants of the Palestinian and Syrian states to proclaim their acceptance of western fashion in quite the novel and deliberate way in which (we have suggested) the Nabataeans did. The proclamation of cultural respectability that the Nabataeans made through the medium of their new pottery would have been meaningless to them; the pottery did not convey its message, and therefore did not appeal to their taste; its visual attractiveness was of no importance in the face of such emotional unreceptiveness. Speculative though this reconstruction is, it does not, we believe, go beyond the bounds of possibility.

There is one final aspect of the Nabataean painted ware to be discussed here. We have noted that the pottery remained fashionable in the Nabataean heartland for several centuries, and we have remarked upon the pronounced development which took place in its style. Quite apart from a certain decline in the standards of both potting and painting (which is in all probability to be explained by the dispersal of manufacture from one individual potter's workshop to a number of mass-production centres), there is an increasing formality and rigidity in the designs, and a tendency to all-over patterning. The lightness and movement of the early style is replaced in the classic period by immobility and darkness, and the *horror vacui* is often revealed. Yet the introduction of new motifs, such as the double cones and the stylized pomegranates, shows that this is not - in the classic period, at least - merely a stylistic degeneration resulting from mass-production or from the misunderstanding of the original motifs and the incompetence to reproduce them. The classic style remains vigorous and inventive, though different from its progenitor; and it is tempting to try and explain this fact.

An analogy may be helpful here, even an analogy which may perhaps appear surprising. To the best of our belief, the resemblance of Nabataean to Islamic pottery has never been remarked upon, yet it is very striking. In the absence of illustrations of Islamic pottery, some quotations from scholars concerning it may make the point. Oleg Grabar has observed that 'there is general agreement on . . . the curious fact that the luxury wares of the early [Islamic] centuries tended to be a production of bowls and plates, i.e. of open shapes which emphasize a single circular surface to be decorated. It has also been generally recognized that interest in surface decoration over generally indifferently shaped bodies is a major characteristic of Islamic ceramics'. [16] Surely nothing could be truer of the classic Nabataean painted ware than this? Pinder Wilson has also drawn attention to the fact that 'Islamic art has been primarily concerned with the problem of surface decoration, with the result that pattern is often of greater consequence than subject . . . Often the scrolling arabesque is used as a background ornament, since the Muslim artist invariably prefers to fill the entire surface with decoration'. [17] And again: 'When organising his decorative scheme the Muslim is careful to avoid giving undue weight or prominence to a single element . . . The principles of balance and symmetry are strictly observed . . . In order to achieve symmetry the artist uses reciprocal ornament in which one element mirrors another . . . A design is either complete and self-contained or a portion of an infinitely repeated pattern. This idea of endless repetition made a strong appeal to the Muslim'. [18] There are, of course, very obvious and important differences between Islamic and Nabataean pottery; the arabesque does not appear on the latter, for instance, and the techniques of manufacture are entirely different. But much of what has been quoted above could be applied, with a fair measure of truth, to the plates and bowls of the classic Nabataean production, and this may be more than coincidental.

It must be made clear, to begin with, that there is no evidence to suggest a direct connection between Nabataean and early Islamic luxury pottery; even though there are hints that the Nabataean style had an influence on Byzantine local painted wares in Transjordan, it is well established that the earliest fine Islamic wares appeared further east, in Iraq and Iran, and were mainly influenced from these quarters. Yet, if artistic style reflects in any way the 'national ethos' and 'sensibility' of a people (to use Read's terms), then the styles of the Nabataean and Islamic ceramic arts are close enough, we suggest, to indicate a definite community of spirit between the two groups responsible for them. What the love of pattern, of symmetry and balance, of closely covered surfaces and endless repetition means in terms of individual or group psychology, is a matter beyond the scope of this paper and the competence of its author; but whatever it means must be as relevant to the study of the psychology of the Nabataeans as to the study of that of the Muslim Arabs. Nothing would, in fact, be more natural than such a psychological link, since both groups were closely related members of the same racial and linguistic stock. There are, needless to say, vitally important differences between the two groups, but they are differences largely emanating from the impact of religious revelation on the Muslims, and they should not be allowed to obscure the close analogies which can be drawn between the early histories of the two peoples, both of whom owed much of their initial importance to their control of the Hejaz trade, and both of whom were confronted by the challenge of a higher material culture among their immediate neighbours in the Levant. The comparative study of Nabataean and Muslim Arab historical and cultural development cannot be pursued here, fascinating though it would be. But, as a small contribution to that study, it is suggested that the Muslim achievement in ceramic art emanated in part from a North Arabian 'sensibility' which had previously, if less gloriously, revealed itself in the classic Nabataean painted pottery.

Much of what has been said in the preceding paragraphs about Nabataean painted pottery has been intentionally speculative. The intention has been to provide a vehicle for the investigation of some of the problems surrounding the relationships between ceramic styles, population groups and political entities, problems which, it seems to the writer, have been largely neglected. Apart from their relevance to Nabataean studies, what lessons of more general interest can be learned from the suggestions that have been made?

In the first place, the restricted area of distribution of the Nabataean ware proves that very distinctive local fashions in material culture could and did exist side by side even in a relatively small area such as Palestine and Transjordan. If this were true in the Hellenistic-Roman period, it would have been even truer in earlier times, This view contradicts that of Albright, for example, who avers: 'There are many serious objections to exaggerating the differences between coeval areas of material culture in such a small country as Palestine . . . It has become absurd to treat Palestine as though it were a land with little movement of trade. The different geographical zones were, furthermore, too small and too easy of access to allow for a situation in which there was little or no exchange of goods. Under such conditions the relative proportion of different types of artifact might change considerably, but there would always be some circulation, and usually quite enough for cross-dating purposes'. In our view every statement in the quotation is disproved by the example of Nabataean pottery. In particular, we have seen that the 'exchange of goods', at least as reflected by the exchange of pottery, does not necessarily depend entirely upon such obvious factors as geographical proximity, trade routes, accessibility, etc.; for although imported sigillata (for example) occurs in the Nabataean realm, Nabataean painted pottery does not occur outside it - or even consistently within it. Whatever factors governed the distribution of Nabataean painted ware - and our suggestions may or may not be acceptable - they are factors which could have been operative at any period of time, and which negate any preconceived model of cultural uniformity, even in an area as small as Palestine.

Secondly, we have seen that a ceramic type, especially a luxury type, can be specifically and uniquely associated with an ethnic and political group, so that the concepts of 'Hurrian ware' or 'Hyksos pottery', for example, are not inherently untenable, although every instance of such an association must naturally be judged on its own merits. But we have also seen that, in the case of the Nabataeans, their real sphere of cultural and political influence was much wider than the distribution map of their 'ethnic' pottery indicates, and this is a fact which should be borne in mind in other situations - when considering, for example, the cultural and political realities of the Philistine settlement in Palestine.

Thirdly, let us consider the matter of the origins of ethnic and political groups in terms of pottery styles. It is a fair assumption that, had the Nabataeans been a prehistoric people, the results of excavations at Petra (where levels spanning the 3rd. and 2nd. centuries BC and containing a typical Palestinian Hellenistic pottery assemblage are followed in the 1st. century BC by the addition of an entirely new ceramic with clear Hellenistic affiliations) would have been interpreted as showing the initial settlement of this area by people from the Levant - i.e., a population movement eastwards, into a marginal zone, followed two centuries later by the influx of a second, even more 'westernised', group. The same conclusions would have been drawn, even more emphatically, from surface surveys of the Nabataean region. Nothing in the ceramic record would have indicated that only one group of settlers was involved, not two, despite the dramatic introduction of a new style, or that the people in question were of Arabian origin. This example must surely throw into question the assumption often made by prehistorians that the direction of origin of a population group is indicated by the direction of origin of the pottery style associated with it. This may in fact often be so; but the deliberate act of borrowing performed by the Nabataeans cannot have been without parallel in the ancient world, and we would do well to bear it in mind when studying such diverse problems as, for example, the origin of the Sumerians and the Ubaid pottery style, or the origin of the 'Amorite' invaders of Palestine in the late 3rd. millennium BC and the associated EB-MB pottery.

If this paper has suggested some ways in which the pottery associated with various ancient political, cultural, or ethnic groups - be they Sumerians, Philistines, Hurrians, Amorites, or whoever - can be reconsidered in the light of the example of Nabataean painted pottery, it will have served its purpose.

References

1.   Sir Mortimer Wheeler, *Archaeology from the Earth* (London, 1954) 13.
2.   J. Deetz (ed), *Man's Imprint from the Past* (Boston, 1971), 219.
3.   See, for the time being, P. J. Parr, 'A Sequence of Pottery from Petra', in J. A. Sanders (ed), *Near Eastern Archaeology in the Twentieth Century. Essays in Honor of Nelson Glueck* (New York, 1970), 348-381.
4.   For a discussion of this, and for a summary of the history of the Nabataeans, see J. Starcky, 'Pétra et la Nabatène', in *Supplément au Dictionnaire de la Bible* Vol. III, fasc. 39 (1964), col. 900 ff.
5.   A few fragments have recently been found much further south in Saudi Arabia, at Qaryat al-Faw, 560 kms. SSW of Riyadh, during the course of excavations by the University of Riyadh. I am indebted to the director of the excavations, Dr. A-R al-Ansari, for this information.
6.   These are unpublished, but were shown to the writer by the late Dr. Lapp.
7.   Nelson Glueck, *Deities and Dolphins* (New York, 1965), 6-7.
8.   J. H. Illife, 'Sigillata Wares in the Near East', *Q.D.A.P.* VI (1938), 15.
9.   The best study of these is still that of G. Leroux, *Lagynoi* (Paris, 1913).
10.   Emily Vermeule, *Greece in the Bronze Age* (Chicago, 1972), 73.
11.   Sir Leonard Woolley, *Alalakh (Society of Antiquaries of London Research Report,* XVIII, 1955), 314-315; ibid., *A Forgotten Kingdom* (London, 1953), 81ff.
12.   Herbert Read, *The Meaning of Art* (London, 1949), 33.
13.   H.C. Thompson, 'Two Centuries of Hellenistic Pottery', *Hesperia* III (1934), 445.
14.   On the fortifications, see P. J. Parr, K. B. Atkinson, and E. H. Wickens, 'Photogrammetric Work at Petra, 1965-68', *A.D.A.J.* XX (1975), 31-45; P. J. Parr, 'Le Conway High Place à Pétra', *Révue Biblique* LXIX (1962), 64-79.
15.   M. Avi Yonah, *Oriental Art in Roman Palestine* (Rome, 1961), 56.
16.   Oleg Grabar, 'Notes on the Decorative Composition of a Bowl from Northeastern Iran', in R. Ettinghausen (ed.), *Islamic Art in the Metropolitan Museum of Art* (New York 1972), 91.
17.   R. Pinder Wilson, *Islamic Art* (London, 1957), 8.
18.   Ibid., 9-10.

Plate XXXI

> *a. Amman – Theatre & Forum area.*
> *b. Details of Capitals and Architrave of South
> Colonnade, from the Southeast*

a.

b.

THE ROMAN TOWN-PLAN OF AMMAN
by Adnan Hadidi

Introduction

In antiquity Amman was the seat of the Ammonites and was called Rabbath bené Ammon. It was re-named Philadelphia for the Hellenistic ruler of Egypt Ptolemy II Philadelphos (285-247 B.C.). In 218 B.C., it was taken by Antiochus III the Great, the Hellenistic ruler of Syria, and became a city in Coele-Syria (Hollow-Syria). For about a century before the Roman conquest of the Near East, Amman belonged to the Nabataeans. When Pompey conquered Syria and Palestine (63 B.C.), Philadelphia became the southernmost member of the Decapolis (League of Ten Cities). In A.D. 106, it became a city in the Roman province of Arabia. Situated on the magnificent *Via Nova Traiana* which joined Bosra with the Red Sea, Philadelphia enjoyed a long period of prosperity during the second century A.D. Amman overlies Philadelphia, just as Philadelphia overlies Rabbath bené Ammon, where David sent Uriah the Hittite to make the beautiful Bathsheba a widow 3000 years ago. Indeed, the springs that still give Amman its water supply have made this place a site of human habitation, as palaeolithic remains show, for more than 12,000 years.

During the last few decades, the city has grown out of all proportions, and an important part of downtown Amman has been built on the major ruins of the Roman city in an area less than a square mile. The crucial area lies at the lowest point in the city, where the Philadelphians built their great forum, beside the *wadi,* or stream, that drains the surrounding hills. On the south side of the forum rises the great Roman theatre, Amman's best landmark, and on the east side is the odeum. The forum area had long been overlaid by a modern street.

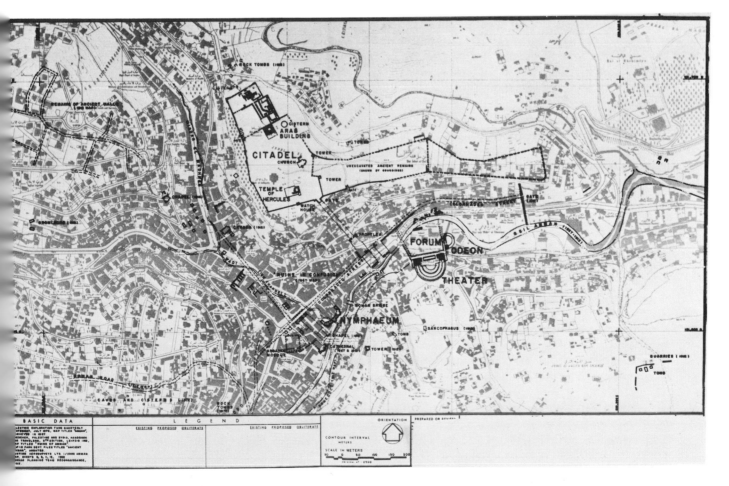

1: *Plan of Modern Amman with Roman Features Superimposed.*

In 1964, the Amman Municipality drafted plans for the development of the forum area into a city park. The time then was opportune for the Jordan Department of Antiquities to undertake a systematic excavation of the site in order to uncover the plan and extent of the Roman forum and to clarify many long-standing points of chronology in the early history of the Roman city. Another aim of the excavation was to discover conclusive evidence that would help in dating more closely the building complex in and around the area.

Fortunately, at the time that the forum was being excavated, the Municipality was laying new sewers beneath the main thoroughfares of the city, overlying the Roman colonnaded streets. These colonnaded streets were still partly exposed, eroded and crumbling but impressive, to a visitor in 1905. The Municipality project has given us, for the first time, the chance to study, record, draw and photograph several sections of these colonnaded streets. These results, together with those obtained from the forum excavation, have helped us to understand and reconstruct more precisely the Roman town-plan of Amman, of which we knew very little before.

Philadelphia is, of course, only one of the hundreds of cities of the Roman Empire. Among these centres of ancient life it ranks comparatively low, and one which is even today only imperfectly known. And yet it has its importance. Its well-preserved buildings and the striking features of its Roman town-plan illustrate various aspects of Roman art and engineering.

Description of the *Cardo* and *Decumanus Maximus.*

Perhaps nowhere in the Roman Empire did the Roman Legionaries feel more at home than in Philadelphia, the name by which they knew Amman. For, like Rome its hills and valleys were embellished with fine paved streets, colonnaded plazas, baths, temples and theatres. Even the climate is similar enough to that of Rome to have made the Legions happy in the thought that they might have been posted to worse places, Londinium for instance with its damp summers and cold foggy winters.

The well organized town-plan of Amman is, however, in complete contrast to the confusion of the Roman capital.[1] Although the urban development of ancient Amman was restricted by the nature of its site, the concept of axial lay-out of streets and buildings is sensibly applied in the greater part of the town-plan (Fig. 1). Two great thoroughfares form the backbone of the plan. The *decumanus maximus,* which is the longer of the two, first ran on a SW-NE axis to a point nearly opposite the wall of the middle terrace of the acropolis.[2] This thoroughfare is designated "Colonnaded Street" on the plan (Fig. 1). At this point, the straight line of the street is broken to follow a short curvilinear course from the northwest to the northeast following the semicircle of the stream which encloses the north side of the forum. The course then gives way to two straight sections, the first running almost due east and the second slightly north east; the two sections form an angle of 130°. The street ends in what was once a monumental gateway at the foot of the south slope of the acropolis. The conjectural plan published by H.C. Butler[3] shows this street in two straight lines meeting at an obtuse angle a short distance to the northwest of the forum, which recent discoveries have shown not to be the case.

The *cardo* is shorter and quite straight, and lies west of the area designated "1912 Channel" on the plan (Fig. 1). Its order was Corinthian, as indicated by the column bases and fallen capitals discovered along its course. The interaxial distance between the colonnades of the street is 11 m. and its width in the clear is 10 m. Each column measures 0.90 m. in diameter and the intercolumniations are 2.20 m. The *cardo* ran from north-west to south-east parallel to the axis of the west wall of the acropolis. The two streets met at a right angle to form a capital T exactly at the point where the *wadi* Amman branches to the north in the east part of the ancient city.

It is assumed that the *decumanus maximus* ended in another monumental gateway at the west end of the ancient city, but the modern buildings erected in this area make it impossible to test this assumption at present. The evidence indicates, however, that the street eventually joined a Roman road that fed the *Via Nova* southward to Petra and to Aila on the Gulf of Aqaba.[4]

The evidence obtained during the course of sewerage construction underneath the modern street overlying the *decumanus maximus* shows that, like the site of the forum, the area of the main thoroughfare was artificially filled and leveled.[5] A retaining wall and a series of arches built of small voussoir blocks laid dry, sealed off the two sides of the stream or *seil* as it is called locally (Fig. 2). The retaining wall is perpendicular and each side flanking an arch is 1 m. wide and 2 m. high with a 0.40 m. off-set from which the arch springs. The arches are of two different sizes; the span of each of the larger arches is 2.50 m. and each of the smaller ones has a span of 1.70 m. Each small arch is set

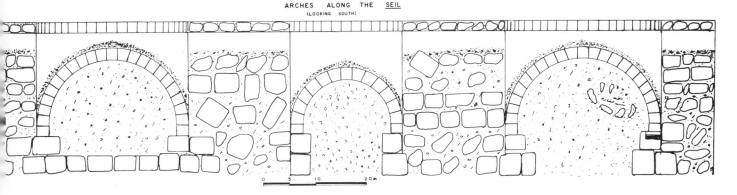

ARCHES   ALONG   THE   SEIL
(LOOKING   SOUTH)

Fig 2: Elevation of the Arches along Seil.

between two large arches. The original level of the ancient city was made by a filling as high as the crown of the larger arches. Evidently, great effort and expense were made to keep the street well up the slope of the *wadi* and maintain it on one level from end to end. Further, the evidence indicates that originally both sides of the stream were kept at a level surface extending from the *decumanus maximus* to the steep hill on the south side of the stream.[6] The stream itself was covered with a series of barrel-vaults and paved from the west to the east end of the ancient city. Unfortunately, the remains of these vaults and pavement have long disappeared and we have to rely on the reports of early travelers who had seen traces of these once beautiful and ingenius works of Roman engineering.[7] The covering and paving of the stream did not only protect the water from contamination, but also provided extra space between the *decumanus maximus* and the south quarter of the lower ancient city.

The best preserved section of the main colonnaded street was uncovered at about 2.5 m. below the level of the present modern street, not far from the northwest corner of the forum. It was found that the colonnades flanking the street on both sides had an interaxial spacing of 11 m., and the width of the street in the clear was 10 m. Judging from the fallen capitals along the course of the street, the order used in the colonnades was Corinthian. The columns were not, however, uniform in dimensions. In the sections discovered between the east gate and a point about fifty metres west of the forum, the columns measure 0.90 m. in diameter each and the intercolumniations were 2.2 m. (Pl. XXXIIb). Beyond this point westward, the columns were much slimmer with a diameter of 0.45 m. Each shaft consisted of several drums and the column bases which were set directly on the stylobate are of the Attic Ionic type like those of the south and east colonnades of the forum. The pavement of the street consisted of well-dressed oblong and square whitish-grey blocks of limestone laid diagonally and closely jointed. The oblong blocks vary from 0.60 m. by 0.40 m. to 0.45 m. by 0.15 m. The square blocks measure 0.45 m. by 0.45 m. Since no architrave pieces were discovered, it is not possible to say whether the colonnades originally supported one. Neither can we know the character and style of the city-gates that once occupied the east and west ends of the street as they have been obliterated a long time ago.

The Siting of the Buildings.

The principal buildings in that part of ancient Amman are all, more or less, oriented in conformity with the axes of the two colonnaded streets.[8] The forum occupies the middle insula of the southern half of the lower ancient city, lying on the south side of the stream which separates it from the main thoroughfare between the east and west gates (Fig. 4). Being so placed, the forum takes full advantage of the space rendered by the natural widening of the valley between the foot of the Citadel hill and the theatre; an important consideration in this rugged topography of the city (Fig. 3).

Stratigraphic evidence indicates that the forum area was in its greater part filled in and leveled artificially. The preparation of the site seems to have involved a deep fill sometimes reaching close to bedrock. This was done in order to raise the level of the forum above that of the stream so that the forum could be kept dry, especially in winter time. Further, the area was provided with a drainage system which consisted of terracotta pipes, about 0.25 m. in diameter, that ran along the inner sides of the stylobates below pavement level and terminated in the north-west corner of the forum, where the water flowed into the stream. The forum and the city quarter south of the stream were connected with the main thoroughfare to the north by stair systems, ramps and bridges.[9] Remains of arches along the south side of the stream were uncovered during the course of sewerage construction at the time of the forum excavation.

Fig 3:   *Plan of Modern Amman, showing location of the Forum.*

Oriented on the diagonal of north-west and south-east, the forum is bordered by porticos on three sides and closed on the north by the arc of the stream and the colonnaded street beyond (Fig. 4).[10] The forum and porticos constitute an irregular ensemble in the form of a trapezium rather than a rectangle.[11] Including the colonnades, the forum measures 100 m. on the south side, 48 m. on the west and 50 m. on the east side. The chord of the arc on the north is nearly 130 m. The total area of the forum as defined by the outer lines of the colonnadés and the arc, including the unexcavated area of the Philadelphia Hotel, is approximately 7620 square m. Thus, the forum at Amman ranks among the largest of Roman Imperial fora. [12]

The south colonnade of the forum traces a straight line parallel to the theatre's stage at a distance of 3 m. to the north. It is also more or less parallel to the *decumanus maximus* which ran east-west on the north side of the stream (Fig. 1; Pls. XXXIb, XXXIIa). On the east as well as on the west end, the colonnade terminates in double columns. Each column is set obliquely on the corner so as to form an obtuse angle with the line of the south

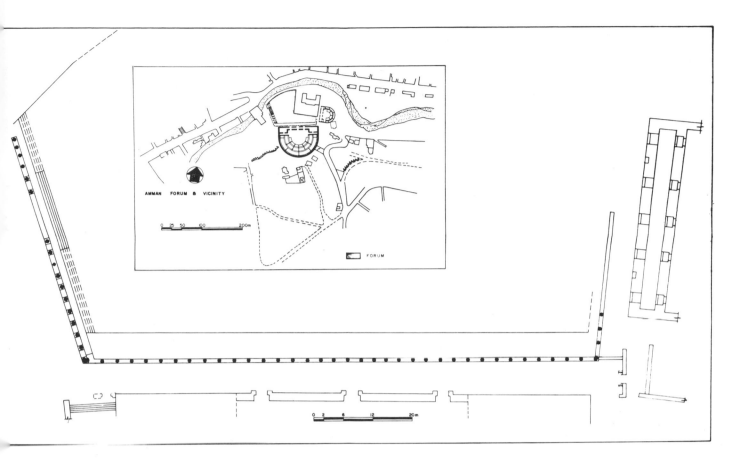

Fig 4: Plan of the Forum Area.

colonnade. The purpose of these double columns apparently was to provide a perfect joint between the architraves when they meet at the corners. Further, these columns help preserve the structural unity of the three colonnades.[13]

In the vicinity of the forum, the odeum is oriented toward the west and its axis is almost perpendicular to the axis of the *decumanus maximus* and to that of the theatre. The structural unity between it and the theatre is provided by the gateway and a small court outside the south-west corner of the forum. The orientation of the theatre is almost perfect; its axis runs 9° west of north thus providing for a minimum of sunlight in the spectators' eyes. The facade of the theatre and the south colonnade of the forum run nearly parallel to the arc of the main street on the north. The diagonal straight line of the west colonnade forms an obtuse angle of 105° with the axis of the *decumanus maximus,* nearly corresponding to the angle formed by the east colonnade and this same street. The trapezoidal shape of the plaza resulting from this arrangement of the colonnades, and the position of the monuments around it seem to have been determined by the configuration of the terrain. The architectural complex is, however, very sensibly conceived. The theatre utilizes the hill on the south for part of its auditorium, and the location of the odeum in close proximity to the theatre offer a striking example of coordinating two recreational centres within almost immediate reach of the main thoroughfare of the city. The peripheral character of the forum on the north side is accentuated by the natural semicircular course of the stream which separates the plaza from the *decumanus maximus.* This accentuation is further enhanced by the curve of the street at this point to make it parallel to the curve of the stream.[14] The arc on the north side of the forum is balanced by the semicircle of the *cavea* of the theatre on the opposite south side and thus in its original shape the area would appear to be symmetrical.[15]

No evidence was discovered of any private houses in the vicinity of the forum. It seems that the area of the forum was restricted for public use.[16]

Axiality is more adhered to in the construction of the *propylaeum* and the *nymphaeum* west of the forum (Fig. 1). Today, the *propylaeum* is completely obliterated and the site is overlaid by modern buildings. Fortunately, in 1887 at the time when C. R. Conder was surveying Amman on behalf of the Palestine Exploration Fund, a small section of the *propylaeum* was still preserved. Captain Conder later published a photograph of this section but describes it mistakenly as part of a forum. [17] The monument was correctly identified by B. Schulz in 1906, [18] and in 1907 H. C. Butler published a more detailed description accompanied by a sketch of the actual remains. [19] From these reports we are able to locate the *propylaeum* in its original position on the ancient town-plan. The front of the structure was exactly aligned on the southwest-northeast axis of the *decumanus maximus,* and its south-north axis cuts through the centre of the south gate of the first terrace of the acropolis above. This gate leads to the *peribolos* of the temple inside the wall. It is, therefore, extremely likely that originally there was a monumental stairway, a *via sacra,* leading up from the *propylaeum* to the temple precincts similar to that of the Artemis temple at Jerash. [20]

Judging from recorded remains, the *propylaeum* at Amman seems to have been truly monumental and highly decorative (Pl. XXXIII). Its front wall seems to have consisted of a wide central doorway flanked by a narrower portal on either side. The front face of this wall, and presumably its back face, were elaborately decorated with columns, pilasters, niches with pediments and friezes. [21] The niches must have originally housed the statues of the city-goddess and her consort. [22] The arrangement and appearance of this *propylaeum* is almost identical with that of the Artemis temple at Jerash dated by inscriptions to A.D. 150. [23]

The *nymphaeum,* which lies further west on the south side of the *decumanus maximus,* is very close to the point where the *cardo* intersects with the main thoroughfare. The building is oriented toward the north-east and its longitudinal axis is parallel to the axis of the *cardo.* The other axis of the monument is perfectly aligned on the southwest-northeast axis of the main colonnaded street. The structure originally stood upon the edge of the main stream. A small branch of this stream flowing from north to south, especially in winter time, passes underneath the middle of the *nymphaeum* where it empties into the main stream. Unfortunately we are not able at the moment to determine the actual extent and complexity of the building, as the area is jammed with modern structures which have sadly encroached upon the ancient remains. The dimensions and architectural elements of the existing southern wall indicate that the building was truly monumental. This wall is built in the form of a half octagon with three large apsidal recessions, each flanked by small niches (Fig. 5A; Pls. XXXIVa XXXIVb). The centre apse measures 8.5 m. in width and each of the side apses is 5.5 m. wide. The width of each of the small niches is 1.25 m. Three partly preserved columns in front of the wall indicate that there was originally a colonnade which ran parallel to the four sides of the wall at a distance of 4.5 m. from it. The intercolumniation of the colonnade is 3.5 m. and its order was Corinthian judging from the few fallen capitals said to have been found in the area. These capitals are similar to the capitals of the south colonnade of the forum. The masonry employed in the building is of two kinds. On the outside, the wall is built up of rusticated bossed blocks of limestone with drafted margins. The inside wall is built of smooth squared blocks of limestone with dowel holes in the lower courses for a marble revetment. The general plan and features of this wall are very similar to the *nymphaeum* at Jerash dated by inscriptions to A.D. 191. [24]

The Acropolis and its Bearing on the Town-plan.

The acropolis of ancient Amman constitutes the upper part of the Roman city. It is built on a prominent strategic natural L-shaped plateau overlooking the forum area in the lower section to the south. This plateau is designated "Jebel el Qal'a" on the plan (Fig. 3), and "Citadel" on the plan (Fig. 1). From very early times this hill had been a fortress of great importance. Recognizing its value for the district now called *Balqa,* the Romans rebuilt the ancient fortress and surrounded it with massive walls which rank among the finest of ancient fortifications. The majority of the remains on this hill are from Roman times. [25] Our primary concern here is with its relationship to the Roman town-plan. It is clear from this plan that the overall scheme for the urban development of Roman Amman was determined, not only by the configuration of the terrain in the lower part of the ancient city, but more decisively by the position of the acropolis hill and the lines of its walls. The *decumanus maximus* follows a straight line which was broken at several points in order to make it conform to the irregular shape of the east-west rectangle of the hill and the axes of the acropolis walls on the south. This orientation of the street is also dictated by the course of the stream. The sensible conception of this lay-out brings the lines of the plateau, the main thoroughfare and the stream into an admirable symmetry. The *cardo,* on the other hand, is nearly parallel to the axis of the north-south rectangle of the same hill. The north-south axis of the east gateway is perpendicular to the east end of the plateau on the north and to the course of the stream on the south. The defensive quality of this gateway was obviously strengthened by its central location between the narrow plateau above and the ravine below taking full advantage of the natural setting at this end of the city and exemplifying a successful case of blending architecture with nature. [26]

The lay-out of the acropolis walls seems to have been determined by the terrain of the plateau. The best preserved section of this wall is in the northwest part of the west rectangle (Pl. XXXVb). The wall was built in straight

b.

Plate XXXII   a. The South Colonnade from the West.
b. Section of Decumanus Maximus showing Stylobate and a column in situ from the North.

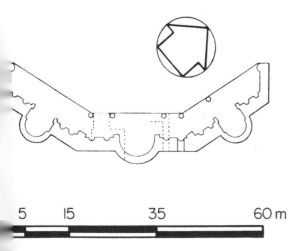

5   15   35   60 m

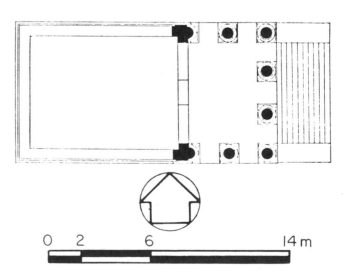

0 2   6   14 m

'ig 5:   A.   Restored plan of Nymphaeum.

B.   Restored plan of Temple.

Plate XXXIII   Remains of the Propylaeum from the Southwest (1898 photograph Bonfils, Lebanon)

Plate XXXIV a. The Nymphaeum from the Southeast.
*   b. The Nymphaeum from the Northwest.*

a.

b.

Plate XXXV   *a. Nymphaeum from the southeast.*
         b. The Northwest corner of the Roman Fortification Wall on the Acropolis from the west.

a.

b.

stretches receding sharply at certain intervals to form nearly right angles. The lower section is built in alternating courses of headers and stretchers. Each course projects slightly beyond the next course above it, giving a shallow stepped appearance to the wall. This lower section is constructed of heavy well jointed limestone blocks, with rough bosses left within wide drafted margins. The higher courses are built of smoothly finished *opus quadratum*. Its thickness varies from 3.25 m. to 3.75 m., and its height varies with the terrain. The outer face of the wall is broken at irregular intervals by towers 5 m. square, built as integral parts of the whole structure. There are remains of two gateways in the south wall. The largest of the two gateways is axial to the *propylaeum* below at the foot of the hill. The scanty remains of this gateway indicate that it was similar in its basic design to the design of the *propylaeum*, but further excavation of this area should throw more light on this question. The smaller gateway to the east is so ruined that its shape is not easily discernible until further clearance has been undertaken, hopefully in the near future.

The temple of Hercules is built close to the south wall. [27] Facing east, its longitudinal axis is parallel to the south wall. This temple is almost completely ruined. Only part of its podium and the column bases of the *pronaos* are still *in situ.* Apparently, the temple was *prostyle tetrastyle* with one column on either side of the portico (Fig. 5B). The antae, which were made of half columns, terminate in rectangular pilasters set at the angles of the cella wall. The podium on which the temple was erected is a rectangle 8 m. by 19 m. [28] A fragmentary inscription discovered in the debris around the temple indicates that it was built during the reign of Marcus Aurelius (A.D. 169-180). [29] Partial excavation near the temple shows that it was built on the site of a sacred rock which, as shown by pottery finds, has quite a long history, beginning in the Early Bronze Age (c. 3000 B.C.). [30]

References

1. For a comprehensive account of Greek and Roman town-planning, see Giuseppe Cultrera, "Architettura Ippodamea", *Memorie della R. Accademia Nazionale dei Lincei, Classe di Scienze Morali, Storiche e Filologiche,* XVII, Fasc. IX (1924), pp. 359-603, esp. Ch. 3, pp. 508ff., and Ch. 4, pp. 540ff.; A. von Gerkan, *Griechische Städteanlagen,* esp. Ch. 4, pp. 123ff.; F. Haverfield, *Ancient Town Planning,* esp. pp. 75ff.; F. Nash, *Roman Towns;* R. E. Wicherly, *How the Greeks Built Cities,* esp. Ch. II, pp. 15ff., and Ch. IV, pp. 50ff.; R. Martin, *L'Urbanisme dans la Grèce Antique;* A. Boethius, in *The Golden House of Nero.* For the topography and monuments of Rome, see H. Jordan & C. Hülsen, *Topographie der Stadt Rom,* I, Pts. 1 & 2; O. Richter, *Topographie der Stadt Rom,* Handbuch der Klassischen Altertumswissenschaft, III; H. Kiepert & C. Hülsen, *Formae Urbis Romae Antiquae,* (2nd Ed.). For a highly technical discussion of the lay-out and monuments of Trajan's Markets, see W. L. MacDonald, *The Architecture of the Roman Empire,* I, pp. 75ff.
2. On the problem of the use of the terms *decumanus* and *cardo* in Roman towns, see F. Haverfield, op. cit., p. 73; M. Wheeler, *Roman Art and Architecture,* pp. 34-35.
3. *Syria (Princeton University Archaeological Expedition to Syria in 1904-5 and 1909)* IIA, opp. p. 34.
4. Cf. *The Archaeological Map of the Hashemite Kingdom of the Jordan,* Sheets 1, 2 & 3, Scale 1:250,000, Department of Lands and Surveys of Jordan.
5. The altering of natural contours, filling valleys and cutting back hills were common practices in Roman building methods especially from Flavian times onward; cf. W. L. MacDonald, op. cit., p. 155; G. Picard, *Roman Architecture,* pp. 12-13; W. J. Anderson, R. P. Spiers & T. Ashby, *The Architecture of Ancient Rome,* p. 52.
6. A very close parallel to the town-plan of Roman Amman is that of Djemila (Cuiculum) in Algeria, where the Roman engineers were faced with similar topographical problems, cf. S. Gsell, *Les Monuments antiques de l'Algérie,* I, pp. 148ff.; G. Picard, op. cit., p. 13; G. Cultrera, op. cit., p. 561.
7. Cf. S. Merril, *East of the Jordan,* 1881, p. 400; H. C. Butler, op. cit., IIA, p. 60; A. E. Northey, "Expedition to the East of the Jordan", *PEFQS,* April 1872, p. 65; Charles Warren, "Expedition to East of the Jordan, July and August, 1867", *PEFQS,* 1869-1870, pp. 284-306.
8. On the principal of axial symmetry in Classical town-planning, see A. von Gerkan, op. cit., pp. 146ff.
9. M. Doughty, *Arabia Deserta,* 1888, p. 18, reports seeing a Roman bridge of one great span on the stream of Amman near the forum area; see also H. C. Butler, op. cit., IIA, p. 60.
10. Two Greek inscribed architrave blocks which were discovered near the eastern vomitorium of the theatre mention the erection of these three porticos of the forum in A.D. 189-190; cf. F. Zayadine, "A Greek Inscription from the Forum of Amman-Philadelphia A.D. 189", *ADAJ,* 14 (1969), pp. 34ff., Pls. XXI-XXIII.

11.   For Vitruvius, V, l, the forum must be rectangular, the width being only two-thirds of the length; cf. R. Cagnat & V. Chapot, *Manuel d'Archéologie Romaine,* 1, p. 114. Although generally speaking most Roman fora follow this rule, exceptions do occur from time to time, as in the triangular forum at Pompeii; cf. Mau, *Pompeii, Its Life and Art,* pp. 134-137, Plan III.

12.   Among fora of more or less similar dimensions are the following: in Rome, the forum of Caesar (*circa.* 160 m. by 75 m), the forum of Augustus (110 m. by 85 m.), the forum Transitorum (120 m. by 45 m.) and the forum of Trajan (118 m. by 89 m.), cf. Giuseppe Lugli, *Roma Antica,* II, pp. 247, 258, 275, 281, pl. V; the rectangular forum at Pompeii (497 ft. by 156 ft.), cf. Mau, op. cit., pp. 45-60, pl. I; the forum at Palmyra (82 m. by 70 m.), cf. Hoyningen-Huene & D. M. Robinson, *Baalbek-Palmyra,* p. 83; the forum of Leptis Magna (1000 ft. by 600 ft.), cf. M. Wheeler, *Roman Art and Architecture,* p. 55, Ill. 40; the forum of Timgad (150 m. by 130 m.), cf. ibid., p. 48, Ill. 27; R. Cagnat & A. Ballu, *Timgad,* p. 178; the forum at Djemila (110 m. by 75 m.), cf. S. Gsell, op. cit., p. 148.

13.   Similar examples to these columns are found in the *temenos* of the temple of Baal at Palmyra dedicated in A.D. 32, cf. Th. Wiegand, *Palmyra,* pp. 144, 150, figs. 169, 175.

14.   A similar arrangement is to be found at Kanawat (Canatha) in Syria dating from the same period; cf. R. E. Brünnow & A. von Domaszewski, *Die Provincia Arabia,* III, pp. 107ff, Fig. 1000; H. C. Butler, op. cit., IIA, Pt. 4, pp. 346ff., pl. XXI; G. E. Rey, *Voyage dans le Haouran et aux bords de la Mer Morte, executé pendant les années 1857 et 1858* (1859), pp. 151-169, Pl. VI.

15.   The combination of rectangles and semicircles seems to have had a special attraction for Roman architects since early in Imperial times, as may be seen in the Forum of Augustus and later the Forum of Trajan; cf. W. J. Anderson, R. P. Spiers & T. Ashby, op. cit., pp. 52-53; G. Cultrera, op. cit., pp. 508-539, Figs. 43-50; W. L. MacDonald, op. cit., p. 8.

16.   On the function and location of the forum in Roman town-planning and the differences between it and the Greek agora, see I. E. Wymer, *Marketplatzanlagen,* pp. 10ff.

17.   Charles Conder, op. cit., Ill. facing p. 32.

18.   B. Schulz, "Bogenfries und Giebelreihe in der römischen Baukunst", *JdI,* XXI (1906), pp. 221-230, Pls. 3-4.

19.   H. C. Butler, op. cit., pp. 43-46, Ill. 28.

20.   C. H. Kraeling, *Gerasa, City of the Decapolis,* pl. XXIV, b.

21.   Cf. B. Schulz, op. cit., pls. 3-4; H. C. Butler, op. cit., p. 44, Ill. 28; C. R. Conder, op. cit., p. 32.

22.   Most probably the Tyrian Herakles and his mother Asteria, who often appear on the coins of the city.

23.   Cf. C. H. Kraeling, op. cit., pp. 52-53, pl. XXIV, b.

24.   Ibid., pp. 54, 406, inscr. 69.

25.   Cf. R. Bartoccini, "Ricerche e scoperte della missione italiana in Amman", *Bollettino dell'Associazoni Internazionale degli Studi Mediterranei,* also under the title, *International Mediterranean Research Association,* 3, (1930), pp. 15-17; "Scavi ad Amman della Missione Archeologica Italiana", ibid., 2, (1932), pp. 16-23; 4-5, (1933-34), pp. 10-15; "La Rocca Sacra degli Ammoniti", *Atti del IV Congresso Nazionale di Studi Romani,* (1938), pp. 3-8.

26.   Although this type of topography, a narrow plateau between two ravines, was a favourite choice for ancient settlements, including Greek, it was usually avoided by the Roman town-planners. However, exceptions do occur from time to time, as can be seen at Djemila in North Africa where the town-plan is similar to that of Amman, see A. von Gerkan, op. cit., pp. 123ff.; G. Cultreta, op. cit., pp. 561ff. & 597ff.; A. Ballu, "Rapport sur les fouilles (1914), Service des Monuments historiques de l'Algérie", *Bulletin Archéologique du Comité des Travaux Historiques et Scientifiques,* (1915), pp. 119ff.; S. Gsell, op. cit., pp. 148ff.

27.   The identification of the deity to whom the temple was erected is not certain. However, the frequency with which the Tyrian Herakles appears on the Roman coins of the city, and the discovery of marble fragments near the building which seem to have belonged to a colossal male statue, make it possible that the temple was built in honour of this god. On the question of the introduction of the cult of Herakles into the Near East, see H. Seyrig, "Antiquités Syriennes; Héracles-Nergal", *Syria,* 24 (1944-45), pp. 62-80, esp. pp. 70 & 72; Susan B. Downey, *The Excavations at Dura-Europos,* III, p. 77.

28.   An evaluation of the restored elevation of the east side of this temple which was published by H. C. Butler, op. cit., pp. 38ff., Ill. 24, must wait until the final report of the excavations on the site by the Department of Antiquities of Jordan, the American Center for Oriental Research in Amman and the University of Jordan is published.

29.   Cf. C. R. Conder, op. cit., p. 33; H. C. Butler, op. cit., III, inscr. 4.

30.   R. Bartoccini, op. cit., (1932), pp. 21ff., fig. 2.

THE STRATIGRAPHY OF CAESAREA MARITIMA
by Lawrence E. Toombs.

The purpose of this paper is to present in summary form the overall stratigraphy of Caesarea Maritima as it appears after four major seasons of excavation.[1]

Method

The study involves four Fields (A, B, C, and H), which are not in physical or visual contact with one another (Fig. 1). The method employed in the attempt to correlate these Fields is comparative stratigraphy, based primarily on the balk sections. Such a method requires a basic reference point; that is, a level common to all the Fields. The latest preserved layer is useless for this purpose, since it varies among the Fields, and sometimes within the same Field, from modern cultivation to Late Byzantine construction. After considerable study, the destruction layers overlying the latest Byzantine occupation were adopted as the stratigraphic key to the site, and the system of General Phases,[2] described in this paper, was developed by working upward and downward in the balk sections from this reference layer. When the stratigraphic similarity between two phases had been established by this method, the result was checked against the ceramic and coin evidence. If this agreed with the stratigraphic conclusions, the two phases were regarded as contemporary.

Correlation of phases across the four Fields is complicated by the physical distance between them, by differences in the history of their use, by the diversity of function of the different areas in the life of the city, and, especially, by the extensive and ruthless robbery to which the site was subjected. For this reason the phasing system is, at several points, conjectural, and must be regarded as tentative. It is most accurate for the Byzantine and Early Arab phases, and least reliable for the Late Arab and Roman levels. In spite of these uncertainties, the system of General Phases, summarized in Figure 4, appears, in its main lines at least, to be soundly based, and to provide a suitable framework for future discussion of the site.

Analysis by Fields

The location of Fields A, B, C, and H is shown in Figure 1.

Field A

Fields A and B were laid out in relation to the Byzantine street or esplanade, uncovered by S. Yeivin in 1951.[3] Because of its impressive dimensions, its fine tesselated surfaces, its well-preserved mosaic inscription, and the two large statues which flank it, this street is familiar to every visitor to the site. Its position part way between the port area and the line of the city wall suggests that it was a civic center of considerable importance. Field A, positioned so as to investigate the northern extension of the street, was located north of the modern road leading to the Crusader Castle. It consisted of four 8 x 8 m. squares, placed side by side in pairs, so that, including the 2 m. wide cross balks, an area 18x18 m. was under excavation.

The earliest remains preserved in Field A belong to the Roman Period. They consist of a rectangular building with a paved porch on the north side (Fig. 2). The room had a heavy plaster floor, into which were set two ceramic bins. Although much of the flooring was destroyed, the sub-floor fill, largely undisturbed, yielded pure Roman pottery, and numerous artifacts.

Coherent structures, belonging to the Byzantine Period, immediately overlie the fragmentary Roman remains. The principal feature of this construction is the continuation northward into Field A of the street first exposed by S. Yeivin (Fig. 2). In the extensive area of Yeivin's excavation the street is clearly not intended to carry vehicular traffic. It is, rather, a civic show-piece, a promenade, embellished with mosaics, statues, arches, and inscriptions. Between Yeivin's excavation and Field A these characteristics have been lost, and the northern extension is an ordinary roadway, a little over 4 m. wide, with a heavy stone pavement. A narrower road enters this main north-south road from the east, but does not cross it. The area west of the road was occupied by housing or shops, with

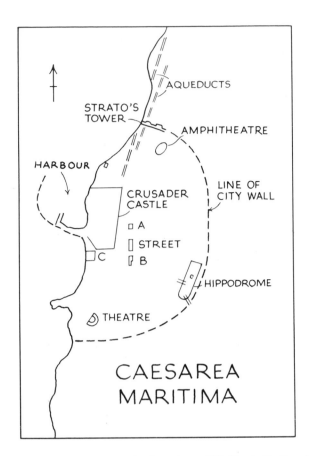

Fig 1: Sketch plan of Caesarea Maritima, showing the location of Fields A, B, C and H in relation to the principal visible monuments on the site.

good quality tesselated or marble-tile flooring. East of the road was an industrial area, with ceramic bins, brick or plaster lined vats, and a well constructed drainage system. The drains are rectangular in cross-section, plaster-lined, and covered with carefully fitted cap-stones.

The Byzantine remains in Field A display at least three construction phases. The latest of these is covered by a thick layer of broken and partly decomposed bright red bricks, mixed with ash, architectural fragments, pieces of marble and plaster, and a high concentration of Late Byzantine pottery.[4] This destruction level can, with a high degree of probability, be dated to the Arab conquest of the city, about A.D. 640. The surfacings immediately below this destruction themselves rest on a thin layer of leveled and worked-over destruction debris. This earlier destruction may, with less certainty, be attributed to the Persian invasions of A.D. 614.

The Arab occupation of Field A begins with evidence of industrial activity, provided by two vats, the larger with a hard plaster lining, laid over potsherds, and the smaller lined with plaster and floored with marble tile. Later Arab occupation in Field A becomes confused by robber trenching from present surface levels. Only fragments of pavements and a deep well survive their depradations, but the balk sections allow us to distinguish four Arab phases, all, on the basis of the pottery readings, pre-Crusader. Of these, phases 1 and 2 are very closely related, and belong to the Late Arab Period.

Field B

Field B was located south of Yeivin's Byzantine street, and consisted of four 8x8 m. squares in a north-south line, with two additional 8x8 m. squares east of the first and second squares of the original line. This arrangement produced an excavated area, allowing for the cross balks, 32 m. long by 18 m. wide in the northern, and 8 m. wide in the southern half.[5]

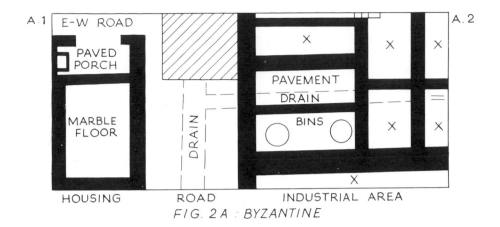

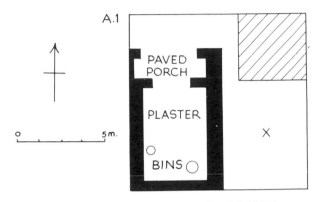

Fig 2: Block plan of Field A, areas 1 and 2, showing the principal architectural features of the Main Byzantine (2A) and Roman (2B) Periods. The Roman remains in A2 are fragmentary and are not illustrated.

Three deep probes in Field B reached levels which produced pure Roman pottery. The two southernmost of these penetrated into sand underlying the earliest Byzantine surfaces, and Roman sherds were found in this sand to a depth of 1.5 to 2.0 m.[6] The northern probe alone indicated the presence of Roman structures.[7] Beneath the Byzantine pavement were seventeen hard-packed layers, closely contiguous with one another. They were probably foundations for earlier Byzantine surfaces, now destroyed. Below them was 1.20 m. of packed fill, resting on a finely-made and extremely hard plaster surface. This plaster was founded on several layers of large field stones impacted in cement. The pottery in the fill above the plaster and among the field stones of the foundation was Roman in date. This northern portion of Field B is, thus, the only place within the Fields presently under excavation where undisturbed Roman structures appear to be preserved.

The Byzantine remains in Field B are both extensive and spectacular (Plate XXXVIa). In a general way, they provide a southern counterpart to the public promenade excavated by Yeivin. It is not so ornate as Yeivin's street, but with its columns, statues, mosaics, and fountains it must have presented a splendid spectacle in its day. An east-west road, surfaced with stone pavers, runs along the north side of the public area. From it two entrances, flanked by stone piers, lead into the southern promenade. From the western entrance an elevated roadway or gently-sloping ramp leads to a tesselated court, 4 m. wide, which extends eastward beyond the limits of the excavation. The tesselation has a design similar to that at the foot of the stairway in Yeivin's excavation.[8] South of the court is a series of rooms with tesselated floors, one of them containing a mosaic inscription. These may have been shops or dwellings. The eastern entrance leads to a lower paved roadway, which terminates at the wall supporting the tesselated court. Along the east side of this road ran a colonnade, giving access to a public square. Within this were a single-roomed building with a mosaic floor, and, to the north, a raised platform, on which stood the plaster bases of several installations, now destroyed. Jutting into the lower road was a massive pedestal of stone. A statue of the goddess Tyche was found, cast down into the destruction debris at the foot of this pedestal. The eastern limits of the complex lie outside the excavated areas.

The entire square described above is overlaid by a thick layer of raw destruction debris, dated by its pottery contents to the end of the Byzantine period. The tesselated floor of the small building in the court, and the raised platform in the northern portion of the square both rest on leveled destruction debris. The pottery is Late Byzantine in date. Here again, as in Field A, two destructions of the Byzantine city are indicated.[9] The evidence for still earlier Byzantine levels, provided by the deep probes, has already been cited. The stratigraphic situation, thus, allows us to distinguish a series of Byzantine levels, terminated by a destruction, after which a rebuilding took place, only to be followed by a second and final destruction. In this report the phase prior to the earlier destruction is called the Main Byzantine phase, and that between the two destruction layers the Final Byzantine phase.

Field B indicates that some halting attempts were made to occupy the city after the destruction of the Final Byzantine Phase. One room, partially cleared of destruction debris, contained a hearth and a shallow stone-lined pit. In addition, slipshod repairs to Byzantine walls — little more than old building stones, daubed into place with mud — and broken fragments of very coarse tesselation, evidence a brief, impoverished attempt to reoccupy the city. The pottery associated with this meagre settlement is Late Byzantine.[10] It seems probable, therefore, that a few Byzantine survivors of the Arab conquest eked out a poor existence for a time among the ruins of their city.

The Arab occupation in Field B began as an exploitation of the destroyed Byzantine city. The new-comers were living on top of a veritable mine of building material, which if it could not be used directly, could be fired to lime.[11] The earliest use of these resources involved a crudely-built industrial area, delimited by a rough wall, and containing a furnace and storage vault. In course of time the industrial area became more sophisticated. It now had regular walls, a well, and a water disposal system. A well-surfaced road ran in the direction of the harbor, and building complexes sprang up to the north and south of the industrial area. Toward the end of the Arab period the industrial complex became restricted in size. The building to the north went out of use, and its site was occupied by a garden area. These developments span the period from Ummayyad to immediately pre-Crusader times.

Field C.

Immediately south of the Crusader Castle, A. Negev had excavated a portion of a large Byzantine building.[12] Field C started as an area clearance of the remainder of this structure, controlled by balks placed at 8 m. intervals.

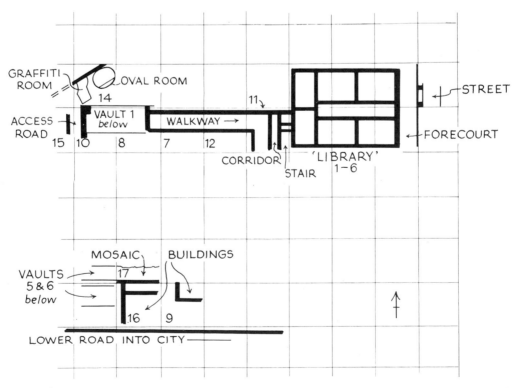

Fig 3: Schematic plan of field C. Zone 1 is represented by the seaward or western ends of vaults 1, 5 and 6; Zone 2 by the buildings surmounting the vaults, by the walkway and corridor to the North, and by the two buildings to the South in areas 9, 16 and 17. The "Library" and street to the East, and the "oval" and "graffiti" rooms belong to Zone 3. Each suare is 10x10 m.

Plate XXXVI

a. *Field B, photographed from a
35 tower looking north*

A. *the E-W road.*
B. *entrances to the complex from
the north.*
C. *the paved ramp.*
D. *the tesselated court.*
E. *shops or dwellings.*
F. *the lower road.*
G. *pedestals for column bases.*
H. *room with mosaic floor*
I. *pedestals for statue*

b. *Segment of the Middle Byzantine
Period city wall, showing earth
layers against its western face.
The surfaces of use were low down
on the wall, where the large stone
is set against the face.*

The Field was then extended as a line of 8 m. squares running westward from the building to the ocean front. These new squares revealed the presence of a system of vaulted chambers, beneath the dunes west of the Byzantine building. The Field was then further enlarged by the establishment of a grid of sixty 8x8 m. squares over the area. To date seventeen of these squares have been excavated in whole or in part. [13]

The structures contained in this complex Field may be divided into three zones: (1) the system of barrel-vaulted chambers lying under the sand dunes along the coast, (2) the buildings erected on top of these vaults, and (3) the large building beyond the eastern limits of the vaults, together with the smaller buildings along their northern edge. Detailed descriptions of the structures will be provided in a forthcoming preliminary report of the Field. For purposes of this report it is sufficient to point out that the three zones do not represent successive chronological phases, but structures in contemporary use at three different physical levels. When the eastern building was in use, possibly as a library or public archive, the rooms and tiled walkways surmounting the vaults were also occupied, perhaps as offices and business establishments. At the same time the vaults below were being employed for a variety of purposes, e.g. warehouse space, drainage, and storage. At one stage of its existence Vault 1, the most northerly in the line, contained a Mithraeum in its eastern end.

Viewed from a ship at sea the waterfront complex must have presented a magnificent sight. The vaulted chambers with their ornate facades towered above the shore to a height of more than five metres. Rising above them were the parapets, walls, and roadways of the buildings built over the vaults, all sheathed in marble and resplendent with brilliant colors. This impressive frontage was pierced at intervals by east-west roads, leading into the city from the waterfront.

Stratigraphically, the basic questions raised by Field C are: (1) at what period were the vaults founded; (2) at what period were the preserved remains in all three construction zones in contemporary use; and (3) what was the stratigraphic history of the area after the vaults went out of use and partially collapsed?

The lowest surfacing in Vault 1 provides an answer to the first question. A heavy layer of plaster spans the vault from wall to wall. The lowest courses of the walls themselves are set in trenches cut into the sandstone bedrock. This sealed locus produced exclusively Roman pottery, and the fill overlying the surface also contained Roman sherds and coins of the first century A.D. Obviously the evidence from a single vault should not automatically be extrapolated to cover the entire Field. Nevertheless, it is a fair inference that the concept of vaulted warehousing along the Caesarea waterfront originated early in the Roman Period.

The answer to the second question comes from the buildings surmounting the vaults. The preserved surfaces are Middle to Late Byzantine in date. They rest on fill layers, which in turn are laid over large stones, set over the vault roofs, in order to provide a solid, level construction platform. The pottery from among these stones and from the lowest layers of the fill is Late Roman in date. Apparently, therefore, the original vaulting of Early Roman times collapsed, or was deliberately broken down, and was rebuilt in the Late Roman era. Subsequently, the surfacing above the vaults was replaced numerous times, the final surfacing being laid in the Late Byzantine period. These final Byzantine surfaces rest on leveled destruction debris, and are overlaid by the massive destruction layers which mark the end of the Byzantine period. They are associated with poorly-constructed rebuilds of earlier Byzantine structures. [14] The final collapse of the seaward ends of the vaults took place in connection with the nearly total destruction of the buildings above.

The eastern public building, "the archive", shows a similar stratigraphic history. [15] Its best preserved surfaces belong to the Main Byzantine Period. This was terminated by a destruction of the building, the debris of which was leveled off and became the base for the surfacing of the Final Byzantine Period. In connection with these surfaces secondary walls were thrown across the large rooms, and destroyed benches were hastily repaired. The heavy destruction layer, characteristic of the close of the Byzantine era, overlies these walls and surfaces.

After the catastrophic destruction of the Byzantine waterfront, squatters camped along the seaward end of vault 1 and in the ruins of the roofless public building, leaving an oven, an installation set on broken roof tiles, and notches in the walls, which supported the roof beams of huts.

The earliest Arab use of Field C was for the mining of building remains from the ruined city. A kiln was constructed in the forecourt of the public building, and an industrial installation was set up at the seaward end of Vault 1. Robber trenches were cut into the collapsed vaults, and into the remains of the buildings over the uncollapsed portions of the vaulting.

After this industrial activity subsided, the ruins quickly filled over with sand, and the area became a cemetery. Three phases can be distinguished in the use of the area for burials. The earliest consists of pre-Crusader Arab burials, in which the bodies are laid on their side with the face toward Mecca. The second is a Crusader cemetery. In this phase the bodies are supine, with the head to the west and elevated on a low stone pillow, so that the eyes are directed to the east. The third level consists of fairly recent Arab burials, usually in stone-built crypts.

In this stage the top of the fill blocking Vault 1 was removed, and a rough ramp constructed, leading down into the vault. Bodies were tossed indiscriminately down the slope of the blocking and over the floor of the vault.

Field H

Field H, the hippodrome area, presents the formidable problem of attempting to excavate a monumental building, some 460 m. long by 90 m. wide, by means of small, stratigraphically controlled trenches - an exercise somewhat like tossing a penny at the moon. The work done in the 1973 and 1974 seasons must be regarded as exploratory, in order to determine the stratigraphic sequence and the position of extant structures - a necessary preliminary to larger area clearances. Four areas were opened in the hippodrome proper: (1) at the assumed location of the starting gates at the north end of the structure, (2) at the northern end of the *spina*, where the obelisk stood, (3) over the track surface and seating on the west side of the arena, and (4) over the seats at the south-east end, where the hippodrome wall begins to curve.

According to plans drawn by the Italian expedition to Caesarea, the city wall runs in close association with the east wall of the hippodrome, diverging from it at the curvature of the seating at the south end (Fig. 1). The trench across the seats was, therefore, extended eastward in the hope of intersecting a part of this wall. The trench encountered a deeply founded wall, of which only the west face was investigated (Pl. XXXVIb).

Since the excavation of the hippodrome is in its initial stages, the full history of the building cannot yet be written, and stratigraphic conclusions are necessarily tentative. The best evidence comes from the excavation over the track and seating on the west side.[16] The balk sections within the seating area show three phases of use of the structure, but the trenches are too small to allow certain separation of the pottery sealed beneath the three levels of surfacing from that contained in the extensive robber trenches cut through them. The middle of the three surfacings appears to have been put in place in the Middle Byzantine Period. No dating evidence is available for the lowest surface, since excavation did not go beneath it, and that associated with the upper surface is ambiguous.

We must, therefore, depend almost exclusively on the successive track levels for stratified pottery. The destruction debris over the upper track level, and the track itself, contained Late Byzantine sherds. The intermediate and lower track levels yielded Middle Byzantine pottery. The sand foundation for the lower track level contained Middle Roman pottery. This stratification is consistent with a founding date for the hippodrome in the second or third century A.D., a period of use, with repairs and reconstruction, extending from the third to the sixth centuries A.D., and an abandonment of the structure as a hippodrome sometime before the end of the Byzantine era in the city as a whole.

Additional supporting evidence for this last conclusion is the presence over the ruined vaulting of the seating area of a tesselated surface, apparently laid after the hippodrome went out of use and had already been robbed of much of its stonework. This tesselated surface is probably, though not absolutely certainly, of Late Byzantine date.

The short fragment of city wall, uncovered to the south-east of the hippodrome, presents a stratigraphic puzzle. Only its inner, or western, face was exposed (Pl. XXXVIb). It consists of an outer facing of cut stones, one row thick, backed by rubble, imbedded in cement. The soil layers against the wall face are deliberately laid fill. The upper of these slope upward against the wall, and contain a few Late Byzantine and two possibly Arab sherds, among a preponderance of Middle Byzantine forms. The lower slope upward away from the wall, and contain no pottery later than Middle Byzantine. The surfacing near the base of the wall also contained Middle Byzantine sherds, while the sand on which the surfacing rested contained only Roman pottery. On the present evidence the wall seems to have been constructed in Late Roman or Early Byzantine times, to have been in use throughout the Middle Byzantine period, and to have been filled over in Late Byzantine or Early Arab times. This history parallels fairly closely that of the hippodrome. It should be remembered, however, that only one face of the wall has been studied, and this may turn out to be a repair on the inner side of an earlier wall.

The Archaeological History of Caesarea

The field-by-field analysis leads to a system of seven General Phases, summarizing the archaeological history of the site: (1) Modern Arab, (2) Crusader, (3) Arab, with three sub-phases, (4) Byzantine/Arab, (5) Final Byzantine, (6) Main Byzantine, with an as yet undetermined number of sub-phases, and (7) Roman, unhappily preserved only in fragments in the excavated areas. Figure 4 outlines this stratigraphic sequence in tabular form. The table also shows the approximate dates assigned to each period, and the type of remains found in each of the Fields investigated by the Expedition.

The chart provides the basis for a brief reconstruction of the archaeological history of Caesarea Maritima.

The Roman Period extends from the founding of the city about 10 B.C. to the removal of the imperial capital from Rome to Byzantium about A.D. 330. In spite of the paucity of Roman remains in the excavated areas, some construction details of Roman Caesarea have become clear. The Herodian engineers faced the formidable task of building a major seaport on sand. Preliminary to the construction of buildings the sand of the dunes had to be leveled and packed. Roman sherds were everywhere encountered to a depth of 1.5 to 2.0 m. in what otherwise appeared to be undisturbed sand. The main drainage and sewage system, consisting of barrel-arched tunnels as much as 3 m. high at their seaward ends, was undoubtedly constructed first. In order to maintain the stability of the buildings, their foundations were cut deep into the sand, and the lower courses, laid in these trenches, were considerably wider than the wall as it appeared above ground. Floors, whether tesselation, flagstone, or marble, lay on beds of large flat, or smaller cobble-like, stones, impacted in cement. The Roman city, with its magnificent port facilities, immense aqueduct system, theatre, hippodrome, and amphitheatre became the commercial and artistic center of the Palestinian coast. It served as headquarters for the Roman high command during the Jewish Wars.

It seems probable that during the Late Roman Period a major catastrophe befell the city, causing a partial collapse of the vaulted warehouses along the waterfront, and the destruction of major buildings within the city. Such a city-wide disaster alone would account for the rebuilding of the warehouse vaulting and the buildings above it, as well as the virtual absence of intact Roman structures in the city proper.

Prosperity and steady growth marked the Byzantine Period until the troubled times at the end of the sixth and the beginning of the seventh centuries. Byzantine control was slackening, and the rise of the Persian and Arab powers posed a mounting threat to the security of the city. In A.D. 614 Persian armies captured Caesarea, but withdrew by A.D. 629. This invasion caused widespread destruction and brought the Main Byzantine Period to a close, but recovery was rapid and the city was restored, although its magnificence was greatly reduced. In A.D. 640 Caesarea fell to Arab invaders. This time the destruction was complete and irretrievable. Battered columns and the empty shells of buildings stood nakedly above heaps of tangled debris. Among these ruins a few survivors attempted to clear enough space among the rubble to make life possible.

Umayyad settlers appear to have moved in relatively quickly, attracted by the wealth of building material available in the ruined city. They kept the port open for the shipment of their products, and elsewhere within the city set up industrial installations and conducted extensive mining operations into the ruins below. Their residences were probably concentrated in the southern part of the site, leaving the Byzantine city centre and warehouse area free for industrial use. The Roman and Byzantine aqueduct system was not maintained. Water was supplied by wells, of which four examples were found in the excavated areas.

During the Abbasid period the industrial use of the city continued, but the industry became more sophisticated and diversified. There is some evidence that major glass and pottery producing establishments existed. The Late Arab Period saw a decline in industrial activity, and a reversion of some of the former industrial areas, even within the city, to agricultural use. Except for the cemetery, remains of the Crusader and later periods have not been found by the Joint Expedition.

It is a source of great personal satisfaction to the author to contribute this stratigraphic study to a collection of essays in honour of Dame Kathleen Kenyon. I was introduced to the fascination and frustration of stratigraphic analysis at Jericho in 1956, and continued the study under Dame Kathleen's direction in the Institute of Archaeology in 1962. It perhaps requires a mild form of audacity to offer a paper on stratigraphy in a volume dedicated to the acknowledged master of the field.

GENERAL PHASE	DATE	FIELD A	FIELD B	FIELD C	FIELD H
I MODERN		Missing	Missing	Arab Cemetery	Placing of debris piles along hippodrome walls to clear area for cultivation.
II CRUSADER	A.D.1200-1300	Missing	Missing	Christian Cemetery	Cultivation and small buildings in track area
III ARAB	A.D.640-1200				
1. LATE		Fragmentary pavements and deep well	Deep well in B4(?) Industrial and garden use.	Arab Cemetery	Agriculture ?
2. MIDDLE (ABBASID)		Fragmentary pavements and deep well	Deep Well in B4(?) Industrial complex: roadway, public buildings or residences, furnaces, storage facilities, drainage systems	Cemetery	Agriculture ?
3. EARLY (UMAYYAD)		Housing and industrial occupation	Crude industrial complex, developing into more sophisticated form in III.2	Lime kiln, and industrial installation	Agricultural use of track area. Crude buildings over seating. Robbery of hippodrome Structures.
IV BYZANTINE/ARAB	A.D. 640	Missing	Impoverished reuse of Phase V walls	Shelters and poor installations in ruins of Phase V building.	Missing
V FINAL BYZANTINE	A.D.614-640	Final use of Phase VI buildings with poor quality walls and tesselation. Sealed by heavy destruction layer.			Missing
VI MAIN BYZANTINE	A.D.330-614				
1		Paved road with shops to west and industry to east. Well-built drains	E—W road, leading to public promenade Complex drainage system	Vaults with buildings above, and public buildings to east and north. Street system.	Hippodrome goes out of use before end of VI.1. Tesselated surfaces built over seating. City wall filled over at end of period.
2		Earlier surfaces associated with same wall system as VI.1			Hippodrome in use with repair and reconstruction. City wall built.
VII ROMAN	10 B.C.-A.D. 330				
1		Deep founded walls, and debris layers over leveled sand. Plaster surface over stone foundation in Field B.		Use of Vault 1 as Mithraeum	Construction of hippodrome
2				Collapse and rebuilding of vaults	
3				Founding of vaults	

Fig 4: Stratigraphic analysis of the results of the first four seasons at Caesarea, tabulated by Field.

References

1.   The Joint Expedition to Caesarea Maritima is under the direction of Dr. Robert J. Bull, Drew
      University, Madison, New Jersey. It is supported by a consortium of twenty-one Colleges, Seminaries, and
      Universities, and is sponsored by the Albright Institute for Archaeological Research. The author served as
      Stratigrapher in the seasons of 1972, 1973, and 1974, and had full access to the records of 1971. Important
      investigations of the sewers and hydraulic installations of the city are not dealt with in this paper, because
      they cannot, at this stage, be integrated directly into the overall stratigraphy of the site.

2.   The assignment of Stratum numbers would be premature at this stage of excavation. The less rigid term
      "General Phase" has been adopted to allow for revision and expansion of the system in subsequent seasons.
      The General Phases are designated by Roman Numerals to distinguish them from the local phases assigned
      in each Area by the Area Supervisors.

3.   "Excavations at Caesarea Maritima", *Archaeology,* 8 (1955), pp. 122-129.

4.   Where pottery dates are given in this paper, they depend upon the field readings of the pottery after washing,
      and follow the dating system adopted by the Expedition. The schema is as follows (dates approximate):

      Roman   -   Early - 10 B.C. - A.D. 100
                  Middle - A.D. 100 - A.D. 200
                  Late - A.D. 200 - A.D. 330

      Byzantine - Early - A.D. 330 - A.D. 450
                  Middle - A.D. 450 - A.D. 550
                  Late - A.D. 550 - A.D. 640

      Arab -   Early (Umayyad) - A.D. 640 - A.D. 750
                  Middle (Abbasid) - A.D. 750 - A.D. 900
                  Late (Fatimid and Seljuk) - A.D. 900 - A.D. 1200

      Crusader - A.D. 1200 - A.D. 1300

5.   Field B, excavated to Byzantine and Roman levels is illustrated in Plate XXXVI. the caption identifies the features
      mentioned in the paper.

6.   The probes are located in Areas B.1 and B.6.

7.   Located in Area B.5.

8.   *Archaeology,* 8, (1955), pp. 122-129. It has been suggested by a number of scholars that the paved area
      described above is an outdoor marketplace.

9.   See above, p. 224.

10.   In the General Phase system (Figure 4) this phase has been given the name "Byzantine/Arab".

11.   Much of the stone and many of the columns used to build Jaffa and Acre were shipped from Caesarea.

12.   "Caesarea" in "Notes and News", *I.E.J.* 10 (1960), pp. 127, 264-265; *Caesarea,* Tel Aviv, 1967, pp. 62-63.

13.   The layout of Field C and its principal structures are illustrated in Figure 3.

14.   These phenomena are best seen in Areas C.10 and C.16.

15.   Pottery and comparative stratigraphy prove the contemporaneity of this public building with the structures
      built on the vaults. The issue is put beyond doubt by the existence of a stairway connecting the hypocaust
      structure under the public building with a ramp-like surface leading to the buildings over the vaults.

16.   Structural details will be presented in a forthcoming preliminary report. A survey of the data relative to the
      hippodrome prior to the 1974 season, has been given by John H. Humphrey in an article soon to be
      published.

ES-SENAMA BIR EL-UAAR: A ROMAN TOMB IN LIBYA
by O. Brogan.

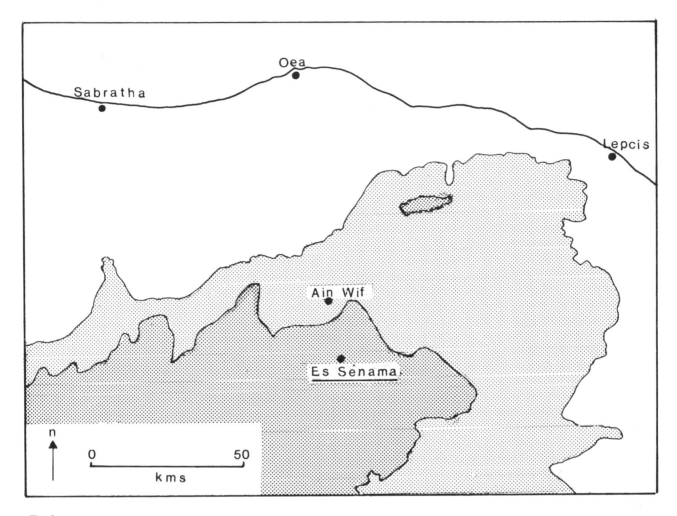

Fig 1.

The tomb here described stands high above the deep narrow valley of the Wadi Bir el-Uaar,[1] in the Gebel, the hilly country that delimits the southern side of the Gefara, the coastal plain behind Tripoli, Libya (see map, Fig. 1). The Gebel rises from the plain as an escarpment and in its central part, south and east of Garian, forms a *massif* about 80 km. square, which constitutes the chief watershed of Tripolitania, deeply seamed by the beds of the great wadis from which in times of heavy rains the waters pour north into the Gefara, or east and south-east into the basins of the Wadi Tareglat and the Wadi Sofeggin. The rainfall of the *massif* is from 300 to 400 mm. a year. The natural coverage is mainly esparto grass and other steppe plants, with here and there, especially along the wadis, little groups of batum trees (*Pistacchio altantica*), which probably represent a more widespread growth in earlier times.

The northern part of the Gebel was, and still is, good olive-growing country and must have made the fortunes of many of the families of the coastal cities of antiquity. Several large mausolea still stand in the region, the best known being the impressive Gasr Doga near Tarhuna and Henscir Soffit near Yefren, described by Heinrich Barth, the famous German traveller.[2] They are evidence of the wealthy landowners of the high Roman period who liked to build their sepulchres on their estates. It would seem from its position that our tomb came within the *territorium* of Oea (Tripoli) which lies almost due north of it, 100 km. (c. 68 Roman miles) distant as the crow flies, and about 100 Roman miles by road which had to traverse much broken country.

Plate XXXVII

a

b

c

d

a. Es Semana Bir el Uaar - southeast and southwest sides.
b. Southeast side showing entrance to tomb-chamber and false doorway.
c. Southwest side.
d. Column base with figure.

The hills around the Senama are now largely covered with esparto grass, though with the coming of modern tractors there has been lately an increase of ploughed land in the neighbourhood. When we look round for a house where the owner of the tomb might have lived when visiting the country, there is nothing apparent that seems in keeping with the wealth so elaborate a mausoleum suggests. There are a few *gsur* quite near, but their visible remains look much too late. The owner probably dwelt for the most part in Oea, going up into the Gebel from time to time to hunt the abundant game. The permanent occupants of his country house would have been his manager and the slaves who worked the estate.

This large and important tomb deserves careful study. The following summary description deals first with the part that is still standing to a height of about 8 m and then with the substantial remains which lie on the ground nearby. A reconstruction of the upper part might be hazarded, but it is to be hoped that before long the necessary study may be undertaken by a competent architect.

The tomb is orientated north-west - south-east, with the false door and the entrance to the tomb-chamber on the south-east side. Three storeys are distinguishable.

I.   A plain podium (height 2.80 m.) on a moulded base below which is an offset. The base of the offset course (5.05 x 5.05 m.) is at ground level, which was probably the same in antiquity as now. Two lower courses are visible in the hollow round the entrance to the tomb-chamber (pl. XXXVIIb). This hollow was probably filled in after placing the remains of the dead in the chamber, but it has since been dug out by treasure-seekers. The chamber is vaulted, constructed of very fine masonry, and measures 2.83 x 1.38 m, with three niches (each 0.51 x 0.52 x 0.51 m.) in the north-west, south-west and north-east walls respectively. It was half full of sand when visited, but the measurement from the bottom of the niches to the top of the vault is 1.66 m. The podium (4.37 x 4.39 m.) is composed of three courses of masonry (heights, 0.77, 0.52, 0.35 m.) above which is a rather shallow moulded cornice.

II.   The second storey stands on a moulded base. The main structure above that has eight courses of masonry, above which was a sculptured cornice, now badly weathered or fallen. The false door in the south-east side has gone, but the lintel and doorposts remain and are carved with several rows of leaves and beads, and a pattern of zig-zags down the inner side of the posts. The stone of the moulding course below the door is carved on its vertical side with a relief of two wine-jugs and, between them, facing right, a beast which seems to hold the head of another animal in its mouth; above this, on the part of the stone sloping down from the threshold and therefore difficult to see from below, are two more beasts, facing left, hunter and hunted. These hunting motifs are familiar symbols of the rape of the soul. On either side of the doorway, level with the lintel, are medallions with busts, presumably of the deceased. That on the right is of a bearded man. That on the left seems to show a woman with a curious headdress covered with flowers (?) and which has two bulges over the temples, and a veil, or tresses of hair, hanging down. Above the door is a large *tabella ansata,* the well-cut *ansae* of which, with their six-petalled rosettes, project beyond the sides of the doorway. If it ever had an inscription this is now completely obliterated.[3]

This storey has four pilasters on each side (pl. XXXVIIc), two at the corners with two between, except on the south-east side where the middle ones are interrupted below the capitals by the false doorway. The handsome capitals come in the course above the *tabella ansata.* They are Corinthian, but the leaves are plain. Each face has five leaves, two below, three above, and volutes and helices carried by long ribbed cauliculi rising between the leaves. The pilaster bases are well-cut Attic forms.

The corner-stones of the abacus have leaf-like ornaments. Above each of the two inner capitals is a female bust in high relief, wearing a pleated garment and with hair falling on to its shoulders. The three intermediate spaces are carved as arches; they have moulded frames, with elegant scallop-shells below. Next above, as Mr. Haynes put it, is 'a debased Doric frieze composed of metopes containing rosettes and single-grooved triglyphs',[4] but this is nevertheless quite handsome. The rosettes, originally thirteen to each side, are varied, with six, eight or more petals; a few have spiralling petals, one or two are plain. The cornice, of which only fragments remain, was richly carved. Above the small dentils came a row of egg-and-dart pattern, then bead-and-reel, and above that an echinus which seems to have had elaborate swelling scroll patterns, though this has almost disappeared, except for the north-west corner.

III.   Part of the bottom of the third storey is still in position, several of the column bases and the plinths on which they stood being well-preserved on the south-west and north-east sides (Pl. XXXVIIa). There are plinths for four columns each side, with gaps between the two middle ones which may have held a plinth for a fifth column, or some other feature (cf. no. 3, below).

Plate XXXVIII   a. Stones fallen from the Tomb.
b. Piece of truncated eave.

a

b

The fallen remains from this upper storey are scattered round the tomb except for a number of pieces of column which have at some time (before 1953) been collected at the foot of the north-west side.
Items noted are:

1)   Pieces of column-shaft, of which the best preserved is 2.05 m. high, diameter at top 0.40 m., at bottom 0.44 m;
2)   Corinthian capitals 0.46 m. high, with carved acanthus, volutes, helices and cauliculi, which would fit the shafts;
3)   Four column-bases (ht. 0.47 m.) (Pl. XXXVIId). On one side of each is a much-battered torso in relief (? female) with a pleated skirt, thin arms, and hands clasped at the waist. These might have gone into the spaces between the second and third columns of the sides, but they are higher than the bases in place on the third storey;
4)   pieces of pillars of square section, of which the highest is 1.50 m. They have a slight moulding on the end. There is no edging along the side to suggest an abacus.

The following items seem to belong to the top of the tomb:

5)   large sculptured blocks with rosettes, belonging to a circular feature, perhaps a drum on the top of the third storey designed to carry a conical roof (Pl. XXXVIIIa);
6)   a piece of truncated cone (diameter 0.60 m. above, 0.80 m. below) with a net-like pattern in relief on it. This fits above a second piece of truncated cone with a somewhat larger net-pattern. The pattern is doubtless intended to give the impression of tiling (Pl. XXXVIIIb);
7)   one large Corinthian capital, resembling those noted above (2), but 0.65 m. high, 0.68 m. across the abacus and 0.58 m. diameter below. This might be a crowning capital which went above the truncated cone; there is, however, no dowel hole;
8)   a few stones which are rounded, as though they formed parts of niches, but it is not possible to suggest where they belonged.

In view of the variety of the remains a search was made for the base of a possible second tomb. There are a few large stones about 28 m. west of the Senama which might be in place to form a base about 3.05 m. square, but clearance would be needed to confirm this. As almost all the stones recorded can be comfortably ascribed to the big tomb, there is not much left for the superstructure of another, hypothetical, tomb. If, however, as seems likely, the conical pieces belong to the upper part of the Senama, there is the question to solve of how the circular part was carried by the columns of which we have the plinths which show that the colonnade was square in plan. There must have been an abacus above the columns, and some kind of a canopy to hold up the circular element, but so far no pieces of anything of the sort have been observed, unless the stone on the left of pl. 4 may belong.

As regards date, Mr. Haynes ascribes the tomb to the third century A.D. It certainly represents the period of the full flowering of the Roman province and the lavish decoration suggests the Severan age, perhaps near the beginning of the century when Septimius had quieted down the troubles on the frontier and established the military posts along the Gebel road. One of them, Ain Wif (probably Thenadassa), is only about 30 km. north of Es-Senama.[5]

A Christian epitaph was found near the mausoleum and taken into Tripoli and published by Romanelli.[6] He makes no claim that it was found on the tomb and an examination shows no place where it could conveniently have gone. There is now an Arab cemetery close to the tomb.

Olwen Brogan

References

1.   *G.S.G.S.* 1/100,000, Libya Sheet 1574, Garian, 595755; *AMS,* 1/250,000 N1, 33-13. UR 4446.
2.   H. Barth, *Travels in Central Africa,* (2nd Edn. 1857), I, pp. 35 and 70. S. Aurigemma, 'Il mausoleo di Gasr Doga', *Quaderni di archeologia della Libia,* iii (1954).
3.   Some other hinterland tombs have well-preserved *tabellae* on which there are no signs that there were ever inscriptions. One such belongs to the tomb at Tigi, in the Gefara (*Libya Antiqua,* ii, (1965) plate XVI, c). Perhaps some of these bore painted epitaphs.
4.   D.E.L. Haynes, *The Antiquities of Tripolitania,* p. 159.
5.   R. G. Goodchild and J. B. Ward Perkins, *JRS,* Lxxxix 1969, pp. 84-88.
6.   P. Romanelli, 'Monumenti cristiani del Museo di Tripoli', *Nuovo Bulletino di archeologia cristiana,* xxiv-xxv (1918-19) pp. 39-42.

THE GOLDEN GATE OF CONSTANTINOPLE
Why and wherefore?
by Mortimer Wheeler †

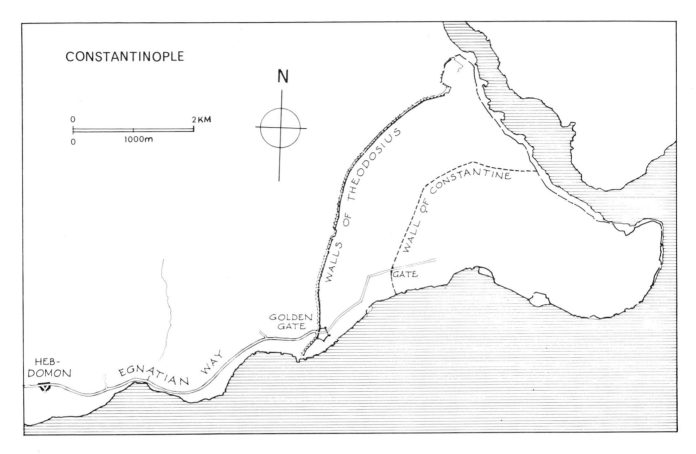

Fig 1.

At a distance of some 500 metres northwards from the acute south-western angle of the great city-wall within which Theodosius II confined Constantinople at its widest extent in the year 413, stands the small but dominant fortress known as Yedikule, "the Seven Towers" (Fig. 1). Five of these towers, with minor auxiliaries, are of limestone and were built by Mahomet the Conqueror when he laid out the enclosure five years after the first and final overthrow of the city in 1453. The other two towers, those on the western side, are substantially of white marble and had already been standing since the year 391 or thereabouts. It is with these and the triple archway which they flanked that the present paper is concerned; a complex which has been known since antiquity as the Porta Aurea or Golden Gate. If some special reason by demanded for my choice of subject in the present honourable context, it must suffice to recall that this embattled monument is an outstanding relic of an Imperial epoch with which Dame Kathleen has been involved elsewhere on at least three notable occasions in her varied archaeological career. And it is a monument which incidentally still calls for rather more consideration than it has yet received.

First, the structure of the Gate (Fig. 2). It consisted originally of a large central archway 8½ metres wide and 15½ metres high, with a smaller archway 5¾ metres wide and 12 metres high on each side. The towers are each 18 metres broad and project 16½ metres west of the line of archways. External faces of the towers are of marble, as was a large part of the facing of the three passages, the remainder being of limestone. Above each arch a slit admitted light, or at least a modicum of air, into the upper part of the interior, and larger slits - now three on the western front of the southern tower and one on that of the northern - made similar provision for the top storeys. The only surviving ornament other than the Corinthian capitals of the framing pilasters is an eagle with spreading wings at the summit of the south-western angle of the northern tower.

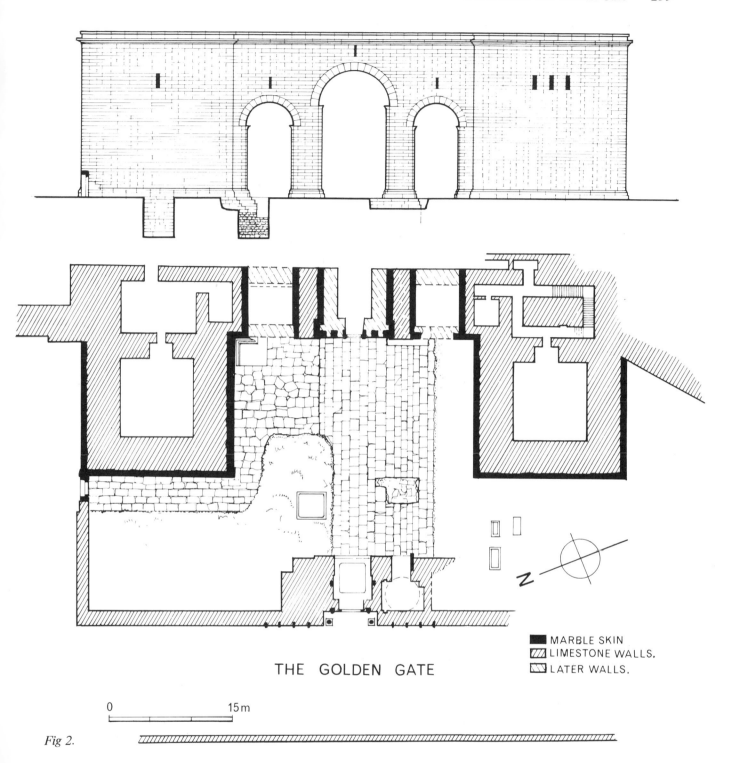

THE GOLDEN GATE

■ MARBLE SKIN
▨ LIMESTONE WALLS.
▧ LATER WALLS.

0   15m

Fig 2.

Internally I have not myself inspected the architectural arrangement of the two towers, but reliable plans show that in the rear (eastern) portions access to the upper floor or floors was obtained by means of a rectangular arrangement of stairways and corridors. It is evident that the towers combined barracks and defensive units; and some of the regiments or detachments which from time to time did duty here may be recognized in the painted *acclamationes* which have been identified on the marble facades of each side of the central archway in black and red paint. They include *numeri-militum [primo] sagitariorum leonum iuniorum* and *numeri militum cornutorum iuniorum,* and are claimed to memorialize parts of the western armies which had been brought to reinforce those in the East in the early years of the gateway's existence.

As to the precise implication of that phrase there is now a sufficiency of agreement. Both on the western and the eastern faces of the central arch the voussoirs, where they have not been replaced in more modern times, still bear holes marking the former attachment of bronze (or gilded bronze) letters. These scars have long been observed, but it was left to Josef Strzygowski in 1891 to verify their significance,[1] more exactly as indicating two hexameters of convincing import:

> HAEC LOCA THEVDOSIVS DECORAT POST FATA TVRANNI
> AVREA SAECLA GERIT QVI PORTAM CONSTRVIT AVRO
> *(This site Theodosius adorns after the destruction of the Tyrant*
> *He displays the Golden Age who builds the Gate with Gold)*

It is unnecessary to recapitulate the arguments that the "Theudosius" here mentioned was Theodosius I, and that the "tyrant" whose overthrow was thus commemorated was the Spanish imposter Magnus Maximus slain at Aquileia in 388 after being welcomed to the Imperial throne by the army of Britain. ("He laughed like a Spanish mule", quoth the author of *Puck of Pook's Hill,* but did not laugh last!) Our triumphal arch was presumably completed in 391 when the victorious Theodosius entered Constantinople for the first time after the death of his rival.

The picture thus presented is a somewhat remarkable one. In 391, and indeed until the enlargement of the walled city by Theodosius II in 413, the walls of Constantinople were those erected by Constantine I in 328 around his newly founded metropolis. They enclosed a little more than half the area of the city of Theodosius II, and their relative position is tolerably familiar. In the region now in question they lay approximately 1½ kilometres within (to the north-east of) the subsequent line of Theodosius II, and the Golden Gate, when built, lay that distance beyond the defended limits of the city, thus presenting two primary questions which have never been completely answered. First, why was this unusual monument sited originally in solitary state amidst a seemingly open countryside so remote from the walled city? And secondly, why the unparalleled association of a garrison with this unenclosed and harmless triumphal archway? I propose to suggest answers to both these conundrums.

There is ample historical evidence that in some special sense the Golden Gate marked the ceremonial entry into the city. To the west of it lay the Imperial suburb and country palace known as the Hebdomon, from the fact that it was seven miles from the city, measured alternatively from the Milion near St. Sophia or the gate of Byzantium near the Column of Constantine. The place was found convenient for imperial inaugurations prior to the triumphal entry along the Egnatian Way, and was so used before the construction of the honorific Gate; for example, by Valens in 364.

The Egnatian Way: this great Way linked the Old Rome and the New, and its worn paving-stones can still be detected amongst the weeds in the forecourt of the Porta Aurea. Here it was that a new emperor or a foreign guest of particularly high distinction (such as a Pope or his Legates) was welcomed by the civic authorities; and there could have been only one reason for the choice of location. Here must surely have been the formal limit of the city's jurisdiction, the outermost fringe of the *pomerium* which, in customary Roman fashion, shielded as an unencumbered military area ("field of fire") the outline of the city-wall. As a likely analogy one may recall the isolated arch of Hadrian which in Jordan bars the highway from Amman to Jerash at a distance of 500 metres from the latter city. Or, more remotely, the ceremonial surrender of the Keys of the City of London to the Sovereign who would pass into the City at the site of Temple Bar. In Roman civic planning there is no evidence of any statutory width of the *pomerium.* No doubt it was varied by circumstances. There is no manifest reason why at the largest and most splendid capital city in the ancient world it should not have been three times as wide as at a provincial *chef-lieu.*

In these understandable circumstances the unique character of the military provision included in the design of the lonely but prestigious monument on the periphery of the inferred *pomerium* becomes perfectly intelligible. The stern square towers which flank the triumphal archway were capable of holding something approaching (in modern terms) a company of troops whose function, both honorific and protective, at the primary focus of high ceremonial on the legal fringe of the city is self-evident.

I offer a partial modern parallel. In London, opposite Hyde Park Corner, a massive archway, isolated at some distance from all neighbouring buildings, marks the summit of "Constitution Hill" and, with it, the boundary of the Royal Park of St. James and the Royal Palace. But, more than that, it is a special kind of police-station. Inspection within the barred archway shows that its broad flanks are in fact an unostentatious barracks; actually the residence of 32 selected members of the Metropolitan Police Force, trained in the niceties of protocol and such other duties as are appropriate to orderly ceremony in the neighbourhood of the Royal precinct. I have no hesitation in finding an organic affinity between the arches of London and Constantinople, with their comparable participation in the control of regal pomp and circumstance across the ages! Of the two familiar monuments, that of London has already enjoyed a long lifetime of honourable utility, whilst that of Constantinople endured little more than a couple of decades of independence, (say) between 391 and 413, when it was swallowed up in the sprawling defences of Theodosius II. Thereafter it retained its status as a formal, if reduced, entry but lost its designed prestige as a self-contained landmark.

In summary, I have proposed the following answers to my questions.

(i)   From the Hebdomon or its harbour the Egnatian Way is known historically to have carried Imperial V.I.P. traffic into Constantinople from the early decades of its metropolitan re-birth.

(ii)   At some point between the Hebdomon and the walls of Constantine the visitor would necessarily enter the *pomerium* or open space which fronted the civic defences and defined the ultimate extent of civic responsibility. It was customary to mark the crucial outer line of the *pomerium* by boundary-marks (*cippi, termini*), and at some appropriate point along the demarcated line the civic authorities would be expected to greet any particularly distinguished arrival.

(iii)   At the conclusion of the critical Maximus episode in 388-391 it was decided to mark this key-point on the Egnatian Way with an imposing marble archway and, in view of its unavoidable isolation, to provide it with flanking towers and a permanent garrison for honorific and protective purposes. The feature was unique, but so were all the attendant circumstances: the outstanding status of the city, the apparent width of its *pomerium,* the consequent remoteness of the monument, the predictable importance of traffic from the Imperial suburb and the West, and the need for the permanent provision of selected troops to deal promptly with a variety of attendant cares in terms of the highest Imperial standards. It might almost be said that, if the Golden Gate were not there in solid fact, it would have been necessary to invent it!

References

1.   *Jahrbuch des Kaiserlich Deutschen Archäologischen Instituts* VIII (Berlin, 1894), 5; and Alexander van Millingen, *Byzantine Constantinople* (London, 1899), pp. 59ff. The most recent examination of the Golden Gate is that by the British Academy and the Museum of Antiquities at Istanbul in 1927, published in *Archaeologia* (Soc. of Antiquaries of London), LXXXI, London, 1931.

Plate XXXIX a. The North Platform
b. Cairn B from the West
c. Cairn A from the South

a

b

c

THE CAIRN OF SA'D.
by G. Lankester Harding

The cairn of Sa'd was one of 50 such examined and recorded from the area north-west and south-west of H4 on the Baghdad road from Amman and Mafraq. In the course of two expeditions to this area organised by Prof. F. V. Winnett, then at the American Schools of Oriental Research in Jerusalem, a total of more than 4000 Safaitic inscriptions were photographed and/or copied, and six of the sites in the Wadi Amqât south-west of H4 have been published by W. G. Oxtoby (480 texts).[1] Two cairns, that of Ghair'el and of Sa'd, had texts claiming the cairn on behalf of the person named in them, but the former was remote and inaccessible to motor traffic and so unsuitable for excavation, hence the cairn of Sa'd, cairn no. 9, was chosen.[2] It comprises two cairns, A and B, only about six meters apart. Both of these were excavated, the supervision and most of the actual work of excavation being carried out by Hasan Awad al Quṭshan of the Jordan Department of Antiquities.

It was originally planned to incorporate this report on the excavation of the cairn in the report on the inscriptions which Prof. Winnett and I are preparing. Since the latter task has taken longer than anticipated, it has been decided to publish the archaeological material without further delay, so it is with great pleasure than I am able to offer it as a tribute to Dame Kathleen Kenyon for her many and great contributions to Near Eastern Archaeology.

This is only the second Safaitic cairn to be excavated, the first being that of Hani',[2] which provided a good deal of information that could never have been obtained from the texts alone. It was hoped that Sa'd would do the same, but I overlooked a basic and serious difference between the two cairns, viz., that the first was in an open, flat plain, the soil of which made it easy to cut a deep grave and seal it off well, whereas the second was on a ridge of basalt and the native soil was full of large rocks and boulders of that stone, making it impossible to dig a grave below surface. The body, therefore, had to be laid on a sort of bench some 50 cms. above natural, with a stone surround, so no grave goods were preserved except possibly for a small iron ferrule (?) (Pl. XL,d), though this came from the fill rather than from the actual burial.

The general layout of the area has not been encountered before (see plan fig. 1). In addition to the two cairns there are some other structures to the east consisting of two roughly circular cobbled platforms constructed on the natural, only one course high, and both about three metres in diameter. The north platform is quite plain (Pl. XXXIXa) but the south had three stones set upright on the east side, the two outer ones on end and the middle one on edge. Their purpose is wholly obscure, but one is reminded of the much larger, square, paved enclosures in Wadi Ramm[3] which have one and sometimes three stones upright in the back wall. The cobbles were removed from both plat-forms, but there was only native soil and boulders below. To the east of these platforms are four rows of stones, of which the two western ones are merely rows of surface stones laid in two roughly straight lines, each a little over six meters long. Level with the north end of these rows and slightly to the east are two more short (one and a half to two metres) rows, but of a very different nature; the more easterly row consists of seven stones set upright on end, while in front to the west are three stones parallel with the seven and one on the north at right angles, all set up on edge. The seven stones remind one of the seven dots, dash, circles or other marks that so often accompany Safaitic inscriptions.

Cairn A (Pl. XXXIX,b) was the first to be excavated as the stone bearing texts 323-334 had been found close to it on the south-west. 323 (fig. 2) reads: *l s'd bn ṣbḥ h rjm*; "The cairn is for Sa'd son of Ṣabâḥ". 329 says that the writer mourns (*wjm*) for Sa'd. These two texts seem to be by the same hand. It was natural to assume from this that the cairn referred to was cairn A, since they were nearer to it than to B, but careful removal of the pile of stones revealed no walled core and no grave, the native soil beneath the cairn being undisturbed and filled with very large basalt boulders. Nevertheless where possible the soil between boulders was dug out to a depth of just over a metre, but nothing was revealed beyond the fact that it was entirely natural, presumably windblown, and previously undisturbed. A significant feature was that no inscribed stone was found either in the mound or underneath it, though some were found upon its surface, so it might have been the dump for surface stones cleared to make room for the east structures and cairn B, but this can only be conjecture. The cairn was a rather flat, amorphous heap of stones, about 1.25 m. high at centre and 8.50 m. in diameter. Among the stones at the edge of the mound were found some sherds of a very rough pottery bowl, probably of mediaeval date.

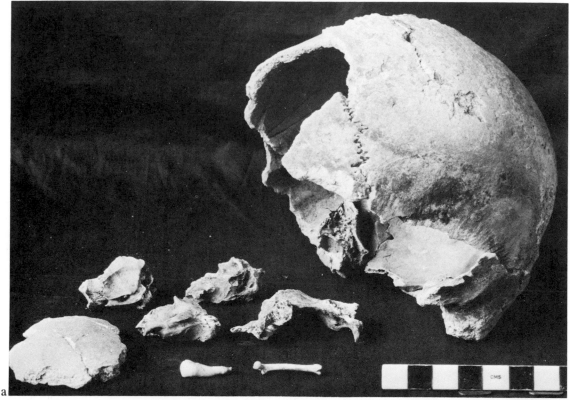

a

b

d

Plate XL

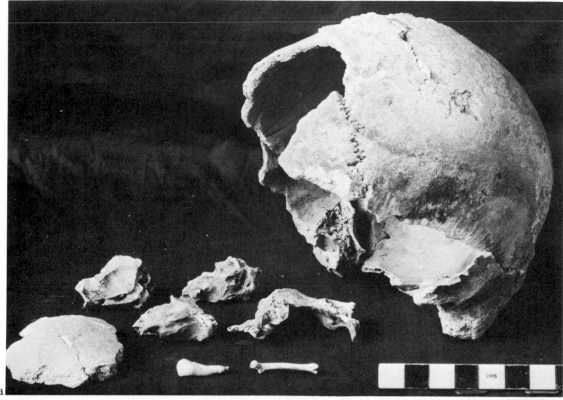

a

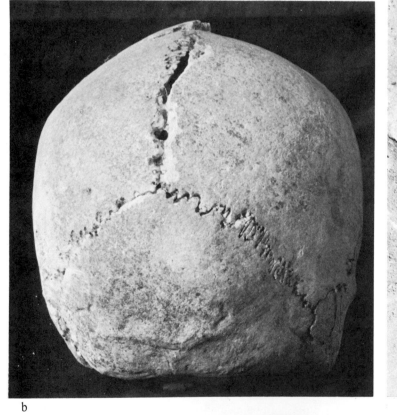

b

d

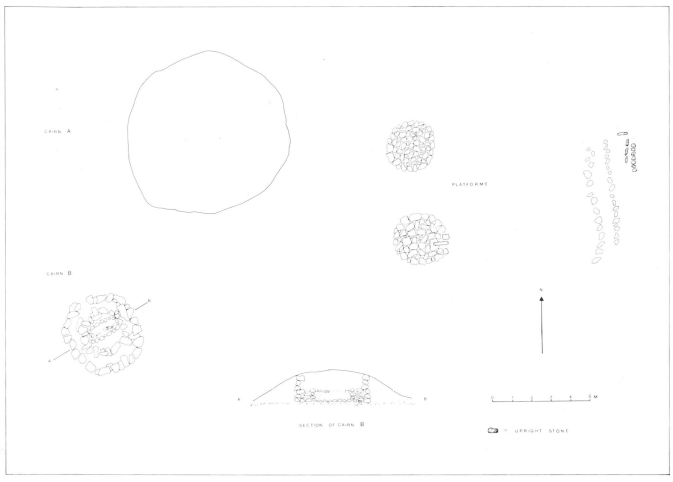

Fig 1.

Attention was then turned to cairn B, and almost at once while removing the outer stones one inscribed with texts 1935-37 was found (fig. 2), of which 1936 again read: "The cairn is for Saʻd son of Ṣabaḥ". 1935 and 1937 both refer to building (*bny*) for Saʻd, while the stone bearing 1933 and 1934 (fig. 2), both of which refer to building and mourning for Saʻd, was found nearby. The association of these texts with cairn B was a strong indication that it and not A was the burial cairn of Saʻd. As clearance continued a circular dry stone wall began to appear (pl. XXXIXb), while with the removal of further loose stones two concentric, roughly circular walls were revealed, the outer being about 4m. in diameter and 1.50 m. high, the inner about 2.50 m. in diameter and only about 0.75 m. high. The space between the two was filled with rubble and in the central well the grave was construct- ed, 1.60 m. long by 0.45 m. wide. The whole structure was erected on a roughly circular cobbled platform similar to those to the east; the workmanship was very rough, even crude, with no attempt made to maintain even lines or courses. The central well had been filled with very fine wind-blown dust (collected, apparently, from the immediate vicinity) to a height of about 0.50 m. above native soil, and on this was laid the grave surround of thin but fairly large slabs of stone, and the corpse laid within this. The orientation of the grave was 250º (cf. Haniʼ, 280º). There was no sign of slabs covering the grave, and apparently no attempt made to protect the body from the filling stones which must have been piled on top of it. It would seem, too, that as the fill rose the outer wall must have been built up to contain it, since it would not be possible to construct a free standing wall one stone thick with stones of very uneven shapes and sizes. The rounding off of the whole thing into the shape of a cairn probably came later and perhaps gradually, as visitors added their quota of stones to the pile, a practice still observed among the Bedu.

There are many curious features about the actual burial, and the only thing it has in common with that of Haniʼ is that the body was laid on its right side, head west (Pl. XLc). But in Saʻd's case the head was separated from the body by nearly five centimeters, and the face, instead of looking south, was pressed against the end (west) stone of the grave. Further, the face itself was entirely missing, as was also the lower jaw and all teeth except one. The last neck bone was still adhering to the skull, but separated from the rest of the neck which curved backwards in a depredations of rodents and insects, the long bones were in so fragile a state that it was impossible to preserve any of them. Only the skull fragments could be collected (Pl. XLa, b).

From these two cairns 500 texts were recorded, nos. 284-675 and 1906-63, 1995-97, 2004-15. Of these 290 were from A and 210 from B, including the two already referred to (329, 1936), which connect Sa'd with the cairn. Nine others (323, 379, 394, 410, 1933, 1934, 1935, 1937) are by people who mourn (*wjm*) or build (*bny*) or both for Sa'd (fig. 2), and the remainder make no mention of him. This is in sharp contrast to Hani', where of 173 texts recorded in the immediate vicinity of the cairn, no less than 99 referred to him by name, and of these 20 were by direct relatives (brothers, cousins and nephews), 13 by relatives by marriage, and 66 by people who can only be identified as friends. They represented between them members of seven different tribes (or families), while the remainder of the texts which do not mention Hani' include four of these seven tribes plus eleven others. Thus members of fourteen different tribes (or families) visited the cairn. In the case of Sa'd it is not possible to tell whether any of those who refer to him were relatives or not, as only his father's name is given, and no one of this group of people mentions a tribe. Only one text out of the 500 from these two cairns (no. 2005) refers to a tribe, and that is a hitherto unknown one. None the less it seems probable that the tribe was that of Ḍaif, as among the 50 cairns there are 25 texts which claim Ḍaif as their tribe and only three claiming 'Awdh, these two being the main Safaitic tribes.[4] It would seem from the smallness of the cairn, the absence of identifiable relatives, the very small number of people who are concerned with him and the apparently casual way he was buried that Sa'd was not a person of any importance as was Hani'. Considering that the grave was only 1.60 m. long, he may even have been a young child.

One text found at B poses a slight problem: no. 646 (fig. 2) reads *l smr bn 'kk h ṣwy*, "The grave (or grave mounds) is for (or by) Sumair son of 'Akkâk". This can hardly refer to the grave of Sa'd, especially as his is in each case called a *rjm*; there was no indication whatever of a secondary or intrusive burial at B, nor were there signs of other burials elsewhere in the vicinity. The work *ṣwy* is probably the Arabic *ṣuway*, grave (according to the dictionary *Al Munjid*), or mounds, grave-mounds (plural of *ṣuwwah*, Salmoné *Arabic-English Dictionary*). Twenty texts refer to various people being on the look-out (*nẓr*), awaiting something (*tẓr*) or keeping watch (*ḥrṣ*), but these are activities indulged in by the Safaites everywhere. Other texts refer to a look-out post (*mẓr*), a shelter (*strt*), place (*dr*), adding a further ten to the total. Of these thirty, twenty were from the vicinity of A.

This, plus the fact that five texts referring to Sa'd are from A, suggests that it is either contemporary with B or perhaps even earlier, but almost certainly not later. There is no evidence to connect the eastern structures with either cairn specifically, nor do they seem to be the kind of structures suitable for keeping watch, being on the look-out and so on. No doubt people were always passing by the site, and most of the texts could have been written at any period before or after Sa'd.

Dr. Jamme's view[5] that no Safaitic cairn is a tomb or burial seems based on a firm denial of all evidence to the contrary both from the inscriptions themselves, archaeology, and the Bedu way of life. As regards archaeology he says (referring to the cairn of Hani'): " . . . . le présence dans ces tombes de chose aussi périssables que des restes de cheveux et de barbe et des morceaux de cuir prouve bien que ces tombes ne peuvent remonter a une antiquité aussi reculée que les temps pré-Islamiques." The "antiquité aussi reculée" is less than 2000 years ago, and conditions of the tomb were peculiarly suitable for the preservation of delicate materials. Under similarly suitable conditions equally delicate materials have been recovered from the Neolithic age, at least 5000 years earlier than Hani'. As regards the Bedu way of life as related to cairns he states categorically (referring to cairns in the 'Ar'ar area): "L'emplacement même de la plupart des cairns [near the crest of a spur of land] définit leur function: ils sont des points de repère pour les bédouins. Les autres sont les restes d'un campement de nomades, . . . ". Anyone who has ever travelled with the Bedu on foot or camelling (*not* in cars and trucks) knows that such artificial landmarks are quite unnecessary; the Bedu relies on entirely natural features to guide him. And surely a nomad camp which included a few specially built cairns (used for what?) would be a very strange sight. Regarding the texts he says (again referring to Hani'): "Non seulment aucun texte safaïtique trouvé dans les alentours ne contient un allusion direct à une tombe, le seul fait qui puisse établir une relation direct entre les tombes et les Safaïtiques, mais encore le présence . . . " (see above). Yet the Arabic word *rujm* or *rajam* (written *rjm* in Safaitic) means both a heap of stones or cairn, or a tomb or grave; Lane, *Arabic-English Lexicon* p. 1048 col. 2 says that *rajam* means "Stones that are placed upon a grave. And hence, a grave." He further says that *rujam* and *rijâm* signify "large stones . . . sometimes collected together upon a grave to form a gibbous covering to it." Two texts from the cairn of Hani' refer to the *rjm* being for Hani', two are by people who claim to have built the *rjm* for Hani', forty two texts refer to "building for Hani' ". All this amounts to fairly strong evidence that Hani' was buried there and the cairn erected over his grave, and there is no archaeological evidence to suggest that the burial cannot be a Safaitic one of not later than the 3rd century A.D.

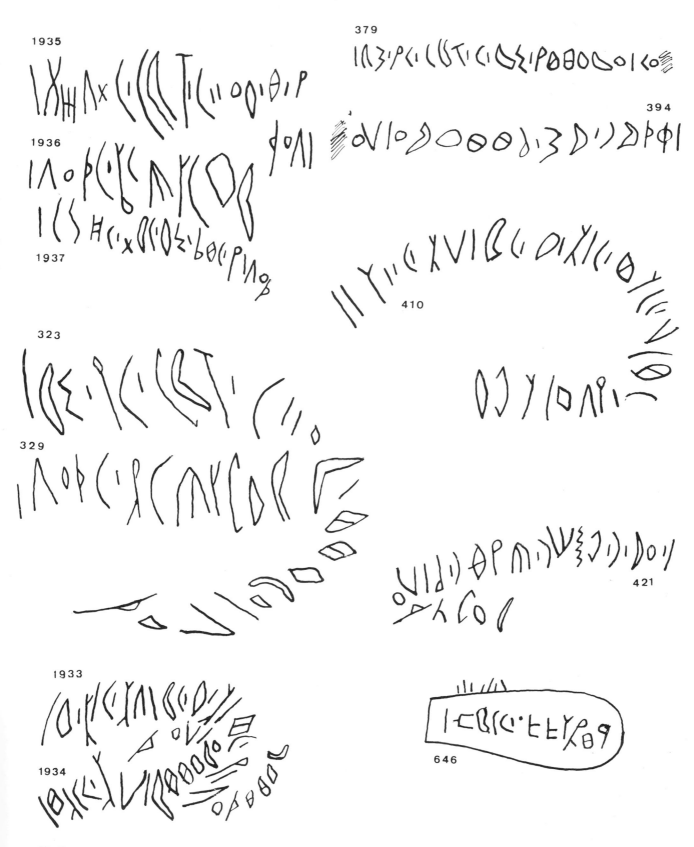

Fig 2.

strange way. Careful examination of the neck bones showed no indications of cutting, so presumably the head had not been severed. Marks on the back of the skull suggested two or three blows with some fairly sharp instrument, though the blows were not powerful enough to penetrate the bone. The skeleton was probably damaged by the weight of stones directly on top of it, and rain must have seeped through to it every year; what with this and the

The cairn of Ghair'el (referred to on p. 243) provides further textual evidence. The information starts with the statement "the corpse belongs to Ghair'el son of RMZN son of MFNY" (no. 931); 930, 932 & 940 record the finding of the corpse of ĠYR'L. Next 933 and 935 record the burying (*qbr*) of ĠYR'L; 929 says "he built the cairn"; 937 "he built for ĠYR'L". 938 and 962 tell us "the cairn is for ĠYR'L". So we have a complete sequence of: finding the corpse of ĠYR'L, burying it, building a cairn, and the statement that the cairn belongs to ĠYR'L, strong evidence that ĠYR'L was interred either under or in the cairn.

It is very desirable now that further cairns should be excavated, some in the plain, like those at Jathum,[6] and some, like the present one, on the ridges. This is the only way one can hope to find objects which would date the burials and hence the inscriptions; archaeology and epigraphy should always be considered as complementary disciplines, and anthropology would not be out of place as a third partner.

The Texts.

Only those few which refer to Sa'd are given here; the remainder will appear in the final publication. The texts are transcribed on figs.

323   This stone, on which 329 also appears, has ten other texts beside these two, but none refers to Sa'd.
l mfny bn rmzn bn n'mn w wjm 'l s'd
By Mufni son of Ramzán son of Nu'mán; and he mourned for Sa'd.
Names and sentiment both well known in Safaitic. A brother of 1935 (see below).

329   *l s'd bn ṣbḥ h rjm*   The cairn is for Sa'd son of Sabah.
The same wording as 1936 (see below).

379   *l mfny bn rmzn bn mfny w wjm 'l (s)'[d]*.
By Mufni son of Ramzân son of Mufni; and he mourned for Sa'd.
Not, apparently, the same person as 323, since the grandfather has a different name. It was a brother of this man, Ghair'el, who was buried at cairn 12 a few kilometers to the north (see p. 243).

394   *l qdm bn mfny w wjm 'l s'd*
By Qadam son of Mufni; and he mourned for Sa'd.
Perhaps a brother of Ramzân of 379. Qadam is common in Safaitic as a name.

410   *l l hnn bn 'slm bn jn'l bn whb bn sr w bny[l] s'(d) h rj[m]*
By HNN son of 'Aslam son of Jann'el son of Wahab son of Sûr; and he built for Sa'd the cairn.

The writer has put two *l*'s at the beginning, and the name should, perhaps, read LHNN, though this is as yet unattested; LHN is, however, known in Thamudic.[7] Vocalisation of both HNN and LHNN is uncertain, but the latter would probably be Lahnân, perhaps from Arabic *lahana* to bring a present. The other names are well-known. The writer must be a brother of 1933 and 1934 (see below). The text is carelessly written, two letters being omitted and one, *d,* incomplete.

421   *l n'mn bn rs̆ḥ bn ḥy w bny l s'd h rjm*
By Nu'mân son of Râshiḥ son of Ḥaiy; and he built the cairn for Sa'd.
Names and formula are well known.

646   See p. 247.

1933   *l jn'l bn 'slm bn jn'l w bny l s'd w wjm*
By Jann'el son of 'Aslam son of Jann'el; and he built for Sa'd and mourned.
A brother of 410 .

1934   *l wnb bn 'slm w wjm 'l s'd*
By Wahab son of 'Aslam; and he mourned for Sa'd.
In all probability another brother of 410.

1935   *l ḥṭst bn rmzn bn n'mn w b ny l s'd*
By Khaṭasat son of Ramzân son of Nu'mân; and he built for Sa'd.
Either writer or copyist has omitted the *b* of the very *bny*.
A brother of 323 above.

1936   *l s'd bn ṣbḥ h rjm*   The cairn is for Sa'd son of Ṣabâḥ.
See 329 above.

1937   *l rg̱d (or bg̱d) bn tm bn mfny w bny l s'd*.
By Raghaḍ (or Baghiḍ) son of Taim son of Mufni and he built for Sa'd.
Raghaḍ (or Baghiḍ) and Taim are well known names; that he is building for Sa'd suggests he is a relation of one of the Mufni's above, but there is no means of knowing which one.

It should be noted that in every text here mentioning building, *bny* (nos. 421, 1933, 1935, 1937) and in all other similar WH texts, the formula is *bny l,* whereas in the cairn of Hani' it is always *bny 'l* (HCH 3-6, 11-15, etc.). It is not clear whether this is of any particular significance, whether the apparent change of preposition changes the meaning and intent of the text, or not, but the problem is being examined.

References

1.   W. G. Oxtoby, *Some inscriptions of the Safaitic Bedouin,* New Haven, 1968.
2.   Map reference approx. CS 9020 on Damascus Sheet of 1: 500,000 World Map.
2.   G. L. Harding, "The cairn of Hani'," *ADAJ,* II (1953) pp. 8-56.
3.   Sir A. S. Kirkbride & Lankester Harding, "Hasma", *PEQ,* 1947, p. 9 & Pl. I, fig. 1.
4.   G. L. Harding, "The Safaitic Tribes", *Al-Abhath,* Beirut, 1969. See particularly the family tree p. 29, in which the following texts from cairn 9 are incorporated: 399, 410, 463, 592, 593.
5.   A. Jamme, "L'article de A. Van Den Branden sur l'expression Safaitique *'tm 'l ḫr',' Al-Michriq,* 1970.
6.   F. V. Winnett, *Safaitic Inscriptions from Jordan,* Toronto, 1957, pp. 5 ff.
7.   G. L. Harding, *An Index and Concordance of pre-Islamic Arabian names and Inscriptions,* Toronto, 1971, p. 521.

a

Plate XLI   a. View from Southwest.
b. Southeast Corner.

b

THE FOUNTAIN OF SULTAN QĀYTBĀY IN THE SACRED PRECINCT OF JERUSALEM

by Christel M. Kessler with the collaboration of Michael H. Burgoyne.

After her last season's excavation in Jerusalem Dame Kathleen initiated the project of surveying and recording the Old City's medieval Muslim architecture. It is in appreciation of this decision that a study of a 15th century A.D. monument of Jerusalem is included here. The Sabil[1] of Qāytbāy happened to be the obvious choice at the time that I was invited to contribute to this volume: with a study of the sculptured masonry domes of Cairo all but completed, this little monument remained intriguing, since the relief decoration of its dome is the only example of that Cairene art found outside Egypt. Thanks to the fact that the Survey of Muslim Architecture was already under way it was possible to deal with the Sabil as a whole. Michael H. Burgoyne, one of the architects engaged in that project, kindly collaborated by giving some of his time to establishing measured drawings and photographs. His survey description, accounting also for features of restoration, is incorporated here to familiarize the reader with the physical appearance of the structure, while I propose to discuss its type, which is unique, and certain aspects of the decoration. A brief assessment of what has so far been said about this monument will serve as an introduction.

Situated in the Sacred Precinct (Ḥaram) which for the pious Muslim is the third holiest place in the world, the Sabil came to be known to the outside world only when it was permitted for non-Muslims to enter that guarded precinct. This new era began sometime after the 1856 concessions agreed upon with the Ottoman Sultan in the peace treaty concluding the Russian-Turkish war. Ever since we find archaeologically minded explorers expressing special appreciation of this little monument and engravings and woodcuts of it published.[2]

The first to devote a monograph to the Ḥaram of Jerusalem, Comte Melchior de Vogüé (1864), singled it out as a "charmante fontaine", the only monument of interest among the small edifices which dot the vast court. His description, though not precise in detail, gives the essentials: it is a typically Mamlūk structure - a small cube surmounted by a transition zone, crowned by a dome of stone, decorated with arabesques in relief.[3] To this other 19th century writers[4] added practically nothing, except Conrad Schick (1887 and 1896) who in his lovingly detailed, though likewise not quite correct accounts provided some measurements and a certain notion of its functioning.[5]

The first to concern himself with an aesthetic appreciation was William Harvey. He devoted a special article to the Sabil which for him was the culmination of an evolutionary series of alterations in style from characteristic Byzantine to characteristic Saracenic forms" (1910).[6] It is an enthusiastic and poetic description which reads like a personal hommage. Equipped with a keen sense for architectural detail, William Harvey was the only one to point out an anomaly of the structure. In 1922, republishing his fine drawing of the Sabil in another context, he stated in the caption that "the axis of the dome and drum is placed somewhat to the west of the centre of the lower storey."[7] Since he did not discuss this further, it was left to the present survey to find out the cause. (For two slightly different interpretations of the findings, see below p. 263).

In 1924 Martin S. Briggs chose the Sabil as frontispiece to his *Muhammadan Architecture in Egypt and Palestine,* obviously making the point that this monument belongs to both the cultural areas dealt with in the book. This visual statement was, however, not put into words; instead his brief text reference brought a long overdue challenge of the traditional dating. For six decades the year "849/1445" was quoted, apparently on the authority of de Vogüé who mentioned it first. Briggs rightly considered the arabesque decoration of the dome as suggesting a later ascription.[8] But the fact that he simply declared the proper date as "not known", showed that he too had not realized that Qāytbāy, the patron usually accorded, did not ascend the throne until 23 years after the objectionable date.

The Sabil is, however, clearly dated by inscription to Shawwāl 887/ beg. 13 Nov. 1482.

To tap this most obvious source of dating, the knowledge of a Max van Berchem in Arabic epigraphy was needed. He read the inscription in 1893. But of his great collection of Arabic inscriptions in Jerusalem only the illustration volume had appeared in 1920;[9] thus, at the time of Briggs' writing, the correct date was published only in

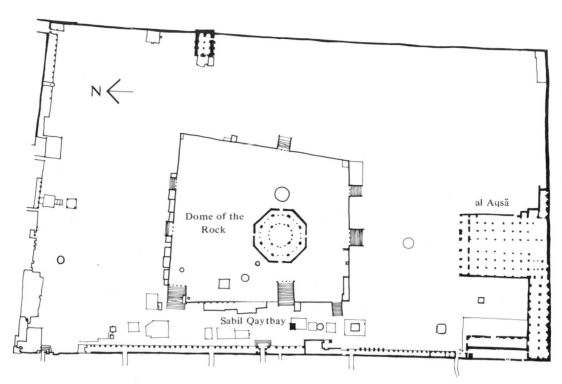

Fig 1: Location Plan.

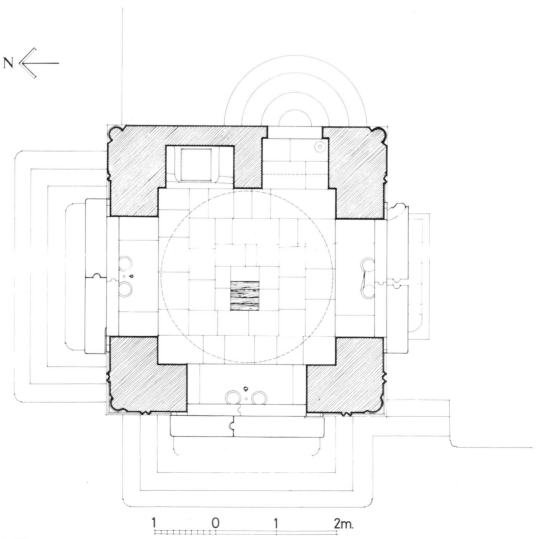

Fig 2: Plan.

so unobtrusive a place as the caption to a photograph of the Sabil [10] and became finally known only in 1925 with the posthumous publication of van Berchem's text volume. [11] From this it was learned that we do not have to do here with a simple foundation inscription, but with a text entirely rewritten to include reference to Sultan 'Abd al-Ḥamīd's restoration of 1300/1883, referring also to a pre-Qāytbāy building stage under Sultan Īnāl (857/1453 to 865/1461). After comparing the inscription with both a pre-restoration attempt in recording the much decayed original [12] and accounts of the contemporary 15th century chronicler of Jerusalem, [13] van Berchem came to the conclusion that the restored inscription was basically a reliable if slightly abbreviated version of the original.

The archaeological question raised by the inscription - what remains of the construction of Qāytbāy? - was also followed up by van Berchem. His answer confirmed that which those less informed had taken for granted: the Sabil, as it stands, is Qāytbāy's building; nothing remains of the previous foundation of Īnāl; and the restoration of 'Abd al-Ḥamīd has changed only the inscription and repaired some of the stone work both inside and outside. [14] Van Berchem's archaeological conclusions, valid as they are, were drawn though from a less broad basis of investigation than his epigraphic ones. For, much against his own inclination, he had imposed on himself the task of concentrating his capabilities on the epigraphic project, which was vast, hoping to find for archaeological problems the collaboration of an architect. [15] Yet it is his great work on epigraphy which set the Sabil, for the first time, into a proper historical context. Based upon a thorough exploitation of Arabic sources and conducted with a true sense for architecture, it remains the best available guidance for archaeological research on the Sabil.

With the advance in knowledge of the medieval architecture of Egypt it had become a point of special interest to stress the similarity of Qāytbāy's Jerusalem Sabil to the contemporary architecture in the capital. Van Berchem is the most explicit in this respect when writing "cette charmante qubba . . . du type égyptien le plus pur, rappelle certains petits mausolées du désert à l'est du Caire". [16] Jean Sauvaget went further (1934); when making the point that after the Crusader occupation Jerusalem had become essentially a religious [rather than cultural] center and buildings of importance followed the style of Syria and Egypt, he illustrated the Sabil as the supreme example of a monument of Egyptian style "without relation to local tradition". [17]

Such a generalisation has become a convenient label for this monument, yet more must be said to prevent it being considered simply an extension of the building traditions of Egypt. No such type of Sabil can be found in Egypt, although it is true that details of structure and decoration are often so similar to contemporary Cairene architecture that one can point to close parallels. [18] And, surprisingly, the sculptured dome decoration, the most obviously Egyptian feature, shows in its technical execution the least resemblance to Egyptian craftsmanship. It is therefore proposed here to take a closer look at the nature of both the Sabil's obvious dependence on Egyptian building traditions and the alleged independence of local ones. But before discussing such questions of style and type it is necessary to introduce the physical appearance of the Sabil as a whole with the description of the present state by Michael H. Burgoyne who has surveyed it.

Survey and Description of the Building
by Michael H. Burgoyne

The Sabil of Qāytbāy is the most ornate of the small domed buildings clustered round the Dome of the Rock in Jerusalem. At the north-western corner of a small open-air oratory (muṣallā), the Sabil is situated between Bāb al-Maṭhara and the central western stair to the platform of the Dome of the Rock (Fig. 1). Directly beneath is a very large cistern, said to have been an ancient gate passage. [19] Built for the Mamlūk Sultan Qāytbāy the Sabil was completed in 887/1482 (see discussion, p. 262). The advent of modern plumbing however, with taps provided at regular intervals throughout the Ḥaram al-Sharīf, has diminished the need for it and it has sadly fallen into disuse. [20]

The Exterior

The Sabil is an often repaired stone structure of three distinct "storeys". A rectangular base (7.65 m. high) supports a transition zone (2.18 m. high) carrying a short drum and pointed dome (3.45 m. high). Thus the overall height is 13.28 m. The south, west and north sides of the base are pierced by large (3.42 m. x 1.94 m.) grilled windows. The east side contains the entrance door. The base storey is not quite square on plan at the exterior, being 4.60 m. x 4.80 m. The extra length is due to the thickening of the eastern side for the well recess. Consequently, while the west facade (Fig. 5) is symmetrical, the north and south facades (Figs. 6 and 4) are asymmetrical with the window placed somewhat west of centre in each. Engaged columns with typical Mamlūk bases and stalactite capitals articulate the four corners.

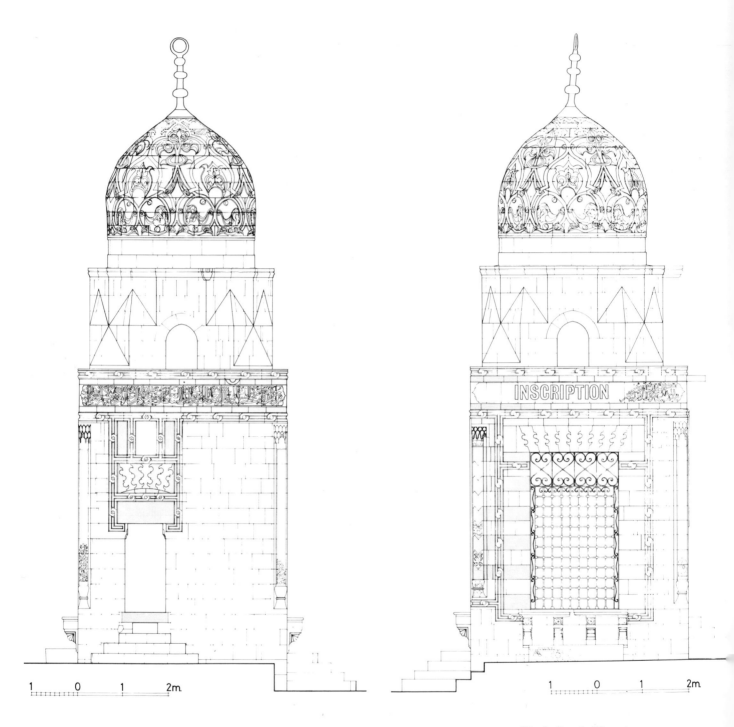

INSCRIPTION

1   0   1   2m.

1   0   1   2m.

Fig 3: East Elevation   *Fig 4: South Elevation*

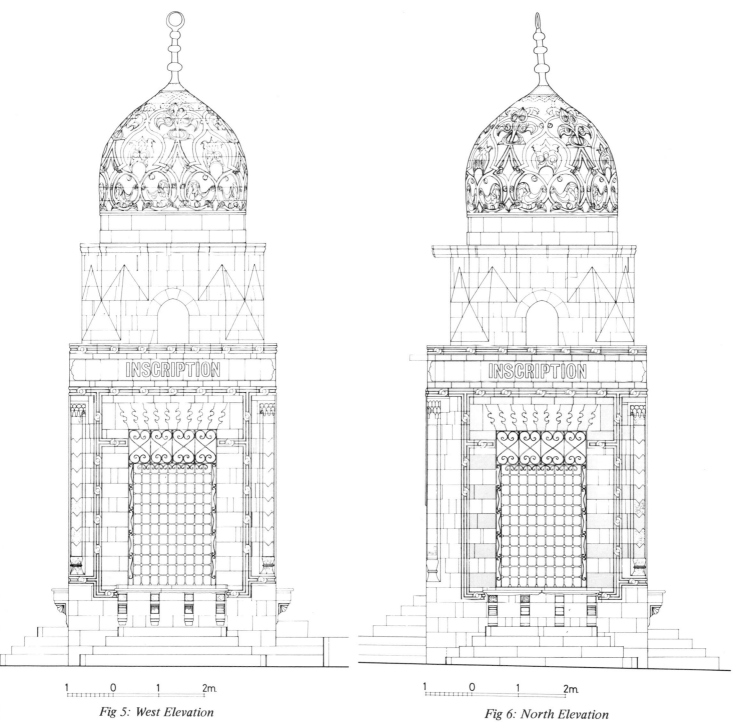

Fig 5: West Elevation

Fig 6: North Elevation

Fig 7: East-west Section

Fig 8: North-south Section

The polychromatic construction (*ablaq*)[21] of alternately red and cream-coloured stone begins immediately west of the vertical double moulding of the north and south facades (Figs. 6 and 4). It continues west, interrupted only by the vertical mouldings (for which cream-coloured limestone is used throughout) through the north-west and south-west corner shafts (Pl. XLIa) on to the west facade. The north-west and south-west corner shafts are composed of alternating courses of red and cream-coloured zig-zag components; the cream-coloured ones are carved with arabesque and strapwork reliefs. The interlocking voussoirs of the window lintels (not original, see below, p. 262) are also polychromatic. A flight of four stone steps leads up to a stone shelf at the base of the north and west windows. On the south side, where there is no need for steps owing to the additional height of the platform of the open-air oratory, an ancient sarcophagus[22] is placed below the window shelf. All three stone shelves are supported by four typically Mamlūk brackets; those at the north and south windows are similar while the two central brackets on the west side are slightly more elaborate (Fig. 11).

The east facade (Fig. 3) is constructed in cream-coloured limestone ashlar which returns through the star-patterned north-east and south-east corner shafts to the vertical moulding of the north and south windows where the bichrome coursing begins. The south-eastern corner shaft is carved with a repeating arabesque arranged round simple eight-pointed and six-pointed star patterns (Pl. XLIb). The north-eastern corner shaft is carved with a now much disfigured pattern of strapwork in which eight-pointed stars play a role (see reconstruction Fig. 9). The plain entrance door (1.95 m. x 0.89 m.) is reached by four semi-circular stone steps (not original, see p. 262) resting on the pavement of the open-air oratory. Above the entrance the double moulding projects 3 cms. more than elsewhere. This moulding frames a red monolithic lintel bearing on small stalactite shoulders, a relieving arch of *ablaq* joggling, and an arrangement of three upright oblong stone tablets. Here the moulding is enriched by hexagonal links enclosing floral bosses (Pl. XLIb). Clearly this moulding, distinct from the rest, is an integral part of the panel of decoration over the door (Fig. 3). The moulding extends to either side with irregularly spaced plain circular links to form the lower border of the band of inscription which runs around the four sides. This inscription, which contains some Qur'ānic verses and details of the foundation and restorations (see below, p. 262), is surmounted by a similar moulding. On the east face, below this moulding, an undecorated water spout (Fig. 3) drains rainwater from the gutter[23] cut into the upper end of this storey at the foot of the receding second storey which is the zone of transition. Square on plan at its base the zone of transition is stepped twice externally. The first step converts the square into an octagon with the corners supported by half-pyramidal buttresses[24] (Fig. 10). The second step, from the octagon to the dodecagon has a half-pyramidal buttress on each of the eight corner facets. A slightly pointed arched window is placed centrally in each side. This storey is crowned by a finely moulded cornice which extends on the east side into a water spout draining the gutter cut into the twelve-sided upper end of the transition zone (Pl. XLIb). On top of this zone sits in recess a plain circular drum of two courses which supports the dome. The exterior of the dome has been somewhat deformed in shape by the action of earthquakes and the effect of unchecked vegetation which has eroded the pointing. The surface of the dome is covered with arabesques. The uppermost details of the arabesque decoration are extremely difficult to distinguish since a later restoration has obscured the carving under a layer of cement. The whole is capped by a typical Islamic crescentic bronze finial which, unlike the others in the Haram, faces east-west rather than north-south.

The Interior [25]

The domed interior is 2.91 m. square and the floor level now stands 1.73 m. above the pavement of the Haram. The base storey is 5.30 m. high, the transition zone 2.02 m. high and the dome 3.32 m high. The total height of the interior is therefore 10.64 m.

In the internal sills of each of the main windows are two circular openings (Fig. 2). Underneath these openings are water troughs. There is a bronze ring between the holes at the north and west windows. It is said that cups (two per window) were chained to these rings. Wooden planks in the middle of the floor of stone slabs (Fig. 2) cover another trough which has now been partly filled with sand and houses a tap.

The window jambs are of *ablaq* construction with a narrow (12 cms.) red stone band extending upwards to frame the decoratively carved limestone spandrels of the internal polychromatic pointed arch over each window. A shallow disk 13 cms. in diameter is cut into the stone above the keystone of each of the three arches (Fig. 7). The recessed tympana of these arches (i.e. the back of the external joggled *ablaq* lintels), are plastered.

The well niche is situated in the east side to the north of the entrance. The well and door recesses, contained by an *ablaq* wall (Fig. 8), are spanned by limestone lintels elaborately carved with star-pattern strapwork in relief

Replaced after 1920

Replaced in 1883

The north–east
corner shaft as
it stands (lower
five courses)

Reconstruction

Analysis

Scale

5 0   10   20   30   40   50cms.

Fig. 9.

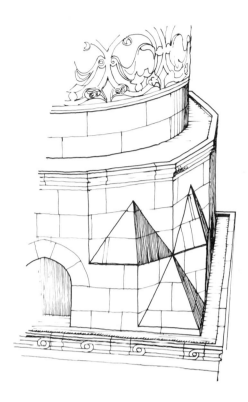

Fig 10: *The Pyramidal Buttresses*

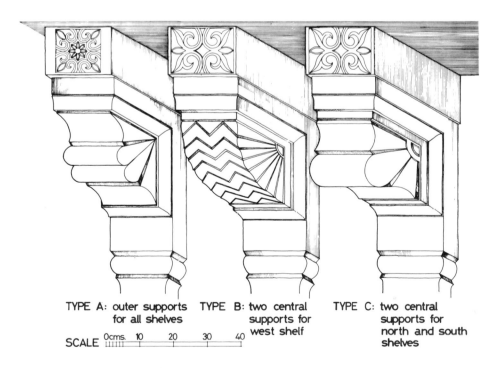

TYPE A: outer supports
for all shelves

TYPE B: two central
supports for
west shelf

TYPE C: two central
supports for
north and south
shelves

SCALE 0cms. 10 20 30 40

Fig 11: *Isometric of Bracket Types.*

a

b

c

d

Plate XLII   a.   *Southwest corner column, basis.*
           b.   *Southwest corner column, capital.*
           c.   *Cupola from the Northwest.*
           d.   *Detail of Qāytbāy's mausoleum dome in Cairo.* (From C. M. Kessler, *op. cit.* in n.55, pl. 34)

Plate XLIII a. Interior of east wall above well recess and door. Each lintel consists of three stones joggled in two steps
to form a flat arch.
b. Interior zone of transition: stone carving.

a

b

(Pl. XLIIIa). Over these lintels are two joggled relieving arches separated by a small panel of strapwork. Continuing upwards we find a plain limestone panel surrounded by a red stone frame (Fig. 8) modelled at each end in a fashion similar to the external inscription tabulae. There is no trace of an inscription on this internal panel.

A red stone band borders the upper end of the walls of the square room immediately below the stalactite pendentives. This device of providing in the interior the transition from the square room to the round base of the dome consists of six tiers; expanding upwards from one niche at the lowest level to six niches at the highest (Figs. 7 and 8). The pendentives are separated by the pointed arched clerestorey windows set in a frame of arabesque (not shown on the Sections, see Pl. XLIIIb). A haphazard array of wooden beams now spans the space between these windows and supports a metal hook probably intended for the attachment of a lamp chain. The whole of the zone of transition is ornamented with an elaboration of relief carving. A simple moulding separates the transition zone from the cupola. Interestingly at a few places there are traces indicating that the interior of the cupola was at one time whitewashed and painted with an artificially regularized network of courses and vertical joints. At the apex is an *ablaq* medallion composed of a central circular red stone surrounded by a cream-coloured limestone border carved with lozenge and spear-shaped reliefs radiating from the centre.

The Sequence of Construction

Little of the early history of the Sabil is known. Mujīr al-Dīn (writing in 1496) tells us that " . . . . . . Among the buildings restored by the Sultan Qāytbāy when he rebuilt his Madrasa was the Sabil facing it in the interior of the Haram, above the well opposite the west stair of the Ṣakhra. A stone dome (*qubba*) formerly stood over this well, like the other wells in the Ḥaram. It was demolished and the new Sabil was built, the floor paved in marble, and it had an elegant appearance."[26] To this we can add the evidence contained in the inscription[27] which runs round the four sides of the building commemorating three stages: firstly, the original foundation of the Circassian Mamlūk Sultan Īnāl (without a date - he died 865: 1460-1), secondly, Qāytbāy's "restoration" in Shawwāl 887/Nov.-Dec. 1482; and, finally, the restoration in Rajab 1300/May-June 1883 by Sultan 'Abd al-Ḥamīd Khān. We must now ask ourselves (1) Is there any trace of Īnāl's original dome? (2) How much of Qāytbāy's construction remains? (3) What is the extent of the subsequent restorations? The existing structure has the appearance of a homogeneous whole which suggests that its overall design dates from one particular period. There is nothing in the present lower courses of the masonry of the Sabil to question Mujīr al-Dīn's statement that Īnāl's *qubba* was completely destroyed. Mujīr al-Dīn's description leads us also to believe that the floor "paved in marble" must have been lifted at some time, probably during the Ottoman period. The present stone floor is therefore a later replacement. From the evidence contained in the inscription it is clear that there was no major restoration between Qāytbāy's original foundation and 'Abd al-Ḥamīd's repairs of 1883. Therefore early photographs might help us to identify those parts, in addition to the inscription, which are not original. Only a handful of pre-1883 illustrations[28] is available but those that do exist confirm that the restorations of 1883 took the form of repairs rather than any major remodelling of the structure. The most obvious and important change is the replacement of the original star-pattern strapwork window lintels by the present *ablaq* joggled voussoirs.[32] Consequently the plastered interior faces of these joggled lintels are not original either. At the same time the steps to the door and the north and west windows were reconstructed. The window grilles are Ottoman in part at least. The cement coating to the top of the dome was almost certainly part of the 1883 repairs, while the painted coursing on the interior cupola, evidently applied in an effort to disguise the unevenness of the stonework, is only presumably so.[29] The next piece of evidence we have at our disposal is the series of fine photographs taken in the 1920s by the late Sir Archibald Creswell. These show that the Sabil was almost identical then to what it is now. But a few minor differences are discernible. The finial faced southwest to northeast rather than eastwest as now. Also, the south-west column base was badly chipped. In fact this damaged base lies amongst the architectural debris scattered around the Islamic Museum in the Ḥaram and so presumably it was removed and replaced by the present one after 1920.[30] Severe erosion of the fifth and sixth courses above the base of the north-eastern corner shaft may be seen in a photograph of the east facade. These stones have since been replaced. A deterioration in the precision of the strapwork design on these two units, and on several parts of the south-eastern corner shaft, serves to confirm the originality of the others. Likewise parts of the moulding over the door are carved differently from the rest.[31] However, examination of the 1920 photographs, which show the slight difference in colour of these stones, suggests that this was part of the 1883 repairs. Missing circular links in the lower half of the vertical moulding at the east end of the north side imply a repair after the restoration of 1883. The absence today of cracks in the masonry of the transition zone shown in Creswell's photographs further evidences some post-1920 repairs. My inquiries failed to discover the exact date of this last restoration although it is likely that a record exists in the archives of the Awqāf Department in Jerusalem. Thus we may conclude that in form the Sabil stands today virtually as it was built in 1482. There is no visible trace of Īnāl's original construction, and the restorations of 1883, altering the inscription, window lintels and steps, and the repairs after 1920, did little to modify the original design.

Thus, although Michael Burgoyne was able to identify further features of restoration, his survey confirms Max van Berchem's conclusions. I should like to stress among the newly identified features of restoration that the so far unsuspected decoration of the window lintels - their Mamlūk type joggling proved to be an Ottoman restoration [32] - is the only drastic change of the original disposition. Likewise interesting to note is the fact that the disarray in the geometric pattern of the south-east corner shaft (Fig. 9) dates from recent repairs and does not have to be considered as incompetence on the part of Mamlūk or Ottoman craftsmen. One of the most welcome results of the survey is the explanation of the eccentricity of the dome: the ground plan (Fig. 2) reveals that the east wall, i.e., the inner rear wall accommodating the well recess, is thicker than the rest. The question now raised is whether increasing the thickness of the rear wall would be the obvious thing to do for adapting a domed edifice to the requirements of a Sabil, [33] or whether we are entitled to suspect here a reuse of part of the previous Sabil structure. The builder, instead of sinking a new well pit may have taken over the existing one together with the wall and recess in which it was accommodated. Yet, even if there were the possibility of proving that the width of the rear wall was determined by the partial reuse of a previous wall, this would not help to clarify questions regarding the type and style of the building.

Before turning to the discussion of the Sabil's mausoleum like type and Cairene style decoration, it is necessary to appreciate the valuable literary evidence we have for the circumstances which gave rise to them.

The circumstances of the construction

The chronicler of Jerusalem, Qādī Mujīr al-Dīn al-'Ulaymī, although contemporary, was not an eyewitness to the construction. [34] He gives little direct news of the Sabil. However, we know from him that it was one of the buildings Qāytbāy constructed in connexion with works at his nearby Madrasa (al-Ashrafiyya). [35] This entitles us to consider the events and circumstances related to these works as equally true for the Sabil. 'Ulaymī amply refers to them. The relevant points shall be briefly assembled here to set the scene:

The building activity goes back to the disappointment Qāytbāy experienced when visiting Jerusalem on 27 Rajab 880/26 Nov. 1474 and finding the Madrasa he had "inherited" [36] and royally endowed [37] much below his expectations. "When he saw it, he did not like it" [38], 'Ulaymi tells us, and his sympathies with the Sultan's reaction transpire from his description that "it was built after the fashion of the Jerusalem madrasas which are not up to much (*laysa fīhā kabīr amrin*)". [39] For, having seen the stately madrasas of the capital during his student days there, he was able to compare. Qāytbāy, consequently, decided to have the Madrasa demolished and rebuilt on a larger scale. [40] Years passed, though, before work began on the site. [41] It seems to have been entrusted initially to local builders, for we learn from 'Ulaymī that the Shaykh of the Madrasa, Shihāb al-Dīn al-'Umayrī, travelled to Cairo (obviously not only impatient to see order restored to his office, [42] but also concerned about the capability of the men at work) "in order to instigate in the Sultan an active interest (*ijtihād*) in the affair of the Madrasa and in expediting reconstruction". [43] Whereupon Qāytbāy dispatched to Jerusalem - in 886/beg. 2 March 1481 - a team composed of builders (*mi'mariyya*), architects (*muhandisūn*), and stone cutters (*hajjārūn*) [44] to rescue the enterprise.

This much can be gleaned from the Chronicle about the circumstances which led to the construction (*'imāra*) (i.e., the remodelling) of Qāytbāy's Jerusalem Madrasa, and, in this connexion, to the construction (*min mā 'amarahu*) (i.e., the annexation and remodelling) of the nearby (older) Sabil. If Qāytbāy's disapproval of the old local-type Madrasa was at the root of the enterprise, clearly his decision to dispatch a team of Cairene builders was largely due to the remonstrances of the Shaykh of the Madrasa. Having stayed earlier in Cairo for several months, Shaykh Shihāb al-Dīn would have appreciated that it was not simply a matter of enlarging the boundaries of the royal Madrasa in the Ḥaram, but rather the question of giving it an appropriately metropolitan style; he would have realized that this could only be achieved by craftsmen from the Cairene building tradition. Certainly, personal ambitions will have played no small role in the initiative of this Shaykh, since he was an exuberant and ostentatious personality who is known to have cultivated high social connexions. [45]

As regards the Sabil, the fact that both the Chronicler and the inscription name the patron Qāytbāy as the builder [46] does not imply that the idea was his. There is archaeological evidence (discussed below p. 265) that neither he nor the Shaykh had envisaged the annexation and remodelling of Sultan Īnāl's Sabil at the time the team of experts was composed in Cairo. Considering on one hand the fact that the old Madrasa had no Sabil, and on the other hand the intense involvement of the Shaykh in the improvement of "his" Madrasa, [47] one may not go far astray in assuming that the Sabil was an afterthought of the Shaykh.

This is what may be inferred from 'Ulaymī's accounts regarding the one who inspired such extension of the building activities; as regards the people who carried it out 'Ulaymī is more explicit, as we have seen. In fact, he even gives, although not mentioning the name, a fair picture of the man who must be held responsible for the design.

The master architect

"There came with them [the Egyptian team]," 'Ulaymī reports, "a certain Christian from amongst the architects (*muhandisūn*) of Cairo equipped with special skill (*hidhq*) in the art of building (*handasa*). When he saw the assembly hall (*majma'*) on the ground floor [recently constructed by local builders] . . . he did not like it and decided to demolish the whole of it. Then demolition of only the southern wall proved to be necessary. He also demolished three arches of the Haram arcade" [48] annexing all for the new Ashrafiyya. Thus the Chronicler describes the leader of the team - unbiased by the fact that he was not a Muslim - as a capable and strong-minded man, apparently entrusted by the Sultan with authority to undertake whatever he deemed right.

Since details of structure and decoration are of the same style and craftsmanship, there is no doubt that the Egyptian team employed at the Madrasa was at work also on the Sabil. The construction works at the Madrasa were finished in Rajab 887/ beg. 16 Aug. 1482 when the marble workers took over, [49] 'Ulaymī reports. Thereafter the master may very well have begun the comparatively small task of demolishing a simple Sabil and rebuilding it on a more grandiose scale, and - with builders, stone masons and material at hand - the work may very well have been completed (or at least almost so, cf. below p. 265) within the three months intervening between Rajab and Shawwāl, the date mentioned in the inscription.

The type

The structural composition was an unusual choice if one considers the Cairene building tradition from which this master came. There is no evidence that in Egypt a free standing square domed edifice was used as a charitable fountain; rather it was the common formula for a funerary monument. As regards the Egyptian Sabil, developed and standardized in Mamlūk times, [50] it was a room in a larger complex, never provided with the emphasis of a dome - not to mention a masonry dome enhanced with sculptured arabesques.

What then has prompted the Egyptian master architect to conceive a sabil in Jerusalem as a free standing monument crowned with a dome? It must have been the shape of the previous construction; for, according to 'Ulaymī this was a "*qubba* built of stone," and he specifies, "like that over other wells in the Haram".[51] Hence so important an aspect as the type was determined by the influence of a local building tradition.

Naturally, the style in which this type was subsequently executed was determined by the craft traditions of the men at work. For them building a stone dome meant applying the current model features of their craft; and these were evolved over a century and a half service in the funerary architecture of the capital's ruling circles. Inevitably, the shape of a dome structure developed in such a context of prestige differed considerably from the simple domes built to cover wells for public water supply in the Haram. The few Sabils still existing there from pre-Qāytbāy times [52] have a low profile - like the exterior of domical vaults - and the transition from the square chamber to the round of the dome is not evident outside. The new Sabil dome, in contrast, was stretched in all its constituent parts: the cupola was given a steep profile ending in a point; it was lifted on a drum, and both cupola and drum were set on a voluminous and decoratively defined zone of transition. Finally, enhanced by an over-all decoration of the cupola in carved relief, the domed Jerusalem Sabil of Qāytbāy came to display all the features particularly evolved in Cairo to raise a tomb chamber to distinction and monumental appearance. The only features which distinguish it from Mamluk mausoleums in Egypt are the large window openings with bracketed shelves in front. They, in their turn, are all but identical to those found in the Mamlūk Sabil architecture of Cairo. Therefore, if one considers its elements of structure and decoration, one can speak - as has deen done so far - of an absolute dependence of the Sabil on Egyptian building traditions. But, in order to do justice in terms of architectural history, one must specify that the particular composition of these elements took place under the influence of a local tradition.

In this context of high-lighting the non-Egyptian aspects of the Sabil, two features of embellishment have to be discussed: the curious lopsided disposition of the decoration on the east wall and the unconventional execution and unfinished aspect of the dome decoration.

The East wall decoration

In general the elements of structure and decoration are disposed symmetrically along the east-west axis of the building. This is true for both the exterior and the interior, except for the outer east wall (Fig. 3). The small entrance

door to one side is enhanced by a top-heavy piece of ornamentation - a monolith lintel with a joggled *ablaq* relieving arch and three upright panels above, framed and interlinked by a double strand moulding, forming a large loose motif which ties the door to the upper decoration of the walls. [53] In contrast to that the other half of the wall is left plain. Why was no effort made to relieve the blankness of the other half? The answer is apparent in days of rainfall when water pours down from the spouts (Fig. 3, Pl. XLI) set exactly above this blank portion of the wall. Any decorative carving would there be exposed to quick erosion.

In the monumental architecture of Islamic Egypt arrangements for rainwater collection and drainage by spouts were known ever since architects from Edessa built the second town wall in the last quarter of the 11th century A.D.[54]; and care was usually taken to set the spouts above undecorated stretches of wall. On Cairene domes, however, gutter grooves and spouts had hitherto not been applied to the narrow projections at the base of drum and transition zone. If they were introduced here, this was in response to the building tradition current in the different climatic conditions of Jerusalem where rainfall was more frequent and water collection more important than in the capital on the Nile.

Thus, if the lopsided decoration of the east wall was due to the installation of rainwater drainage from domes, the adoption of such local building practice was indeed of no small consequence aesthetically.

The dome decoration

The feature which most obviously marks the Sabil's dependence on Egyptian traditions is the relief decoration of the dome - an art developed and flourishing in Cairo during the 15th and early 16th centuries A.D. Its design reflects the stage of refinement this art had attained in the capital under Qāytbāy's patronage: grooved arabesque relief was first used on the two domes of Qāytbāy's funerary complex. [55] It is therefore surprising to find, on closer inspection, that this most Egyptian type of decoration bears the least resemblance to Egyptian craftsmanship in the technique of its execution: not only is the "apex seeking" pattern less evenly and elegantly adapted to the dome surface than in the two Cairene examples, but also a basic rule, hitherto observed by all builders of sculptured masonry domes, was not applied: there is no consistent coordination of the vertical axes of the pattern (as visible, e.g., in the detail of Qaytbay's own mausoleum dome, Pl. XLIId).

Such non-conformity in a building which otherwise conforms in detail to Cairene practices, [56] can only be for the simple reason that there was no specialist at hand to work out the usual coordination between structure and design; that is, no dome decorator was included in the team when it was composed in Cairo, since sculptured dome decoration was exclusively used there for funerary architecture. He would have been superfluous for remodelling a madrasa which was all that the Sultan (and the Shaykh) had in mind at that time.

Thus the idea of replacing Īnāl's domed Sabil by a more grandiose one in the name of the reigning Sultan will have emerged only during the works on the site. According to the Cairene building practices where stone domes were built only for the sake of enhancing the cupola with a sculptured decoration, [57] it was naturally for the master -although not fully equipped - not to neglect such elaboration at the stone dome of the royal Sabil. The builders at hand, although not expert in sculptured dome decoration, have done their best.

Such a deviation from Cairene techniques may therefore still be attributed to the Egyptian team. There are, however, deficiencies in the dome decoration for which they cannot be held responsible: the design is not fully interpreted (see e.g., the large upright leaf in the center zone of the dome, Pl. XLIIc); that is, not all parts of the foliage are carved out in the oblique cutting technique usually applied to give it a filigran refinement. On the other hand, where the carving was executed, it is often handled in such a way as to obscure rather than enhance the motif (e.g., the pairs of large leaves at the lower rim of the cupola, Pl. XLIIc). Such imperfections are not found in any of the other arabesque decorations elsewhere on the Sabil, and therefore give the impression that the carving of the dome, or at least part of it, was left to hands unfamiliar with this kind of work.

Archaeological evidence thus can be adduced for supposing that the Egyptian team was prevented from seeing the work through to its proper conclusion. What circumstances intervened must remain the subject of mere speculation until evidence from other sources comes to light. It is not impossible, though, that the team was recalled for other work - their original assignment, the Madrasa, having been completed three months earlier.

While only precious bits of the ruined Madrasa [58] - once called the "third jewel of the Ḥaram" [59] - remain to give a small impression of the original splendour (dryly described in its endowment deed [60]), the Sabil for which no such description has yet been found, survives as a fairly intact witness of the remarkable performances of the Cairene builders and their master: in order to achieve a truly representative monument to the charitable generosity of the royal patron in the Sacred Precinct of Jerusalem, a local type Sabil was recast according to the grandest fashion Cairene craft had developed for enhancing a single room.

In no less holy a place than this could the master have dared to disregard the fact that a sculptured masonry dome was an embellishment restricted to the funerary architecture of the capital's ruling circles. It is the holiness of the site which must be regarded as the most significant "local" influence which shaped this unusual kind of Mamlūk Sabil. [61]

References

Abbreviations

CIA Jer. Ville - CIA Jer. Haram - CIA Jer. Planches:
Max van Berchem, *Corpus inscriptionum arabicarum*, 2e partie, Syrie du sud. I. *Jérusalem "Ville"*; II. *Jérusalem "Haram"*; III. *Jerusalem, Planches*. Mém. de l'Inst. franç. d'Archéol. orient., XLIII-XLV, Le Caire, 1920-27.
Uns (1866); *Uns* (1973): Mujīr al-Dīn al-'Ulaymī, *al-Uns al-jalīl bi-ta 'rīkh al-Quds wa'l-Khalīl*, Būlāq, 1866; 'Ammān, 1973 2 vols.

1.   A *Sabīl* is a public fountain founded as a charitable act pleasing to God. The Arabic term is retained here since no translation adequately expresses the religious connotations it implied for medieval Muslim society. Literally *sabīl* means "way"; this is an abbreviation of *jihād fī sabīl Allāh*, "fight on the way to God". This abbreviation came to be applied to a building through a double transfer of meaning. The first step was an extension of the originally rather militant sense of the term *jihād* (fight with weapons) to a wider moral concept comprising the performance of any charitable act well pleasing to God (cf. I. Goldziher, *Muhammedanische Studien* II (1890) p. 390; Engl. trsl. ed. by S.M. Stern (1971) p. 354). Since the free dispensing of water was considered one of the most meritorious charitable acts the architectural unit developed to house it was subsequently called in short *sabīl*. By the beginning of the 14th century this usage was so commonly accepted that the term appeared in epigraphy (*CIA, Jer., Haram*, p. 100).

2.   Bibliography of 19th c. authors. 1864: de Vogüé, Comte Melchior, *Le Temple de Jérusalem*, p. 105-6; - 1876: Baedeker, Karl, *Palestine and Syria*, p. 175; Sauvaire, Henry, *Histoire de Jérusalem et d'Hebron. Fragments de la Chronique de Moudjir-ed-Dyn traduits sur le texte arabe*, p. 144; - 1880: Wilson, Ch. W., *Picturesque Palestine*, vol. I, ill. p. 53, p. 70; - 1882: Saulcy, F. de, *Jérusalem*, ill. facing p. 96; - 1883: de Vaux, L., *La Palestine*, ill. p. 193; - 1884: Warren, Ch. and Conder, Cl.R., *The Survey of Western Palestine. Jerusalem*, p. 82; - 1887: Schick, C., *Beit el maqdas oder der alte Tempelplatz zu Jerusalem*, p. 34-5; 1891: Oliphant, Mrs., *Jerusalem*, ill. p. 33 subtitle "The tomb of Elias"; - 1893: Gayet, Al., *L'art arabe*, ill. p. 131 subtitle "Tombe du Qarafah", p. 134; Lees, G. R., *Jerusalem illustrated*, p. 115 and ill.; - 1896: Schick, C., *Die Stiftshütte, der Tempel in Jerusalem und der Tempelplatz der Jetztzeit*, pp. 261-2; - 1899: Clermont-Ganneau, Ch., *Archaeological Researches in Palestine during the years 1873-4*, pp. 138-9. As the first pictorial record of the Sabil may be regarded the panoramic views taken from the "Governor's Palace" on the high grounds outside the north-west boundary of the Ḥaram by Francis Bedford, dated 6 April 1862, publ. as mounted photographs by Day & Son, *Holy Land and Syria*, [1863] Section II, nos. 53 and 54; no. 54 publ. in print in 1865 in Mrs. Mentor Mott, *Stones of Palestine*, facing p. 68); the same view taken by Sergt. J. McDonald publ. in 1865 in Ch. W. Wilson, *Ordnance Survey of Jerusalem - Photographs*, pl.6b. For the earliest close-up illustrations of the Sabil - 1880 from north/north-west (Ch.W. Wilson) and 1882 from east/south-east (F. de Saulcy) - see Bibliography above.

3.   Loc. cit.

4.   Cf. Bibliography, n. 2.

5.   Loc. cit.

6.   "The Fountain of Kaït Bey. Jerusalem", *The Builder*, XCVIII, 1 Jan., pp. 16-17, 1 ill.

7.   "The geometrical decoration of Domes", *The Builder*, CXXII, 14 Apr., ill. p. 551. The sole reference in the text calls it an example of a successful - "apex seeking" - adaptation to the domical surface.

8.   Op cit., p. 125.

9.   The manuscript was ready for print since 1919, according to E. Herzfeld "Max van Berchem geb. den 16. März 1863, gest. den 7. März 1921", *Der Islam* XII (1922) p. 212.

10. *CIA Jer. Planches,* Pls. LXXXVII, other photographs of the Sabil LXXXVIII.

11. *CIA Jer. Haram,* fasc. 1 (1925) pp. 159-62.

12. By H. Sauvaire. According to *CIA Jer. Ville,* p. 5 his copy was made about 1865.

13. Mujīr al-Dīn al-'Ulaymī, a Ḥanbali Qāḍī of Jerusalem. He began his chronicle *al-Uns al-jalīl fī ta'rīkh al-Quds wal-Khalīl* on 25 Dhū'l-Ḥijja 900/18 Sept. 1494 finishing it in less than 4 months.

14. Op. cit. p. 162.

15. Cf. E. Herzfeld's obituary notes,loc. cit.

16. Op. cit. p. 159.

17. "L'architecture musulmane en Syrie", *Revue des Arts Asiatiques,* VIII, no. 1, p. 20, Pl. XIII b. and

18. See below note 56.

19. Warren Report No. XLI "Bab el-Mathara" in *P.E.F.Q.St.II* (April - June, 1869) p. 107.

20. Although no longer providing water for drinking or ablution, the Sabil, by virtue of always having two sides in shade still serves as a meeting place for local worthies. The interior is used as a store by one of the Haram cleaners and the roof provides a useful wiring post for cables carrying electricity to the Dome of the Rock. Since the insulation of these cables is far from adequate, surveying at this level was a somewhat hazardous exercise.

21. The dotted shading on the drawings indicates red coloured stones and is not intended to suggest any tonal variation. The hatching at the apex of the dome implies that the detail of the carving is obscured while the broken line indicates a tentative restoration.

22. Clermont-Ganneau, C.,*Archaeological Researches in Palestine,* (London, 1899) pp. 138-9. Clermont-Ganneau supposes that this antique sarcophagus, like others around the Ḥaram, must have come from the cemetery of "K'bûr es Sâlatîn" to the north of the city (better known as the Tombs of the Kings).

23. One stone from a fine Kufic inscription has been reused near the water spout to pave this gutter. The epigraphical style strongly resembles that of the inscriptions found in Madrasa Fakhriyya and Qubbat al-Mi'rāj; it is probable that these fragments belong to the 6th/12th century, possibly from an inscription for Saladin in the Dome of the Rock - *C.I.A. Jer. Haram,* pp. 55-56, 133.

24. The sloping sides of these buttresses would have the advantage of shedding water directly into the gutter below.

25. The interior of the Sabil is normally kept locked. I am indebted to the Supreme Muslim Council in Jerusalem, particularly Mr. Tahboub and Mr. Dakkak, for their kindness in enabling me to enter and to make a complete survey.

26. *Uns* (1866), pp. 388 and 661; *Uns* (1973) II, pp. 36 and 330.

27. *CIA Jer. Haram,* pp. 162-163.

28. In addition to the illustrations in 19th century publications cited above (note 2) should be noted the earliest close-up photograph published: Hanauer, Rev. J. E., *Walks in and Around Jerusalem,* second edition (London, 1926) p. 295 (Pl. 166) - a pre-restoration photograph of "Sebil Kaiet Bai from Temple platform" by an anonymous photographer. On p. 239 (Pl. 140) and p. 252 (Pl. 147) are later, post-restoration photographs of the Sabil.

29. At the same time the vegetation which was weakening the structure was removed. Once again a proliferation of Golden Henbane and Syrian Golden Drop is beginning to break up the fabric of the Sabil.

30. Also in the debris around the Museum lies a single carved stone evidently intended to replace the badly eroded neck below the capital of the north-west shaft, but for some reason never fitted.

31. It should be observed that the carving of specific groups of architectural ornament by obviously different hands does not necessarily indicate a restoration. Undoubtedly several masons, each with his own cutting style, would have been employed on the construction of the Sabil.

32. On the only pre-restoration photograph of a window - Wilson's Ordnance Survey, pl. 6b (cf. n.2) - one can recognize with a strong magnifying glass remains of a lintel with 10-pointed star-pattern strapwork.

33. As implied in the above description, p. 262

34. He went to Cairo in 880 for studying law and seems to have still been there in 887, according to *al-Shaṭṭī* al-Baghdādī, *Mukhtaṣar ṭabaqāt al-Ḥanābila* (Damascus 1339/1921) p. 73.

35. *Uns* (1866) 388 and 660; *Uns* (1973) II, 36 and 330.

36. After his accession in Rajab 872/Jan. 1468, the Superintendant of the Ḥaram "offered" the unfinished Madrasa (claiming to have built it from his own funds for Sultan Khushqadam) to Qāytbāy who accepted without, however, reconfirming the Amir in his Superintendant position, *Uns* (1866) p. 387 and 618; *Uns* (1973) II, p. 35 and 284.

37. Cf. the Waqf deed of 17 Rabī' II 877/21 Oct. 1472 publ. in extract by 'Abd al-Laṭīf Ibrāhīm 'Alī, "Wathīqat al-Sulṭān Qāytbāy - al-madrasa bil-Quds wal-jāmi' bi-Ghazza", in *al-Mu'tamar al-thālith lil-āthār fī bilād al-'arabiyya, Fās 1959* (1961). The list of recipients of grants (p. 411) includes as many as

60 Sufis, i.e. 20 more than at his own madrasa-mausoleum complex in Cairo (cf. L. A. Mayer, *The buildings of Qāytbāy as described in his endowment deed* (1938) pp. 66-67).

38. *Uns* (1866) pp. 387 and 647; *Uns* (1973) II pp. 35 and 315.

39. *Uns* (1866) p. 618; *Uns* (1973) II, p. 284.

40. By incorporating other buildings *Uns* (1866) 656; *Uns* (1973) II, 325.

41. *Ibid.*, a couple of lines further on.

42. The Waqf stipends had been cut when the demolition was decided upon, *Uns* (1866) 628; *Uns* (1973) II, p. 295.

43. *Uns* (1866) p. 656; *Uns* (1973) II p. 325.

44. *Uns* (1866) p. 657; *Uns* (1973) II p. 326.

45. *Uns* (1866) p. 555; *Uns* (1973) II p. 216: among his influential friends was the Secretary of State in Cairo; he was generous (*'indahu sakhā'*), lived luxuriously with good food and dress (*'āsha . . . mun 'iman mutafarrihan bi-ḥusni 'l-ma'kali wa'l-malbasi*), he lived long and enjoyed life with his senses (*'ammara wamatta'a bi-ḥawāssihi*). Cf. also the incident of his unjustifiedly assuming a more honourable place than his position allowed at a reception in Jerusalem and his subsequent complaint at the court in Cairo which ended with Qāytbāy officially confirming and investing him as Shaykh of his Jerusalem Madrasa, *Uns* (1866) pp. 622-5; *Uns* (1973) II, pp.288-291 (the Chronicler being present at that ceremony describes it in detail).

46. Since it was the patron to whom the charitable foundation was credited as an act relieving from The Fire.

47. *Uns* (1866) p. 664; *Uns* (1973) II, p. 333.

48. *Uns* (1866) p. 657; *Uns* (1973) II, p. 326. He likewise annexed an area in front of the arcades from the court of the Ḥaram (not specified by 'Ulaymī).

49. *Uns* (1866) p. 659; *Uns* (1973) II, p. 328.

50. Cf. Sophie Ebeid, *The Formation and Standardization of Sabil Architecture in Mamluk Cairo*, unpublished M.A. thesis, American University, Center for Arabic Studies, January 1976.

51. *Uns* (1866) pp. 388 and 661; *Uns* (1973) II, pp. 36 and 330.

52. There is a shallow stone dome above the angle of the L-shaped cistern room called Sabil Sha'lān, but it is not clear whether this dates from the foundation of 613/1216 or the restoration of 832/1429 or rather of 1037/1628 (*CIA, Jer. Haram*, pp. 98-102; ill. *CIA, Jer. Planches*, pl. XLI). Only one further example exists from pre-Qāytbāy times near Bāb al-Nāẓir (op. cit., pl. XVI, in the foreground); it is the ancient qubba over a well which Sultan Barsbāy restored in 839/1435-6.

53. Note that the circular loops of the double strand moulding are replaced here by hexagons with insets and that the horizontal band at the upper end is given for the width of the motif a slight forward projection.

54. E.g., the spouts at Bāb al-Futūḥ, 480/1087, ill. K.A.C. Creswell, *Muslim Architecture of Egypt*, I (1952) Pl. 62.

55. I.e., the dome of Qāytbāy's own mausoleum, fin. 879/1474, the masterpiece of all Cairene domes, illustrated in all relevant books on Islamic architecture, and the smaller one he built before ascending the throne at the advanced age of 56 (hitherto known under the name of the later proprietor as "Gulshānī Mausoleum" and dated to the end of Qāytbāy's rule). - On the sequence in which Cairene dome decoration evolved, C.M. Kessler, *The Carved Masonry Domes of Medieval Cairo*, AARP/American University in Cairo Press, 1976.

56. E.g., several patterns are taken from the Sabil at Qāytbāy's caravanserai near al-Azhar mosque of 882/1477; for example, the strapwork pattern rolled onto the north-east corner shaft (see the reconstitution of its original lay-out by M. H. Burgoyne, Fig. 9) and the pattern on the flat arch above the door recess (Pl. XLIIIa, right panel), both appear in the decoration above a door leading to the dependencies of Qāytbāy's caravanserai Sabil (ill. in Jules Bourgoin, *Les arts arabes* (1873) pl. 1). Also the corner shafts with courses joggled in a zig-zag fashion (see Pl. XLII a, b) occur there for the first time. As regards the outer shape of the intermediary zone with its prismatic corners which provide transition from the square base to a dodecagonal rim, this was modelled after the intermediary zone of Amir Qijmās al-Isḥāqi's mausoleum in Cairo, finished in 886/1481, i.e. at the time that the team was composed for Jerusalem.

57. A single exception is the small dome (probably built 748/1348 against the twin mausoleum complex of Amir Sanjar al-Jawlī (703/1303), cf. C. M. Kessler, op. cit., p. 4.

58. Cf. Shmuel Tamari, "Al-Ashrafiyya - an Imperial Madrasa in Jerusalem", *Bar Ilan Departmental Researches* 1 (1973), in Hebrew pp. 9-64, 40 pls., 5 plans (in pocket); English summary pp. LI-LII.

59. *Uns* (1866) pp. 388,660; *Uns* (1973) II, pp. 36, 329.

60. See n. 37.

61. The Sabil of Qāytbāy figures as no. 112 in the chronological Index of the Muslim monuments of Jerusalem, by M. H. Burgoyne, in: The British School of Archaeology in Jerusalem, *The Architecture of Islamic Jerusalem, an Exhibition prepared on the occasion of the World of Islam Festival, London, 1976* (Jerusalem, 1976). Mr. Jalal Nasir kindly informs me that the Sabil is also dealt with in his unpublished M.A. thesis on Qāytbāy's buildings in Jerusalem, Cairo University, 1974.

SYRIAN TILES FROM SINAI AND DAMASCUS
by John Carswell

In the Oriental church, records of individual acts of patronage often combine pious expressions of faith with details of a more temporal nature. This is especially true in centres of pilgrimage, such as Jerusalem and Bethlehem, where many of the objects given to churches are inscribed not only with the donor's name, but also with details of their date and provenance, and even of their manufacture. This passion for recording the circumstance of each donation is invaluable to those seeking clues to the evolution of different crafts. Moreover, the information is not confined to a purely Christian context, for many of the objects were commissioned from non-Christian craftsmen.

So it is not surprising to find the same pattern repeated in the Church of St. Catherine, on Mount Sinai. Here, inscriptions on metalwork, icons, carved and inlaid woodwork and other objects all contain detailed information. And in the little Chapel of the Burning Bush, where it is said that a shaft of sunlight penetrates only once a year, the walls are covered with Syrian glazed tiles. A Greek inscription on four of them records that they were made in 1680 A.D., probably in Damascus.[1]

But when one begins to look closely at the Sinai tiles, it is clear that there is more to be gleaned from them than evidence for the date and place of their manufacture. Their use in this sacred spot contrasts so strongly with the use of similar tiles in an Islamic setting, that for comparative purposes details of tiles in a *zâwiya*[2] in Damascus are described first. The Syrian tiles in Sinai and Damascus, so similar in many respects, differ fundamentally in the way they serve as vehicles for two distinct types of religious expression.

The *zāwiya* in Damascus is that of Sa'd ad-Dīn 'Omar al-Taftazānī, in the quarter of Damascus known as *maidan fauqāni*, just south of the city on the old road to Palestine. The building is rectangular in plan, with a square central area surmounted by a dome on four arches, preceded by a narrow entrance-way with raised platforms on either side, and a gallery above at the rear. (Figure 2) Outside, the wall facing the road is carved with a large panel of ornament in low relief.

The *zāwiya* is still used by the followers of Sa'd ad-Dīn for the *dhikr*, once a week. On entering the building, facing one is the south-west wall. (Fig. 1a; Pl. XLIV). This is set with wide horizontal bands of light and dark stone, to the height of the springing of the arches. In the centre is a simple *miḥrāb* with a slightly pointed arch, which on closer inspection is seen to be set at an angle to the alignment of the wall. (Fig. 2). This has been ingeniously achieved by adding an extra vault on the right side, which tapers off to the left; the wide bands of contrasting stone passing across the *miḥrāb* help to create the illusion of the plan being symmetrical, and conceal the irregularity. On either side of the *miḥrab* there are recesses, now filled with glass-fronted cupboards and drawers, with arched panels of tiles above.(Pl. XLVIII, *D, E*). Dark bands of stone radiate from these arches and the *miḥrāb* vault. Above, there are two horizontal panels of stone, inlaid in three colours with a pattern of scalloped and spiked zig-zags; between them there is a panel of tiles painted with an inscription from the Qur'ān. (Pl. XLIV). The whole facade is framed in stone carved with an interlocking pattern, extended to the left and right at the level of the springing of the arches. Here, the irregular spaces between the arches and the Qur'ānic inscription are filled with tiles painted with floral motifs (Fig. 1b, *L, M*). Below the carved frame there are tiles painted with dated inscriptions in verses (Pl. XLV, *H, I*), and elaborate floral medallions (Pl. XLVI, *J, K*). Above the *miḥrāb* a round glazed plaque (*O*) has been set in the stonework (Pl. XLVI,*top*). In the centre, at the top of the whole facade of stone and tiles, there are three tiles painted with a dated inscription (*F*), and above them there is a much later inscription painted on the wall, dated 1365 H. /1945-6 A.D. (Pl. XLVI,*top*). There is also a collection of flails, double-headed axes, cymbals, spikes and a *subḥa*,[3] hanging on the wall; and a frame of electric lights serves to add an emphatic contemporary note to the Qur'ānic inscription.[4]

On the south-east wall there is a similar but less elaborate facade of light and dark stone courses, inlaid at the top with three decorative panels, two square and one rectangular. (Fig. 1a). There are two windows, each with tile panels above (*B, C*), and there is an enclosing frame of carved stone similar to that on the south-west wall. Hanging on this wall are three shallow drums and a flail. At the north end of this wall, in the raised section of the building, there is a third window set in a panel of contrasting stone, with another panel of tiles above it (*A*). The floor of the main part of the *zāwiya* is thickly carpeted, and carpets hang on the north-west wall facing the windows. (Pl. XLIV).

Fig 1a: Zāwiya of Sa'd ad-Dīn, Damascus. The south-east wall.

That the tiles were mostly part of the original scheme for the decoration of the *zāwiya,* is clear from their integration with the stonework. On the south-west, *qibla* wall, the long Qur'ānic inscription is the dominating feature, sandwiched between the two animated bands of zig-zag. The five inscribed tile panels above the windows and the recesses serve to accent these features, and supply more quotations. Other tiles are purely decorative; two large panels (Pl. XLVI, *bottom,J, K*) are painted with formal medallions of interwined floral motifs, and look very carpet-like, particularly so with real carpets hanging close to them. Above, the two irregular floral panels (*L, M*) are painted in a freer and more naturalistic style

The south-west wall of the *zāwiya* is actually irregular, being narrower on the left side between the carved stone frame and the end of the wall; and it is evident that the designer of the tiles was aware of this irregularity. In striving for a symmetrical composition, he has designed the floral panels (*L, M*) to fit the differently shaped spaces. He faced an even greater problem with the carpet-like panels (*J, K*); here he balanced the designs by contracting the pointed medallion at the centre of (*J*) and making the vertical borders narrower; at the same time, the borders at the ends of both panels are varied. A reconstruction shows how the two panels were originally conceived (Pl. XLVI, *bottom*).

But the workman who set the tiles was apparently ignorant of the designer's intention. In setting (*J*), the tassel border meant for the top has been mistakenly placed at the bottom. The bottom right tile (Pl. XLVII, *above*) is obviously a corner tile, and could only have fitted at the top left hand corner, where it would have continued the pattern of the left border, as it does in the reconstruction. When he came to set panel (*K*), his error caught up with him, and further complications arose. If he had proceeded and set (*K*) as it was originally designed, the pointed medallion would then have fallen one tile lower than the medallion in (*J*). He solved his dilemma by removing the top border completely; but to have re-inserted it at the bottom would not have made sense, as it would have resulted in a double border. His solution was a desparate one; he inserted two upper border tiles in the third row from the bottom, and another in the centre of the lowest row. He then set into the panel four tiles of completely arbitrary design. His final mistake was to reverse one of the central tiles of the panel, and mix up the floral border of the central medallion.

Fig 1b: Zāwiya of Saʻd ad-Dīn,Damascus. The south-west wall.

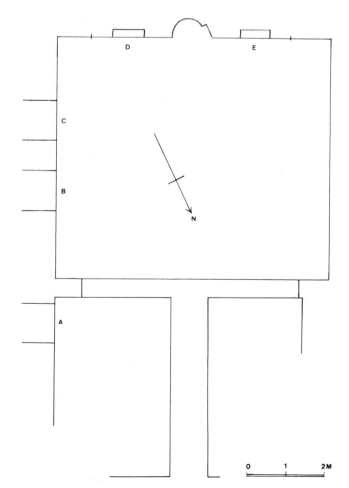

Fig 2: Zāwiya of
Saʻd ad-Dīn,
Damascus;
sketch plan.

0   1   2M

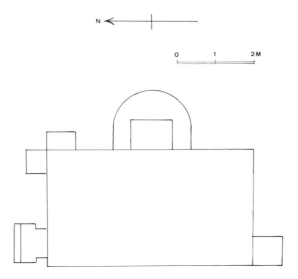

Fig 3: The Chapel of the Burning Bush, Church of St. Catherine, Mount Sinai; sketch plan.

Could the designer of the tiles, who had taken so much trouble to conceal the irregularity of the *miḥrāb*, have allowed the tiles to have been set wrongly in the wall? This would seem hardly likely, and the answer lies in the three inscribed and dated panels (*F, H,* and *I*). These three panels are dated 982 H/1574-5 A.D., 995 H. /1586-7 A.D., and 1005 H./1596-7 A.D. respectively, by chronograms at the end of each inscription,[5] and are all later than the date of the building of the *zāwiya,* which Wulzinger and Watzinger give as about 970 H./ 1562-3 A.D.[6]

Accepting the dates of the three panels (*F, H* and *I*) as accurate, they must then have been later additions to the wall. Indeed, (*F*) does have an extraneous air, stuck on the top of the whole composition, outside the frame. The inscriptions (*H*) and (*I*) are not only different in style, but also in colour, to all the other tiles; and the style of lettering also differs from that of the main Qur'ānic inscription (*G*), and that of the five arched panels (*A - E*). Comparing (*H*) and (*I*), made ten years apart, although they are similar in style, a closer inspection of the lettering again reveals two different hands at work; the calligraphy of (*I*) is much less assured than that of (*H*). (Pl. XLVI).

Allowing that these three panels were later additions, this would leave the rest of the tiles as part of the original design. That the Qur'ānic inscription (*G*) was part of the original concept is evident from the way it relates to the stonework as a whole. The manipulation of the tile panels (*J, K*) and (*L, M*) to fit their differently shaped contexts shows an ingenuity on the part of the designer similar to that displayed by the architect when he concealed the irregular alignment of the *miḥrāb* with visually distracting bands of stone, and would again suggest that these tiles were part of the original design of the facade. It was only when the panels (*H*) and (*I*) were inserted later, and the panels (*J*) and (*K*) below them had to be re-set, that the designs of the latter were confused.

Considered as a whole, the tiles play an important part in the decoration of the *zāwiya*; apart from their obviously decorative function, they are also an important adjunct to the religious purpose of the building. The Qur'ānic inscription marches sturdily across the facade, echoing the rhythmic pattern of the bands of coloured stone above and below it, and occupies a central position. The arched panels (*A-E*) project their religious quotations against a rich background of decorative detail. The little plaque (*O*) above the *miḥrāb* acts as a kind of ceramic talisman. Contrasting decorative effects are obtained by the other panels; the carpet-like panels (*J* and *K*) help to stabilise the two sides of the wall, with the floral panels above (*L* and *M*) providing lively accents at the springing of the arches. In sum, the designer drew on a variety of different styles to suit different purposes.

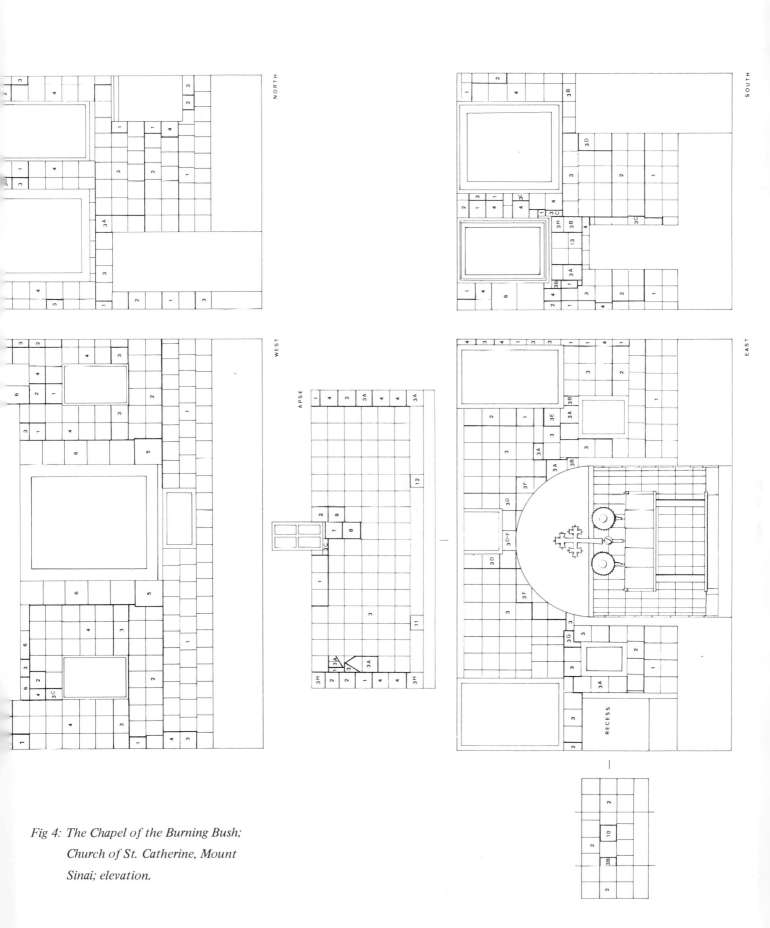

Fig 4: The Chapel of the Burning Bush;
Church of St. Catherine, Mount
Sinai; elevation.

The tiles in the Chapel of the Burning Bush on Mount Sinai are conceived in quite a different spirit. (Figures 3, 4; Pls. XLIX, L, LI). With the designs confined mostly to single tiles, they are much less sophisticated than the tiles in the *zāwiya* in Damascus, and they simply serve to provide a decorative background for the other objects, such as the icons, many of which are actually set in the wall. In order to fill the spaces between the various icons, doorways and recesses in the wall, the tiles are somewhat haphazardly placed, particularly in the upper registers. At the bottom of the walls there is a marble dado, above which the walls are tiled to the ceiling. The curved recess behind the altar is also decorated with a frieze of tiles, as is the recess at the north end of the east wall. The area immediately behind the Episcopal chair, which stands against the south wall, is not tiled but covered instead with marble.

The tiles are of thirteen different types, and vary considerably in quality of execution and design (Pls. L, LI).[7] *Types 1, 2* and *3* are all competently painted, in the usual range of colours associated with Syrian tiles: cobalt blue, turquoise, green, purple, and black for outlines. Numerically, *type 3* tiles are in the majority, and they are used in quantity on the east wall round the arch above the altar.[8] There are several variations in the design of the borders of this type, and tiles with borders which follow the curve of the arch are the only indication that the designer had any idea of the actual setting for which the tiles were intended. (Fig. 4, Pl. XLIX) *Type 4* tiles are both diffuse in design and imperfect in firing, as are the two large *type 5* tiles with crosses painted on them. On the other hand, the ten *type 6* tiles are the most precisely painted of all the tiles. Six of the types, 7, 8, 9, 10, 11 and 12, are only represented by single examples. Of these, the *type 7* tile set at the back of the altar and painted in a linear style with a vase of flowers, is similar to a type of tile found in large quantities in a house in Aleppo, and which are now in a private collection in Beirut. (Pl. LVI).[9] Indeed, with the exception of the *type 3* tiles painted to fit the arch above the altar, there is nothing to show that any of the tiles are other than stock types commonly available in Damascus in the seventeenth century and later.

The four inscribed tiles form a panel set above the Episcopal chair on the south wall. (Pl. L) The two upper tiles are square, and the two below are rectangular. The upper pair are painted with clumsy floral borders at the sides, and the four tiles are painted with an inscription in Greek, in six lines, which reads:

ΑΡΧΙΕΡΑΤΕΒΟΝΤΟΣ / ΚΥΡΙΟ͞Υ ΑΡΧΙΕΠΙΣΚΟΠΟΥ / ΙΩΑΝΝΙΚΙΟ͞Υ Κ͞ΑΙ
ΗΚΟΝΟΜ(Ο)Σ / ΟΗΤΟΣ ΕΝ ΠΟΛΕΙ Δ͞ΑΜ͞ΑΣΚ͞ΟΥ / ΓΕΡΟΝΤΟΣ ΚΥΡΙΟ͞Υ
Φ͞ΙΛΟΘΕΟ͞Υ / ΕΤΕΛΕΙΟΘΗ Τ͞Ο ΠΑΡΟΝ ΕΡΓΟ/Ν Α͞ΧΠ ΕΝ ΜΥΝΗ ΑΥΓ͞ΟΥΣΤ͞ΟΥ

While the Lord Archbishop Iōannikios was archbishop and the elder Lord Philotheos was steward in the city of Damascus, this work was completed. 1680 in the month of August.[10]

The inscription is very poorly written and betrays all the signs of having been executed by a workman who had been given a model to copy which he did not understand. Indeed, considering that these tiles were to be placed as a permanent record in the Sinai chapel, the disparity in size and the ineptitude of their execution lead one to presume that whoever commissioned them never saw the finished work, or was very easily pleased.

The inscription itself is ambiguous; it does not actually say *what* work was completed. It could as easily refer to the Episcopal chair below it, or the painting above it; but there are some grounds for thinking it refers to the tiling of the chapel, for it is set between four *type 3* tiles with borders (*types 3a, b, h*); and as already noted, *type 3* tiles are in the majority, and are the only tiles which were specially designed for part of the chapel. It seems that an attempt was made to decorate the east wall with *type 3* tiles in a coherent fashion, but difficulties soon occurred owing to the irregularity of the wall, and the attempt was abandoned in the lower registers. In the recess behind the altar, the tiles are mostly *type 3* type, but there are also other types at the sides and in the centre, and four *type 3* tiles with borders were clearly meant for some other position. It is also odd that whilst the *type 3* tiles are well drawn and utilise the full range of colours of Syrian tilework of the period including green and purple, the inscription which appears to be associated with them is so poorly done, in cobalt blue, turquoise and black alone.

Nor do the inscribed tiles, with the mention of the date 1680 A.D., really help to determine the date of the tiles in the chapel as a whole, from which they differ considerably in style. All they can provide is a *terminus ante quem* for the panel itself; and the mention of Damascus serves only to reinforce the probability that they were made in that city. The Episcopal chair, which stands below the inscribed tiles, does not help much in clarifying the issue. Pls. L, LII).

The chair is one of several pieces of inlaid wooden furniture in the chapel, including the altar, outer doors of the north entrance, a candelabra, and a footstool (Plates XLIX, LII). The chair has finely worked panels of mother-of-pearl and tortoise shell inlay, and is a splendid example of this type of craft. It is inscribed, in Greek, on the back of the chair,[11] and in Arabic written in detached characters on the post on either side of the head-rest. (Pl. LII).

The Arabic inscriptions read:

ل د ى ر ط و ر س ى ن ا ال

م ع م و ر سنة ١٧١٣

[لدير طور سينا المعمور سنة ١٧١٣]

To the monastery of Mount Sinai, the flourishing, in the year 1713

ا و ق ف ا ل ف ق ى ر ب ر ا ه ى م

م ر س ع د ا ل ح ل ب ى

[أوقف الفقير [ا] براهيم مرسعد الحلبي]

He made it as a waqf [I] brāhīm Marsaʻd from Ḥalab, who is in need [of god's grace].[12]

As the date of the chair is 1713 A.D., this means that it arrived in Sinai thirty-three years *after* the inscribed tiles on the walls above it. Either it replaced an earlier chair, or we are faced with the possibility that the tile inscription was once set elsewhere, and not, as present, in conjunction with the empty marble space below, and the chair in front.

That the tiles may have been moved around after their original distribution is suggested by a bilingual marble inscription on the west wall; a translation of the Greek reads:

> This wall was constructed at the expense of the Metropolitan of Homs, the lord Gerassimos, in eternal memory, and so that he has the Burning Bush as an invincible wall and salvation, with the help of the Monk Raphael, of Homs, during the Archbishopric of Kyrillos, of Crete, in the year of salvation 1770.

- whilst the Arabic reads:

> This paving, bearing an inscription on tiles, is a testimony to the faith of brother Raphael, of Homs, known to the holy father the lord Gerassimos, Metropolitan of Homs, who is of most honourable descent, hoping that Our Lord his Divine Father will protect, defend and save him, and for which reason he joins the number of monks in retirement from this world, under the Archbishopric of the holy father, the Archbishop of Mount Sinai, the venerable lord Kyrillos, of Crete, in the year of the Messiah, 1770.[13]

From these inscriptions we learn that Gerassimos, Metropolitan of Homs, financed the paving of the Chapel (including presumably the marble dado and the tiles above), work which was carried out with the assistance of the monk Raphael, also from Homs, in 1770 A.D. during the time that Kyrillos of Crete was Archbishop of Sinai. There is no tile inscription on the west wall now; and indeed if it had existed it would have made the marble inscription redundant.

But there is part of tile inscription dated 1770 A.D. elsewhere in the monastery; this is in the Chapel of St. George, perched on the outside wall of the monastery. Again, there is a bilingual Greek and Arabic inscription, this time on Damascus tiles. The left tile is missing, and what remains can be translated thus:

> ... of the most reverend [Metropolitan of] Homs, the lord Gerassimos ... Archbishop, the lord Kyrillos, in the year 1770.[14]

This may be the tile inscription referred to on the marble text, though why it should have been moved is not at all clear. The important point is that tiles were specially made in 1770 for the restorations. These restorations also included the addition of a pair of magnificent inlaid doors, leading into the Chapel of the Burning Bush (Pl. LIII). These are inscribed in Greek:

(left)　ΚΥΡΙΛΛΟΥ ΑΡΧΙΕΠΙΣΚΟΠΟΥ ΤΟΥ ΚΡΗΤΟΣ ΑΨΟ
Of (or to) Kyrillos, Archbishop, the Cretan, (A.D.) 1770

(right)　ΜΝΗΣΘΗΤΙ ΔΕΣΠΟΙΝΑ ΤΟΥ ΔΟΥΛΟΥ ΣΟΥ
Remember, Lady (= BVM), thy servant [15]

All this points to considerable activity in the monastery in the year 1770, and to return to the Chapel of the Burning Bush, the marble inscription would indeed suggest that the tiles on the walls were at least partly re-arranged in that year. It is to be observed that *type 3* tiles are relatively few in number on the west wall, where the inscription is placed; on the other hand, the rows of *type 1* and *2* tiles just above the marble dado repeat a sequence found right round the chapel (*Fig. 4*). In consideration of this, all that can be safely said about the tiles in the chapel is that they *may* have been all part of a donation made in 1680 A.D., but that the donation could have included some earlier tiles, and also some that arrived later, used in the re-shuffling of the icons. Nor was 1770 A.D. the final date for adaptions to the chapel. Two marble inscriptions on either side of the apse tell of repairs to the mosaic decoration in 1847 A.D.; and a Greek inscription on a metal plaque says that the interior of the chapel was completely restored as late as 1911 A.D. [16]

What does remain consistent as far as the tiles are concerned, is that whenever they were installed, they only served as one of several decorative elements in the chapel as a whole, like the lamps and the inlaid furniture. The spiritual component was provided by the icons. The tiles in Sinai do not, as the tiles in the *zāwiya* of Saʻd ad-Dīn do, serve to proclaim the Faith through the Word; nor do they serve as an extension of the basic architectural form of the chapel; indeed, any original architectural concept in the Chapel of the Burning Bush has long since sunk below the crust of surface decoration.

The tiles in these two widely different buildings serve to illustrate several points that can be made about Syrian tiles in general. In the fifteenth century, tiles made in Syria were close in spirit to similar tiles being made in Egypt and Turkey; nowhere can this be better seen than the tiles on the walls of the tomb chamber of Tawrīzī (d. 1430 A.D.) in Damascus. [17] But in the sixteenth century, the Ottoman conquest made its mark on the development of the decorative arts in Syria, and Syrian potters became aware of the work of the Turkish tile-makers at Iznik. In Aleppo, both the Adiliya mosque and the Bahrāmiya mosque are decorated with fine panels of Iznik tiles, which must have been specially made for them. (Pls. LIV, LV). [18] Such panels provided a stimulus for Syrian craftsmen to experiment with similar designs. But here occurs a difference, which goes beyond the inability of the Syrians to reproduce either the colours, or the flawless technique of the Turkish tiles. The Syrian designers developed a certain individuality, and their designs broke with the magnificent but severe discipline of the Iznik product. This new quality can be seen to best advantage in five buildings in Damascus erected between 1550-1585 A.D. [19] Instead of the unreal refinement of the Turkish designs, there is a primitive, but lively naturalism at work, painted in the different key of the Syrian palette. [20]

In the seventeenth century and later, Syrian tiles declined in quality in much the same way as their Turkish counterparts. [21] The Syrians continued to produce tiles, but the designs are cruder and the technique less sure. Just as the Iznik craftsmen took to working for non-Muslim patrons, so did the Syrians. Tiles continued to find a place in the decoration of interiors in the eighteenth century, but they were assembled as a *collage* of available types, rather like a child who sticks stamps indiscriminately in his album, oblivious of the country from which they come. The guiding hand of the architect/designer was lost, who alone could control the tiles as an extension of the building. The integration of glazed tiles and architectural form, one of the great achievements of the Islamic world, swiftly disappeared, like the shaft of sunlight that briefly pierces the Sinaitic darkness.

References

1.　My record of the tiles on Mount Sinai was made possible thanks to a travel grant from the Arts and Sciences Research Fund, of the American University of Beirut. I visited Sinai before 1967; since then, the monastery has lain in Israeli-occupied territory. A general account of the monastery and its treasures is given by M.H.L. Rabino, *Le Monastère de Sainte-Catherine (Mont Sinai)*; Cairo, 1938. Details of the tiles are given in the Catalogue at the end of this article.

2.   A *zāwiya* is a mosque-like structure, with a *miḥrāb,* where members of religious fraternities meet for the *dhikr*; the *dhikr* is the repetition of certain fixed phrases, repeated in a ritual order, for the glorification of 'Allāh. See *Encyclopaedia of Islam,* under *zāwiya, dhikr.*

3.   The *subḥa* may be compared with the rosary in the Catholic church; it is used for the counting of *dhikrs,* and consists of a varying number of beads on a string; see *Encyclopaedia of Islam,* under *subḥa.*

4.   Although the electric lights might at first glance appear inappropriate, it is worth recalling that Ibn 'Atā 'Allāh noted that spiritual progress in the performance of the *dhikr* is matched with the vision of coloured lights; - *Encyclopaedia of Islam, dhikr.*

5.   Here I acknowledge my debt to Dr. Heinz Gaube, lately of the German Oriental Institute in Beirut, who generously supplied me with translations of the various texts in the *zāwiya,* and who first noticed that three of the tile inscriptions were dated by chronograms. The dates are contained in the last words of each inscription, the Arabic characters each having a numerical value.

      Some of the inscriptions have already been published; H. Gaube, *Arabische Inschriften aus Syrien,* Beirut, 1975.

      I am also indebted to Dr. Gaube for his advice and criticism of a number of aspects of this article.

6.   K. Wulzinger and C. Watzinger, *Damaskus, Die Islamische Stadt,* Berlin, 1924; p. 101.

7.   For details of each type of tile, see the catalogue at the end of this article.

8.   There are 675 tiles and tile fragments in the chapel.

      Type 1, 152; *2,* 113; *3,* 232; *3a,* 10; *3b,* 10; *3c,* 8; *3d,* 9; *3e,* 1; *3f,* 10; *3g,* 1; *3h,* 3; *3d/f,* 3; *4,* 97; *5,* 2; *6,* 10; *7,* 1; *8,* 1; *9,* 1; *10,* 1; *11,* 1; *12,* 1; *13,* 4.

      Type 3 tiles and its variants total 287.

9.   These now belong to *H. E.* Henri Pharaon, who kindly allowed me to reproduce three of them here.

10.   Rabino, op. cit., p. 33, gives a French translation.

11.   The Greek text has so far defeated attempts at translation.

12.   Dr. Gaube's translation.

13.   Rabino, op. cit., p. 32, gives the Greek and Arabic texts, with a French translation.

14.   Rabino, op. cit., p. 35.

15.   Rabino, op. cit., p. 33, gives a French translation of the inscriptions.

16.   Rabino, op. cit., p. 32.

17.   John Carswell, 'Six Tiles', *Islamic Art in the Metropolitan Museum of Art,* ed. R. Ettinghausen, 1972; - 'Some Fifteenth-century Hexagonal Tiles from the Near East', *Victoria and Albert Museum Yearbook,* 3, 1972.

18.   According to As'ad Talas, *al-Athār al-islāmiya wa-t-tārikhīya fi Ḥalab* (Damascus, 1956), (p. 127) the Adiliya mosque in Aleppo was built when Mohammed Pasha was *vali* (from *c.* 957 A.H./1550 A.D.); and above the entrance is a date, 974 A.D. / 1566-7 A.D.

      The Bahrāmiya mosque (p. 129) was built when Bahrām Pasha was *vali,* (from 988 A.H./1580-1 A.D.; he died in 995 A.H./1586-7 A.D.); However, a carved stone inscription above the *miḥrāb* (Pl. XVII, *centre*) gives the date 1003 A.H./ 1594-5 A.D. The tiles in the Bahrāmiya mosque are not so fine as those in the Adiliya, and may well be a few years later.

19.   The buildings are:

      1. The Suleymaniya mosque; 1550-4 A.D.

      2. The Selim II *madrasa*; 1555-70 A.D.

      3. The *zāwiya* of Sa'd ad-Din; Wulzinger and Watzinger, op. cit., p. 101, give the date as about 970 A.H./ 1562-3 A.D. As already noted, the three tile-panels with chronograms give the dates 1574-5, 1586-7 and 1596-7 A.D.

      4. The Darwichiya mosque; 1574 A.D.

      5. The Sinaniya mosque; 1585 A.D.

20.   Arthur Lane, *Victoria and Albert Museum, Guide to the Collection of Tiles,* H.M.S.O., 1960, *Plate 17, C, D,* illustrates two groups of Syrian tiles of this period.

21.   An interesting intermediary phase is to be seen in the tiles in the tomb-chamber of Saladin in Damascus. Here, stock types are used with others specially made for the setting, including a panel at the centre inscribed and dated 1027 A.H./ 1618-9 A.D. See Carswell, 'Some fifteenth-century tiles . . . ', loc. cit., *Plate 15.*

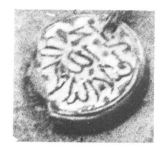

O

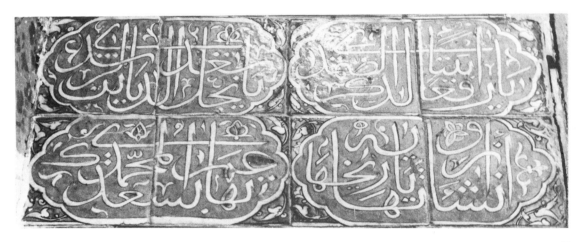

H

I

Plate XLV: (top) *Glazed plaque, O;* (centre, bottom) *Tile panels H, I; south-west wall, zāwiya of Sa'd ad-Dīn, Damascus.*

F

J

K

Plate XLVI: (top). *Tile panel F, with painted inscription above; south-west wall, zāwiya of Saʿd ad-Dīn, Damascus.*
(bottom). *A reconstruction of the tile panels J and K; south-west wall, zāwiya of Saʿd ad-Dīn, Damascus.*

Plate XLVII: Details of tile panel J; south-west wall, zāwiya of Saʻd ad-Dīn, Damascus.

D

A

E

Plate XLVIII: Tile panels D, A, E; zāwiya of Sa'd ad-Dīn, Damascus.

Plate XLIX:
(top)
The altar, of inlaid woodwork
(bottom)
South-east angle, Chapel of the
Burning Bush, Church of St. Catherine
Mount Sinai

Plate L: (top). *The Episcopal chair, dated 1713 A.D.*
              (bottom). *Tile panel (13) dated 1680 A.D. Chapel of the Burning Bush, Church of St. Catherine, Mount Sinai.*

Plate LI: *Tiles, types 1-10. Chapel of the Burning Bush, Church of St. Catherine, Mount Sinai.*

Plate LI: *Tiles, types 1 10. Chapel of the Burning Bush, Church of St. Catherine, Mount Sinai.*

Plate LII: The Episcopal chair; detail of the inlaid inscription, dated 1713 A.D. Chapel of the Burning Bush, Church of St. Catherine, Mount Sinai.

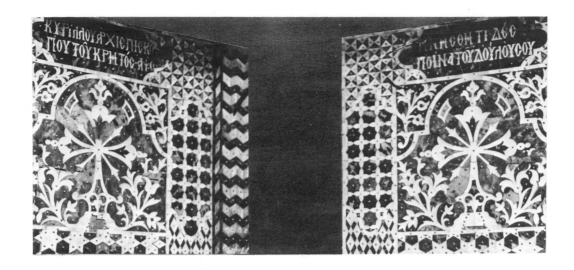

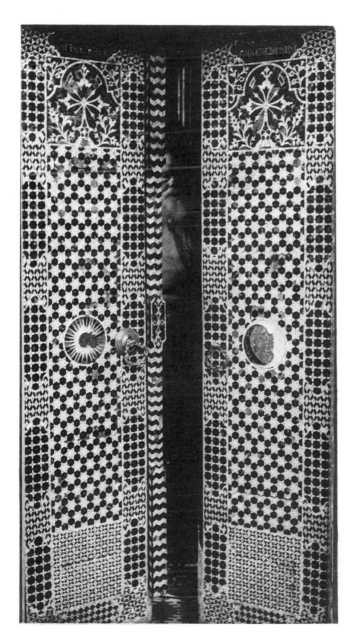

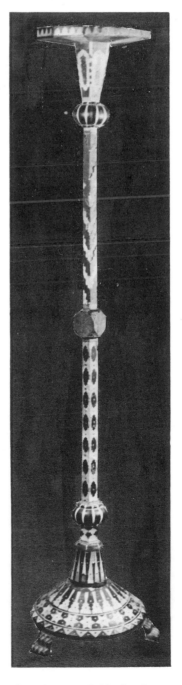

Plate LIII: *Chapel of the Burning Bush, Church of St. Catherine, Mount Sinai.* (top, bottom left) *the doors on the north side.* (bottom right) *inlaid candelabra.*

Plate LIV: *Ādilīya mosque, Aleppo.* (top) *the portico.* (bottom) *panel of Iznik tiles; approx. 35 cms square; painted in cobalt blue, turquoise and red, with black outlines.*

Plate LV: Bahrāmīya mosque, Aleppo. (top) *Iznik tile panel; tiles measure 25 cms. square, painted in cobalt blue, turquoise, red, with black outlines.* (centre) *carved stone inscription above the miḥrāb, dated 1003 H. /1594-5 A.D.* (bottom) *the interior.*

Plate LVI: *Syrian tiles, from an old house in Aleppo. Collection of* H. E. *Henri Pharaon, Beirut.* (top left)
25 by 29 cms., painted in dull blue, apple green, olive green. (top right) *22.5 by 31 cms., painted
in cobalt blue, pale blue, olive green.* (bottom) *22.5 by 31 cms., painted in pale blue, olive green,
pinkish grey.*

CATALOGUE

Tiles in the *zāwiya* **of Sa'd ad-Dīn, Damascus**

Panel A. Four square, and eight shaped tiles, forming an arched panel on the east wall (*Plate XLVIII*).
Square tiles, 23.5 cms. Painted in dark cobalt blue, turquoise, pale green, with black outlines.
The lower part of the panel with an inscription in a cartouche, within a rectangular frame; at the corners are wild tulips.
The inscription reads:

صدق الله العظيم

Allāh, the mighty, speaks the truth

The rest of the panel is a symmetrical design of interlacing spiral stems, bearing a variety of flowers; pointed, lobed and serrated leaves, and palmettes.

B. Similar to *panel* A. Square tiles, 23.5 cms. (*not illustrated*)
Painted in dark cobalt blue, turquoise, pale green, with black outlines.
The corners of the rectangular panel are painted with leaves.
The inscription reads:

وسبحو بكره واصيلا

(Qur'ān, XXXIII, 42.)

C. Similar to *panel* A. Square tiles, 23.5 cms. (*not illustrated*)
Painted in dark cobalt blue, turquoise, pale green, with black outlines.
The corners of the rectangular panel are painted with leaves, and there is a single white tulip at the end of the inscription.
The inscription reads:

الله ذكرا كثيرا

(Qur'ān, XXXIII, 41: end)

D. Two square, and five shaped tiles, forming an arched panel, to the left of the *miḥrāb*. (*Plate XLVIII*).
Square tiles, 23.5 cms.
Painted in dark cobalt blue, turquoise, pale green, with black outlines.
The lower part of the panel with an inscription in a cartouche, and sprays of flowers and leaves.
The inscription reads:

يا يها اذين آمنوا آذكروا

(Qur'ān, V, 11: beginning)
The rest of the panel filled with a loose design of flowers and leaves on arabesque stems; at the top, a large flower against a spray of feathery leaves.

E. Two square, and five shaped tiles, similar to *panel* D, to the right of the *miḥrāb*. (*Plate XLVIII*)
Square tiles, 23.5 cms. Painted in dark cobalt blue, turquoise, pale green, with black outlines.
Similar in design to D; the large central flower is different. The cartouche contains an inscription, and wild tulips.

The inscription reads:

بسم الله الرحمن الرحيم

In the name of Allāh, the Merciful, the Compassionate

F.   Three tiles, approx. 22 cms. wide. (*Plate XLVI*)
Painted in cobalt blue, turquoise and black.
The tiles are painted with six cartouches with scalloped ends, the upper and lower three cartouches separated by a horizontal hand. The inscription incorporates decorative foliate details.
The inscription reads:

حل سعد الدين في دار

البقاء وجاور الحق مولاه

الكريم ان

تر نقلا له

تاريخه   [:]   قبر زاهي

بجنات النعيم

(1)   Sa'd ad-Dīn is in the house of eternity and is approaching his noble Lord.

(2)   If you look on it [you see] his date[:] a blooming grave is the paradise of happiness.

The inscription is dated by a chronogram, which consists of the last four words, 982 H. /1574-5 A.D. Above the tiles is a painted inscription (Qur'ān III, 37) with the date 1365 H./ 1945-6 A.D.

G.   Panel of forty-two tiles, set in two horizontal rows, above the *miḥrāb*; (*Plate XLIV*)
22.5 cms. square. Painted in dark cobalt blue, turquoise, pale green, with black outlines.
The panel bears a long inscription from the Qur'ān, II, 255, in two rows of characters, reserved on a dark blue ground with touches of turquoise. There is a border of pale green overlapping palmettes.

H.   Panel of eight tiles set in two horizontal rows, on the upper left of the south wall; (*Plate XLV*).
22.5 cms. square. Painted in pale cobalt blue, turquoise, with grey-black outlines.
The tiles are painted with an inscription in verses, in four cartouches with scalloped ends, with decorative leafy details and turquoise touches.
The inscription reads:

يا رافعا بيتا لذكرى العميد

يا نجل سعد الدين بالرشدى

أنشأتها زاوية تاريخها

عمرتها بسعدى المحمد

(1)   You, that you erected a house to remember the Eternal, oh, spiritual son of Sa'd ad-Dīn.

(2)   You erected it as a *zāwiya,* its date [:]
       You erected it with the aid of the praised

The inscription is dated by a chronogram, which consists of the last three words, 995 H. /1586-7 A.D.

I.   Panel of fifteen tiles, set in three rows of five, similar to *panel* H, on the upper right of the south wall;
      (*Plate XLV*)
      22.5 cms. square. Painted in pale cobalt blue, turquoise and grey-black.
      The tiles are painted with an inscription, in eight cartouches with scalloped ends, reserved on a blue
      ground. At the centre is a pointed medallion with a *bismallāh* in grey letters, surrounded by wild tulips;
      at the corners of the cartouches are leafy details.
      The inscription reads:

أورى غياث الوجود شمس محمد

في الشيح سعد الدين دامت معاليه

بقيتم لأهل الأرض آخر ملجأ

وطيب الثنا   عنكم له المسك زاوية

بسم الله الرحمن الرحيم

عمر تم لأهل الورد والود زكية

فها هى با الحسن في الحالين جالية

تخيرتها الوردين فأرخت

بنيت لهم بالشام زاوية لله

(1)   The gift of creation, the son of Muhammad has been buried in the person of the sheikh
       Sa'd ad-Dīn. His dignity lasts. You continue to be the last impetus for the people of the earth.

(2)   To honour you is perfume, which is represented by the zāwiya. Bismallāh. You erected to
       the people of devotion and love a benefaction.

(3)   See now that it has been completed, it appears in ever lasting beauty. I had to choose
       bctween two wishes and I date: You erected for them a zāwiya for Allāh in Damascus.

The inscription is dated by a chronogram, which consists of the last five words, 1005 H. / 1596-7 A.D.

J.   Panel of forty tiles, set in horizontal rows of four, on the left of south wall; (*Plates XLIV, XLVI, XLVII*). 22.5 cms. square. Painted in dark cobalt blue, turquoise, pale green, manganese purple, with grey-black outlines. The panel is painted with a large medallion filled with intertwined arabesque leafy stems reserved on a blue ground, with a scalloped and pointed border. The central medallion is set within a larger vertical pointed medallion of floral bands. Inside and out are feathery leaves and flowers of various types. The corners are filled with quarter-medallions. At the bottom is a narrow rectangular band, with interlocking leaves scratched through the black ground. The whole panel is framed with a border of palmettes, extended at the top (now mis-placed at the bottom) with a wider frieze of trefoil and tassel motifs.

K.   Panel of fifty tiles, set in horizontal rows of five, on the right of the south wall: (*Plates XLIV, XLVI*). 22.5 cms. square. Painted in dark cobalt blue, turquoise, pale green, manganese purple, with grey-black outlines. The tiles are similar to *panel* J; it also has several tiles now placed out of sequence. The border is wider and of different design, again extended at the top with a narrow fringe. Four unrelated tiles are painted with a floral spray within a medallion of scalloped and pointed leaves.

L.   Panel of three square, and five shaped tiles, between the left end of the facade and the springing of the arch, on the upper part of the south wall; square tiles, 22.5 cms. (*Plate XLIV*).
Painted in dark cobalt blue, turquoise, pale green, with grey-black outlines.
At the bottom of the panel is a spray of serrated leaves; from this spring undulating stems bearing a variety of flowers and leaves reserved on a dark blue ground.

M.   Panel of seven square, and seven shaped tiles, between the right end of the facade and the springing of the arch, on the upper part of the south wall; square tiles, 22.5 cms. (*Plate XLIV*).
Painted in dark cobalt blue, turquoise, pale green, with grey-black outlines.
Like *panel* L, decorated with flowers and leaves on thin curving stems springing from a spray of serrated leaves, reserved on a dark blue ground.

N.   Two rows of border tiles, set horizontally above and below *panel* H. 10 by 22.5 cms.
Painted in cobalt blue, turquoise, pale purple, and dark olive green. (*Plate XLIV*) 10 by 22.5 cms.
Decorated with a palmette frieze.

O.   A glazed pottery plaque, set into the stone above the *miḥrāb*. Damaged on the left side; originally 11.5 cms. in diameter, it projects 1.5 cms. from the stone. (*Plates XLIV, XLV*).
Painted in cobalt blue and black. At the centre are the words:

لا اله الا الله محمد رسول لله

[the Muslim confession of faith]

The side of the plaque is decorated with a chevron band.

Tiles in the Chapel of the Burning Bush, Church of St. Catherine, Sinai

Type 1.   Crackled glaze, sometimes pitted; white ground; 22.5 cms. square. (*Plate LI*).
Painted in uneven cobalt blue, turquoise, grey-green, purple, with brownish-black outlines.
A four-pointed medallion, composed of four iris-like flowers symmetrically disposed, stems springing from a central square enclosing a little flower. Smaller flowers and curving stems intertwine within the medallion, with pointed scalloped leaves. The medallion is enclosed in a roughly circular scalloped frame; at the corners of the tiles are quarter-flowers.

2.   Crackled glaze, sometimes pitted; white ground; 22.5 cms. square. (*Plate LI*).
Painted in uneven cobalt blue, turquoise, grey-green, purple, with brownish-black outlines. The use of colour is not always consistent on each tile.
A pointed, scalloped medallion encloses a spray of pointed, scalloped leaves, on a blue ground. The medallion is enclosed with a wreath of white leaves with curving blade-like stems.

Around the central motif white petals float on a blue ground; at the corners of the tile are quarter-flowers.

3. Glaze sometimes crackled; white ground; 22.5 cms. square. (*Plate LI*).
    Painted in cobalt blue, pale turquoise, grey-green, purple, with dark brown outlines.
    A central flower, from which radiate eight smaller flowers on interlacing stems, four flowers pointing inwards and four outwards, with pointed leaves, the whole forming a basket-like design. The designs is enclosed in a scalloped frame, linked to scalloped circles at the corners enclosing quarter-flowers.
    Of this type, there are nine variants:

    3 *a*   22.5 cms. square. (*Plate LI*).
            The side of the tile is painted with a border of arabesque leaves and palmettes, and the rest with three-quarters of the basic pattern.

    3 *b*   22.5 by 16.5 cms.
            Painted with a border like 3*a*, and half of the basic design.

    3 *c*   Rectangular tile.
            Painted with a border like 3a, only.

    3 *d*   Square tile.
            The basic pattern the same as 3, but with a different, narrower border of palmette design.

    3 *e*   Square tile.
            Like 3*a,* but with the border pattern painted diagonally across one corner.

    3 *f*   Square tile, specially shaped on one side to incorporate a curved section of border pattern.

    3 *d-f* Square tiles of same basic pattern as 3, with curved border pattern like 3*a* at the bottom, and narrow pattern like 3*d* at the top. The three tiles of this design are above the apse.

    3 *g*   L-shaped corner tile.

    3 *h*   Square tile of 3*a* type, with inside border pattern at one corner.

4. 22.5 cms. square. (*Plate LI*).
    Off-white ground.
    Painted in cobalt blue, turquoise, pale green, some with purple. The colour is diffused in firing.
    At the centre a flower with eight pointed petals, inside an eight-pointed star. At the base of the points of the star, eight trefoils; at the points of the star, four tulip-like motifs alternate with four larger flowers in profile. The corners and centre of each side painted with pairs of arabesque leaves.

5. Rectangular tile, 32.5 cms. wide by 35 cms. high. (*Plate LI*).
    Crackled, thick glaze.
    Painted in smudgy cobalt blue and turquoise with grey-black outlines.
    The tile is painted with a cross, with a trefoil design at the end of each arm, two rings on either side of the stem, and a triangular base. Above the horizontal arm of the cross are two smaller crosses with equal arms set diagonally. From the base of the cross spring symmetrical branches of arabesque flowers and leaves. The upper and side margins of the tile are painted with a border of crosses between double lines.

6. 31 cms. square. (*Plate LI*).
    White ground.
    Painted in light cobalt blue, sage green, turquoise and purple, with black outlines.
    From a central flower of peony type spring curving, interlacing stems bearing smaller round flowers with scalloped petals, hyacinth, carnations, campanulas, and pointed leaves some with twisting tips. At the centre of each side, a half-flower of peony type. Above and below the centre of each vertical side, a half-tulip. At the corners, quarter-flowers with scalloped petals.

7. 23 cms. square. (*Plate LI*).
    Painted in dark cobalt blue, pale purple, light green, with dark outlines.

In the centre of the tile is a two-handled vase with a fluted globular body and flaring tall neck, containing a bouquet of flowers of carnation and tulip types, with long pointed leaves; the stems are clasped at the centre; The vase and bouquet are flanked on either side with symmetrical sprays of flowers, including hyacinth. At the corners, quarter-flowers with radiating scalloped petals.

8.   23 cms. square. (*Plate LI*).
Painted in dark cobalt blue, pale purple, light green, with dark outlines.
A central rosette with eight pointed petals and two rings of scalloped petals, surrounded by four flowers in profile placed symmetrically, with interlacing thin stems and four tulips between them. At the corners, quarter-flowers of the same type as the rosette at the centre.

9.   23 cms. square. (*Plate LI*).
Painted in light and dark cobalt blue, pale green, with dark outlines.
Placed diagonally across the tile is a hybrid flower with arabesque petals, on a curving stem; it is surrounded by intertwining stems bearing smaller flowers and long scalloped leaves with twisting tips. At the centre of the top and bottom sides are half-flowers like that in the middle of the tile; at the centre of the vertical sides are half-flowers of peony type.

10.   22.5 cms. square. (*Plate LI*).
Off-white ground.
Painted in dark cobalt blue, dark purple, and turquoise, in colours diffused in firing.
A symmetrical design with a large flower at the centre of the bottom side, from which spring two diagonal stems bearing tulip-like flowers. On either side, pointed, serrated leaves and two flowers curve inwards; above is a carnation-like flower at the centre, and below a pair of campanulas on either side of the main flower. Half flowers on the upper borders of the two vertical sides. Quarter-flowers with pointed petals at the top corners of the tiles.

11.   (not measured; approx. 18 cms. wide)
(colours not noted)
Painted with a pattern of interlocking palmettes; *see Plate XLIX, top*.

12.   (not measured; approx. 12.5 cms wide)
(colours not noted)
Painted with large flower placed diagonally, with two split arabesque petals, and smaller assymetrical flowers; see *Plate XLIX, top*.

13.   Panel of four inscribed tiles. The upper two tiles are approximately 22.5 cms square; the lower two tiles, 22.5 cms. wide and 16 cms. high. (*Plate L*)
Painted in cobalt blue and turquoise with black outlines.
The tiles are painted with a crude Greek inscription in seven lines (see p. 274, *supra*). The upper two tiles have a floral border at either side.